1776
Year of Illusions

1776
Year of Illusions

BY

THOMAS FLEMING

CASTLE BOOKS
Edison, New Jersey

This edition published in 1996 by
CASTLE BOOKS
A Division of Book Sales, Inc.
114 Northfield Avenue
Edison, New Jersey 08837

Published by arrangement with and permission of
W.W. Norton Co.

ISBN 0-7858-0724-1

MANUFACTURED IN THE UNITED STATES OF AMERICA.

"God from this Wilderness will cause a
light to break forth more and more unto
the perfect day."
   —Anne Hutchinson

"We must . . . make the best of mankind as
they are, since we cannot have them as
we wish."
   —George Washington

"I believe . . . that though the American
people have been favored by providence
above all others in many ways, this luck
does not mean we were chosen by God to
be immune from unoriginal sin, foolishness,
and irrationality—*and* perhaps disaster."

   —Douglass Adair

Contents

Illustrations

General Israel Putnam, by John Trumbull (Wadsworth Atheneum, Hartford; on loan from Putnam Phalanx)

Sir Henry Clinton, watercolor on ivory by Thomas Day (R. W. Norton Art Gallery, Shreveport, Louisiana)

Miss Carolina Sullivan, English engraving, 1776 (Chicago Historical Society)

Sir Peter Parker's Attack on Fort Moultrie, June 28, 1776, detail of a painting by James Peale (Colonial Williamsburg)

Representation du Feu Terrible à Nouvelle Yorck, line engraving by Francois Xavier Habermann (Eno Collection, New York Public Library)

Hanging of Nathan Hale, after an anonymous painting of 1820 (Culver Pictures, Inc.)

Benedict Arnold, mezzotint by Thomas Hart, 1776 (Anne S. K. Brown Military Collection, Brown University Library)

British Naval Squadron at Lake Champlain, by H. Gilder (Royal Collection, Windsor Castle, by gracious permission of Her Majesty The Queen— Crown copyright reserved)

The Turtle, sketch of interior profile of David Bushnell's submarine boat (Submarine Force Library and Museum, Groton, Connecticut)

View of the Attack against Fort Washington, watercolor drawing by Thomas Davies (I. N. Phelps Stokes Collection, New York Public Library)

The Phoenix and the Rose, aquatint in color by Dominick Serres after Sir James Wallace (I. N. Phelps Stokes Collection, New York Public Library)

The Landing of the British Forces in the Jerseys, watercolor drawing by Lord Rawdon (I.N. Phelps Stokes Collection, New York Public Library)

Joseph Reed, by James Peale (The Historical Society of Pennsylvania)

Major General Charles Lee, by Alexander H. Ritchie after B. Rushbrooke (Prints Division, New York Public Library)

Major General Philip Schuyler, by John Trumbull (New-York Historical Society, New York City)

William Franklin, by Mather Brown (Collection of Mrs. James Manderson Castle, Jr.)

Frederick Philipse, by John Wollaston (New-York Historical Society, New York City)

Joseph Galloway, miniature by an unknown artist (Courtesy of David Stockwell, Inc.)

William Smith, miniature by Henry Stubble (New-York Historical Society, New York City)

William Byrd III, by an unknown artist (Virginia State Library)

British satire of American soldiers, 1776 (The British Museum)

Robert Morris, by Charles Willson Peale (Independence National Historical Park Collection)

Jacques Necker, French engraving (Culver Pictures, Inc.)
Benjamin Franklin, by Joseph Siffrèd Duplessis (The Metropolitan Museum of Art, The Michael Friedsam Collection, 1931)
The Capture of the Hessians at Trenton, detail of a painting by John Trumbull (Yale University Art Gallery)
Charles Earl Cornwallis, by Thomas Gainsborough (National Portrait Gallery, London)
Battle of Princeton, by William Mercer (The Historical Society of Pennsylvania)
George Washington at Princeton, by Charles Willson Peale (The Pennsylvania Academy of the Fine Arts; Gift of the Executors of the Elizabeth Wharton McKean Estate)

Maps

Acknowledgments

In a book based on research which began ten years ago, it is impossible to acknowledge all the help I have received from librarians, editors, research assistants, and friends. I can only hope to mention a few library staffs whom I found particularly helpful. Among these are the William L. Clements Library at the University of Michigan, the New-York Historical Society, the American History Room of the New York Public Library, the Yale University Library, the Olin Library at Wesleyan University, the Library of Congress in Washington, D.C., and two private libraries with remarkably good historical collections, the New York Society Library and the University Club Library. Among many friends who lent me books and articles from their private collections, I would like to thank Edward O. Mills, Samuel Cohen, Ted Rowland, and Robert Kammer, fellow members of the New York American Revolution Round Table. Also, I'd like to express special thanks to Joan Paterson Kerr for her expert advice and assistance with illustrations for this book. Finally, I am grateful to my sons, Thomas J. Fleming, Jr., David J. Fleming, and Richard L. Fleming, who helped me find and Xerox some 350 periodical articles, diaries, etc., and indexed them. Jayne K. Tomkins was also helpful in providing me with research materials from the Library of Congress during my final year of work on the book. Perhaps most valuable was the contribution of my secretary, Mrs. Joseph Daffron, who patiently typed and retyped the manuscript.

THOMAS FLEMING

New York
December 19, 1974

1776
Year of Illusions

Soldiers Far from Home

A mixture of sleet and snow hissed ominously out of Canada's polar north. In the lanes and fields outside the city of Quebec, the darkness was total. It was almost 2 A.M. on December 31, 1775. Around a table in a slope-roofed stone house in the suburb of St. Roch sat a group of grim-faced Americans. Their leader was Richard Montgomery, a tall, elegant Irishman of thirty-seven, who, fifteen years before, had helped to conquer Canada for England. Now Richard Montgomery was a brigadier general in the Army of the United Colonies of North America, and already the conqueror of two-thirds of Canada for the Continental Congress. Himself an aristocrat, the son of a baronet and member of Parliament, he had become converted to the American cause by two of Parliament's finest orators, who were also his personal friends: Edmund Burke and Charles James Fox. But never did they dream, when they discussed the folly of the English government in general and George III in particular, that this current of emotion and opinion could carry their magnetic young friend to this climactic moment, in the dawn of such a climactic year.

In the nine months of semi-war that had begun at Lexington, Massachusetts, on April 19, 1775, British power had been driven off the North American continent, save for a few square miles in and around the town of Boston, some scattered, feeble outposts in Florida, and the jumble of narrow streets and battered buildings and crumbling walls a short walk away from Montgomery and his circle of listeners—the fortress city of Quebec. With his unique combination of personal charm and military magnetism, Montgomery went over once more a plan that was certain to spell death for many of these listening men. Armed with nothing but muskets, hatchets, and pikes, they were going to attack a walled and fortified city, garrisoned by an army twice their size, backed by two hundred cannon. As a professional soldier, Montgomery knew what he was asking these men to do. He also knew that he was going to ask them to do it long before he revealed the desperate gamble to them. Well over a month ago, he had written to his brother-in-law, wealthy Robert R. Livingston of New York, mournfully admitting that it would come "to storming the place . . . at last." To his immediate commander, Major General Philip Schuyler, waiting anxiously at Albany for good news, he wrote in the same elegiac way about his decision. He was "very sorry to be reduced to this mode of attack" because he knew "the melancholy consequences." [1]

Other thoughts which Montgomery revealed to his brother-in-law and to his fellow aristocrat, Schuyler, he also concealed from his troops. One was his low opinion of them. He told his brother-in-law that the New Englanders were "the worst stuff imaginable for soldiers." He could find among them no "zealous attachment to the Cause." As for the New Yorkers, they were "the sweepings of the York streets." Their morals were "infamous" and they had no more spirit than the New Englanders. Never again, Montgomery told his brother-in-law, would he "hazard my reputation at the head of such ragamuffins. . . . Would I were at my plow again." [2]

Why was he now hazarding not only his reputation, but his life? It was *not* for American independence. In his last letter to Robert Livingston, Montgomery made it clear that he shuddered at the "melancholy necessity" of separating from England. Instead, he was convinced that an American conquest of Canada would force the British Parliament to reverse their policy toward America. Behind his mask of cool, seemingly unillusioned courage, Montgomery was a captive of one of the major illusions of 1776. [3]

The men who sat around the table with Montgomery listening to his plan of attack were also aware of the harrowing gamble they were about to take. One of Montgomery's aides, Captain Jacob Cheesman of New York, had dressed himself with special care and put five gold pieces in his pocket, enough, he hoped, "to bury me with decency." Another aide, diminutive nineteen-year-old Aaron Burr of New Jersey, was equally convinced that the assault was virtual suicide, but he was a gambler by nature, with faith in his own lucky star—and in nothing else. A third aide, twenty-one-year-old Captain John McPherson of Philadelphia, summed up the prevailing mood in a letter to his wealthy father. He told him that the letter was probably "the last this hand will ever write you." He added, "I experience no reluctance in this Cause, to venture a life which I consider is only right to be used when my country demands it." [4]

If we pause to think about those words, they become rather strange. What country was demanding John McPherson's life? His native colony, Pennsylvania? There was nothing to gain and a great deal to lose in a Pennsylvanian attempt to conquer Canada. McPherson was obviously talking about America, the country that was at best a shadowy entity in the minds of the two and a half million white inhabitants of North America. At this point in time, it was little more than a word. It had no flag, no constitution, no laws, no legal existence. If there was a voice demanding McPherson's life, it emanated from a fluctuating group of some fifty to sixty men who met each day at the Pennsylvania State House in Philadelphia to pass resolutions, exhortations, and decrees in the name of the Continental Congress.

This extralegal body had sent Richard Montgomery, John McPherson, and their fellow Americans into Canada in pursuit of another illusion—the notion that the Catholic French-Canadians were ready and willing to revolt against their British conquerors and join the Protestant Americans in a united front that would make Congress truly continental. Alas, most French-Canadians had no interest whatsoever in joining the *Bostonnais,* as they called the Americans, unless it became very, very clear that they were the winning side.

Congress's illusion about the French-Canadians was piled on top of an even more fatuous illusion—the idea that British power, once swept off the continent of North America, would never be able to gain a foothold on it again. That Congress could take seriously such a notion about a government with the world's most powerful navy and an army that had perfected amphibious operations in previous wars was melancholy evidence of their military ignorance—an ignorance they were to demonstrate repeatedly in the next twelve months.

This does not mean that they were fools or knaves, worthy of nothing but contempt. On the contrary, as the year 1776 began, men on both sides of the Atlantic were in the grip of illusions that were hurtling England and America down a collision course to a military and political convulsion that would shake the civilized world. It is a convulsion about which contemporary Americans know amazingly little and contemporary Britons know even less. As for the rest of the world, their knowledge can be filed under "Infinitesimal."

Subtracting everything but sheer size, the dominant figure at Montgomery's table was Daniel Morgan, the huge Virginia rifleman. He sat glowering, impatient as always with words and plans, his big fists clenched on the tabletop like primitive symbols. Morgan seemed born to make war. His face and body bore the scars of numerous encounters with violence. In 1758, he had been hit by an Indian bullet which smashed all the teeth on the left side of his mouth and exited through the back of his neck. Earlier, he had punched an English officer who had slapped him with the flat of his sword. For this he acquired five hundred lashes and an undying grudge against England.

But not even the massive Morgan or the suave Montgomery could overshadow the man who sat at the opposite end of the table. Blue-gray bulging eyes shining with tense ardor, the heavy lower lip thrust out belligerently, Benedict Arnold hunched his broad, powerful shoulders and absorbed once more each minute detail of Montgomery's plan of attack. Without Arnold's leadership, this moment would never have come. True, with only 1,200 men and a tiny fleet, Montgomery had strung together a series of amazing victories since he had advanced into Canada in late August on orders from the Continental Congress. He had captured two British regiments, the fort they were defending, and finally Montreal. But most of his troops had turned around and gone home, ignoring the general's pleas that until Quebec was taken, Canada would never join the Revolution.

Then out of the Maine woods had materialized Benedict Arnold and 675 survivors of one of history's greatest marches. They had defeated 350 miles of wilderness thanks largely to Arnold's indomitable will and astonishing energy. From a military point of view, the expedition had been a fiasco. It had been launched without any serious attention to the accuracy of the maps they were using or the difficulties certain to be encountered along the Kennebec and Chaudière rivers in winter. It was the first but by no means the last example of atrocious American planning in what was not yet styled "the Revolution."

Half starved, their clothes in tatters, their shoes in shreds, Arnold's men had laid siege to Quebec. This former New Haven apothecary and merchant turned soldier had been a familiar figure in the Canadian capital in more peaceful days, when his ships carried on a brisk trade in "large, genteel fat horses, pork, oats and hay." More than any other man in the room, Benedict Arnold wanted to enter Quebec in triumph.

When he and his ragged legion had demanded the city's surrender on their emergence from the Maine wilderness, insulting remarks about a "horse jockey" posing as a general had been hurled from the city's walls.[5]

For Arnold, the clash with England was an opportunity to unleash fantastic amounts of energy and ambition surging inside his bulky body and vivid mind. Previous generations of Arnolds had been leaders in Rhode Island, but the family had a history of meteoric rises and equally precipitous falls. His father was the impoverished grandson of a governor of Rhode Island. Beginning life as an apprentice barrelmaker, he had married a wealthy widow from Norwich, Connecticut, and become a ship captain and a rich man. For no apparent reason, he took to drink and lost everything. Benedict Arnold went from a pampered scion in an expensive boarding school to an apprentice druggist in the course of a year.

Moving to New Haven, Arnold soon prospered as a ship captain and then as the owner of a small fleet. But the business world was too humdrum for this man. He plunged headlong into the Revolution the moment he heard the news of the fighting between Minutemen and British regulars at Lexington and Concord. More than any other single person, he was responsible for the American invasion of Canada. On May 10, 1775, with Ethan Allen's help, Arnold seized the great fort at the foot of Lake Champlain, Ticonderoga, and then surged up the lake with a ragbag collection of volunteers to capture the fort at St. John's, opening the gate to Canada. A dazzled Congress, after some soul-searching hesitation, allowed itself to be swept in Arnold's wake, and ordered Montgomery and his men to bring Canada into the defiant American confederacy. Arnold had retired to American army headquarters at Cambridge and persuaded the leaders there to let him and 1,100 picked troops make their mad, heroic march up the Kennebec.

Montgomery's plan of attack was as simple as it was daring. Quebec was divided into an Upper and a Lower Town. The Upper Town was practically impregnable, its lofty walls surrounded by snowdrifts six to eight feet deep. The Lower Town, fronting on the St. Lawrence River, was far more vulnerable. The walls were incomplete and poorly fortified. If this part of Quebec could be seized and threatened with destruction, the French-Canadian majority inside the city would almost certainly force the British to surrender.

One column was to attack under Benedict Arnold's leadership, and fight its way into the Sault au Matelot, a narrow, twisting street that ran deep into the Lower Town from the northern side of the walls. Montgomery was to attack along the river's edge, over the southern walls, and link up with Arnold in a kind of pincer movement that would envelop the whole Lower Town. To distract the British, two feints were simultaneously to be made, one at St. John's Gate by Colonel James Livingston, a Canadian citizen who had talked about two hundred fellow Canadians and a few Indians into joining the Americans. The other feint attack was to strike the "Diamond Bastion," the most heavily fortified part of the Upper Town's walls. Montgomery hoped it would pin down the heavy concentration of British and Canadian defenders there.

By now it was 4 A.M.—time to march. Outside in the driving snow, the men waited in well-formed companies, under the eyes of their lieutenants and sergeants. In little more than the three weeks since he had joined Arnold, Montgomery had done his utmost to create a spirit of pride and discipline in these amateur soldiers. It had taken all his skill at cajolery and command to lead them to this moment. Benedict Arnold's tactless, imperious style had created a spirit of mutiny in his men, and on December 27 three of his captains had declared that they were "averse to storming" and refused to fight under Arnold's leadership. Montgomery had calmly outmaneuvered them by excusing them. He wanted no man with him who "went with reluctance." [6] Twenty-two-year-old Dr. Isaac Sentner, who had marched with Arnold through the Maine wilderness, was so incensed he offered to replace one of the captains as a battle commander. But the heart of the problem was in Montgomery's explanation to General Schuyler. "The three discontented companies are within a few days of being free from their engagements. I must try every means to prevent their departure; and in this matter I am much embarrassed." [7] This was another reason why he was committed to the desperate tactic of frontal assault. The enlistments of almost all Arnold's men were on the point of expiring. No wonder Dr. Sentner noted that on the climactic night Montgomery was "extremely anxious." [8]

Other emotions prevailed among the men outside in the snow. Montgomery had fired them with a sense of destiny. When four soldiers refused to muster on December 28 and feigned sickness, their fellow privates put nooses around their necks and marched them around the camp. Captain Simeon Thayer of Massachusetts considered it "a punishment due to their effeminate courage," and scorned them for "timorously withdrawing from the laurels" they were about to gather.[9] Earlier, Montgomery had ordered each regimental commander to prepare a list of the men who promised "to distinguish themselves by activity and bravery in the attack." The almost unanimous response had played no small part in convincing Montgomery that the gamble was worth taking.

Listing volunteer heroes was also another shrewd way of creating a committed warrior spirit in these amateur soldiers. Twenty-two-year-old Abner Stocking of Connecticut confided to his journal, "The attempt to storm a place so strongly fortified, I thought was rash and imprudent, but did not think proper to make any objections, lest I should be considered wanting in courage." Yet even this Doubting Thomas was reached by Montgomery's leadership. The General was, he said, "resolved on victory or death." [10]

This heroic rhetoric, and the mood on which it was based, suggest that the conquest of Canada had become virtually an end in itself. It had acquired its own momentum, its own purpose for all these soldiers, from Montgomery to the lowliest private. Another motive, not visible in the rhetoric, was Montgomery's promise that every man would have a share in the booty of captured Quebec. But none of these motivations answer the larger question: What did these Americans think they were doing in Canada in the first place? Primitives like Morgan, farm boys like Stocking could not possibly have the same motivation as the sophisticated Montgomery, who was intimate with members of Parliament.

A thorough search of their numerous journals and many surviving letters from Canada in 1775–76 fails to turn up a trace of the slogan that was supposedly the heart of the Revolution, "No taxation without representation." Nor is there a line about independence. On the contrary, there are good reasons for supposing that almost every one of the attacking Americans would have declared himself a loyal, dutiful subject of George III, precisely as Richard Montgomery believed himself to be. Perhaps these men were responding to the harsh imperatives of class distinction and economic oppression, those vague entities which, according to Marxist historians, are the inspiration of most revolutionaries? Statistics and a modest knowledge of human nature reject this possibility. Recent studies have demonstrated that British taxes cost the average American in 1776 about $1.20 a year.[11] Men do not charge cannon under the banner of "Victory or Death" to save a dollar twenty a year. For the time being, this larger question must remain unanswered.

Silently, Montgomery and his officers moved to their positions, and the four detachments vanished into the howling snowstorm like so many ghosts. Adding to their invisibility were the uniforms they wore— white overcoats and sealskin moccasins, into which they had stuffed hay to keep their feet dry and warm. Beneath the overcoats, they were wearing woolen coats of bright red. All this standard winter equipment for British troops in Canada had been captured by Montgomery at Montreal. Without this borrowed clothing, there would have been no assault on Quebec. Arnold's incredible Americans had invaded Canada wearing summer clothing.

Each detachment had two hours to reach its jumping-off point. The signal was to be rockets from the feint attackers, who had the longest marches to make.

As they fought their way through the savage, driving snow and sleet, only Montgomery, Arnold, and probably the young aides, McPherson and Cheesman, knew something else that made the assault totally desperate. "Masters of our secret, we may select a particular time and a place for attack," Montgomery had told his brother-in-law, Robert R. Livingston. But on December 27, a New York sergeant named Singleton had deserted to the enemy, carrying with him, if not the exact date of the attack, its natural signal—the first snowy night.[12]

Inside Quebec was a soldier ready to use this vital information with deadly effect. Guy Carleton, Royal Governor and captain general of the province of Quebec, was, like Richard Montgomery, born in Ireland. Like Montgomery, he had fought in Canada. He had been quartermaster general of the army commanded by the legendary James Wolfe, who had died on the Plains of Abraham while conquering the fortress city and thereby capturing Canada for the Empire.

Governor of Canada since 1766, Carleton had assiduously wooed the French majority, especially the semi-aristocratic *seigneurs* and the even more powerful clergy. He had spent four years in England—from 1770 to 1774—lobbying through Parliament the Quebec Act, which guaranteed their continued dominance of the lowly *habitants*. The act, which passed during the flood tide of American nonviolent resistance in 1774, provided the other thirteen colonies with a key grievance. Its favoritism of the Catholic Church drew explosive denunciations from the American Protestant majority, particularly in New England. The omission of an elected assembly, or any other vestige of a free government, also raised American hackles.

Carleton's four-year absence, during which he had repeatedly assured London officials and MPs of the loyalty of the conquered French, and the need to create a government suited to their religion and autocratic political past, had left him badly out of touch with Canadian realities. While he was gone, the resident English went to work on their long-range goal—a thorough takeover of the Canadian economy. This created resentment, even among the *seigneurs*. As for the *habitants,* they thought the possibility of escaping the heel of the *seigneurs* and the thumb of the priests was a rather attractive idea, and decided to sit on the sidelines and see if the Americans could deliver on their puissant promises. At Montreal, the Canadians ignored Carleton's pleas to rally to the royal cause. The stunned Governor had been forced to disguise himself as a *habitant* and flee downriver to Quebec. He arrived there just in time to rescue the situation from collapse. The appearance of Arnold and his men from the Maine wilderness had struck the Canadians as a kind of miracle, and aroused all their latent discontent against their British conquerors. The city, with its uneasy blend of perhaps 5,000 French and 500 English, was seething with division and discontent.

The lieutenant governor, Hector Cramahe, had turned the town over to a tough old Scotsman, Allan Maclean, and retired to his house in an alarmingly neutral posture. Maclean had settled in Canada in the 1760s. When the troubles between mother country and colonies thickened, he had received the King's permission to raise a regiment of loyal Highlanders. He had scratched together little more than 200 fellow Scots when Arnold appeared before Quebec. The only other man with comparable military rank in the city was Henry Caldwell, a retired artillery major, who intensely disliked Carleton because he felt that he favored the French in his administration of the Canadian government. With these two headstrong, opinionated characters in command, Quebec would have handed itself over to the Americans through an internal revolution in a matter of weeks.

But Carleton's presence changed everything. His astute handling of the French paid dividends now. Spurred by their bishop, Jean Olivier Briand, who wholeheartedly backed the British, they rallied behind the desperate Governor. To conserve his supplies, Carleton ordered every potential traitor—a surprising number of them British—driven beyond the walls. No wonder loyalist Thomas Ainslie wrote in his diary when Carleton arrived, "We saw our salvation in his presence." [13]

Under the threat of exile, Carleton persuaded 200 British and 300 French to volunteer for militia duty. To these he added 37 marines and

271 sailors from British warships in the St. Lawrence, 74 sailors from other British ships, Maclean's 200 Highlanders, about 180 Royal Fusiliers of the Seventh Regiment, and a scattering of military specialists, such as artillerymen and engineers, to form a makeshift army of about 1,300 men. By continuing pressure on the civil population, this number had been raised to 1,800 by the last weeks of December. Carleton thus had more than twice the number of the attacking Americans, but only the Fusiliers, the marines, and the Royal Scots, 425 in all, came close to being regulars. Maclean himself admitted that a minimum of 3,000 men were needed to defend Quebec's walls. The discovery that the Americans were planning an attack on the first snowy night was therefore a godsend to Carleton. When the last night of the old year brought a blizzard, he instantly put the garrison on full alert. Every available man was ordered to his post.

Montgomery, committed and betrayed, played his last card magnificently. By waiting until 4 A.M., he knew that there was a good chance that Carleton's amateur soldiers would fall asleep, get drunk, or simply desert to the warmth of the nearest fireplace. So there was still this small flickering hope in the American commander's mind as he led his 300 New Yorkers down the steep road to Wolfe's Cove. Sixteen years before, the famed British general had landed here for his ascent to the Plains of Abraham and the conquest of Quebec. Perhaps Montgomery thought for a somber moment of Wolfe's fate, so ironically prophesied by that line in the general's favorite poem, Gray's "Elegy": "The paths of glory lead but to the grave." But he had his own motto, as he had told his brother-in-law, Robert R. Livingston, a few weeks ago: *"Audaces fortuna juvat*—Fortune favors the brave."

From Wolfe's Cove, the path wound along the edge of the frozen river. The going had been bad enough for Montgomery and his men as they fumbled their way down the cliff face. But now forward movement became a nightmare. The northwest wind whirled the sleety snow around them with ominous howls. The swirling currents of the St. Lawrence had thrown onshore "enormous and rugged masses of ice," forcing the men to claw their way as much as thirty feet up the face of the cliff to get around them. For the two-man teams carrying scaling ladders, this was a herculean feat, beyond their strength and endurance. Again and again, they had to call for help, stopping the column and losing precious minutes of darkness. Montgomery, aides McPherson and Cheesman, and young Aaron Burr, who was along to serve as liaison with Arnold's men, a role he had already skillfully played, pushed ahead with some thirty volunteers and a half dozen carpenters.[14]

This left the rest of the column under the command of Colonel Donald Campbell, Montgomery's quartermaster general. He was a tall, handsome man who ostentatiously wore a large claymore—a two-edged Scottish broadsword—at his waist. A big-talking blowhard, Campbell was fighting for the Americans for only one reason. He owned twenty thousand acres of New York land given to him by the British Crown as a reward for his father's services in putting down the Scottish rebellion of 1745. Campbell had used this inheritance to persuade a number of Englishmen, including a member of Parliament, to stand surety for his numerous debts, for which he was on his way to jail. With exquisite ingratitude, he then decamped for America. His ex-friends were furiously suing for the title to his swath of New York, to recoup their losses. If there was one man who was hoping that the capture of Quebec would lead to American independence, it was Campbell. There was no other way for him to avoid paying his bills by the surrender of his lordly estate.

About halfway down the two-mile path, Montgomery and his volunteers found their way blocked by a twenty-foot-high palisade. Above them loomed the blockhouse of Cape Diamond, with enough cannon and muskets to blast them all into the frozen St. Lawrence if the defenders were aroused. With numb fingers and palpitating hearts, the carpenters went to work on the palisade with saws. The storm swallowed the rasping sound of iron on wood, but the work went so slowly in the sub-zero cold that Montgomery impatiently ripped away a few of the half-sawed poles near the rocks, and climbed around the rest to continue the march. Leaving half the carpenters there to finish the job for the main attack force, the rest of his little detachment followed him.

On the other side of the city, Arnold and his 500 men struggled through snow six feet deep. Seventeen-year-old John Joseph Henry of Lancaster, Pennsylvania, found the storm "outrageous" and the wind "extremely biting." Stoically, he noted that "in this northern country the snow is blown horizontally into the faces of travelers on most occasions—this was our case." [15] Like Montgomery, Arnold led the way, accompanied by some thirty picked volunteers—the "forlorn hope" in the military terminology of the day. Beside Arnold trudged young Mathias Ogden of New Jersey, a Princeton classmate of Aaron Burr. No one could accuse either Arnold or Montgomery of avoiding the risks to which they were exposing their men. Both knew that it was absolutely vital when leading raw troops to take such reckless chances, so foreign to most modern generals.

Behind Arnold and his advance party came Captain John Lamb of the artillery, with a company of men hauling a six-pound cannon on a sled. Few men in the column had more to do with bringing on this moment of climax in the long quarrel between England and America. For a decade, Lamb had been a leader of New York City's riotous Sons of Liberty. His quarrel with England was intensely personal. His father had been deported as a criminal, had married well in New York, and had prospered, first as an optician and instrument maker, and later as a wine merchant. His son inherited both his scientific skills and his deep grudge against the mother country. Unfortunately, Lamb was as insubordinate in the army as he had been at the head of the New York mob. Montgomery at one point became so exasperated with his "bad temper" he denounced Lamb in a letter to their superior officer, Major General Philip Schuyler, as "turbulent and troublesome." But he also admitted his "bravery, activity, and intelligence." [16]

Behind Lamb and his men came the huge figure of Morgan at the head of his riflemen. As with Montgomery, the two-man scaling-ladder teams slowed the march to a crawl; it was just as hard to maneuver them through the heavy drifts as it was for Montgomery's men to juggle them on the icy path from Wolfe's Cove. The sled with the cannon was even more trouble. Again and again it sank into the snow-drifts, and finally the exhausted artillerymen and their captain abandoned it and pushed forward to fight as infantry. All of the men, as they floundered through the drifts, struggled to keep their muskets dry by holding the priming pans of their guns under the lapels of their overcoats. Attacking with guns that would not fire was the ultimate nightmare that tormented them every step of the way.

On the other side of the St. Charles River, Captain Henry Dearborn of New Hampshire was frantically mustering his company. The twenty-four-year-old veteran of Bunker Hill was gaunt and hollow-cheeked, having barely recovered from one of those devastating camp fevers that riddled eighteenth-century armies. Not until 4 A.M. had Dearborn learned that an attack was to be made. His sergeant major was supposed to get word to him. But the man claimed that the extremely high tide had made it impossible for him to cross the shifting ice of the frozen river. Dearborn's men were sleeping in three different houses, one a mile away from his own quarters, and it took him an hour to pull them out of bed and get them ready to march. It was 5 A.M. before he got them across the river and began slogging through the snowdrifts. "We marched—or rather ran as fast as we could," he later recalled. But they were still a mile and a half from Arnold and his men when all Quebec seemed to explode.[17]

Arnold and his forlorn hope had escaped detection. But a sharp-eyed sentry had spotted the rest of the Americans as they advanced Indian file past the Palace gate, the northern entrance to the Upper Town. "A horrible roar of cannon . . . and the ringing of all the bells in the city, which are very numerous and of all sizes" momentarily numbed the brain of young John Joseph Henry. Moments later, rockets soared up from St. John's Gate and from the Diamond Bastion, as Livingston's Canadians and a hundred Connecticut men led by Captain Jacob Brown began their feint attacks on these strongpoints. The American five-gun battery in the suburb of St. Roch opened up, although its twelve-pound balls were useless against Quebec's ten-foot-thick walls.

Carleton's defense went into instant operation. Lanterns were swung out over the walls to detect attackers, and mortars looped shells filled with burning pitch into the snow beyond the Americans, illuminating them in stark and deadly outline. Dr. Sentner, watching from the hospital three miles away, noticed that this secret weapon "burnt notwithstanding the depth of snow with amazing advantage to the enemy." [18]

For a third of a mile, Arnold's men had to run this gantlet of fire to reach their objective—a British barricade on Drummond's Wharf, which barred the way to the Sault au Matelot, the street that led into the heart of the Lower Town. "Here we lost some brave men," young Henry said, bitterly noting that he and his companions were "powerless to return the salutes we received, as the enemy was covered by his impregnable defenses. They were even sightless to us—we could see nothing but the blaze from the muzzles of their muskets."

Racing on the heels of his lieutenant, Henry escaped this first fire and legged it along the edge of the St. Lawrence to get in position for a flank attack on the Drummond's Wharf barricade. A number of ships were pulled up on the shore, moored to the houses by long cables. One of these hawsers caught Henry under the chin, and sent him hurtling into a drydock some fifteen feet deep. "My descent was terrible," he said. "Gun and all was involved in a great depth of snow. One of my knees received a most violent contusion." No one stopped to help him. They were still receiving deadly fire from the ramparts of the Upper

Town. "Scrabbling out . . . without assistance," Henry shook the snow off himself and his gun and tried to get back into line. But his own company had vanished, and the men passing now "knew me not. We had not gone twenty yards in my hobbling gait, before I was thrown out," Henry said. The teen-age soldier was discovering that men under fire "lose the compassionate feeling." [19]

Nineteen-year-old Simon Fobes of Massachusetts saw his sergeant shot down beside him. "I am a dead man," he choked. "I wish you would turn me over." Fobes turned him on his face and raced on, in obedience to the "strict orders, before we marched, not to stop for the wounded or the dying." [20]

Suddenly the fire from Quebec's walls slackened. Panic was mounting inside the city as officers and men rushed in all directions to repel the apparently four-pronged American attack.

By now, Montgomery and about a third of his men had reached their jumping-off point, the Potash or Prés de Ville section of the Lower Town. A second palisade barred their way, and the carpenters went to work on it. Again, the impatient Montgomery ripped aside the half-sawed logs with his own hands. Stepping inside the barrier, he peered through the snowy murk at what lay before him. It was a simple frame house, which had been converted into a strongpoint by loopholing the walls for muskets and mounting four small cannon in the windows. Inside was a motley garrison, most of them in the sort of condition Montgomery had hoped to find them.

There were 30 French and 9 British civilians, plus 9 seamen commanded by a ship captain named Barnsfare. To pass the long night and to keep warm, the amateurs had been drinking heavily. By now, most of them were drunk. But one man was icily sober. He was John Coffin, a symbolic name if there ever was one. Fiercely loyal to his King, he and his family had been driven out of rebellious Boston and had settled in Quebec, "expecting to find there peace and quietness." Coffin was enraged to find the rebellion on his doorstep once more. When the explosion of cannon and bells erupted behind them in the dark city, he was the only man in the house who kept his head.

Someone else, one of the Canadians perhaps, saw the shadowy forms of Montgomery and his men filtering through the barrier and unleashed a choked cry of panic. There was a wild rush for the rear door, but John Coffin drew his sword and barred the way. Carleton had offered him a commission, but as a man of peace he had declined it. Now he decided that the offer gave him the authority to take charge

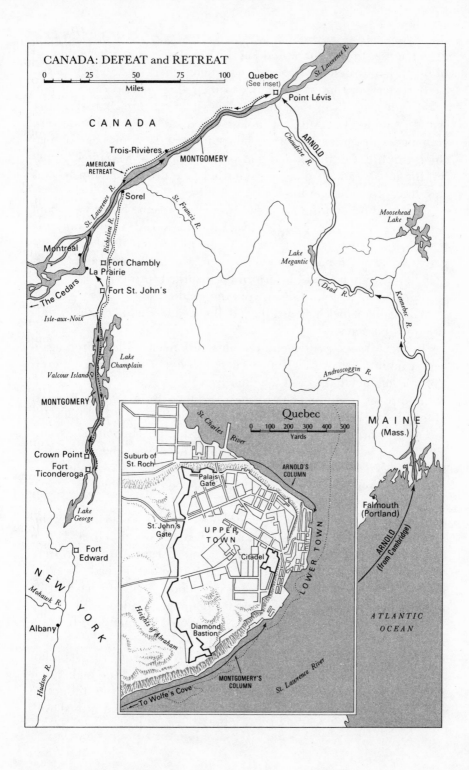

CANADA: DEFEAT and RETREAT

Miles
0   25   50   75   100

CANADA

Quebec
(See inset)
Point Lévis

Trois-Rivières
MONTGOMERY

AMERICAN
RETREAT

Sorel

St. Lawrence R.
St. Francis R.
Chaudière R.
ARNOLD

Moosehead
Lake

Lake
Megantic

Montreal
Fort Chambly
La Prairie
Fort St. John's
Richelieu R.

The Cedars
Isle-aux-Noix

Dead R.
Kennebec R.

Androscoggin R.

Lake
Champlain
Valcour Island

MONTGOMERY

Crown Point
Fort
Ticonderoga

Lake
George

Fort
Edward

MAINE
(Mass.)

Falmouth
(Portland)

ARNOLD
(from Cambridge)

ATLANTIC
OCEAN

NEW
YORK
Mohawk R.
Albany
Hudson R.

Quebec inset

St. Charles River

Quebec

Yards
0   100   200   300   400   500

Suburb of
St. Roch

Palais
Gate

ARNOLD'S
COLUMN

St. John's
Gate

UPPER
TOWN

Citadel

LOWER
TOWN

Heights of Abraham

Diamond
Bastion

MONTGOMERY'S
COLUMN

To Wolfe's Cove

St. Lawrence River

of the house. Vowing he would kill the first deserter and have the rest
of them shot by General Carleton, he ordered them back to their posts.

Barnsfare and his sailors slunk to their three-pound cannons and
stood with matches in their hands. He would not fire, Barnsfare declared, "till he was sure of doing execution." The cannon were
crammed with grapeshot—the eighteenth-century equivalent of ma-
chine-gun fire. Coffin nodded and posted himself at a window, assuring the jittery captain that he would not give the order until he was
sure the guns could not miss.

The road beyond the barricade running up to the house was about
twenty-four feet wide. Montgomery drew his sword, threw away the
scabbard, and turned to his men. "Come on, my good soldiers, your
general calls upon you to come on." Then, with McPherson and Cheesman beside him, he and his forlorn hope surged forward.

"Fire," snarled John Coffin from the window.

The cannon belched death, and the militia followed suit with a
volley of musketry.

In their frantic excitement, the amateurs reloaded and fired again
and again into the swirling snow. Then, in a total panic which not even
Coffin could quell, they ran for their lives.[21]

Two paces from the bank of the river, his arms extended, Richard
Montgomery lay on his back, with grapeshot in his brain. To his left lay
Jacob Cheesman, to his right John McPherson, forming a tragic trian-
gle. Twelve other members of the forlorn hope lay in the snow a few
feet away. The dazed survivors fled. Aaron Burr may have paused for
a moment to try to carry off Montgomery's body. But there is no evidence for the claim, made years later by his admirers.

On the other side of Quebec, Benedict Arnold was marshaling his
confused, battered companies for the assault on the barrier that
blocked their way into the Sault au Matelot. At least two cannon were
behind the barrier. The breathless Lamb gasped out the bad news that
he had abandoned the only American cannon. It would have to be
muskets and bayonets against twelve-pounders loaded with grape.
Roaring, "Now, lads, all together rush," Arnold charged into the cannon's mouth.

One gun went off with a belch of fire. A hurricane of grapeshot
whistled over Arnold's head. The gun had been aimed too high. Snow
had wet the powder of the other gun, and it sputtered and did not go
off. The cannon were reinforced by at least thirty men armed with

muskets, and they fired a fusillade of their own. Arnold pitched forward into the snow, writhing in agony. A bullet had ricocheted off one of the stone houses and ripped into the calf of his leg. Chaplain Samuel Spring rushed to his side and pulled him to his feet. A frantic conference ensued. Who would take command? The men called out for Morgan, and the other officers agreed. The chaplain begged Arnold to retreat to the hospital, but he furiously refused to leave.[22]

While his blood stained the snow, Arnold watched Morgan fling himself at the barrier, men with scaling ladders racing beside him. Muskets flamed through the barrier's loopholes, and men toppled into the snow. But one ladder reached the barrier, and Morgan went up it roaring, "Now, boys, follow me. Follow me." As his head cleared the fifteen-foot barrier, a blaze of cannon and musketry erupted behind it. For a moment, Morgan wavered there, illuminated in the fiery glare. Then he toppled backward off the ladder into the snow. Could any man have survived that point-blank blast?

Morgan did it, turning every American in the army into an instant fatalist. Powder from the cannon had blackened his face, and bullets had cut away part of his whiskers and his hair, but he was on the ladder again within a second, and this time he dived over the top before the astonished British had a target. Bouncing off a cannon, he rolled under it, while a dozen British bayonets lunged for him. Most of the blades glanced off the cannon, and before the soldiers could lunge again, other Americans were firing through the loopholes and leaping from the top of the barrier. A British soldier went down screaming with a wound in his head. Morgan was on his feet swinging his long rifle like a club. Other Americans drove homemade pikes at the astonished British, while Morgan roared, "Down with your arms if you want quarter."

The British fled into the nearest houses, but the Americans followed them and they swiftly surrendered. Surging up the narrow, twisting street, the Americans met a company of French-Canadian militia, wearing green provincial uniforms. Their captain was drunk, and the amateur soldiers threw down their arms and cried, *"Vive la liberté!"* [23]

Within five minutes, Morgan and his men had captured over a hundred prisoners. About three hundred yards ahead of them, they could see a second, higher barrier, blocking the way to Mountain Street and the Upper Town. Behind him, an exultant Arnold permitted

Chaplain Spring to talk him into retiring to the hospital. He did his best to hurry forward the men from other companies to support Morgan and his surging handful.

The sight of Arnold wounded upset many of the rank and file. John Joseph Henry heard, "We are sold," passed up and down the line. Nevertheless, their officers did their best to find their way down the confusing streets to where Morgan and his men were waiting for them. Henry Dearborn, still floundering through the drifts in the suburb of St. Roch, met Arnold on his way to the hospital. The Connecticut leader assured him that the town was practically captured. By now, Arnold was so weak from loss of blood two men were carrying him. Dearborn also met "wounded men very thick."

Struggling forward, Dearborn "got bewildered" in the winding streets of the Lower Town. He asked several men to help him, including some officers. They all refused. Finally, one of Benedict Arnold's waiters plodded past, leading some men with scaling ladders. They followed him. He had lived for years in Quebec, but he got lost, too. He finally confessed he did not know where they were and left them. "We were all this time harass'd with a brisk fire," Dearborn ruefully noted.[24]

Up ahead, Morgan and his men studied the next barrier, and debated what to do. A British lieutenant named Anderson came charging through a doorway in the barrier, calling upon the Americans to surrender. Morgan picked up his rifle and shot him through the head—a fantastic feat of marksmanship in the semi-dawn.

Anderson's panicked men dragged his body back through the barrier. Now, Morgan said, now is the time to charge. But his fellow officers disagreed. Their orders were to wait at this point for Montgomery and his men. The barrier was formidable, and less than half of their own detachment had reached them. The rest were blundering around the Lower Town. A repulse here could change the whole momentum of the battle. Wait for the New Yorkers, they argued, and when the men at the barrier saw a second column striking in from the flank, there was a good chance that they too would panic and surrender. Against his deepest instincts, Morgan agreed.

Down at the Potash, the stunned survivors of John Coffin's blockhouse blast shuddered on the other side of the palisade, beyond the range of those deadly guns. Coffin's blockhouse was now deserted and their route to the Lower Town was wide open. But none of the Americans knew this. Colonel Donald Campbell quickly made it clear that he had no interest in imitating Montgomery's example of daring leader-

ship. After a hasty conference with some company officers, Campbell
ordered a retreat. Within minutes, the whole column was in undig-
nified flight down the icy path to Wolfe's Cove.[25]

For a crucial half hour, Morgan and his men waited for Montgomery to appear. If they had pushed forward, Major Henry Caldwell later
admitted, they could have seized the entire Lower Town, even without
the aid of the New Yorkers. Caldwell had rushed to defend St. John's
Gate, and Allan Maclean had dashed to the Diamond Bastion, stripping
Carleton of his two best field officers. When word reached Carleton
that the Americans had penetrated the Lower Town, he almost collapsed. The widespread disloyalty among the Canadians made him fear
the worst.

Then Maclean returned from the Diamond Bastion to report that,
in his professional soldier's judgment, the attack there was nothing
more than a feint. Caldwell hurried back from St. John's Gate to tell
the shaken commander that the attackers there had vanished like so
much smoke after a few volleys of musketry and cannon. Next came
word from John Coffin that the Potash assault had been beaten off.
Carleton realized that the Americans in the Sault au Matelot were the
only threat. He threw the full weight of his 1,800-man garrison at
them.

When Morgan and his men tried to advance up the narrow street,
they met sheets of musket and cannon fire, pouring not only from the
barrier but from windows of houses along the way. Yet they fought
their way to the barrier, and Morgan actually mounted it. But what he
saw beyond it did not inspire him to repeat the heroics of the first barrier. At least seventy Royal Fusiliers waited with drawn bayonets, their
backs to the house walls. Muskets blazed from every window. When the
Americans fired back, nine times out of ten their triggers clicked fruitlessly. In spite of all their efforts to protect their priming pans, the
snow had wet their powder. In their desperation, many seized muskets
from the captured British and Canadians, but there were not enough
of them to go around.

Then the Americans noted that one house, a big stone structure
that was part of the barrier, had a door that opened into the end of the
street they held. At the other end of the house was a gable window that
looked down on the British side of the barrier. Here was a unique opportunity. The Americans seized the first floor of the house.

But Major Henry Caldwell was on the scene now, and he saw the
danger. He ordered a sailor to grab a ladder which the Americans had

placed on the inside of the barrier. The sailor planted it against the gable window, and a squad of bayonet-wielding regulars charged up it and into the house. In ten minutes of gory hand-to-hand fighting, they drove the Americans into the street, and the barrier was now impregnable.[26]

Their momentum gone, the Americans saw their best men toppling before the ferocious British fire. Captain John Lamb fell with half his face torn away by grapeshot. John Joseph Henry saw one of his officers lose three fingers from his hand as he was raising his gun to fire. Another officer reeled against the side of a building with a mortal wound, and young Simon Fobes asked him if he could help him. He was told to move forward.

Dawn was beginning to pale the sky, and it was obvious to all that they were targets in the narrow street. More and more men took refuge in houses—not exactly an offensive tactic. But even here the British fire had deadly effect. A captain from Pennsylvania, one of the most popular of Arnold's officers, was aiming his gun out a window when a bullet struck him in the heart. He stumbled back and fell dead upon a bed. At least fifty or sixty other men were dead or dying in the streets.

Carleton, now in complete control of himself and the battle, called for the coup de grâce. He sent 500 men out the Palace gate to attack the Americans from their rear. They collided with Dearborn and his lost company, still fumbling through the streets of the Lower Town. The British hailed him, and asked who he was.

"A friend," he said.

"Who are you a friend to?" they asked.

"A friend to liberty," Dearborn replied.

"God damn you," replied the questioner, and leaped out to fire at Dearborn.

"I clapt up my piece which was charged with a ball and ten buckshott," Dearborn said, "but to my great mortification my gun did not go off." The veteran of Bunker Hill discovered that not one gun in ten in his company would fire. It soon became obvious that he was surrounded and outnumbered six to one. There was no choice but to surrender.[27]

The British, led by Captain George Laws of the Royal Highland Emigrants, pushed on to attack Morgan's men. Laws charged up the street, sword in hand, and roared, "You are all my prisoners."

"How your prisoners? You are ours," the Americans answered.

For the first time, the excited Laws noticed that he was alone. The rest of his men were far behind him, struggling through the drifts. "Make yourself easy about that matter. They're all about here, they'll be with you in a twinkling," he said.²⁸

Some of the more skeptical Americans were inclined to shoot Laws on the spot. But their officers uneasily told them to hold their fire. In a few minutes, just as the captain had predicted, the street below them was swarming with British soldiers.

The heart went out of the surviving Americans. Only Morgan insisted that they could hold out until nightfall, when they could cut their way out with ease. Major Caldwell made this a dubious proposition by mounting a cannon in a nearby house, which began blasting holes in their houses of refuge. Then the shrewd Carleton sent them his personal promise of "good quarters and tender usage." The British moved up the Sault au Matelot, and in house after house exhausted, dispirited Americans gave up their guns. Finally, there was only Morgan, still in the street, his back to a wall, weeping tears of rage. A hundred British moved toward him with drawn bayonets. The officer in charge stepped forward and demanded his sword.

"Come and take it if you dare," Morgan roared.

The officer warned that he was thoroughly prepared to shoot him.

"Shoot if you will."

Morgan's appalled men pleaded with him. French-Canadians swarmed to gape at the spectacle of one man defying an army. Morgan's eye caught a man in black.

"Are you a priest?"

"I am."

"Then I give my sword to you. No scoundrel of these cowards shall take it out of my hands."

Even as this American Achilles was surrendering, Carleton sent another detachment charging into the suburb of Saint Roch to seize the American artillery battery. They captured it handily, the artillerymen running for their lives. Fired by the scent of total victory, the King's men raced through the suburb toward the general hospital, shouting, "Damn the dogs, we'll take them all." But one of the artillery officers from the abandoned American battery scratched together some stragglers, found a brass six-pounder, and replied, "You lie! Take that!" using a charge of grape for punctuation.

At the same moment, two reserve American regiments appeared, marching to replace Arnold's men at the general hospital. The British fled back into Quebec, while the Americans, aware by now that disaster had befallen Morgan and his men, ran in the opposite direction to warn Arnold and Dr. Sentner of an oncoming assault. Sentner had barely finished extracting the ball from Arnold's leg. It had lodged in the "muscle at the rise of the tendon Achilles," the doctor noted, not bothering to comment on the agony the operation without anesthesia must have caused the colonel.

In spite of his pain and the imminence of total disaster, Arnold was indomitable. He had just lost 454 of his best men inside Quebec—48 killed, 34 wounded, and 372 captured. The New Yorkers were in a state of panic only a step away from collapse, and Livingston's Canadians were in even worse shape. Dr. Sentner begged Arnold to retreat upriver to Montreal, or at least back into the country, where Carleton would be less inclined to pursue him. Instead, Arnold ordered a gun issued to every wounded man in the hospital. He loaded his pistols and told Sentner to place his sword on his bed. "He was determined to kill as many as possible if they came into the room," the awed young doctor later recalled.[29]

Carleton, unsure of how many men Arnold still had, declined to attack, remembering that this was the blunder by which the French had lost Quebec in 1759. He remained inside his walls, thoroughly satisfied with the victory he had achieved. The following day, January 1, 1776, he had the body of Richard Montgomery carried into Quebec and buried, along with his young followers, McPherson and Cheesman. Inside Quebec, behind the bars of the city jail, Captain Simeon Thayer of Massachusetts listed in his diary the thirty-nine officers besides himself who had been captured and "were all together in prison on the first of January, being a bad method to begin the New Year." [30]

II

Their Country— Rights and Wrongs

The defeat of those Americans who flung themselves at Quebec's icy walls shouting "Victory or death" underscores one of the least-known, least-absorbed aspects of the year 1776: the repeated failure of slogans and ideals in the face of determined opposition by men with opposing slogans, opposing ideals. But the question remains. What aroused city men like John Lamb, frontiersmen such as Daniel Morgan, aristocrats such as Richard Montgomery, boys like John Joseph Henry to this pitch of ferocity and daring? We have discounted the possibility that a subtle, all but metaphysical faith in their ability to change the mind of the British Parliament had much to do with it. Or that the $1.20 a year they paid in British taxes drove them to desperation.

Even if some of them were sufficiently learned to take a continental view of the situation, there was little statistical support for the charge of economic oppression. British taxes cost the 2,250,000 Americans of 1776 at most 3 percent of their over-all national income—between $3 million and $7 million a year. Moreover, most of these taxes were invisible, paid by seaport merchants as part of the cost of doing business and passed along to consumers as the price of that particular item when it was sold over the counter.

Since most of these items were what moralistic Americans called superfluities—expensive china and jewelry and furniture, the latest London fashions in ladies' dresses, cloaks, and wigs—unless a man was extraordinarily henpecked and could not stop his wife from buying such things, he could get along without them, and most people did. No reason here for daring death by frostbite and gunshot. Tea, a very popular beverage, did have a British tax on it—of threepence to the pound. But immense amounts of Dutch, Danish, and French tea— about £500,000 worth a year—were smuggled into America, and no doubt tasted all the sweeter for being drunk without paying the British tax. If a man had to buy British tea, he would have had to drink about a gallon a day before the threepence tax cost him as much as a dollar a year. It is hard to believe that any American was that addicted to tea.

By and large, taxation was the last thing the Americans had to worry about in 1776. Only one other nation in the western world enjoyed a lower tax rate—Poland. The explanation there was extreme poverty. This is hardly surprising if—again—we stop to think about it. The Americans had no navy and no standing army, nor did any of their cities possess more than a rudimentary part-time police force. The fire departments, where they existed, were manned by volunteers. There was no central government with an ever-expanding bureaucracy.[1]

Moreover, in the middle 1770s, the thirteen colonies were extraordinarily prosperous. Contemporary Americans simply have no concept of this thriving eighteenth-century economy. New England's balance of trade with the mother country was heavily in the colonials' favor. A few colonies, notably in the South, had an unfavorable trade balance, but this was because the gentleman plantation owners and their ladies could not resist buying those English "superfluities"—silver, porcelain, Chippendale furniture, superfine broadcloth and laces, silks and satins to decorate their houses and themselves. A hundred million pounds of tobacco—worth £800,000 sterling—were shipped to England each year, largely from Virginia and Maryland. The Carolinas and Georgia exported 150,000 barrels of rice and 750,000 pounds of indigo each year. In 1774, a single port—Philadelphia—shipped 200,000 bushels of wheat and 280,000 barrels of flour to England. The export-import trade between England and Virginia and Maryland alone totaled as much as £1,500,000 sterling in a single pre-revolutionary year. These are 1776 pounds, which translate into at least one hundred dollars in contemporary currency.[2]

Already southern Europe depended heavily on American rice and wheat for its burgeoning population. One out of every three ships for imperial commerce was being built in America (for about half the price of the cost of construction in England). The American iron industry was producing more pig iron and bar iron than Great Britain. A great merchant such as Philadelphia's Robert Morris had a fleet of ships and agents acting for him in all the major ports of the western world, and utilized the most sophisticated credit techniques with an acumen that would dazzle a contemporary international banker.[3]

The total value of English exports to the colonies in 1774, the last normal year, was £2,590,000 sterling. This was, in round figures, 20 percent of all the exports from England, Wales, and Scotland. Colonial exports to England totaled £1,920,950. America was a rich country in 1776.[4]

But none of the men at Quebec—Americans of such widely different colonies as Connecticut, New York, Pennsylvania, and Virginia—was fighting to overthrow the existing class structure, the goal of most modern revolutionaries. In the diaries and letters of the men who made the assault on Canada, there is not a single word about changing the social status quo. This should disturb the Marxist assumption that class consciousness is a prerequisite for revolutionary action. It may even surprise those who are not particularly interested in historical theory, but have absorbed a general assumption that a potentially revolutionary enmity inevitably exists between the rich and poor. Most Americans have not applied this assumption to the American Revolution, because of another equally vague and equally erroneous assumption—that the Americans of 1776 were more or less equal.

On the contrary, in each of the thirteen colonies a highly stratified society already existed, not much different from the one that exists today. In the northern colonies, the wealthiest 10 percent of the population owned about 45 percent of the property. In the South, although the upper class was larger, wealth was more concentrated in the hands of the well-to-do. In some parts of Virginia, North Carolina, and South Carolina, 10 percent of the taxpayers owned 75 percent of the property. This was hardly surprising. In 1776, American society was over one hundred and fifty years old. This was more than enough time for the ambitious and the gifted to accumulate wealth and pass it on to ambitious and gifted children.[5]

In fact, class distinctions were more obvious in 1776 than they are in contemporary America, two hundred years later. In the center of a major city such as Boston today, one would find it hard to distinguish at a glance the rich from the barely affluent, unless one has an expert knowledge of tailoring and fabrics. Not so in eighteenth-century Boston. Gentlemen like John Hancock were as conspicuously rich, not as they dared, but as they wanted to be. They, and their wives and chil-

dren, wore elegant imported silks and satins. Their homes were decorated with expensive wallpaper and furniture, and they rode around
the city in carriages worth the annual wages of a dozen workers. There
was very little criticism of this ostentation. In fact, most Americans
seemed proud of the fact that they had gentlemen who could rival the
splendor of English lords.

This kind of social distinction existed even on the frontier, contrary
to the American myth that the pioneers were the harbingers of equality. A typical frontier community in South Carolina, part of the district
called "East of the Wateree," was dominated by two men, John Chesnut
with 126 slaves and 10,000 acres of land, and Joseph Kershaw with
over 20,000 acres of land and 70 slaves. In the Mohawk River valley of
New York, Sir John Johnson ruled a colony of Highland Scots whom
his father, Sir William Johnson, had imported as tenants of his immense tract of land, on which his family lived like English nobility.
Presiding over western North Carolina were the Persons and the
Joneses, each of whom owned ernormous swaths of the countryside—
80,000 acres in the Persons' case. A young New Jersey minister of the
gospel, Philip Fithian, was amazed to find similar conditions prevailing
on the Pennsylvania frontier in 1775. At Sunbury on the forks of the
Susquehanna was a village of some hundred log cabins—except for the
house of William McClay, "which is of Stone, & large & elegant." [6]

Much more significant than this concentration of wealth was its
dispersion through the rest of the population. Some 40 percent of the
people were small independent farmers who largely supported themselves from their own land. When artisans, shopkeepers, innkeepers
were added to this group, there emerged a thriving middle class who
owned property worth about £400 on the average. This was modest
wealth in an economy where the average landless laborer earned £30 a
year. Above this pivotal group was an upper middle class of substantial
farmers, prosperous artisans, and professional men, largely doctors
and lawyers, who were worth between £500 and £1,000 a year. Less
than 20 percent of the population—in some states only 10 percent—
were on the poverty line, with less than £50 of property to their names.
Even in southern states such as Virginia, some 30 percent of the white
men owned farms of between 100 and 500 acres, the average being 230
acres.

Moreover, even between the extreme upper level of American society and the very lowest, there was not an overwhelming gap. A great
landowner, such as Robert Livingston of New York or Charles Carroll

of Maryland, might earn £1,800 a year from his estates, but there were lawyers in Charleston, Boston, and New York who earned twice as much from their practice, and a prosperous tavern keeper might easily clear £1,000 a year. Because aristocracy was not a legal reality, there was no built-in awe to add to the distance between the rich man and the poor man. In one section of New Jersey, for instance, three land-owners, each worth about £16,000, were far and away the richest and most prominent people in the neighborhood. But they associated freely with the "poor and industrious farmers and mechanics" who were their neighbors and on their farms set "a laborious example to their domes-ticks." The less wealthy neighbors were often seen "at the tables & in the parlours of their betters enjoying the advantage & honour of their society and conversation." [7]

One reason for this familiarity was the fact that poor or middling men had the power to vote for or against the rich man if, as many of the well-to-do did, he sought the right to represent them in the colony's assembly or become the town's first selectman. Contrary to the wide-spread idea that property qualifications limited the voters in colonial America, more recent research has inclined historians to conclude that almost anybody could vote if he was so inclined. In Massachusetts, for instance, anyone over the age of twenty-one who owned land yielding 40 shillings in rent a year or property worth £40 could vote. In states ranging from Massachusetts to New Jersey to Virginia, between 80 to 90 percent of the adult males could easily scrape together sufficient property to qualify as voters.

As Thomas Hutchinson, the governor of Massachusetts, informed a British official in 1772, the £40 "may be in clothes, household furniture or any sort of property . . . And even into that there is scarce ever any inquiry and anything with the appearance of a man is admitted [to vote] without scrutiny." An equally strong disinclination to challenge anyone who wanted to vote prevailed in the rest of America. Even in New York, where aristocrats were supposedly dominant, the latest re-search shows between 50 and 60 percent of the adult white males vot-ing in New York City. Previous generations of American historians were confused by the relatively small number of voters in American co-lonial elections. Only recently has there been a focus on the turnout in heavily contested elections, particularly in towns and cities where it was easy for men to get to the polls. The light turnout in the countryside was primarily attributable to the difficulties of traveling over wretched roads and more than normal voter inertia induced by rural isolation.

Even in our highly urbanized and overcommunicated society, seldom do more than 70 percent of Americans vote, and in state and local elections the percentage often slips below 50 percent.[8]

But there was a remarkable tendency throughout colonial America to elect men of distinction—which usually meant men of wealth—to political office. Even in Massachusetts, the most vigorously democratic of all the colonies, this was a visible fact. "Go into every village in New England," one revolutionary leader admitted, "and you will find that the office of the Justice of the Peace and even the place of [Assembly] Representative, which has ever depended only on the freest election of the people, have generally descended from generation to generation, in three or four families at most." [9]

In Virginia, to seek election to the House of Burgesses was to stake a distinct claim to social rank. Elections were often fiercely fought, but the contestants were invariably members of the gentry. Even among this class, the rule of deference prevailed. Of some hundred members who regularly attended the House of Burgesses in Virginia before the Revolution, only about twenty took an active part in the proceedings. Three families, the Robinsons, the Randolphs, and the Lees, provided most of the leaders. This tradition of deference was a kind of shadow cast by the aristocratically dominated society from which America had sprung. But politically there was an enormous difference between the New World and the Old World—and it is symbolized by that earlier description of the big New Jersey landlords setting "a laborious example to their domesticks" and sitting down to dinner with their laborers and less affluent neighbors. The American leaders were in intimate contact with the people they represented. The average American in a colonial assembly was elected by 1,200 people.

These figures make more understandable one of the first rallying cries of American resistance to British policy—"No taxation without representation." But by 1776 this idea had long since dropped out of the revolutionary debate. In fact, it was to some extent a fake even when Americans first shouted it. Americans never did have the least desire to be represented in the British Parliament, for reasons which will soon be clear. By 1776, both sides understood very well that Americans meant no taxation by England, period.

What did Americans have to complain about in 1776? The answer: Very little. With minimal taxes, they were living in the freest civilized society in the world. This pre-revolutionary freedom is something that many Americans no longer understand or remember. We have been bemused by revolutionary rhetoric from other traditions—from France, from Russia, and lately from China—into thinking that revolutions create freedom, an idea that a little historical knowledge of the French Revolution and a mild acquaintance with current events in Russia and China should refute. The American Revolution was fought for a different reason—to defend a free society which had been existing and slowly maturing for a hundred and fifty years.

In 1722, sixteen-year-old Benjamin Franklin wrote in his brother's Boston newspaper, "I am . . . a mortal enemy to arbitrary government and unlimited power. I am naturally very jealous for the rights and liberties of my country." On July 4, 1774, a Massachusetts farmer named William Prescott wrote, "Our forefathers passed the vast Atlantic, spent their blood and treasure, that they might enjoy their liberties, both civil and religious, and transmit them to their posterity. . . . Now if we should give them up, can our children rise up and call us blest?" Less than a year later, Prescott led fellow Americans against British cannon and bayonets at the battle of Bunker Hill.

The conviction that this free society was being threatened—this was the essential motivation that underlay the mixture of illusion and impulse and bravado in the minds and hearts of Montgomery and Arnold and Morgan and the men who followed them through the snow into the blood-spattered streets of Quebec. They were responding to an idea they had heard and read about for over a decade—an idea that had become a conviction. It had been declaimed in both houses of the British Parliament and pasted on the damp walls of London's twisting streets, repeated in pamphlets and sermons in America until it had inflamed thousands. The idea can be stated quite succinctly: There was a conspiracy by men in England to deprive America of her freedom, step by devious step.[10]

Was there anything to it? For the time being, let it suffice to say that a lot of intelligent Americans thought there was something to it. They could point to a fairly impressive collection of facts to support their suspicions. Since 1765, when the British passed the Stamp Act, their first attempt to tax the colonies directly, there had been a series of laws and regulations from London which seemed to point toward a comprehensive program aimed at the control and exploitation of Americans. True, the English repealed the stamp tax when Americans defied them, but they were back two years later with a wide-ranging set of taxes on paint, lead, tea, and other American imports. With these came a new customs organization, backed by vice admiralty courts in which

Americans were tried by royally appointed judges without a jury. Worse, the judges and the customs men were often little more than racketeers, and Americans who refused to pay them off—such as John Hancock of Boston and John Laurens of South Carolina—had their ships seized and their freedom threatened.[11]

Fierce American resistance, including massive boycotts of English imports, forced the mother country to back off once more and repeal all taxes but the one on tea. But the British returned to the contest by trying to give a government monopoly on tea sales in America to the financially pressed East India Company. The result was the Boston Tea Party, to which the British responded with a series of repressive laws that not only punished the entire city of Boston by closing the port, but changed the charter of the entire colony of Massachusetts. Almost all Americans found this hard line intolerable, and the confrontation between the two countries began.

Not all Americans agreed that this concatenation of men and events added up to a conspiracy. In the dawn of 1776, some thoughtful men were breaking their skulls studying the history of the relationship between Britain and America, the acts of Parliament, the decrees of the Privy Council and the Board of Trade, the actions of heterogeneous Royal Governors, trying to decide the question by looking carefully at the evidence. These were a distinct minority—hardly surprising— scholars have always been a minority in every country. Their influence was negligible in America for a psychological reason.

In 1776, England was still "the mother country," the English were still "our parents" for most Americans. But these terms no longer provided the sense of security that the child draws from his parents when he is small and helpless. America was neither small nor helpless in 1776, and for ten years the mother country had been acting like a domineering parent determined to keep a turbulent adolescent in line.

Benjamin Franklin summed up this prevailing American perception in a song which he wrote in 1771.

> We have an old Mother that peevish has grown,
> She snubs us like Children that scarce walk alone
> She forgets we're grown up and have Sense of our own
>   Which nobody can deny, deny
>   Which nobody can deny.[12]

This widespread feeling of resentment and unconscious anger led a vast number of Americans to believe in a British plot against America, without bothering to examine the evidence very closely. We shall see how these feelings were exploited more or less consciously by some and inadvertently by others to sustain the revolutionary impulse. Ultimately, we shall see that, like all emotional motivations, they had a built-in backlash which threatened the Revolution with extinction.

The men who assaulted Quebec compose a drama in miniature of the entire year 1776. There are Montgomery and his forlorn idealists, charging the cannon's mouth; there are the venal Campbell and his cowardly New Yorkers, running for their lives; there is Arnold, that volcanic combination of anger and energy, for whom the Revolution is an expression of his rage-ridden self. There is Morgan, the original primitive, ready to fight for almost any cause, and Henry, the seventeen-year-old in search of adventure.

But one man, essential to an understanding of 1776, was not at Quebec. George Washington summed up in his large frame a remarkably high percentage of the elements that composed the Revolution. This was as true on January 1, 1776, as it would be seven years later, when an exhausted England and a shaky United States of America signed a treaty of peace. Except for one thing: on January 1, 1776, George Washington was almost as much a captive of illusions as Richard Montgomery and the Continental Congress.

III

A General and His Illusionary Army

On January 1, 1776, one of Philadelphia's leading newspapers, the *Pennsylvania Packet,* compiled a list of the remarkable occurrences of the year 1775. One of them was an extremely biased account of the fighting that took place during the British retreat from Concord and Lexington on April 19.

> Two thousand veteran British soldiers were attacked and defeated by 300 peasants, and were saved from total destruction by running forty miles in one day.

The American peasants actually numbered 3,763. This bit of propaganda was followed by a slightly more accurate item.

> An army of Americans commanded by a Virginia FARMER locked up 10,000 British troops, commanded by three of the ablest generals in the British service.[1]

George Washington was considerably more than a Virginia farmer. He was the closest thing to a professional soldier that Americans had to offer in 1776. True, he had never run anything larger than a regiment, and had diffidently warned Congress that he did not think he was qualified to command an army in a war for a continent. But he had borne the title of Colonel in Command of Virginia's Armed Forces, and had briefly served as an aide-de-camp to the ill-fated British general, James Braddock, who declined to take the twenty-six-year-old colonel's advice about forest warfare, and was shockingly defeated in an ambush in western Pennsylvania. At the end of that imperial war, Washington had settled down to sixteen peaceful years as a farmer, contentedly married to one of the richest women in Virginia.

Thanks to his astute management of Martha Custis's estates, and his own not unsubstantial wealth both earned and inherited, by 1776 George Washington was one of the richest men in America. He owned 12,463 acres of prime Virginia soil and claimed 24,100 acres of unimproved western land along the Kanawha and Ohio rivers. He rode to hounds in a black velvet hunting cap decorated with a silk band and handsome silver buckle and a waistcoat of a superfine scarlet cloth and gold lace. He was, on the face of it, an unlikely candidate to lead a revolution.

At forty-three, Washington was rather far from being a young hothead. But he was somewhat younger than the average age of revolutionary leaders from the thirteen colonies, which was 47.6 years. His age was almost the exact average of the leaders of his home state of Virginia—43.6 years.[2] Washington's experience as a soldier, local Virginia politician, and landowner had given him several opportunities to see some of the glaring deficiencies and inequities of British government in North America. As a colonel in command of 700 Virginians, he had found himself unable to give orders to a man with a captain's commission in the British Royal Army. Washington was so infuriated he rode from Virginia to Boston in midwinter to settle the question with the British commander in chief. Washington won the argument, but when he asked for regular army commissions for himself and his fellow provincial officers, he was tartly informed, "His Majesty sends over officers to the various regiments that are to be raised." [3]

Another officer whom His Majesty had sent over, John Murray, Earl of Dunmore, the present governor of Virginia, had abruptly informed the retired colonel that all the titles to western lands won by himself and his men as bounties from a grateful Virginia legislature for their defense of the colony in the French and Indian War were null and void. The ostensible reason was that the man who surveyed the lands did not qualify as a surveyor, according to a strict interpretation of the statute. The real reason, of course, was Colonel Washington's determined stand with those Virginians who were resisting the British government's policy in North America.

From the very beginning of the clash with England over taxation and the power of royal government in the colonies, Washington had been a leader of the resistance in Virginia. In 1769, while Patrick Henry and others made speeches, he got on his horse and personally persuaded some one thousand Virginians to sign a solemn pledge not to import any item from England on which Parliament had levied a tax. A letter which he wrote to his neighbor, George Mason, during this year gives an even clearer glimpse of Washington's attitude. "At a time when our lordly masters in Great Britain will be satisfied with nothing less than the deprivation of American freedom, it seems highly necessary that something should be done to avert the stroke and maintain the liberty which we have derived from our ancestors . . . that no man should scruple or hesitate a moment to use a-ms in defense of so valuable a blessing on which all the good and evil of life depends is clearly my opinion. Yet a-ms, I would beg leave to add, should be the last resource, the dernier resort." [4]

The inner motivating force of the American Revolution is in that letter. The sarcastic reference to "lordly masters" reflects the encounters of Washington—and hundreds of other Americans in the upper level of colonial society—with the condescension too frequently displayed by royal officials and army officers.[5] The reference to a plan by these lordly masters to deprive Americans of their freedom is an equally apt summation of the firm American belief in a conspiracy among the men around the throne in England. Finally, the reference to "a-ms"—six years before a shot was fired—reflects the self-confidence generated by personal observation of the British army in action—an experience that had convinced Washington, and thousands of other Americans, that if the British resorted to force to settle the argument, the Americans were more than a match for them.

In the general orders that Washington issued to his men, there are other glimpses of American motivation. Urging discipline on them, he noted that "our unnatural Parent is threatening us with Destruction from every Quarter." The parent-child psychological dynamics already discussed and decades of American resentment against being treated as colonials, second-rate citizens, are submerged in that sentence. Exhorting the men to take more pride in their appearance, Washington pointed out that British troops were mercenaries fighting for "twopence or threepence per day only." Surely Americans could match them in neatness when they were fighting for "Life, Liberty, Property, and our Country." [6]

This direct formulation of American goals, with its unabashed use of the word "property," may make twentieth-century Americans uncomfortable. But the word meant to Washington and to thousands of Americans who owned far less land something much different from mere possession, self-aggrandizement. It meant control over their own lives, control over this vast rich continent, their country, which they and their ancestors had wrested from the wilderness over the previous hundred and fifty years. They also saw with an acuity which twentieth-century Americans have to some extent lost that the liberty of a man who did not control some property was a tenuous thing at best. This was the heart of American resistance to British taxation, and no one summed it up in more downright fashion than George Washington when he wrote to a friend in 1774, "The Parliament of Great Britain hath no more right to put their hands into my pocket, without my consent, than I have to put my hands into yours for money."

At the beginning of 1776, this tough stand involved Washington and most of his fellow Americans in a curious psychological balancing act. Although they were now most defiantly and aggressively using "a-ms" against the mother country, they stoutly maintained that this did not disqualify them as loyal subjects of the King. Washington was one of a growing number aware that this position was something of an absurdity. As he was soon to admit in a forthright letter, from the time he arrived in Cambridge on July 2, 1775, and learned the details of the savage battle fought on Breed's and Bunker hills on June 17, he was convinced that it was time "to shake off all connections with a state so unjust and unnatural." But Washington was also aware that the word "independence" had an unnerving effect on most Americans. This awareness in part explains General Washington's rather odd behavior on January 1, 1776.

Early in the day, he left his comfortable headquarters on Brattle Street in Cambridge, Massachusetts, mounted his horse, and rode to nearby Prospect Hill, where he presided at the raising of a new flag. It was a huge banner with thirteen alternating red and white stripes. But there were no stars in the upper corner. Instead, the combined crosses of England and Scotland gleamed in the brisk morning sunlight. Thirteen cannon roared a salute to this complicated symbol, clearly visible to every eye in British-occupied Boston. It testified to the uncertain stance of these thirteen united colonies, who were simultaneously fighting a war in Canada and waging a kind of nonviolent siege and blockade against 10,000 of the King's regulars in Boston. The flag affirmed America's determination to resist Britain's authoritarian pretensions—and at the same time somehow to maintain an allegiance to the ideal of a united British Empire.

For the commander of the "Grand American Army," as it was

sometimes called, the flag was "a compliment to the United Colonies," as he explained it to his friend and former secretary, Joseph Reed, who had recently left him for the politics of Philadelphia. The flag was also an act of bravado to conceal from the British the fact that his Grand American Army had almost ceased to exist. On this first day of the new year, Washington had exactly 5,582 men to man a ring of forts and batteries in a sprawling semicircle that ran from Prospect Hill through the town of Cambridge to Roxbury—some eight miles. Last night, the roads west and south were thronged with departing Americans, and many points in the lines were totally undefended.

For George Washington, the last days of the year 1775 had been a waking nightmare. "It is easier to conceive than to describe the situation of my mind for some time past," he told Reed, "and my feelings under our present circumstances. Search the vast volumes of history through, and I much question whether a case similar to ours is to be found; to wit, to maintain a post against the flower of the British troops for six months together, without ———, and at the end of them to have one army disbanded and another to raise within the same distance of a reinforced enemy. It is too much to attempt." [7]

The missing word, which Washington wisely omitted lest the letter be captured in transit by the British, was "powder." Major General John Sullivan of New Hampshire was with Washington on the day an aide rushed into his headquarters to report that there had been a miscount of the powder barrels. Instead of a reserve of 305, there were 90. "He was so struck he did not utter a word for a half hour," Sullivan said.

When Washington had taken command of the Grand American Army, it had numbered 16,667 men. But all of them were New England men, and they had volunteered, in the military tradition of their colonies, for a specific enlistment. Nothing was more sacred to a Yankee than a contract, and when their terms were up, they simply went home. The Connecticut men had gone first, on December 10, and then, on January 1, as Washington put it bitterly to Joseph Reed, "the same desire of retiring to a chimney corner seized the troops of New Hampshire, Rhode Island and Massachusetts."

This mass defection underscores one of the forgotten oddities of 1776. Although contemporary Americans celebrate it as the year of their national birthday, and the date has become synonymous with the Revolution and all its patriotic emotions, for Americans who lived through the revolutionary experience 1775, not 1776, was the year of great patriotic outpouring. Numerous witnesses testify to the frenzy of emotion that swept the continent when Americans heard that fighting had broken out at Lexington and Concord on April 19, 1775, and then escalated to the carnage of Bunker Hill two months later. From Massachusetts to Georgia, in cities, towns, and villages, militia companies assembled and drilled, and preachers and politicians hurled oratorical defiance against the British butchers.[8] But when the butchers retired timidly inside Boston and dug forts, and the army of volunteers that rushed so eagerly to the outskirts of the town did nothing but dig forts of their own, this ardor inevitably cooled. By January 1, 1776, helped by the winds of winter, the thermometer of patriotism dropped to something very much like its standard peacetime low.

This explains why Washington did not waste much time in emotional exhortations to his departing troops, although he let other generals try such appeals with no success. Instead, the American commander in chief tried to persuade Congress to head off the mass exodus by offering a bounty for re-enlistment. Continental privates were getting only $6.50 a month. But $40 for putting themselves on the line for another year might have worked wonders. Moreover, a bounty was traditional in New England to sign up troops.

But New Englanders were a minority in Congress, and they simply could not convince the delegates from the middle and southern states that they should part with the extra money. Congress swore that "before they would give a bounty they would give up the dispute." The majority of the nation's leaders were in the grip of the greatest American illusion of 1776—the belief that patriotism alone would inspire men in every walk of life to make heroic sacrifices—above all, to fill up the ranks of the army. Washington knew better. As a frontier military leader in the French and Indian War, he had learned that the average man thought in terms of his own self-interest as long as total disaster did not seem imminent. At one point in his attempts to recruit men, Washington had come close to being shot by his fellow Virginians. Now, fighting to defend America's freedom, he had voluntarily placed himself and his fellow soldiers under the command of the civilians in Congress, and he could only wearily submit to their myopic judgment.

When the harassed commander in chief tried to get permission from Congress to enlist his new army for the duration of the war, he got another barrage of criticism from the politicians in Philadelphia. New Englanders had supported him on the bounty. Now they were ferociously against him. John Adams said that only the "meanest, idlest, most intemperate and worthless New Englanders" would sign such a contract and give up "better living, more comfortable lodgings, more than double the wages." His cousin Samuel Adams declared that standing armies were "always dangerous to the liberties of the people." So Washington was ordered to limit the enlistment to a single year. Aside from the fears of the New Englanders, Congress adopted this policy because most of them were convinced that the war could not possibly last beyond a single campaign. Even Benjamin Franklin shared this delusion—in his case, he was sure that the British government would fall because Parliament would never vote the money for a second round. Washington and the men around him gave this one-year-war illusion a military twist. They saw the quarrel being decided in one titanic battle.

When regiment after regiment responded to the no-bounty policy by going home almost en masse, Washington feared that this titanic battle would be fought while he had only half or one-third an army. He asked Massachusetts to call out 5,000 militia to serve for one month in his denuded lines. Aside from their undependability, these militiamen added discord to the army because they got paid $36 a month, while his new regulars got $6.67.

Washington sent some officers from his skeleton regiments home to their districts, with the faint hope that they could recruit more effectively there. Yet, by calling up 5,000 militia, he was skimming away many of their potential volunteers. This was only the beginning of Washington's woes. He was having at least as much trouble with his top-ranking officers. On January 5, Major General Philip Schuyler wrote him from Albany, informing him that he wanted to resign. The reason: "Troops from the colony of Connecticut will not bear with a general from another colony. . . . I sincerely lament that a people of so much public virtue should be actuated by such an unbecoming jealousy, founded on such a narrow principle. . . . It tends to alienate the affections of numbers in this colony."

Like many intra-American quarrels in 1776, this one had an economic base. New Englanders disliked Schuyler's aristocratic style. He was one of the great Dutch patroons of New York, owner of thousands of acres of land in the Mohawk and Hudson River valleys. The Yankees also resented and disliked New Yorkers like Schuyler because they had beaten the New Englanders in a legal battle over the so-called New Hampshire Grants—the present state of Vermont. The area had been settled by New Englanders under grants from the Royal Governor of

New Hampshire in the 1750s and '6os, but George III in council had repudiated New Hampshire's claims and declared the land part of New York. Schuyler and many other prominent New Yorkers had made large speculative purchases of these disputed lands. But the Yankees refused to give up their farms and had exhibited an unlovely tendency to take potshots at any New Yorker who tried to claim them.

Schuyler was also disturbed by recruiting troubles in his Albany bailiwick. "I tremble lest Canada should be lost," he wrote, still unaware of the disaster of December 31 before Quebec. "If I could procure any men, I would send them to Canada immediately; but I know not where to get any. . . . The officers to whom I issued warrants to raise four companies meet with no success."

Washington's gorge must have risen at Schuyler's report of Yankee hostility. He had had a bellyful of intercolonial rivalries in the last six months. To his friend Reed he had written almost in despair early in November, "Connecticut wants no Massachusetts men in her corps; Massachusetts thinks there is no necessity for a Rhode Islander to be introduced into hers; and New Hampshire says it is very hard, that her valuable and experienced officers, who are willing to serve should be discarded." Three weeks later, after watching the Yankees jockeying for positions in the new army, he was even more depressed. "Such a dearth of public spirit and such a want of virtue, such stock jobbing, and fertility in all the low arts to obtain advantages of one kind or another . . . I never saw before, and pray God's mercy I might never be witness to again. . . . Could I have foreseen what I have, and am like to experience, no consideration upon earth should have induced me to accept this command." [9]

Anyone who thinks that patriotism and devotion to the Cause inspired the revolutionary generation to forget the differences and dislikes which have divided later Americans will abandon this myth after a brief reading of the correspondence of the leaders in the army and in Congress. At the beginning of 1776, Washington was typical in this respect, as he was in so many others. He had imbibed an antipathy for New Englanders before he reached Cambridge. Virginians in Congress found the delegates from Massachusetts and her satellite colonies very hard to take. Their self-righteousness, their stiff-necked argumentative ways, and their bigoted religiosity had been a stumbling block to revolutionary unity at the meeting of the First Continental Congress in 1774. One of Washington's best friends in Congress, Benjamin Harrison, wrote to him sympathetically. "Your fatigue and various kinds of trouble I dare say are great, but they are not more than I expected, knowing the people you have to deal with by the sample we have here."

Washington told Richard Henry Lee—a very bad choice for a correspondent, because he was intimate with many New Englanders, especially Sam Adams—that there was "an unaccountable kind of stupidity in the lower class of these [New England] people which, believe me, prevails too generally among the officers of the Massachusetts part of the army who are nearly of the same kidney with the privates." Either Lee or Joseph Reed, who was to prove himself anything but discreet later in 1776, was probably the source of the rumor in Congress that Washington and many others were bad-mouthing New Englanders. Congressman Eliphalet Dyer of Connecticut grumbled that his state's troops had "lost . . . all their fame and glory. You will scarce hear anything but execrations against them." Early in 1776, John Adams asked a Massachusetts officer, "Does every man to the southward of Hudson's River behave like a hero, and every man to the northward of it like a poltroon, or not? . . . I must say that your amiable general gives too much occasion for these reports by his letters, in which he often mentions things to the disadvantage of some part of New England, but seldom any thing of the kind of any other part of the continent." [10]

The New Englanders evened the score by querulously asking what was wrong with the famous Virginia general. Six months after he had taken command of the New England army, the British were still sitting in Boston unmolested. Why hadn't they long since been driven into the harbor?

If Washington had any shreds of illusions about patriotism as a motivating force left, a letter from Congressman Thomas Lynch of South Carolina dissipated them. Lynch inveighed against the "unaccountable and amazing supineness of all our state governments. Not a single individual anywhere . . . seems to consider himself as interested in public matters unless he can get money by them." Aside from the "continuance of the favor of Heaven," the only hope Lynch saw was "your vigorous exertions" and "the weakness of our enemies." He then reiterated the illusion that motivated the Americans before Quebec and Boston. "Should they [the British] lose footing in America this winter, I should despise their 30,000 Russians [rumored to have been hired by George III] scattered by storms, arriving, one transport after another, fatigued and debilitated by the fatal effects of a long voyage, without a spot to collect and recruit themselves for the field, and depending for every necessary on supplies from a country 3,000 miles distant." [11]

In his devotion to this fallacious strategy, Washington had been far more eager to storm Boston than Richard Montgomery had been to assault Quebec. But his fellow generals, in the councils of war he called, dissuaded him. Now, as his army dissolved in front of his eyes, the American commander cried out to Reed, "Could I have known that such a backwardness would have been discovered in the old soldiers to the service, all the generals upon earth should not have convinced me of the propriety of delaying an attack upon Boston till this time. When it can now be attempted, I will not undertake to say; but this much I will answer for, that no opportunity can present itself earlier than my wishes." He remained deeply pessimistic about when this opportunity would come. "Few people know the predicament we are in on a thousand accounts; still fewer will believe, if any disaster happens to these lines, from what cause it flows."

Still short of powder, Washington was now informed that the army was out of muskets. Attempts had been made to buy guns from the men who marched home, but the inspecting officers were ordered to buy only muskets that were worth the money. It was dismaying to discover how many of these soldiers had been on duty with old and defective guns for the previous six months. Only 1,620 muskets were considered worth buying, from almost 10,000 that were inspected. Now, musketless men, numbering over 2,000 by the end of January, were sent into the lines with spears.

What redoubled the grimness of the situation was the arrival, a day or two after the raising of the Grand Union flag, of the King's speech from the throne at the opening of the fall session of Parliament. Congress had, in the summer of 1775, sent a plea to the King—their second—asking a redress of American grievances. In Congress, and in the minds of George Washington and most other Americans, the argument was not with the King, or with the ideal of a united Empire, but with the greedy ministry, who had attempted to inflict their wrongheaded policies on America to expand their patronage and power. Since he had taken command, Washington consistently referred to the British in Boston as "the Ministerial army." Now Washington and his friends read the grim, threatening words uttered by the man whom they had been taught to revere as the lodestar, the center of gravity of the English world, the "father of their country." George III informed Parliament that he was determined to end "that desperate conspiracy" and "rebellious war . . . manifestly carried on for the purpose of establishing an independent empire." In a letter to John Hancock, the

president of Congress, Washington said, with something close to surprise, that the speech was "full of rancor and resentment against us,
and explicitly holds forth his royal will to be, that vigorous measures
must be pursued, to deprive us of our constitutional rights and liberties. These measures, whatever they may be, I hope will be opposed by
more vigorous ones."

As if the problem of trying to bottle up a 10,000-man British army
with half that number of men was not enough, Washington was constantly harassed with warnings, cries for help, and unsolicited advice
about crises in other parts of the continent. From distant Georgia came
a worried inquiry from Colonel Lachlan McIntosh. With 15,000 slaves
to control and a hundred miles of coast cut by eight rivers, Georgia had
less than 3,000 potential soldiers. Just across the border in the province
of East Florida, there were 500 British regulars "and 1,000 more expected there daily from Europe." To the west, there were the Creek,
Choctaw, and Cherokee Indians, "supposed to have at least 10,000
gun-men, brave, intrepid and eager for war, whom we shall have the
utmost difficulty to keep at peace." Already five British ships of war
and transports with 300 men were lying at the mouth of the Savannah
River. Georgia desperately needed men, but South Carolina was "already drained of such people as will enlist by their provincial regiments." North Carolina was their only hope, but, aside from distance,
how to persuade them was the problem. "Our currency passes in no
other colony but our own," McIntosh glumly noted, "and we have
received very little Continental money yet."

In fact, Georgia had received little of anything. "No kind of orders
or instructions from the General Congress, or Your Excellency; nor
have I yet been able to obtain even a copy of the American Articles of
War, which makes me at a loss how to act in many cases." Yet McIntosh
and his fellow Georgians were convinced that "our fine harbors, makes
the security of this colony, though weak in itself, the utmost consequence to the whole continent of America." [12]

Canada, especially Quebec, was constantly on Washington's mind.
He had given Arnold some of his best troops, and his reputation was,
to some extent, committed to that northern adventure. After a British
squadron burned Falmouth, Massachusetts (now Portland, Maine), in
November, half the towns and cities along the New England seacoast
had implored him for men and guns to defend them. He had refused
to fragment his army, but he had sent his second in command, Major
General Charles Lee, to advise them on defense.

From Rhode Island, Lee suddenly wrote to Washington about an entirely new worry. "The consequences of the enemy's possessing themselves of New York have appeared to me so terrible, that I have scarcely been able to sleep from apprehensions on the subject." Lee urged Washington not to wait for the approval of Congress to occupy New York. Send him there, he begged, with a regiment of Connecticut volunteers, which he could easily raise, if Washington would "lend me your name." Congress, Lee assured Washington, expects, in fact hopes, that he would "step in to their relief" on this delicate matter of interfering in the internal affairs of a sovereign state. "The delay of a single day may be fatal," Lee trumpeted.[13]

Washington, still nursing the bruises he had received in his struggle with Congress over re-enlistments, was not so sure about what they expected him to do. He asked Congressman John Adams, who happened to be back in Massachusetts, what he thought. Adams gave him a crisp go-ahead. New York was, he said, "the nexus of the northern and southern colonies . . . a kind of key to the whole continent."[14] Washington thought it over, added it to information he had from Boston that the British were fitting out transports with the obvious intention of sending one or two regiments somewhere, and information he had from New York that loyalists on Long Island were organizing military companies and defying the patriots, and other loyalists in New York City were boldly doing business with the King's ships anchored in the harbor. He decided to take the risk. He gave Lee the orders he wanted.

Then, on January 17, he opened another dispatch from Philip Schuyler in Albany. Washington's eyes leaped past the first sentence, with its apology for sending "this melancholy account," to the stunning words, "My amiable friend, the gallant Montgomery, is no more; the brave Arnold is wounded; and we have met with a severe check in an unsuccessful attempt on Quebec."

With Arnold hanging on in front of the city with only 700 men, there was desperate need for an "immediate reinforcement that is nowhere to be had but from you."[15] Washington may well have groaned with anguish at those words. Although his recruiting officers had brought in some more men, on January 10 he had to ask his Massachusetts militia to stay for another two weeks, instead of letting them go on the fifteenth, as he had planned. Then, to complete his own sense of personal humiliation, he had to ask the New England governments to call out thirteen more regiments of militia, to serve until April 1, when he vowed that he would have 10,500 men enlisted (although he felt he needed 20,000) or give up and retire to a wigwam in the west.

On January 9, when Washington still had only 5,582 men present and fit for duty, he slaked part of his passionate wish for an assault by ordering Major Thomas Knowlton of Connecticut to make a night attack on the British outworks at Bunker Hill. Knowlton and his men set fire to some houses which the British were using in Charlestown, just below Bunker Hill, took some prisoners, and returned before dawn without losing a man. Not only did the action raise American morale; it threw the baffled British off balance, and convinced them all over again that only an army with superior numbers would dare such risky, aggressive tactics.

Yet this minor victory did little to assuage the worries that gave Washington "many an uneasy hour when all around me are wrapped in sleep." It was not merely the insanity of his position and his very real fear of failure and disgrace that tormented him. Almost as troubling was his isolation. Although Martha Washington had arrived on December 15 to handle the not unimportant problems of entertaining visiting congressmen and local New England politicians, she was not someone with whom Washington could discuss the problem of sending reinforcements to Canada. To one of her lady friends at home, Martha wrote, "I confess I shudder every time I hear the sound of a gun." [16] Surrounded by New England men, Washington clung to the only Southerner in his household, thirty-year-old Robert Hanson Harrison of Maryland. But this obliging young man was in danger of being overwhelmed by the mountain of correspondence he was grappling with daily. Washington wrote to Joseph Reed expressing hope for his early return. Reed had told him he was only going to Philadelphia for a week or two to check up on a few law cases. He had succumbed to friends who told him he had a brighter future in politics than he could ever hope to win in Washington's military shadow.

In the third week in January, Harrison informed Washington that family problems were likely to call him home, too. Almost pathetically, the commander in chief wrote to Reed telling him that if Harrison should go, "I shall really be distressed beyond measure, as I know no persons able to supply your places in this part of the world, with whom I would choose to live in unbounded confidence. . . . At present my time is so much taken up at my desk, that I am obliged to neglect many other essential parts of my duty. It is absolutely necessary, therefore, to have persons who can think for me, as well as execute orders."

Reed stayed in Philadelphia.

Not burdened enough with the problems of trying to run his almost nonexistent army, Washington was also forced to become an admiral. From the moment he arrived in Boston, he saw that control of the sea was essential if the British were to be driven off the continent. He soon detached seafarers from his army and put them aboard ships with orders to go to work. The first of these vessels sailed under the most peculiar orders ever issued to a naval commander. "You," Washington told Nicholson Broughton, "being appointed a captain in the army of the United Colonies of North America, are hereby directed to take command of a detachment of said army and proceed onboard the schooner *Hannah* at Beverly."

Washington sent Colonel John Glover and men from his regiment of Marblehead sailors aboard two other vessels. By the middle of December, 1775, six more members of Washington's impromptu fleet were at sea. They were soon grabbing British supply ships by the dozen. The biggest capture, made by the most aggressive of his seafaring army captains, John Manley, was the brigantine *Nancy*. In her hold were 2,000 muskets, 31 tons of musket shot, 3,000 round shot, several barrels of powder, and a thirteen-inch brass mortar, which was called "the noblest piece of ordnance ever landed in America" and promptly christened the "Congress."

Manley made the headaches Washington had with other ships and crews worthwhile. He reported to the president of Congress that the crews of two ships had actually deserted them, and "every time they come into port we hear of nothing but mutinous complaints. . . . I do believe there is not on earth a more disorderly set." Always eager to reward talent, on January 1, 1776, Washington appointed Manley commodore of his fleet, and sent him aboard the schooner *Hancock*. Like the army, the crews of the ships had gone home at the end of their enlistment, and Manley had to find new seamen. Washington also had to find new commanders for practically all his ships. This was not easy. The success of Manley and other captains emboldened numerous sailors in Massachusetts, Rhode Island, and Connecticut ports to ship out aboard privateers, hoping not only to strike a blow at the British, but to make their fortunes. It was the beginning of a business that soon obsessed avaricious New Englanders to the point of stripping Washington's army of badly needed men. Why sweat or freeze as a private for $6.67 a month when with a little luck a man could make twenty times that aboard a privateer? For the time being, Washington was pleased by this New England aggressiveness at sea because it applied economic screws to the British in Boston. On February 26, 1776, no less than fifteen British ships were advertised for sale at Ipswich alone. The following month, twelve others went under the hammer at Plymouth.[17]

Washington's inclination to pessimism and his disillusionment with New Englanders made him less enthusiastic about the naval project of a Connecticut man named David Bushnell. He supported it halfheartedly by allowing Bushnell's brother, Sergeant Ezra Bushnell, to go home on special leave to Saybrook, Connecticut—actually to the western portion of that town now known as Westbrook. Ezra was needed by his brother David to operate a secret weapon that he believed could win the war for America before it really started. At Yale, David Bushnell had displayed remarkable mathematical and scientific talent. While still a freshman, Bushnell had demonstrated to several members of the faculty that gunpowder could be exploded under water—a fact which they refused to believe until they saw it.

During the summer of 1775, David Bushnell journeyed to Boston, trying to decide whether he should join the American army. Surveying the situation from one of the hills overlooking the occupied city, he instantly saw that the existence of the British army depended on the British fleet. What if those men-of-war riding at anchor suddenly blew up and sank, one by one, destroyed by underwater torpedo attacks? The panic-stricken British would flee the American continent instantly. What was the best way to get a torpedo—the term to Bushnell meant simply a cask of powder timed to go off under water—beneath a British ship? By submarine. All right, said David Bushnell to himself, he would go home to Saybrook and build a submarine.

Before the end of 1775, he had completed the outer hull and stored it on an island in the Connecticut River. It was shaped like a top, measuring seven and a half feet in length and six feet in width. The hull was made of oak timbers six inches thick, bound with iron bands and thoroughly coated with tar to make it watertight. Bushnell described it as resembling "two upper tortoise shells of equal size, joined together; the place of entrance into the vessel being represented by the opening made by the swell of the shells at the head of the animal." Bushnell christened her the *Turtle.*

Inside the *Turtle,* a transverse beam served as a seat, and also reinforced the sides against the pressure of the water during a deep dive. A broad iron band was sunk into the wood of the hull at the hatch, to give additional support against potentially deadly pressure. A brass hatch cover was hinged to the iron band. The hatch could be screwed down until it was thoroughly watertight. In the collar of the hatch were some six glass portholes, each about the size of a half dollar. These gave the one-man crew of the *Turtle* enough light to see his navigating instruments. In the darkness beneath the surface, he could still see his depth gauge and compass because they were illuminated with a phosphorescent weed known as fox fire.

To maintain the *Turtle*'s stability, Bushnell had built 700 pounds of lead into the base. Two hundred pounds of this ballast was detachable, which meant the submarine could surface instantly if she got in trouble. Ordinarily, she could be brought to the surface by pumping her bilge tanks dry. For propulsion, the *Turtle* had a screw propeller twelve inches long and four inches broad, which was revolved by a crank turned by the operator inside the craft. A vertical propeller, slightly smaller than the horizontal one, was fitted to a shaft in front of the conning tower, providing the *Turtle* with stability under water, achieved by modern submarines' hydroplanes. There was enough air in the *Turtle* to stay under water for a half hour.

In December, 1775, David and Ezra Bushnell began making test dives with the *Turtle* in the Connecticut River. Bushnell himself was a frail man physically, in contrast to his husky brother Ezra. This is why he persuaded Ezra to become the *Turtle*'s crew. It required a lot of energy to propel the craft through the water.

The Bushnells tried to keep their work a secret. But they did tell one friend, Dr. Benjamin Gale of Killingworth, what they were doing. Gale, carried away by local pride, wrote to Congressman Silas Deane in Philadelphia, describing the submarine in detail and discussing the inventor's difficulties in perfecting her. The tavern keeper and postmaster in Killingworth was a loyalist, and he opened Gale's letters, made copies, and forwarded them to Governor William Tryon of New York. Tryon did not take the threat very seriously. He wrote to Vice Admiral Molyneux Shuldham, commander in chief of the British squadron in North America, "The great news of the day with us is now to Destroy the Navy, a certain Mister Bushnell has completed his Machine. . . . You may expect to see the Ships in smoke." Apparently Admiral Shuldham did not think the letter worthy of a reply.

Early in 1776, Bushnell and his brother took the *Turtle* out into Long Island Sound, where, they assumed, they would have conditions approximating those of Boston Harbor. The *Turtle* was lowered into the water from the deck of their sloop, and Ezra Bushnell entered it, screwed shut the hatch, and slowly submerged. He sank to the bottom, rose, circled the sloop, and bumped the nose of the *Turtle* against its hull under water. Ten minutes later, he emerged from the hatch, smiling confidently. The two brothers shook hands. The world's first submarine was a reality. Now all they had to do was figure out how to attach the torpedo to the hull of a British man-of-war.[18]

Another New Englander who stirred more enthusiasm in George Washington was also far away from Boston. In fact, if someone had chanced to observe Henry Knox, the burly, two-hundred-and-fifty-pound commander of the American artillery on New Year's Day, 1776, he would have wondered what in God's name he thought he was doing, boring holes in the ice of the frozen Hudson River near Albany. But the self-taught artilleryman, who had learned his trade largely by reading about it in his Boston bookshop, knew precisely what he was doing. He had 119,900 pounds of cannon to get across the Hudson, and boring holes in the ice was, paradoxically, a way of strengthening it by allowing the river to flood over the already formed shell.

For the better part of December, artilleryman Knox, with the help of his brother William and some eighty-two sleds and eighty yoke of oxen, had been shipping, shoving, and dragging fifty-nine cannon from Fort Ticonderoga, at the head of Lake George, down to Albany, where, freezing weather permitting, they hoped to cross the Hudson and haul these iron monsters over the Berkshires and across western Massachusetts to Washington's army at Cambridge. Without these guns, Washington's hope of driving the British out of Boston was practically nil.

Optimistically, Knox had guaranteed the commander in chief that he could get the guns to Boston in seventeen days. They had now been on the road for more than three weeks, and there was still the Hudson to cross. More alarming was a shortage of available teamsters and oxen for the wagon train. As usual, the source of the scarcity was money. The local folk wanted considerably more for each span of horses or oxen than the twelve shillings per day Knox was authorized to pay. Only the patrician authority of Philip Schuyler enabled him to beat down the twenty-four shillings a day that was being asked, and by December 31, 124 pairs of horses and sleighs were gathered from the countryside around Albany.

A "cruel thaw" made the crossing a dubious risk. But the impatient Knox, thinking of Washington practically stripped of men before Boston, decided to take a chance. It was jittery work all the way. As each gun crossed behind the straining horses, a teamster with a hatchet walked alongside it, ready to cut the rope to save the horses if the ice started to crack. Almost miraculously, all the guns, even a monster that weighed 5,500 pounds, got across except one, a "noble 18," as Knox called it, which plunged through weakened ice at Half Moon or Lansings Ferry, near the present town of Waterford.

Knox abandoned a sumptuous New Year's Day dinner at General Schuyler's mansion and rushed to the scene. Summoning reinforcements of men and horses, he dragged the gun out of the relatively shallow water. A few days later, another gun broke through, in deeper water, and it took a day and a half of herculean labor in freezing weather to drag it out. Knox, grateful for the help of Albanyan volunteers, christened the gun the "Albany."

By January 5, Knox was organizing his line of march for the push through the Berkshires. In some ways, this was more harrowing than the Hudson crossing. It was bad enough struggling up the snow-covered hills, but going down the other side with a sled carrying several tons of cannon always threatening to run over you was terrifying. On the steeper slopes, the teamsters had to lash ropes to the heavier sleds, and continually throw drag chains and poles under their runners, while they moved the ropes from tree to tree, literally inching down the roller coaster-like hills. At one point, a group of teamsters threw up their hands and swore that they would not risk another foot. But Knox, with that combination of tact and leadership which every American military man needed so badly at this time, argued and pleaded for three hours, and cajoled them into staying with the job.

The artillery inspired delusions of military grandeur as it moved through the small towns of western Massachusetts. The locals fondled the guns and talked excitedly about the punishment they would give the British. The favorite was the Old Sow, as everyone called a huge, fat twenty-four-pound mortar. Occasionally, hoping to heighten patriotic fervor, Knox fired the monster. But no one was shocked into volunteering for Washington's army. "What a pity," Knox told a group of militia officers at Westfield, "that our soldiers are not as numerous as our officers."

At Springfield, most of Knox's New York teamsters quit in spite of all his powers of persuasion. Another thaw had turned the roads into mud, nullifying his usual plea of "just a few days more." So he had to recruit another brigade of Massachusetts teamsters, who made the rest of the haul to Cambridge by the end of January. Proudly, Knox pre-

sented to his beaming commander in chief "a noble train of artillery,"
plus a carefully itemized bill for £520.15.8¾—a small price to pay for
such a feat of military engineering and leadership. For his reward,
Washington handed Knox his official commission, approved by
Congress in his absence, making him commander of the American artillery.[19]

The rest of the American army, which Washington earnestly called
"Continental" in spite of the fact that statistics showed it to be 90 percent New England, inhabited a world considerably different from the
one that harried their commander in chief. The privates and junior
officers had more mundane things to worry about, such as where to get
firewood to cook their food and where to find shelter from the Massachusetts winter. By the end of the year 1775, the army had consumed
every fence post and tree within a square mile of Cambridge, and
Washington worried about the possibility that they might start on
houses. With 117 cords of wood being burned each day and men
scarce, it was difficult for the army to chop its own wood. Nearby
townships had been ordered to supply 88½ cords daily, and this was
soon raised to 120. "Many regiments have been obliged to eat their
provisions raw, for want of fuel to cook it," Brigadier General Nathanael Greene informed the former governor of Rhode Island, now a
Continental Congressman, Samuel Ward. Worse, Greene noted, "the
barracks have been greatly delayed for want of stuff. Many of the
troops are yet in tents and will be for some time, especially the officers." It was hardly surprising that "a multitude of soldiers [were]
heartily sick" of army life.[20]

Confirmation of the general's observation can be found in the numerous diaries and letters of the ordinary Americans who were serving
in the ranks. Ex-shoemaker Joseph Hodgkins of Ipswich, Massachusetts, a thirty-two-year-old lieutenant in the Twelfth Massachusetts Regiment, told his young wife that his tent "smocked
[smoked] very bad in the storme . . . for the rane runs douen the
chimbely so that we cannot keep any fire." Of the fifty-one men whom
Hodgkins and his captain, Nathaniel Wade, had led from Ipswich the
day fighting broke out at Lexington, on April 19, 1775, only twenty-
eight remained in the company. For a while, toward the end of the
year, Hodgkins was as worried about the future as George Washington.
"If we due not exarte ourselves in this gloris cause our all is gon and we
made slaves for ever." Yet Hodgkins stuck to his job, although he was
still living in a tent on February 12, when he wrote to his twenty-five-

year-old wife, Sarah, "I must be short for the weather is very cold and our tent smoks so that it is with defelty that I can stay in it." [21]

Hodgkins had fought at Bunker Hill, where "one ball went under my arme and cut a large hole in my coate & a buckshot went throue my coate & jacket." He feuded constantly with Captain Wade, a bachelor, because the captain tended to hog the furloughs, leaving poor Hodgkins nothing to do but write to his Sarah, "I whant to see you very much." But he continued to ship Sarah his laundry, as well as socks and shirts that needed mending. "I fear I shall weary you," he wrote nervously. But Sarah, who was his second wife, assured "Mr. Hodgkins" that she was returning a mended "shirt and pair of briches" and pledged herself "your most afectionate companion till death."

There were times when Sarah could not conceal her feelings about their long separation. At one point, she warned him that if he did not "alter your mind about staying all winter" it would be "such a disappointment that I can't pute up with it." With that relaxed eighteenth-century frankness which makes one wonder about our so-called sexual revolution, she did not hesitate to tell him why she could not "pute up with it." A few weeks later, she added in a P.S., "Give regards to Capt. Wade and tell I have wanted his bedfellow prety much these cold nights that we have had." [22]

Her spirits were certainly not raised by the letter which Hodgkins wrote to her on January 7. "It is a good deal sickly among us we bured Willeby Nason last Thusday John Sweet is very sick in camp and Josiah Persone . . . is just moved to the hospittle. John Holladay died last Thusday night. There was five buried that day . . ." The following day, he wrote her more of the same bad news. "A grate many die verry sudden." He could only hope that "God will apear for us and remove the pestelance."

Benjamin Thompson, the brilliant twenty-three-year-old Harvard-educated scientist who deserted to the British on October 13, 1775, after Washington declined to give him a commission in the American army, explained in scathing terms why the "mortality" among the Americans was "very great." Without women to do their washing for them, they "choose rather to let their linen, etc., rot upon their backs than to be at the trouble of cleaning 'em themselves. And to this nasty way of life, and to the change of their diet from milk, vegetables, etc., to living almost intirely upon flesh, must be attributed those putrid, malignant and infectious disorders . . . which prevail with unabating fury." [23]

Twenty-four-year-old Joseph Perry, chaplain to a Connecticut militia regiment, "found the hospital a disagreeable place; a dead man at
the door. . . . Groans from within from distress both of body & mind.
. . . Prayd at four places at the desire of the sick." The following week
he presided at the funeral of one of the men for whom he had prayed,
a "sarjant" from Southington. During his sermon at the grave, he noticed "a young lad about sixteen who appeared much affected; wept
some tho silently." The sympathetic chaplain asked who he was. The
answer: the sergeant's son.

It was that kind of war. Fighting so close to their homes, the soldiers
had a steady stream of sons and nephews and cousins pouring in and
out of camp. They sent home for items in short supply, such as sugar
and coffee. One ensign asked for "a young pig to roast." In general,
however, the food was the one consolation of these amateur soldiers.
Captain Wade's orderly book shows him issuing one pound of fresh
beef or three-quarters of a pound of pork or one pound of salt fish per
day, a pound of bread or flour, three pints of peas or beans per week,
and a quart of beer per man per day. Lieutenant Hodgkins' letters
frequently speak of "a fine peas of beaf," and on January 2 he told his
wife, "We have ben to supper on a fine turky."

Such feasting would soon be a thing of the past for American soldiers. Like almost everyone else, Massachusetts farmers had lost the
1775 glow and were charging the army higher and higher prices. On
December 31, 1775, Brigadier General Nathanael Greene raged to a
friend, "We find many articles of merchandise multiplied four fold
their original value . . . the farmers are extortionate wherever their
situation furnishes them with an opportunity." [24]

Another officer who stayed to greet the New Year was twenty-year-
old Lieutenant Nathan Hale of Connecticut. A teacher in a prosperous
school in New London, he had not rushed to Massachusetts with the
first regiments that marched within a few days of the fight at Lexington
and Concord. He had waited until school closed and then obtained a
commission in the Seventh Connecticut Regiment as a first lieutenant.
The motive for his volunteering was similar to that of many other intelligent Americans of the time. Not a wild rush to the barricades, but a
thoughtful commitment, tinged with reluctance. One of his Yale class-
mates, Benjamin Tallmadge, wrote a letter to Hale shortly before he
joined the army discussing the situation and undoubtedly echoing
many of Hale's feelings. Tallmadge, too, was teaching school, and had
gone to Boston to survey the situation personally before he wrote his

advice to Hale. He began by discussing with his "brother pedagogue" the difficulties of abandoning a profitable career and "so agreeable a circle of connections and friends" to join the army. "On the other hand, when I consider our country, our land flowing as it were with milk & honey, holding open her arms & demanding assistance . . . I think the more extensive service would be my choice."

The letter strikes a theme that was repeatedly echoed in the diaries and letters of other thoughtful Americans. They were keenly aware that they were in possession of rich country. It made the argument for a British plot to get their hands on this wealth seem all the more plausible.

Hale chose the more extensive service and arrived at Cambridge late in September, 1775. He was soon criticizing the disorganized state of the army. "It is of the utmost importance that an officer should be anxious to know his duty, but of greater that he should carefully perform what he does know," he wrote in a diary he kept sporadically. "The present irregular state of the army is owing to a capital neglect in both of these." He also fretted about being separated from a dark-haired young widow named Alice Adams. But otherwise, Hale, a convivial young man, enjoyed camp life and admitted it. After reading his cheerful letters, friends such as Gilbert Saltonstall of New London were soon wishing they could join him. But Saltonstall's father did not think the emergency warranted sparing him from the family business.

When the re-enlistment crisis struck at the approach of the New Year, Hale did everything in his power to persuade the men of his company to stay. He noted in his diary that he "promised the men if they would tarry another month they should have my wages for that time." After a visit home over Christmas and New Year's, he was back in camp on January 4, itching for action. He wrote to his ensign, George Hurlbut, on that day, "Sir, I hope the next time I see you, it will be in Boston, a Drinking a glass of wine with me. If we can but have a Bridge we shall make a push to Try our Brave courage." [25]

If more of the officers were like Hale, Washington would not have despaired of creating a professional army. Unfortunately, too many other New Englanders seemed more interested in making money or playing politics. Joseph Hodgkins was constantly asking his wife to send him some "shothread" because he had a buyer for a new pair of boots. Lieutenant Jabez Fitch of Connecticut had a neighbor drive two fat oxen from Norwich to his post at Roxbury, where he sold them for £13.3. Fitch frequently joined his fellow officers to petition Washington against the appointment of a certain lieutenant, or inform him that in their opinion they should be permitted to cut wood on Tory land. Washington, unacquainted with the New England town meeting, condemned "this mode of associating and combining, as subversive of all subordination . . . and order." Fitch found it almost impossible to discipline his men. He was always ready to argue on behalf of the offenders. When one man was put in jail for firing his gun in camp, an offense which Washington had forbidden at least a dozen times, Fitch did his utmost to get the sinner out of the jug. "Yet after all poor Bedwell lay confined till morning," Fitch informed his diary.

Fitch was often at gatherings where "the gin sling passed very briskly" and on two occasions was "catched" by the officer of the day carousing with his fellow lieutenants and captains in the guardhouse. Although the atmosphere of the camp, with its abundance of preachers, was intensely religious, Lieutenant Fitch was not above ranging "beyond the Punch Bowl Tavern to find . . . some white-stockinged women, etc." Seventeen-year-old David How, a leatherworker from Methuen, noted in his diary that a man was "found dead in a room with a woman this morning. It is not known what killed him." He also noted the story of a "drinking bout" between two men in Cambridge who "drinkd so much that one of them died in about one hour or two after." [26]

The Reverend Joseph Perry informed his diary of "a merry story" which he decided was "for substance undoubtedly true." It seemed that a certain soldier was put under guard for some minor infraction of duty. His captain found that the delinquent had performed well at the battle of Bunker Hill, and had been a reliable soldier throughout the rest of the year and—even more admirable—had re-enlisted. À la Lieutenant Fitch, he therefore went to Washington to "plead the delinquent off." Washington listened with his usual gravity, and decided to grant a pardon. Whereupon the delinquent made a curtsy. The astonished commander in chief and the captain started asking questions, and discovered they had a female volunteer on their hands—"a poor woman from Boston enlisted into the service to gain a subsistance &c."

Women who attempted to accompany their men to camp in skirts found the military routine a dreary experience. The wife of Fitch's colonel, wealthy Jedediah Huntington, became so depressed she killed herself. Martha Washington seldom ventured from headquarters, the comfortable house of loyalist John Vassal. She devoted herself to planning dinners for visiting politicians and generals. She was seen in public only on Sundays, when she and the general went to church.

At Martha's request, a special service was held on January 1 in Christ Church. Instead of a prayer for the King, which most ministers had abandoned, Mrs. Washington had Colonel William Palfrey read a special exhortation: "O Lord, our Heavenly Father, High and Mighty King of Kings and Lord of Hosts, who has made of one blood all the nations upon earth . . . most heartily we beseech Thee to look down with mercy upon His Majesty George III. Open his eyes and enlighten his understanding, that he may pursue the true interest of the people over whom Thou in Thy providence has placed him. Remove far from him all wicked, corrupt men and evil councilors, that his throne may be established in justice and righteousness . . ."

The church was a grim comment on the chances of this prayer being heard. Because it had been identified with loyalism, as most Episcopal churches were throughout the continent, soldiers had been quartered in it; doors had been ripped off, windows shattered, and the organ destroyed. All but two of the congregation had fled into Boston to the dubious protection of the British army.

IV

All the King's Unhappy Men

For the men in the ranks of the British army in Boston, the New Year began in the gloomiest possible way—with courts-martial. Privates Thomas Owen and Henry Johnston were sentenced by General William Howe "to suffer death by being hanged by the neck until they are dead." They had broken into and robbed the store of another branch of that staunch family of loyalists, the Coffins. Other sentences were almost as grim. Private Thomas MacMahon learned that he would receive one thousand lashes on his bare back with a cat-o'-nine-tails "for receiving sundry stolen goods, knowing them to be such." His wife, Isabella, who was a partner in the crime, was allotted "a hundred lashes on her bare back, at the cart's tail, in different portions and the most conspicuous parts of the town, and to be imprisoned three months."

MacMahon's agony was equaled by Private Timothy Spillman, who was also sentenced to a thousand lashes for "an assault on the person of Mrs. Moore" and "beating her almost to death."

Privates Thomas Jones and William Eves were given eight hundred lashes each for breaking and entering a private house, and stealing from it. Private John Witherspoon got five hundred lashes for lifting a piece of linen from the shop of Archibald Wilson and a shirt from a sergeant of the marines. Private John Brown got the same dose for "mutiny," and probably considered himself lucky, since this was a hanging charge in time of war.[1]

The bitter weather, and the constant duty on the lines, added to the somber mood of officers and men. Gloomiest of all were the regiments stationed upon Bunker Hill. From this long, narrow ridge, better known as Charlestown Neck, guarding the garrison's right flank, officers and men could look down upon the slopes of Breed's Hill and the rail fence where their comrades had suffered over a thousand casualties attacking entrenched Americans on June 17, 1775. It was the memory of Bunker Hill, more than anything else, that kept the British inside Boston on a strict defensive.

Captain Francis Rawdon, a twenty-one-year-old Irish nobleman, very much in love with martial glory, had distinguished himself on that bloody field, leading the grenadiers of the Fifth Regiment forward after an American bullet felled his company commander. There was little of martial fire or glory in the letters Rawdon wrote home from Bunker Hill in the last months of the year 1775. "It is very bleak at present upon these heights, and the duty of the officers is severe. At our lines neither officer nor man have the smallest shelter against the inclemency of the weather, but stand to the works all night. . . . In general every man goes to his own tent very soon after sunset, where those who can amuse themselves in that manner read; and others probably sleep. . . . We hear with some envy of several little balls and concerts our brethren have had in Boston. Many officers as well as private men have been very ill with fluxes, agues and other disorders . . . from the damp and cold." [2]

In Boston, to which Lord Rawdon returned on December 13, he soon discovered there was a more absorbing topic than balls and theatricals: food. One officer told friends in London, "With regard to diet, we are obliged to live on salt beef and salt pork, much the greater part of which is hard as wood, rotten as carrion, and as rusty as the devil. Could we have good beer, it would in some measure, prevent their pernicious effects and alleviate the hardships we labour under; but that is impossible, our only beverage being new rum or spruce liquor, which soon throws us into the bloody flux and runs us off our legs in a few days, and has made the remains of our famished army look like so many regiments of skeletons." [3]

Lieutenant Martin Hunter, another officer who had distinguished himself at Bunker Hill, told of one officer killing a foal, roasting it, and inviting a party to dinner. A major's fat mare was stolen, "killed and sold in the market for beef." [4]

Worse off were the civilians, especially those who supported the American cause. John Andrews, who had sent his wife, Ruth, into the country and stayed behind to protect his property, was comparatively lucky. He had enough money "to eat fresh provissions, while it was to be got, let it cost what it would." He was able to boast that "since October I have scarce eat three meals of salt meat," but he admitted that he was living at "the rate of six or seven hundred [pounds] sterling a year." He told of being obliged to pay a shilling for a loaf of bread "of the size we formerly gave three pence for . . . butter at two shillings. Milk, for months without tasting any." Yet Andrews maintained that he "never suffered the least depression of spirits." A conviction "that my country would eventually prevail" kept his morale high.[5]

Only about 3,500 civilians remained in Boston, and of these some 2,000 were loyalists, who had fled to the city from many parts of New England. Their motives were as mixed as their backgrounds. Lawyer Samuel Fitch considered the British system of government "the most perfect that human wisdom ever adopted." Joshua Loring, on the other hand, discovered an intense enthusiasm for the British cause on the morning of the battle of Lexington. "I have always eaten the King's bread and always intend to," he said. Mather Byles, descendant of Cotton Mather, pastor of the Hollis Street Church for over forty years, considered George III a tyrant, but said he preferred a tyrant three thousand miles away to the tyrannical rule of three thousand or so upstart rebel committeemen within three miles. Dr. John Jeffries, one of Boston's best-known doctors, was remaining loyal, although his father was treasurer of the rebel Massachusetts government. Oddest of all, perhaps, was Dorcas Griffiths, John Hancock's former mistress. When the president of the Continental Congress left Boston shortly before the battle of Lexington, Dorcas had found consolation with a marine captain who was wounded at Bunker Hill. She nursed him back to health and abandoned both herself and her political principles to her suffering British hero.

The prevailing note among the loyalists was neither idealism nor opportunism, but a sadness bordering on despair. As 1776 dawned, it had become evident to the most intelligent of them that there was no hope of dispersing the American army. Some of the more naïve thought that the King's speech, with its maledictions on rebellion, might bring the rebels to their knees, and these clutchers at straws actually thought that Washington's raising of the Grand Union flag on January 1 was an act of submission. But most had long since abandoned optimism. Peter Oliver, whose father was the lieutenant governor without a province to govern, wrote to his friend Elisha Hutchinson, who was in London with his father, deposed Royal Governor

Thomas Hutchinson, "Your wife braves it out; by the last accounts from her in September, she is president of a club composed of eight ladies. They meet over a tea table once or twice a week, in opposition to the rebells. They keep up their spirits strangely." [6]

Equally common among the loyalists was a deepening rage. Stephen Kemble, on the last day of the year 1775, wrote in his journal a searing portrait of the rebel government. Born in New Jersey, Kemble was deputy adjutant general of the British army. His sister was married to Thomas Gage, who had been commander in chief of the British army in North America until he was summoned home in October.

> A Portrait of the American leaders taken from facts.
> They openly avow that they have a right to oppress others; but they complain, without cause, being oppressed themselves. They acknowledge, in words, subjection to the King; but they will not submit to his government.
> They will have a right to ravage and murder all that stand in their way . . . but the King's calling them to an account for it is insult and oppression. . . . Their breaking the laws to serve their purposes is being at liberty and free; but their being forced to keep them is slavery and chains. Their flying in the face of authority and declaring themselves independent of our government shows their duty, love and affection to the King; but His Majesty not supporting them in it, as they would have him, makes him a tyrant to them. . . . They were peaceful and quiet on the 19th of April last, when they attacked the King's troops; but the King's troops were savage and brutish in meddling with them. . . . Their leaders take refuge in, and support themselves, by falsehood, lying and deceit; and make fraud, violence, insurrection and rebellion the distinguishing badge of their liberty and freedom . . . these are the men that our modern patriots have in the highest veneration, and cry up for the only lovers of truth and the natural rights of mankind: but even humanity calls, away with such fellows from the earth, for it is not fit they should live. [7]

The same attitude toward the rebels was also becoming widespread among the British-born officers. "The infamous falsehoods they circulate in their papers, which we sometimes see," Lord Rawdon wrote home, "relative to the behavior of our army or navy fill me with indignation. . . . These misrepresentations may perhaps influence the spirits of the lower class against the troops, but they will have a most pernicious effect . . . when our men are let slip against a parcel of wretches whom they hate and despise, when no officer will interpose to rescue the victim from their rage." Rawdon wrote this in September, before the winter winds had further sharpened his resentments. By December, he was predicting that the next campaign would be "carried on with an inveteracy unparalleled in the history of modern wars." Rawdon and most of his fellow officers were convinced that the American talk about negotiation was sham, and that all the patriot leaders, to the last man, were involved in a gigantic plot to declare their independence.[8]

To buoy their spirits, several of the officers wrote a farce called "The Blockade of Boston." It featured Washington as a country bumpkin, with a huge sword that dragged along the ground. Washington knew in advance the date of the first performance, and it may have influenced his choice of the night he attacked the British outpost on Bunker Hill. He was inclined to this sort of dry humor. At any rate, the play was just beginning when a rattle of gunfire drifted across the water from Charlestown. An Irish orderly sergeant standing outside the playhouse door heard the guns and charged inside. He did not stop until he was onstage. "Turn out! They are hard at it, hammer and tongs," he roared. The audience thought he was playing a part and paid him the compliment of "a general clap," in Lieutenant Martin Hunter's words.

The sergeant, close to apoplexy, screamed, "What the deuce are you all about? If you won't believe me, by Jasus, you need only go to the door, and there you will see and hear both." By now, the roar of cannon was added to the crackle of musketry, and the playhouse emptied, the ladies trembling and crying, the officers racing to their regiments bawling orders without bothering to take off their farce costumes, their faces blackened with soot, and some of them wearing skirts.[9]

Among the audience on that tumultuous night was the British commander in chief, William Howe. The disruption of his evening's entertainment was, for him, one more frustration in a situation that must, at times, have made him wonder if the world had gone mad. A man who valued his popularity with enlisted men and junior officers, he could not have enjoyed inflicting harsh punishments on lawbreakers or sending men to bleak duty on Bunker Hill. Seven months ago, Howe had arrived in Boston with two fellow major generals, Henry Clinton and John Burgoyne, confident that a little deft manipulation of the sword and the olive branch would end America's troubles overnight. As the senior major general, Howe personified the ambiguities of Britain's stumbling, fumbling policies at that time. Yet in Howe's own limited mind, the idea of his mission to America seemed logical enough. He was, from the viewpoint of English politics, a friend of the American cause. In Parliament, where he sat as a member from Nottingham, he had regularly voted with the opposition against the taxation-or-the-sword policy of the administration. In fact, when he had stood for re-election to Parliament in 1774, he had promised Nottingham's voters that he would never under any circumstances accept a commission to serve against "our American brethren." When he did an about-face and accepted the King's call, he insisted he was still a friend to America, and was putting aside his "private feelings" because of the "delicate nature in which our affairs stand at present." [10]

Howe felt himself uniquely qualified to deal with the delicate situation, because he was not only a political opponent of the men in power; he had a name which was respected and even admired by Americans. He had led Wolfe's advance guard up the narrow path to the Plains of Abraham, overwhelming the French outposts and clearing the way for the capture of Quebec and the extinction of French power in America. His brother, George Lord Howe, had died fighting beside American rangers in the advance on Fort Ticonderoga. The people of Massachusetts had erected a plaque in Westminster Abbey in his memory.

But before he had had time to proffer his olive branch, Howe found himself, sword in hand, leading 2,500 picked British troops against Americans entrenched along the foot of Bunker Hill and on top of Breed's Hill. In the ensuing carnage, Howe lost almost 50 percent of his attacking force, and he, the daredevil par excellence, "had a moment I never felt before"—a sudden searing doubt in the infallibility of his lucky star, which had guided him smoothly to the top of the British military establishment without so much as a wound or a blemish on his reputation. A gambler by nature—there were strong rumors that his real motive for taking the assignment in America was the need to pay off some heavy faro debts—Howe had had more than confidence in his own luck destroyed at Bunker Hill. The image of himself as a peacemaker was also shattered by those American bullets. When Howe replaced Gage as commander of the British army in Boston, he made no attempt to talk reconciliation with Washington or anyone else.

Although dribbles of reinforcements gradually raised Howe's strength to 8,906 men, he could see no point in attacking the entrenched Americans in their semicircle around Boston. Bunker Hill had taught him that, raw as the American militia might be, they had an ominous supply of officers who had acquired at least a semiprofessional military background fighting the French. Not that Howe had grossly underestimated the Americans at Bunker Hill. The real story of that battle has no resemblance to the comic-opera version in the minds of most Americans. The redcoats did not march blithely up to the American barricades, presenting the whites of their eyes like targets in a shooting gallery. Howe had tried to execute a thoroughly professional battle plan, which would have enabled him to outflank the stationary American defenses and envelop the badly exposed American regiments. But the American commanders had swiftly divined his plan, blocked his flank attack, and forced him to choose the desperate alternative of frontal assault. There was no reason to assume that the same thing would not happen if he committed his regulars to an attack on Washington's better entrenched army. So the daredevil general was forced to sit in Boston in a humiliating defensive posture, while the rest of the continent slipped away from British control.

But this fact was only the beginning of Howe's frustrations. He was soon far more worried about the sheer survival of his army in blockaded Boston. The impromptu American navy organized by George Washington wreaked havoc with British attempts to send food from the West Indies and England. Even the ships that escaped the American privateers only underscored the difficulties of trying to supply an army across three thousand miles of ocean. One ship that arrived in December had 744 barrels of good flour and 813 that had spoiled. Twenty-six provision ships sent out by the government wound up at Antigua, driven there by Atlantic storms. Many of them had jettisoned their cargoes to survive, and in others the food had rotted. Another ship arrived with 600 barrels of flour, only five of them usable. Even more irritating, the hand of the war profiteer was visible in barrels that were only half full.

To Howe, it was almost incredible that the British navy could not guarantee him adequate supplies. He and his brother officers spent not a little of their time castigating the navy. The admiral in command, Samuel Graves, had been relieved on January 1. Old and timid, Graves personified the decline of the navy that had smashed France and Spain and won a worldwide empire for England thirteen years ago. His captains and his crews were as decrepit as he was. One captain who resigned because of "great age" complained that aboard his ship his carpenter was "infirm and past duty." His gunner "was made from a livery servant, neither seaman nor gunner." His only petty officer "owns himself mad at times." Graves' replacement, Admiral Molyneux Shuldham, could do little to solve Howe's dilemma. He brought a few more ships, but the navy was still scandalously short of vessels and men to patrol the immense American coast.[11]

Another source of embarrassment for Howe was the lack of money in the army's war chest. Major General John Burgoyne complained to London that they were "destitute" not only of fresh meat "but of the most important of all circumstances in war or negotiacion—intelligence. We are ignorant, not only of what passes in congresses, but want spies for the hill half a mile off." Thus, inadvertently, Howe's brother general explained why George Washington was able to recruit a new army and disband his old one without a British attack.

In this situation, a man of action like Howe could only think of one way to console himself. If he could not make war, he would make love. He found a willing companion in blond, beautiful Mrs. Joshua Loring. The lady was married to one of Boston's staunchest Tories. He was also, as we have seen, a man to think first of where his bread was buttered. For an ample opportunity to satisfy his acquisitive instincts, he was apparently prepared to overlook a great many other difficulties. By promising Mr. Loring the lucrative job of commissary of prisoners, General Howe persuaded him to ignore where his wife was spending her nights. Shocked Bostonians promptly saw Samson waylaid by Delilah, or Anthony by Cleopatra. But General Howe, noted for saying as little as possible, ignored the gossip and enjoyed the lady.

Like Washington, Howe, too, was bombarded with requests for aid and advice from other parts of the American continent. John Moultrie, the South Carolina–born lieutenant governor of East Florida, wrote to one of Howe's field officers, Major General James Grant, a former governor of the same colony, assuring him that East Florida had no intention of following "our foolish young sisters, Georgia and Carolina." Then he moved to the subject that absorbed every loyalist on the continent. "I am surprised to find you and the army in the state you have been in. I flatter myself you will move to advantage soon." [12]

These and other letters from royal officials in Quebec, Virginia, and North Carolina assumed that the British foot soldier was some kind of miraculous military machine, which Howe was holding back for utterly mysterious reasons. Gazing at a map of the American continent, Howe could only become depressed by the size of the task confronting him. Like his American opposite, George Washington, Howe had never before commanded anything larger than a regiment under wartime conditions. Although he had performed his previous military assignments with daring and skill, his forte was not strategy—plotting military movements on a grand scale—but tactics—the quick thinking which wins single battles once they are joined.

Even before Howe was given command of the army inside Boston, he wrote a letter to his brother in London, telling him he felt unequal to directing the reconquest of America. In that letter, he sketched out a fairly viable strategic plan. An army of 15,000 men would seize New York from the sea, while 4,000 regulars, Canadians, and Indians descended from Canada and 5,000 additional men remained inside Boston. He urged the appointment of a viceroy with unlimited powers to coordinate these operations.

Surprisingly, Howe eliminated himself from contention for this job. In fact, reading the letter, one gets the distinct feeling that Howe was performing an expected function in forwarding this plan. The policy he really preferred came toward the end of the letter, where he remarked that if the government could not furnish this many men—which in his opinion was the minimum number necessary to have any hope of victory—then the British army and navy ought to withdraw from the colonies and leave them to quarrel with each other until one by one they fled like prodigal children to the protection of the mother country.

Basing his estimate on the political situation when he left England, Howe probably told himself that there was a very good chance of this last suggestion's being adopted. The cost and difficulty of feeding his 8,906 men in Boston was enough to undo any minister who had to tell such bad news to a parsimonious Parliament. The thought of equipping and supplying almost three times that number might persuade England to abandon a war that Howe could only view with dismay.[13]

But the temper of the British government had undergone a significant change since Howe had departed for America almost a year ago. The King and his advisers no longer had any doubts about how to settle the quarrel with the thirteen rebellious colonies. In the government offices at Whitehall, determined men were planning to give Howe an army twice as large as he requested. Force, massively, savagely applied, was to be Britain's answer to the Americans. Let us visit the capital of the British Empire and see why and how its rulers reached this fateful decision.

A Not Very
Merrie Mother

At first glance, London newspapers on January 1, 1776, seemed more interested in the forthcoming trial of the Duchess of Kingston for bigamy than in the American Revolution. The Duchess, born Elizabeth Chudleigh, was one of those remarkable women who appear from time to time in English history. Beginning as a maid of honor to the Princess of Wales, she progressed by horizontal leverage to the summit of society. George II was among her conquests. Other maids of honor, although "not of maids of the strictest," were appalled by her behavior, which included an appearance at a masquerade as Iphigenia in a gown that anticipated the nude look by some two hundred years. She eventually settled down with the second Duke of Kingston, who built Kingston Palace for her. There, one witty chronicler of the era declared that "every favor she has bestowed, is registered by a piece of Dresden china."

In the course of her earlier nocturnal peregrinations, the lady made the mistake of marrying one John Hervey, a Royal Navy lieutenant from whom she soon separated. The Duke of Kingston paid Hervey £14,000 to swear before a church court that no marriage had ever taken place. His Lordship then married his "fair injured innocent," as the gossips ironically called her. There is considerable evidence that the Duke had no alternative. The lady had a habit of threatening to shoot him with a pistol. Four years later, the Duke died of natural causes, leaving her in possession of the Kingston estates.

A disinherited nephew instantly brought suit, charging that the

Duchess was legally married to Hervey and her marriage to the Duke
was therefore null. There was more than money at stake. Bigamy was
punishable by death. But there was a wrinkle that made this threat
nonexistent. Lieutenant Hervey had in the meantime succeeded to a
title which made the Duchess a countess at last. It was therefore impossible for the House of Lords, where her trial was to be held, to pronounce a death sentence. If found guilty, the lady could still claim im-
munity as a peeress. The entire trial was therefore motivated by
nothing but malice—and the anticipation of seeing the Duchess
stripped of her slight veneer of respectability.[1]

The decision to prosecute the Duchess, willy-nilly, was symptomatic
of a society where a small, enormously wealthy group of men and
women were used to having their own way. Remarkably few in
number—there were only 184 English peers as 1776 began—they had
at their disposal immense incomes from landed estates. In an era
when the average workman lived on £30 to £50, a landed lord had anywhere from £4,000 to £30,000 pounds a year at his disposal, almost all
of it in rents and revenues for which he had scarcely to lift a finger.
This tended to create an extraordinary life style, a combination of
complacence, arrogance, and prodigality. The Duke of Somerset, for
instance, ordered his daughter to watch him every day while he took an
after-dinner nap. One day he woke up and found that she had left the
room. He forbade all the members of the family and all his servants to
speak to her for a year. The Duke of Montague gave a dinner party at
Bath composed entirely of people who stuttered—and sat at the head
of the table enjoying the confusion.

These men were descended from fathers, grandfathers, and great-
grandfathers who had been running England for a hundred years.
They were the heirs of the "Glorious Revolution" of 1688, which
ousted the Stuarts, with their Catholic sympathies and inclination to
rule by divine right, rather than "constitutionally" with the advice and
consent of Parliament. From where the rulers of England sat in 1776,
they—or their fathers—had done pretty well. True, there was some
heavy weather setting in from North America, but England had survived worse storms. In 1763, she had taken on her two great Catholic
rivals, France and Spain, and trounced them in the first truly world
war, a conflict that made Great Britain the dominant power on the
globe.

The victory made London more than the capital of Great Britain. It
became an imperial city. Sprawling along the Thames in a five-mile

oblong, it supported one-eighth of all the people in the realm—1,500,000 souls. Into its countinghouses and stock exchange and banks flowed profits from an empire that already included a huge swath of India, lucrative chunks of Africa, and the islands of the West Indies, where sugar was synonymous with cash. "Nabobs" came home from India to build great houses, deck their wives in diamonds, buy their way into Parliament, and convince honest men like Richard Montgomery that they could never compete with them or their sons. West Indian planters, such as "Rum" Atkinson, who had the contract for supplying the British army with much of that vital liquor, were equally rich. When it came to net profits, the trade of the Indies, West and East, far outweighed the commerce of the thirteen American colonies.

High taxes would hardly seem to bother such a wealthy nation. But taxation troubled the British in 1776 almost as much as it vexes Americans in 1976. How much money the government—which in effect meant the King—should spend was a touchy question. In the preceding century, Charles I had lost his head debating it with Parliament and the people. By 1776, thanks to a series of wars with France and Spain, the national debt had reached what seemed to be astronomical proportions—over £150,000,000. There were no Keynesian economists around to tell everyone that this was perfectly all right. The interest on this borrowed money cost the government over £4,000,000 a year, and national bankruptcy was a frequent topic of conversation among businessmen and politicians. To keep things going, the British paid more money to their government in taxes than any other people in the western world. Only the Dutch came close to them.[2]

The standard levy was the land tax, which was maintained at two to three shillings to the pound in time of peace, and four in time of war. The tax was not on the net worth of the land but on the income from it. However, there was no Internal Revenue Service to investigate the real income a landowner made, and there had been no reassessment of the value of land in England since 1692. Thus, it was ridiculously simple for everyone from great lords to country gentlemen to conceal their real income and pay about half of what they really owed the government. Instead of paying a fifth of his income, the average landowner paid a tenth or a twelfth.

Money raised from the land tax accounted for only a modest proportion of the government's total revenue. Most of the taxes paid by the British fell on the general population, through indirect levies on official documents, which required a government stamp, on luxuries such as liquor, and on imports and exports. The approximate annual tax rate in England was 26 shillings per head, a rather startling contrast to the estimated one shilling paid by citizens of Massachusetts and the fivepence paid by those of Virginia. It was easy for the government to focus resentment on the lightly taxed Americans. No one responded to this propaganda more readily than the country gentlemen in Parliament, who were paying all the indirect taxes, including a few new ones invented by the current ministry, such as a tax on the number of windows in a house, and the land tax as well.

Few wealthy Englishmen were troubled by the contradictions and paradoxes that abounded in the society over which they presided. John Wesley roamed up and down the land, preaching religious revival among the middle and lower classes. Rampant skepticism was the prevailing religion of the upper classes. The streets of London swarmed with prostitutes, and the sons of the nobility seemed interested in only two things, sex and gambling. At clubs such as Almack's, White's and Boodle's, directly across Hyde Park from St. James's Palace, immense sums changed hands nightly. One young nobleman sat for twenty-four hours at faro, losing £500 an hour. The nephew of Sir Joshua Reynolds, the leading painter of the era, won £34,000 at a single sitting from Sir John Bland, who walked out of the club a ruined man and committed suicide.

It was an age of invention and experiment. The great manufacturing centers in the Midlands churned out millions of yards of linen and wool, thanks to machines such as the spinning jenny, which multiplied the labor of a single individual a hundred times and ironically reduced his wages. James Watt had patented his steam engine in 1768, and men were already thinking about adapting it to factory machines. Steel and iron poured from furnaces, thanks to a new method of smelting iron ore with coke, and striking improvements in furnaces and blast techniques. Farming had become scientific, and great lords such as "Turnip" Townshend experimented with crop rotation and trooped to the Leicestershire kitchen of burly Robert Bakewell, to learn how to breed more profitable sheep.

In other respects, England was still living in the Middle Ages, or, at best, the Reformation. Dissenters—Presbyterians, Methodists, Quakers, and other Protestants who refused to take an oath of allegiance to the Church of England—were denied the right to vote, and many other rights. Roman Catholics were treated even more barbarously. By law, they were forbidden to travel more than five miles from home without a special license, they could not bring a lawsuit in any court in England, and a Catholic caught running a school, or a priest found saying Mass, was liable to a life sentence in prison. This was tantamount to a death sentence, since few survived more than a year or two in a British prison.

The barbarity of the English penal code was almost unbelievable. Men, women, and even children were sentenced to be hanged for the most trifling crimes, such as stealing a loaf of bread or a few yards of cloth. Most of the death sentences were, it is true, commuted to "transportation" to the American colonies. In 1776, these had ceased to be a convenient dumping ground for felons, and hundreds of men sentenced to transportation were being held on hulks in the River Thames, where they were dying by the dozen every week.

In spite of the severity of the laws, crime was rampant. People set traps in their gardens to catch thieves. One man's leg was torn off by one of these devices. "It were to be wished that these machines could be so contrived as to secure the offender without disabling him and thereby rendering him not only useless but a burthensome member of society," remarked one commentator on the passing scene. At the top of the crime list was smuggling. In the year 1776, no less than 141,300 pounds of tea were confiscated by the British revenue agents, and sold at customhouses.[3] The newspapers regularly reported running battles between revenue cutters and smugglers. Highwaymen were at work on almost every road around London. The King's first, or "prime," minister, Frederick Lord North, was held up on Hounslow Heath while en route to a weekend at his country house.

The reason for this lawlessness was visible to many—although few were inclined to do much about it. Outside the great lords, the wealthy upper stratum of English society was equally small. Recent studies by economists suggest there were some three hundred families with incomes of £4,000 a year. Then there were perhaps two hundred families of merchants and bankers, who earned in the vicinity of £2,500 a year. It should be noted, however, that an eighteenth-century family represented a web of relationships that ranged far beyond the father, mother, and children of the twentieth century's nuclear family. It included cousins, servants, even friends, all of whom had a claim on the family exchequer or at least on its political and business connections.

After these men of worth were perhaps seventy thousand people with incomes of £1,500 a year and another two hundred and fifty thou-

sand who earned about £700 a year. Another million and a half Englishmen were comfortable farmers or shopkeepers. But almost half
the nation of seven million lived on or below the poverty line.[4]

There was a constant fear of the uneasy, often resentful poor.
Workmen regularly smashed up new machines in the manufacturing
towns. In 1765, the pitmen of the Tyne went on violent strike, wrecking the mining machinery and setting fire to the coal under ground. A
few years later, riots swept Lancashire as the poor attacked spinning
jennies and other machinery that they thought were depriving them of
jobs. In 1773, the sailors of Liverpool staged something very close to a
revolution, training their cannon on the town's stock exchange, wrecking and looting the houses of prominent shipowners, and even hoisting
a "bloody flag." [5]

On July 10, 1776, a mob marched on the town of Shepton Mallet to
destroy some new weaving machines. Three justices of the peace ordered the crowd to disperse. They refused, and when two of the justices
went home, the mob attacked the poorhouse where the machines had
been operating, destroyed the machines, and all but wrecked the building. The remaining justice called out the local regiment of the army,
and five ringleaders were arrested. The mob rioted as they were being
led to jail. The troops, after firing two rounds over the heads of the
mob, let it have a full volley, killing one man and seriously wounding
six others. The coroner ruled the death "accidental." [6]

When Parliament convened in the fall of 1775, a pamphlet urged
the people of London to rise and prevent the corrupt members from
continuing to defraud them. The government rushed additional troops
into the city. Protesting the American war had nothing to do with this
threatened uprising. America was too far away and the grievances of
the poor in the city of London too real and immediate to make the
Americans a primary concern for most Englishmen in the early days of
1776.

The government had labored hard to utilize the average Briton's in-
stinctive combative patriotism, which was almost synonymous with gul-
libility, to bolster its position and intimidate opposition in and out of
Parliament. Late in 1775, the nation was swept by rumors of a plot to
kidnap the King. Stephen Sayre, an American working as a banker in
London, was arrested for high treason and confined to the Tower. The
government announced that Sayre had planned to seize the King as he
walked in procession to the opening session of the House of Lords and
somehow spirit him out of the kingdom. All England seethed with in-

dignation over the story. The King was deluged with loyal addresses from dozens of cities and towns, denouncing the conspiracy and vowing loyalty to His Majesty and the British Constitution. Sayre was never brought to trial—in fact, he sued Lord Rochford, the secretary of state on whose order he was jailed, for £1,000 and eventually won—but meanwhile the government had scored a major propaganda victory.[7]

There was evidence that some Englishmen were disturbed about the trouble in America if the reader looked into the middle pages of the newspapers. English papers in 1776 did not arrange the news in the order of importance. Few editors thought in terms of headlines or front-page news. Papers were small, and readers were expected to read them thoroughly.

The problem was not only finding the news, but deciding what to believe. Almost all the newspapers mixed facts and rumors with a severe political bias, and most were opposed to the government. Only three papers supported British policy toward America. One of these, the London *Gazette,* was owned outright by the secretaries of state. Most opposition papers were edited by London radicals, who represented only a tiny minority of the English people.

The moderate *Morning Chronicle and London Advertiser* published a New Year's ode on January 3, 1776. It declared that America's "aching eyeballs" sought in vain for a sign of peace from England. The final stanza urged reconciliation on the mother country.

> Let peace and plenty smile again
>   And let fair Freedom shine;
> Thine was the fault; Britannia, then
>   Be reparation thine.[8]

In the January 3 issue of the anti-government *Morning Post and Daily Advertiser,* one entire column was devoted to officers being appointed to command of regiments and companies. The second column on the same page reported the situation in Boston with an odd combination of accuracy and rumor, purporting to have received the information from Major General John Burgoyne. It declared the army "in very good health and good spirits and better affected to the service than has been lately reported." It noted that the American army "is cantoned within strong entrenchments, forming a blockade rather than a siege, and amounting to 27,000 men"—a figure that George Washington would have been ecstatic to embrace in reality. On January 4, the *Chronicle* reported "from good authority" that Quebec had been captured by the Americans, who were pictured as having "plenty of arms and ammunition but are almost destitute of the necessary provisions for the camp." [9]

The *Morning Chronicle*'s writers seldom missed an opportunity to score on Americans. One writer contributed an anecdote about "an eminent American merchant" who held forth at a coffeehouse near the Royal Exchange, declaring his support of his rebellious countrymen, and avowing that he would take paper currency established by "the grand American Congress" as readily as he would an English guinea. This prompted "a brother merchant" to offer him a thousand pounds' worth of American Continental dollars at 10 percent discount. The American stuttered, spluttered, and said that he would take paper money in America but not in England.

America was often a convenient stick which radical newspapermen used to thump government supporters and attack other political targets. On January 4, 1776, the *Morning Post,* the paper with the largest circulation in England, carried a front-page attack on Chief Justice Lord Mansfield, one of the ministry's most outspoken supporters. They accused him of having "driven the colonies into a resistance by a series of measures equally cruel and absurd." Now he told the British people that they "must conquer them or they will conquer you. I do not remember an argument, which from the beginning to the end, so completely begs the question. Why not treat with them? What sort of a war is it to which no end can be put by treaty?

"America is and will be united," the writer declared, "and you had better make that union a means of conciliation . . . ." Instead of refusing to recognize the Continental Congress, the administration "ought to have rejoiced at its existence, as the only possible means of negotiating a firm and lasting union with America." [10]

The writer proceeded to become even more angry about the politics of the East India Company. Ruling a territory larger than England, with a revenue of £1,000,000 a year, it seemed about to collapse into the arms of the government to avoid bankruptcy. This meant its enormous holdings in the Orient would become royal possessions, raising the power of the throne to overwhelming proportions. "Machinations are already upon the anvil among the Scotch Junto," declared the *Morning Post* writer.

The reference to Scottish influence was a favorite theme of opposition papers, such as the *Morning Post*. Two of the most hated members of the current ministry were Scots, Solicitor General Alexander Wed-

derburn and Attorney General Edward Thurlow, as was Lord Mansfield. George III's tutor, Lord Bute, was a Scot and had been named by
the young King as his first prime minister. He was a failure, but the opposition persisted in seeing him as a secret influence behind the throne.
Basically, English liberals feared that the Scots, having failed to seat
Bonnie Prince Charlie on the throne as an absolute monarch in the
rebellion of 1745, were now attempting to convert George III into a
smoothly working model of the same thing. "It is a . . . fact that some
of the members of the present administration, with no great attention
to the company they are in, speak openly in favor of an absolute government," the *Morning Post* writer declared, "and throw all the misfortune attendant on the public affairs of England on the too great freedom of the Constitution. These are the men who want to govern
America by a standing army, and who will bye-and-bye throw Bengal
[India] into the hands of the Crown." [11]

More important than the newspaper debate was the pamphlet war.
The government had thrown into this effort to marshal public opinion
some of the best writers of the day—James Macpherson, the author of
the highly popular poems of Ossian, and Dr. Samuel Johnson, creator
of the first dictionary and the leading literary name in England. Johnson had a pension of £300 a year from the King, but there was no need
to purchase him to belabor the Americans. He once maintained vehemently to the Irish poet and playwright Oliver Goldsmith his complete
agreement with the statement, "The King can do no wrong."

Johnson's pamphlet was entitled *Taxation No Tyranny*. It was a
tough, rough job, aimed at the prejudice and patriotism of country
squires and local parsons. He denounced the American reluctance to
pay taxes as hypocrisy. The fact that they were able to resist the mother
country so vigorously was proof in itself that they were anything but
weakened by British policy. As for representation, he insisted that the
rich Americans had lost their right to vote by a voluntary exile. "If by
change of place they have less share in the legislature than is proportionate to their opulence, they, by their removal, gain that opulence
and had originally and have now their choice of a vote at home or
riches at a distance." Johnson was also quick to point out the paradox
of the Americans fighting for liberty while they kept several hundred
thousand Negroes in slavery.

None of the government productions came close to matching the
popularity of a pamphlet attacking the war written by Dr. Richard
Price, a dissenting minister and close friend of Benjamin Franklin. En-

titled *Observations on the Nature of Civil Liberty and the Justice and Policy of the War in America,* it was published on February 10, and in London alone ran through fourteen editions, selling over 60,000 copies. The author was granted the freedom of the City of London on March 14, and he suddenly found himself a national figure.

Richard Price was a member of the tiny group of London-based English radicals who worked for a total reform of the current political system. They wanted annual parliaments, universal suffrage, moderation of the penal code, and many other changes which were a hundred years away from achievement. Price's view reflected his friendship for Franklin. He argued that the Americans were not "our subjects" but "our fellow subjects." But Price's reputation as a radical reformer, and the enthusiasm with which many of his radical friends rushed to praise the pamphlet, did the American cause in England more harm than good. Also, while Price's intentions were good, his logic was poor. For instance, he argued that every state "in which a body of men representing the people make not an essential part of the legislature, is in slavery." This was hardly an accurate definition of slavery. Such overheated rhetoric was unlikely to impress the complacent aristocrats who were running the government.

Moreover, in the same month that Price published his pamphlet, the government recruited—with no effort on their part—a far more valuable ally. John Wesley was already the most famous preacher in England. He was deeply disturbed by the American war, and began reading widely on it in order to decide whether or not he should support the government. In February, he read Johnson's pamphlet, *Taxation No Tyranny.* It convinced him of the rightness of the British cause, and he immediately "judged it my duty" to impart the "light" he had received to others.

Wesley considered Dr. Price's effort "that dangerous tract" and decided to answer it. As a veteran debater on public platforms, Wesley had no difficulty making Price look foolish. He hit hard at his loose use of terms such as "slavery." He scoffed at the idea of majority rule, insisting that there was no precedent for it in British history. He echoed Johnson, declaring that Americans were plotting to declare their independence, in the hope of getting richer than they already were.

Another book was published early in 1776 that ostensibly had nothing to do with the American war. But the threat of the imminent dismemberment of the British Empire undoubtedly helped Edward Gibbon's *The Decline and Fall of the Roman Empire* to sell "like a three penny pamphlet on current affairs," from the day of its publication on February 17, 1776. The hot sale indicates how seriously the British took the idea of their own empire. It is also clear from the text that Gibbon saw a great resemblance between second-century Rome, at the height of its affluence and power, and eighteenth-century England. He lauded the five "good emperors" of the second century and the "rational freedom" which the Roman upper classes enjoyed under their benevolent rule. The historian distinguished this freedom from "wild democracy" and "savage independence." Gibbon was also a member of Parliament, where he usually supported the King and Lord North and was eventually rewarded by a pension.

The success of Gibbon's history, with its curious combination of praise for imperial rule abroad and liberty at home, sheds light on another reason why George III and his government had little difficulty rallying the English people behind them to oppose the Americans. Although the upper and middle classes were the only ones who enjoyed any of the privileges of this native liberty, every Englishman from the highest to the lowest was intensely proud of being a free man. In fact, for a hundred years the ruling class had used liberty as a kind of pep pill to produce the courage that English soldiers and sailors displayed in the century's numerous wars.

It took an observer with an unillusioned eye and a subtle wit to see the irony in the average Englishman's infatuation with liberty. Irish-born Oliver Goldsmith qualified in both departments, and more than once in the brilliant journalism he practiced between his poetry and plays he exposed this social contradiction. In one series of sketches, Goldsmith reported on England through the eyes of a Chinese philosopher who found "liberty is echoed in all their assemblies, and thousands might be found ready to offer up their lives for the sound, though perhaps not one of all the number understands its meaning."

In the course of his travels, Goldsmith's Chinese philosopher stops near a prison window to hear a debtor, a porter, and a prison guard talking about the threat of an invasion from France. The debtor says, "The greatest of my apprehensions is for our freedom; if the French should conquer, what will become of English liberty?" The two listeners, who are just as much in jail as the debtor although not legally incarcerated, solemnly agree with him. Later, the Chinese philosopher meets a soldier who has lost a leg fighting the French and is forced to beg for a living. The crippled warrior tells the story of his misfortunes, which include captures, beatings, starvation. But he cheerfully insists that it was all worthwhile, because it was in defense of English liberty. "O liberty, liberty, liberty!" he declaims. "That is the property of every Englishman, and I will die in its defense!" [12]

But only an outsider like Goldsmith could see this contradiction. Samuel Johnson, in contrast, could write a solemn essay, "The Bravery of the English Common Soldiers," and blandly attribute this fact to "the equality of English privileges, the impartiality of our laws . . . and the prosperity of our trade." The Englishman, Johnson serenely declared, "was born without a master, and looks not on any man, however dignified by lace or titles, as . . . inheriting any qualities superior to his own." This blindness of the English to the parlous state of their own freedom, its degeneration into abstraction and slogans, became enormously important in 1776. It explains their national deafness to the fears of Americans about the future of their far freer society under British direction. At the same time, the pride of the British in their own freedom and their readiness to use the word "liberty" as their personal property gave them a prompt reply to the Americans' revolutionary ideology. It also enabled them to plan the conquest of the Americans with a clear conscience.[13]

VI

Father (of the Country) at Work

On January 1, 1776, George III was at his desk in Queen's House, as Buckingham Palace was then called, writing to his ailing prime minister, Frederick Lord North. The King urged him to take a few days' rest. "I trust to see you well on Wednesday when I will certainly return you MG Howe's papers," he wrote. This intense interest in Howe's latest reports was evidence that God was not answering Martha Washington's prayer and sending George III the guidance she felt he needed.

Preceding his letter to North in the papers of the King is more evidence—a mass of memoranda in the royal handwriting. One page listed all the ships in his fleet ready for action, with notes beside their names estimating each as first, second, or third rate. Another list told His Majesty the number of "ships building and repairing." Another memorandum discussed the number of troops in Ireland, and specified the regiments that were to be sent to America. Still another memorandum neatly summed up the "effective strength of the infantry" at his command (18,255). Another listed all the available generals, lieutenant generals, and major generals. The artillery in North America was the subject of another list, which noted which guns were brass, which were iron, and distinguished between cannon, mortars, and howitzers. Another list annotated the regiments on foreign garrison duty and when they were last rotated home. There was a memorandum on supplies, which estimated that 52,000 blankets and 4,200 watch coats (overcoats) would be needed by the troops in North America. Finally, there was a long memorandum on the "organization of the army in America," which listed the regiments and most of their commanders.

There is no doubt from these papers that George III was preparing to fight war. Nothing was too large or too small for his attention. He selected the generals for America and "maturely weighed the advantage of a winter expedition against the four Southern colonies." Deciding in favor of it, he ordered "the 15th and 37th regiments of infantry to embark on the second week in December." Around the same time, he was worrying the secretary of war about AWOL officers in another regiment. "By the return the Lord Lieutenant has sent me of the 68th Regiment of foot on their landing in Ireland I have the pleasure of seeing that it wanted only fourteen: but in this return, Lieutenant Richard Taylor, Ensign Molly Barbizon, Ensign James Bixby, and Surgeon Calibarber are returned absent without leave. You will therefore write to Lieutenant General Lambton to direct them immediately to join the regiment in Ireland . . ."

On December 20, the King had written to Lord North, "I shall not fail to order everything for my going on Friday to the House of Lords to pass the bills that shall be ready for my assent." On that Friday, December 22, 1775, George III journeyed from Queen's House to receive from his assembled nobles their approval of a bill already passed by the House of Commons "to prohibit all trade and intercourse with the North American colonies now in actual rebellion." The bill authorized the British navy to blockade the American coast and seize as contraband any American ship on the ocean.

The Prohibitory Act was a declaration of war, and no one had any illusions about it, least of all George III. It was the logical next step from the denunciation of the "desperate" American conspiracy that the King had made in his speech opening the session of Parliament. While Americans clung to the belief that this ferocity had been foisted on their benevolent father by his ministers, the King was writing to Lord North, "I am certain any other conduct but compelling obedience would be ruinous and culpable, therefore no consideration could bring me to swerve from the present path which I think Myself in Duty bound to follow." His goal, he made it clear, was "to force these deluded people to submission." [1]

But a king who is involved in a civil war must display some magnanimity toward those who are opposing him. So George III permitted his ministers to wrap the Prohibitory Act around a clause that proposed in a very indirect way that the government would send peace commissioners to negotiate a truce with the Americans. This "person or [these] persons" would be "authorized by His Majesty to grant pardons" to all Americans who were "disposed to return to their duty." As soon as a whole colony exhibited this disposition, its ships were exempt from the seizure and blockade provisions of the Prohibitory Act. Little did George III realize that this innocuous clause, which he saw as a mere placebo, would undo his prescription of all-out force as the cure for the Empire's American illness.

The King found it inconceivable that anyone in England could disagree with his policies. When the Lord Mayor and aldermen of the City of London presented him with a protest against war with America, George III replied "with the utmost astonishment" to find "any of my subjects capable of encouraging the rebellious disposition which unhappily exists in some of my colonies in North America. Having entire confidence in the wisdom of my Parliament, the great council of the nation, I will steadily pursue those measures which they have recommended for the support of the constitutional rights of Great Britain, and the protection of the commercial rights of my kingdom."

For generations, Americans have been schooled to regard George III as a tyrant. Those last words illustrate why he and the men around him thought that the accusation was unjust. As George III saw it, he was the working partner of Parliament, duty bound to confer and reach agreement with the "council of the nation" on policies foreign and domestic. To an external observer—a visitor from China, perhaps, who could not read English newspapers—this may have looked like what he was doing. But to insiders the picture was reversed. By 1776, George III had reduced Parliament from a working partner to an obedient servant.

To assess George's government requires a modest knowledge of the early years of his reign and the reign of his predecessor, his grandfather, George II. During George II's reign, the cabinet system had evolved to the point where no group of ministers could run the government without majority support in Parliament. The standard modes of obtaining this support were the devices used by politicians since the dawn of history—jobs, favors, and money. Throughout his growing years, George III was told by his mother and the moralistic men who undertook his education that this system was bad for two reasons. One, it was corrupt and was corrupting the English nation. Two, it made the king a captive of his ministers. George's experience as Prince of Wales, when he gathered around him at his residence, Leicester House, a

group of supposedly pure politicians and advisers, led by his tutor,
Lord Bute, seemed to confirm these ideas. Neither choleric George II
nor the politicians around him showed the least interest in supporting
the young Prince's candidates for office, nor even in listening to his
naïve suggestions.[2]

As a result of this experience, when George ascended the throne in
1760, he saw himself as a "patriot king" fighting to break the grip of
greedy politicians on the Crown. His goal was the freedom to make
decisions with the welfare of the whole Empire in view, and not the interest of a small faction. Party and faction were synonymous in
George's mind—and in the minds of many of his contemporaries—and
both terms were equally reprehensible. Nobody combined to do anything, from this narrow—and at bottom very cynical—point of view,
without the ultimate goal of a lavish amount of butter on his bread.

By 1772, twelve years after he mounted the throne, George III felt
he had almost achieved his goal. He was able to write that he had "put
an end to those unhappy distinctions of party called Whigs and
Tories." This left George free to "countenance every man that supported my administration." When we look behind the words "countenance" and "supported," we discover why many Englishmen saw
George III as a menace.

Those whom the King countenanced almost invariably found themselves considerably richer for it, thanks to that endless well of royal benevolence known as the Civil List. This corresponded to the civil service in modern governments in only one respect: it was controlled by
the executive arm of the government—the King. Early in his reign,
Parliament had voted George III £800,000 a year from government
revenues to support his Civil List. This gave the King tremendous leverage in dealing with parliamentary politicians, who, like most politicians, always needed money, and had untalented, impoverished, or im-
portunate relatives and friends who wanted jobs.

George, not content with this stupendous sum—remember, the
average workman lived on about £50 a year—spent much more than
£800,000 a year "countenancing" his supporters. In 1769, he was
£500,000 in arrears, but persuaded Parliament to pay it off. By 1776,
he had accumulated another £600,000 of red ink. One critic of the
King warned that if the House of Commons continued to pay for the
Civil List without an accounting, "it must establish such a fund of rewards and terrors as will make Parliament the best appendage and support of arbitrary power that ever was invented by the wit of man."

Another leader of the opposition warned that the Civil List could be used to "spread corruption through the people, to procure a Parliament, like an infamous packed jury, ready to acquit the ministers at all adventures." In response to these remarks, Lord North, the prime minister, expressed the King's point of view. "Upon the whole, sir, as the Civil List is entirely the revenue of the Crown, the Crown has the right to dispose of it at will." North scolded the critics for giving the King "£800,000 a year to spend as he pleases, and then ask him what he does with it; this is neither decent to him nor sensible to yourselves." [3]

A fantastic number of jobs on the Civil List paid handsome salaries and required no work whatsoever. The office of chief clerk of the King's Bench or a mastership in chancery could earn a man over £6,000 a year, while the duties were performed by a deputy who might be paid £200 or £300 a year for the work. The functions of the Master of the Jewel Office or Master of the Buckhounds had long since been absorbed by the king's servants. This was equally true of the Groom of the Bedchamber, which paid £500 a year, or the Lord of the Bedchamber, which paid £1,000 a year, or even Groom of the Stole, which paid £2,000 a year. There were hundreds of similar jobs in the households of the Queen and princesses for widows, sisters, and other female connections of politicians. [4]

George, although he saw himself as a patriot king, was never shy about using the Civil List and his £800,000 slush fund to engineer elections. In the fall of 1774, when the Parliament that was sitting in 1776 was elected, the King spent £50,000 making sure that people he "countenanced" got into the House of Commons. The government's role is clearly visible in the papers of the man who managed the King's money, an obscure treasury official named John Robinson. A very efficient man, Robinson compiled long lists of jobs and jobholders. One, a list of "offices tenable with seats of lords in Commons," fills two and a half printed pages. Here is a sample: ". . . 13 Lords of the Bedchamber, 11 Grooms of the Bedchamber . . . 4 Gentlemen Ushers, Privy Chamber; 4 Gentlemen Ushers, Daily Waiters . . . Master of the Robes."

Another Robinson list totted up all the peers who held offices. This, too, fills two and a half printed pages. There was the Duke of St. Albans, who was Grand Falconer; the Earl of Berkeley, Constable of St. Bruvel's Castle in the Forest of Dean; the Earl of Ashburnham, Keeper of the Great Wardrobe; and Lord Hyde, Chancellor of the Duchy of Lancaster, a nonexistent political entity.

A third Robinson list noted all the members of the House of Commons who held "offices, commands, contracts, lieutenancies or governments." George Selwyn was Paymaster of the Works and Surveyor of the Mint, two jobs at which he never worked a day. Richard Vernon was Clerk of the Green Cloth, William Edgerton was Clerk of the Jewel Office, Charles Scudamore was Deputy Ranger of Whittlebury, Hans Sloane was Deputy Cofferer. After name after name, Robinson simply wrote "a contract," meaning that the MP was doing business with the government. This list fills three and a half printed pages.[5]

The correspondence between Prime Minister North and Robinson is a study in the business of corruption. Here is a sample, written after the 1774 parliamentary election: "Let Cooper know whether you promised . . . £2,500 or £3,000 for each of Lord Edgcumbe's [parliamentary] seats. I was going to pay him £12,500 but he demanded £15,000 and said that he had settled it with you."

Some historians maintain that Robinson and North operated in this style with perfectly clear consciences and were not even aware that they were corrupt. Undoubtedly, the King's warm approval of their actions did allay their qualms. But numerous members of Parliament repeatedly denounced corruption in government and warned—as we have seen—of the pernicious effects of the Civil List. It is hard to believe North and Robinson were not aware that their dealings were, at the very least, questionable. In fact, one letter from North suggests they were aware of their critics. "Perhaps it may be considered that the sums paid to gentlemen who have command of [parliamentary] boroughs for their interests, are to be considered as bribes. But these bargains are not usually called by that name and the money disbursed in that manner does not exceed what has been disbursed on all former occasions." [6]

This is the kind of thinking that third-rate American politicians have long used to justify stealing from the public. It boils down to the cheap, easily disproved claim that everybody does it, and has always done it.

Those historians who have tried to argue that George was only a constitutional monarch trying to do his job are fond of pointing out that the eighty to one hundred independent country gentlemen who constituted the swing vote in Parliament were not susceptible to bribery or corruption in the mass. The claim becomes a quibble if we stop and think for a moment about the nature of parliamentary politics in a free society. No political leader has ever succeeded in buying up *all* the votes in a representative assembly. Not only is the notion economically impractical, it is psychologically unsound. The very effort would offend the ideas of dignity and independence which the House of Commons possessed almost as vigorously in 1776 as today.

Like any political leader who is reasonably astute, George III or his alter ego Lord North used corruption selectively to pick off potential leaders of the opposition, and to guarantee themselves a formidable base of votes, from which they could readily build a bridge to the independent country gentlemen, who were almost always inclined to vote with the majority.

Rose Fuller, a West Indian–born MP who was one of the most outspoken critics of the government's American policy in 1774, was given a secret pension which reduced him to silence. The historians who attempt to defend their thesis that corruption was not the prime source of George III's power piously declare that only fifteen or sixteen of these pensions were ever in force at one time during the 1770s. Anyone with some political sophistication can only blanch at the naïveté of this argument. From an opposition which numbered only perhaps a hundred to a hundred and fifty at the outside, the King had fifteen or sixteen of these invisible arrows to pick off those members too embarrassed to surrender their independence publicly by taking a royal sinecure.

Typical of the way the King recruited parliamentary adherents, no matter how dubious their reputation, was his enlistment of Thomas Lord Lyttleton in late 1775. Son of a highly respected but impoverished peer, known as the "good" Lord Lyttleton, Tom Lyttleton had won a reputation as one of the wildest rakes of his day. His father's death elevated him to the House of Lords, where he pursued political fame by attacking both the government and the opposition, whenever they presented a target. His Lordship had also advanced his career considerably by promoting a regatta on the Thames in June of 1775, the combined effort of the Savoir Vivre, Almack's, White's, and Guthrie's clubs, where he regularly gambled for thousands. An estimated 200,000 Londoners turned out for this event.

On November 18, 1775, Lyttleton was appointed to the sinecure of Warden and Chief Justice in Eyre of all His Majesty's parks, chases, and warrens beyond [the river] Trent, a title which carried with it a handsome salary, a seat on the Privy Council, and no requirement whatsoever for work. Only a few days before, he had spoken vehemently in Parliament on behalf of the Americans. Two days later, he was on his feet damning the Americans in general and the Duke of Grafton in particular, for demanding from the ministry a statement on the number of troops now in America.[7]

While he stopped at nothing to maintain and increase his political power, personally George III was the ultramoral paragon of a patriot king. "Farmer George," as they called him, hated London, and preferred to spend most of his time at Kew or Windsor, where he practiced experimental agriculture, rode, and played husband and father to his large family. His queen, homely Charlotte, a German princess whom George's mother had selected for him, bore him children in rapid succession. His sober life style made him popular with the average Englishman and gave him reserves of energy to draw upon for his royal mission. George's passion for exercise matched his appetite for hard work and made him a kind of marvel in an indolent age. Often, en route from Windsor to London, he would walk twelve or thirteen miles beside his carriage. Some mornings, he rode for as much as three hours, beginning at 4 A.M. A thirty- to forty-mile ride was routine for him, and usually at a horse-killing pace. At his desk, he doggedly slogged through reams of detail to keep up with his ministers.[8]

Aside from the political power and wealth at his command, the King's ability to control Parliament in 1776 was simplified by the almost incredible imbalance between representation and population. The county of Middlesex, which included London and Westminster, returned eight members to Parliament, while Cornwall, with only a fraction of London's 1,500,000 population, was represented by no less than forty-four MPs. Many of these members came from so-called rotten boroughs, which were literally owned by a great lord, or were completely under his influence. In some constituencies only members of the municipal council were permitted to vote. At Bath, for instance, the franchise was limited to the mayor, ten aldermen, and twenty-four councilmen. At Salisbury, it was the mayor and the corporation—a total of fifty-seven persons—who sent the town's representative to Parliament. In the borough of Gatton, there were only seven voters, in Tavistock ten, and in St. Michael's seven. Perhaps seventy members were returned by thirty-five boroughs in which there were no visible electors. "Voters" were moved into the houses by the man who owned the borough on election day, cast their votes as directed, were given lavish amounts of food and drink and a few pounds for their trouble, and moved out that night.

Seats from rotten boroughs were often purchased as a commercial speculation, the way a twentieth-century financier might invest in real estate. By 1776, the price for a "safe" seat—one guaranteed to support the government—had risen to £3,000. Even the corporation of Oxford, where one might expect a little more probity, was not exempt from playing the game. In 1768, they offered to re-elect their two members only if they paid the town's debts, amounting to £5,670. The members indignantly reported the offer to the House of Commons, and the mayor of Oxford and one of his aldermen were thrown into Newgate Prison. There they continued their negotiations, and by the time they were discharged—with a reprimand from the Speaker of the House— they had sold the two seats to the Duke of Marlborough and the Earl of Abington.

As for Wales and Scotland, which returned only twenty-four and forty-five members respectively, they were totally subservient to the King's will. Edinburgh had only thirty-three voters. At the election of 1774, one of the candidates from that city promised never, except on a point of principle, "to clog the wheels of government by voting against the Ministry."

To get an idea of just how much Parliament was a closed corporation, ponder the following statistics. More than 50 percent of those who sat in it between 1734 and 1832 had a close blood relative in the parliaments immediately preceding them. There were, for instance, seventeen Townshends and thirteen Grenvilles. Although a nobleman could not sit in the House of Commons, this rule only applied to those who formally held the title. Brothers and sons of nobles could and did seek election in the so-called popular chamber. One out of every four was either a baronet (a rank below the highest peers but still hereditary) or the son of a peer who was waiting for his father to die.[9]

The system was designed, developed, and defended by the upper class because it guaranteed their continuing control of the government. When the Americans protested that they had no representatives in the British Parliament and therefore Parliament had no right to tax them, they were blandly informed that "nine-tenths of the people of Britain" had no representatives in Parliament either, and they were not threatening rebellion. Whether or not a citizen voted for representatives to Parliament was really beside the point. Every citizen of the realm was "virtually represented" because, in the words of one government pamphleteer, "Every member of Parliament sits in the house not as representative of his own constituents but as one of that august assem-

bly by which all the commons of Great Britain are represented." The
idea that a man was in Parliament mainly to represent the needs of the
constituents who voted for him was rejected as "a departure from his
duty."

If the MP voted new taxes, or committed the nation to a foreign
war, went the argument, the burden fell on him and his friends and
electors just as heavily as it did on those who had no representatives in
Parliament. The MPs were excellent guardians against the danger of a
king's turning into a tyrant, because they and their friends and electors
would be victims of the same tyrant as the non-electors. This argument
was outrageously specious, ignoring the possibility that in a nation of
enormous wealth, such as England had become, a king could buy up
Parliament or Parliament could sell itself to the king at irresistible
prices, and create an oligarchy as tyrannical and arrogant in its own
way as any absolute monarch. More important—and the chief irony in
the entire situation—this smug British sophistry in defense of their corrupt electoral system was the root of the quarrel with America. It was
thus no accident that many reformers, such as Richard Price, saw the
American problem as a reflection of similar trouble at home.

When government spokesmen huffed that Americans were virtually
represented in Parliament, American pamphleteers made them look ridiculous. Virtual representation might, they conceded, work for Englishmen living on the home island—although they doubted it. Americans found themselves unimpressed when they were told that Manchester, Birmingham, and Sheffield, all large manufacturing cities, were
not represented in Parliament. Their answer was, "They ought to be."
But when it came to arguing that Americans were virtually represented, this was, in the words of one American pamphleteer, "witch-
craft."

America and England were different countries, and a Parliament in
England could blithely vote taxes on America without the slightest
worry that their friends, constituents, or nonconstituents would suffer
a dent in their pocketbooks. Who, one American pamphleteer asked, is
the Americans' virtual representative in England? "Does he know us?
Or we him? No. Have we any restriction over his conduct? No . . . Is
he acquainted with our circumstances, situations, warrants, &c.? No.
What then are we to expect from him? Nothing but taxes without end."
Another pamphleteer sarcastically summed up the British argument
from the American point of view. "Our privileges are all *virtual,* our
sufferings are *real.*" [10]

By now it should be clear that Richard Montgomery's dream of using the conquest of Canada to shock Parliament into changing its collective mind was a pathetic illusion. It should also be possible to answer the question raised by the widespread American conviction that the British were plotting to destroy their freedom. There was no such plot—in the sense that George III, his ministers, and his supporters in Parliament gathered by night in secret conclaves to think up new ways to browbeat and traduce the Americans. But in another sense, the entire system over which George III presided was a plot against America's free society. The resentment felt by Englishmen who were paying twenty-five times heavier taxes than the Americans heightened the probability that if the English had their way, they were going to remodel colonial America into a closer resemblance to the mother country—not only by insisting they share a hefty hunk of the tax burden but by insisting on that "subordination" and "submission"—two of George III's favorite words—they felt colonies and colonials should display vis-à-vis the mother country. This undoubtedly would have meant the creation of an apparatus similar to the one used to subdue Ireland—and milk that hapless nation for all it was worth: a local aristocracy, an established church, and as many meaningless but well-paying jobs as the ingenuity of the King's bureaucrats could devise.

Benjamin Franklin, who spent twenty years in England before the war, saw this clearly. It was why he rejected the suggestion of his friend, Joseph Galloway, for a written constitution which would unite Britain and America. Franklin predicted "more mischief than benefit from a closer union." He went on to give incisive eyewitness testimony of England's unplotted but nonetheless dangerous conspiracy against America. "I fear they will drag us after them in all the plundering Wars which their desperate Circumstances, Injustice, and Rapacity, may prompt them to undertake; and their wide-wasting Prodigality and Profusion is a Gulf that will swallow up every Aid we may distress ourselves to afford them. Here numberless and Needless Places, enormous Salaries, Pensions, Perquisites, Bribes . . . false Accounts or no Accounts, Contracts and Jobs devour all Revenue, and produce continual Necessity in the Midst of natural Plenty. . . . To unite us intimately will only be to corrupt and poison us also." [11]

VII

Father's Dangerous Friends

In spite of his wealth and energy and attention to details large and small, George III could never have achieved the enormous power he had acquired by 1776 without the help of his prime minister, Lord North. The son of the Earl of Guilford was that rare thing in eighteenth-century politics, a politician who had the views and attitudes of a courtier. Part of this was explained by his intimate relationship with the King. North had been one of the few playfellows permitted George III during his lonely childhood. His father had been a close friend of both George's father and his mother—in fact, he was so friendly with George's mother that more than a few wiseacres noted that there was a decided resemblance between the prime minister and his royal master. Both had the same fair hair, bushy eyebrows, gray eyes, and light complexion.[1]

But George presented a much more striking appearance than his prime minister. North seemed at first glance extremely unqualified for the role of government leader. Sitting on the ministry's front bench in the House, he always looked half asleep and frequently was fast asleep. One contemporary who disliked him intensely described North's face as "two large, prominent eyes that rolled about to no purpose—for he was utterly shortsighted—a wide mouth, thick lips and inflated visage gave him the air of a blind trumpeter." But North was a gifted parliamentary leader in his own peculiar way. His somnolence made him all but unflappable in the face of attacks that would excite the average American congressman of today to violence. North also had a great deal of personal charm and a first-class wit. Toward the end of 1775, one friend told Samuel Johnson, "It is the fund of natural humor which Lord North possesses, that makes him so much a favorite of the House, and so able, because so amiable, a leader of a party."

An opposition leader admitted that in North Parliament had "no more complete master of language," and another opposition leader described him as "a man of admirable parts, of general knowledge, of a personal understanding, fitted for every sort of business," but "he wanted something of the vigilance and spirit of command that the time required." This was one of history's great understatements.

A favorite North trick when the opposition was haranguing him was to fall asleep and then wake up at an opportune moment with a funny remark which deflated serious opponents. One of these, declaiming on the extravagance of the government, declared, "I shall draw attention of the House to revenues and expenditures of the country in 1689." As these words were spoken, one of Lord North's aides had nudged him in the ribs. "Zounds, sir," declared North, "you have woken me up near one hundred years too soon." Another time, when an opposition leader was making a seemingly interminable harangue, he stopped and accused the Prime Minister of being asleep. North, with his eyes still closed, said, *sotto voce,* "I wish to God I *were.*" [2]

North was not a warlike man. He frequently disclaimed all knowledge of military matters and often expressed severe doubts about the wisdom of a collision with America. An astute politician, he was aware that many thoughtful Englishmen did not believe that England could win the war. Late in 1775, Lord Barrington, the secretary of war, had warned North, "There are no more troops in England than are absolutely necessary for securing the peace and collecting the revenue." Barrington was particularly worried by the "leveling spirit among the people."

On the American question, North functioned less as a prime minister than as a secret advocate of peace in a government where the majority—including the King—wanted war. He called the Prohibitory Act, which threatened America with economic strangulation, "a preparatory step to the sending our Commissioners, who are to restore trade to any province which they can declare to be at peace with us." Earlier in 1775, he had submitted to Parliament a "Bill for Conciliating the Differences with America," which stated that if America agreed to raise a just portion of the Empire's military budget by self-taxation, Parliament would suspend its exercise of the taxing power. But the atmosphere in

which North had introduced this bill was as unpropitious for peace as
the one created by the Prohibitory Act. He had just finished fighting
for two hard-line measures, declaring the New England colonies in
rebellion and barring them from one of their greatest sources of food
and trade, the Newfoundland fisheries.

The country gentlemen at first could not believe their ears when
they heard the prime minister giving up the right to tax the colonies.
They almost voted North into oblivion. Only when they were assured
that the bill, which specified that each colony had to approach the
mother country separately, might shatter colonial unity, and in no way
countenanced that illegal body, the Continental Congress, did they
reluctantly support it. But North really meant what he said about giving up the taxing power. He even told the King that it was "precisely
the plan which ought to be adopted by Great Britain; even if all
America were subdued." [3]

This was one of the best kept secrets of 1776—and in fact has seldom been underscored by any historian of the Revolution—that the
British prime minister had persuaded Parliament tacitly to surrender
its right to tax America. The Americans barely noticed it because they
saw it arrive on their shores wrapped in more punitive measures, as
with the peace commission in the Prohibitory Act. North never had the
courage—or the King's permission—to make this concession the leading edge of Britain's policy toward America. Instead, it was trailed
along in the wake of denunciations and prohibitions.

Always at the back of North's mind was the threat of an Irish rebellion which would be far more dangerous to Britain's survival than the
loss of America. In that neighbor across the Irish Sea, some three
million disfranchised Catholics were ruled by an uneasy veneer of Protestants who had by now acquired an Irish nationalism of their own. A
standing army had to be maintained at all times in Ireland. Bands of
White Boys, a kind of secret guerrilla army, roamed the countryside by
night, attacking landlords and police posts. On January 1, 1776, the
Morning Post and Daily Advertiser reported an attack on the county jail in
Kilkenny by a squad of White Boys.

Abroad, the prospect was equally alarming. On January 5, 1776,
Lord North rushed to the King two letters from Paul Wentworth, head
of the secret service in France, which left "no doubt of the essential assistance that France and Spain had promised and are upon the point of
affording the Rebels." Since 1763, when the English had won the Seven
Years' War against France and Spain, George III's ministers had pur-

sued a complacent nonpolicy of neglect toward former allies on the European continent, Austria, Prussia, and Holland. All of them were now estranged, and even Russia, the one nation that George III had made a pretense of wooing, was jealous of England's ever-growing commercial power. Diplomatically, England stood alone.

Whenever North tried to communicate his doubts to the King, he was shushed as a fond parent might shoo aside an inarticulate small boy who was trying to tell him that his house was on fire.

Long before 1776 dawned, the King saw that North was not the war leader that he needed to supplement his own efforts. Energetic though a patriot king might be, he could not be everywhere at once. There were too many people to spur in the creaky administrative machinery of the army, navy, and other branches of the government. To handle this job, the King needed a man who possessed his energy—and his confidence in the rightness of his course. He found him in the person of tall, imperious sixty-year-old Lord George Germain.

Descended from a line of noblemen who had played commanding parts in the reigns of a half dozen previous kings, Lord George was also the possessor of one of the worst public reputations in England. But in George III's mind, this reputation was only another reason to elevate Germain to power. The King had been longing to make such a gesture on Lord George's behalf since he had ascended the throne. George III was convinced that Germain's terrible reputation was the result of party malice.

Born a Sackville, Lord George could trace his lineage to William the Conqueror. One of his ancestors had written the first English tragedy, *Gorboduc*. Another had been the champion spendthrift of his time, living in "the greatest splendour of any nobleman in England" and dying a half million pounds in debt. It was a family tradition that no Sackville ever did anything halfway. Lord George grew up at Knole, one of the great houses of England, once the private retreat of the archbishops of Canterbury and for a while the favorite country house of Henry VIII. Knole had 365 rooms and 52 stairways, 42 indoor servants, and a small army of outdoor workers who tended the vast gardens and woods, called, then as now, the Wilderness. George I had been Lord George's godfather, and had come to his christening. The miserly old king had looked with envy on the mighty house, its magnificent furniture, paintings, silver, and statuary.

Perhaps any man growing up in such surroundings, with such a lineage, would inevitably be arrogant. But Lord George elevated this tendency into a habit that gave offense, even among his fellow peers, where arrogance was hardly unusual. He chose the army as his career, and advancement was swift. A major general at thirty-nine, he commanded the British troops in one of the great battles of the Seven Years' War, Minden. By this time, he was also a member of Parliament, with large political ambitions, and had become an intimate friend of Prince George, the heir apparent to the throne. The Prince and his circle disliked on principle everything that George II did, and Lord George Sackville was more than ready to play this dangerous game.

In Germany, he spent most of his time before the battle of Minden writing letters home criticizing his commander in chief, the Prussian Prince Ferdinand. A close relation of the King of Prussia and a distant cousin of George II, Ferdinand was a talented soldier who was as high-handed as Lord George. At Minden, the British infantry won an astonishing victory, repulsing four charges by the French cavalry and infantry. As the French reeled back, Prince Ferdinand ordered Lord George, who was in command of the cavalry, to attack immediately. It took him a half hour to obey the order, and by that time the opportunity to destroy the French army was lost. Censured in Prince Ferdinand's official reports, Lord George demanded a court-martial. George II packed the fifteen-man jury with generals who were his yes-men, and while his grandson Prince George looked on with helpless indignation, Lord George Sackville was found guilty of disobeying the orders of his commander in chief and was adjudged "unfit to serve His Majesty in any military capacity whatsoever." The King ordered the sentence, with its imputation of cowardice, read before every regiment in the British army. "So finishes the career of a man who was within ten minutes of being the first man in the profession in the kingdom," wrote one of Lord George's contemporaries.[4]

Essentially, this personal disaster was the result of political miscalculation, rooted in turn in that persistent arrogance which was the hallmark of Lord George's character. He assumed that young Prince George had far more influence on the politicians around aging George II than the timid prince actually possessed. Lord George had displayed a similar lack of judgment six years earlier, when he had served as his father's chief adviser during the latter's term as Lord Lieutenant of Ireland. The two Sackvilles had attempted to ram through the Irish Parliament a bill that would have given the English government the power to annex any surplus revenue left in the Irish exchequer at the end of the fiscal year.

The Irish House of Commons, ordinarily the most docile of parliamentary bodies, rebelled at this insult to their slender prerogatives. Lord George attempted to buy them off by offering Henry Boyle, the Speaker of the House, a peerage and a pension of £1,500 a year. Boyle denounced him in public, declaring, "If I had a peerage, I should not think myself greater than now that I am Mr. Boyle; for t'other thing, I despise it as much as the person who offers it." Lord George had to retire to London for safety, and the British government, retreating for the first time in decades before Irish wrath, removed his father as Lord Lieutenant.[5]

Lord George's experience in Ireland—and his inability to learn from it—is perhaps the most ominous, and least noticed, of the shadows cast by his emergence as the second most powerful man in the British government in 1776. Americans and the rest of the world have heard a good deal about British oppression in Ireland, but the details have always been distressingly vague. Arthur Young, a British agricultural expert, toured Ireland in 1776. Here are a few of his observations.

"It must be very apparent to every traveler through [Ireland] that the labouring poor are treated with harshness, and are in all respects so ill considered, that their want of importance seems a perfect contrast to their situation in England." Young castigated the "oppressive conduct of the little country gentlemen, or rather vermin of the kingdom," who "bear still very heavy on the poor people, and subject them to situations more mortifying than we ever behold in England."

A landlord of an Irish estate, Young found, was "a sort of despot who yields obedience, in whatever concerns the poor, to no law but that of his will." There was no point in consulting the law of the land, which supposedly protected the average man. "To discover what the liberty of a people is, we must live among them, and not look for it in any of the statutes of the realm," Young wisely noted. In Ireland, Young found that "many very ill-judged laws have brought landlords into a habit of exerting a very lofty superiority, and their vassals into that of an almost unlimited submission. . . . A landlord in Ireland can scarcely invent an order which a servant, laborer or cottar dares to refuse to execute. Disrespect or anything tending towards sauciness he may punish with his cane or his horsewhip with the most perfect security; a poor man would have his bones broke if he offered to lift his hand in his own defense. . . . Landlords of consequence have assured me that many of their cottars would think themselves honoured by having their wives and daughters sent for to the bed of their master; a mark of slavery that proves the oppression under which such people must live."

Young even heard anecdotes of landlords murdering their tenants without "any apprehension of the justice of a jury." He saw "whole strings of carts whipped into a ditch by a gentleman's footman to make way for his carriage." If a poor Irishman lodged a legal complaint against a gentleman, and the justice of the peace, almost all of whom Young found to be corrupt, issued a summons, the Irishman's life was literally in danger. "The colors of this picture are not charged [exaggerated]," Young insisted. There was little or nothing that "an unfeeling landlord" could not do with impunity. "What is liberty but a farce and a jest," Young asked, "if its blessings are received as the favor of kindness and humanity, instead of being the Inheritance of Right. . . . By what policy the Government of England can for so many years have permitted such an absurd system to be matured in Ireland, is beyond the power of plain sense to discover." [6]

It may have made no sense to a fair-minded man such as Young, but it made perfect sense to the aristocrats who were running England and Ireland. Bereft of all leadership since the exile of the Catholic nobility after the battle of the Boyne in 1690, Ireland was a perfect example of how aggressive governments such as England could first crush and then exploit another nation.

The example of Ireland could not have been lost on Lord George Germain. Nor was America so different from Ireland from his point of view. The Americans were all non-aristocrats, and as government pamphlet writers pointed out, they were no longer purebred Englishmen but a mingling of Irish, Scotch, German, and other peoples. If it proved to be politically suitable, the Americans could be treated as foreigners, even barbarians, a term which the British fastened on the Irish in the sixteenth century and used to justify any and every enormity. As early as 1767, Lord George was telling one of his closest friends, "Nothing but military power [can] make the Americans in their present temper submit." He denounced "the fatal consequences of yielding to riot and ill-grounded clamour." He traced all the troubles in America to the repeal of the Stamp Act in 1765. When Americans threw taxed tea into their harbors, Lord George's hard line became even harder. He called for the abolition of town meetings, commenting, "I would not have men of a mercantile cast every day collecting themselves together, and debating about political matters." He called colonial assemblies "a downright clog upon all the proceedings of the Governor." [7]

Manly perseverance was Lord George's formula for restoring things in America to "a due obedience to the laws of this country." He also made a point of condemning "that mob of people, which, under the profession of liberty carried dark designs in its execution." After Bunker Hill, he had no doubt whatsoever about the policy that should be pursued. "As there is no common sense in protracting a war of this sort, I should be for exerting the utmost force of this kingdom to finish this rebellion in one campaign." [8]

This was the kind of talk that made George III glow. Here was a man who had been one of England's best generals before his disgrace; here was an opportunity to right one of the many wrongs which George II and his coterie of party politicians had inflicted on those who opposed them. To a very minor extent, Lord George had also enhanced his appeal by changing his name. An old friend of the Sackville family, Lady Betty Germain, died in 1769, leaving him a handsome country house, Drayton, and an estate of £20,000, with the provision that he change his name to Germain. Lord George had no difficulty persuading Parliament to let him make the change, and he had legally become Lord George Germain. But he was still the detested Sackville to most Englishmen, and it was an act of considerable courage—and arrogance—on George III's part to make him the American secretary of state, and give him command of the war.

Taking office in November of 1775, Lord George began displaying that vigor and decision which the King hoped to see. He exuded confidence in a swift end to the war. "Lord G. Sackville seems in very good spirits—is quite persuaded that all this will end after the first campaign, and that he himself, as I take it for granted, shall establish his reputation as a minister by it," wrote one parliamentary observer.

On January 5, while Parliament was still in recess, Lord George sent his first communication to his commander in chief in the field, William Howe. He told Howe he could expect reinforcements of 15,000 men, bringing his total strength to some 23,000 for the 1776 campaign. An additional 10,000 men were going to Canada, to relieve Carleton in Quebec. The undersecretaries in the American Department were impressed by the energy Germain displayed and the clarity of his thinking. One secretary, Richard Cumberland, wrote later that there was "no trash in his mind." Lord George's letters were concise, he was punctual and demanded punctuality from others. He moved into a house in Pall Mall, only a short walk across the park from his offices in Whitehall.[9]

But Germain was in office only a few weeks when he also demonstrated his talent for being difficult. First, he proceeded to hold a great ball at his London house to which he invited every friendly politician of any importance—except Lord North and his wife. Instead of requesting a meeting of the cabinet, he "summoned it," which only the king or the prime minister usually did. When a sinecure, the Receiver General of Jamaica, became vacant on the death of a Scottish nobleman, he asked the King to give it to his son—who was only six years old. It paid £600 a year. The right to dispose of the job was not even attached to Lord George's department—it belonged to Lord North at the treasury. But little details like that never troubled Lord George Germain. The King, knowing North was in financial straits (he eventually accepted an outright gift of £20,000, which guaranteed his total subservience), gave it to one of his sons instead. But Lord George bullied North and the King into accepting his man as Lord Lieutenant of Ireland.[10]

For the moment, these portents of trouble could be dimissed as minor irritations. The King was vastly pleased with Lord George Germain, and felt free to concentrate on diplomatic negotiations that were equally essential to victory in America—the hiring of German mercenaries to do Britain's fighting for her.

VIII

Another King, Another Country

Throughout the summer and fall of 1775, George III had been hunting troops throughout Europe with growing desperation. For a while, there seemed to be a good chance of obtaining 20,000 men from Russia. This vast, secluded country, ruled by the empress Catherine the Great, had been wooed by the British to replace Austria-Hungary and Prussia, the major continental allies which England had lost. But Catherine the Great was shrewd enough to see that England was using her to play, somewhat halfheartedly, its traditional balance-of-power game in Europe. Moreover, in 1774 Catherine had had a revolution in southern Russia which reached alarming proportions. She decided she could not spare 20,000 of her veteran troops. She also did not think that the British decision to fight America made sense. France and Spain inevitably would join the conflict, and this might embroil Russia in a European war. The abortive revolution of 1774 had, it was rumored, been started by French agents. Catherine told George III that she was doing him a favor by refusing him troops. It was poor policy for the King to admit he was too weak to put down his rebellious subjects without foreign aid.

The so-called principality of Hanover, which George III theoretically still ruled as Elector, formed five battalions and garrisoned Gibraltar and the island of Minorca, releasing British regulars stationed there for service in America. But this was only a tiny percentage of the men Britain needed. A brigade of Scots had been serving as mercenaries in the Dutch army for the better part of a century. An attempt to per-

suade the good burghers of the Netherlands to part with these first-
class fighters failed. So George III and the Earl of Suffolk, his European secretary of state, turned to the next best market for hired
troops—Germany.

In 1776, the German nation existed largely as a language. The
kingdom of Prussia, ruled by the enlightened (in his opinion) despot,
Frederick the Great, occupied the north. In the southeast were the territories of Austria-Hungary. Between these two great powers was a
jumble of 300 sovereignties and 1,400 estates of Imperial Knights, who
claimed the right to rule by inherited titles from that even vaguer entity, the Holy Roman Empire. These mini-countries were called elector-
ates, duchies, bishoprics, free cities, counties. Almost all of them were
ruled by aristocrats who did their best to imitate the real kings and emperors by living on an absurdly extravagant scale. For generations,
many of them had been in the business of renting their troops to war-
ring powers to pay for their conspicuous consumption.

Among the best-known body merchants were the landgraves of
Hesse-Cassel. Their soldiers had been fighting for strangers in various
parts of Europe since 1687, and had fought for the British monarch on
the Continent in 1739, 1740, and 1742. A contingent of Hessians had
helped George II smash the last attempt of the Stuart kings to win back
the throne of England in the Scottish revolt of 1745. The present
landgrave of Hesse-Cassel, Frederick II, saw no reason to change the
national policy when he was approached by George III's emissary, Colonel William Faucitt, late in 1775. By this time, Frederick was working
on his second wife and reportedly had at least a hundred illegitimate
children. He maintained a French theater and opera and a French
corps de ballet. The possibility of paying for all this with British pounds
sterling did wonders for his *joie de vivre.* He cheerfully signed a contract
to rent 12,000 soldiers for £7.4.4½ per man. To keep the corps de
ballet dancing, he also persuaded Colonel Faucitt to part with an annual subsidy of £108,281.5 to be continued for a year after his troops
returned. The Landgrave also managed to extract from the British
treasury payment for an old claim dating from the Seven Years' War,
which had long since been disallowed. It amounted to a neat
£41,820.14.5.

Colonel Faucitt concluded a similar treaty with the Duke of Brunswick, whose brother, Prince Charles William, was married to a sister of
George III. The Duke had an Italian theatrical director receiving a salary of 30,000 thalers a year, and at one point had hired an alchemist in

a vain attempt to replenish his exchequer. For 3,964 infantrymen and 336 unmounted dragoons, he got the going rate per man plus a subsidy of £11,517.17.1½ while his troops were in service, and twice that amount for two years after their return to the dominions of "His Most Serene Highness." He also managed to get a clause which gave him the price of a new recruit for every man killed. The agreement also stipulated that "three wounded men shall be reckoned as one killed."

Faucitt managed to scrape up a few thousand more men by negotiating similar treaties with the tiny principalities of Hesse-Hanau, Waldeck, Ansbach-Bayreuth, and Anhalt-Zerbst. Prince Frederick August of Anhalt-Zerbst was a brother of Catherine the Great. But there is no evidence that she declined to send her Russians in order to feather Prince Frederick's little nest. He had only 20,000 subjects and spent most of his time in Basel and Luxembourg, letting privy councilors govern in his name. He is said to have issued a formal printed order that any servant who troubled him with the political or social problems of Anhalt-Zerbst was subject to immediate dismissal.[1]

By the time Colonel Faucitt completed his tour of Germany, he had 18,000 men. The princes were gleefully rubbing their well-oiled palms, and their recruiting agents were scouring the countryside for practically anything on two legs. Students were waylaid on their way to universities, the jails were emptied of bankrupts, deserters from other nations were taken into protective custody. A nineteen-year-old poet, Johann Gottfried Seume, was among those forcibly recruited in Hesse-Cassel. His university matriculation certificate was torn up and he thus lost "the only instrument of my identity." He found himself in a Hessian recruiting center, the fortress of Ziegenhain, where there was "a real medley of human beings." His comrades included a poet from Jena, a bankrupt merchant from Vienna, a haberdasher from Hanover, a dismissed postal clerk from Gotha, and a monk from Würzburg. But many other young men, bored with the peasant society of Germany, volunteered. More than a few were lured by promises that a man might make a fortune conquering such a rich country as America.[2]

The British purchasing effort inspired a good deal of acrid comment in Europe. Frederick the Great, who bore a grudge against the English for deserting him to sign a separate treaty with France at the end of the Seven Years' War, expressed his contempt for the German princes in a letter to Voltaire. It was "an unbecoming trait in the character of a prince," Frederick declared, to sell his subjects to the English "as one sells cattle to be dragged to the shambles. . . . Such conduct is caused by nothing but dirty selfishness." Frederick could have stopped the whole business with a curt order. After all, the English were stripping Germany of men that he might need if he went to war with either of his traditional enemies, France or Austria-Hungary. On the other hand, such were the twists and turns of international politics, there might come a time when Frederick needed England, or England's money. So he confined his opposition to sneers.

Moreover, though he had a grudge against the English, the King of Prussia liked the American revolutionaries even less. Enlightened though Frederick claimed himself to be, he was still a despot, and frowned on any and all tendencies to alter the present order of things, which placed him and his fellow aristocrats firmly in charge of Europe.[3]

But Frederick was a minor power compared to the nation that bestrode the heart of Europe—France. If France had chosen to interfere, Colonel Faucitt could never have bought his Germans—nor would George III, his ministers, and loyal followers in Parliament have dared to concoct their dream of smashing the Americans. This illusion was rooted firmly in the larger illusion that France would remain a cool— even cowardly—spectator of the American imbroglio. There were good reasons for believing this in the early months of 1776, but it was to prove a disastrous illusion before the end of the year. To find out why, we must spend some time in the nation that was to be shaken more fundamentally by the American Revolution than any other country in the world.

Paris was the only city in Europe that rivaled London in size and wealth. Its 600,000 people were three times the population of Amsterdam or Vienna. In the city's government offices and in the halls and salons of the palace of Versailles, the men in power greeted the year 1776 with gloating anticipation. More and more, it looked as if it would be a year in which their hated enemy, those detestable, perfidious English, finally got what the laws of God and economics decreed they deserved. For most of the century, France had been fighting England's growing power, and in between the wars predicting her collapse. To France, possessed of an immense swath of Europe's most fertile land, with its population of twenty-six industrious millions to England's seven, the English ascendancy was both a terrible goad and an infuriating mystery. The average Frenchman was fond of portraying England as a little frog that was trying to inflate itself to the size of an ox. Eventually it was certain to explode.[4]

Twenty-two-year-old Louis XVI was a popular king in early 1776. Not so much because he had done anything spectacularly wise or good to merit the confidence of the nation in his eighteen months on the throne, but because his grandfather, Louis XV, had done so many spectacularly wrong and despicable things. There were celebrations in the streets of Paris when Louis XV died. His funeral procession was showered with offal and indecent remarks. His reign had been a long decline into moral and political disgrace. Politically, the ultimate insult was the 1772 partition of Poland between Russia, Prussia, and Austria, without even consulting France, once the greatest power in Europe.

Morally, the indulgent—indeed, indifferent—monarch was ruled by his mistresses, whose extravagance was monumental. The King had trended down from Madame de Pompadour, a charming bourgeoise, to Madame Du Barry, who began her career in a Paris brothel. She spent money at the rate of a million livres a year, mostly on diamonds and dresses. In the course of his fifty-year reign, the King's income had risen from 120 million to 300 million livres, yet he still operated at an enormous deficit. In his will, Louis XV summed up his reign: "I have governed and administered badly because I have little talent and I have been badly advised."

Louis XVI began his reign resolving, not unlike George III, to give his nation a new age, free of the previous regime's corruptions and extravagances. One of his first gestures was a gift of 200,000 livres to the poor of Paris. Next, to everyone's amazement, he renounced the *joyeux avènement* (the "joyful accession"), a special grant usually given to the king on his coronation day to enable him to launch his reign in style. It had cost the French taxpayers 20 million livres for Louis XV. His young queen, Marie Antoinette, renounced a similar gift, known as the *droit de ceinture* (the "right of the girdle"), which is puzzling until we recall that in the eighteenth century women wore their purses tied to a belt around their waist. These gestures had won cheers from the fickle Paris mob.

But like George III on the other side of the Channel, Louis XVI was already on his way to proving that hell is paved with good intentions. George III's priggish view of politics made it impossible for him to work with anyone who was not a yes-man. Louis XVI's approach to politics was at the opposite extreme—so vapid and formless that he was inclined to sway before every passing influence.

There were powerful contradictory influences at work in France. The King had three aunts, all of whom were ready to advise him on national policy. Around them clustered a circle of cardinals, bishops, and true believers known as the *Dévots,* who were convinced that all-out support of the Catholic Church and its policies was the only thing that could save France. Next came the spokesmen for the nobility, led by the princes of the blood royal who fought to maintain aristocratic rights and privileges against the rising bourgeoisie and the restless masses. There was also a circle around Louis's nineteen-year-old queen, Marie Antoinette, who was determined to emulate her mother, Maria Theresa of Austria, one of the great politicians of her era. The Queen backed the Duke de Choiseul, who was, until he was fired in 1770, the dominant minister of Louis XV's reign and the architect of the policy of perpetual war against England. Finally, there were the men of the Enlightenment, determined to break the grip of the established church on the mind and spirit of the masses and convinced that a heady dose of rational thinking could reform the regime and set France on a course to true greatness.

Trying to keep all of these people happy, Louis XVI first surrendered to the importunities of his aunts and appointed as his prime minister Jean Frédéric Phélippeaux Maurepas, a septuagenarian incompetent who had been discarded by Louis XV decades ago, in one of his few discerning gestures. To satisfy his queen, the crucial post of foreign minister went to the Count de Vergennes, a moderate disciple of Choiseul. To appease the philosophers and his own conscience, Louis chose as his minister of finance Baron Anne Robert Jacques Turgot, a reformer who was convinced that the future of France lay not in fighting with England but in trading with her.[5]

Turgot belonged to a group of economic thinkers called Physiocrats. They were somewhat naïvely convinced that all wealth came from the land, and the future of a peaceful world order was perceivable in the doctrine of free trade. Like most sweeping ideas in any era, this was rooted in the experience of preceding decades. Most of the wars fought in the eighteenth century, particularly those between France and England, were for commercial advantages, thinly disguised as political principles. Turgot and his circle of thinkers concluded that the cost of the wars exceeded the worth of the trading rights, islands, and colonies for which they were fought.

When he became minister of finance, Turgot had little interest in foreign policy. As he saw it, his mission was to create a French nation whose wealth surpassed England's to the precise degree that France's numbers and the fertility of her soil exceeded those of perfidious Albion. Then, if the King so decided, the Crown could create a French army and navy second to none—especially a navy—and challenge England for world dominion once more. But Turgot was determined to create this wealth the French way—not the English way. It would not be based on credit, on paper loans floated by the Bank of England. It would be rooted in the potentially enormous productivity of the French land. In order to enhance that fertility and tap that productivity, drastic reforms were needed.

Although the actual revenues of the monarchy approached 500 million livres (a livre was worth about twenty-five cents) a year—larger than those of the King of Great Britain, twice as large as those of the Hapsburgs, three times those of Russia, Prussia, Spain, or the Dutch Republic—the government was operating at a deficit of 37 million livres a year. The total debt was at least 235 million—as far as Turgot could determine. Government accounting was incredibly bad. Accountants more or less owned various taxes, collected them as individual entrepreneurs, and invested the money for their own profit, getting around to paying the government five or six and even twelve years later.[6] In this situation, Turgot was forced to warn the King that unless the budget was balanced and 20 million livres reserved to reduce longstanding debts, "the first gunshot will drive the State to bankruptcy." [7]

Turgot's primary goal was the reform of France's tax structure. This was organized around the Farmers General, a corporate entity that was virtually a state within a state. They advanced to the King the money he needed to keep the court at Versailles functioning and the wheels of government turning. The Crown already owed the Farmers some 130 million livres at outrageous interest rates. In return for their cash, the King gave the Farmers the right to collect his taxes—at an enormous profit. On a single contract, a man could make 60 million livres. There were sixty farmers plus hordes of associates, all among the wealthiest people in France. Each farmer had a list of *croupiers,* parasites who attached themselves to the operation through various forms of political influence. From the farm of 1774, for instance, the controller general got 300,000 livres (the *pot de vin*) simply for signing the contract. Marquises and dentists were side by side on the list of *croupiers* with the nurse of the Duke of Burgundy, a singer at the Queen's concerts, discarded mistresses of Louis XV, and the ex-King's daughters, each clipping one or two thousand livres.

Over the centuries, the tax system had accumulated endless exceptions that permitted the nobility and high bourgeois—anyone, in short, with money or influence—to avoid paying the various levies. As a result, the tax burden fell on the peasantry, leaving them in a perpetual state of economic underdevelopment. Turgot announced plans to equalize the tax structure and eliminate some aristocratic privileges. This sent the French aristocracy into hysteria.

A substantial difference between France and England was the numbers of the nobility. In England, the word "noble" was limited to the great lords. Baronets and knights were called "sir," but unless they had the money to buy respect, they had no additional claim to distinction or privileges. In France, the *noblesse* were much more numerous. Tens of thousands of families had the right to put *"de"* between their first and last names. Sometimes the king, in a sweeping decree, added whole groups to the nobility. Louis XV, for instance, gave 4,000 bourgeois officers in the army noble papers and tax exemptions after thirty years' service.[8]

None of the aristocrats were in the least inclined to surrender their tax exemptions on Turgot's demand. In fact, since 1760 they had been aggressively asking—and often getting—more and better favors from the regime. This aristocratic resurgence was common throughout Europe, and it made the American Revolution—on the surface, at least—an attempt to swim against a very strong international tide.[9]

Turgot also attempted to break up various monopolies that were inhibiting France's economic growth. He ordered a free trade in grain—instead of the traditional policy of the government's setting the price and instantly creating a black market, which led to immense corruption, house-to-house searches, and vast public resentment. He abolished the guilds, which had become closed corporations, like some contemporary American unions. Each year, thousands of France's best artisans left the country to seek work elsewhere because they could see no future bucking the nepotism and narrow self-interest of the guilds. Turgot also abolished laws which prevented foreign craftsmen from settling in France. He even tried to lure across the Channel English textile workers made jobless by the loss of American markets.

Unfortunately, Turgot was no politician. His tough approach to France's problems soon coined an ominous *bon mot*. Insiders compared him to the Abbé Terray, the minister of finance in the closing days of Louis XV's reign, who operated largely by letting France go bankrupt in stages, defaulting on government debts whenever he thought he could get away with it. Terray, they said, did everything wrong in the right way, but Turgot did everything right in the wrong way.

Throughout 1775, Turgot's enemies attacked him from all directions. They fomented a mini-revolution in Paris by artificially driving up the price of bread, then blaming it on Turgot's free trade in grain. Turgot defeated them by dismissing the minister of police and moving 25,000 troops into the Seine River valley. The *Dévots* accused him of being an atheist. He still declined to go to mass on Sunday. The aristocrats called him a revolutionist in disguise. Marie Antoinette and her hawks called him a coward for frowning on war with England. The American Revolution gave them a chance to shout this accusation. Turgot ignored this cacophony and reiterated the warning he had given the King when he first took over France's finances—*the first gunshot will drive the state to bankruptcy.* He urged the King to let the British and the Americans fight each other into exhaustion, with no assistance from France to either side.

In the first months of 1776, Turgot was by far the most powerful man in the French government, in spite of his widespread unpopularity. He dominated the young King with his blunt ways and forthright honesty. If he could not be persuaded that war—or a flirtation with war—to help the American colonies was a sound move, there would be no move. The Count de Vergennes, the French foreign minister, was edging toward intervention—ironically impelled by growing confidence in France's finances created by Turgot's reforms. In a letter to a friend, Vergennes echoed the standard French opinion about the English. "These people can go on as much as they like about the wealth of England, but I still regard it as an unnatural growth, a sort of bloated dropsy; I prefer the healthy plumpness of France, even if it does come from overindulgence. At least it is real: fertile lands, valuable produce, hard cash. No amount of credit crises can bring that down." [10]

From England, the French ambassador, the Count de Guines, sent his government a steady stream of information about the American revolt. This fascination with America was a fairly recent development. When Guines returned to London in the late spring of 1775, Foreign Minister Vergennes was much more concerned about settling the ten-year-old dispute over French fishing rights off Newfoundland and another long-running argument between the French and British East India companies. Guines was ordered above all to maintain good relations with England. Vergennes was worried about the possibility that the English would start a war with France to divert the Americans. In fact, he even told Guines that France really desired to aid Great Britain in suppressing the American revolt, if it could do so discreetly. France had colonies, too, and the revolution was a dangerous example.[11]

But on July 1, 1775, Vergennes received an excited dispatch from his ambassador that changed his mind about America. Guines reported that fighting had broken out, and supposedly impregnable Fort Ticonderoga, over which the French and British had fought more than one bloody battle, had fallen to the amazing Americans. Vergennes ordered Guines to start pounding on tables to make his points. Guines tried this with Lord Rochford, the English secretary of state for the Southern Department, demanding (not asking) an immediate concession of broad French rights to store boats and other fishing equipment along the northern portion of the Newfoundland coast.

Although the British had conceded this right in the treaty that ended the Seven Years' War, they had been systematically sabotaging the French fishing fleet ever since, hoping to further cripple France as a naval power. Instead of caving in to Guines's belligerence, Lord Rochford replied that if the Frenchman meant what he was saying, his King had better prepare for war. This remark caused an enormous flap in Versailles and almost frightened Vergennes out of his job. He told Guines to assure the British that war was the last thing France wanted.[12]

When the Americans invaded Canada, captured Montreal, and invested Quebec, Vergennes switched back to an aggressive policy, but with much more discreet execution. A trusted naval officer, Achard de Bonvouloir, was sent to America to reconnoiter the situation. Vergennes wrote a series of *Considerations* designed to convince the King, the French cabinet, and, above all, Turgot that it was time to embark on a more aggressive policy toward England. The *Considerations* recommended that France and Spain, united by the Bourbon family compact—the King of Spain was Louis XVI's uncle—should begin rearming. At the same time, France should make elaborate efforts to assure the British government that it had no intention of helping the Americans. Finally, France should funnel secret assistance to the Americans.

Turgot wrote a long, vigorous reply to these *Considerations* in which he deplored all flirtation with a war with England at this time. He had managed to reduce the annual deficit to a projected 24 million livres in 1776 without raising a single tax. He was in the midst of negotiating a 60-million-livre loan from Dutch bankers which would free the King from some of the murderous interest he was paying to French financiers of the Farmers General. All his reforms would be undone by war with England. The most Turgot would concede was a policy of secret assistance to the Americans on a very small scale. The King, trying to please everyone as usual, waffled. He expressed grave scruples of conscience against stabbing George III in the back while pretending to be his good friend. To arouse the King, Vergennes decided that he needed a more impassioned pleader than he was in person or on paper. Where was he to be found? Reading his diplomatic mail, Vergennes suddenly realized the man he needed was in England— Pierre Augustin Caron de Beaumarchais.

Most people know Beaumarchais as the author of two famous plays which became even more famous operas, *The Barber of Seville* and *The Marriage of Figaro*. A watchmaker's son, he had risen from obscurity to considerable wealth and not a little notoriety in France. But he did not win either the wealth or the notoriety by writing plays. His wealth was built on solid business ability and a connection with Joseph Pâris-Duverney, one of the great merchant-bankers of the era. Beaumarchais had worked as Pâris-Duverney's right-hand man—practically an adopted son—and together they had made a fortune supplying the French army during the Seven Years' War. Simultaneously, Beaumarchais was carving out an influential career at court. For 85,000 livres, he purchased a title in the lower ranks of the nobility, which included the office of *Secretaire du Roi* and gave him the rank of *écuyer*—squire. There was nothing unusual about this—it was done all the time in a France where almost all the bourgeoisie yearned to be included in the *noblesse*.

In 1774, Beaumarchais had won his notoriety in a spectacular battle with the heirs of Pâris-Duverney over his benefactor's will. He had already won the confidence of high officials in the French government, serving as an unofficial envoy to Spain, and next as a secret agent on a special mission for Louis XV in London. As January, 1776, dawned, Beaumarchais was within twenty-two days of celebrating his forty-fourth birthday. He was a solid, responsible, sophisticated man with a reputation for shrewd judgment and remarkable energy. It was this reputation which sent him back to London on another mission for the new king, Louis XVI.[13]

Beaumarchais's first mission to London, in March of 1774—and the current one—were intimately connected with the follies of Louis XV. A French blackmailer named Morand had written a life of Madame Du

Barry that was certain to cause a scandal if published. Since even the truth about Du Barry was malodorous, it is not difficult to imagine what this hack biographer had poured into his bit of diplomatic pornography. Acting as the King's agent, Beaumarchais bought up the three thousand copies already printed, burned them in a plaster furnace outside London, and secured Morand's future silence for an annuity of 4,000 livres.

Beaumarchais's second mission to London involved an even more fantastic situation. This time, he was negotiating with Chevalier Charles Geneviève d'Éon de Beaumont. This son of a Burgundy nobleman had been circulating in London for thirteen years as a living mystery. No one knew whether he (she) was a man or a woman. The Chevalier smoked black cigars and was one of the foremost duelists of Europe. But he (she) had a sweet, delicate voice, no sign whatsoever of a beard, and the rounded contours of his physique suggested femininity. Wearing a skirt, he had gone to St. Petersburg in 1755 as a secret envoy of the French King, talked her (his) way into the confidence of the Tsarina, and was the conduit of a secret correspondence that eventually led to an alliance between Russia and France against England and Prussia.

The Chevalier put on his trousers for the Seven Years' War and distinguished himself as a captain in a regiment of dragoons. Thereafter, he was sent to England as a secret envoy of the King, with the promise that he would be made ambassador. But court intrigue handed this plum to another nobleman, and Éon remained undercover with a salary of 12,000 livres a year. Louis XV continued to correspond with him, and with almost unbelievable indiscretion sent him a series of letters outlining plans for a surprise invasion of England.

Éon was ordered to gather technical information on landing beaches, roads, local militia strength, and other pertinent data. When Louis XV died, Éon's salary died with him, but he was soon knocking on Louis XVI's treasury door with a polite request for 318,477 livres— his price for handing over Louis XV's compromising letters. Beaumarchais was sent to London with orders to extract the letters from Éon at a more reasonable price and get him out of England before the British bought him. For nine months, April to December, 1775, Beaumarchais negotiated with Éon. Simultaneously, he spent a great deal of time talking with two men who changed him from a loyal servant of the King to a semi-revolutionary. Their names were John Wilkes and Arthur Lee.

John Wilkes was the Lord Mayor of London. He told Beaumarchais, "The King of England has long done me the honor to hate me. I, on my side, have always done him the justice to despise him; the time has come to decide which of the two has shown the best judgment, and on which side the wind will blow off the most heads."

This braggadocio echoed an American illusion which had flowered in 1774–75 and was wilting in 1776—the belief that a revolution in America would be supported by a revolution in England. To America, watching from three thousand miles away, Wilkes seemed to be the logical leader of the Cause in the mother country. In the 1760s, he had clashed with George III and the political establishment over his right to a seat in Parliament, in spite of a conviction for impious and seditious libel. Elected from Middlesex in an orgy of riots and drunkenness and expelled again and again by Parliament, Wilkes had become a popular hero of the London poor. But he was a hollow man who loved publicity more than principles. He expressed his real purpose when he made his first run for Parliament after his conviction: "I must raise a dust or starve in a gaol." He had nothing but contempt for his London followers who paid off his gambling debts by subscription. He often ridiculed them in public. When a political associate told him not to treat his friends that way, Wilkes replied, "I never laugh at my *friends*, but these are only my followers." [14]

With such a leader, it was inevitable that by 1776 the Wilkites had receded from a movement to a faction. Wilkes's eye was not on revolution but on the lucrative office of chamberlain of the City of London, which he finally won on a fourth try in 1779. As Wilkes put it later, mocking himself as much as his followers, "I was never a Wilkite." Basically, Wilkes was only a step removed from the French pornographer, Morand, with his use of blackmail or the threat of blackmail for his own aggrandizement. Only at a distance did Wilkes emerge as a political hero.

But for Arthur Lee a close examination of an issue or a man only seemed to increase his political myopia. A Virginia-born graduate of Eton with an M.D. from the University of Edinburgh, Lee returned briefly to America, but was soon back in London to study law—an early sign of his basic instability. He got deeply involved in Wilkes's brawl with Parliament and became a passionate, no-holds-barred foe of the British establishment. The Revolution was made to order for his temperament, which was a strange blend of acrimony and idealism.

While Wilkes filled one of Beaumarchais's ears with vituperation against George III and his minions in Parliament, Arthur Lee was pouring into the other ear a heady combination of American defiance and pugnacity. By the time 1776 dawned, Beaumarchais was convinced that revolution in America was not only inevitable—it would be inevitably successful. It was therefore imperative, he believed, for France to participate in the event and reap all possible benefits from it. Beyond this calculation, Arthur Lee's declamations on American rights and his descriptions of American freedom stirred in the soul of Beaumarchais an idealism which he had never known before. Soon he was no longer merely a diplomatic proponent of the American Cause, he was America's passionate advocate in the court of Louis XVI.

On February 29, 1776, with Vergennes's encouragement, Beaumarchais wrote a letter entitled "Peace or War." It was directed "To the King alone," and began:

> SIRE—
> The famous quarrel between America and England, which will soon divide the world and change the system of Europe, imposes upon each power the necessity of examining well in what manner the event of this separation can influence it, and either serve it or injure it. . . . I am obliged to warn Your Majesty that the preservation of our possessions in America, and the peace which Your Majesty appears to desire so much, depends solely upon this one proposition: the Americans must be *assisted*. I will now demonstrate it.

Beaumarchais, with the skill of a born writer, played on the King's natural resentment against the English style in war and diplomacy. "Have the . . . outrages of this people ever had any limit but that of its strength? Has it not always waged war against you without declaring it? . . . The most solemn treaty of peace, to this usurping nation, is merely a truce demanded by exhaustion and from which it always issues through glaring hostilities."

In several thousand more words, Beaumarchais told the King that if the Americans and the British composed their differences, they would almost certainly attack the islands of the French West Indies to recoup the losses which their dispute had already caused them. The Americans would be glad to join in this war because they would be furious at France for her refusal to assist them. The only way of preserving peace and French prosperity, Beaumarchais argued, was by "secretly assisting the Americans without compromising ourselves." [15]

At the same time, Beaumarchais descanted on the tense political situation in London, as described to him by the highly nonobjective Wilkes. "The slightest reverse of the Royalists in America, strengthening the audacity of the people and of the opposition, may bring matters to a head in London when least expected, and should the King find himself obliged to yield, I do not believe his crown safer on his head than the heads of his ministers on their shoulders."

In Versailles, Vergennes backed up Beaumarchais's assault on Louis XVI's emotions with another cold-blooded analysis of why France should get involved in the Revolution. These *Reflexions,* as they were called, summed up the goal of French assistance to the Americans as follows: "First of all, it will diminish the power of England and increase in proportion that of France. Second, it will cause irreparable loss to English trade, while it will considerably extend ours. Third, it presents to us as very probable the recovery of a part of the possessions which the English have taken from us in America, such as the fisheries of Newfoundland and of the Gulf of St. Lawrence. . . . We do not speak of Canada."

As for the Americans becoming dangerous if they win their independence, Vergennes dismissed it. The war would exhaust them, and if they set up a republican government—as they seemed inclined to do—few republics in history had showed much appetite for or ability at conquest. To soothe the King, Vergennes emphasized the importance of keeping French aid as secret as possible. Under no circumstances should France risk a war with England until it was clear that the Americans were going to win. For the time being, arms and munitions should be supplied clandestinely, disguised as transactions between businessmen.

While Vergennes was moving France toward war in Versailles, strange things were happening in the French Embassy in London. Toward the end of January, 1776, Vergennes ordered the Count de Guines to renew his demand for the proper treatment of French fishermen on the Newfoundland shore. Guines talked twice with Lord Rochford's replacement, Lord Weymouth, one of the most aggressive French-hating aristocrats in the British administration. Weymouth insulted Guines in so many different ways the incensed ambassador told Vergennes he doubted if the whole history of diplomacy would furnish anything like the two conferences he had just endured. Guines himself was, of course, one reason why Weymouth thought he could get away with such arrogance. He was dissolute, incompetent, and weak. Even while Guines was taking his lumps from Weymouth, Vergennes was trying to get him replaced—no easy task, because he was a favorite of Queen Marie Antoinette.[16]

The British undoubtedly thought they could get away with almost anything when dealing with Guines, because they knew everything he was doing and thinking. His private secretary had sold them Guines's secret diplomatic ciphers for £500. The British had also planted in the French Embassy a fantastic character named Pierre Roubaud, an ex–Jesuit missionary to the Abenaki Indians who had attached himself to the English after Canada fell, rather than return to France and face charges of stealing some 66,000 livres from his mission treasury. Roubaud was a total scoundrel, who peddled documents from the Jesuit archives in Canada as military intelligence, and talked himself into an English pension of £100 per year, plus a job as secretary to the British ambassador at The Hague. In 1774, when the American crisis exploded, he rushed back to London, hoping to make his fortune. The witless Guines was a perfect foil for this fast-talking con man. When Roubaud told him that he was intimate with John Pownall, the undersecretary for American affairs, and was a confidant of Lord Dartmouth, then the American secretary, Guines agreed to pay Roubaud £500 a year for information. Roubaud was, of course, doing and saying all this as a double agent, with the complete knowledge and approval of the British.

But Roubaud was too greedy and unstable to be satisfied with taking Guines's money and making a fool of him. The ex-Jesuit had dreams of glory. Like too many fertile brains working on the fringes of power politics, he had an exaggerated confidence in his own ingenuity. So, in the last weeks of 1775, he dropped into Guines's lap a document that was to have an explosive future. It was, he told the gullible ambassador, the product of Undersecretary Pownall, who had a well-known reputation as an American hater. The document propounded nothing less than a British-French alliance to suppress the American rebellion. Guines swallowed the bait whole. He saw himself as the hinge on which a vast historical maneuver was about to swing. He rushed news of the proposal to France. Meanwhile, Roubaud was working the other side of the street. He went to almost every minister in the British cabinet and presented him with the memoir, telling him he was doing so at Guines's request.

Incredibly, the British believed him. In their arrogance, they saw this as proof that they had no need to worry about French intervention. It made them more high-handed than ever in their approach to the American quarrel. Guines helped fuel this illusion by talking up the idea all around London. He even went so far as to suggest that the

Bourbon compact between France and Spain was a bagatelle which could be ignored at the prospect of an alliance with England. The infuriated Spanish complained to Versailles, and this gave Vergennes the excuse he was looking for to dismiss Guines as ambassador.

Meanwhile, although not a word had come from France to support Guines's aborted diplomacy, Roubaud's memoir was taking on a life of its own. Among its readers was Lord Sandwich, the First Lord of the Admiralty. He decided to send twenty copies to the colonies "to convince the Americans that France, far from wishing to help them, was prepared to join itself to England to subjugate them." This was the way Roubaud proudly described it to the French chargé d'affaires, Charles Garnier, on April 2, 1776. This comic-opera combination of deception and fantasy would rebound on the British with historic impact.[17]

Nothing illustrates more cogently than Roubaud's caper the difficulties involved in controlling men and events with the feeble resources of human intelligence. In Versailles, another event was about to illustrate this maxim in even more mordant terms. The combination of Vergennes and Beaumarchais, with some help from Marie Antoinette, coached by the followers of Choiseul, had convinced Louis XVI that he could with a good conscience help separate the American colonies from the domain of his fellow monarch, George III. On April 22, the King ordered the navy to begin rebuilding and the army to begin purchasing new equipment. On May 2, he agreed to supply one million livres to Roderigue Hortalez & Co., a new enterprise headed by a delighted Caron de Beaumarchais, whose sole business was to be the sale of guns, ammunition, and the other sinews of war to the Americans. To make these decisions, Louis XVI had to discard the one man who might have saved his crown—Turgot.[18]

On May 10, Turgot journeyed to Versailles to see the King. "What do you want?" said Louis abruptly. "I have not time to see you."

The next day, the minister of finance was in Versailles again. He was curtly told that Louis was hunting. He called later in the day and was told even more curtly that Louis was dressing. On May 12, a courtier informed Turgot that the King wanted his resignation.

Turgot wrote the King a letter in his bluntest style. He denounced virtually everyone in the cabinet for intriguing to wreck his reforms. With or without his help, Turgot begged Louis XVI to be a real king. "Do not forget, Sire, that it was weakness that placed the head of Charles I [of England] on the block; it was weakness that made Charles

IX [of Spain] cruel; it was weakness . . . that made Louis XIII and makes the King of Portugal today crowned slaves; it was weakness that led to all the unhappiness of the last reign."

Mournfully, a few days later, Turgot wrote to his friend, the Abbé Veri, "I shall part with the regret of seeing a good dream disappear, of seeing a young King, who deserves a better fate, and a kingdom lost entirely by one who ought to have saved it. But I shall depart without shame and without remorse." [19]

The dismissal of Turgot left as the most powerful man in the French government Foreign Minister Vergennes, proponent of intervention in the English family quarrel. He quickly persuaded Spain to add another million livres to the resources of Roderigue Hortalez & Co. Thus, before a single American diplomat reached Paris, the French had decided to support a revolution that would eventually inspire a far more destructive imitation at home.

IX

Politicians
in Search of a Policy

Three times during the month of December, 1775, Benjamin Franklin and John Dickinson of Pennsylvania, Thomas Johnson of Maryland, John Jay of New York, and Benjamin Harrison of Virginia left their Philadelphia residences and traveled by circuitous routes to a rendezvous with the French agent Achard de Bonvouloir. His contact was the French-born librarian of the Philadelphia Library, Francis Daymon, who arranged for a preliminary meeting between Franklin and the self-styled "Antwerp merchant," who insisted he had come to America "out of curiosity." Franklin, Dickinson, Jay, et al. were members of a secret committee created by the Continental Congress for "the sole purpose of corresponding with our friends in Great Britain, Ireland, and other parts of the world." Another secret group, later called the Committee of Commerce, headed by the merchant Robert Morris, was formed about the same time to buy war matériel.

Bonvouloir spoke to the Committee of Secret Correspondence, through a cloud of double meanings. He insisted he had only oral instructions and spoke of "acquaintances" in France to whom he could pass on requests. Franklin asked him bluntly if France would help America. Bonvouloir zigzagged. "France wishes them well." Whether she would aid them—"That might happen." The secret agent winced at Franklin's suggestion that Americans send a deputy with full powers to France. This might arouse the English lion. But he was willing to pass on the inquiry. After all, he was only "a traveler," but if his "acquaintances" turned out to be of service, he would be "much pleased."

Franklin all but blew Bonvouloir's cover by remarking that the Americans were thinking of asking Spain for help, instead of France. Bonvouloir argued vehemently against this idea. Convinced that he was dealing with a French government agent, Franklin gave Bonvouloir a thorough briefing on American plans to resist the British army and navy. The Frenchman was soon convinced that the Americans were determined to defy Britain and declare their independence. He rushed a report to Vergennes, stating these conclusions in unqualified terms.[1]

These midnight meetings of the secret committee would seem to more than substantiate the conviction of George III and his ministers that the American leaders were plotters aiming at independence. But a poll of the Committee of Secret Correspondence would have exploded this illusion. Franklin was the only member committed to independence. The rest were either strongly opposed or at best lukewarm to the idea. One of them, Thomas Johnson of Maryland, would soon enter into secret discussions with the Royal Governor of his colony about ways to resolve the crisis peacefully and keep America in the Empire. The conduct of the committeemen and their opinions were typical of the schizophrenia afflicting most Americans in the early months of 1776.[2]

One of the reasons for this confusion was the way the Continental Congress operated. A visit to the first-floor room of the Pennsylvania State House, where Congress met—with the royal coat of arms still conspicuously displayed above the building's front door—is an educational if not exactly edifying experience.

Nothing was too large—or too small—for the attention of this haphazardly selected body of men, who found themselves fighting a continental war. Early on January 1, 1776, they voted for an adjutant for a battalion of infantrymen from Pennsylvania, and elected one John Patterson. A few minutes later, they were embarked on more of the fuzzy strategy that had led to the disaster at Quebec.

> *Resolved,* that the seizing and securing the barracks and castle of St. Augustine [Florida] will greatly contribute to the safety of these colonies; therefore it is earnestly recommended to the colonies of South Carolina, North Carolina and Georgia, to undertake the reduction of St. Augustine, if it be thought practicable.

The following day, the congressmen were worrying over barracks and stockings for Continental battalions in New Jersey. They ordered the convention of New Jersey to pay the "Colony of New York" a thousand dollars for furnishing New Jersey troops with a hundred muskets. Then, scarcely drawing a breath, Congress plunged into fundamental policy again. They urged the "different assemblies, conventions, and committees or councils of safety in the United Colonies" to take "speedy and effectual measures to frustrate the mischievous machinations and restrain the wicked practices" of "unworthy Americans" who were spreading "erroneous opinions respecting the American Cause and the probable issue of the present contest." Congress recommended that "the more dangerous" should be "kept in safe custody"— that is, jail—or forced to post bonds to guarantee "their good behavior."

In this and other maledictions on the loyalists, Congress tacitly admitted that revolutionary fervor in the United Colonies was by no means universal. They also made it plain that they did not consider freedom of speech a luxury which Americans could enjoy in 1776.

The following day, January 3, Congress played purchasing agent.

> *Resolved,* that the following goods and stores ought to be imported, as soon as possible, for the use of the United Colonies, viz: 60,000 striped blankets; 120,000 yards of 6–4 broadcloth, the colors to be brown and blue, from 3 s. to 6 s. sterling per yard; 10,000 yards of ditto, different colours, for facings, at 4 s.; . . . 100 M sorted needles . . . 20,000 stand of arms; 300 tons of lead; one million flints; 1,500 boxes of tin and iron wire, properly sorted . . .

A few minutes later, they were pondering whether to pay Robert Erwin, wagonmaster, $222.60 for carrying clothing and medicine to Dobbs Ferry and Cambridge. They decided to pay him.

Then back to politics. Queens County, New York, was populated almost exclusively by Americans loyal to the King. They declined even to send deputies to the New York [revolutionary] provincial congress. The gentlemen in Philadelphia resolved that all those who voted against sending deputies should have their names published and patriotic Americans should henceforth cease "all trade and intercourse with them." They were forbidden to leave Queens County without a certificate from the New York congress or committee of safety, and they were to be immediately disarmed with the help of 600 militiamen from New Jersey.

The next day, the solons were back to small beer, selecting lieutenant colonels for Pennsylvania regiments, repaying James Whitehead $64 for his expenses in feeding prisoners captured aboard a British ship, and paying $1,165.70 to the "sundry persons" who signed the Continental money before it was issued.[3]

Thus did the Continental Congress attempt to grapple with the task of organizing and running a government along a thousand miles of the North American coast, while simultaneously fighting a war. The policy in regard to enlisting free Negroes, the pay of assistant engineers, the number of chaplains per regiment, the request of Ibbetson Hamar, a captured British officer, "for leave to reside with Mrs. Hamar" were all duly pondered, resolved, and ordered. That the net result was not total confusion was rather miraculous.

It was hard work. John Adams told his wife, Abigail, in December, "The whole Congress is taken up, almost in different committees, from seven to ten in the morning. From ten to four or sometimes five, we are in Congress, and from six to ten, in committees again. I don't mention this to make you think me a man of importance, because it is not I alone, but the whole Congress is thus employed, but to apologize for not writing to you oftener."

"I rise at six," Silas Deane of Connecticut wrote to his wife, "write until seven, dress and breakfast by eight, go to the Committee of Claims until ten; then in Congress till half past three or perhaps four, dine by five, and then go into the Committee of Secrecy or Trade till nine; then sup and go to bed by eleven. This leaves little room for diversion or anything else . . ."

No wonder more than a few delegates showed signs of strain. Joseph Hewes of North Carolina groused that "we grow tired, indolent, Captious, Jealous, and want a recess."

Even more alarming at this early stage was news of financial anemia. The first three million dollars in paper money which Congress had voted six months ago was spent. Three more million had to be voted, and on January 11, Congress resolved that any person "so lost to all virtue in regard to his country" as to refuse to accept this new money was to be treated "as an enemy of his country and precluded from all trade or intercourse with the inhabitants of these colonies."

On January 8, Congress confronted by far the most important question on their crowded agenda. A copy of the King's speech had been received, and they were now aware that His Majesty had accused them of rebellion aimed at independence. Sixty-six-year-old Samuel Adams, his palsied hands shaking, thin voice quavering, denounced the speech and the King and called on Congress "to act the part which the great law of nature points out" by declaring independence then and there.

But Adams was not the man to lead Congress. He did not blush to admit to Dr. Benjamin Rush, soon to be a delegate from Pennsylvania, that "the independence of the United States" had been "the first wish of his heart" for the previous seven years. He was also fond of remarking that if 999 Americans out of a thousand perished in a war for liberty, he would still vote for the war rather than see his country enslaved. He had the characteristic sharp tongue of the Yankee, and was never shy about using it. On January 7, in a letter to his friend James Warren, he attributed to certain members of Congress "the vanity of the ape, the tameness of the ox, or the stupid servility of the ass." Many of his fellow delegates returned these compliments by privately referring to him as "Judas Iscariot." [4]

The following day, stolid James Wilson of Pennsylvania, one of the more eminent legal scholars in Congress, rose to call upon his fellow delegates to deny the King's accusation in respect to independence. He received some strong support, although several members declared that if the rumor was true that the King was hiring foreign troops to fight Americans, they would change their minds. John Adams, supported ably by Benjamin Franklin of Pennsylvania and George Wythe of Virginia, managed to get Wilson's motion for a reply to the King postponed. Instead, Adams suggested that Congress propose a day to consider the plan of confederation which Benjamin Franklin had submitted in July, 1775.

This brought Adams' chief opponent onto the floor. John Dickinson was tall and thin to the point of emaciation. He looked as if he might expire imminently from consumption or some other wasting disease. But beneath his expensive waistcoats and aristocratic manner lived a spirit that was as unyielding as steel. For nine months, Mr. Dickinson had led Congress, and he was not about to surrender his leadership now. Even after the bloody explosion on Bunker Hill, he was able to persuade his fellow delegates, with his peculiar combination of sensibility and certainty, to sign one more humble petition to the King, begging him to redress their grievances. Stumpy John Adams, whom many considered—incorrectly—the alter ego of his cousin Samuel, had written home that "a certain great fortune and piddling genius . . . has given a silly cast to our whole doings." The letter was captured by the British and published in the papers, and Mr. Dickinson stopped speaking to Mr. Adams.

Earnestly, Dickinson called on Congress to defeat Adams' proposal, and once more they obeyed. Franklin, who had feuded with Dickinson more than once in the complex politics of Pennsylvania, had the mortification of seeing his plan of confederation rejected for the second time.

Nor was Dickinson through. On January 24, he persuaded Congress to select a committee composed of five outspoken anti-independence men to draft the reply to the King which Wilson had proposed. On February 9, Dickinson proposed a seemingly innocuous resolution to invite the Reverend Dr. William Smith, rector of the Pennsylvania Academy, to deliver an oration in honor of the slain Montgomery. Smith was an artful little man who had double-crossed Franklin, the founder of the Academy, by joining his political enemies in Pennsylvania and incidentally abandoned Franklin's program to create a science-oriented curriculum. He loved to dabble in politics and was a first-class expert in dirty tricks. Franklin once characterized him with a couplet from a contemporary English poet.

> Full many a peevish, envious, slanderous elf
> Is in his works, benevolence itself.

Smith proceeded to deliver a sonorous oration on Montgomery. Interlaced with quotations from Cicero, Milton, Livy, and Isaiah was some ingenious anti-independence propaganda. Even at the moment of his death, Smith declared, Montgomery's "principles of loyalty to his sovereign . . . remained firm and unshaken. . . . In the full triumph of success, he most ardently joined his worthy friend General Schuyler in praying that 'Heaven may speedily reunite us in every bond of affection and interest; and that the British Empire may again become the envy and admiration of the universe, and flourish' till the consummation of earthly things."

Had Montgomery evidenced "a contrary sentiment, or gone forth in the rage of conquest instead of the spirit of reconciliation," Smith piously declared, "not all his other virtues . . . could have induced me to appear in this place, on this occasion. God forbid that any of the profession to which I belong [the clergy] should ever forget their peculiar character, exercise a turbulent spirit, or prostitute their voice to inflame men's minds to the purposes of wild ambition or mutual destruction." [5]

This was a calculated swipe at the Congregational and Presbyterian clergy of New England, New York, New Jersey, and Pennsylvania, who had been specializing in inflammatory pulpit oratory since the crisis with England began. They feared that part of the British plan for

American subordination included an established church in the style of the mother country which would soon disfranchise them.

William Livingston of New Jersey proposed that the thanks of Congress be voted to Dr. Smith, and that his address be printed at their expense. This seemingly innocuous bit of courtesy aroused a terrific brawl. John Adams, George Wythe, Edward Rutledge of South Carolina, and Oliver Wolcott and Roger Sherman of Connecticut refused to countenance the idea. Pennsylvania delegate James Smith recorded their reason in his diary. "The Doctor declared the sentiments of the Congress to continue with a dependency on Great Britain, which doctrine this Congress cannot now approve." The argument soon descended from this momentous statement to the gut level of personal accusation and sectional rivalry. Oliver Wolcott bellowed that Smith claimed land in the Wyoming valley, where Connecticut and Pennsylvania were fighting a sporadic civil war. Smith was also one of those middle-state snobs who looked down his nose at New Englanders, Wolcott roared. Livingston's motion was finally put to a vote, and for the first time Dickinson and his followers knew the harsh taste of defeat. Congress declined to thank Dr. Smith or publish his sermon.[6]

It was a sign, a very small sign, of a shift in the political wind. But Congress's prevailing mood remained far from fiery defiance. On February 4, Edward Tilghman, member of a prominent Pennsylvania-Maryland family, wrote his father that a large majority in Congress were "abhorrent from independency." Only the New Englanders and the Virginians were "what we call violent." All the other colonies "breathe reconciliation." [7]

John Adams, arriving on February 11 from a visit to Boston, wrote his wife, Abigail, "There is a deep anxiety, a kind of thoughtful melancholy, and in some, a lowness of spirit approaching to despondency, prevailing throughout the southern colonies, at present, very similar to what I have often observed in Boston, particularly on the first news of the Port Bill" (the British act which closed the port of Boston as punishment for the Tea Party).

The bad news from Canada had dampened the martial spirit of Congress and left the majority of the members swaying on a pendulum between independence and reconciliation. Even Adams had to admit that he saw no hope of changing direction "until late in the spring, when some critical event will take place, perhaps sooner." Then, he confidently declared, the Cause would "roll on to dominion and glory though the circumstances and consequences may be bloody." This was rather close to bombast. The leader of the independence party was obviously trying to keep up his wife's spirits—and probably his own.[8]

Even inside the Massachusetts delegation there was tension, temper, and disunity. The reason was another intercepted letter, this one from the powerful Massachusetts politician James Warren to John Adams, containing some critical remarks about Adams' fellow delegate, Robert Treat Paine. The Adamses had already irritated the conservative Paine by engineering the replacement of another anti-independence man, Thomas Cushing, in December. "It seems we are not men to suit them," Cushing had told Paine. "We are not subservient enough. We do not pay an implicit obedience to their sovereign dictates." [9]

Now Paine wrote a fierce rebuke to Warren, denouncing his "malevolent disposition" and implacable temper and accusing him of "laboring for my disgrace." He had almost as many nasty things to say about John Adams. The president of Congress, John Hancock, another Massachusetts man, was soon involved in the argument, and he sided with Paine and Cushing against the Adamses. With his penchant for living in the grand style—he rode to Congress each day in a magnificent coach drawn by four horses—Hancock found the anti-independence gentry of Pennsylvania and Maryland far more congenial than his fellow Bostonians. He had also not forgiven John Adams for nominating George Washington as commander in chief of the American army, a job Hancock had passionately desired.

The American people knew nothing about these personality clashes and power struggles. The proceedings of Congress were secret. While the politicians waffled, people were reading an argument for independence far bolder than any yet made in the Pennsylvania State House. In a pamphlet titled *Common Sense,* Tom Paine, an Englishman in America less than two years, assaulted the whole idea of reconciliation with rhetoric that sent loyalists into shock and William Smith and other Dickinson men racing for their pens to scribble agitated replies. The heart of the moderate position was an emotional loyalty to the King. They joined the most fervent independence men in their denunciations of Parliament as a corrupt and wrongheaded, avaricious, and arrogant body. But the King remained inviolate. Even his speech from the throne, condemning the Americans as rebels and independence plotters, could be excused as the product of his corrupt advisers.

As symbol even more than reality, the King invoked deep emotions. He was the focal point of the immense and triumphant British Empire, which was not only the most powerful nation but the wealthiest protected trading area on the globe. Patriotism, profits, reverence for law and order were all inextricably mingled in the word "king." Reinforcing these motivations was an even more powerful metaphor. George III was the father of the country. In the years before the Revolution, colonial assemblies regularly referred to "the paternal Care" of the King, his "paternal regard," his "paternal Care and Tenderness." They addressed him as "our most gracious Sovereign and father." Mayors, college presidents, chambers of commerce, and ministers regularly used similar expressions. The Continental Congress itself had petitioned George III in 1774 as "the loving father of your whole people."

Closely intertwined with this idea was the image of England as the mother country. This image was fairly easy to reject on an emotional level. Every man had to break away from his mother in order to achieve his masculine identity. But breaking away from a father was a different matter. As long as a father lived, he was the ruler of the family in the highly paternalistic society of eighteenth-century England and America. Men loved their mothers in a sentimental way, but in a male-dominated era they seldom took them seriously as thinkers. They identified with their fathers and took their opinions, their life styles, their sense of the past from them. Only one thing freed a man from his father's grip: death. Without consciously admitting it, even to himself, Thomas Paine went to work on George III with murder in his mind and heart.

Paine later confessed he took most of his arguments in his book, *Common Sense,* from two political tracts written by the great English poet John Milton, defending the execution of Charles I by Puritan revolutionaries. In these tracts, Milton had insisted that "fathers and kings are very different things," and went to great lengths to distinguish "the rights of a father from those of a king." One more evidence of the enormous power of kingship in the mind of the average man was this tendency to identify regicide and patricide.

In order to kill the king, all reverence for him had to be destroyed first. Paine assaulted this sentiment with verbal bludgeons. George III was "the royal brute of Great Britain." The whole idea of kingship as something to be revered was absurd. "Of more worth is one honest man to society and in the sight of God, than all the crowned ruffians that ever lived." An English king's right to rule was ordained by God? The present rulers of England claimed their power from William the Conqueror, "a French bastard, landing with an armed banditti and establishing himself King of England against the consent of the natives."

Such a claim "certainly hath no divinity in it." Anyone "so weak" as to believe in hereditary right ought to "promiscuously worship the Ass and the Lion, and welcome." Morever, "government by kings was first introduced into the World by Heathens." It was not until three thousand years after the Creation that the Jews, who had been living in a "kind of republic," yielded to "national delusion" and requested a king.

Paine's rage at George III was fueled by English, not American grievances. A failure as a businessman, a tax collector, a husband, he was a perfectly named symbol of an Englishman defeated by the aristocracy-dominated society of the mother country, yearning for revenge on his complacent tormentors. As an intellectual exercise, *Common Sense* was not especially impressive. Paine's comments on world history and the lessons of the Bible were superficial at best. Paine was not writing for intellectuals. His target was the minds and hearts of average Americans, already inflamed by two years of political and economic turmoil. It was a historic symbiosis between a revolutionary situation and the greatest pamphleteer of his time.

Paine hacked away at the idea that the mother country had nurtured America and enabled her to grow rich within the protected trading area of the British Empire. "Nothing can be more fallacious than this kind of argument," he declared. "We may as well assert that because a child has thrived upon milk, it is never to have meat, or that the first twenty years of our lives is to become precedent for the next twenty." As for Britain's present conduct, "the more shame upon it. Even brutes do not devour their young, nor savages make war upon their families."

Far more to the point was evidence that America had *suffered* through her connection with Britain. "Europe is too thickly planted with kingdoms to be long at peace, and whenever a war breaks out between England and any foreign power, the trade of America goes to ruin, *because of her connection with Britain.*" The very distance between England and America was "a strong and natural proof that the authority of the one over the other was never the design of heaven." It may make some sense for a powerful nation to take a small island under its care, "but there is something absurd in supposing a continent to be perpetually governed by an island." The present arrangement between England and America reversed "the common order of nature."

But above all was the transcendent fact that the matter had passed "from argument to arms, a new era for politics is struck—a new method of thinking has arisen." All the plans and proposals for recon-

ciliation that had some validity prior to April 19, 1775, "are like the al-
manacks of the last year." Quoting Milton, "Never can true reconcile-
ment grow where wounds of deadly hate have pierced so deep," Paine
said Americans could no more forgive "the murders" of the men slain
at Lexington and Concord and Bunker Hill than "the lover forgive the
ravisher of his mistress." This, if we remember that Paine was working
on the image of the King as father, was a uniquely powerful combination of metaphors.[10]

From here, *Common Sense* became something that most admirers of
Paine would prefer to forget—an argument for war. He assured the
Americans that they could easily wallop the British. Americans had no
national debt to hold them back. They had all the tar, timber, iron, and
cordage they needed to produce a fleet, and there was no need to
worry about trained sailors. Twenty experienced seamen could tell two
hundred amateurs what to do aboard ship. Besides, England's long list
of men-of-war was fake. Less than 10 percent of the ships on it were
seaworthy. As for the English outnumbering the Americans—nothing
to worry about. The British were too interested in business to join the
army, whereas America, a young country without a thriving commerce,
could inveigle almost everyone into putting a gun on his shoulder.
Moreover, underpopulated America had plenty of land to reward its
soldiers, so it could fight the war without running up a big debt. Ninety
percent of this would be proven nonsense by the end of 1776.[11]

A hundred and twenty thousand copies of *Common Sense* poured
from American presses in three months—the equivalent of a ten-
million-copy sale today. Like numerous contemporary authors, Paine
found fault with his publisher. "The book was turned upon the world
like an orphan to shift for itself. No plan was formed to support it," he
later said. But George III proved to be an unintentional collaborator.
The King's speech denouncing the American rebellion was published
in Philadelphia the same day that *Common Sense* appeared.

A glimpse of *Common Sense*'s impact on the younger generation is
visible in a letter which one of Nathan Hale's friends wrote to him on
February 19, 1776. After commenting on the fact that war seemed to
be inevitable, the writer says, "Whether we ought in point of advantage
to declare ourselves an independent state and fight as independents or
still continue to resist as subjects is a question which has of late very
much engross'd in these parts the conversation of every rank more
especially since the appearance of a little pamphlet entitled *Common
Sense*. . . . Have you seen it? Upon my word 'tis well done—'tis what

would be common sense were not most men so blinded by their prejudices that their *sense* of things is not what it ought to be—I confess a perusal of it has much reform'd my notions upon several points & I hope it may have the same effect upon many others—I own myself a staunch *independent* and ground my principles upon almost innumerable arguments." [12]

X

Petticoat Despotism and Other Democratic Terrors

With his empty pockets, worn clothes, and growling hostility to inherited wealth and established privileges, Tom Paine was a spokesman for a part of America that made many independence men nervous. Particularly alarming were his suggestions for governing the independent nation that he envisioned. Paine wanted equality of representation and annually elected assemblies in every colony and a constitutional convention to draft an American Magna Charta, setting up Congress as a permanent government, "drawing the line of business and jurisdiction" between them and the states and "securing freedom and property to all men."

John Adams, while praising Paine's "manly and striking" style, condemned his "very inadequate ideas of what is proper and necessary to be done in order to form constitutions for single colonies, as well as a great model of union for the whole." In fact, Adams worriedly confided to his friend James Warren that he feared that *Common Sense*, with its "crude, ignorant notion of government by one assembly, will do more mischief in dividing the friends of liberty than all the Tory writings together. He is a keen writer but very ignorant of the science of government." [1]

This was an opinion widely shared by the ruling class of Pennsylvania. In the previous November, moderates, led by John Dickinson, had specifically ordered their delegates to the Continental Congress, also led by John Dickinson, to reject all proposals that would lead to a separation between America and Great Britain. Many people thought the Pennsylvania assembly was unrepresentative. A heavy proportion of the delegates came from the city of Philadelphia and the nearby eastern counties, while the western counties, where independence sentiment was strong, were underrepresented. Paine took dead aim at the situation when he wrote in *Common Sense:* "A small number of electors or a small number of representatives are equally dangerous, but if the number of representatives be not only small but unequal, the danger is increased." Paine avowed that the assembly's instructions to the delegates "ought to warn the people at large how they trust power out of their own hands." He declared the instructions would "in point of sense and business . . . have dishonored a schoolboy." They had been approved "by a *few,* a *very few,* without doors, and were carried in the House and there passed in behalf of the whole colony."

There was a word for the kind of government Paine was pushing— a word that made most independence men flinch and reconciliationists shudder—"democracy." *Plain Truth,* by Marylander James Chalmers, attacked Thomas Paine as "a political quack," and prophesied that America would "immediately degenerate into democracy" if it took his advice. Even John Adams had a dread of "the leveling spirit" in the revolutionary local conventions that were replacing the old colonial assemblies. Adams feared that "members will obtain an influence, by noise not sense, by meanness not greatness, by ignorance not learning, by contracted hearts not large souls." Along with the importance of carefully designing the government, "there must be a decency and respect and veneration introduced for persons in authority of every rank, or we are undone. In a popular government, this is the only way of supporting order." There were grounds for hesitating before "the measure of independency," Adams admitted in private. "No man living can foresee the consequences." [2]

If Honest John, as he called himself, did not have enough trouble, he received around this time a letter from Abigail, declaring that along with independence she expected a new code of laws which would be "more generous and favorable" to women than the English Constitution. "Do not put such an unlimited power into the hands of the husbands. Remember all men would be tyrants, if they could. If particular care and attention are not paid to the ladies, we are determined to foment a rebellion, and will not hold ourselves bound by any laws in which we have no voice or representation."

Adams proved himself equal to this challenge. With his usually solemn tongue in cheek, he replied, "We have been told that our struggles loosen the bonds of government every where; that children and apprentices were disobedient; that schools and colleges were grown turbulent; that Indians slighted their guardians, and Negroes grew insolent to their masters. But your letter was the first intimation that another tribe, more numerous and powerful than all the rest, were grown discontented." Coolly he assured his "saucy" wife, "Depend upon it, we know better than to repeal our masculine systems. Although they are in full force, you know they are little more than theory. We dare not exert our power in its full latitude. We are obliged to go fair and softly, and, in practice, you know we are the subjects. We have only the name of masters, and rather than give up this, which would completely subject us to the despotism of the petticoat, I hope, General Washington and all our brave heroes would fight." [3]

No one loved an argument more than John Adams. He had a natural talent for the rough-and-tumble of debate, as his opponents in the Continental Congress found out to their grief more than once. Early in February, the opponents of independence tried to get rid of him by taking the low road. As he told it in his autobiography, "I soon found there was a whispering among the partisans in opposition to independence, that I was interested; that I held an office [chief justice] under the new government of Massachusetts; that I was afraid of losing it, if we did not declare independence." These whisperers managed to get the ears of the leaders of the Maryland legislature, who passed a resolution warning their delegates against "listening to the advice of interested persons." Adams tried to laugh off the implication. But he could not ignore the slur when a congressman whom he described as "a gentleman of great fortune and high rank" made a motion that "no person who held any office under a new government" should be permitted to vote on the question of independence.

Adams arose and solemnly seconded the gentleman's motion. "I recommend it to the honorable gentleman to second another which I should make," he said, "namely that no gentleman who holds any office under the old or present government should be admitted to vote on any such question as they were interested persons." This, Adams said, "flew like an electric stroke through every countenance in the room." Practically every man in Congress—especially the reconciliationists—had held prominent offices in the previous governments of their colonies.

The reconciliationists were "mortified," Adams said. Sensing he had the majority with him, Honest John made them squirm even more. He was ready to cheerfully consent to a resolution "before we proceeded to any question respecting independence" that would forbid any man in Congress from accepting or holding any office of any kind in America after the Revolution.

George Wythe of Virginia leaped up to deplore the idea. Adams agreed that it was deplorable, and said that he was only attempting to reply to "personal attacks" that were being made on him. His countenance darkening, Adams defended his acceptance of the "unmerited and unsolicited" job of chief justice of Massachusetts. It was, he said, "a post of danger" and that was why he had not "dared to refuse it," although it meant relinquishing another office—his law practice—which was more than four times as profitable. Duty and a conviction of an honest cause, not ambition or hopes of honor or profit, had drawn him into this struggle in which they were now engaged. He had already seen enough to know that the American Cause was not the most promising road to profits, honor, power, or pleasure. "On the contrary, a man must renounce all these, and devote himself to labor, danger and death, and very possibly to disgrace and infamy, before he was fit to take a seat in this Congress." Licking their wounds, Adams' foes went back to abusing him "in their secret circles." [4]

Around the central issue of independence, there was a host of minor decisions that lacerated the nerves of Congress. High on the list was the question of opening the ports of America to commerce with the whole world. As colonials, Americans had heretofore been permitted to trade only with the mother country or other colonies in the Empire. Even when they sold rice or wheat to southern Europe, the commodities had to be shipped to England first and then reshipped to foreign destinations. In early February, Congress resolved itself into a committee of the whole—where decisions reached and motions made were not officially recorded—and decided against opening the ports. It was considered "a bold step to independence," as John Adams later recalled, "and I urged it expressly with that view." But the party against him "had art and influence . . . to evade, retard and delay every motion that we made." The constant use of the committee of the whole enraged Adams and his fellow independence men because they felt that it enabled the "cold party," as Adams called them, to evade the appearance in the journals of Congress of any subject they disliked.[5]

For two weeks, Congress wrangled over this decision. Even pro-independence men were weary. "I fear we shall maintain the armies of our enemy at our own expense with provisions," said Roger Sherman of Connecticut. "We can't carry on a beneficial trade as our enemies will take our ships."

Stout James Wilson of Pennsylvania replied that the merchants ought to judge for themselves the danger and the risk. Lean, intense George Wythe of Virginia shoved the argument toward the larger question of independence. He urged Congress to follow the example of the Virginia convention, which had passed a resolution urging the opening of America's ports to all nations except ships of Great Britain, Ireland, and the British West Indies. There were two ways of getting American produce to market—authorizing American ships to arm themselves and issuing letters of marque which would permit American vessels to sail as privateers and make reprisals on British commerce. The other alternative was "inviting foreign powers to make treaties of commerce with us." This in turn might lead to protection for American ships.

But how, asked the canny Wythe, could or should Congress approach foreign powers? Were they subjects of Great Britain—or rebels? If they came as subjects of Great Britain, the Court of France, for instance, would regard it as an absurdity—"Bristol or Liverpool" might as well offer their trade. It also made no sense to suggest that the offer of foreign commerce be temporary, "that after a season, we would return to our subjection to Great Britain." A foreign court wanted a permanent arrangement, or nothing. Why, asked Wythe, were so many members of Congress so fond of calling themselves dutiful subjects? "We must declare ourselves a free people." [6]

But the reconciliationists declined to take this advice. Instead, as John Adams recalled it, "this measure of opening the ports &c. labored exceedingly." The anti-independence men shoveled into the committee of the whole all sorts of other business, letters from Generals Arnold, Wooster, Schuyler, Lee, and Washington, as well as numerous minor matters, down to dispatching single companies of riflemen to guard New York. "Postponement was the object of our antagonists," Adams said. He declaimed at "the frivolous importance" of the business being transacted, in comparison to "the great concerns." Fortunately, the debate had a cut-off point. On March 1, the Nonimportation Acts, which Congress had passed in the previous year with the hope of boycotting Britain into submission, were to expire.

On February 26, the reconciliationists received news which must have struck them as the unkindest possible cut. While they were supporting the principle and the profit of union with Great Britain, Parliament had passed the toughest piece of anti-American legislation yet. Robert Morris, thanks to his worldwide trading contacts, received a copy of the Prohibitory Act, and laid it before Congress, along with letters reporting that Great Britain was raising an army of 25,000 men to crush the rebellion in a single campaign.

The harshness of the Prohibitory Act staggered the moderates. Robert Alexander of Maryland wrote that it had extinguished "every idea of reconciliation," and he now saw the struggle as having two alternatives, "absolute slavery or independency." This letter was written on February 27, the day after Morris had reported the Prohibitory Act to Congress. Two days later, into Philadelphia came a letter which gave new hope to the reconciliationists. There was a British peace emissary already in America. His name was Thomas Lord Drummond, and he had been secretly conferring with three members of the Continental Congress who had been sent to New York to deal with lack of enthusiasm for the Revolution in that vital state. Drummond had sent a letter to the British army in Boston, asking them to arrange for passports for American negotiators who might go to England to talk with peace commissioners appointed by the King. As a committed independence man, Washington opened the letter and, not liking the sound of it at all, forwarded it to Congress for instructions, commenting that he suspected it was a plot to divide the Americans.[7]

The reconciliationists ignored this cautionary advice and seized this straw of peace like drowning men. They even reread the Prohibitory Act and found the minor clause authorizing the King to appoint such peace commissioners. This, in John Adams' words, "was a fine engine to play cold water on the fire of independence. They set it in operation with great zeal and activity." For five hours on March 5, Congress discussed the Drummond mission while the independence men groaned and fumed. March dribbled away and the wrangling continued, with no decision in sight. "We do not treat each other with that decency and respect that was observed heretofore," Joseph Hewes of North Carolina, an opponent of independence, wrote home. "Jealousies, ill-natured observations and recriminations take the place of reason and argument. Our tempers are soured." [8]

Congress seemed deadlocked. But the secret committees of commerce and of foreign correspondence were operating as if war had already become a fatal certainty. The commerce men held several meetings with two French merchants named Penet and Pliarne, who were eager to supply munitions of war and anything else the Americans wanted. Other Frenchmen offered gunpowder by the ton. More important was the decision of the Secret Committee of Correspondence to send a representative to France. Their choice was Silas Deane of Connecticut, an ambitious merchant who dreamed of becoming the Robert Morris of New England. Until recently, he had been a member of Congress, but his constituents had replaced him, and he was in search of a job.

In Paris, Deane would have to function as a merchant, buying munitions and other supplies on credit. At thirty-nine, Deane had the mercantile background but was otherwise anything but a prime choice. He spoke no French, had not an iota of previous diplomatic experience, and was temperamentally unstable. To guide him, Franklin had to write a kind of primer on how to deal with French diplomats such as the Count de Vergennes. If Deane found Vergennes reserved, under no circumstances was he to argue with him. Instead, he was told to "shorten your visit." Above all, he was urged to be deferential—not an easy task for an aggressive Connecticut Yankee. He was to tell the Count that he knew "how precious his time is, you do not presume to ask another audience, but that, if he should have commands for you, you will, upon the least notice, immediately wait upon him." As for diplomacy, Deane was to tell Vergennes that "there is a great appearance that we shall come to a total separation from Great Britain." Moreover, Congress already regarded France as "the power whose friendship it would be fittest for us to obtain and cultivate." By way of bait, Deane was to dangle in front of the French the prospect of winning "a great part of our commerce." Deane was given his commission and Franklin's wise advice during the first three days of March, and he immediately departed for France. Difficulties at sea delayed his arrival until June.

Meanwhile, in Congress, the constant pressure of the independence men created a seemingly significant breakthrough. A large number of Philadelphians had asked Congress for letters of marque—legal recognition as privateers—so they could seize British ships in retaliation for the Prohibitory Act. On March 18, seven colonies—the four New England states, New York, Virginia, and North Carolina—had voted in favor of a resolution to grant this request. But the real battle over this issue erupted a few days later, when the preamble to this privateering resolution, defending it to the world, was debated.

George Wythe and Richard Henry Lee demanded a preamble

"wherein the King was made the author of our miseries instead of the Ministry." John Jay of New York, Pennsylvanian James Wilson, and other reconciliationists vigorously opposed this idea as "effectually severing the King from us forever." After considering it overnight, the following day Congress voted once more with the reconciliationists and rejected Wythe's motion. Instead, the preamble declared that the step was being taken only to provide for "the defense and security" of American ships. Congress hoped their friends in Great Britain would blame "the authors of our common calamities if their ships were seized or destroyed."

A disgusted John Adams wrote, that same day, to Major General Horatio Gates, "I agree with you that in politicks the middle way is none at all. If we finally fail in this great and glorious contest it will be by bewildering ourselves by groping after this middle way. We have hitherto conducted half a war; acted upon the line of defense, &c., &c. But you will see by tomorrow's paper that, for the future, we are likely to wage three-quarters of a war. The Continental ships of war and provincial ships of war and . . . privateers, are permitted to cruise on British property, wherever found on the ocean. This is not independency, you know; nothing like it.

"If a post or two more should bring you unlimited latitude of trade to all nations, and a polite invitation to all nations to trade with you, take care that you do not call or think it independency. No such matter. Independency is a hobgoblin of such frightful mien that it would throw a delicate person into fits to look it in the face."

Then, like too many of his colleagues, Adams slipped from irony to spleen. "All our misfortunes arise from a single source—the reluctance of the southern colonies to republican government. . . . Each colony should establish its own government, and then a league should be formed between them all. This can be done only on popular principles and axioms, which are so abhorrent to the inclinations of the barons of the South and the Proprietary interests in the middle states." [9]

John Adams was a great congressional politician and is justly famed as the architect of the decision for independence, but he was not a reliable reporter. It never seemed to occur to him that substantial numbers of people in the middle states and the South did not *want* independence. This was evident to anyone who spent time in these parts of America.

XI

The Cautious Men
of Gotham

Nowhere was this reluctance to embrace independence more visible than in the city of New York. Its strategic position as the very center of the thirteen colonies, and at the mouth of the Hudson River, the beginning of a broad water highway up to—or down from—Canada, its magnificent harbor, made the politics of New York a crucial issue in 1776. On January 16, Sam Smith, the Albany post rider, arrived with the news that the Americans had been repulsed at Quebec; New York's hero, Montgomery, was dead; and Lieutenant John McDougall, son of Colonel Alexander McDougall, one of the most radical New York politicians, was captured. A younger McDougall boy, Ranald, had been captured five weeks earlier in another action in Canada. The city's morale sagged, and it tottered still further two days later when it was learned that some three hundred cannon which New Yorkers had collected in three gun parks in Westchester County, just north of the city, had been wrecked. Steel-pronged plugs had been driven into their muzzles, and their touchholes had been smashed by sledgehammers. The city watch, a rudimentary police force, had been supposed to guard these guns. Their commander, Town Major William Leary, had been warning the revolutionary Committee of Safety for weeks that most of the watch were untrustworthy, either leaning to the British side by conviction, or ready to sell their loyalty for a few gold coins.[1]

On the same day that the news of this depredation spread through the city, the British warships in the Hudson River, H.M.S. *Asia, Phoenix,* and *Viper,* fired a series of salutes in honor of Queen Charlotte's thirty-second birthday. The booming cannon were also a reminder that the King's men had the firepower to blast New York off the map if they were so inclined, or were given sufficient pretext.

Some people feared this pretext was at hand when 600 New Jersey militiamen under the command of Brigadier General Nathaniel Heard arrived to disarm 788 loyalists in Queens County who had signed a statement deploring the rebellion. They managed to collect over three hundred guns without violence and arrest nineteen ringleaders. The New Jersey men had been sent by the Continental Congress at the request of the New York provincial congress, because they could not muster enough rebellious New Yorkers to do the job. Heard marched his nineteen captives to Philadelphia. The Continental Congress, with no prison facilities and not much in the way of ideas about how to handle loyalists beyond issuing orders to arrest them, sent them back to New York. There they remained under a sort of embarrassed house arrest—because their state's provincial congress did not know what to do with them, either. Meanwhile, there were rumors that other Long Island loyalists whom Heard had failed to arrest had an arsenal of cannon and small arms concealed somewhere along their marshy shores.

Aboard another British ship in the harbor, H.M.S. *Duchess of Gordon,* was the Honorable William Tryon, Royal Governor of New York. He was doing everything he might be doing in ordinary times, except living ashore in his handsome town house, built for him at provincial expense in 1774. He regularly conferred with members of his council and the mayor of New York City, and did business with everyone from vegetable peddlers to gunsmiths in his cramped cabin. If there were touches of make-believe in Boston and Philadelphia, New York was the quintessence of unreality. The Revolution was taking place, but few people seemed willing to admit it or show much enthusiasm for it.

Into this combustible situation came Major General Charles Lee with orders from General Washington to occupy New York. A retired colonel in the British army who had won the nickname "Boiling Water" from the Indians during the Seven Years' War, Lee was inclined to dramatic gestures and imperious manners. He was in many ways a classic English eccentric, son of a somewhat deranged mother who made a point of never showing him the slightest affection. A radical in politics, he had quit England in disgust and wandered through Europe in search of employment in foreign armies, eventually winning a major general's rank in Poland where, paradoxically, he made war on Polish patriots who were fighting the Russian puppet who was ruling the country. After some service with the Russian armies fighting the Turks, he returned to England, which he found as politically unpalatable as when he left it. He had developed a particular animosity for George III, whom he considered to have welched on promises to promote him in the British army. Still a lieutenant colonel on half pay, Lee departed to America, where he had acquired various tracts of land as a result of his service in the Seven Years' War. Settling in Virginia, Lee leaped into the revolutionary upheaval and won the second highest rank in the Continental Army by dazzling Congress with fusillades of political and military advice.

Lee fancied himself a military genius, a great politician, and a philosopher all in one explosive package. Unfortunately, he neither looked nor acted the part. He was, for one thing, an incredible slob, regularly appearing in public with the dirtiest imaginable shirts and waistcoats. He was thin to the point of reediness, with a huge beak of a nose and almost no chin. He professed to love dogs more than people, and invariably traveled with a pack of them numerous enough to stage an impromptu fox hunt, if the fancy struck him. His favorite dog, Spada, was a Pomeranian, which one American said "I should have taken for a bear had I seen him in the woods." [2]

Lee had found the inaction of the Cambridge camp maddening. He bombarded Congress with demands for a decision on independence, lecturing leaders such as John Dickinson that if Congress did not "act more decisively we shall be ruined, decision, decision ought to be our word. . . . I demand and expect that the legislature of my country shou'd lay aside all childish attachments and prejudices, and make it the sole aim of their politicks—to insure the welfare and safety of this community of which I am an adopted member—" Enraged by his failure to produce action in Congress, Lee declared that the members would be too timid to take a stand, even if they found their wives in *flagrante delicto* with General Howe.[3]

Simultaneously, Lee sought to escape from Washington's shadow to the potential glory of an independent command. He was ambitious as well as impatient. His five-day tour of Rhode Island, at the request of local patriots, had given him dreams of political glory. He inspected fortifications, frightened waverers, and arrested loyalists who refused to take an oath to support the Continental Congress. Lee was hardly back in Cambridge before he began suggesting a similar treatment for New York. Although his letters to Washington and others professed "distraction" at Congress for failing to fortify and garrison the city, his

real fear was not seizure by the British—he knew the Americans had
the short supply of redcoats thoroughly pinned down or bottled up
throughout the continent. New York's supposed profusion of loyalists
was his real worry. Lee thought he was the perfect man to intimidate
and disarm and if necessary arrest them, as he had done in Rhode
Island.

The man behind the man behind this plan was a character almost as
strange as Charles Lee—Isaac Sears, considered by some people the
most dangerous agitator in America. The forty-five-year-old Sears was
the leader of the New York mob, a phenomenon which played a vital,
not always positive, role in the city's politics. He had made a fortune as
a privateer captain in the French and Indian War, and become a leading figure along the New York waterfront. All Sears had to do was
shout the word "liberty" or "taxes," and two hundred brawlers were at
his heels, ready to smash windows, apply tar and feathers, or wreck a
printing press. Sears supplied so much ammunition for the Tory claim
that the Revolution was synonymous with anarchy that moderate New
Yorkers such as John Jay, James Duane, and Robert Livingston ran
him out of town, back to his native Connecticut. There letters and
reports from henchmen only convinced him that New York was in
danger of being seized by a conspiracy of open and secret loyalists, and
he traveled to Cambridge to pour his story into Charles Lee's ears.

When John Adams assured Washington that he had the authority
to send Lee on this rescue mission, the commander in chief wrote out
the necessary orders and Lee, Sears, Spada, the bear-sized Pomeranian,
and his fellow canines were on their way. Washington even arranged
for Lee to pick up two regiments of militia from Governor Trumbull of
Connecticut. With 1,200 Yankees under his command, Lee paused in
Stamford to write a letter to Congress and make sure they approved his
mission. Before he heard from Philadelphia, he got a panicky letter
from the Committee of Safety of New York. The last thing they wanted
in Gotham was 1,200 contumacious New Englanders eager to start
shooting at the British and, incidentally, ready to define patriotism for
New Yorkers. Simultaneously, the New York provincial congress
lodged a strong protest with Congress, denouncing such intercolonial
interference. The patriots on the Committee of Safety explained to Lee
that they feared the sight of 1,200 Connecticut musketeers would bring
on a naval bombardment that would reduce the town to ashes. Lee
replied that "the first house set in flames by their guns shall be the funeral pile of some of their best friends." [4]

In spite of this bombast, Lee assured the touchy New Yorkers that he was not "one of those who have entertained a bad opinion of the virtue of N. York or made it my business to asperse them; on the contrary, I have condemn'd loudly the illiberal, impolitic and unjust reflections I have heard frequently thrown out." This only rubbed salt in the wound. Since Lee had just spent the better part of two weeks in Connecticut, the men of Gotham had little difficulty divining whose opinions the general had been condemning. Meanwhile, Lee was telling Washington that the letter from the Committee of Safety was "woefully hysterical" and asking him what to do about the recent resolution by the Continental Congress, which declared that Continental troops were to be under the direction of local assemblies or their representatives. "It is impossible, having two sovereigns," wrote the ex–British colonel.[5]

To his relief, Lee learned three days later (January 26, 1776) that Congress had decided to appoint a committee of three members to go to New York and work with him, thereby superseding the authority of the New York provincial congress and Committee of Safety and extricating themselves from the cul-de-sac into which their own resolution had thrust them. Before Lee could march, he came down with an attack of the gout, which left him feverish and bedridden for eight days. Then came a letter from Washington that galvanized him into action, in spite of his indisposition. William Howe's second in command, Major General Henry Clinton, had sailed from Boston on January 23, reportedly with four or five hundred men. There was a strong rumor that he was headed for New York. This made it necessary for Lee to be "decisive and expeditious" in his operations in that quarter. The Tories should be disarmed "immediately," and their "principals" seized. "They must be so notoriously known, that there will be little danger of your committing mistakes," Washington wrote, in an uncommon burst of optimism.

This was, of course, music to Lee's ears, and even more lyrical to Isaac Sears. Appointing the mob leader his adjutant general, Lee marched for New York, his own transportation a litter carried by relays of his soldiers. If the loyalists had had a good satirist in their ranks, and a printing press at their disposal, they could have made wonderful propaganda out of the sight of the American general arriving in town like a Turkish pasha on the shoulders of his freedom-loving "Connecticutians," as he called them.

Within the hour that Lee arrived, on February 5, word spread through the jittery town that Major General Clinton and his redcoats were in the harbor. It was Sunday, a perfect day for a panic. Everyone assumed that Lee and Clinton would open fire immediately, and people fled into cellars and nearby woods. Then came a message from the man who was still theoretically the ruler of the province of New York— the Royal Governor, William Tryon. From the deck of the *Duchess of Gordon,* he assured the agitated citizenry that General Clinton was only paying him a social visit, and had no troops with him, other than those on a single transport which was remaining in the lower harbor.

Lee, still rather skeptical, sent a messenger to the visiting general, asking him if he planned to assault the city. They were old friends; when Lee had quit the British army to wander Europe in search of adventure, Clinton had written him letters of introduction to some of the most important politicians in Germany. Clinton answered with disarming candor. The Governor was telling the truth. He was acting under orders to investigate Governor Tryon's situation, and had no intention of attacking New York. The only troops he had with him were two companies of light infantry. His destination was North Carolina, where he expected to meet five regiments from England, and pacify that province in a winter campaign.

Few things underscored the unreality that pervaded America in these first months of 1776 more than this message. "This is certainly a droll way of proceeding," Lee wrote to Washington. "To communicate his full plan to the enemy is too novel to be credited." Yet Clinton was telling the truth; apparently he could not quite bring himself to believe that his old friend Lee was wholeheartedly committed to the American cause.[6]

Governor Tryon added not a little to this fantasy atmosphere by continuing to hold meetings of his American councilors aboard the *Duchess of Gordon,* appointing judges and mayors and issuing decrees with—sometimes without—their approval. He declined to accept the reassurances of the Committee of Safety that he would be perfectly safe onshore. To make the situation completely bizarre, Clinton, Tryon, and the three-man committee of the Continental Congress found themselves involved in a peace negotiation.

Thomas Lord Drummond, the center of this episode, which almost ended the Revolution before it began, was a thirty-four-year-old Scotsman who came to America in 1768 to look after an estate near Perth Amboy, New Jersey, which belonged to a kinsman. He claimed to be the heir of the earldom of Perth, which was attainted during the Scottish rebellion of 1745. The Amboy estate was one of the few pieces of property belonging to the Earl of Perth which had not been forfeited to the Crown, and Drummond (or his brother James) obviously hoped someday to own it. By 1773, Lord Drummond was sufficiently well known in New York to be elected president of the St. Andrew's Society. As the quarrel with England escalated, he became intensely concerned about it, no doubt because he feared that he would be forced to choose sides in another rebellion, and the Drummonds might lose the last remnants of the earldom of Perth.[7]

Drummond also saw an opportunity to restore his family's shattered fortunes. The British government would, he reasoned, be more than grateful to any man who gave them a solution to the crisis that was threatening the dismemberment of the Empire. In September, 1774, as the Continental Congress prepared to meet for the first time, Drummond sailed to England as a self-appointed mediator. He was related to Lord Mansfield, the chief justice of England and a power in the North ministry, and apparently had no difficulty obtaining audiences with a number of leading officers of the government, including Prime Minister Lord North. Drummond submitted to North six propositions that he thought could lead to peace.

The propositions as we know them parallel to a remarkable degree the ideas North put into his Conciliatory Bill six months later. The similarity is so remarkable it forces one to wonder if Drummond convinced North, or vice versa. North may have put Drummond on the secret-service payroll, as he did another Englishman, Gilbert Barkly, whom he sent to Philadelphia around the same time. At least, Drummond seems to have become a North peace missionary, working more or less under cover—which, as we have seen, was the way North was forced to operate because of the appetite for war prevailing with the King and the rest of the cabinet.

Drummond's propositions simply spelled out in detail the basic conception of the Conciliatory Act—that Parliament would give up the right to tax America if each colony agreed to make an annual grant to meet the expenses of maintaining the army and navy to defend the Empire. The assessment would be by "calculation"—it would take into account the wealth and trade of each colony. There would be nothing arbitrary about it. Money for the annual grant would be raised by taxes voted by the Americans themselves on items that would "keep pace with the growth or decline" of the colony. No one wanted the taxes to become "accidentally burthensome."

That Drummond was no wholehearted friend of America is evident in the advice which he gave Lord North along with these propositions. He pointed out that even if they were only "loose or incompetent," they could certainly be used to begin a negotiation "which if once set on foot cannot but ultimately tend to the advantage of England in either terminating a peace, or in giving her the intermediate time to prepare for war." Drummond knew the parlous state of the British army in America. "Armed but in threats and not in preparation as is our present case," he said, "we may irritate but cannot carry into their country a serious distress."

North seemed more interested in how to start a negotiation with the Americans. He could not do it personally, as prime minister, without arousing the war party. Nor, at that point, could anyone else appointed by the government. To advise him, North called in Sir Gilbert Elliot, another Scot, whose brother Andrew was collector of the Port of New York and a friend of Drummond's. Elliot concurred with Drummond's belief that it was "the aim of the leaders of Faction in America to hurry on the Contest to that Stage which is to break off all Intercourse between the two Countries." But Elliot also disapproved of the ultras in Parliament and in the North ministry, who would, he said, refine any set of propositions to the point where they were "obnoxious to the People of America." There was only one way to silence these arrogant violents—the proposal for peace had to come from America. Drummond had to return to America and persuade some leading colonists to sail to England with these peace propositions in hand.

Drummond was reluctant. His health was fragile, and another eight or ten weeks at sea might be fatal. But Elliot urged him to risk the voyage. He was the ideal negotiator. He had property in America and possessed the confidence of some of the American leaders. More important, Elliot told Drummond as one Scotsman to another, if he succeeded, he could look forward to "the indulgence of government" toward re-establishing his family to the power and prestige they once enjoyed as earls of Perth.

Lured by this promise of rewards, Drummond decided to make the return voyage. In New York, picked up Andrew Elliot, a man known for both his conservativism and his caution. They proceeded to Philadelphia, arriving in that city on January 3, 1776. Drummond was soon closeted with delegates from the southern colonies, as well as John Jay and James Duane of New York, Andrew Allen of Pennsylvania, and Jay's future father-in-law, William Livingston of New Jersey. All were impressed by Drummond's propositions and his confident assertion that they were approved by Lord North. Revealing a deep cleavage behind the façade of American unity, the Southerners and middle-staters told Drummond they were not prepared to "plunge themselves into . . . [a civil war] merely to humor a set of people [the New England delegates] who were obnoxious to them." Jay, meeting secretly with Drummond at night, said the young Scot had "undeceived" the southern delegates about the true state of affairs, and they were now satisfied that they "could not embrace too early an opportunity of availing themselves of the present disposition of [the ministry] in England."

The Americans wanted to send Drummond back to England with this message. He suggested that it would be better if they sent a deputation from Congress. He argued that if the English government sent commissioners to America, they would probably make only one offer, which the Americans would have to accept or reject. The English were obsessed with saving the honor of the nation. If the Americans took the initiative, the British could consider their honor more or less tacitly assuaged, and could then begin negotiating reasonably. The Americans agreed with Drummond's logic, but they feared that if they appeared in England as delegates of the Continental Congress, they might be arrested for high treason. Drummond tried to resolve this problem by a courageous gesture. He offered himself as a hostage to Congress "to be held responsible in all respects" for the fate of such a peace delegation.

In his eagerness to get American negotiators moving toward England, Drummond said that the British wanted "but a show of revenue to hold up to Parliament." In South Carolina's case, as little as £5,000 sterling a year would settle the matter. This made Thomas Lynch of South Carolina think twice. He knew that the duties paid in an average year on goods moving in and out of Charleston averaged £10,000. It seemed incredible to him that the British were ready to give away half of the income they already possessed. Lynch, who served on the Army Committee, mentioned Drummond's mission in a letter to Washington on January 16, 1776, expressing his skepticism. Yet the South Carolinian was sufficiently impressed by Drummond's assurances to more or less agree to head the American peace delegation, with either John Jay of New York or Andrew Allen of Pennsylvania as his partner.

Because Drummond had signed a parole of honor before the Pennsylvania Committee of Safety, promising not to correspond with England or any English representatives while he was in Philadelphia, he retreated to New York. Apparently no mention was made to anyone else in Congress about the plan to send American peace seekers to England, because they feared the opposition that the idea would arouse among New England delegates. As a cover, Lynch and Allen volunteered to be part of the three-man committee sent to survey the defenses of New York and cooperate with General Charles Lee.

While Lee was writing contentedly to Washington, telling him that he had obtained permission to build fortifications "in some commanding part of the city" and plant cannon at Hell Gate and on the heights of Brooklyn, Allen and Lynch were huddling with Drummond, hoping to further explore his proposals and allay their suspicions.

At this point, Drummond brought into the picture New Yorker William Smith, one of the few Americans who were trying to maintain communications across the gulf that was widening between the belligerents. Smith, forty-eight years old and a Yale graduate, was married to a Livingston, and was a former law partner of William Livingston, who was representing New Jersey in the Continental Congress. John Adams, who visited him in New York during one of his many journeys between Philadelphia and Boston, described Smith as "a plain composed man . . . a consistent unshaken friend to his country and her liberties." Long a political power in New York, Smith was a member of Governor Tryon's council, and regularly met with him aboard the *Duchess of Gordon*. There he frequently lectured the Governor on the folly of the British ministry. Smith was convinced that stupid mistakes and belligerent ultimatums on both sides had produced the present crisis.

When Drummond sought his help for his peace mission, Smith asked him if he had discussed it with Governor Tryon. Drummond objected that it would "inflame his jealousy" because a basic part of Drummond's appeal to the Americans was the confession that the ministry had been deceived by their crown servants in America. Since Tryon had been one of the most active and outspoken of these crown servants for more than a decade, there was a good chance that such a remark would indeed inflame the Governor, who was described by one New York loyalist as "generous, perfectly good natured, and no doubt brave, but weak and vain to an extreme degree." When Drummond asked Smith to intercede with the New York provincial congress to prevent Charles Lee from occupying New York, Smith told him that he "did not intermeddle in their affairs nor seek their confidence." But Smith did introduce Drummond to Colonel Alexander McDougall, who had in previous years been a compatriot of Isaac Sears in mob leadership.[8]

1776

Published in England on January 26, 1776, this cartoon underscores the psychological importance of the parent-child image in the relationship between England and America. The Indian dress of Miss America hints at another, more ominous image in the British mind. The Americans were savages, barbarians, and only ruthless force could subdue them.

The Father of the Country, George III, found it hard to understand why the Americans called him a tyrant. Stubborn, hard-working, idealistic, the King thought he was defending the British Constitution against an "unnatural" conspiracy. In England, the King's sober, ultra-moral life style made him popular with the average man. "Farmer George" hated London, and preferred to spend most of his time in the country, where he practiced experimental agriculture, rode, and played paterfamilias to his large family. This 1778 portrait by Gainsborough emphasizes the King's mildness. But in politics he could be as ruthless and pragmatic as Machiavelli.

Frederick Lord North was the King's first, or "prime," minister. According to the Americans, he was also the architect of a sinister plot to deprive them of their liberty, step by devious step. Actually, North was opposed to a war with America. But he was a weak man, dependent on the King financially and emotionally. A witty debater in Parliament, he skillfully defended a policy in which he had little faith, guaranteeing majority support by buying off the opposition with secret pensions and well-paying jobs which required no work.

France's king, Louis XVI *(right)*, had been on the throne only eighteen months when 1776 began. At twenty-two, he was earnest, idealistic, and easily influenced by his queen, Marie Antoinette *(left)*, and his ministers. The Queen and Foreign Minister Count de Vergennes wanted to risk war with England by aiding the American rebels. They were assisted by Caron de Beaumarchais *(below, right)*, playwright and secret agent, whose vivid dispatches from England portrayed the Americans as unbeatable. Baron Turgot *(below, left)*, the minister of finance, opposed aid. "The first gunshot will drive the state to bankruptcy," he warned the King.

As 1775 ended, ex–British officer Richard Montgomery *(below)* led some 900 Americans in a frontal assault on Quebec, defended by his former comrade in arms, Guy Carleton *(above)*, governor-general of Canada. Montgomery was killed by a blast of grapeshot as the attack began. His death inspired numerous poems and the dramatic painting by John Trumbull *(right)*. With 1,800 men and 200 cannon, Carleton smashed the Americans and captured over 400 of them. It was, wrote one glum Yankee from his jail cell on January 1, 1776, "a bad method to begin the New Year."

In the South, Scottish illusions led to British disasters. Lord Dunmore *(left)*, Royal Governor of Virginia, saw himself as a warrior and tried to suppress the sputtering rebellion by starting a slave insurrection. He alienated moderates such as Edmund Pendleton *(below)*, chairman of the Committee of Safety, and played into the hands of independence men such as Patrick Henry *(above)*. In North Carolina, Flora MacDonald *(right)*, a heroine of the Scottish rebellion of 1745, switched sides and urged recently arrived Highlanders to fight for the King. The Scots were smashed at Moore's Creek Bridge on February 27, 1776. A few weeks later North Carolina became the first state to vote for independence.

In Philadelphia, where the Continental Congress was meeting, acrimony flared behind apparent unanimity. John Adams *(facing page, top)* called John Dickinson *(right)* a "piddling genius" who gave "a silly cast to our doings" because he favored reconciliation with England. Samuel Adams *(bottom, left)* scorned "half way patriots" such as John Jay *(bottom, right)* for the same reason and attributed to them "the tameness of the ox or the stupid servility of the ass." They nicknamed him Judas Iscariot. Thomas Paine *(facing page, left)*, author of bestselling *Common Sense*, attacked George III as "the royal brute" and demanded immediate independence. Virginia grandee Landon Carter *(facing page, right)* disliked the way Paine called "every man a damned scoundrel that didn't think as he did."

pound a Magpie, drown an Eel,
many Things of worthy Note
esent much too long to quote,
District was both far and wide
not a little swell'd their Pride
bove all that they possess'd
a fine Goose, by all confess'd,
n Avis to behold
aid each Day an Egg of Gold
made them grow immensely rich
them an avaritious Itch.
ase belongs to many more

This Glorious purpose to obtain
About her Neck they put a Chain,
And more their Folly to compleat
They Stampt upon her Wings & Feet
But this had no Effect at all.
Yet made her struggle, flutter, squa
And do what every Goose would de
That had her Liberty in view.
When one of more distinguis'd Note
Cry'd D——n her, let us Cut her Throat
They did, but not an Egg was foun
But BLOOD came pouring from ye Woun

NORTH AMERICA

Opposition to the British government's American policy produced this
1776 satiric print *(left)*, *The Wise Men of Gotham* (each here a member
of the British cabinet) killing the golden goose, America. In Parliament,
Lord Rockingham *(above, right)* was the chief opposition leader, with
Edmund Burke *(above, left)* his spokesman in the House of Commons. But
Rockingham was lazy and Burke's Irish brogue was a major handicap.
They found it hard to unite with other opposition leaders, the secretive
Lord Shelburne *(bottom, right)* and the disreputable Charles James Fox
(bottom, left). "The public," lamented Rockingham, was "but a silly echo"
of the government's hard line.

From Boston, on January 24, 1776, British engineer Archibald Robertson sketched "the Heights of Dorchester" south of the city *(above)*. A few months later, George Washington *(bottom, right)* put troops and cannon on these heights, hoping to tempt the British into an attack. He planned a surprise assault of his own across Back Bay, which might have ended the war. Instead, William Howe, the British commander *(bottom, left)*, decided to evacuate the city, which he did without the loss of a man. Overconfident Americans hailed it as another victory.

Behind this serene portrait of Thomas Jefferson, Benjamin Franklin, John Adams, and the other members of the committee presenting a draft of the Declaration of Independence lay a fierce revolutionary upheaval in Pennsylvania, in which radicals overthrew the moderate government of the state with mob violence. Even after the vote, some American leaders were ready to trade independence for "British liberty, well secured."

Drummond pleaded with McDougall to persuade the New Yorkers not to exasperate the captains of the two line-of-battle ships in the harbor, the *Asia* and *Phoenix*. Lord Drummond vowed that the captains knew "peace would take place soon," and that the administration would not "thank any servants of the crown for irritating men's minds." He swore that General Howe also knew "the amiable desires of [the] government."

On the day that Lee and Clinton arrived, Thomas Lynch called on William Smith. This fifty-one-year-old grandson of an Irish immigrant was one of the wealthiest men in South Carolina. Yet his Irish ancestry had prompted him to take the lead in defying the British government since 1765. Unlike many of his fellow South Carolinians, who followed the Charleston style and dressed in splendid silks and satins, Lynch preferred "the manufacture of this country"—plain simple clothes. But a fellow congressman said that he "carried with him more force in his very appearance than most powdered folks in their conversation." The feverish climate of South Carolina's bottom lands, where Lynch grew the rice that made him wealthy, had taken a toll of his health, and he had frequently vacationed in the North on the advice of his doctors. In these journeys, he had met Smith several times. Now Smith could see at a glance that Lynch was a sick man. The grinding twelve-hour Congress workday had exhausted him. But his mind was still clear, as he demonstrated by getting instantly to the point.

"What do you and other New Yorkers think of Lord Drummond?"

"A man of faith and honor," Smith replied, who had "conducted himself with more prudence than common to people of his years."

"What do you think of his accounts concerning the intentions of the ministry?" Lynch asked.

"I believe them," Smith said. "It is very natural to suppose the administration is alarmed at the consequences of the present quarrel."

Lynch asked him what Drummond thought of the Continental Congress. Smith assured him that "nothing dropp'd by them" had dimmed Drummond's hopes for "a happy reconciliation." Lynch then asked Smith to relate what Drummond had told him of the North ministry's plan. He listened closely to Smith's concise summary, and nodded, relieved to find that it was essentially the same thing the young Scot had said at Philadelphia.

Now it was Smith's turn to pump Lynch. He admitted that the men he represented in Congress "did not dislike the proposal of a duty to raise a revenue for the common defense of the empire." More impor-

tant, Lynch revealed the deep reluctance with which he and other delegates confronted the possibility of separation from England. "We shall
be obliged to set up a republic," he said, "and that is a form of government . . . which I think reads better than it works."

Lynch asked Smith what he thought of sending commissioners to
England to negotiate with the ministry face to face. Smith approved
wholeheartedly. The weary Lynch shook his head. He knew England's
treacherous record in Ireland. Drummond's whole mission might be a
trap. "They may hang our commissioners, and we must send our best
hands. They are not to be spared. How can we persuade any man to
such a risk?" Yet Drummond said that if the commissioners were not
dispatched, Britain would certainly "arm at all points for war." What to
do? asked this sick, worried man. "We can trust nobody not of the
Congress," and sometimes "it is too much to trust even them." He
begged his old friend to think all this over "and let me know the result." [9]

The day after Clinton arrived, Drummond rushed aboard ship to
meet him. He assured him that sentiment in Philadelphia was strongly
for peace and wanted to know if Clinton had the power to negotiate. If
he could wait four days, the excited young Scot declared, he might get
a formal offer from Congress. This was an indication of how far Drummond thought he had progressed in his discussions with Lynch and
Allen. Lynch, who thought that Clinton had come to New York to continue the negotiations on a more official level, was baffled by Howe's
choice. "It is mysterious to me how such a man should be sent on such
an errand," he said in a letter to Washington.

Clinton was anxious to establish contact with William Smith. He
carried with him a letter from Major General James Robertson, who
had served as barracks master in New York for over a decade. Robertson was convinced that Smith was the crucial figure in the peace negotiations. Through his friendship with Lynch, he was in a perfect position
to convince the Southerners that they had better save themselves from
Clinton's imminent attack by seizing Drummond's olive branch. In the
letter of introduction, Robertson tried to galvanize Smith by painting a
grisly picture of the havoc Clinton would wreak in conquering the
South. "Try to save America, try to save Mr. Clinton from a measure
his brave but humane soul shrinks at," he wrote.[10]

Drummond was crushed by Clinton's coolness, and by his confession that he had no power to negotiate. In the memoranda which he
was fond of writing to himself, the British general lamented that he

lacked this power, and conjured up a wild image of himself as America's peacemaker. Meanwhile, he picked the brain of Governor Tryon for his expedition to North Carolina; Tryon had been governor of that province for six years. It was another example, centered in a single individual, of the schizophrenia which was afflicting the entire continent. Neither side was sure whether it was committed to fighting a war or bluffing one.

Disappointed in Clinton, Drummond returned to his original plan—to send Lynch and Allen as a deputation to England. But the still suspicious Lynch requested Drummond to get passports from the British army. He thought this would protect him and Allen from arrest if Drummond turned out to be a far-out optimist about British intentions. On the same day that he talked to Clinton—February 5, 1776—Drummond wrote a letter to General Robertson asking for the passports, and cautioning him to be sure the matter was kept a secret. Unfortunately, Drummond sent the letter by land to General Washington's headquarters, asking that it be forwarded to General Howe. Washington decided the letter was possibly dangerous, opened it, and read it. He sent it to Congress with a number of negative comments. As we saw in the previous chapter, the letter was seized by the moderates as an excuse to delay a vote for independence.

Led by John Adams, the independence men opened a fierce attack on Drummond, precisely as Lynch and his fellow moderates had feared and predicted. Adams sneered that Drummond "pretended to have had conversation with Lord North; and talked warmly of Lord North's goodwill and desire for reconciliation, but had no authority to show, and no distinct proposal to make." George Wythe of Virginia offered a set of propositions to the effect that "no public bodies or private persons other than the Congress or the people at large ought to treat for peace." Congress declined to deliver this rebuff to Lynch and his friends, voting down Wythe's proposition by eight colonies to three. But a majority of the delegates mollified the independence men by voting that Lord Drummond had broken the parole to which he had sworn in Philadelphia, and he was ordered placed under arrest.[11]

Released on another parole, Drummond seems to have suffered a nervous and physical collapse. He asked for permission to retire to Bermuda to recover his health, and, accompanied by a doctor, he sailed for that island colony late in April, 1776, after signing a pledge that he would have no communication whatsoever with "any ship or vessel of war belonging to Great Britain or any vessel with troops or officers of that government," and would not even go into any fort or harbor where British troops or vessels of war were likely to be. Within a few weeks, Lynch, the only man with the prestige and courage to maintain the momentum for peace on the American side, had collapsed with a stroke which proved fatal before the end of the year.

Hope for peace from the New York negotiations fell apart before Drummond was arrested by Congress. On February 9, Sir Henry Clinton's transport with his two companies of regulars aboard came up the harbor. Although the mayor had informed the city that the transport was expected, "the fears of the multitude," as William Smith put it in his journal, "made them forget the Mayor's message . . . & conceiving that they were betrayed, Mr. Clinton and the Governor were calumniated as false villains, liars and deceivers. The river was full of ice and the cold intemperate and yet the inhabitants flew into the country with their effects & nothing could restrain them from escaping at every possible outlet." [12]

Smith accused the Committee of Safety of adding to the panic by refusing to transmit a message from Governor Tryon that no attack on the town was contemplated. The next day, while refugees still streamed from the city, Charles Lee made a move which might have produced the bombardment everyone feared. With 1,000 New Jersey men reinforcing his 1,200 Connecticutians, he decided he was strong enough to defy repeated British warnings not to touch a number of cannon and a large quantity of stores at the Battery, only yards from the water's edge and practically under the muzzles of the warships. Lee organized groups of "men and boys of all ages" who proceeded to haul away the guns by hand, and pile the stores in carts which were in turn dragged to "the fields" in the interior of the island. "With an astonishing uproar and shouting . . . the work continued all day long with an almost intire neglect of all public worship," the disgusted William Smith reported.

Lee made fun of Captain Hyde Parker of the *Phoenix,* the senior British naval officer, for his failure to deliver on his threat of "perdition to the town after his weaponry was removed." The intemperate general did not know how close he came to igniting a conflagration. One of the Governor's council, William Axtell, had gone out to the *Duchess of Gordon* to warn Tryon that the removal of the stores would be attempted. The captain of the ship came into the cabin and, when he heard the conversation, cried exultantly, "Then the ball will begin," and began gloating over the prospect of flattening the city.

Axtell turned on him and cried, "I am surprised, sir, to see you pleased. You may be safe but there are 16,000 souls in that town in danger who can neither prevent the removal nor firing of the cannon." The abashed captain said nothing. Axtell, describing the scene to Smith, said, "The fellow was as gay at the thought of an attack as a giddy girl at the invitation to a dance."

The following day, Colonel Alexander McDougall invited Smith to meet him at a local tavern and told him how grateful the New York Committee of Safety was for the forbearance the navy had displayed. "The captains acted wisely," McDougall said, and added bitterly that the New England troops and people "wish to render a reconciliation impossible and to bring on the destruction of the town as conducive to that end." The reason for this attitude, according to McDougall, was "the Susquehanna Scheme," the Connecticut land company that claimed huge tracts in the Ohio Valley. The "chief men" in Connecticut were all shareholders and had decided that its success depended on "a total separation" from Great Britain. "A word to the wise is sufficient," said McDougall.

Smith replied by warning McDougall that the populace, "excited by the war," might insist upon independence or, worse, turn their wrath upon Congress and seek peace "hastily in their own way." Smith added that he "had reason" to suspect that the administration was ready to make "capital concessions," and intimated that it would be wise for McDougall to "have an eye to peace & so to act as to be in reputation under the restoration of government."

McDougall replied that he was opposed to independence. This was not the first time he had told this to Smith. The wily councilor parted company with the "Wilkes of America," as McDougall had been called during his days as an agitator, speculating that "Lord Drummond has led him to suspect there might be a sudden peace & this was a device to secure his reputation with one for whose friendship he has always been solicitous." Lamenting the disruption of Drummond's peace negotiations, Smith confided to his diary the fear that "the delay of the peace commissioners will make it the interest of many to fight for an eternal separation. O Britain! O America!" [13]

Two days later, Smith boarded the *Duchess of Gordon* for another meeting of the Governor's council. The Governor proceeded to appoint a new mayor of New York and make the old mayor a judge. After dinner, Smith argued with the Governor and the rest of the council, condeming the British ministry for its devious policy. He insisted that Lord North's so-called Conciliatory Act of February 20,

1775, actually gave up the claim of taxing the colonies, but the administration had managed to smother the surrender in so much verbiage and indirection that no one on either side of the argument recognized it. In one of the most astonishing exchanges of the American Revolution, Smith appealed to Governor Tryon to admit whether Lord North had not informed him that the taxing power was given up.

"Yes," replied the Governor.

Was there any explicit written declaration of this? asked Smith.

The Governor admitted that he would have "declared the surrender with more liberality."

No wonder Smith wrote in his diary, "O Britain! O America!" [14]

Onshore, Charles Lee, his audacity increasing as his gout declined, suddenly interdicted all communication with the Governor's ship. He declared that Tryon had "inveigled some of the gunsmiths" aboard his ship, and was endeavoring to seduce as many as he could to cripple America's fighting power. The provincial congress investigated the accusation and found that there were only two gunsmiths missing from the city. One of these had gone back to England on the last packet, and the other had emigrated to some other part of the state. The following day, February 17, General Clinton sailed for North Carolina. The *Asia* and *Phoenix* hauled anchor to escort him to sea. The *Asia* ran aground opposite the Exchange, and Lee began preparing cannon to fire on her. "We flattered ourselves that we should have been able to have destroyed or much damaged her," he said in a letter to John Hancock, president of the Continental Congress, but "unfortunately" the warship got afloat before his artillerymen could go into action.

If Lee had stayed in New York another month or two, he might have driven the state out of the independence movement. He continued his quarrel with the provincial congress, addressing them in a tone which barely concealed his contempt. The congress returned the compliment by sending him letters which they left unsigned—a calculated insult which further infuriated Lee.

The Continental Congress unwittingly rescued the situation by appointing Lee the commander in chief of the troubled army in Canada. With the order came flattery that Lee did not need. "I tremble for your health," John Adams wrote. "We want you at N. York—we want you at Cambridge—we want you in Virginia—but Canada seems of more importance than any of those places and therefore you are sent there." Benjamin Franklin was more temperate, saying, "I rejoice that you are going to Canada," and went on to introduce the bearer of his letter, Thomas Paine.

The following day, Lee once more interdicted all supplies to Governor Tryon on his warship. This time he claimed the British had seized several provision vessels crossing from New Jersey. Lee described his action to Washington in his own inimitable way. "It has pleased His Excellency, in violation with the compact he had made, to seize several vessels from Jersey laden with flour. It has, in return, pleased *my* excellency to stop all provisions from the city and cut off all intercourse with him—a measure, which has thrown the Mayor, Council and Tories into agonies. The propensity or rather rage for paying court to this great man, is inconceivable. They cannot be weaned from him. We must put wormwood on his paps or they will cry to suck, as they are in their second childhood." [15]

Eleven days later, Lee got another letter from Congress. Displaying a vacillation which was more than a little alarming, they gave him command of the "Continental forces in the Southern Department, which comprehends Virginia, North Carolina, South Carolina and Georgia." This was more to Lee's liking. His attack of the gout had made him dread Canada's freezing winds, and he had delayed departing for his new command, pleading the necessity of completing the fortification of New York. He now departed with alacrity for the South.

Before Lee left, he took a parting shot at New York's loyalists. He ordered Isaac Sears to proceed across the East River to Queens County and Long Island, and administer the oath Lee had concocted to silence loyalists in Rhode Island. One of its clauses was a promise to take up arms in defense of their country if called upon by Congress. Sears went to work with his customary energy, and on March 17, 1776, he sent the following report to his commander.

Sir,
Yesterday afternoon I arrived at Newtown, and tendered the oath to four of the grate Torries, which they swallowed as hard as if it was a four pound shot, that they were trying to git down. On this day at 11 o'clock, I came here, whare I sent out scouting parties, and have ben able to ketch but five Torries, and they of the first rank, which swallowed the oath. The houses are so scatering it is impossible to ketch many without hosses to rid after thim. But I shall exert myself to ketch the gratest part of the ringledors, and beleve I shell effect it, but not less then five days from this time. I can asure your honor they are a set of villins in this country, and beleve the better half of them are wateing for soport and intend to take up arms against us. And it is my oppinion nothing else will do but removeing the ringledors to a place of secuerty.
From your most ob Hum Sir
ISAAC SEARS [16]

With New York's Tories chastised—so he thought—Lee turned southward. En route, he received a sharp rebuke from New York's provincial congress. "It may not be improper to remind you, sir, that the right of apprehending, trying, and punishing citizens who violate the resolutions of Congress, or act inimical to the liberties of America, is by the Continental Congress, delegated to the Provincial Conventions of the respective colonies." In the Continental Congress, the New York delegates persuaded that body to declare on March 9 that "no oath, by way of test, be imposed upon, exacted, or required of any inhabitant of these colonies by any military officers." When Colonel Sears presented a bill to the New York Committee of Safety for feeding and housing his men on their expedition to Long Island, the committee refused to pay it. In spite of General Lee's inflammatory rhetoric and brinkmanship, New York remained lukewarm to independence. Let us follow Charles Lee south and see what he finds there.[17]

XII

Nervous Masters,
Restless Slaves,
and a Flaming Argument

On January 12, 1776, the Maryland provincial convention voted to raise a force of 1,444 troops. It issued $535,111.50 in paper money to pay and equip them. Next, the convention resolved that their delegation to the Continental Congress should not "without the previous knowledge and approbation of the convention of this province consent to any proposition to declare these colonies independent of the Crown of Great Britain." The vote on this resolution was unanimous.[1]

William Eddis, a peaceable man who had come out to Maryland as a crown customs officer in 1770, reported to his wife, whom he had sent back to England, "Our Governor is in perfect health. He still continues to receive every external mark of attention and respect; while the steady propriety of his conduct, in many trying exigencies, reflects the utmost credit on his moderation and understanding." [2]

There was a considerable stretch of the truth in these words. Governor Robert Eden was anything but the model royal official that Eddis, a flatterer who later published his letters, portrayed. In fact, Eden was a vivid example of the kind of government servant the British too often sent to America. He was a dissipated spendthrift who took the job to escape squadrons of creditors in England. He used the perquisites of his office to push his own business interests in Maryland, borrowed money from local planters with no apparent intention and even less ability to repay it, and threw wild parties at which he made advances to the wives of leading planters, such as Charles Carroll. The continued presence of Governor Eden in Annapolis was not to be explained by either his personal charm or his political ability. The reason was fear of independence.

On January 15, one of the firebrands of Maryland, Daniel of St. Thomas Jenifer, invited a number of his friends to join him in a series of conferences with Governor Eden. A day later, Eden wrote his superiors in London that Marylanders were "so far from desiring an independency that if the establishment of it were left to their choice, they would reject it with abhorrence."

The gentlemen of Maryland saw alarming signs that independence might become synonymous with anarchy. They had discovered in the preceding six months that they were sitting on a restless volcano composed of poor whites, secret loyalists, and Negro slaves. Tax collectors had been mauled and beaten by armed bands, and debtors had marched on jails to free fellow bankrupts who were behind bars. In the files of the Dorchester County Committee of Safety was testimony from one James Mullineaux, who told of asking a poor white whom he met fishing if he was going to the militia muster at Cambridge, on the Eastern Shore. The fisherman's answer displayed harsh unenthusiasm for "gentlemen" who were "intending to make us all fight for their lands and Negroes."

"Damn them," growled the angler, "if I had a few more white people to join me, I could get all the Negroes in the country to back us, and they would do more good in the night than the white people could do in the day."

The motive of this potential Robespierre was simple. "If all the gentlemen were killed, we should have the best of the land to tend and . . . money enough." The Dorchester County Committee of Inspection had already disarmed numerous slaves, and denounced "the malicious and imprudent speeches of some among the lower classes of whites, who had led the blacks to believe that their freedom depended on the success of the King's troops." [3]

In Maryland, this threat of a slave uprising was only a mutter for the present. But just across Chesapeake Bay the British government was doing its utmost to incite a slave rebellion. John Murray, Fourth Earl of Dunmore and Royal Governor of Virginia, was the man responsible for this policy. Irritable and impulsive, Dunmore had begun quarreling with the Virginians the moment their House of Burgesses showed an inclination to take the American side in the revolutionary dispute. A better politician would have tried to soothe and humor the Virginians by admitting at least the partial justice of their defiance.

The Old Dominion had a tradition of quarreling with the mother country and royal officials that was a hundred years old. In 1676, a young planter, Nathaniel Bacon, led an authentic rebellion against the aging Royal Governor, Sir William Berkeley, when they disagreed over Indian policy. In the ensuing warfare, Jamestown, the capital, was burned, and 1,000 royal troops were required to restore order. So touchy were the Virginians over their rights for a number of years at the turn of the eighteenth century they refused to use the royal mail, regarding the high fees charged by the post office as a tax. Virginians had been the leaders of the opposition to the Stamp Act in 1765. In a speech that went through the colonies like an electric shock, a backwoods Demosthenes named Patrick Henry rose to cry, "Caesar had his Brutus, Charles the First his Cromwell—and George the Third may profit by their example." But moderates and conservatives had risen to rebuke Henry and dismiss or emasculate his most defiant resolutions.

Dunmore chose to ignore this fact of recent history and see violent revolution where none thus far existed. He was a warrior. The Governor had almost started a war between Pennsylvania and Virginia over the ownership of a vast tract of land along the Ohio River. When the Shawnee Indians tried to block settlement in the area, Dunmore fought a war with them—a contest that was climaxed by the battle of Point Pleasant in the fall of 1774. There, at the junction of the Kanawha and the Ohio, for the first time in the century, an American-supplied, officered, and commanded army defeated an Indian army of approximately the same size and strength.

The news of this victory, won by frontiersmen from the Valley of Virginia, had another electric effect on American self-confidence. George Washington was so impressed he suggested making Andrew Lewis, the architect of victory at Point Pleasant, commander in chief of the American army. The following year, Virginia commissioners at Fort Pitt used Point Pleasant to cow the southern Indians into neutrality. They scoffed at the idea of the British beating them. "We are not afraid these people will conquer us. They can't fight in our country and you know we can; we fear not them nor any power on earth."

The pugnacious Dunmore learned nothing from this experience. Instead, he renewed the process of building Virginian—and American—self-confidence by fleeing from his palace in Williamsburg

to the shelter of the man-of-war *Fowey* at Yorktown, declaring his fear
of "hostile appearances around me." The Virginians warned the Governor that they knew what he was thinking. They urged him not to
prosecute "a scheme most diabolical . . . to offer freedom to our slaves
and turn them against their masters." Dunmore had been thinking out
loud about such a possibility since April, 1775, and on May 1 he had
proposed it to his superiors in London without receiving a word of
demur. Throughout the summer, he used numerous sloops from his
large fleet—at one time, he had as many as 103 ships—to lure Negroes
from tidewater plantations. On board his ships, Dunmore had 150 men
from the Fourteenth Regiment, whom he had wrangled from Florida.
To these, he added some sailor volunteers and a sprinkling of the few
loyalists he was able to muster from the largest American colony.[4]

By early November, 1775, Dunmore had 350 men under arms, and
he felt strong enough to take the offensive. Hearing that 170 militiamen from Princess Anne County were marching to join other
Virginians massing for an attack on Norfolk, Dunmore surprised them
at Kemp's Landing on the Elizabeth River. Two of the three militia
companies took to their heels after firing a single volley. The third,
composed largely of gentleman volunteers, fought bravely but soon
sought the safety of nearby swamps under the pressure of Dunmore's
superior numbers. The Governor let his black soldiers hunt their
former masters through the muck, and the colonel in command of the
regiment had the disagreeable experience of finding himself eyeball to
eyeball with one of his own slaves. He fired his pistol at him, missed,
and the black man clobbered him with a cutlass. Covered with slime
and streaming blood, he was dragged into the Governor's camp as an
ignominious captive.

Elated by his success, Dunmore issued a proclamation declaring
martial law and summoning "every person capable of bearing arms
. . . to His Majesty's standard, or be looked upon as traitors to His
Majesty's crown and government." Then came the words that sent a
chill of fear through every white man and woman in Virginia, Maryland, and the lower South. "I do hereby further declare all indented
servants, Negroes, or others (appertaining to rebels) free, that are able
and willing to bear arms, they joining His Majesty's troops as soon as
may be."[5]

Virginians were advised by letter writers in the *Virginia Gazette* to
counter Dunmore's appeal with psychology. There was no point in try-

ing to conceal Dunmore's proclamation. Instead, Negroes should be told they would be much worse off under the English flag than under Virginia masters "who pity their condition, who wish in general to make it as easy and comfortable as possible, and who would willingly, were it in their power, or were they permitted, not only prevent any more Negroes from losing their freedom, but restore it to such as have already unhappily lost it." Another writer urged masters to warn their Negroes that if the Americans were defeated, the British would sell all the slaves to the West Indies, as part of a general confiscation policy. The West Indies was tantamount to a death sentence for a Virginia slave.[6]

The Virginia convention, the revolutionary legislature that had succeeded the House of Burgesses, quickly hammered out a policy to deal with Dunmore's threat. All runaways who returned within ten days would be pardoned. The customary patrols on the colony's roads were doubled, and anyone who owned a boat was asked to guard the tidal rivers that flowed so conveniently down to the Chesapeake and Dunmore's fleet. Slaves captured on the run were simply returned to their masters, with advice that they be sent into the interior of the state as soon as possible. Those taken in arms were to be sold to the foreign— French and Dutch—West Indies.

In spite of these precautions, some 500 Negroes had joined Dunmore by the end of November, 1775. The Governor outfitted 300 of them in makeshift uniforms, with "Liberty to Slaves" boldly printed on their coats. They were called "Lord Dunmore's Ethiopian Regiment." Attention now focused on the town of Norfolk, where Dunmore centered his forces, hoping to set up an enclave into which white loyalists and rebellious Negroes could flee.

For a few weeks, Dunmore seemed fabulously successful. Most of the citizens of Kemp's Landing had rushed to take the oath in the midst of His Lordship's black and white soldiers. The same performance was repeated by even larger numbers in Norfolk a few days later. From the printing press aboard his warship headquarters, Dunmore published an issue of his own *Virginia Gazette,* declaring that "now upwards of 3,000 men, determined to defend this part of the country against the inroads of enemies to our King and Constitution" had rallied to his side. In a confidential letter to the American secretary of state, Dunmore admitted, "Of this number not above three or four hundred at most are in any degree capable of bearing arms, and the greatest part of these hardly ever made use of a gun." Dunmore was hoping that a show of force would by some miracle generate the real thing.

The motivation of many oath takers can be glimpsed from a story told in later years by Mrs. Helen Maxwell, a resident of Kemp's Landing. Dunmore gave each of his loyalists a red strip of cloth to wear on his breast. When Mrs. Maxwell saw her husband appear with one of these badges of loyalty, she cried, "Believe me, I would rather have seen you dead than to have seen you with this red badge."

"Phast!" he replied. "Do you think that it has changed my mind? Don't you see how Dunmore is carrying all before him, and if I can save my property by this step, ought I not in common prudence to wear it, for your sake and the children?" [7]

In Norfolk and Princess Anne counties, Dunmore had the potential for a formidable base. Separated from the rest of Virginia by swamps, the area was within easy striking distance of the richest parts of both the Old Dominion and North Carolina. It provided an excellent harbor from which the British fleet could control the sea lanes off Cape Hatteras. It was, in the words of one worried North Carolinian, "perhaps the most noble place of arms for them that the world ever produced."

By early 1776, Dunmore had become one of George Washington's major worries. "If, my dear sir," he wrote to Richard Henry Lee, "that man is not crushed before spring, he will become the most formidable enemy America has." Washington believed that the "fate of America" depended on forcing Dunmore "to evacuate Norfolk this winter." [8] Whether the Virginians could do the job seemed dubious.

The only approach to Norfolk was across a causeway, Great Bridge, which ran through several hundred yards of swampy forest land some nine miles from the little port. Dunmore hastily threw up a fort at his end of the Bridge and equipped it with cannon that swept the causeway.

Five hundred Virginians, led by a cautious veteran named William Woodford, gathered to drive Dunmore back to his ships. When Woodford arrived at the causeway, he wisely decided against a frontal assault on Dunmore's fort. Not long after Woodford had taken command of one of Virginia's two Continental regiments (the colonel of the other regiment was Patrick Henry), he had asked Washington for advice and received a wise letter urging him to be strict in his discipline, but "to require nothing unreasonable of your officers and men." Woodford saw that time and terrain were on the side of the Americans. Neither men nor supplies could reach Dunmore in any quantity as long as the Virginians retained control of their end of the causeway. He was betting that the Royal Governor would lose his head and attack. The strategy of Bunker Hill had made a great impression on all Americans. It was so much easier to sit back and wait for the British to present the whites of their eyes.

Woodford's caution soon had him in trouble with his compatriots. Patrick Henry was the commander in chief of Virginia's armed forces, but the Virginia convention thought it was better to put the experienced Woodford in charge of this military confrontation with the Governor. The chagrined Henry sent Woodford nagging letters asking him for information, and implying that the colonel should have long since driven the British into the Chesapeake. Woodford replied that he was responsible to the Virginia convention, and not to Henry, as long as he was exercising an independent command. If Henry had been in command, there is little doubt that he would have ordered a headlong charge at Dunmore's fort—which would have produced a Bunker Hill in reverse. Yet even the members of the colony's Committee of Safety seemed to think that Woodford was something less than a soldier because he was halted by a fort that was little more than a heap of sticks propped on swampy ground, and manned by a handful of Tories and Negroes. It was a miniature replay of the civilian judgments being passed on Washington, before Boston.

Woodford sent out a series of strong patrols to probe Dunmore's flanks, and asked for more men, ammunition, and artillery. This was supposed to arrive shortly with reinforcements from North Carolina, under the command of Colonel Robert Howe. Meanwhile, Woodford did his best to occupy his grumbling, restless men, many of whom were sleeping on the bare ground in the cold, wet December weather. He threw up a breastwork on his end of Great Bridge, and decided to concoct a plan that might persuade Dunmore to attack him.

In the Virginia ranks were Major Thomas Marshall and his son, Lieutenant John Marshall, the future chief justice of the United States Supreme Court. They persuaded one of their slaves to become a pretended runaway. He made it to the British fort and told Dunmore that Woodford had no more than 300 raw "shirt men," as the British contemptuously called the Virginia militia, for the hunting shirts they wore in lieu of uniforms. Dunmore snapped at the bait, and immediately ordered an attack. Captain Charles Fordyce led 120 of Dunmore's 150 regulars across the causeway. American sentries met them with buck and ball. One, a free Negro named William Flora, fired no less than eight shots at them, holding up the attack for precious minutes, before hotfooting it to the American breastwork through a volley of British musketry.

Whirling his hat over his head and shouting, "The day is ours!" Captain Fordyce led his men through the haze of gun smoke and early-morning mist. Ninety men on duty in the redoubt, commanded by a very cool young lieutenant named Travis, waited for the redcoats to reach point-blank range, then fired. Fordyce went down with fourteen bullets in his body, and twelve privates followed him into eternity. A lieutenant and seventeen other privates became wounded captives, and the surviving redcoats ran for their lives. Before they could rally, Woodford sent part of his men through the swamp to make a flank attack which drove Dunmore's Ethiopians and the remaining redcoats back into their fort in total confusion, abandoning two cannon. "This was a second Bunker's Hill affair, in miniature," Woodford said proudly, "with this difference, that we kept our post and had only one man wounded in the hand." [9]

A few days later, the British abandoned the fort and fell back to Norfolk. Woodford crept closer, but still declined to go over to the offensive. The jittery Dunmore, with so many of his regulars dead or wounded and his hopes of raising blacks all but crushed by his defeat, abandoned the town, and retreated to his ships. This was a fearful blow to the 3,000 residents of Princess Anne and Norfolk counties who had taken the oath of allegiance. Many of them joined Dunmore on the water in whatever they could find to float them. Some took to the woods and swamps. Most ripped off the red ribbons of loyalty they had pinned to their coats and the doors of their houses and begged for mercy.

Woodford, joined by Colonel Robert Howe and some 500 North Carolinians, was not inclined to be sympathetic. Whenever he found a loyalist who had been active on Dunmore's behalf, he handcuffed him to one of his "black brothers," which, he declared, "is the resolution I have taken, shall be the fate of all those cattle." When three of Woodford's men were shot during their first night in Norfolk, he wrote to the Virginia convention, "The town of Norfolk deserves no favour." [10]

The weather remained cold, with snow and rain intermingling. Lord Dunmore wrote of the "melancholy sight . . . of gentlemen of very large property with their ladies and whole families obliged to betake themselves onboard of ships, at this season of the year, hardly with the common necessaries of life, and great numbers of poor people without even these, who must have perished had I not been able to supply them with some flour."

In Norfolk, Woodford relinquised command of the little North Carolina–Virginia army of 1,275 men to Robert Howe. They had compared commissions, and found that Howe was the senior officer by a few months. This sudden elevation of the North Carolinian to commander in chief did not help Woodford control his men. He was soon having many of the troubles Washington was facing on a larger scale. In late December, he wrote the Virginia convention, "I am extremely sorry to think it my duty to inform the Convention that the service begins to be very irksome to some of the officers & I have several applications to day for leave of absence, which I thought inconsistent with the good of the service to grant—upon which they desired leave to resign—this I likewise thought it my duty to refuse. . . . One gentleman thinks himself ill used if he is not allow'd to do this, another chuses to judge for himself in other instances, the men I fear will follow this bad example & where it will end is hard for me to say."

Patrick Henry was still trying to take command of the Virginia army. The Committee of Safety and the Virginia convention were doing everything in their power to prevent this disaster from occurring. Woodford, who seemed to be in on the secret, continued to evade and equivocate when he answered Henry's peremptory letters.

Woodford and his fellow Virginians managed to keep before their eyes the most important problem—what to do with Norfolk. Woodford already had inquired whether he should fortify the town as an American base or whether it should be "totally distroy'd to prevent its furnishing the enemy with good barracks for six or seven thousand troops." This was a clear indication of what he was thinking, and he found the Virginia convention in fundamental agreement. Between them, the soldiers and the civilians launched a policy of trying to provoke the British into destroying the disloyal seaport for them. They permitted their restless men to take potshots at the British ships and to parade up and down the wharves making defiant noises and gestures.

Once more, the bellicose Dunmore proved a perfect foil. He found a ready partner in Captain Henry Bellew of the frigate *Liverpool,* who had recently arrived from London accompanied by a brig. This gave Dunmore four major warships, and he stationed them in a semicircle just off Norfolk's wharves. Bellew, in need of provisions after his long voyage, demanded the right to buy some from shore. Colonel Howe declined to permit him to do so. Notes of varying degrees of courtesy passed back and forth between the military men, with Howe usually insisting that a final reply had to come from the Virginia convention in Williamsburg. Captain Bellew, who did most of the writing, kept insisting that he had no wish "to shed the blood of any of His Majesty's subjects," and Colonel Howe kept regretting that "under the force of reciprocal feelings consequences may ensue which each of us perhaps may wish to avoid."

Finally, at a quarter after three on January 1, 1776, Captain Bellew gave the signal from the *Liverpool,* and the four ships opened fire. Over a hundred guns poured hot shot and flaming "carcasses" (incendiary projectiles) into Norfolk. Boatloads of men went ashore with torches and other combustible materials to make sure the flames burned briskly.

The British intended only to destroy the warehouses and wharves along the waterfront to discourage sniping. But the Virginians and North Carolinians were not going to allow the opportunity to burn Norfolk to pass without a little cooperation from their side. While some of them skirmished briskly with the British landing parties, others set fire to the houses of leading Tories, and soon the entire town was one enormous blaze. It burned for over fifty hours, consuming 913 houses valued at £122,455. Americans were responsible for an estimated £118,807 of this damage. When Robert Howe wrote to the Virginia convention on January 2, the town was still burning. A British midshipman aboard a ship in Dunmore's fleet noted on January 9 that the flames were "still visible here and there, and no more of Norfolk remains but about twelve houses." Colonel Howe, ignoring the share that his men had had in the holocaust, wrote of "women and children running through a crowd of shot to get out of town, some of them with children at their breasts," and asked, "Does it not call for vengeance, both from God and man?" [11]

If there were any loyalists left in Virginia after Norfolk stopped burning, they were wise enough to keep their heads down for the rest of the war. Dunmore seemed incapable of understanding what more astute governors, such as Robert Eden of Maryland and William Franklin of New Jersey, saw—there was no hope of rallying the loyalists without backing from the British army and fleet. It was better to let the rebels have their way and hope they would blunder.

In Virginia, it was the British who blundered. Dunmore's "flaming argument" radicalized thousands of moderates. Edmund Pendleton, the gentle, genial man who was head of both the Committee of Safety and the Virginia convention, had skillfully sidetracked Patrick Henry and his adherents. Henry, by opting for a military command, had temporarily turned himself into a political zero. But Dunmore had turned Pendleton, who at heart yearned for reconciliation with Britain, into an active rebel by forcing him to raise troops and back a ruthless suppression of Toryism and slave rebellion.

Perhaps the saddest man in Virginia in the opening months of the new year was William Byrd III, scion of one of the oldest and most distinguished families in the colony. In his magnificent house, Westover, on the James River, he watched the drift toward war with mounting agony. He had been offered command of Virginia's Continental troops by the state's leaders—but had refused the opportunity to join the Revolution. Writing to his friend Sir Jeffrey Amherst, the famed British general who had refused to serve against the Americans, Byrd said it was "impossible now to avoid civil war" and reported that he had "met with insults and been given offense" because of his refusal to command the armies being raised by "this Convention [the Virginia convention] to oppose the King's troops." Byrd told Amherst he did not want to be "considered one of the American traitors." He was "ready to serve His Majesty and would be glad of the opportunity to convince the Virginians of their error and bring them back to loyalty and duty."

Bryd was a living refutation of the canard advanced by a generation of American historians infatuated with economic explanations for everything men thought and did. These historians noted Virginians owed some £5,000,000 to British merchants and suggested that George Washington and his friends joined the Revolution in the hope of repudiating these debts. No one in Virginia owed more money to British creditors than William Byrd III, yet his loyalty to the King made him a foe of the Revolution.

Byrd had two sons, one in the British army, the other in the navy. On February 25, 1776, his son Thomas joined Dunmore's forces off Norfolk, sent by the British at Lord Dunmore's request in the hope that his name might inspire some Virginians to espouse the royal cause. Thomas told his father in a brief note, "I can talk no other language but that of a Soldier & am determined to support that character as long as I have the honour to belong to the Army."

Byrd had inserted in his will a clause disinheriting any of his children who joined the Revolution. Yet the son in the navy, Otway Byrd, chose to risk his father's wrath and the loss of his share of the Westover estate by jumping ship off the North Carolina coast, swimming ashore, and joining the Virginia branch of the Continental Army. Otway's decision only deepened his father's gloom, and increased William Byrd's already strong penchant for hard liquor.[12]

Almost as sad as Byrd was a man at the other end of Virginia's social scale. Twenty-five-year-old English-born Nicholas Cresswell had no visible means of support. Unhappy with his severe, bad-tempered father, he came to America as a half runaway, half tourist in May, 1774, and found himself involved in the Revolution. He took a trip down the Ohio River, and wandered around Virginia for the next eighteen months, growing more and more unhappy. On the last day of 1775, he wrote in his diary, "The New Year bears a forbidding aspect. I am here a prisoner at large. If I attempt to depart and don't succeed, a prison must be my lot. If I do anything to get a living, perhaps I must be obliged to fight against my King and country, which my conscience abhors."

Within two weeks, he was noting nervously, "Many of my old acquaintances look very cool upon me because I will not be as great scoundrels as themselves." The next day, he read Tom Paine's *Common Sense,* which was making "a great noise." Cresswell called it "one of the vilest things that ever was published to the world. Full of false representations, lies, calumny and treason, whose principles are to subvert all kingly governments and erect an independent republic." By the end of the month, when news of Norfolk's burning had spread throughout Virginia, Cresswell noted in his diary, "Nothing but independence will go down. The devil is in the people." [13]

Cresswell was not the only man in Virginia who disliked *Common Sense.* Colonel Landon Carter, a grandee of the old school, called it "quite scandalous," and in his diary concluded that it "disgraces the American Cause much." A few days later, in an argument with a fellow Virginian who praised the pamphlet as a "most incomparable performance," Carter said it was "as much the random of a despot as anything could be." Carter especially disliked the way Paine called "every man a damned scoundrel that didn't think as he did, a coward and sycophant." But this quintessence of conservatism changed his mind about the British government being the best on earth when ten of his slaves looted his silver and stole a new boat from his wharf to join Dunmore. Carter was, as he put it wrathfully, "compelled to independency." [14]

Thanks to the confrontation tactics of Lord Dunmore, more and more men found themselves persuaded by *Common Sense*. The moderates, led by Edmund Pendleton, were firmly in control of the Virginia convention, but they had nowhere to go. As long as the royal government was represented by Dunmore, any attempt to take even a small step toward reconciliation was out of the question. In a few weeks, news from North Carolina made it clear that this situation was not unique to the colony of Virginia.

XIII

King George
and Broadswords

Governor Josiah Martin of North Carolina seemed to be duplicating Governor Dunmore's experience, as the year 1776 dawned. A former major in the British army, married to an American-born Long Islander, he became governor in 1771, inheriting a gorgeous palace built by his predecessor, William Tryon, at New Bern, and a colony split by civil war. For well over a decade, the more than 40,000 Scots, Irish, and German settlers in North Carolina's back country considered themselves underrepresented and overtaxed, in comparison to the wealthier, more settled seacoast. They had attempted to set up a semi-independent government, which took over the courts, beat up tax collectors, and started to "regulate" taxes and fees. Governor Tryon had led a seaboard army that routed the back-country men at the battle of Alamance Creek in 1771. After hanging six of their leaders, Tryon had sailed off to more trouble in New York.[1]

Governor Martin made a tour of the Regulator country. His conclusion, secretly conveyed to the British government, was startling. "I now see most clearly that they [the Regulators] have been provoked by insolence, and cruel advantage taken of the people's ignorance by mercenary tricking attorneys, clerks and other little officers, who have practiced upon them every sort of rapine and extortion, and who have enlisted the aid of government in order to cover their own transgressions." Part of this conclusion was pique. The assembly continued to send Tryon state papers even after Martin was installed in the Governor's Palace. But there was a good deal of truth in Martin's contention that North Carolina seaboard leaders had been exploiting the back-country people.

On his opulent estate, Hilton, near Wilmington, lived Cornelius Harnett. Josiah Quincy of Boston, traveling for his health, visited him in 1773 and called him "the Sam Adams of the South." Nearby were men who had been commanders of the army that crushed the Regulators—James Moore, Alexander Lillington, John Ashe, and Richard Caswell. Harnett became Martin's hair shirt. As the confrontation between England and America mounted, his men caught a messenger from the Governor with a letter asking for royal troops. Harnett published it with a comment about "diabolical schemes." When the Governor summoned the state assembly, Harnett called a meeting of the extralegal provincial congress for the same day. Practically every man was a member of both bodies. The jittery Governor retreated to Fort Johnston at the mouth of the Cape Fear River.

This ramshackle structure threatened to collapse every time someone fired a cannon from it. It was guarded by one Captain John Collett and a handful of British soldiers. Offshore bobbed the eight-gun sloop, H.M.S. *Cruizer,* which began looking much safer to Martin than Fort Johnston. When plans for a slave uprising on the Tar River were discovered early in July, Martin was implicated. He vowed he had nothing to do with it, but decided it was time to seek the safety of the *Cruizer's* main deck, and got aboard the sloop just in time. A force of 500 men under orders signed by "The People" burned the fort, ignoring the Governor's proclamation threatening death to anyone who attacked it.

But Martin was by no means out of action. For the next six months, he bombarded the British government with assurances that he could raise a formidable army in North Carolina, thanks to his support among the ex-Regulators. What convinced the statesmen in Whitehall more than anything else was the Governor's ability to invoke one of the most romantic names of the century in his behalf—Flora McDonald. Those who are inclined to see history as a crazy quilt without meaning or pattern can make a good argument out of the appearance of this heroine on the banks of the Cape Fear River in 1776. Thirty years before, when Flora McDonald was an unmarried, delicately beautiful Scottish lassie, she had fired the imagination of the world by risking her life and reputation to save Charles Edward Stuart, the pretender to the throne of England.

Bonnie Prince Charlie was a man on the run after the defeat of his Highlanders at the battle of Culloden in 1746. For two months, the fair

Flora guided him through the hedgerows to the coast, where a French ship rescued him. Flora spent a few weeks in the Tower of London, but the cold realism of the power brokers in Whitehall for once compromised with romance. When it was obvious that Scotland's spirit was crushed, they let Flora go home to marry her distant cousin Allan McDonald and read the ballads and poems hustling hacks churned out about her exploit.

Thirty years later, Flora and her husband decided to follow their many countrymen fleeing a ruined, rack-rented Scotland to the fertile hills of North Carolina. By now, Flora was a buxom matron of fifty-four with seven children to her credit. The McDonalds were welcomed with reverence by their Scottish countrymen in western North Carolina. As the United States discovered after World War II, a defeated ex-enemy often makes a loyal ally. The Governor persuaded Flora and her husband to support his threatened—not to say extermi-nated—royal authority in North Carolina. The excited Martin was soon assuring his superiors in London, "The people are in general well af-fected and much attached to me." He estimated that no less than 20,000 fighting men would rally to the King's standard in the back country.[2] This was fantasy. Most of the Scots had arrived after the battle of Alamance Creek and had only a tenuous relationship with the Regulators. Governor Martin ignored this fact in his determination to build a backfire against Cornelius Harnett and his friends.[3]

While Lord Dunmore off Norfolk begged and wheedled for a single regiment, Martin's report inspired George III to send no less than 2,000 redcoats and two batteries under the command of Henry Clinton to Martin's support. The King and his advisers saw the strategic advantages of Martin's dream. Cape Fear was a magnificent deepwater base for the British fleet, so vital, in fact, that when Parliament prohibited all American trade with Great Britain and the West Indies, they had exempted North Carolina from this ban. Control of the Cape Fear River valley would split the southern colonies and create an enclave to which loyalists throughout the back country of both North and South Carolina could rally. Martin was playing for the highest possible stakes. Even the recapture of a single colony might silence the independence men in Congress by swinging the relatively few bellicose Southerners back to the reconciliation side of the argument.

The North Carolina patriots watched Allan McDonald, Flora's husband, closely. They were equally jittery about her son-in-law, Alexander McLeod. They sent them a letter demanding to know whether they planned to "raise troops to support the arbitrary measures of the Ministry against the Americans in this colony." McLeod and McDonald did not bother to reply. They had already met secretly with Governor Martin and urged him to form a battalion of "good and faithful Highlanders" from the McDonald and McLeod clans. Also under surveillance were two British officers from Boston, Lieutenant Colonel Donald MacDonald and Captain Donald McLeod, who said they had been wounded at Bunker Hill and were thinking about retiring to peaceful North Carolina. They were not watched very closely. In a few months they had recruited 300 men for a Royal Highland Emigrant Regiment.

Early in January, 1776, word arrived from London about the dispatch of 2,000 troops and Major General Clinton. The Governor was told that the troops would sail from Ireland by December 1, which meant that they should reach the North Carolina coast by late January or early February, 1776. The message from London breathed confidence "in subdueing, with the assistance of the Almighty, the said impious and unnatural rebellion."

The ecstatic Martin lost his head. He appointed Donald MacDonald brigadier general of the militia and Donald McLeod second in command with the rank of lieutenant colonel, and sent messengers hustling into the back country ordering the Highlanders and Regulators to muster early in February. The Regulators, who had boasted of producing 5,000 or 6,000 men at a nod from the Governor, turned out to be a paper army. When Donald McLeod arrived in their district to lead them to the loyalist rendezvous, Cross Creek, barely 500 men appeared, and they vanished like smoke when they heard a rumor that a rebel army was marching on them.

At Cross Creek on February 15, acting Brigadier MacDonald found approximately 1,400 men, almost all Scots. Only 520 had guns. Another 130 weapons were hastily confiscated from local rebels. This still left half the army, if it even deserved that name, without muskets.[4]

Meanwhile, Cornelius Harnett and his friends were not idle. On February 9, when Harnett heard that the clans were gathering, he ordered his military leaders into action. Within a few days, Colonel James Moore was on the march toward Cross Creek with 1,100 men. Two other columns, led by Colonels Lillington and Caswell, also converged on the loyalists. Donald MacDonald had no appetite for a battle before joining forces with Clinton and his regulars. Neither did his men. Two companies from Anson County marched home in a body at the mere prospect of a fight, taking their badly needed guns with them. Trying to bluff Moore into retreating, MacDonald sent him a note ordering him to lay down his arms or "suffer the fate of an enemy of the Crown." Moore, his confidence bolstered by five cannon, declined to scare. He continued to block the most direct route to the seacoast, and told MacDonald and his men to "take oath to support the Continental Congress or be treated as enemies of the constitutional liberties of America." *

MacDonald ferried his army across the Cape Fear River, sank his boats, and tried a bolt down the opposite bank to Wilmington. But Caswell and Lillington were moving up this side of the river, and after some five days of marching and countermarching, the loyalists discovered that the rebels had blocked their last route to the sea—the bridge across a little meandering stream called Widow Moore's Creek. By now, Brigadier MacDonald was both exhausted and desperate. He was well over fifty—some accounts place him in his seventies—and he really had been wounded at Bunker Hill. He had less than two barrels of flour left to feed his men. A sick man, MacDonald took to a bed in a nearby farmhouse. Command of the army passed to Donald McLeod.

At a council of war on Sunday night, February 25, 1776, the Scots decided to attack Caswell and Lillington at dawn. But the forty-seven-year-old Maryland-born Caswell was a canny soldier. By night, he withdrew his army to the safe side of the creek, ripped up the only bridge, and greased the sleepers with soft soap and tallow. He dug in his thousand-man army, ordered all fires to be doused, and waited.

At dawn, shouting "King George and broadswords!" eighty Highlanders led by McLeod came storming out of the woods, hefting the two-edged weapons that had almost broken the British lines at Culloden. Behind them, bagpipes skirling, came the rest of the clans in three columns. If Caswell had stayed on the wrong side of Moore's Creek, there is a good chance that this eighty-man phalanx might have crumpled his amateur soldiers and sent them fleeing. But the impact of the Highland charge evaporated as they struggled to cross the greased, semi-demolished bridge. Many toppled off into the freezing water. Those who made it had to reform behind McLeod, and before they could regain any kind of momentum, Caswell's men cut them down with a blast of swan shot and musket balls. It was Great Bridge all over again, with even worse carnage. McLeod was dead before he hit the

* Map on page 240.

ground, with more than twenty bullets in him. The survivors fled back across the creek.[5]

Caswell sent one of his lieutenants across the stream to strike the Scots in the flank and rear and sallied across the bridge with his main force. The loyalist army dissolved. Eight hundred and fifty slower-footed fugitives were taken prisoner, and thirteen wagons, one carrying a war chest with £15,000 in gold, were captured. Included in the haul were Brigadier General MacDonald and Flora's husband, Allan McDonald, and two of their sons.

Down on the lower Cape Fear, a confident Josiah Martin had ordered the guns of the sloop of war *Cruizer* trained on Wilmington, to enforce a demand for one thousand barrels of flour. Cornelius Harnett, hoping to save the town, had been permitting the sale of fresh meat and vegetables to the Governor and his floating entourage. But one thousand barrels of flour could only mean that the Governor expected either a British squadron and army or his loyalist supporters. Harnett replied that he could see no reason why "His Majesty's servants" required one thousand barrels of flour, and ordered the people of Wilmington to throw up breastworks and get the women and children out of town. Late on February 28, a footsore fugitive from the battle of Moore's Creek Bridge rowed out to H.M.S. *Cruizer* with news of the disaster. The next day, a note, signed by the captain of the *Cruizer,* came ashore humbly requesting "a few quarters of good beef."

The clash at Moore's Creek Bridge had consequences extending far beyond the swampy little battlefield. Loyalism in North Carolina was as crushed by this mini-victory as if the dead and wounded numbered 7,000, instead of 70. The explanation for this impact was not pure terror. Showing an imagination which Governor Martin, with his gasconades about impious, seditious rebellion, conspicuously lacked, the North Carolina provincial congress issued a proclamation in which they assured the loyalists that if they repented, all would be well. "We have their security in contemplation, not to make them miserable," declared Cornelius Harnett and his followers. "In our power, their errors claim our pity, their situation disarms our resentment. We shall hail their reformation with increasing pleasure, and receive them to us with open arms."

Not all North Carolinians espoused this official benevolence, especially when most of the loyalists, including the sons and husband of romantic Flora, stubbornly declined to switch sides. But the impact of the publicly proclaimed mercy, which won approval and funds from the Continental Congress, undoubtedly made more than one wavering loyalist in other colonies think twice about reaching for his gun.

The warrior spirit of the rebel North Carolinians soared to hitherto unknown heights. "Since I was born I never heard so universal an ardor for fighting prevailing, and so perfect a union among all degrees of men," reported one native. "You never knew the like in your life for pure patriotism," said another in a letter to a northern friend. When the North Carolina provincial congress met on April 4 at Halifax, Cornelius Harnett was named head of a committee "to take into consideration the usurpations and violences committed by the King and Parliament of Great Britain against America, and the further measures to be taken for frustrating the same, and for the better defense of this province."

Three days later, Harnett returned with a resolution which more than justified his admirers' claim that he was the Samuel Adams of the South. *"Resolved,* that the delegates for this colony in the Continental Congress be empowered to concur with the delegates of the other colonies in declaring independency, and forming foreign alliances . . . " Thus the explosive word "independence" for the first time was urged upon the hesitant Congress by one of the thirteen sovereign states. Those two military gamblers, Lord Dunmore and Josiah Martin, had taken a long stride toward losing a continent for their master, George III.[6]

XIV

How to Celebrate
a Non-Victory

The victory at Moore's Creek Bridge played a major part in North Carolina's fervor for independence. But some of the bravado was also explained by good news from Boston. The British army had been driven out of that beleaguered city. Not a single redcoat remained on the soil of the thirteen colonies.

On February 16, as the loyalists of North Carolina mustered at Cross Creek, George Washington had counted heads in his Cambridge headquarters. He found he had 8,797 privates fit for duty and another 1,405 near enough to be summoned to camp if needed. Militia numbered 7,280, officers included. Against these 17,482 men, the American general estimated Howe had little more than 5,000 regulars. Moreover, the frigid winter had made "some pretty strong ice" in South Bay and Back Bay. Before a council of war Washington laid a daring proposition: a frontal assault across this slippery natural bridge to take Boston by storm. The generals voted against it. Washington could only swallow hard and try to digest the rebuff. Congress, taking him at his word when he modestly protested that he lacked the ability to be commander in chief, had directed him to rely on councils of war to make decisions. Washington felt bound by this foolish directive. His diffidence about his ability was real, and his deference to civilian authority was equally genuine. Out of these two realities rose a monstrosity—an army with a half dozen heads.

Sounding more like a sergeant than a general, Washington groused to his favorite confidant, Joseph Reed, still playing politics in Philadelphia. "Though we had been waiting all the year for his favorable event, the enterprise was thought too dangerous." [1]

But Washington was also learning to live with frustration, and slowly adding to his Indian fighter's fondness for surprise attack a reluctant acceptance of American limitations. The council of war may have been right, he admitted to Reed. "Perhaps the irksomeness of my situation led me to undertake more than could be warranted by prudence." Always the realist, Washington had to admit that the council was correct when they pointed out that they still lacked enough powder for an effective bombardment. To send men against the entrenched British without artillery support was almost asking them to commit suicide. Moreover, although Howe might be short on enlisted men, there was an ample supply of British officers in Boston, and this could be a great advantage to an army fighting on the defensive.

The plan to attack the city and annihilate the British army in one fierce stroke was set aside—but by no means abandoned by the American commander in chief. For the next few weeks, hints and rumors circulated through the American army and the surrounding countryside, raising everyone's hopes of an early end to the war.

On February 20, 1776, Sarah Hodgkins wrote to her husband, Lieutenant Joseph Hodgkins, complaining mightily because he had defaulted on his promise to see her once a month,"& it is now a-month & I think a very long one" since his last visit." But she added that she was sure his failure was not "for want of a good will." Ipswich was full of rumors "that there will be something done amongst you very soon." This was an interesting commentary on the state of security in Washington's army. That the American general planned an attack on Boston was one of the worst-kept secrets in the history of warfare.[2]

Everyone from lieutenants to chaplains even seemed to know exactly where the attack was going to be made. On January 21, 1776, Lieutenant Ebenezer Huntington of Connecticut wrote slyly to his father, "I wish to tell you something about Dorchester but cannot, tho expect to be able to by the first of Feby." Ebenezer David, a Rhode Island chaplain, wrote to his friend, Nicholas Brown, father of the man who gave Brown University its name, that a captain who was cozy with Brigadier General John Sullivan of New Hampshire had offered to "lay a bett that we shall be in possession of Boston in fifteen days' time." On January 29, David dined with Isaac Foster, the senior surgeon of the American hospital at Cambridge, who told him that "he was in expectation of Dorchesters Neck being seised by our people in a few days—which will be likely to bring on a general engagement." [3]

If George Washington in his Cambridge headquarters had been omniscient, the knowledge of these letters would only have caused him additional pain. His sensitivity to criticism, demonstrated many times during his life, was particularly acute during these months. His favorite correspondent in Philadelphia, Joseph Reed, had told him that there were more than a few nagging tongues in Congress and out—"chimney corner heroes," Reed called them—who were criticizing the American commander for his inaction. For a moment, Washington relapsed into his anti–New England attitude, and exclaimed, "These people—among friends—are not to be depended upon if exposed; and any man will fight well if he thinks himself in no danger." But he hastily added, "I do not apply this to these people only. I suppose it to be the case with all raw and undisciplined troops." [4]

The reason for Washington's inaction was not the courage of his troops, but the lack of powder. "Why will not Congress forward part of the powder made in your province?" he asked Reed. "They seem to look upon this as the season for action, but will not furnish the means." As for attacking Boston, Washington insisted that he had "the same opinion of the attempt now, which I have ever done. I believe an assault would be attended with considerable loss, and I believe it would succeed, if the men should behave well."

Some two weeks later, Washington wrote a chatty note to Martha's brother-in-law, Burwell Bassett, in which he remarked, "We are preparing to take possession of a post (which I hope to do in a few days if we can get provided with the means) which will, it is generally thought, bring on a rumpus between us and the enemy." In the same letter, Washington dropped a hint that this "rumpus" might be much more serious than he made it sound. He thanked Bassett for watching over the prime western land he had bought along the banks of the Kanawha and Ohio rivers. The title to these lands was being disputed by speculators from other colonies. Washington promised to be more careful of his interest in them in the future. "In the worst event," he wrote, "they will serve for an asylum." [5]

The post which Washington planned to take had been accurately foreseen by Lieutenant Huntington and Chaplain David. Dorchester Heights was a peninsula, or "neck," of land about a mile long and a mile and a half wide, reaching around the south shore of Boston like a giant arm. Charlestown peninsula, where the battle of Bunker Hill had been fought, duplicated this semi-encirclement on the north. Lieutenant Samuel Webb of Connecticut, writing in his diary on March 1, 1776, rather effectively summed up what the American commander in chief had in mind.

"Dorchester Point," as he called it, reached some six hundred yards within the outer lines which the British had constructed on Boston Neck—the narrow stretch of land which linked the town to the mainland. "A strong battery erected on this point would enable us to cut off the communication between the town and their outworks on the Neck, at the same time annoy the ships and town. . . . Our commander in chief is determined to lose no time in putting into execution this plan." Webb even seemed to know what General Howe was thinking. " 'Tis said their commander has swore if we brake ground . . . he will sally on us—if he was sure of loseing two-thirds of his army. This is what we wish for." Here Webb revealed—as Woodford in Virginia had done before him—how Bunker Hill had mesmerized America's soldiers. They would pay a fearful price for this self-hypnosis before the end of 1776.[6]

Webb and the other rumor swappers were dealing in half-truths. Only a handful of men knew that Washington was hoping to attack and destroy the entire British army. His correspondence with Charles Lee, which put him in close touch with the situation in New York, had convinced Washington that the British intended to seize this strategic city as their base of operations. The fact that the British were "watering and fitting up their vessels," as he told his brother-in-law Burwell Bassett, caused no exultation at American headquarters. The commander in chief was convinced that this was only a prelude to a dash for New York. It was this and other information which he got in a steady stream from Boston, thanks to his efficient intelligence system, that convinced him that he should make his move toward Dorchester at this unpropitious season of the year, when the ground was still frozen.

Here, too, Washington knew something that neither the British nor the rumor spreaders knew. Colonel Rufus Putnam, one of the American army's engineers, had been summoned to headquarters for a conference on how to build fortifications in spite of frozen ground. Putnam borrowed a book called *Muller's Field Engineer,* and found in it the answer to Washington's dilemma. Wooden frames called "chandeliers" could be set on the frozen ground and filled with fascines—bundles of twisted sticks and hay—and gabions—barrels filled with dirt. To bind everything together, the Americans cut marsh turf, which had some of the consistency of peat.[7]

This problem solved, Washington ordered a crash program to prepare the needed matériel. Lieutenant Isaac Bangs of Harwich, Massachusetts, noted in his journal, "Great preparations were making for some new enterprize, such as fashienes, gaboreenes, barracks ready framed [no doubt the chandeliers] & boards cut. All imagine that Dorchester Hill is the object of our attention." [8]

Washington made no attempt to conceal his interest in Dorchester—it was impossible anyway, because it was such an obvious move. But the seizure of these heights was, for him, only a first step in a daring battle plan. He was hoping that Howe would make good the boast which Webb had reported in his diary—and attack the American regiments on Dorchester. While a third or even half of the British army was absorbed by this assault, Washington planned to send 4,000 men in 45 batteaux, supported by twelve-pound cannon on rafts, swarming out of the Charles River to attack the west side of Boston. The first division of 2,000 men were to seize Beacon Hill and Mount Horam (or, as it was sometimes called, Whoredom), high ground near the Boston Common. The next wave was to wheel and attack the rear of the British lines on Boston Neck, clear this key position, and open the gates of the city for reinforcements waiting at Roxbury. The man whom many people had been accusing of timidity and inaction was preparing for a battle certain to be as bloody and hair-raising as any ever fought in America.[9]

Washington's plan was as daring as Montgomery's smash at Quebec. Committing raw troops against professional soldiers fighting from fortifications was desperate business. It underscored the conviction in Washington's mind that all hope of reconciliation had vanished. Military victory was the only hope of preserving America's freedom. The destruction or capture of Howe's army would cripple the British war effort. Although others, including Continental Congressmen, might still talk of reconciliation, for Washington the King's speech had been the end of all such hopes. Early in February, he had written to Joseph Reed, "I have never entertained an idea of an accommodation since I heard of . . . the King's speech. . . . If every man was of my mind, the ministers of Great Britain should know, in a few words, upon what issue the cause should be put."

He had no illusions about what he was risking. On February 27, he told his army, "The season is now fast approaching when every man must expect to be drawn into the field of action." He urged each sol-

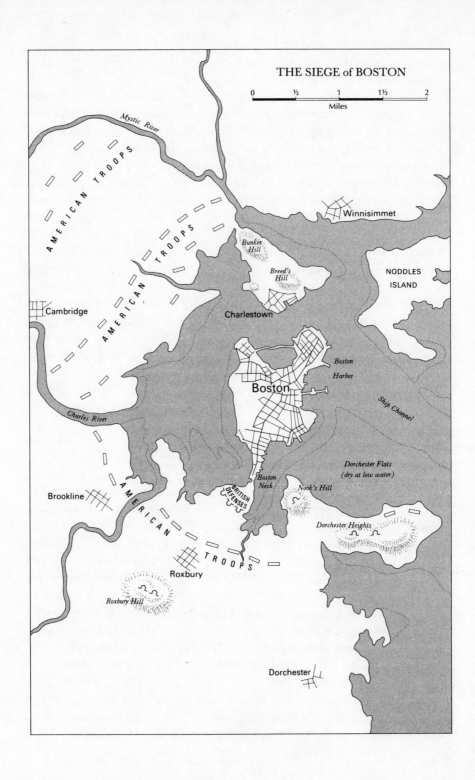

THE SIEGE of BOSTON

0   ½   1   1½   2
Miles

Mystic River

AMERICAN TROOPS

AMERICAN TROOPS

AMERICAN TROOPS

Winnisimmet

Bunker Hill

Breed's Hill

NODDLES ISLAND

Cambridge

Charlestown

Boston Harbor

Boston

Ship Channel

Charles River

AMERICAN TROOPS

Dorchester Flats (dry at low water)

Brookline

BRITISH DEFENSES

Boston Neck

Nook's Hill

Dorchester Heights

AMERICAN TROOPS

Roxbury

Roxbury Hill

Dorchester

dier "to prepare his mind" for the challenge. "It is a noble cause we are engaged in; it is the cause of virtue and mankind. . . . Freedom or slavery must be the result of our conduct. There can therefore be no greater inducement to men to behave well." He added that "if any man in action shall presume to skulk, hide himself, or retreat from the enemy, without the orders of his commanding officer, he will be *instantly shot down,* as an example of cowardice." [10]

Massachusetts militia were called up to man the lines. Huge, unwieldy mortars were dug into laboriously constructed beds in Roxbury and at Lechmere Point on Back Bay. Once more, Washington counted his barrels of powder, and decided he could issue twenty-four rounds to every man, including the militia. That would leave him with about a hundred barrels—a far from reassuring amount if anything went wrong and the army had to defend itself against a British counterattack.

On March 2 and 3, Washington ordered bombardments, carefully limited to save powder, against British positions far away from Dorchester Heights. The British blasted back, and Abigail Adams in nearby Braintree, writing to her husband, John, groaned, "No sleep for me tonight." Lieutenant Webb pitied the "poor inhabitants, our friends" in Boston, whose houses were on the receiving end of the American bombardment. But the fiery Abigail, after listening to the thunder for a while, decided it was "of the true species of the sublime." Chaplain Ebenezer David feared the worst. After assuring his friend Nicholas Brown once more that Dorchester was the American objective, he predicted "a warm & general action." But he felt that the "profanity of our camp" made it almost inevitable that "GOD should frown upon us."

On the first night, the American artillery fired only twenty-five rounds, and the inexperienced gunners split three mortars, including the mighty thirteen-inch Congress, which had been captured in the *Nancy.* The second night, they fired only a few more rounds, but spaced them at wide intervals, so that the bombardment lasted until dawn. On the night of March 4, however, "a more furious fire was began than ever," noted Lieutenant Bangs in his journal, and was returned by the British "with eaqual vigour." Lieutenant Bangs took refuge in a small, uncompleted American battery to the right of the Roxbury forts to watch the show. Mortar shells were the chief entertainment. These crude forerunners of contemporary explosive shells were hollow balls of iron filled with powder. A fuse sent a trail of sparks through the night, and the excited young lieutenant saw "4 & sometimes 5 of their Boms flying in the air at a time." One of them took a wild bounce and came toward him. Aghast, the lieutenant watched it bounding along the ground. "If it had hopped again before it broke . . . it would have come, as near as I can judge, to the very spot where I was; it broke about twenty-five yard distance, and one of the pieces came with great rapidity about two yards above my head." [11]

While all this excitement was being provided by the artillery, a long procession of men, guns, and carts under the command of Brigadier General John Thomas was toiling across the causeway that connected Roxbury and Dorchester. For the first—and not the last—time, Washington was to have the best possible sign of a lucky general—the weather in his favor. It was, Lieutenant Bangs noted, "a very light moonshine evening." A screen of hay bales was placed along the vulnerable passage to protect the Americans from British fire. But it was not needed. A ground fog shrouded the causeway and peninsula from the view of the already disconcerted British soldiers on Boston Neck.

First came a covering party of 800 men, who took up positions along the Dorchester shore, and on the outer point of the peninsula. Following them were 1,200 workers lugging picks and shovels, and after them 360 ox teams hauling the chandeliers, fascines, and gabions. On the two high hills directly above the anchorage of the British fleet. Richard Gridley, the chief engineer of the American army, Rufus Putnam, and several assistants had already sketched the outlines of the forts on the frozen earth. For Gridley, it was a familiar experience. Some nine months ago, he had directed another brigade of pick and shovel men, who built a momentous fort on Breed's Hill, which brought on the battle of Bunker Hill. There was very little doubt in the American army that they were about to have a replay of that blood-drenched drama. Lieutenant Huntington, scribbling a hasty note to his father before he marched to Dorchester, said, "My cloaths and papers are properly secured in case that my maker should in His great good Pleasure so ordain that I should not live to Come off the Hill. . . . Pray that we may succeed as we trust that we are fighting the Lords Battle."

In spite of ground that was frozen a foot and a half deep, the men soon had the chandeliers firmly planted, and they were swiftly filled with the fascines and gabions and the smelly chunks of marsh turf. Nearby, some 250 axemen were demolishing an orchard to make abatis, long pointed spears of wood that would jut from the fort to impale attacking British. Beneath these, they piled hundreds of specially built "well Naild" barrels filled with dirt and stones. They would look to the attacking British like part of the fortification. But at a signal they were to be turned over and sent hurtling down the hill into the British ranks. At 10 P.M., Brigadier General Thomas took out his watch and noted with satisfaction that the six forts under construction were already solid enough to protect the men from small arms and grapeshot.

But this was only the first step. Twice, three times, the oxen and carts returned across the causeway for more gabions and fascines and barrels. Among them now came horses hauling heavy cannon to be emplaced in the forts. The working parties, once they got below the frost line, made the dirt fly at a prodigious rate to build emplacements for these cannon. On either side of the causeway and up on the Dorchester hills, in the shadowy moonlight, the toiling men more than once glimpsed a big man on a bay horse, watching their efforts with silent approval. It was Washington.

At 3 A.M., the exhausted men shouldered their tools, and the covering party was withdrawn from the shore. Back marched General Thomas at the head of his men, while 2,400 fresh soldiers, with guns primed and twenty-four rounds in their pouches, strode into the forts. Companies of riflemen swarmed down to take up positions along the shore. The precision, the organization, must have struck more than one veteran of Bunker Hill, when he remembered the haphazard planning and helter-skelter orders that turned that battle into an American defeat.

Through the long night, not a sound of alarm came from Boston or the ships in the harbor, beyond the steady crash of their cannon and mortars, replying to the American fire. Only one British officer seems to have been alert enough to detect what was going on. A lieutenant colonel named Campbell reported, at ten o'clock, that "the rebels" were at work on Dorchester Heights. Unfortunately for the King's arms, he made his report to Brigadier General Francis Smith, who had commanded the British troops at Lexington and Concord. A fat, stupid, slow man, Smith seems to have done nothing with the information except sleep on it.

In the morning, the British awoke to stare in disbelief at what the Americans had accomplished. William Howe, when he studied the American forts through his field glass, was said to have exclaimed, "Good God, these fellows have done more work in one night than I could have made my army do in three months." Later, he wrote to his superiors in London that the Americans "could not have employed less than twelve or fourteen thousand men." The British army's chief engineer, Archibald Robertson, guessed as high as twenty thousand. Another high-ranking redcoat was convinced that the Americans possessed "the genie belonging to Aladdin's wonderful lamp." The British admiral informed Howe that if the rebels were allowed to stay, the fleet would be required to leave.[12]

The Americans who had taken charge of the forts were themselves "prodigiously surprised" by the "vast works that had been carried on in so little time," according to Lieutenant Bangs. But they saw that the forts called for more digging, and set up fatigue parties. "We expected a salute immediately from the ships in the harbor as also from their works," Bangs wrote, "and they must have greatly annoyed us had they fired when our forts were thus weak, being then little beside fashiens about six feet thick." Fortunately for the Americans, the British could not elevate their guns high enough to reach the crest of the two hills. "They fired a few shot upon us as we were seting the fatigue partys," Bangs said, "and brok 6 or 8 small arms in our rigiment; but as their balls struck chiefly before they reached us, we could avoid them."

In Boston, General Howe, racked by memories of Bunker Hill, nevertheless ordered Brigadier Daniel Jones with five regiments—about 3,000 men—to drive the Americans off Dorchester Heights. His battle plan revealed not a little desperation. Jones was ordered to board ships which carried him out to Castle William, the fortified island in Boston Harbor not far from the outermost point of the Dorchester peninsula. Two more regiments, bolstered by picked companies of grenadiers and light infantry, were ordered to prepare for an amphibious landing from flatboats on the shore below the forts. Simultaneously, Howe planned to assault the American lines at Roxbury with 4,000 men, whom he would lead personally. A breakthrough here would enable him to trap the Americans on the Dorchester peninsula between his two forces. This plan left only 400 men to guard the side of Boston where Washington was planning to make his amphibious assault. The stage was set for a titanic showdown.

On Dorchester Heights, Major John Trumbull said his men were "in high spirits" and "waited with impatience for the attack, when we meant to emulate, and hoped to eclipse, the glories of Bunker's Hill." They had some twenty pieces of cannon in the fort, and were "amply supplied with ammunition." Washington visited them, and urged them to remember the date.It was March 5, commemorated since 1770 as the anniversary of the Boston Massacre. "Avenge the death of your brethren," he urged them.

All day, civilians crowded the roofs of Boston and the nearby hills, waiting for the battle to begin. In Cambridge, Washington's 4,000-man amphibious force waited even more tensely. But the day dwindled away with no sign of an aggressive move from the British. Probably, Howe was planning a night—or at least a dawn—attack. Among the orders issued to his troops was a prohibition against loading their muskets. The bayonet was to be the weapon of choice. He hoped the darkness would shield his ranks from the American marksmanship, which had wreaked such havoc on Breed's Hill.

Just as darkness fell, the mild weather began to undergo a sea change. Out of the south whistled a cold, biting wind that soon became mixed with snow and hail. One Boston diarist called it "a hurrycane." Lieutenant Bangs, shivering on the exposed Dorchester hills with "nothing to cover us excepting apple trees," called it "the most violent storm . . . that ever I was exposed to . . . what I suffered this night I shall ever bear in mind."

In Boston, General Howe was holding another council of war. All day, engineer Archibald Robertson had been going about the town, buttonholing influential officers and urging them to persuade Howe to abandon the attack. "The fate of this whole army and the town is at stake, not to say the fate of America," he insisted. As he read the size and solidity of the American position, he could foresee nothing but disaster for the British. Finally, at about eight o'clock, while Robertson lurked in an empty room at headquarters, General Howe made his decision, backed by unanimous agreement from his ranking officers. The attack would be abandoned. In his diary, Robertson noted that "the General said it was his own sentiments, from the first, but thought the honor of the troops concerned." To protect his image and salve the army's pride, Howe dictated an order to be published the following morning. "The General desires that the troops may know that the intended expedition of last night was unavoidably put off by the badness of the weather." [13]

There was no need to soothe the pride of the enlisted men. The news that they were not to attack inspired nothing more formidable than profound relief in most of them. An American who had watched them embark the day before noted that they looked "pale and dejected, and said to one another that it would be another Bunker's Hill affair or worse." [14]

The same general orders that published Howe's excuse for not attacking carried the news that Boston was to be evacuated. The general requested "The following working parties to be furnished by the troops

at the hours specified . . ." Artillery, barracks furniture, baggage were
to be collected on the wharves. Even in the eighteenth century, 8,906
soldiers carried with them an immense amount of paraphernalia. While
the city swarmed with sweating redcoats, two groups of civilians
watched them with drastically different emotions. Those who were
loyal to the American cause—the Whigs—silently rejoiced, but dreaded
the very real possibility that when the last British soldier left the
wharves, the ships would open fire and Boston would go up in flames.
Three selectmen went to General Robertson and asked him if Howe
planned to burn the city. Robertson went to Howe and came back with
the reply that the general had no intention of destroying the town
"unless the troops under his command are molested during their embarkation or at their departure." [15]

On Dorchester peninsula, Washington was planning a step that
would force the British to give battle or face destruction. Hundreds of
men labored along the safe side of the peninsula, carrying fascines as
close as possible to Nook's Hill, an outlying point of Dorchester peninsula that curved to within three-quarters of a mile of the city. Once that
was fortified, cannon would be able to fire into the rear of the British
positions on Boston Neck. While the soldiers toiled, three selectmen,
accompanied by a British major, appeared on Boston Neck under a
flag of truce. They gave Washington a letter begging him not to attack
Howe's army. Washington was anything but pleased by this request for
inaction. He pointed out that the letter put General Howe under no
obligations whatsoever. It was not even addressed to him, Washington
complained. As far as he was concerned, he had never recieved it.

That same day—March 9—Washington began building fortifications on Nook's Hill. The men worked in daylight, easily visible to the
British in Boston. Washington was trying to gall Howe into attacking
him. Instead, the British commander decided to make Nook's Hill a
very uncomfortable place. Every available cannon raked the site with
mortars and round shot. Four men were killed with a single ball, and
that was enough to discourage the rest of the amateur American soldiers. The project was abandoned. The next morning, Lieutenant
Bangs noted that the ammunition-short Americans "picked up 700
balls that they had fired upon us."

Aside from this defensive gesture, Howe made no attempt to attack.
Instead, soldiers continued to lug baggage and equipment to the
wharves. As long as Howe declined to divide his army by attacking
Dorchester, Washington hesitated to assault Boston. Perhaps he was

more influenced than he cared to admit by the feeling that he was commanding an alien (New England) army, who might resent an aggressive move that resulted in the destruction of the city. At any rate, he did nothing but watch and wait during the next eight days, while Howe and his soldiers struggled to strip Boston of everything that might be valuable to the American army. What could not be carried away was destroyed. Heavy cannon were pushed off the wharves. Even General Howe's coach vanished into the cold, murky waters of the harbor.

Howe did his best to preserve order. He told officers to sleep in the barracks with their men. Anyone selling liquor to the troops was to be arrested. All the army's rum beyond the amount needed aboard ship was to be poured into the harbor. We can be sure that this order was obeyed halfheartedly at best. A few days later, Howe forbade the soldiers to do any further work for civilians, "as much drunkenness arises from it."

This order hinted at the agony of the second group of Americans who were watching the British evacuate Boston. According to a pro-American journal, the loyalists were "thunderstruck" when Howe announced he was departing. They had been "many hundred times assured, that such reinforcements would be sent, as to enable the King's troops to ravage the country at pleasure." Another American, watching the loyalists hiring soldiers and sailors to transport their possessions, said they "carry'd death in their faces." For one, at least, this was literally true. John Taylor committed suicide. Others, said the same letter writer, ran about "distracted." [16]

More than a thousand of these stunned people chose to leave with Howe's army rather than face the wrath of their countrymen. Contrary to the general impression that all Tories were aristocrats or royal officials, only 102 were members of the Governor's council, commissioners, customs officers, and similar servants of the Crown. Two hundred and thirteen were merchants, 382 were farmers, traders, and mechanics. But there were enough aristocrats to make those sensitive to class distinctions wince or gloat, depending on their predilections. Wealthy Benjamin Hallowell was forced to share a cabin with thirty-six others, "men, women and children; parents, masters and mistresses, obliged to take together on the floor, there being no berths."

Outside Boston, George Washington was becoming more and more uneasy. He was concerned about the possibility that once Howe got most of his stores and his loyalists on board ship, he might risk a final smash at the American lines, or, worse, land his troops outside the circle of American forts and attempt a pitched battle in open country. Washington was even more worried about Howe's destination. He was convinced that Howe was heading for New York, and he began making plans to detach a hefty portion of his army and start them on the march for that city. Ahead of them, he rushed messengers urging Governor Trumbull of Connecticut to send 2,000 men there without delay.

Still the British lingered in Boston. Washington decided to give William Howe one more excuse either to fight or to run. On the night of the sixteenth, he sent fresh working parties onto Nook's Hill, and this time, in spite of a sporadic bombardment from the redcoats' greatly diminished supply of cannon, by morning there was a fort frowning down on Boston. Before another night was over, there would be cannon in it, ready and able to blast the British into the harbor if they declined to go.

Howe chose to depart. Early on Sunday morning, March 17, the garrison abandoned Bunker Hill and took to their boats. Around the same time, no doubt on a prearranged signal, a vast number of boats shoved off from the Boston wharves. It was the last of Howe's army— picked companies of grenadiers and light infantry who had been chosen for his rear guard.

Along Boston Neck, an Irish lieutenant of the marines was spreading caltrops, ingenious booby traps also known as crow's-feet. They were of twisted iron, with four sharp points. No matter how they landed, one point was always facing up. The purpose was to delay a possible American dash to the waterfront to give the men in the boats a farewell volley. But the lieutenant, like a house painter in a slapstick comedy, made the mistake of scattering his booby traps as he walked *toward* the British fortifications on the Neck. Only when he reached the abandoned lines and looked behind him did he realize that he would have to negotiate the obstacle course he had just created. It took him an extra half hour to come panting down to the wharves. There, British engineers stood by with a handful of men, ready to set fire to some houses if they saw American regiments heading toward them with murderous intentions. About 9 A.M., they shoved off and rowed to their ships, admiring the balmy early spring weather. "The finest day in the world and fair breeze," Archibald Robertson told his diary, once he was safely aboard his transport.[17]

Other British officers were in a far less sunny mood. By now, they knew that Howe was sailing for Halifax, Nova Scotia, to get rid of his loyalists and to re-equip and revivify his army, if possible. "Neither hell,

Hull nor Halifax can afford worse shelter than Boston," one officer wrote home. "The necessary care of the women, children, sick and wounded," another man said, "required every assistance that could be given. It was not like the breaking up of a camp, where every man knows his duty; it was like departing your country with your wives, your servants, your household furniture and all your encumbrances. The officers, who felt the disgrace of a retreat, kept up appearances . . ."

That was about all they kept up. "Bad times, my dear friend," wrote another unhappy Briton. "The displeasure I feel from the very small share I have in our present insignificancy is so great, that I do not know the thing so desperate I would not undertake, in order to change our situation." [18]

Meanwhile, small boys came racing across Boston Neck, picking their way expertly through the crow's-feet and bounding over the British fortifications to dash into Roxbury and inform the Americans that "the lobsters" were gone at last. Brigadier General John Sullivan, studying the British works at Bunker Hill, was puzzled to find sentries still visible in the eye of his field glass. But high-spirited Thomas Mifflin of Pennsylvania, the quartermaster general of the American army, suspected the truth. With two men, he went boldly down to the foot of Bunker Hill and ordered his corporal's guard to make an assault. They found scarecrows standing to attention with laced hats and red coats, and for a gorget—the silver breastplate which a British officer wore into battle—a horseshoe. Their shirts were made of paper ruffles, and on the red breast of each dummy was pinned a note which read, "Welcome, brother Jonathan." [19]

Washington might have made a triumphal entry into Boston. But he showed how much he had learned in the last nine months by giving the honor to the senior Massachusetts general in his army, Artemas Ward. Because there was smallpox reported in Boston, Ward was told to select 500 men who had already experienced this dread eighteenth-century plague. Washington stayed in Cambridge, and went that afternoon to the meetinghouse, where the Reverend Abiel Leonard preached from Exodus 14:25: "And they took off their chariot wheels, that they drove them heavily: so that the Egyptians said, Let us flee from the face of Israel; for the Lord fighteth for them against the Egyptians."

An equally exultant Jedediah Huntington wrote to his brother Andrew at Norwich, Connecticut, "Never was joy painted in higher colors

than in the faces of the selectmen of Boston & other of the inhabitants
of that distressed town when we first had an interview this forenoon—
Where the enemy will get another such foothold I know not." Again we
see the persistence of this illusion, that the British, once forced from
the continent, could never re-establish themselves.

The next day, Washington cantered casually into the city. He
seemed primarily interested in checking John Hancock's house for possible damage—there was none—and studying the British fortifications.
He was a little awed by their strength. "The town of Boston," he admitted,"was almost impregnable." Yet he refused to abandon his conviction that a battle might have decided the war. By the change in weather
on March 5, "much blood was saved," he told his brother John Augustine (Jack) Washington. "This remarkable interposition of providence is
for some wise purpose, I have not a doubt; but as the principal design
of the Manouvre was to draw the Enemy to an Ingagement under
disadvantages, as a premeditated Plan was laid for this purpose, and
seemed to be succeeding to my utmost wish, and as no Men seem'd better disposed to make the appeal than ours did upon that occasion, I can
scarce forebear lamenting the disappointment, unless the dispute is
drawing to an accommodation, and the Sword going to be
Sheathed." [20]

Washington said nothing about a disappointment to anyone else.
He let his countrymen convert Howe's bloodless withdrawal into a
glorious victory. He politely accepted the flattering oratory showered
on him by the selectmen of Boston and the Massachusetts assembly.
The president and overseers of Harvard College gave him an honorary
degree of Doctor of Laws, and the Continental Congress voted its
thanks and a gold medal. Praise poured in from all parts of America.
Washington was hailed as a general on a par with Julius Caesar and the
Duke of Marlborough.

Self-satisfaction was the order of the day. "How are Parliamentary
pretensions to be reconciled?" crowed Elbridge Gerry, the influential
Massachusetts politician. "Eight or ten thousand British troops, it has
been said, are sufficient to overrun America; yet that number of their
veterans, posted in Boston (a peninsula fortified by nature, defended
by works the product of two years' industry, surrounded by navigable
waters, supported by ships of war and commanded by their best generals) are driven off by about one-thirtieth of the power of America.
. . . I am at a loss to know how Great Britain will reconcile all this to
her military glory."

Gerry seemed to be implying that the parliamentary pretensions, as exemplified by the British army in America, would now be repudiated by the people of England, and they would humbly negotiate peace. Washington, with his comment about sheathing the sword, hinted at a similar hope. This was another primary American illusion in the early days of 1776—one that underlay the formation of the Continental Congress in 1774—the conviction that a determined resistance on the part of the Americans would topple the North-Germain ministry, with their talk of a swift, easy conquest. The opposition in Parliament had repeatedly warned the nation against this idea. Didn't Great Bridge, Moore's Creek, the evacuation of Boston prove the opposition was right? Didn't that mean they would soon replace North and Germain and negotiate a generous peace? The Americans would not have answered these questions with a hopeful yes if they knew more about George III's determination and the dimensions of his grip on Parliament. They would have abandoned optimism entirely if they could have read the correspondence between two leading members of Parliament's opposition about the evacuation of Boston.[21]

XV

Discouraged Peacemakers and Revenue-Hungry Gentlemen

MY DEAR LORD,

What say you to the News? I take it for granted that you have heard in detail the matter which engages a few of the few in Town whom any thing can engage. Genl Howe is driven from Boston, By a Cannonade and Bombardment of a fortnight's continuance, acting in concert with a scarcity of provision of much longer standing. The Ministers triumph in his escape; and all things considered it is surprising that he should have been able to effect it with so much advantage. They say that he has brought off every thing with him, Cannon, Military Stores, and a vast quantity of useful Goods of all kinds, with about eighteen hundred of the inhabitants. I saw a letter today which says, that they were obliged to quit, partly from want of provision, partly that the place was made too hot for them. . . . The Office folks tell us that Genl Howe writes, that he would have gone to New York; but from tenderness to the women and children of whom he has such Numbers onboard—he thought it better to proceed to Halifax where his landing would not be opposed. In that nook of Penury and cold, the proud conqueror of America is obliged to look for refuge. The Provincials entered the Town [of Boston] on the 24th of March, Drums beating and colors flying. There is reason to believe from some letters by way of Ireland that the Cannonade began almost immediately on receipt of the separation act [Prohibitory Act]. That before that time they did not choose to proceed to extremities. Since then, the most moderate are become eminently outrageous. . . . I wish Newmarket may perfectly agree with you.[1]

This letter was written by Edmund Burke to Charles Watson-Wentworth, Marquess of Rockingham, who was the leader of the opposition in Parliament. With a little explication, its contents reveal several reasons why the Americans who saw him as a potential peacemaker were hopelessly wrong. One is Burke's bitter opening sentence, in which he admits that no more than "a few of the few" in London really care what is happening in America. (Among other things, the trial of the Duchess of Kingston for bigamy continued to fascinate the ruling class until her conviction in mid-April. The House of Lords strenuously debated whether each peer should have seven or eight tickets of admission to the trial. Conservatism prevailed; the vote was for seven.) Next is Burke's sarcastic tone, referring to General Howe as "the proud conqueror of America." Third is the egregiously bad information with which Burke had to work. As we have seen from our session with the Continental Congress, the Prohibitory Act did not make most moderate Americans outrageous, nor did it have the slightest influence on George Washington's timetable to drive the British from Boston. Finally, there is the reference to Newmarket, where His Lordship was more interested in racing his blood horses than he was in fighting Lord North and his battalions in Parliament.

Generations of American children have been taught to revere Edmund Burke as the great defender of America in the House of Commons. Seen from an English viewpoint, Burke becomes a quite different figure, a lost political metaphysician wandering through a landscape of ironies, a pathetic Irishman seeking his fortune in a foreign land, ultimately a victim of the England he was struggling to rescue from its folly.

In American textbooks, Burke has been portrayed as a lone hero, pouring forth his eloquence on an arrogant, unfeeling Parliament. In actuality, he was the spokesman of Lord Rockingham. The House of Commons heard Burke's rolling periods as another bid by Rockingham for power.

Moreover, Burke had a heavy Irish brogue which made much of what he said unintelligible. His magnificent rococo style was totally unsuited for his audience, the hard-riding, hard-drinking English country gentlemen who possessed the swing vote in Parliament. Essentially, Burke was a literary man who strayed into politics and found it irresistibly fascinating to his Irish temperament. Perhaps the best contemporary view of Burke, one that sums up all the reasons for his failure, was written by his good friend and fellow Irishman, Oliver Goldsmith. Toward the end of his life, Goldsmith wrote a series of mock epitaphs for Burke and other theatrical and literary friends who dined regularly at St. James Coffeehouse.

Here lies our good Edmund, whose genius was such
We scarcely can praise it, or blame it too much;
Who, born for the universe, narrowed his mind
And to party gave up what was meant for mankind.
Though fraught with all learning, yet straining his throat,
To persuade Tommy Townshend to lend him a vote:
Who, too deep for his hearers, still went on refining,
And thought of convincing, while they thought of dining;
Though equal to all things, for all things unfit,
Too nice for a statesman, too proud for a wit;
For a patriot too cool; for a drudge disobedient;
And too fond of the *right* to pursue the expedient.
In short, 'twas his fate, unemployed, or in place, sir,
To eat mutton cold, and cut blocks with a razor.[2]

Burke—and Rockingham—also labored under a fatal political defi-
ciency. Rockingham had been prime minister once before—in
1766—and he had persuaded the House of Commons to repeal the
Stamp Act, the first parliamentary tax that caused Americans to riot
and rebel. This gesture of benevolence had not improved the Americans' attitude toward Parliament one whit, as far as the average
member could see, and they tended to blame Rockingham for being
soft when he should have been hard. George III was emphatically of
this opinion.

In order to repeal the Stamp Act, Rockingham and Burke had
mollified Parliament by linking it to the Declaratory Act—a pronun-
ciamento which reiterated that Parliament had the right to make any
and all laws for the internal and external regulation of America and
any other colony in the Empire. The Declaratory Act became part of
Rockingham's party baggage, and Burke was forced to do more than
one agonized rhetorical dance to explain why the Marquess and his followers still supported parliamentary supremacy in principle, but insisted that in fact Parliament should not tax America or pass any laws
that were liable to arouse the colonies or alienate them from the
mother country. Partly because of this stance, and partly because they
were both devoted to the ideal of a united British Empire as a liberal
counterweight to the despotism of France and Spain, the idea of American independence was as abhorrent to Burke and Rockingham as it
was to George III.

Worse, as far as Burke was concerned, Rockingham shared that passion for country life which pervaded the feelings of all wealthy Englishmen of his era. His health was rather delicate, and he was convinced that the fresh air of his great estate at Wentworth Park in Yorkshire was essential to his life. With other property in Northamptonshire and Ireland, Rockingham had an income of £20,000 a year from his rent rolls. He put a great deal of time into improving his estate, which required him to become something of an expert on breeding horses, draining and fertilizing land, and even inventing agricultural instruments. Arthur Young, an apostle of scientific farming, visited Wentworth Park and declared that he "never saw the advantages of a great fortune applied so nobly to the improvement of the country." All this took time and inclined Rockingham to have a rather passive attitude toward national politics.[3]

Where Burke yearned for vigorous leadership, Rockingham was seldom eager to fight the tide of public opinion. As far as America was concerned, Rockingham was convinced that only the failure of Britain's attempt to coerce the colonies could change the public mind. Burke did not agree. Again and again, he pleaded with his patron to take a strong stand. "We are called to rouse ourselves, each in his post, by a sound of a trumpet almost as loud as that which must awaken the dead," he told the Marquess.

A few weeks later, Burke restated his opinion in aphoristic terms that had profound political truths in them, as pertinent today as they were in 1776. "I do not think that weeks or even months or years will bring the monarch, the ministers or the people to feeling. To bring the people to a feeling, such feeling I mean, as tends to amendment or alteration of system, there must be plan and management. All direction of publick humour and opinion must originate in a few. . . . Events supply materials. Times furnish dispositions. But conduct alone can bring them to bear to any useful purpose. I never yet knew an instance of any general temper in the nation, that might not have been tolerably well traced to some particular persons. If things are left to themselves, it is my clear opinion, that a nation may slide down fair and softly from the highest point of grandeur and prosperity to the lowest state of imbecility and meanness."[4]

Burke admitted that there were "many, many difficulties in the way, but . . . this is no time for taking publick business in its course and order, and only as a part in the scheme of life, which comes and goes at its proper periods and is mixed with other occupations and amusements. It calls for the whole of the best of us; and every thing else however just or even laudable at another time ought to give way to this great urgent instant concern. Indeed, my dear Lord, you are called upon in a very peculiar manner. America is yours. You have saved it once; and you may possibly save it again." [5]

But Rockingham refused to heed this trumpet call. From Yorkshire, he wrote that he saw no point in doing more than taking "the step of a protestation" after Parliament met. "When once that measure is taken, I think we need not be tied to residence in London. I have hopes of returning here and passing some months quietly, I really want recess, for the bad weather and the frequent sultry heats, have prevented me receiving either much benefit to my health from the country air, or much relaxation to my mind, from the various amusements which residence in the country affords me." [6]

These words must have stirred mordant reflections in Burke's mind. In the summer of 1773, the government had passed a law imposing a tax on the rents which absentee landlords received from Ireland. It was in part a device to raise money, and in part an attempt to force more Englishmen to live on their lands in Ireland and keep their tenants more contented than they had been lately. At least £732,000 a year went out of Ireland to these absentee landowners. One of the largest was Lord Rockingham. The news galvanized His Lordship to feverish action. He moved into London, and with four other noble lords with equally large Irish estates—their combined rents totaled £66,000 annually—launched a day-and-night campaign against the measure. The Marquess' house in Grosvenor Square became the headquarters of a full-scale protest movement. Copyists worked from 9 A.M. until midnight pouring out letters to other large Irish landowners and remonstrances to members of Parliament. English companies with property in Ireland were enlisted. After a month of such pressure, the North administration collapsed and abandoned the measure. It must have seemed a pity to Burke, during the first months of 1776, that Lord Rockingham did not own large estates in America. [7]

Depressed by Rockingham's failure to act, Burke turned to Ireland. He asked another member of the Rockingham opposition, Charles Lennox, the Duke of Richmond, to help him swing the Irish to America's side. "Ireland . . . has the ballance of the Empire and perhaps its fate forever, in her hands," Burke wrote. He wanted the Irish Parliament to interpose "a friendly mediation" and send a "pathetic address" to the King. If they added to these a "suspension of extraordinary grants and supplies for troops employed out of the Kingdom," he was convinced that the North ministry would reverse their American policy. It was, Burke argued, to Ireland's interest, because North's policy "tends to its own ruin by enslaving all its dependencies."

Burke admitted that he did not have "the most enthusiastick opinion of the dignity of thinking which prevails in Ireland." But he could not believe the Irish Parliament would continue their subservient support of a policy aimed at "the exhausting of their own purses for the purpose of destroying their own liberties." [8]

Richmond was closely connected by marriage and blood with several powerful members of the Irish Protestant establishment. But he declined to act because he was in despair over the current state of British opinion toward America. Burke lectured him in vain. "This speculative despair is unpardonable. . . . I cannot think the people at large wholly to blame; or if they were, it is to no purpose to blame them. For God's sake, my dear Lord, endeavour to mend them."

To Burke's mortification, the Irish Parliament, instead of opposing the American war, backed the North government by voting 2 to 1 to view the rebellion "with abhorrence and indignation." George III then felt free to withdraw 4,000 troops from Ireland for the army in America. On January 7, 1776, Burke discharged his anger and frustration in a letter to his friend, Charles O'Hara. ". . . Your general politicks in Ireland . . . are so sublimely profound, there is such a grandeur of meanness in them, that they pass my expression and indeed my comprehension." [9]

A few members of the opposition had not yet abandoned all hope of defeating the North–George III majority. Best known was the one Englishman who could match Burke's Irish eloquence—Charles James Fox. In the Parliament of 1775–76, this magnetic twenty-six-year-old politician emerged as the most vigorous opposition voice outside the Rockingham party. But the very brilliance of his oratory, the savagery of his wit, only added to his already grave liabilities as a parliamentary leader. Even less than Edmund Burke with his thick brogue was Charles Fox suited to seduce the conservative country gentlemen from their support of the King's ministers.

For one thing, Charles, as everyone called him, was the son of Henry Fox, one of the most corrupt politicians of the eighteenth century, a man who made an immense fortune out of his job as paymaster of the forces. Spoiled by his indulgent father, who bought him a seat in Parliament at the age of nineteen and made him a Lord of the Admiralty at twenty-one, Fox spent most of his time campaigning for the

title of the most dissipated man in England. He spent all night, every
night, gambling at Almack's, Brooks', or White's, frequently losing
£10,000 between midnight and his usual quitting time, 5 A.M. In the
winter of 1773–74, his father paid off his debts—which totaled
£140,000. He died a few months later, reportedly of grief at his son's
seemingly hopeless determination to destroy himself. Fox went right on
gambling. A wit composed the following poem.

> At Almack's of pigeons I'm told there are flocks;
> But it's thought the completest is one Mr. Fox.
> If he touches a card, if he rattles a box,
> Away fly the guineas of this Mr. Fox.[10]

A Londoner who visited Fox in his rooms left the following description of how the young firebrand looked on arising from one of his all-
night gambling sessions. "His complexion was of the dirtiest colour and
tinged with a yellowish hue; his hair is exceedingly black, uncombed,
and clotted with the pomatures and small remnants of powder of the
day before; his beard was unshaved, and together with his bushy eyebrows increased the natural darkness of his skin; his nightgown was old
and dirty; the collar of his shirt was open and discovered a broad chest
covered with hair; the knees of his breeches were unbuttoned; his
stockings were ungartered and hung low upon his legs; his slippers
were down at the heels; his hands were dirty; his voice was hoarse like
that of a hackney coachman who is much exposed to the night air. Yet
under all these various disadvantages his countenance was mild and
pleasing." [11]

"Squalid and disagreeable" was how a reporter in the *Public Advertiser* described Fox. He replied that "he never cared what was said of his
person." He had, another man said, "an infinite contempt" for the conventions which govern most people's conduct. Charles also admitted to
"a natural partiality to what some people call rebels." This and his admiration for Edmund Burke as a man and a speaker were more than
enough to convert Fox into a fierce critic of the North government's
policy toward America. He declared he could not consent "to the
bloody consequences of so silly a contest about so silly an object, conducted in the silliest manner that history, or observation, had ever furnished an instance of; and from which we were likely to derive nothing
but poverty, misery, disgrace, defeat and ruin."

On February 20, Fox rose to ask Parliament to create a committee
to inquire into the causes of British defeats and retreats in North

America. "He painted in the strongest colours," wrote one reporter, "and held to view in the most striking lights, such a scene of folly in the Cabinet, servile acquiescence in Parliament, and misconduct and ignorance in office and in the field, as never before disgraced this nation, or indeed any other." But the unflappable North turned aside Fox's eloquence by assuring the members that he had no objection to such an inquiry at the right time. But now was not the right time. Parliament agreed, 240 votes to 104.

Fox's support of the Americans sometimes veered close to treason. On March 11, 1776, in a debate over a request to vote an additional £845,165 for "extraordinary expenses" of the army in America, Fox delivered a eulogy of his fallen friend, Richard Montgomery. Lord North pounced on what he thought was a gaffe. He said he disliked hearing praise of such "unqualified liberality" bestowed upon a rebel. Montgomery's death was hardly a public loss. North admitted that he was "brave, able, humane, generous," but he was "only a brave, humane and generous rebel." In fact, the verse of the tragedy *Cato* might be applied to him: "Curse on his virtues, they've undone his country."

Fox rose a second time to inform North that the term "rebel" was no "certain mark of disgrace." He was therefore uninterested in clearing his dead friend of the imputation. On the contrary, Fox cried, "All the great asserters of liberty, the saviors of their country, the benefactors of mankind, in all ages, had been called rebels."

But Lord North had the last word. Parliament voted, 180 to 57, to give the army its £845,165.[12]

With the energy and optimism of youth, Fox labored to bolster the sagging, discouraged opposition. He persuaded the Duke of Grafton, a former prime minister who was holding the sinecure of Lord Privy Seal, to resign and become a public critic of the ministry. Fox spent even more time negotiating with another supporter of America in his great house on Berkeley Square.

William Petty, the second Earl of Shelburne, was thirty-nine years old. The great-grandson of a brilliant economist, himself an intellectual who cultivated French *philosophes* and American and British freethinkers such as Benjamin Franklin and Joseph Priestley, Shelburne was a very wealthy man who had a clear vision of what was wrong with England, and a strong desire to reform it. But he was frustrated by a personality which seemed to force him almost against his will to be cold and aloof, and to play a lone wolf's game. His contemporaries called him "the Jesuit of Berkeley Square."

Basically, Shelburne was a shy idealist, marked like so many Englishmen before him and since by an atrocious childhood. He was also enormously rich. His Irish rent rolls alone totaled £13,000 a year. His great country house, Bowood, was decorated by Robert Adam, the leading architect of the day, and the gardens were designed by the chief landscape architect, Capability Brown. In 1761, he bought the entire borough of Calne near Bowood for £97,000. This gave him control of three seats in the House of Commons, a good base for any young nobleman who sought to build a political career. But his following never expanded much beyond the three men whom he regularly named to these seats. One of these was the Irishman Isaac Barre, "Shelburne's bulldog," an orator who almost matched Fox and Burke.

Early in 1776, Shelburne saw that there was no hope of stopping the North juggernaut in Parliament without more information. He hired a team of clerks who worked long hours at Shelburne House in Berkeley Square copying details of government accounts. He purchased the papers of a former secretary of the treasury, and was not above bribing civil servants in the government to get the kind of information he wanted. With Barre as his spokesman in the House of Commons, Shelburne hoped to rouse the country gentlemen by pointing to the fantastic expense—and inevitable corruption—which the war was certain to cause. But this, Shelburne conceded, would be a long, slow process. A government fighting a war was always able to refuse information on the grounds of security.[13]

Fox failed to persuade Shelburne to join him and the Rockinghams in a united opposition. Shelburne resented Rockingham's insistence on his followers' hewing more or less to a party line. Shelburne believed that Parliament should surrender all its pretensions to tax Americans, and ridiculed the Rockingham compulsion to cling to the Declaratory Act.

During the first six months of 1776, there was really only one point on which all the oppositionists agreed. Independence was an unacceptable solution to the crisis. Almost to a man, they rejected the government argument that there was a conspiracy in America to set up an independent state. Shelburne went so far as to tell Richard Price that he was prepared to risk his head on the Americans' proving themselves "not only faithful subjects, but faithful colonists to the parent state."

Divided and outnumbered, the opposition was helpless to stop Lord George Germain and the King from organizing to strike the massive blow against the Americans which would end the war in one campaign.

A single day's debate toward the end of the spring session is perhaps the best example of the frustrations which Burke and his colleagues had to endure. The day opened with a demand by General Henry Seymour Conway, whose brother, Lord Hertford, was an intimate friend of George III, for the instructions which the government had given to the peace commissioners which Lord North had recently announced they were sending to America. The peace commissioners happened to be Admiral Richard Lord Howe, commander of the British navy in America, and his brother William, commander of the British army. This was enough in itself to make many people wonder about the sincerity of the government, and Conway, heretofore a North supporter, now publicly joined the doubters. He apologized for making a motion "at this late period of the [parliamentary] season," but "the alarming and dreadful situation of this country" impelled him to trouble the House. He wanted to know by what right the ministry was giving instructions to peace commissioners to negotiate with the Americans without "the previous consent of Parliament."

Specifically, Conway wanted to know if the government planned to give up the right to tax America "entirely." One member of the cabinet had told him this was the case. Another member had denied it. Conway wanted to know if the House of Commons was in agreement on "that fundamental point." First the government had maintained that nothing but unconditional submission by the Americans was acceptable. If that was the policy, Conway said, "I have no more to say—throw away the scabbard!" But he hoped this was not the case. "The wisest of men, the wisest of nations have treated, have receded, granted the concessions asked by rebellious subjects." He cited a long list of examples from the Romans to the French under Louis XIV.

Conway insisted that the Americans were defending the same principles which had precipitated England's "glorious revolution of 1688." They were defending their fundamental rights. "Who is there among you that would not combat any power on earth, invading in the same manner . . . what God and nature had given them and no human power can justly wrest from them?" Conway accused the administration, with its talk of unconditional submission, of using "the language of vengeance and not of sense; of violence, not of reason . . ." He pointed out that France and Spain were arming and there had been a dramatic change—the dismissal of Turgot—in the French ministry. The influence of the war party, the avowed enemies of England, had grown great.

Did it matter that Spain and France had assured England of their "pacifick intentions?" Who made those assurances, "the last or the present administration?" Conway said he was asking these questions because his "duty to my country, paramount to every obligation, obliges me to seize the only moment which remains between you and destruction." The war, he said, was "horrid," with "German mercenaries carrying desolation along with them; slaves excited to cut the throats of their masters." He regretted his "inattention to public concerns" over the last five years—a soft way of saying he was sorry he had supported the government.

Lord John Cavendish, leader of the Rockingham party in the House of Commons, seconded Conway's motion. He declared that Lord Howe and General Howe were fine officers, but "they have now got a character which they are entire strangers to"—peace commissioners. Since they could not make peace without the "interposition and sanction of Parliament," Cavendish thought it was only common sense that Parliament should know their instructions.

Lord North replied for the government. He opposed "the communication of any instructions previous to their execution"—which meant that both the Americans and Parliament should remain ignorant of the Howes' powers. North maintained that "he never was of opinion that no rebels were to be treated with," but he insisted that the government had a right to keep secret "the modes by which any commissioner may be instructed to carry any powers into execution." He was willing enough to discuss the general powers of the act of Parliament which made the Howes peace commissioners. They had the right to grant general and special pardons, to confer with any of His Majesty's subjects without exception, inquire into causes of their complaints, but they could not offer any peace terms. None had yet been settled by Parliament.

North pointed out that neither "the Congress nor any of the Americans [has] ever yet offered any [peace terms] which Parliament could listen to." The commissioners were to "confer and to sound for grounds of peace; but all must be referred to Parliament." North insisted that the Americans would never come to terms "unless they have some proof of our resolution and power." He said it would be dangerous "even to peace itself" to hold out any proposition which might not succeed. Therefore, the full extent of the ministry's peace plan, while it has been "suggested" to the commissioners, cannot be revealed.

Edmund Burke rose to denounce this double-talk. As far as he could see, the commissioners were empowered only to feel America's pulse. It was "downright nonsense" to talk of conferring without "some instructions on what terms the persons conferring are to meet." Lord North seemed to be contradicting "another noble lord who, it is said, has the confidence and the lead in these American measures." Burke was referring to Lord George Germain. "Between the various jarring opinions of ministers themselves," Burke declared, "more opposite at times than those of opposition itself are to them, the object of the war or the ends of peace have never yet been clearly fixed." At one point, the ministry said the goal was America's unconditional submission. At another point, they said it was to guarantee a revenue from America. Now was the ministry sending out commissioners to "give up taxation and all expectation of a revenue and to make peace without any notion of conditions?" Burke ridiculed the idea of a general and an admiral as peace commissioners, picturing them "offering pardons both general and special when they were beat" and burning and slaughtering where they were supposed to bring peace.

Up leaped Robert Vyner. With a revenue of £8,000 to £10,000 from an estate in Lincolnshire, he was one of the more outspoken country gentlemen upon whose continuing support the North administration depended. "Landed gentlemen came into these measures [to suppress the rebellion] in expectation of a revenue from America," Vyner declared. If taxing the Americans was not the "fixed and determined object of the war, they had been led into a fine scrape." Vyner was a quintessential hard-liner. On May 3, 1775, he had declared he was "willing to pay [taxes of] not only four shillings but fourteen shillings in the pound" to see Great Britain's supremacy maintained over her colonies. Vyner had also said he was "not for offering any conditions for peace while an American had a musket on his shoulder." Now was the time to be explicit, Vyner bellowed. It was time for country gentlemen to declare "that they could not go on any further with such ministers unless they abided by the plan which these ministers first held out to them."

Lord North, for once more than a little agitated, replied, "Taxation was not to be given up: it was to be enforced. But whether at present or hereafter was a point of policy which the commissioners would learn by sounding the people upon the spot."

Charles James Fox ridiculed the confusion into which Vyner had forced North. "According to the noble lord's explanation," Fox cried, "Lord Howe and his brother are to be sent out as spies, not as [peace] commissioners." As for taxation, "the noble lord has not reconciled

what gentlemen might think absolute contradiction." The country gentlemen were promised a revenue. But the tea duty, the only tax on
America extant, made no revenue, and it was clear from American
statements that they would never consent to future parliamentary taxation. In fact, in a previous administration, the government had issued a
circular letter to all thirteen colonies, solemnly promising that there
would be no more taxes. Therefore, they were fighting a war and
spending millions of pounds to preserve a tax that raised no revenue.
The real purpose of the war, Fox cried, was "to annihilate and over-
turn the liberties of *this* country [England]." This plan had been unre-
mittingly pursued by the minister, and it mattered very little who was
the deviser of this unnatural conspiracy. Lord North was responsible
for the "desperate scheme his traitorous and concealed employers
chalked out for him."

Another outspoken member of the opposition, Thomas Townshend
of Frognall, Kent, observed that "Parliament had talked in a high strain
against America; but what Parliament thought or resolved one way or
the other was of very little consequence for administration would act
just as they liked." Townshend maintained that Parliament had been
degraded "into a mere engine of government, one day to bully, another to conciliate," and the next he foresaw would be to sue for terms
to America. This was precisely what Townshend was hoping Parliament would do, but he said it at this point to further exacerbate the
country gentlemen.

Lord George Germain rose to shore up the government's sagging
case. He denied that he ever said he required America's unconditional
submission. Anyone who read the act of Parliament empowering the
peace commissioners should realize that the commissioners would
never "treat with rebels in arms." The commissioners were empowered
to "restore either whole colonies or any bodies of them or even individuals to the King's peace whenever they returned to their duty." But
they had no power to discuss "the sovereignty of the supreme legislature [Parliament], the colonies' duty to this legislature or the right of
taxation." This, said Germain, was what Lord North intended to say.

The country gentlemen were soothed, but the opposition was even
more infuriated by Germain's bland explanation. Colonel Isaac Barre,
Lord Shelburne's spokesman, declared that Germain had in fact admitted that the Americans must submit unconditionally. The commissioners could not treat with them until they laid down their arms, and

there was no mention of any condition upon which they could be received into the King's peace. What else could Parliament deduce?

George Johnstone, a former governor of British West Florida, closed the opposition's argument. He was noted for his "ardent, impetuous, half savage eloquence, restrained by no delicacy of language." He denounced "the numerous infamous jobs that were every day going on" and enumerated the various methods North used to create "corrupt majorities" in Parliament. He spoke of licenses granted by the Admiralty Board, such as a recent one for ten thousand gallons of rum at four shillings a gallon when the going price was two shillings. One of the principals in the contract was Sir James Cockburn, a rich Scot who sat in Parliament and owned extensive plantations in the West Indies. No wonder the American war had become a favorite with the majority of the House, cried Johnstone. No wonder Parliament could sit and listen to the two chief ministers of the government contradict each other on the same day with scarcely a comment.

Conway's resolution was put to a vote. It lost, 171 to 85.

On the following day, May 23, 1776, the opposition made a last attempt to deflect the government's course. A Rockinghamite, David Hartley, friend of Benjamin Franklin, an expert on public finance, a man known for his "unsullied probity, indefatigable perseverance and labour," which was unfortunately combined with one of the dullest speaking styles in Parliament, recommended an address to the King which, he said, "would record a testimony for himself and for his friends of their anxiety and apprehensions for the important events of this year."

Hartley feared that the "unlimited confidence" which Parliament had put in ministers who were known to be averse to America would "alienate the Americans from the hopes of reconciliation." He wished to show the Americans "that they still had some friends left who thought no anxiety or labour too much to take the least chance of improving any favourable event that might happen towards the restoration of peace and to prevent the effusion of blood." Hartley then read an appeal to the King, which recounted the drift toward war with America and asked His Majesty to be "graciously pleased not to prorogue the Parliament, but that he will suffer them to continue sitting by adjournments during the summer that they may be ready to receive from time to time such information of the transactions in America as His Majesty shall think proper to lay before them."

The idea of giving up their summer recess appalled the country gentlemen and probably dismayed most of the opposition. Hartley's idea was buried in a negative avalanche and Parliament began its usual four-month holiday, leaving Lord George Germain and George III in unchallengeable control of the war.[14]

XVI

Profitable Islands
in the Sun

Although the King and Germain exuded confidence, they were already learning what many politicians before them and since have also learned the hard way—that war unleashes forces and energies and reveals or revives old conflicts that are extremely difficult to control. Especially was this true when the warmakers presided over a global empire which made them vulnerable to their enemies in many parts of the world. While the French, guided by the Count de Vergennes's fine diplomatic hand, continued to assure the English of their peaceful intentions—and there was little evidence in France of anything beyond a modest rearmament program to contradict these protestations—reports reaching London made it clear that France was playing a much more dangerous game in another part of the world—the West Indies. Even more alarming was the news that the Americans were invading these crucial islands in startling numbers to work with England's old enemy.

Few contemporary Americans have heard of Abraham van Bibber, Richard Harrison, Thomas Burch, or William Bingham. Without their vigorous exertions, the American army would have been forced to go into battle in 1776 armed largely with spears and bows and arrows, an idea actually suggested by Benjamin Franklin early in the year, when shortage of gunpowder was acute. Thanks to these unknown Americans and their work in the West Indies, by the middle of the year 1776 George Washington's frantic cries about lack of powder disappeared. By July 4, 1776, Washington had more powder than his army could fire off if they worked steadily at it for the rest of the year.[1]

Van Bibber, Harrison, Bingham, et al., were merchants, and some modern Americans, for whom the word "profit" has a vaguely immoral sound, may think less of these forgotten patriots because they made a handsome return on their war efforts. Beguiled by nonsense about the purity of more recent revolutions, forgetting that power and ruling-class status can appeal to a man's self-interest as much as or more than cash, we may be shocked to learn that supplying the sinews of war for 1776 usually turned a handsome dollar for the suppliers.

Most of the contracts for importing gunpowder went to the firm of Willing & Morris. Thomas Willing was the first chairman of the secret committee organized in September, 1775, to procure war supplies around the world. He was replaced in December by his partner, Robert Morris, also a prominent member of the Pennsylvania congressional delegation. Other powder contracts were handed out to firms controlled by members of the committee from Connecticut and New York.

Some congressmen carped when they discovered that Willing & Morris were guaranteed profits of £12,000 sterling on their powder contract.[2] It was the beginning of fierce strife between the purists and the realists in Congress. The realists did their best to ignore, or at least outmaneuver, their critics. Robert Morris, who sat with them in Congress, understood their motives perhaps better than anyone else. "Some of them do not like to part with power," he wrote a fellow businessman, "or to pay others for doing what they cannot do themselves." [3]

In a realist tradition that has been honored by endless imitation in succeeding congresses, Morris and his committee also made sure that the contracts for procuring other war matériel were carefully distributed throughout the colonies from Massachusetts to South Carolina. An Otis in Massachusetts, a Braxton and a Harrison in Virginia were soon "improving some Moneys," as the expression went, sometimes to an incredible extent. Along with gunpowder and muskets, these merchants always managed to include in their ships several hundred pounds of goods for civilians to replace the woolens, laces, silks, spices, wines, coffee, and tea no longer flowing from England. By mid-1776, they were selling these at 500 or 600 percent markup.[4]

But the men who did the real work, who risked more than their investments, were the daring American ship captains and aggressive agents operating throughout the West Indian islands.

There was nothing new about Americans doing business in the West Indies—frequently illegal business. Although the British had run

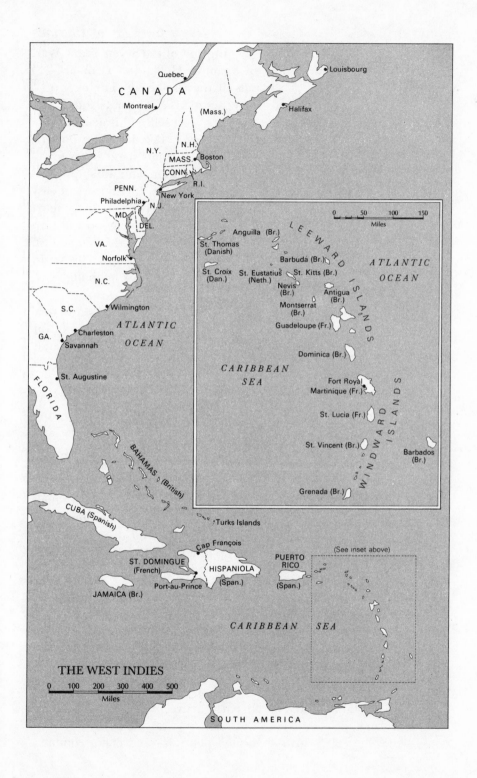

THE WEST INDIES

the French off the continent by 1763, the end of the Seven Years' War, no one could persuade France—or Spain or Holland or Denmark—to part with the fabulously rich islands of the Caribbean. The export of their basic crop, sugar, earned them the title the "Sugar Islands," and the profits were as sweet as the brown spice itself, cultivated beneath the broiling sun by brutally driven slave labor. The dominant powers, France and England, made sure they had strong island bases in all parts of the Caribbean, with plenty of forts, cannon, and warships. This supposedly guaranteed each other's good behavior. It also made it easy for fast-sailing American captains to island-hop. It was only a short haul from the chief British island, Jamaica, to the thriving port of Cap François in present-day Haiti. The Dutch islands of St. Martin and St. Eustatius were within a day's sail of British Antigua, St. Kitts, or Nevis, and then French Guadeloupe and Martinique, with its booming port, Fort Royal, appeared on the horizon.

According to imperial policy, the Americans were supposed to deal only with the British West Indies. But Dutch and Danish sugar sold for 25 or 40 percent less than the British product, and the British islands did not produce enough to keep New England's busy rum distilleries going in the first place.

So an American captain became adept at cruising the Caribbean, stopping off at St. Kitts or Nevis, paying off a customs official to prove that he had sold his cargo of rice or wheat to British traders, and hauling on to Cap François or St. Croix, where he traded his cargo for French sugar or sometimes for British goods sold at a discount. Even during the Seven Years' War, these Americans kept right on trading with the imperial enemy, France, using Spanish ports to transship their goods, as long as Spain remained a neutral. When Spain entered the war, the Yankees were undaunted. They transferred their operations to St. Eustatius, or, as she was called up and down the American coast, "Statia." [5]

This was the seven square miles of sand and volcanic rock that, in the words of a choleric English admiral, "alone supported the infamous American rebellion." Actually the tip of an extinct volcano, St. Eustatius was a tribute to the Dutch talent for survival. Technically, Protestant Holland was allied with England, and in the closing years of the previous century had supplied the English with a badly needed king, William of Orange. But France brooded on Holland's border, and there was a well-financed French party active in the councils of the Dutch government.

By 1776, the Dutch were dedicated neutrals—and major commercial rivals of England. The English governor of the Leeward Islands frequently complained that St. Eustatius was the place through which American provisions and lumber reached the French islands. It was hard to stop because Statia was an international free port to which ships of all nations had access.

St. Eustatius was an ugly little place, with the houses of the more successful merchants built around the volcano's extinct crater and the crowded lower town scooped out of the volcano's slopes. The rocky soil was virtually barren. It did not produce more than 600 barrels of sugar a year. But its one-mile main street produced enough mercantile wealth to rival the richest of the sugar islands, Jamaica or Guadeloupe. Statia's warehouses bulged with goods from the entire civilized world. A Scotswoman who visited the place in 1775 marveled at being able to buy "excellent French gloves" and English stockings below London prices.

On barren Statia, and also on almost all the other islands, particularly the tiny Leewards, people had one large worry—starvation. They depended on American farmers for their food, and when the quarrel between Great Britain and America grew hot, it caused intense anxiety throughout the Caribbean. Jamaica was so alarmed it sided with the Americans, petitioning George III to avert the "approaching horrors of an unnatural contest . . . in which the most dreadful calamities to this island . . . are involved." The Jamaicans informed the King that they believed that "no one part of Your Majesty's English subjects can ever or ever could legislate for another part." The Bahamas were equally panicked. The governor wrote home that the Continental Congress had cut off "every kind of Succour, not even a sheep being permitted to be sent us."

On the northernmost British island, Bermuda, sympathy for the Americans—and fear of starvation—was so strong that the island's leader, Colonel Henry Tucker, sailed to Philadelphia in mid-1775 to seek an exception against the Congress's resolution to prohibit American exports to the West Indies. Realist Robert Morris persuaded Congress to pass another resolution, declaring that every vessel that brought gunpowder or the essential ingredients for making gunpowder, saltpeter and sulfur, to any American port could exchange the explosives for "the produce of these colonies." Colonel Tucker was so enthusiastic he invited some friendly Americans back to Bermuda and assisted them in looting 1,800 pounds of powder from the island's arsenal.

Bermudians controlled another commodity which enabled them to bargain very effectively with the Americans. One of the few natural resources lacked by the rebellious colonies was salt. Americans needed no less than 1,500,000 bushels a year to preserve fish and meat in peacetime, and they would need even more to keep their armies supplied with meat. Well over half of this vital stuff came from the West Indies, most of it from the Turks Islands in the Bahamas, to which the Bermudians had access in their fast-sailing sloops of close-grained cedar. In return for a steady flow of American provisions, the Bermudians ran tons of salt and a lot of other contraband from the Turks to the mainland throughout the war.[6]

Obviously, corruption—perhaps survival would be a better word— was a way of life in the West Indies. They were anything but enthusiastic supporters of Britain's policy of confrontation with the Americans. As for the French, they shared the national desire to settle old scores with England. Most important, the neutralist Dutch were the last people in the world to pass up a chance to "improve some moneys." The States General of the United Netherlands, at the request of the British ambassador, issued a proclamation forbidding the exportation of arms or ammunition to the British colonies in America. But there was no attempt whatsoever to enforce this edict. Instead, the chagrined ambassador was soon reporting a "prodigious increase" in the trade to and from St. Eustatius.

Secret agents informed the ambassador that tons of powder and thousands of muskets were pouring out in Dutch ships, consigned to the coast of Africa, a normal destination—the Dutch were very active in the slave trade. But their real destination was St. Eustatius "where their cargoes . . . are instantly bought by the American agents." By April, 1776, the profit on gunpowder sold at Statia had leaped to 120 percent. French powder, shipped to Martinique, also flowed from that island to St. Eustatius. A single American agent, Marylander Richard Harrison, exultantly shipped 6,000 pounds from Martinique, then 14,100 pounds from Statia, then another shipload of 10,000 pounds to Charleston, and 10,000 more to Philadelphia. Harrison and his fellow Marylander, Abraham van Bibber, who spent most of his time on St. Eustatius, soon formed a profitable co-partnership which funneled tons of gunpowder and other goods to the continent.[7]

By May of 1776, the English ambassador to the Netherlands was calling St. Eustatius the rendezvous of everything and everybody clandestinely shipped to America. Abraham van Bibber reported to the Maryland Council of Safety that he was on "the best terms with His Excellency, the Governour [of St. Eustatius]," and in another letter added, "Our Flag flies current every day in the road [roadstead or harbor]," Although American tobacco, rice, indigo, and other products paid for much of the purchased powder, a lot of it was bought on borrowed French money. Isaac van Dam, one of the principal St. Eustatius merchants, bought powder directly from France and admitted to friends that he carried out much of the trade on behalf of Frenchmen.[8]

The Count de Vergennes had refused British men-of-war the right to search merchant vessels plying between France and her colonies. This made it simple to ship quantities of war matériel to the French West Indies. The British navy could only watch the French captains sail serenely past their gun ports without a challenge. Vergennes backed this policy with a French squadron which he sent to the West Indies with instructions to protect "insurgent" vessels when they were pursued by British cruisers—if they sought asylum under the French flag.[9]

Individual states pursued the hunt for powder vigorously. Massachusetts set up a special Board of War which had thirty-two vessels prowling the Caribbean, and even crossing the Atlantic to French and Spanish ports. South Carolina, Virginia, Maryland, and Connecticut were also active. The British fought this flow of contraband with all the guile and strength they possessed. Their ambassador to the Netherlands prodded the Dutch to enforce the edict forbidding arms shipments. Lord Rochford, British secretary of state for southern Europe, accused France of gunrunning to America, claiming she had violated an agreement to make England's interest her own. The Count de Vergennes replied that he was "not acquainted with this agreement" and asked how Lord Rochford could say that "we ought not to sell any article of commerce to any person, because it might possibly pass, at second hand, into America?" [10]

More and more British warships were ordered on West Indies patrol. American agents on St. Eustatius were soon reporting that the islands were "infested with Men-of-War." But it was not necessarily fatal to be seized by a man-of-war if your ship had the right papers. Thomas Burch, head of Thomas Burch & Co., who shipped 50 tons of gunpowder to the Groton, Connecticut, merchant, Thomas Mumford, a relative of Silas Deane, advised his client to make sure his captains got "neutral" papers from "say St. Croix, St. Martin's etc." Another American, John Crohon, who did business with North Carolina, believed in covering all possible bets and sent his ships out with British, French, Spanish, and Dutch clearance papers.

Complicating matters were the privateers. These men-of-war, commissioned by individual states and by Congress to attack British ships anywhere on the high seas, wreaked havoc with the West Indies trade. One frantic Englishman wrote from Grenada that 35 out of 60 ships sailing from Ireland with provisions had been picked off by the profit-hungry Americans. By the end of 1776, no less than 733 British vessels, representing a loss of £2,600,000 sterling, had been seized by the Americans. A heavy proportion of these captures took place in or around the West Indies.

It was the beginning of the end of the Sugar Islands as one of the great and more awful enterprises of eighteenth-century British capitalism. Paradoxically, it was also the first blow struck against New World slavery. For generations, the West Indies had devoured four-fifths of the slaves shipped to the Americas. The collapse of their economy would expose the flank of the slave system to attack.[11]

But this possibility was far from the minds of the Americans who struck the blow. They were primarily interested in making money. Appeals for privateering crews barely mentioned patriotism. They concentrated on the heart of the matter—cash. One notice in Wethersfield, Connecticut, summoned "all gentlemen volunteers who are desirous of making their fortunes in eight weeks." In Boston, "Jolly Fellows, who love their country, and want to make their Fortune at one stroke" were urged to "repair immediately" to John Hancock's wharf. Congress, wrongheaded as usual, had ruled that sailors of the embryonic regular navy could keep only one-third of the value of any ship they captured. The rest was to be donated to the nation. Aboard a privateer, it was winner-take-all. This policy, plus the ineptitude of the naval commander in chief, Esek Hopkins of Rhode Island, practically guaranteed the navy's impotence for 1776.[12]

The British West Indians took to privateering themselves early in 1776, even though Great Britain had not yet authorized this free-enterprise branch of naval warfare. Numerous American merchantmen were seized and sailed into Antigua, where they were sold as prizes. Vice Admiral Sir James Young, in command of British naval forces in the Leeward Islands, denounced these counterprivateers, most of them Antiguans, as pirates. The Admiral's moral indignation is open to question. The Antiguans were cutting into his prize money. He got 12.5 percent of every American ship caught, and the British Parliament, unlike the romantics in the Continental Congress, let the sailors keep every cent. When Young tried to stop a privateer from leaving the harbor, the Antiguans arrested the admiral. He was forced to send home a sloop asking for instructions.

Meanwhile, the trade on Statia boomed. People began calling it "the Golden Rock." In thirteen months, 3,182 vessels cleared the port. The warehouses overflowed and mountains of sugar, tobacco, and cotton covered the "very extensive beach." Stevedores worked day and night ferrying goods from the beach to the hundred-odd ships in the crowded harbor. Even British merchants, trying to protect themselves against the losses being inflicted by American privateers, opened branch houses on the island and traded with the enemy. Nothing, raged First Lord of the Admiralty Sandwich, "could restrain the rapacity of merchants." [13]

Worse news was to reach London from Martinique. On June 3, 1776, the Committee of Commerce dispatched twenty-four-year-old William Bingham to represent Congress on that pivotal island. He was a sophisticated, wellborn young Philadelphian, who had made the Grand Tour in 1773 and had been serving as secretary of the Committee of Secret Correspondence. While working as a clerk in the countinghouse of Thomas Wharton, another prominent Philadelphia merchant, Bingham had been the owner-manager of two profitable merchant ships. He had convinced Robert Morris that he had "abilities & merit both in the Political & Commercial line."

While operating as an agent of Congress, Bingham was also assured he could do business for himself, and Robert Morris cheerfully guaranteed him it would be "rich." As befitted a representative of the United Colonies, Bingham sailed to Martinique aboard an American ship of war, the swift, slim three-masted sloop *Reprisal,* commanded by Marylander Lambert Wickes, who had previously captained merchant ships for the firm of Willing & Morris.

The *Reprisal* reached broiling Martinique, with its paradoxically cool-looking green peaks, on July 27. En route, Wickes had captured three British merchantmen and sent them to Philadelphia under prize crews. He was able to persuade many of the British seamen aboard these ships to volunteer for duty aboard the *Reprisal.* The entire crew of the merchant ship *Friendship* signed on, including all the officers except the captain. This meant that almost forty of Wickes' original American crew were now British—a fact which gave him no cause for alarm until he stood in to the harbor of Saint-Pierre at Martinique and encountered the British sloop of war H.M.S. *Shark,* commanded by Captain John Chapman. He was carrying a message from Vice Admiral Sir James Young to the governor of Martinique.

The *Reprisal* carried 18 six-pounders, the *Shark* 16 nine-pounders—giving the British sloop a clear superiority. Captain Chapman called his crew to general quarters and stood out of the harbor to challenge the *Reprisal.* Ordered to heave to, Wickes replied with a broadside. The French in Saint-Pierre poured down to the shore to root for the American rebel against the hated British. Wickes handled the *Reprisal* superbly, never giving his opponent a chance to rake him, swooping in to hurl a port or starboard broadside and winging away before his opponent could damage him with his heavier guns.

William Bingham was with the French spectators ashore. Wickes had ordered him and his baggage off the ship as soon as he saw that the British captain planned to challenge him. The young merchant wrote a few days later that he never felt "a sensation of joy in a more lively degree" at the sight of Wickes' seamanship. Dusk was settling over the harbor. The two lean, swift ships were almost invisible, the smoke of their cannons adding to the murk. As they began maneuvering for another round, a heavy cannon in the French fort boomed once, twice. Two huge, screaming shots straddled the *Shark.* A single direct hit from a gun of that caliber could demolish a sloop. Captain Chapman cut for the open sea.

When Wickes and his crew came ashore at Saint-Pierre, a carnival atmosphere prevailed. They were, Bingham wrote, "complimented and caressed beyond Measure." The next day the *Shark* returned with a furious complaint from Vice Admiral Young. The governor of Martinique replied by denouncing the British captain for fighting a war in his harbor. He declared that he was only defending "the rights of my country." This was bosh and the British knew it. So did the exultant Wickes and Bingham.

A few days later, the French told Bingham that American privateers could bring captured British ships into any French port in the Caribbean. Bingham could also issue "neutral" French papers for American ships. The French hinted broadly that if an American vessel got close to Martinique, she would be assured of French naval protection. Best of all, the ecstatic Bingham learned that he could issue letters of marque for privateers sailing out of Saint-Pierre and Fort Royal.

Wickes asked if he could haul his ship ashore at the local dockyard to clean his hull. The governor gave him the run of the place. This produced another angry message from Admiral Young, demanding the surrender of "the American pirate." The admiral threatened to send a frigate to England immediately to "acquaint His Britannic Majesty" of the governor's outrageous violations of France's purported neutrality. The governor replied that he would inform "His Most Christian Majesty Louis XVI" about the impertinent British attack on an American ship in a French harbor.[14]

The ultimate insult to Great Britain's presumed dominance of the seas came later in 1776 in the harbors of Danish St. Croix and Dutch St. Eustatius. An American schooner standing out of St. Croix with a small cargo of powder aboard saluted the fort overlooking the harbor. In the words of a Briton who reported the incident to harried Vice Admiral Young, the fort returned the compliment "the same as if she had been an English or Danish ship." A few weeks later, the Continental man-of-war *Andrea Doria* stood in to St. Eustatius flying the Grand Union flag. She saluted Fort Orange with eleven guns, and the Dutch cannon boomed nine times in return—the standard salute for a merchantman. British indignation exploded all over the Caribbean. Saluting an unnamed schooner with a single gun might be mere politeness, but replying to the eleven-gun salute of a rebel man-of-war was an insult.

Shock waves of British indignation were soon reverberating in The Hague. While they were at it, the British also complained that in the *Andrea Doria* was a Barbadian, John Trotman, who had been studying at Princeton. He had been seized by a press gang while vacationing in Philadelphia. For good measure, the British reported that within range of the guns of Fort Orange, the sloop *Baltimore Hero,* half owned by Abraham van Bibber, had captured a British brigantine and brought it into the port, with the Dutch cheering.[15]

The British ambassador to the Netherlands warned the Dutch not to expect George III any longer to "suffer himself to be amused by mere assurances, or that he will delay one instant to take such measures as he shall think due to the interests and dignity of his crown." The Dutch disavowed any intention of recognizing America as a separate state, and made a great production of summoning the governor of St. Eustatius home for an explanation. Meanwhile, Thomas Burch, Abraham van Bibber, and their American friends went right on wheeling, dealing, and privateering. "All American vessels here now wear the Congress colours," van Bibber reported. "Tories sneak and shrink before the Honest and Brave Americans here."[16]

On Martinique, William Bingham exuded similar cheer, with good reason. He had his own fleet of privateers operating out of Saint-Pierre. The ships had American captains and French and Spanish crews. The profits, which he shared with Robert Morris, were fantastic. A single captured cargo of coffee, rum, sugar, and molasses sold for £13,780. Bingham's share was £4,953. In one wild week, his captains picked off fourteen prizes. Captain Lambert Wickes carried back to Philadelphia a cargo of gunpowder and civilian goods on which Bingham cleared a neat £742.13 profit. Bingham was on his way to becoming an early example of that unique social phenomenon—the American millionaire.[17]

XVII

A Retreating, Raged, Starved, Lousey, Thevish, Pockey Army

In America, the British evacuation of Boston and the small victories in North Carolina and Virginia had created an illusion of military prowess. In no place was it more illusory than Canada. Before Quebec, Benedict Arnold with about 500 men maintained a siege that was a compound of his own legerdemain and Governor-General Carleton's caution. In Montreal sat sixty-five-year-old Brigadier General David Wooster of Connecticut, drinking enormous quantities of hot flip, damning the Catholics who were all around him, and marveling, as he wrote in letters to Congress, that "General Arnold had . . . kept up the blockade of Quebec, and that with half the number of the enemy." Wooster marveled away the winter, but declined to send Arnold more than a dribble of men and equipment. He was convinced that the treacherous Catholics who abounded in Montreal were ready to butcher him and his men at the first opportunity.

Even more remarkable, until the end of February Arnold performed his legerdemain while flat on his back. Not until the first week in March was he able to limp about and begin to look like a general again. Besides Carleton inside Quebec, he had to cope with temperatures that sank to 24 degrees below zero, smallpox in his army, and bankruptcy—which required him to force unwanted Continental paper money on the Canadians. Priests loyal to the Crown circulated among the inhabitants urging treachery against the Americans. Arnold arrested them. Several hundred Canadians staged an uprising on the southern bank of the St. Lawrence. Arnold not only crushed the mini-revolt but persuaded many of the insurgents and their friends to join his army. He was not so successful when he tried to persuade his men to build artillery batteries. They pointed to five feet of snow and told him to go to hell. "We labor under almost as many difficulties as the Israelites did of old, obliged to make bricks without straw," he wrote to one of his many correspondents.[1]

Congress, still in the grip of the illusion that the British must be driven off the continent before reinforcements arrived, committed thousands of additional men and even more thousands of paper dollars to the Canadian effort. They also sent three commissioners to romance the Canadians. They chose the best men they could find for this unpalatable task—Benjamin Franklin, for his supposed influence with the French; Charles Carroll of Maryland, because he was a Catholic; and Samuel Chase of Maryland, who apparently was supposed to represent the Protestant Americans and deny all the nasty things that Congress had said about the Quebec Act and Catholic supremacy in Canada.

Winter travel and the reluctance of Washington to part with any of his shaky army until the British evacuated Boston slowed the arrival of reinforcements. Less than 1,000 had reached Arnold by the end of March. Many of them caught smallpox as soon as they arrived. The remainder did little more than replace the 400 sick and wounded on Arnold's muster rolls.

On April Fools' Day, Brigadier General Wooster arrived in Arnold's camp and announced that he was taking charge of the siege of Quebec. He predicted that he would have the town and General Carleton in his power within the month. How? asked Arnold. Wooster declined to confide in the second ranking brigadier general in Canada. Arnold foresaw a fiasco and asked Wooster if he would mind letting him take command at Montreal. Wooster said it was a matter of indifference to him, and Arnold departed. Within a few days, Wooster's feet were as cold, psychologically, as they were physically numb from an inspection of Arnold's snowbound army. There now seemed to be somewhere between 2,000 and 3,000 Americans around Quebec. Regiments lacked muster lists, and officers were reluctant to give an accurate count because they were embarrassed to admit that their men were deserting continuously. At any rate, only half the men Wooster saw were fit for duty.[2]

While Arnold was traveling to Montreal, that city's acting commander, Canadian Moses Hazen, was predicting imminent disaster. In their four months' occupation of Canada, the Americans had managed to alienate the French clergy with their outspoken Protestantism, the Indians by neglect, and almost everyone else by appropriating thousands of dollars' worth of food and clothing on credit or with paper money, which amounted to the same thing as far as the Canadians were concerned. "We have brought on ourselves by mismanagement," Hazen declared, "what Governor Carleton himself could never effect." [3]

Congress's determination remained unshaken. They resolved "that the reduction of Quebec and the general security of the Province of Canada are objects of great concern," and appointed Major General John Thomas of Massachusetts, the man who commanded the advance onto Dorchester Heights, to replace the vacillating Wooster. A few weeks later, they added another general, Baron Frederick William de Woedtke, a thirty-five-year-old ex-major in the Prussian army who had managed to impress Benjamin Franklin—and conceal the fact that he was a drunk. Congress commissioned him a brigadier and sent him north to assist Thomas.

The politicians in Philadelphia also ordered Washington to add six additional regiments to the four he had already shipped up the Hudson River to Canada. Washington pointed out that sending some four thousand of his best men to the other end of the continent was a little risky, because at present they did not know "the designs of the enemy." If the British ordered Howe and his entire army up the St. Lawrence River to relieve Quebec, the men he was sending would "be insufficient to stop their progress." On the other hand, if the British attacked New York, "the troops left here will not be sufficient to oppose them." [4] Congress ignored him.

In Montreal, Benedict Arnold greeted Benjamin Franklin, Charles Carroll, and Samuel Chase at his headquarters, the Château de Ramezay, the residence of a wealthy British merchant, Thomas Walker. He had joined the American cause not because he was an enthusiast for the rights of man but because he cordially hated Carleton and the British regime in Canada for their supposed favoritism toward the French. The three congressmen were impressed by the "genteel company of ladies and gentlemen" whom Arnold and Walker assembled for a welcoming dinner.

The purpose of this largess on the verge of bankruptcy, although the three ambassadors did not seem to be aware of it, was to impress the French. Philip Schuyler had advised Congress (and presumably Arnold) that "the committee, if any be sent, should be enabled to live in splendor, which, with Frenchmen, creates respect." As for the Walkers and their genteel friends, they were among the welcomers because they thought the committee was bringing hard cash. When the Americans turned out to have nothing to offer but soft promises, the enthusiasm of all concerned plummeted to zero.[5]

Attempts by the commissioners to conciliate the Catholics were in vain. Charles Carroll had brought with him his brother, John Carroll, a former Jesuit who had been living on the Carroll estate since the Jesuit order was disbanded by papal decree in 1774. The one or two French-Canadian priests who received Father Carroll were instantly suspended by Bishop Jean Briand, the ruling Catholic prelate in Canada. Briand had remained inside Quebec throughout the American siege, issuing strident pastorals forbidding the sacraments to any Catholic who sided with the *Bostonnais*. The commissioners were soon reporting to Congress that "it seems improper to propose a federal union of this Province with the others as the few friends we have here will scarce venture to exert themselves in promoting it, till they see our credit recovered, and a sufficient army arrived to secure the possession of the Country." [6]

Before Quebec, the man who was supposed to bring the bayonets, Major General John Thomas, arrived virtually unescorted. Most of the American reinforcements had yet to reach Albany. The day that he arrived, May 1, Thomas learned that British men-of-war and transports carrying reinforcements had appeared at the mouth of the St. Lawrence River. Thomas surveyed the make-believe army Arnold had perpetrated around Quebec and decided an immediate retreat was the only alternative. By his count, there were still only 500 reliable soldiers besieging Quebec, with its 5,000 inhabitants, 200 cannon, and 1,600-man garrison. Some reinforcements reached Thomas in the next few days—the Second New Jersey Regiment and six companies of the Second Pennsylvania Regiment. But he was still planning a retreat when fifteen British ships appeared in the still ice-choked St. Lawrence. The British navy had done the heretofore impossible, turning one of their ships into an icebreaker, which plowed a path for the rest of the flotilla, enabling them to appear weeks ahead of schedule.

Reinforced by 200 men from the first two ships to arrive, Carleton sallied from the city with 900 men and four fieldpieces. Thomas tried to pull together his still dispersed army, which a more experienced general would have concentrated the moment he heard about the British reinforcements. After a brief exchange of fire, the Americans broke and fled in all directions, abandoning two tons of gunpowder, 200 sick men in the hospital, 500 muskets, and all their cannon. Although Thomas kept a somewhat organized force around him, most of the American army became a mob of fugitives fleeing down the road along the river, without supplies or hope. Food was ripped from the hands of the French-Canadians without even a proffer of Continental money. At times, it seemed that half the army was carrying the other half, so many men were ill with smallpox. More than one man was left to die in the woods when his companions became too weak to carry him. Enterprising captains from British ships moving up the river landed marines who captured or killed stragglers, but were beaten off when they attacked the men around Thomas.[7]

Carleton did not pursue Thomas. He had no interest in capturing any more Americans. He just wanted to get them out of Canada. On May 10, he issued a proclamation.

> Whereas I am inform'd that many of his Majesty's deluded subjects of the neighboring Provinces laboring under wounds & diverse disorders are dispers'd in the adjacent woods and Parishes & in great danger of perishing for want of proper assistance; all Capts: & other Officers of Militia are hereby commanded to make diligent search for all such distress'd persons and afford them all necessary relief, & convey them to the General Hospital, where proper care shall be taken of them. All reasonable expenses which shall be incurr'd in complying with this Order shall be paid by the Receiver General.
>
> And lest the consciousness of past offences shou'd deter such miserable wretches from receiving that assistance which their distress'd situation may require, I hereby make known to them, that as soon as their health is restor'd, they shall have free liberty to return to their respective Provinces.[8]

When the entire British fleet reached Quebec, Carleton learned he was expected to do much more than restore order in Canada. With the fleet was Major General John Burgoyne and some 10,000 men. Burgoyne produced orders from the American secretary, Lord George Germain—a name that sent Carleton into shock. If he had an enemy in England, it was Lord George. Carleton had sat on the court-martial that condemned him. Germain ordered Carleton and Burgoyne to take the offensive as soon as possible. They were to advance down Lake Champlain into the Hudson River valley as far as Albany. Carleton had little enthusiasm for an offensive war and even less for one that would add to the power and glory of Lord George Germain. But he was a soldier, and he began obeying the King's orders.

Meanwhile, General Thomas and his men struggled on to Sorel at the junction of the Richelieu and St. Lawrence rivers. Thomas left one regiment behind at Trois-Rivières on the north bank of the St. Lawrence to cover the retreat. Sorel was a pleasant village in the center of level country thickly populated by French-Canadians. It was no place to make a stand, but reinforcements coming up the lakes could be met and organized there.

Waiting for Thomas at Sorel was Irish-born Brigadier General William Thompson of Pennsylvania, another veteran of the French and Indian War, with four regiments from Washington's army. The first remnants of Thomas's retreating army reached Sorel on May 12, and the story they told considerably dampened the morale of the men who had marched to Canada with confidence born of their pseudo-victory at Boston. Dr. Lewis Beebe wrote in his diary, after listening to the story of "great numbers sick with the smallpox" and other hardships of the siege, "No person can conceive the distress our people endured the winter past, nor was it much less at the time of their retreat." These last words were true enough. Thomas's men had to endure the closing weeks of the Canadian winter on their retreat. Beebe himself, sailing up Lake Champlain on May 6, encountered "a hard snowstorm . . . which continued the evening and the greater part of the next day." [9]

Bad news aside, the situation was not encouraging in the American camp at Sorel. At least fifty men were already in the hospital, most of them retching and sweating with smallpox. On Thursday, May 16, Benedict Arnold had arrived in camp. He had hurried from Montreal to join Thomas and his retreating men. Arnold ordered every man in the army who had not had smallpox to be inoculated immediately. The following day, General Thomas arrived and countermanded the order. It would be "death for any person to inoculate," he snarled to Beebe, and he ordered every person inoculated to be sent to Montreal. In a letter to Congress from that city, Benjamin Franklin and his fellow commissioners had noted in the last sentence, "The small pox is in the army, and General Thomas has unfortunately never had it." Beebe took one look at Thomas and saw a sick man. Two days later, he told his diary that the general was "this day . . . under great indisposition of body." Thomas was also showing signs of hysteria. He issued an order that "it should be immediate Death for any person to fire a gun in the Camp.[10]

More bad news arrived. Arnold had stationed some 400 men under Colonel Timothy Bedell of New Hampshire at the Cedars on the St. Lawrence some thirty miles west of Montreal. Operating in the vicinity was an adventurous British captain named George Forster, who had volunteered to head a force of about a hundred British regulars and 400 Indians. When Bedell heard rumors of Forster approaching, he decided a visit to Montreal was a necessity. Later, he claimed that he had gone to seek reinforcements—an odd task for the commanding officer of the post. Still later, he changed his story to claim he was en route to an Indian council to enlist their support. Neither story was an excuse for abandoning his post when it was threatened with attack.

The Americans had a small fort at the Cedars. The Indians informed Captain Forster that they had no interest in a frontal assault. Forster was about to retreat when he heard about the American rout at Quebec. He sent a message to the Americans at the Cedars, demanding their immediate surrender. Otherwise, he said, the Indians would give them no quarter when they carried the fort by storm. The man Colonel Bedell had left in command, Major Isaac Butterfield, surrendered.

Unaware of this act of cowardice, the American commander at Montreal, Moses Hazen, ordered Major Henry Sherburne and 140 men to reinforce the Cedars. Forster and his regulars and Indians ambushed Sherburne on the march, surrounded him, and, after some hard fighting, forced him to surrender. This meant that 500 Americans—a quarter of the American army in Canada—were lost. Benedict Arnold decided this was unacceptable. Rushing back to Montreal, he rounded up a hundred men and pursued Forster. He sent ahead of him friendly Indians who told Forster's braves that he had 1,500 men and eight cannon, and another thousand were en route. The Indians decided it was time to go home. So did a sizable number of Canadians who had joined the victorious Forster. The appalled British captain found himself with only about 80 regulars and 500 prisoners.

When some of his Indians drifted back, Forster sent Arnold a warning that if he attacked, the warriors would butcher the prisoners. Forster said he was ready to exchange his captives for an equal number of British redcoats—with one catch. The Americans must agree to go home and stop fighting the King. Arnold rejected both ideas. He had his Indian emissaries warn Forster's Indians that he would hunt them down to their villages if they harmed so much as a single American. As for exchanging prisoners, he was ready to do so, but only on equal terms.

This dickering took most of a day. When the negotiations collapsed,

Arnold, indifferent to the difficulties of a night attack, prepared to do battle. But he could not persuade his field officers, notably Colonel Moses Hazen, and eighteen-year-old Major James Wilkinson, who persuaded Colonel John de Haas of the First Pennsylvania Regiment to agree with him. At one point, the four were close to a fist fight. Arnold finally abandoned his plan for a night attack, but forced the others to agree to an assault across the St. Lawrence the following morning.

At 2 A.M., Forster sent another message to Arnold's camp, announcing that Butterfield and Sherburne had accepted the "cartel," as he called the exchange. Their signatures were on the document to prove it. Arnold said he refused to accept the agreement and planned to attack at once. He repeated his threat "to sacrifice every soul who fell into our hands," if American prisoners were murdered. Captain Forster swallowed hard, counted his numbers, and decided the signatures of Butterfield and Sherburne were all he needed. He sent back the prisoners and decamped. Arnold had rescued 500 men from captivity and very possibly from death at the hands of the unstable Indians. He marched them back to Montreal, where they gave that town a respectable garrison once more.[11]

At Sorel, General Thomas was by May 21 "evidently suffering from smallpox." He decided to retreat to the town of Chambly, ten miles south along the Richelieu River. Thomas was well enough to walk a half mile to his lodgings after the trip on the river, and the next day, May 24, Dr. Beebe found "every Symptom appeared very favorable." Thomas ordered all smallpox victims to join him there. His order countermanding Arnold's policy of inoculating those who had never had the disease guaranteed him a lot of company. Within a day or two, Dr. Beebe was writing, "If ever I had a compassionate feeling for my fellow creatures, I think it was this day, to see Large barns filled with men in the very heighth of the small pox and not the least thing, to make them Comfortable." It was enough, Beebe wrote, "to excite the pity of Brutes." [12]

The army drifted into inertia. "Very few General Orders, and they usually countermanded within a few hours after given," Beebe wrote in his diary. Four regiments arrived in Chambly and milled around, catching the smallpox and doing nothing else but mounting one thirty-two-pound cannon and a four-and-a-half-inch brass mortar. This in spite of the fact that three messengers had arrived from Trois-Rivières on May 26 reporting that 5,000 British regulars, reinforced "by a large body of Canadians," were moving up the St. Lawrence to within five miles of this vital junction. General Thomas's favorable symptoms began to turn ominous, and the gloomy Beebe wrote, "Things go on after a confused manner as usual." By May 31, it was clear that General Thomas was dying.

That evening, in what seemed like a miraculous apparition to the sick and dispirited men at Chambly, boats began appearing on the river. By the time darkness fell, no less than fifty-seven had arrived, bringing with them Brigadier General John Sullivan and most of the six additional regiments Washington had sent from New York—some 3,300 men. The son of an Irish schoolmaster, Sullivan had been a lawyer in New Hampshire and a leader in the revolutionary party of that state. At thirty-five, he had energy, courage, and ambition. He saw himself as the reconqueror of Canada, and did not waste any time getting the message across to his men. On June 1, 1776, he put the soldiers under his immediate command at Chambly through the manual of arms and maneuvered them about the parade ground, where Dr. Beebe thought they showed "Surprising dexterity and alertness." But Beebe did not like ambitious men. He had already taken an intense dislike to Arnold. On the following day, General Thomas died, and Beebe confided to his journal:

> Thomas is dead, that pious man,
> Where all our hopes were laid.
> Had it been one, now in Command,
> My heart should not be grievd.[13]

This was typical of the dissension and disorganization raging within the American army. A few days later, when one of Beebe's patients died, "among hundreds of men it was difficult to procure 8 or 10 to bear the corps about 15 rods." Beebe himself was suffering from dysentery, and he asked another doctor for "A little physic." The man replied, "I have a plenty of physic but God Damn my soul if I let you have an atom."

At Sorel, Sullivan's ambition began blinding him to reality. As early as May 31, Arnold was writing from Montreal to Major General Horatio Gates in northern New York, "My whole thoughts are now bent on making a safe retreat out of this country." Sullivan, ignoring smallpox and frequent reports that the British reinforcements amounted to as many as 10,000 men, took the offensive. He placed Brigadier General William Thompson of Pennsylvania in charge of some 2,000 men, al-

most all of them Pennsylvanians except William Maxwell's Second New
Jersey Regiment, and ordered them to attack Trois-Rivières.[14]

No attempt was made to reconnoiter the enemy or to use friendly
Canadians to spy on them. Thompson put his men aboard boats and
rowed to within three miles of the river town. There they formed into
four columns and moved overland, relying on a Canadian guide. He
was probably a double agent. The next thing the Americans knew, they
were floundering through a swamp full of bone-chilling water and
muck that sucked the shoes off their feet. It was daybreak when they
stumbled back onto the road, where they were spotted by British ships
in the river. They ran a gantlet of grapeshot and round shot for three-
quarters of a mile, and dived into the woods—to find themselves in
another swamp.

One of the colonels, Anthony Wayne, who had not yet won his nickname "Mad Anthony," admitted that by now "a Surprise was out of the
Question." But the largely Pennsylvanian army pushed forward. It took
them three hours to wade, stumble, crawl, and stagger through the
swamp. They emerged to discover that they were confronting not a
small body of regulars and Canadians under one of the defenders of
Quebec, Colonel Allan Maclean, but Major General John Burgoyne
and most of the British army in Canada—8,000 men. It took some time
for the Americans to realize this. Wayne, for instance, thought he was
winning when his men attacked "a large body of regulars" and forced
them to retreat. But the Americans were suddenly engulfed by blasts of
fire from both flanks—as Wayne wryly put it, "our Rear now becoming
our front."

Wayne found himself with 200 men "exposed to the whole fire of
the shipping in flank and full 3,000 men in front with all their artillery." The Pennsylvanians and their handful of New Jersey allies
broke and ran. Wayne and Colonel William Allen struggled to rally
them, while another colonel attacked the British with some 200 men
who had been held in reserve. Wayne and Allen managed to organize
about 800 men. In the confusion, General Thompson and most other
field officers had disappeared. Two companies of riflemen kept the
British at bay, assisted by the swamp, which was "so deep and thick with
timber and underwood that a man ten yards in front or Rear would not
see the men Drawn up." Unfortunately, the Americans grew as confused as the British, and when they began retreating, regiments passed
each other in the gloom without realizing it.

Colonels Wayne and Allen soon found themselves "left on the field with only twenty men & five Officers." While the British continued to pour ammunition into the swamp "from Great and small guns," they stood their ground, "keeping up a small fire in Order to gain time for our people to make good their retreat." They continued this make-believe battle for about an hour, then "cut loose" and caught up to the rest of the army, which fluctuated between 600 and 1,500 men, depending on how many were out looting the countryside for food. The British sent a detachment of about 1,500 men in pursuit, but Wayne and Allen beat them off and "Continued our march, and the third day almost worn out with fatigue, Hunger & Difficulties . . . arrived here [Sorel] with 1100 men." [15]

"I believe it will be Universally allowed that Col Allen & myself have saved the army in Canada," Wayne wrote home. The real savior was Governor-General Guy Carleton. He could easily have bagged the retreating Americans. He had a strong detachment posted at a bridge across the Rivière de Loup, blocking the only overland route to Sorel. But he ordered the major in command at the bridge to withdraw. He still thought it was better to let these deluded rebels go home, defeated, dispirited, eager for pardon and peace. The wilderness, the Indians, starvation, and smallpox would do enough damage to them, he reasoned, to make them thoroughly disenchanted with making war. Loading his men aboard his ships once more, he headed up the St. Lawrence for Montreal. He was in no hurry to take the offensive on behalf of Lord George Germain. Order had to be restored in Canada first.

A neutral eyewitness would have been inclined to agree with Carleton's policy. Wayne's men stumbled into Sorel, their faces and hands ravaged by "musketoes of a Monstrous size." Dozens of stragglers had met grisly deaths in the woods from stalking Indians and revengeful Canadians. From Montreal, Benedict Arnold sent Major James Wilkinson to Sorel to ask Sullivan for some men to cover his line of retreat. Wilkinson "found every house and hut on my route crowded with straggling men without officers, and officers without men." Finally, he found Colonel William Allen, who told him, "Wilkinson, this army is conquered by its fears, and I doubt whether you can draw any assistance from it." [16]

At Sorel, Sullivan had plunged from brainless optimism to equally brainless despair. He wrote to Major General Schuyler at Albany that the enemy's force was "exceedingly superior to ours." He was in command "of a dispirited Army, filled with horror at the thought of seeing their enemy." No less than forty officers were trying to resign. Typical of these was Colonel Jeduthan Baldwin of Massachusetts, who had spent most of his time in Canada sweating out a case of smallpox which he had received by inoculation. For Baldwin, the last straw was robbery. Someone pulled up his tent pins, dragged out his chest, and looted everything from a "jacoat [jacket?] full trimd with a narrow Gold lace and a pair of silk breeches" to "silver shoe and knee buckles," his compass, and his money. The Colonel was "Stript to my Shirt, my breeches & watch that lay under my head." He sat down and wrote to Sullivan, requesting a discharge from "this Retreating, Raged, Starved, lousey, thevish, Pockey Army in this unhealthy Country." [17]

On June 13, Benedict Arnold wrote to Sullivan that "the junction of the Canadians with the colonies . . . is at an end. Let us quit them and secure our own country before it is too late; there will be more honor in making a safe retreat than hazarding a battle, against such superiority. . . . These arguments are not urged by fear for my personal safety. I am content to be the last man who quits this country and fall so that my country rise—but let us not fall altogether." [18]

Sullivan was already retreating from Sorel when he received this letter. The American army disintegrated as it fell back by boat to Chambly. There, baggage and sick men had to be unloaded from batteaux into carts and hauled around the rapids, then loaded again into boats for the trip to St. John's. Colonel Baldwin was in charge of this operation, and he complained about "savere fateague" caused by "the vast No of Men sick & in the most distressing condition with the Small pox." He denounced "many offficers Runing off Leaving there men by the Side of the river to be taken care of by me or others." About 1 P.M., a report reached these toilers that the regulars were at Chambly. This sent "great Numbers of officers & Soldiers upon the run to St. John's, & some . . . could not be stopt till they got to Crown Point," which was over a hundred miles down Lake Champlain. [19]

On June 18, at a council of war, Sullivan's officers advised him to destroy the fort at St. John's and retreat to the Île-aux-Noix. This was a low, flat, brush-covered island full of mosquito-infested swamps in the middle of the Richelieu River near its outlet into Lake Champlain. Strategically, it made sense to cling to this last bit of Canadian soil. It blocked the British invasion route down the lakes into the Hudson River valley. But from every other point of view, the Île-aux-Noix was a disastrous choice. Only a mile long and four hundred yards wide, it lacked almost everything the smallpox-racked American army needed to survive.

Dr. Lewis Beebe arrived there about 3 P.M. on June 17 and was "struck with amazement . . . to see the vast crowds of poor distressed Creatures. Language cannot describe nor imagination paint, the scenes of misery and distress the Soldiery endure. Scarcely a tent upon this Isle but what contains one or more in distress and continually groaning & calling for relief, but in vain! Requests of this nature are as little regarded, as the singing of Crickets in a Summers evening." On the island's lone farm, Beebe found "a large barn Crowded full of men . . . many of which could not See, Speak or walk—one nay two had large maggots one inch long, Crawl out of their ears."

Brigadier General de Woedtke took to the bottle and drank himself into a state of stupefaction which proved fatal. He was carried down the lake a dying man and expired near Lake George on July 28. Other officers imitated his example with less fatal results. It was the only escape from the charnel house of Île-aux-Noix. Each day, twenty, thirty, forty men were buried in a common grave. Black flies and mosquitoes swarmed over the sick, the dying, and the dead.[20]

Indians prowled in the vicinity of the army. A number of officers went across the Richelieu to a house about a mile below the island to drink spruce beer. A party of Indians attacked them, killed and scalped one ensign, one captain, and two privates, and took several prisoners. Indians also attacked boats on the lake, killing three men and wounding six others.

The last of Sullivan's army had left St. John's when Benedict Arnold and young James Wilkinson rode into the town. Arnold had executed a masterly retreat from Montreal with his three-hundred-man garrison. He had broken down bridges and felled trees across the road to slow the pursuing British. After making sure his men were safely embarked in boats, he had ridden back with Wilkinson to reconnoiter the enemy's advance. By now, St. John's was a burning wreck. Docks and houses had been smashed and set ablaze by the retreating Americans. At the water's edge, Arnold paused. Through the roar and crackle of flames, he and Wilkinson could hear the beat of drums and the skirl of fifes. The British army was very close. In a few moments, through the billowing smoke they caught a glimpse of scarlet and white, light infantrymen moving in a skirmish line. Arnold stripped the saddle from his horse and threw it into the boat. Then he whipped out his pistol and shot the horse in the head. Young Wilkinson followed the brigadier general's example. The American invasion of Canada was over.[21]

Benedict Arnold had by no means abandoned his determination to "secure our own country." But he must have wondered—as did many others in the dying army at Île-aux-Noix—whether it was already too late. Only one thing stood between the Americans and disaster, a schooner named *Liberty,* a large sloop named *Enterprise,* and the schooner *Royal Savage.* All three ships had been captured by the Americans in the spring and fall of 1775. Armed with cannon, these ships dominated Lake Champlain, making a British invasion by water impossible for the moment. The rapids between St. John's and Chambly isolated the British navy in the St. Lawrence River. But what if Guy Carleton built ships of his own to protect the batteaux and longboats in which his men had heretofore been traveling?

By June 25, the Americans were staggering south from Île-aux-Noix to Crown Point, where an irate John Sullivan discovered he had been replaced by Major General Horatio Gates. While this British-born volunteer tried to bring some order out of his chaotic command, Benedict Arnold kept scouts and spies watching the enemy at St. John's, and they brought him "undoubted intelligence" that the British had with them "a large Number (it is said One hundred) Frames for Flat Bottom Boats design'd to be made use of on Lake Champlain." Arnold warned Washington that "their Industry & Strength will doubtless" make them "masters of the Lake, unless every nerve on our part is Strained to exceed them in a Naval armament. I think it absolutely necessary that at least three hundred carpenters be immediately employed." Arnold recommended building at least twenty or thirty "Gundaloes, Ro Gallies & floating Batteries." Who was going to command them? Admiral Benedict Arnold.[22]

XVIII

A Commodore
Loses His Breeches

While the Americans in Canada teetered toward total collapse, Charles Lee was discovering that patriotism was not exactly rampant in the Southern Department. In spite of the "flaming argument" Governor Dunmore had given the independence men at Norfolk on January 1, Virginia and Maryland remained reluctant to admit they were fighting a war, and act accordingly.

Accompanied by his dogs, Lee had peregrinated to Williamsburg in his usual eccentric fashion. From here, he aroused the wrath of rebels and loyalists alike in Maryland, where signs of counterrevolution were growing more ominous daily. Letters from Lord George Germain to Maryland's governor, Robert Eden, had been intercepted and presented to Lee. They indicated that Eden had been urging a military landing in Maryland or Virginia. Lee fired off a letter to Samuel Purviance, the leading hothead of the Committee of Safety of Baltimore "not to lose a moment and in my name (if my name is of consequence enough) to direct the Commanding Officer of your Troops at Annapolis immediately to seize the person of Governor Eden—the sin and blame to be on my head." [1]

Instead of forwarding this order to Annapolis, Purviance, who did not trust the moderates in charge there, ordered Samuel Smith, captain of the Baltimore militia, to march his men to Annapolis and arrest Eden in person. Smith obeyed, but when he reached Annapolis, he found Eden unarrestable. The Governor said he had no intention of running away, so why incarcerate him? The Maryland Council of Safety agreed and gave Purviance a sharp rebuke.

To cover himself, Purviance had sent Lee's order and Eden's intercepted letter to Congress in Philadelphia. When Congress heard that Eden was still unarrested, they sent a reprimand to the Maryland Council of Safety and ordered him seized. The Council refused to arrest the Governor as long as he promised not to leave the province without their permission. The Marylanders then turned on Lee, and in the style of the New York provincial congress accused him of forgetting that military authority was subordinate to civil authority in America—a tendency which was soon to grow more flagrant in the second ranking American general.[2]

In a letter to Richard Henry Lee (no relation) in Congress, General Lee denounced the "namby-pambies of the senatorial part of the Continent" for growing "timid and hysterical." Not even Virginia measured up to Lee's expectations. He told the congressman that the Old Dominion's Committee of Safety was "as desperately and incurably infected with this epidemical malady [namby-pambyism] as the Provincial Congress of Maryland."[3]

Lee had set himself up in the Governor's Palace at Williamsburg, a bit of self-indulgence which one member of Congress correctly foresaw "will not be much approved of by the gentlemen of that country." Lee described the distribution of Virginia's relatively few troops—dispersed throughout the huge state—as "a masterpiece—I wonder they did not carry it further and post one or two men by way of general security in every individual gentleman's house." As for getting cooperation from the local politicians, Lee told Washington that "the Provincial Congress of New York are angels of decision when compared with your countrymen." Trying to head off a confrontation between Lee and the sensitive Virginians, Washington wrote a letter to his brother Jack, assuring him that Lee was "zealously attached to the Cause, honest and well meaning, but rather fickle and violent, I fear, in his temper."

Lee had some legitimate complaints. The economy of the Virginia Committee of Safety, he raged, was "of a piece with their wisdom and valor; to save money, we have no carriages to our guns; to save money, we have no blankets for our men, who are, from want of this essential, dying by dozens." Lee soon took ruthless charge of the Virginia war effort. He concentrated the state's nine regiments in and around Williamsburg. Advancing to Norfolk, he fought a brisk skirmish with Lord Dunmore and his ships and drove them from their anchorage off that town. They retreated up the bay to Gwynn's Island, where Negroes and whites began dying by the dozens of scurvy and smallpox. Lee now went to work on Virginia's comparative handful of loyalists. He ordered the arrest of anyone suspected of supplying Dunmore with food and information. Houses were burned, farms were stripped of livestock for several miles around Portsmouth and Norfolk. Lee then bullied the Committee of Safety into ordering the entire population of Norfolk and Princess Anne counties moved inland—an order which punished the innocent and guilty. It was only halfheartedly enforced.[4]

By this time, Otway Byrd had become a Lee aide. His brother Thomas was still aboard Dunmore's ships. The two young Virginians came close to shooting at each other while Lee was supervising his scorched-earth policy along the shore.

But organizing Virginia did not solve Lee's larger problem. His department comprised Virginia, North Carolina, South Carolina, and Georgia. The British were capable of striking at any one of these states. Where should he set up his headquarters? "I am in a damned whimsical situation," he wrote to Robert Morris. "I know not where to turn, where to fix myself. I am like a dog in a dancing school. . . . I may be in the north, when as Richard III says, I should serve my Sovereign in the west." North Carolina and South Carolina kept sending Lee messages, pleading for his presence. Lee sent Brigadier General John Armstrong to South Carolina to investigate the situation and advise them.[5]

Lee himself continued to bombard Congress with advice. He urged them to conquer the British posts at Niagara and Detroit and stop wasting money on "our damn'd fleet." When bad news began arriving from Canada, Lee went into a frenzy. "Your idea of quitting Canada from want of specie is to me inconceivable, when you can or ought to command plate sufficient to purchase ten Canadas," he told Richard Henry Lee. Above all, Lee urged the delegates to vote for independence. "You will force at last the people to attempt it without you—which must produce a noble anarchy," he warned Robert Morris in April. To Richard Henry Lee, he played the part of Brutus and cried, "Ah, Cassius, I am sick of many griefs." He denounced the "poorness of spirit and languor" in Congress's recent proceedings, and vowed that if they did not "declare immediately for positive independence, we are all ruined." When some Virginians, such as Edmund Pendleton, spoke out against separation from England, Lee said their arguments would have disgraced "an old midwife drunk with bohea [tea] and gin." [6]

On May 8, Lee received a letter from North Carolina, telling him that British warships were gathering off Cape Fear. He immediately began marching south with 1,300 Virginia regulars. On the road, he received a frantic message from President John Rutledge of South Carolina, telling him the enemy fleet was off Charleston bar. "For God's sake," wrote Rutledge, "lose not a moment."

Charleston! If the British captured the queen city of the South, it would be a fearful blow to the American cause—and to Charles Lee's reputation. Leaving his foot soldiers behind him, he galloped south at top speed, wondering how and where the British had accumulated enough men to attack such a formidable place.

The British attack had evolved, like many things the British did in 1776, from a combination of accident, illusion, and overconfidence. Major General Henry Clinton had sailed south in March to cooperate with the loyalists in North Carolina. He arrived at Cape Fear only in time to discover that the Scotsmen and ex-Regulators had been smashed at Moore's Creek Bridge. Clinton and his two companies of regulars had spent most of March and April bird watching, fishing, and pursuing oysters along the beaches of Cape Fear, wondering if everyone in England had forgotten they existed.

Between mid-April and the end of May, the fleet and army that would have guaranteed a loyalist triumph in North Carolina finally straggled over the horizon. Delays of every conceivable sort had wrecked their timetable. The nervous Lord Lieutenant of Ireland did not want to let some of the regiments out of that restless country; when the ships were at sea, they found that the transport captains had crammed aboard so many packing cases full of goods they hoped to sell in America that no one could reach the cavalry horses to feed them. Winter storms blew a quarter of the ships back to England. The 2,000 men in the transports were exhausted by the long, rough voyage. At first, Clinton was inclined to return to Virginia and assist Lord Dunmore in setting up a loyalist enclave there. The Virginia governor was still clinging to the island in the Chesapeake to which he had retreated.

But in command of the fleet was an aggressive, ambitious sailor, Commodore Peter Parker. With him was an equally ambitious and aggressive general, Charles Lord Cornwallis. Parker urged Clinton to tackle a state that would be, if conquered, a far more prestigious plum than North Carolina—South Carolina and its capital, the immensely wealthy city of Charleston. Parker was probably thinking about the money that he and his officers could make if the city capitulated and all the merchandise in its warehouses, the silver plate and opulent furnishings of the leading rebels, became prizes of war. Clinton was dubious. Two thousand men were hardly enough to conquer a town, much less a major city with a population of perhaps 20,000 people. But he allowed Parker to send two junior officers to reconnoiter Charleston Harbor.[7]

The sea scouts returned declaring that the city was easy pickings. The rebels were constructing a fort on Sullivan's Island at the entrance to the harbor, but it was unfinished, and they were confident that a few broadsides from the fleet would send the defenders scurrying. Charleston would then have no choice but to surrender under the threat of a naval bombardment which could easily reduce it to ashes.

To this siren song were added the pleas and assurances of the Royal Governor of South Carolina, Lord William Campbell. Like most other governors, he had fled to the safety of a British man-of-war. Like Governor Josiah Martin of North Carolina, he vowed that the back country of South Carolina was largely loyal and only waiting for some support from the royal government to rise against the pretensions of the men of Charleston.

There was some truth to Campbell's claim. South Carolina was badly divided in its enthusiasm for the Revolution. The leaders were, as in North Carolina, mostly from the long settled coastal part of the state. When they formed their own government in March, the back country was virtually unrepresented. A motion to declare the provincial congress "a full and free representation of the people" was seriously questioned by many delegates. But the radicals in charge of the proceedings ignored these protests, and demonstrated even more arrogance and bad judgment. They loaded all future elections in their favor by apportioning two-thirds of the election districts to the low country.

The vice-president of the state, Henry Laurens, admitted in a letter to his son, John, in England, that there had been a "dangerous Insurrection by thousands of the back country people." The low-country leaders had suppressed it by a combination of force and persuasion. Aided by troops from North Carolina, they had taken "hundreds or more properly thousands . . . prisoners," and "informed [them] truly of the nature of the dispute between Great Bitain and the colonies." A hundred back-country leaders were imprisoned in Charleston until they "confessed their errors [and] united in the American Cause." [8]

Even among the low-country men, there was little enthusiasm for the idea of independence. Laurens, one of the wealthiest merchants and planters in the South, admitted that he had been reluctant to "lay his fingers upon his nose" at the British, and he told his son that he still felt "a Tear of affection for the old country [England] and for the people in it whom in general I dearly love." [9]

When gaunt, choleric Christopher Gadsden, South Carolina's Sam Adams, returned from the Continental Congress waving a copy of *Common Sense* and calling for independence, the reaction was explosively negative. John Rutledge, who soon after was elected president of the new government, rebuked Gadsden and called the idea treasonable. Everyone applauded when Rutledge declared that he was ready to ride day and night to Philadelphia to reunite Great Britain and America.

The sight of the fifty-five-ship British fleet produced momentary panic in Charleston. "All was hurry and confusion . . . men running about the town looking for horses and carriages and boats to send their families in the country." Militia began digging trenches and throwing up breastworks in the streets. An alarming shortage of ammunition was discovered, and lead was requisitioned from the windows of churches and houses to be melted down and cast into musket balls. Horsemen pounded into the country to summon reinforcements. If the British had attacked immediately, they might have been able to fight their way past the fort on Sullivan's Island and capture the town.[10]

But foul weather kept the British from entering the harbor for three days. Commodore Parker fretted about getting his flagship, the fifty-gun *Bristol,* and another fifty-gun two-decker, the *Experiment,* over the bar. The *Bristol* drew 18 feet 7 inches of water and the *Experiment* 17 feet, and these figures were attained only when both ships were lightened by removing several tons of round shot, casks of powder, and other heavy cargo. Not until June 8 was the whole fleet over the bar, and Henry Clinton began reconnoitering to see where he could land his regulars. By this time, Major General Charles Lee had arrived in panicky Charleston.[11]

Lee's European reputation tremendously heartened the shaky South Carolinians. As stout, florid William Moultrie, commander of the fort on Sullivan's Island, put it, "It was thought by many that his coming among us was equal to a reinforcement of a thousand men." The reason, Moultrie added, was that Lee "taught us to think lightly of the enemy." But Lee was not thinking lightly about his immediate prospects in Charleston. He thought the city's defenses were nonexistent.[12]

Briskly, Lee began demolishing warehouses and homes along the waterfront to provide fields of fire. When Clinton landed his troops on Long Island, which was separated from the mainland by a narrow inlet known as the Breach, Lee became seriously alarmed. The British army was between Moultrie's fort on Sullivan's Island and the city. There were 1,200 men—the best troops in the state—on the island, in danger of being cut off. Crossing to Sullivan's Island, Lee was not encouraged by a conversation with the stubborn, pipe-smoking Moultrie. Lee pointed out that there was no line of retreat. He looked over the fort and called it "a slaughter pen." His opinion was backed by an ex-British sea captain who inspected the fort and told Moultrie that the fleet would knock it down in half an hour. "Then," said Moultrie, "we will lay behind the ruins and prevent their men from landing." [13]

Lee thought this was idiocy. He urged President Rutledge and his council to abandon Sullivan's Island. The South Carolinians refused to a man. President Rutledge swore he would cut off his right arm before he would write such an order. The frantic Lee ordered Moultrie to build a bridge from Sullivan's Island to the mainland. A makeshift affair was knocked together, two planks wide, floating on empty hogsheads and boats. It sank when two hundred Carolinians tried to cross on it.

The more Lee studied the fort, the more appalled he became. On the west, it was open to cross fire from any ships that worked around a bend in the island. Although it had been planned as a square with bastions at each angle, it was finished only on the front—the southeast side—and on the southwest. There were neither walls nor bastions on the northeast and northwest. Guns were mounted only on the southeastern and southwestern fronts. In short, the fort had only two walls worth mentioning.

To bolster the fort's right flank, Lee ordered Moultrie to build screens high enough to protect the men on the gun platforms. He also ordered the colonel to build a trench to protect the garrison from potential attack from Clinton from the rear. The easygoing Moultrie disregarded both orders. Digging and building in the South Carolina sun was hot work, and he was afraid that his men might desert as numerous carpenters had already done during the several months he had been building the fort. Lee began talking about relieving Moultrie from command. This was difficult, since South Carolina had not yet placed its armed forces under the control of the Continental Congress. Technically, Lee had no power to make Moultrie do anything.[14]

On the British side, Clinton was as unhappy as Lee. In the fleet were several Negroes who had served as pilots in Charleston Harbor, and claimed to know the area well. They had probably been enticed aboard Governor Campbell's frigate by offers of freedom. Henry Laurens wrote of "hundreds" of blacks "stolen and decoyed by the servants of King George III—Captains of British ships-of-war and noble lords." The loyalist Negro pilots had told Clinton that there were only eighteen inches of water between Long Island and Sullivan's Island at low tide.

Instead, the British discovered that in most places the water was seven feet deep with just enough eighteen-inch shoals to frustrate an attack by boat. By the time they found this out, the Americans had moved cannon to the northern end of Sullivan's Island facing Long Island and were entrenched behind breastworks. Clinton thought about attacking the mainland, but needed naval support—which Peter Parker could not give him because the channel was not deep enough for his frigates. Besides, Lee had fortified the most likely landing place—Haddrell's Point—and reinforced it with a thousand men. For days, Clinton and Parker exchanged notes proposing and dismissing various plans of attack. It never seemed to occur to them that they were giving the Americans two weeks to build up their defenses and their nerve.[15]

On the morning of June 28, Lee was so annoyed with Moultrie for failing to execute his orders that he informed President Rutledge that he was crossing over to Sullivan's Island to relieve him. Before he could make this mistake, the boom of cannons told him that the British were attacking. It was a hot sultry day, with a soft wind blowing from the south. Moultrie, who had been up most of the night suffering from an attack of gout, was inspecting the defenses facing Clinton on Long Island. He saw "the men-of-war loose their topsails" and raced back to the fort to order "the long roll to beat." [16]

Officers and men dashed to their posts. The British fleet outgunned them 270 cannon to 25. There was only enough powder and shot in the fort for about twenty-eight rounds per gun. From Long Island, Clinton launched a diversionary attack with a few hundred men aboard boats. They were driven off by cannon and rifle fire. Thereafter, the redcoats remained mute spectators to the duel between the fleet and the fort.

Parker and his captains were confident that the battle would be over within the hour. During previous wars in the West Indies, the British navy had won simular duels with French and Spanish forts constructed by skilled engineers. Surely they would have no trouble wiping up this homemade American affair. The bomb ship *Thunder* began the attack, hurling mortar shells into the fort from about a mile and a half. These primitive explosives did little damage. They fell into the soft sand and mud in the center of the fort, where the fuses of many of them went out. The sand swallowed the flying pieces of those that exploded.[17]

The two fifty-gun ships, Parker's flagship *Bristol* and the *Experiment,* accompanied by the frigates *Active* and *Solebay,* formed a line 400 yards from the fort's southwestern bastion. They left enough room between them to allow three more frigates, the *Syren,* the *Actaeon,* and the *Sphynx,* to form a parallel line a few hundred yards to their rear and fire between them. Broadside after broadside blasted into the fort. Moultrie's men, conserving their ammunition, returned the fire at a much slower pace.

To the amazement of the British, their cannonballs thudded into the fort's palmetto logs with virtually no effect. The soft wood absorbed the flying metal with a minimum of deadly splinters. Nor did the walls give the slightest sign of crumbling or cracking. Too late, the British sailors—and Charles Lee—were discovering that Americans knew how to build a fort. There were not one but two sets of palmetto logs in the walls of the fort in parallel rows. In between were tons of sand, making walls sixteen feet thick. After about an hour of furious broadsides, it dawned on the British that they were not going to knock the fort down.

Commodore Parker ordered the three frigates in the second line to swing around the fort and open fire from the west. Guided by Negro pilots, the British captains hauled their anchors and began obeying the order. Charles Lee, watching from the shore, shuddered. If those frigates got into position, a few broadsides would make the gun platforms of Fort Sullivan run red with the blood of Moultrie's men.

But once more the Negro pilots proved they knew much less about Charleston Harbor than they claimed. Swinging wide around the four ships still dueling with the fort, they ran into the shallow water of the harbor's middle ground. The *Actaeon* and the *Sphynx* collided, and all three were soon stuck fast on a shoal which later became the foundation for Fort Sumter. It was an almost unbelievable piece of good luck for the Americans. On Long Island, Henry Clinton and Lord Cornwallis must have stared in disbelief. British men-of-war colliding and running aground in what was once one of the busiest harbors of the Empire. It was incredible.

Inside the fort, the courage of Moultrie's men rose astronomically as they saw how little damage the British could do to them. Moultrie made sure their enthusiasm for the fight remained high by serving rum

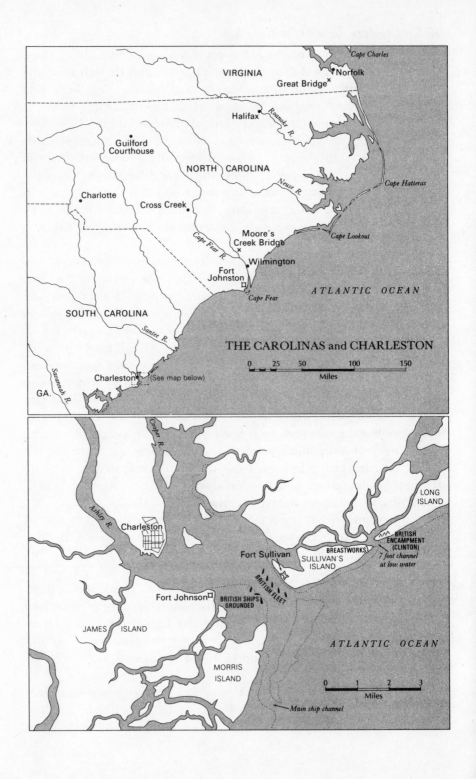

THE CAROLINAS and CHARLESTON

0   25   50   100   150
Miles

Cape Charles
VIRGINIA
Norfolk
Great Bridge
Halifax
Roanoke R.
Guilford
Courthouse
NORTH   CAROLINA
Neuse R.
Cape Hatteras
Charlotte
Cross Creek
Cape Lookout
Cape Fear R.
Moore's
Creek Bridge
Wilmington
Fort
Johnston
ATLANTIC OCEAN
SOUTH   CAROLINA
Cape Fear
Santee R.
Charleston   (See map below)
GA.
Savannah R.

Cooper R.
Ashley R.
LONG
ISLAND
Charleston
BRITISH
ENCAMPMENT
(CLINTON)
BREASTWORKS
7 foot channel
at low water
Fort Sullivan
SULLIVAN'S
ISLAND
BRITISH FLEET
Fort Johnson
BRITISH SHIPS
GROUNDED
JAMES   ISLAND
ATLANTIC OCEAN
MORRIS
ISLAND
0   1   2   3
Miles
Main ship channel

in fire buckets along the gun platforms. The liquor did not seem to affect the Americans' accuracy. Aboard the British ships, Moultrie's slow-firing guns began inflicting murderous damage. The captain of the *Bristol* had his arm torn off. Another shot inflicted the same fearful wound on the captain of the *Experiment*. Twice, the *Bristol*'s quarterdeck was cleared of every man but Commodore Parker. An explosion ripped Parker's uniform to shreds, and he bled freely from two wounds, but refused medical attention. He also refused to quit the fight. All afternoon the duel continued.

From the Charleston shore, thousands of soldiers and citizens watched the battle, which shrouded fort and warships in thick smoke. At one point, a cannon shot carried away the fort's flag, which had the word "Liberty" embroidered upon a field of blue. Sergeant William Jasper of the Second Carolina Regiment, no doubt considerably emboldened by one of Colonel Moultrie's rum-filled fire buckets, leaped up on the fort's wall, tied the flag to the staff of a cannon sponger, and planted it once more to wave defiance to the enemy. Onshore, Charles Lee contemplated sending Moultrie an order to spike his guns and retreat. He could not believe that untrained troops could stand up under the British barrage. He later said it was "the most furious fire I ever heard or saw." Lee sent aide Otway Byrd to the fort, but he did not believe him when he returned and said that the garrison was in high spirits and there was nothing to worry about. In midafternoon, Moultrie ordered his men to cease firing. Lee dashed across from the mainland to see what was wrong. Moultrie and his officers hastily put aside the pipes they were smoking and tried to look like professional soldiers. They told Lee that they were winning the battle and let him aim and fire two or three of their guns. The visiting major general was embarrassed. "Colonel," he said, "I see you are doing very well here. You have no occasion for me. I will go up to town again."

About 5 P.M., President Rutledge sent 500 pounds of powder over from Haddrell's Point, and the Americans resumed firing. By this time, two of the three frigates that had run aground had extricated themselves with the flood tide and were back in the battle. The British kept on blasting away until 9:30 P.M. By that time, both sides were firing at the belches of fire from the muzzles of their opponents' guns. Men continued to die, or lose arms and legs, from the whistling 12- and 18- and 32-pound shot. Finally, Commodore Parker was told by his officers that their supply of powder was running dangerously low.

Parker ordered a retreat. Aboard the *Bristol* alone, there were 46 killed and 86 wounded. The *Experiment* had 43 dead and 75 wounded. There were a few more killed and another 170 wounded aboard other ships and among Clinton's troops on Long Island. The *Bristol* had taken 70 hits, many of them below her waterline. If a high sea had been running, the British later admitted, the ship would have sunk.

The next morning, the British tried to get the frigate *Actaeon* off the shoal. The Americans in the fort began cannonading her. The British set her on fire, and the crew fled in small boats. A party of South Carolinians under an Irishman named Milligan rowed out to the abandoned ship and boarded her. But the blaze was out of control. They fired three of her guns at the departing British, grabbed the ship's bell, some sails, and stores, and fled. Moments later, the *Actaeon* blew up.

Military self-confidence and war fever soared in South Carolina. So did independence fever when Charleston learned that the Cherokee Indians, instigated by the British in Florida, had attacked the back country, burning several towns and killing about sixty pwople. This news turned even the loyalists imprisoned in Charleston into rebels. Several of them swore an oath of fidelity to the United Colonies and marched to join state troops protecting the frontier. Henry Laurens wrote his son that there were "few men . . . who had not lost all inclination for renewing our former connexion with your King and his Ministers." [18]

This did not guarantee an upsurge of self-sacrifice, however. Lee was soon complaining to President Rutledge, "The inhabitants of this town begin or rather continue to fleece the army most unmercifully." The citizens were demanding £6.1.3 to bury a single Virginia soldier. Lee was also outraged that the South Carolinians would not send a single man to defend Georgia. "Is it just that other colonies should be obligated to march" to your assistance, Lee asked Rutledge, while you "refuse in . . . turn to assist others?" He denounced the whole idea of provincial troops and hoped that Congress would abolish them.

Lee lost no time spreading the news of the British repulse. He claimed little credit for it, freely admitting his astonishment "that so much coolness and intrepidity could be displayed by a collection of raw recruits." He told Washington that he had urged the creation of a 1,000-man cavalry corps to give the Americans the mobility they needed to defend the southern states. Some members of Congress had resented the proposal. Lee truculently maintained it was a soldier's duty "to propose and adopt anything, without other authority than the public safety." Already Lee was eager to shake off the authority of

Congress. Because of this lack of cavalry, "we had infallibly lost this Capital [Charleston] but the dilatoriness and stupidity of the enemy saved us." [19]

Lee might have added atrociously bad British luck to that list of causes. But for the time being, no one in South Carolina—or in the other United Colonies—was inclined to attribute their military success to luck. Ignoring the growing cloud of bad news from Canada, they saw the British repulse at Charleston as one more proof of America's invincibility. It did not make them receptive to a proposal for peace that was coming their way in a British warship.

XIX

A Sailor Sights
an Olive Branch

While the South Carolinians were thumping Sir Peter Parker, another far more important British sailor was aboard his flagship, *Eagle*, somewhere between Halifax and New York, fretting and fuming over the ship's slow progress. The admiral was Richard Lord Howe, the British peace commissioner about whom the members of Parliament had wrangled so fiercely. Admiral Lord Howe is rarely mentioned as an architect of American independence. But without him the nation would not have survived the year 1776.

Swarthy and uncommunicative like his brother, the general, Howe shared the family knack for popularity with the average man. After a battle, he would go below decks to visit the wounded, and often shared wine and food from his personal provisions with them. He shook hands with sailors who had distinguished themselves—behavior which may not seem remarkable to twentieth-century readers, but was rare in the eighteenth century, when the names of seamen (and soldiers) were not even mentioned in casualty reports and the average officer regarded enlisted men with a mixture of hostility, contempt, and fear. Howe's sailors called him "Black Dick," a tribute to his swarthy complexion and their sense of comradeship with him.

Another emotion which has become somewhat foreign to twentieth-century readers moved Admiral Richard Lord Howe and his brother into the center of the quarrel between England and America—family feeling. It is essentially an aristocratic emotion. To the Howes, America was not merely a word or a distant semi-mythical place peopled by rebellious ingrates. It was a land imperishably connected with the honor and the valor and the destiny of the Howes. When their oldest brother, George Lord Howe, was killed by a random French bullet a few miles from Fort Ticonderoga in 1758, a bond was created between the Howes and America.

His brother Richard, who inherited the title, personally supervised the selection of the monument to George Augustus in Westminster Abbey paid for by the colony of Massachusetts Bay. When it was unveiled in 1762, he announced his intention to erect a companion obelisk testifying to both "his love and veneration for his brother's virtues" and "his gratitude and respect for that public and patriot voice, whose generous applause has adorn'd their memory." [1]

Howe never forgot that this "public and patriot voice" was American. Throughout the decade of controversy that preceded the outbreak of war, he had been a consistent supporter of America in Parliament. In 1766, he was one of a handful of prophetic voices who urged the King and Parliament to receive the petition of the Stamp Act Congress. The advice was rejected. Instead, the majority chose the posture, absurd for Parliament and outrageous for the King, of refusing to hear petitions of supposedly illegal assemblies—a posture that eventually convinced many Americans that petitions were a waste of time and war was the only alternative.

Howe became directly involved in the American quarrel when he attempted to negotiate a settlement with Benjamin Franklin during that American patriarch's last months in London. Franklin had petitioned in the name of the Massachusetts assembly for the removal of the Royal Governor, Thomas Hutchinson. He had been given a hearing before the Privy Council in which he was insulted and denounced as a rebel and a liar. Franklin's enthusiasm for the idea of a united Empire vanished that day, and Howe was unable to revive it, even though he spoke with the tacit support of Lord North. Franklin's insistence on the abandonment of all claims to parliamentary taxation power was unacceptable to the majority of the cabinet and Parliament. But the two negotiators parted with sincere expressions of regard. [2]

In the course of their conversations, Franklin and Howe had discussed the possibility of creating a peace commission to inquire into America's grievances. Howe originally envisioned it as an Anglo-American affair, with himself and Franklin as its leaders. But Howe made the mistake of suggesting to Franklin that anyone who succeeded in such a mission could look forward to a generous reward from his sovereign. This, of course, was only standard practice, the combination of fear and favor which the British had used so successfully to destroy rebellions in Ireland and Scotland during the preceding hundred years.

Here Howe revealed his first weakness as a peace negotiator. He did not understand Americans, for the simple reason that he did not know very many of them and had never been to America. Thus he could not see why neither fear nor favor tempted them. Howe could not comprehend the defiant impregnability that Americans felt as possessors of a continent—an impregnability that was both martial and financial. They did not need British money, and they had no need to truckle to British power as weak men in Ireland and Scotland did repeatedly.

Although Franklin bristled at Lord Howe's talk of rewards, considering the remark an attempted bribe, he was sincere enough in his desire for reconciliation (on American terms) to tell Lord Howe that "a Person of Rank and Dignity who had a Character of Candor, Integrity and Wisdom, might possibly, if employed in that service, be of great use." In spite of the way the negotiations had collapsed in the face of Franklin's American intransigence, Lord Howe seized on these words and proposed himself to the North government as the Person that Franklin had described. But the King and his councilors had by this time decided on war. For the better part of six months in 1775, Lord Howe got nowhere, while Lord George Germain took charge of the effort to settle things with round shot and musket balls.

But the ambivalent North still hoped to settle things short of war. In the autumn of 1775, with the government readying the show of force the hard-liners demanded, North revived the idea of a peace commission. He first tried to offer it to Lord George Germain—a gesture which revealed both his pessimism about its chances of success and his desire to get Germain off his back. Germain refused. His predecessor as American secretary, North's half brother, Lord Dartmouth, pushed Lord Howe forward once more. North decided to make Howe his candidate too—in part to maintain his position against Germain. North knew in advance that the King, though very lukewarm to the idea of a peace commission, favored Howe over all other contenders. Thus Howe was the man North had in mind when he slipped a clause about a peace commission into the Prohibitory Act.[3]

For a while, Lord George Germain demurred. Howe was one of the many navy and army officers who considered the former Lord George Sackville a living blot on England's honor, and had let him know it more than once. But Lord Howe, in his eagerness to play the peace-maker, had broken twenty years of frosty silence between him and Lord George by sharing confidential reports he received from his brother in Boston. Parenthetically, he assured Lord George that he favored a vigorous repression of the rebellion if the Americans persisted in fighting.

At the same time, through close friends, Howe advanced the proposition that he should be not only commissioner in charge of making peace in America but commander in chief of His Majesty's navy there. On January 10, 1776, Howe declared in Parliament, "However he suffered, if commanded his decided duty was to serve [in America]." He then paradoxically added that "if it was left to his choice, he should certainly decline to serve." This sounded like double-talk. But Howe was separating himself from officers like Admiral Augustus Keppel and General Lord Jeffrey Amherst, heroes of the Seven Years' War who had said they would refuse to go to America, even if directly ordered by the King. Since they publicly made these statements in stentorian tones, the King was careful not to command them.[4]

The First Lord of the Admiralty, Lord Sandwich, opposed Howe as commander of the American fleet, pointing out that he had just appointed a new admiral there. North and the rest of the cabinet, including Lord George Germain, backed Howe strongly. But the man who finally got him the job was George III himself. The King was extremely fond of the Howes for much the same reason that prompted him to look with filial-like favor on Lord North. George I was generally assumed to be the Howes' maternal grandfather. Their mother received a pension of £750 a year from the King when she married, later increased to £1,250 and renewed in favor of her daughter. It was this connection as well as his brother's sacrifice at Ticonderoga that permitted Howe to champion America vehemently, even to the King's face.[5]

During 1775, while having dinner with him at a public inn, Lord Howe excoriated His Majesty's "persevering and invincible obstinacy" toward America. All the King did was mildly remind the admiral that he was damning his sovereign in public. On February 2, after a talk with Lord Howe, George III summoned Lord Sandwich to Buckingham Palace, and told him to dismiss the admiral he had just appointed and give Howe command of the American squadron. The King let Sandwich make the announcement that evening at a cabinet dinner, pretending that he had voluntarily yielded to the pleas of his fellow ministers.

By February 5, Lord Howe was officially commander in chief of His

Majesty's fleet in North America. The appointment was almost universally acclaimed. Government critics such as the editor of the *Morning
Post* and hard-liners such as Thomas Hutchinson, the deposed Royal
Governor of Massachusetts, were in agreement that scarcely a man
could have been found who was "more generally satisfactory to the
kingdom." [6] Howe did not realize it yet, but by accepting the naval appointment first, without waiting to hammer out the terms of his peace
commission, he had made a fatal mistake. He was now committed to go
to North America as more or less the creature of Lord George Germain and the King. He evidently thought that his powers of persuasion
were stronger than their bellicose intentions. Howe had succeeded in
picking up the olive branch which had been shot out of his brother's
hand at Bunker Hill. But he had done it without finding out how
serious the King and a majority of the cabinet were about smashing the
Americans first and talking peace later.

First, Howe found himself locked in combat with Lord George Germain on the composition of the peace commission. Germain wanted to
make it a two-man team—with one of his followers, opposed to all concessions, as the second man. Howe angrily reminded North that the
original plan called for him to be the sole commissioner. Finally, after
much wrangling, someone, probably Germain, suggested that the admiral's brother, Major General William Howe, might do as a second
man acceptable to both sides. Germain had been reading General
Howe's letters, and they seemed to express a tough determination to
prosecute the war if he got the men and guns. Lord Howe agreed,
because he knew that the general looked to him as the leader of the
family and would do whatever he told him.[7]

In this first round, Lord Howe emerged as the winner—although
the government inflicted on him as secretaries two hard-liners. Ambrose Serle, a former solicitor and clerk of reports for the Board of
Trade, had written a number of pamphlets on America, including one
entitled, *Americans against Liberty; or, An Essay on the Nature and Principles
of True Freedom, Shewing That the Designs and Conduct of the Americans
Tend Only to Tyranny and Slavery.* Henry Strachey, a Foreign Office bu-
reaucrat, was described as an "artful and insinuating man" and an experienced diplomat who would press hard for every point.[8]

But Lord George Germain and the hard-liners had only begun to
fight. On February 22, the government's top lawyers, Edward Thurlow,
the attorney general, and Alexander Widderburn, the solicitor general,
distributed a draft of Howe's peace commission to the cabinet. It did

not give Howe much power, but it at least authorized him to discuss with the Americans the basis of a reunion, grant pardons, and, most important, suspend the Prohibitory Act for any colony he declared to be at peace. But these powers could only be revealed to colonies that had formally submitted to royal authority once more. In short, Howe had to win the war before he could start talking peace.

Shocked, Howe complained that the ministry wanted him to beat the Americans so thoroughly they would scarcely be worth conciliating. He informed Lord George Germain on March 26 that he was prepared to resign his naval command if he did not get a commission that truly empowered him to make peace. Alas, Lord Howe did not know that Germain was already hard at work reducing his slender olive branch to a toothpick.

The peace commission draft would be acceptable, declared the American secretary, only if it stipulated that the rebellious colonials must "formally acknowledge Parliament's right to make laws binding the colonies in all cases whatsoever" before any peace talks could begin. North, trying to please everybody as usual, agreed with Germain but then proposed the precise opposite approach—the peace commission would convene an assembly of negotiators from all thirteen colonies and suspend the Prohibitory Act before getting the total verbal submission Germain demanded. Germain said no. North, goaded by Dartmouth, threatened to resign. Germain countered with a resignation threat of his own. The government seemed on the point of coming apart until the King intervened and ordered North and Germain to work out a compromise.[9]

On March 17, the day that William Howe was successfully evacuating Boston, Germain achieved a less spectacular but far mare fateful victory in a conference with North and Chief Justice Lord Mansfield, whom the King had appointed as arbiter—knowing he was thoroughly in favor of Germain's policy of force. The compromise was a total capitulation to Germain's smash-them-into-submission-first policy. If North had an iota of integrity, he would have resigned on the spot.

When the Germainized version of the peace commission reached Lord Howe, he threatened to resign—and this time he meant it. This threw the government into another flap. But Germain, who, in the words of a subminister, had "now collected a vast force and having a fair prospect of subduing the colonies . . . ," stood his ground and advised the King to find a replacement for Lord Howe. For a while, the King seemed inclined to agree with him. But he feared that Howe

could make good on his threat to order his brother the general to resign with him—decapitating the government's armed forces in America
with a stroke of his pen. At the King's request, Germain agreed to negotiate with Howe. Utilizing the shrewd advice of the government's solicitor general, Alexander Wedderburn, he totally outmaneuvered the
admiral.[10]

Germain agreed to forgo his insistence on a formal acknowl-
edgment of Parliament's supremacy. But he forced the admiral to accept so many stipulations for declaring a colony at peace—the Americans had to be all but inert beneath the royal standard, their arms
surrendered, all royal officials restored—that it was a practical impossibility for Lord Howe to talk about anything more serious than the
weather with a rebel American.

He was also forbidden to negotiate with any extralegal American assemblies—especially the Continental Congress. For a crusher, Germain
saw to it that nothing of even medium importance could be decided by
the commissioners without final approval by London. The wording of
this ultimate hamstring is worth repeating. "It is our will and pleasure
that in the discussion of any arrangement that may be brought forward
into negotiation . . . you do not pledge yourself in any act of consent
and acquiescence that may be construed to preclude our Royal determination upon such report as you shall make to us." [11]

Why Howe accepted this revision can only be explained by two
things: He knew by now that the King was standing behind Germain
and there was no hope of getting anything more substantial from the
government. And he still knew nothing about America and Americans,
much less what they would accept as peace terms. He had not learned
much from his months of negotiation with Benjamin Franklin.

A glimpse of Howe's uneasy state of mind is visible in the diary of
Thomas Hutchinson, the refugee Royal Governor of Massachusetts.
After talking with Lord Howe, perhaps at the King's suggestion,
Hutchinson concluded, "He seems unacquainted [with America]."
Howe even admitted that he wished he was as well versed in American
affairs as Hutchinson. At this point (in mid-April), Howe was clearly
uncertain about accepting the mangled peace commission.[12]

Lord Howe spent the rest of the month struggling with North, Germain, and the King for more power. He did manage to wring from
them one major concession—the right to state categorically that Parliament was prepared to abandon taxation in America and replace it with
a system of negotiated contributions to imperial defense from each

colony based on its ability to pay. This was, of course, the heart of the North-Drummond peace plan. But it was a far different matter for a peace commissioner to have the power to work out such an arrangement with all the colonies at more or less the same time. Howe may have hoped that it could become the basis of the peace convention North had proposed and then abandoned in the face of Germain's intransigence. But Howe was still hamstrung by his fundamental concession to Germain—that he would not, in fact could not, talk reconciliation in this or any other way until a colony had manifested George III's favorite words, submission, subordination and obedience.

When Howe attempted to get some additional minor powers, the King told North to tell the admiral to take the peace commission or leave it. The unhappy admiral decided to take it. He apparently reasoned that even with an unsatisfactory commission, it was more important to have men of good will such as himself and his brother as the executors of imperial policy than a general and an admiral who would take Germain literally and aim at a Carthaginian peace.

To justify his decision to accept the shriveled olive branch and to bolster his dwindling hopes, Howe persuaded various friends to write to influential Americans, describing his mission in the most benevolent possible terms. David Barclay, an old friend of Benjamin Franklin, unaware that the philosopher was talking with French agents and sending feelers to other nations as head of the Committee of Secret Correspondence, declared in a letter that "it will not be for want of inclination in [Lord Howe] should the olive branch not rise superior to the . . . din of war." Others wrote to Washington's absentee secretary, Joseph Reed, and other influential Philadelphians, hinting that Howe had powers to "compromise and adjust" and reiterating their faith that he would "return with the olive branch." [13]

In ironic contrast to these optimistic letters was the package of orders that Lord Howe received from the ministry as commander in chief of the North American squadron. All orders to previous admirals were included in this thick packet. These documents made it clear that the King and Lord George Germain expected Howe to scour the American coast from New Hampshire to Georgia, destroying every American vessel that dared to show a sail and bringing devastation to every seaport that defied the British flag.

Nursing an olive branch that now existed almost entirely in his troubled mind, Lord Howe raised his vice admiral's flag to the foretop masthead of the *Eagle* and set sail for America at dawn on May 11,

1776. His hope was to arrive at Halifax, Nova Scotia, in time to join his brother William and the fleet that was to escort his army to attack New York. But foul weather, head winds, and icebergs slowed the *Eagle,* and it took six weeks to reach Halifax. There Howe discovered that General William and his army and naval escorts had already departed for New York.

Although Lord Howe only spent a day in Halifax, he probably heard enough about the politics of that jumpy province to raise his hopes for peace. Nova Scotia was largely settled by New Englanders who had rushed to grab the lands of the Acadian French when they were deported by the English for supporting France in earlier colonial wars. Not surprisingly, in 1775 stay-at-home New Englanders, particularly Massachusetts men, did their utmost to communicate their revolutionary ideas to the Nova Scotians, and an encouraging number of them proved responsive. The province's only newspaper, the *Nova Scotia Chronicle and Weekly Advertiser,* was decidedly sympathetic to the Revolution. When the governor, Lieutenant Colonel Francis Legge, collected a large quantity of hay to be shipped to the British in Boston, it went up in smoke one dark night. Next, a fire was discovered in the navy yard. Legge arrested two suspects, and the provincial assembly promptly declared them to be "dutiful and loyal subjects of King George."

Attempts to enlist enough men to raise a provincial regiment, the Royal Fencible Americans, got nowhere. The jittery governor began threatening—and sometimes arresting—anyone who talked against the British government, and he ordered anyone coming from the rebellious colonies not only to take an oath of allegiance but to declare his submission to the King and Parliament and his detestation of the rebellion. Legge also tried to force the assembly to give him power to declare something very much like martial law. The assembly told him off in strong words. "Dictatorial powers may be necessary to quell insurrections or to rule a disaffected people," they declared, but these conditions did not exist in Nova Scotia.

Governor Legge complained to London that there was a conspiracy against him in the legislature. Other Nova Scotians told the same royal officials that the Governor had "disgusted almost all the inhabitants, from whom His Majesty might otherwise receive the strongest assurances of fidelity and loyalty." In January, 1776, the principal officers of the government, the prominent merchants, and almost every influential man in Nova Scotia joined in a petition to the King demanding

Legge's removal. Otherwise, they declared, "there is abundant reason to fear this, Your Majesty's valuable province, may be irrecoverably lost."

The Nova Scotians spoke with confidence because they had already accepted the British government's formula to make an annual lump-sum contribution to the Crown in return for the promise to abandon all levies and duties heretofore paid under various acts of Parliament, including the tax on tea. They were in the process of negotiating the lump-sum payment and how it would be raised. Their confidence was not misplaced. The warning note in those words, "irrecoverably lost," sent a tremor through the colonial offices in Whitehall. Not even Lord George Germain, that proponent of unbridled imperial prerogative, could ignore it. Within a month, a packet boat was on the high seas with orders for Legge to come home for a hearing on the charges against him. The Governor was in the process of departing for London when Lord Howe arrived.

Here was proof that the King and his ministers were prepared to eat a good deal of humble pie and listen attentively to colonial complaints and act on them promptly. Lord Howe may have meditated for a moment on the ironic contrast between the government's reaction to Nova Scotia's demand for the Governor's removal—and the petition sent to London in 1773 for the removal of Thomas Hutchinson, the Royal Governor of Massachusetts.[14]

On Lord Howe's voyage to New York, the winds were again remarkably contrary. It took him three weeks to complete a trip which normally the *Eagle* should have made in six days. The chagrined officers of the *Eagle* vowed that "they never remembered an instance of the kind since they had been to sea."

Aboard the *Eagle*, Lord Howe's secretary, Ambrose Serle, was filling a diary with sentiments which were far more typical of the prevailing English attitude toward America than the thoughts and hopes of his leader. As Serle saw it, nothing less than the Constitution of the British Empire itself was at stake. He was convinced that the Americans, by abandoning what he called "British freedom" or "freedom of law," were declaring themselves "open enemies to the public and general liberty of the British Empire." Serle considered all revolution a sin of disobedience to God and "His substitute, the King."

In his valuable journal, Serle gives us several glimpses of Lord Howe's determination to take a far different attitude toward the Americans. On Sunday, July 7, off Nantucket, the *Eagle* overtook a whaling vessel returning to that island from the coast of Brazil. The captain was in despair, certain his ship was about to be destroyed or at the very least captured and sold as a prize of war. But Lord Howe found a loophole in the Prohibitory Act and let him continue his homeward journey. To show him "that Englishmen had not quite lost their usual generosity," he gave the relieved captain a bottle of brandy from his private stock.[15]

The following day, Howe caught and released another ship, although this one was clearly liable to seizure. Howe was more interested in preparing with Serle's help a declaration of the appointment of himself and his brother as peace commissioners and their strong desire to make this the primary purpose of their mission in America. He also wrote a letter to Benjamin Franklin in which he declared his eagerness to resolve the differences and remove the prejudices that kept "us still a divided people."

On Friday, July 12, the *Eagle,* the wind finally in her favor, crossed the bar at Sandy Hook. By 6 P.M., they were dropping anchor off the east side of Staten Island. Above them, the hillsides were white with British army tents. General Howe had revealed the folly of Congress's no-foothold policy by landing his army on this island without a shot fired at him. All around the *Eagle,* guns boomed as the ships of the fleet saluted Admiral Howe. Sailors lined the decks to cheer "Black Dick," and equal numbers of soldiers joined them onshore. "A finer Scene could never be exhibited," Ambrose Serle wrote in his journal, "both of country, ships, and men."

A few minutes after the anchor touched bottom, General William Howe came aboard to embrace his older brother while an honor guard came to attention and a band played a brisk march. The general brought Lord Howe a document that considerably dampened their family reunion—a copy of the Declaration of Independence.[16]

XX

Labor Pains,
Real and Imaginary

If Admiral Howe had reached America during the third or fourth week in June of 1776—as he had hoped to do—the vote for independence might never have been taken. Throughout the month of May, the leader of the independence movement, John Adams, admitted that congressmen were continually wincing at what he called "the dismals from Canada." Yet Adams himself burbled with confidence. On May 20, he wrote a famous letter to his friend James Warren: "Every Post and every Day rolls in upon Us, Independence like a Torrent." Surveying the continent, Adams declared that the "four colonies to the Southward" were "perfectly agreed now with the four Northward"—he admitted that the five in the middle were "not yet quite so ripe; but they are very near it." [1]

In the past, this has been taken as an accurate assessment of what most Americans thought and felt about independence. Actually, it was the statement of a party politician, relentlessly pushing a program through Congress. John Adams had not been outside Philadelphia for five months. He was not in touch with what the rest of America was thinking.

In the four colonies to the southward, the revolutionary party in Georgia was so miniscule that the delegates to Congress could fairly be said to represent no one but themselves. The rebels of South Carolina had, as we have seen, denounced the idea of independence, until Commodore Parker and General Clinton changed their minds on June 28. The state's assembly had done no more than authorize its delegates to vote with the majority on any measure judged "necessary for the defense, security, or welfare of this colony, in particular, and of America in general." That Adams could see in this commission an endorsement of independence was proof of his wishful thinking, and nothing else.[2]

Only in Virginia and its satellite, North Carolina, was there any evidence of a torrential impulse for independence. On May 15, the Virginia convention, under the leadership of Adams' alter ego, Richard Henry Lee, had ordered its delegates in Congress to propose a declaration of independence. The source of this decision lay not in a great outburst of patriotism or a widespread change of heart among his state's moderates—but in panic. Virginians—in particular, Richard Henry Lee and Patrick Henry—were convinced that France and England were about to sign a treaty to make joint war on America and partition the defeated colonies between them. Most men in the Old Dominion thought they had hard evidence to prove it. The bogus scheme of a partition treaty, perpetrated in London by the ingenious ex-Jesuit Roubaud to further mulct the French ambassador, had, you will recall, been forwarded to the colonies by First Lord of the Admiralty Sandwich to discourage American hopes of a French alliance. In Virginia, it had paradoxically produced a frenzy for independence.

The progress of the partition treaty story can be traced almost schematically. On April 16, 1776, the *Pennsylvania Evening Post* published an article asking "Serious Questions Addressed to the Congress and All the Legislative Bodies of America." Among these was the question of whether America might fall victim to what the writer called "the partition spirit of the times." The writer pointed out that France was shipping an extraordinary number of troops to its West Indian islands. Various newspapers had printed figures which added up to 30,000—about ten times the actual number of reinforcements which the cautious, financially strapped French government had actually sent.

The writer went on to note that the tyrants of Europe "think they have a right to dispose of their subjects in the same manner the farmer in this country disposes of his livestock." Poland had been partitioned in 1772 by Russia, Prussia, and Austria. Corsica had revolted against the kingdom of Genoa. The Genoese gave the island to France, who quickly smashed the uprising. Now the writer warned that France might "grow weary in listening to our whining cries after our mother country, and instead of striking a blow to draw off the British armies and fleets from our coast" would instead join the British war effort and accept Canada as a reward. Even Spain might be induced to join the slaughter if the British promised to restore Florida to Madrid's empire.

On April 20, 1776, Richard Henry Lee wrote to Patrick Henry echoing practically every one of these ideas. Lee worked himself into near hysteria over "the despotic aims of the British Court" and their readiness to promote them by "treaties of alliance with foreign states." He asked Henry "to judge, whether whilst we are hesitating about forming alliances, Great Britain may not, and probably will not, seal our ruin by signing a treaty of partition with two or three ambitious powers that may aid in conquering us . . . When G.B. finds that she can not conquer us alone and that the whole must be lost, will she not rather choose a part than have none? Certainly she will. . . . Nothing in this world is more certain than that the present Court of London would rather rule despotically a single rod of earth, than govern the world under legal limitations."

On May 11, the Williamsburg *Gazette* reprinted the *Pennsylvania Evening Post* story, and the partition scheme became a topic of passionate discussion in Virginia. With Patrick Henry's help, Lee used it to push the resolution for independence through the Virginia convention on May 15.

On May 20, Henry was still so worried about the partition threat that he rushed a letter to Lee warning that France, "ignorant of the great advantages to her commerce we intend to offer and of the permanency of that situation which is to take place," might be lured into the partition scheme before they heard that America had declared her independence. He urged Congress to send American ambassadors to France "instantly." The same day, Henry wrote a similar letter to John Adams, who replied that he was in complete agreement on "the importance of an immediate application to the French Court." [3]

The four New England colonies did not need the partition treaty to tilt them toward independence. But they were not as unanimous or as enthusiastic as John Adams claimed in his misleading letter. The Rhode Island assembly had refrained from using the dangerous word in its instructions to its delegates, and the New Hampshire legislature was dragging its feet as late as May 20, the date of Adams' letter. On May 16, 1776, Oliver Wolcott of Connecticut told a friend, "A strange infatuation has possessed the British Councills to drive Matters to the length they have gone. Everything convinces me that the Ability of a Child might have governed this country, so strong has been their attachment to Britain." [4]

As for the middle colonies being "very near" ripe—this was pure

Adams dreaming. In New Jersey, Royal Governor William Franklin still sat in his handsome mansion in Perth Amboy, and the colony continued to pay his salary. Timid New York was meeting loyalist resistance and threats of counterforce in the Mohawk Valley, around Albany, in Westchester County, and in Queens and Kings counties on Long Island. In Maryland, on May 15, the people's elected delegates meeting in convention had unanimously resolved "that a reunion with Great Britain on constitutional principles would most effectually secure the rights and liberties, and increase the strength and promote the happiness of the whole Empire." [5]

But the biggest obstacle—the middle state that virtually exercised veto power over a declaration of independence—was Pennsylvania. This province at the center of the confederated thirteen, third largest in population, with the wealthiest, most protected port, was to the other colonies, in the words of a contemporary, "what the heart is to the human body in circulating the blood." In this heart, contrary to Adams' wishful thinking, enthusiasm for independence was almost invisible.

Unlike many other colonies, where revolutionary conventions and provincial congresses had replaced the royal assemblies, the Pennsylvanians had clung to their old assembly. They justified this conservative stance by arguing that Pennsylvania was not a royal colony. There was some evasion and some truth in this argument. Assemblymen, judges, and other officials took an oath of allegiance to the King before being seated, and the royal coat of arms hung above the State House door. But the King and Parliament were the remote, rather than the immediate, rulers of Pennsylvania. The real power belonged to the sons of William Penn, known as the Proprietors. Over the years, the Penns had used the huge sums they extracted from Pennsylvania in rents and land sales to build up a very sophisticated political machine, which was now almost completely committed to John Dickinson. The independence men in Congress gradually began to realize that until this machine was destroyed and Dickinson's grip on the assembly broken, Pennsylvania— and America—would never declare independence. While John Adams led the public fight on the floor of Congress, his cousin Sam and his friends began working to overthrow Pennsylvania's legal government.

Tom Paine had fired one of the opening shots in this war in *Common Sense,* where he went out of his way to attack the assembly as unrepresentative. This cry soon became a chorus, and the assembly finally gave ground. On May 1, 1776, it held special elections to fill seventeen additional seats. If the independence men won these, they would control the assembly, and could change the instructions to Pennsylvania's delegates to the Continental Congress.

The Adamses and their party in the Continental Congress watched the election with intense interest. It was fiercely fought, with meetings held night after night on corners and in the taverns and coffeehouses of Philadelphia and in the churches and taverns of the country districts. The result was a crushing defeat for the independence party. In the city of Philadelphia, they elected only a single man. In Northampton County, moderate James Allen, son of the Penn-appointed chief justice of the colony, won 853 to 14. James was also the brother of Colonel William Allen, who had helped save the Americans at Trois-Rivières, and of Congressman Andrew Allen, the peace negotiator with Lord Drummond. Some independence men were elected from western Pennsylvania. But John Dickinson still retained a majority in the assembly.[6]

The independence men screamed foul. Their best propagandist, Thomas Paine, who had been attacking the assembly in the Philadelphia newspapers ever since he had blasted it in *Common Sense,* declared that the Whigs, as he called the independence men, had lost the election only because so many of their voters were fighting for their country in Canada.

In the Continental Congress, the independence men revealed their growing desperation with a maneuver that tried to render the Pennsylvania election null and void on the first floor of the State House. John Adams moved "that it be recommended to the several Assemblies and Conventions of these united Colonies who have limited the power of their delegates in this Congress by any express instructions, that they repeal or suspend these instructions for a certain time." Adams argued that Congress needed "power, without any unnecessary obstruction or embarrassment, to . . . order such measures as may seem to them necessary for the defense and preservation, support and establishment of right and liberty in these colonies." The motion was vigorously criticized by the anti-independence men, who argued that Congress should never cut itself off from the voice of the people in such arbitrary fashion. Independence, they declared, could only be maintained if the people wholeheartedly backed the idea. The change of heart had to be thorough, and proof had to be displayed by flourishing local governments fully ready to support the idea before Congress could take such an enormous step. Adams' proposal was voted down.[7]

During these first days of May, the parliamentary leader of the anti-independence men, John Dickinson, had retired to his country estate to rest from his strenuous exertions in the Pennsylvania election. He was confident that he had dealt the independence movement such a setback that there was little to worry about for a week or two. The absence of this able man may have encouraged the independence men to launch another counterattack in the Continental Congress on behalf of their friends in Pennsylvania. It was preceded by an intriguing coincidence. For some time, a British frigate, the *Roebuck,* had been patrolling the lower Delaware River. On May 9, the ship was attacked by a flotilla of gondolas manned by Philadelphia sailors. The *Roebuck* beat them off with a few broadsides and retreated down the river. The boom of cannon was distinctly heard in Philadelphia—the first time that the sounds of war had penetrated the city. The sailors—like the soldiers in the ranks of the city militia—were controlled by wholehearted independence men.[8]

When Samuel Adams heard the sound of gunfire on Lexington green a year before, he had reportedly exclaimed, "Oh, what a glorious morning this is—a glorious morning for America." In his letters, John Adams had often noted that the middle colonies "have never tasted the bitter cup; they have never smarted." He meant they had seen and heard nothing of the war and were, therefore, lukewarm for independence. Did one or both the Adamses hint to a Phildelphia independence man the potential value of a little cannon fire on the Delaware? [9]

The next morning, May 10, Richard Henry Lee, John Adams' alter ego from Virginia, introduced the following proposal: "*Resolved,* that it be recommended to the respective Assemblies and Conventions of the United Colonies, where no governments sufficient to the exigencies of their affairs have hitherto been established, to adopt such governments as shall, in the opinion of the representatives of the people, best conduce to the happiness and safety of their constituents in particular, and America in general." Adams seconded the motion. John Dickinson, shrewd politician that he was, might have seen where Adams was going. But he was reclining in Delaware, and no one else among the anti-independence delegates was aroused.[10]

As John Adams recalled later, the resolution was adopted "with remarkable Unanimity." Congress had received a number of requests from state governments asking for their advice on replacing various aspects of the old royal government which had fallen in abeyance—such as courts and county sheriffs. With studied innocence, John Adams next suggested that a preamble should be published to explain and justify this important resolution. Congress agreed, and without any objection from the anti-independence men the minutes duly recorded that *Mr. J. Adams, Mr. Rutledge, Mr. R. H. Lee* were appointed to prepare the document.

Mr. J. Adams was promptly asked to do the writing by the other two members of the committee. On May 15, the stunned anti-independence men heard John Adams read his handiwork. It began with a ferocious swipe at George III. Adams declared that "his Britannic Majesty was, with the lords and commons of Great Britain," responsible for excluding the inhabitants of "these United Colonies from the protection of his crown." No answers had been given to the Colonies' humble petitions. Instead, "the whole force" of Great Britain "aided by foreign mercenaries" was being exerted for "the destruction of the good people of these colonies."

Then came the projectile, aimed squarely at the Pennsylvania assembly. It was, Adams declared, "absolutely irreconcilable to reason and good Conscience, for the people of these colonies now to take the oaths and affirmations necessary for the support of any government under the Crown of Great Britain, and it is necessary that the exercise of any kind of authority under the said Crown should be totally suppressed, and all the powers of government exerted, under the authority of the people, for the preservation of internal peace, virtue, and good order, as well as for the defense of their lives, liberties, and properties, against the hostile invasions and cruel depredations of their enemy." [11]

The anti-independence men were on their feet instantly, shouting denunciations. But Dickinson, who might have rallied numerous wavering moderates, was still absent, and the sound of cannon fire on the Delaware was only five days old. James Duane of New York insisted that Congress was interfering in the affairs of individual colonies. Peace commissioners were on their way from England. "Why all this haste? Why this urging? Why this driving?" he cried. James Wilson of Pennsylvania revealed a more personal fear. "In this province, if that preamble passes, there will be an immediate dissolution of every kind of authority. The people will instantly be in a state of nature."

Six colonies voted for the preamble, four against it. Maryland's delegates walked out, declaring they needed instructions from their convention.

After the vote, James Duane told Adams that the preamble was "a machine for the fabrication of independence." With a smile, Adams said that he thought it was independence itself, then added, "But we must have it with more formality yet." In a letter to his wife, Abigail, and other correspondents, Adams called the preamble "the most important resolution that ever was taken in America." He said it was "a complete separation from [Britain], a total absolute independence, not only of her Parliament but of her Crown." [12]

Adams refrained from telling Abigail the real purpose of the maneuver. But everyone in Pennsylvania knew exactly what it meant. Anti-independence man James Allen wrote in his diary, "The 20th of this month the assembly meets but I believe we shall soon be dissolved. The Congress have resolved to recommend it to the different colonies to establish new forms of Government, to get rid of oaths and allegiance &c." The result, Allen predicted, would be a "convention chosen by the people" which would "consist of the most fiery Independants."

Yet opposition to the radicals remained intense. Hopefully, Allen noted that "yesterday the resolve of Congress was read . . . at the Coffee-house. One man only huzzaad; in general it was ill received. We stared at each other. My feelings of indignation were strong, but it was necessary to be mute." [13]

On the very day that Congress passed the preamble, the Philadelphia Committee of Inspection met to urge the calling of a state convention. On May 18, the committee summoned a mass meeting "to take the sense of the people." The Philadelphia committee had once been controlled by John Dickinson. But by February, 1776, other men with more radical ideas were rising out of the popular ferment. Among them were Christopher Marshall, a retired druggist; James Cannon, eccentric instructor of mathematics at the College of Philadelphia; and Timothy Matlack, a debt-ridden ex-brewer. In April they were joined by the most radical American of them all—Dr. Thomas Young of Boston, a foe of just about everything that could be called established, from religion to royalty to governors, admirals, generals, and assemblies. Young had been agitating on behalf of "we, the common people" for twenty years and had been run out of several cities for his rhetoric. He had been arrested in Dutchess County, New York, for calling Jesus Christ a knave and fool, quarreled with patriot leaders in Boston over his medical theories, and was present, "a sword in his hand," the night of the Boston Massacre.

Young's talents as an agitator won the admiration of Sam Adams, who delegated him to become one of the principal organizers of the Boston Tea Party. As early as May, 1774, Young was rejoicing at "the perfect crisis of American politics." It was almost inevitable that he should gravitate to Philadelphia, now the red-hot center of political action. Sam Adams made sure he met Matlack, Marshall, Cannon—and, of course, Thomas Paine. In the coffeehouses and taverns and on street corners, Dr. Young soon became an effective advocate for independence and a major social overhaul.

Today's Americans, increasingly isolated in single-family homes or huge apartments, have difficulty imagining the life style of eighteenth-century Philadelphia which enabled Dr. Young and his friends to be so influential. It was a city of small, cramped houses, which often doubled as stores, offices, and workshops. This meant that people spent a remarkable amount of each day on the streets, in the style of the later nineteenth- and early twentieth-century immigrants. Housewives shopped every day. Artisans worked in the large front rooms of their houses and spent an hour or two a day chatting with passersby. There were ninety-three tavern keepers and seventy-two innkeepers in the city—which meant one watering place for every hundred and forty persons. Each constituted an informal community cell.

As this gossipy, volatile society discussed John Adams' coup of May 15, George III—with an assist from George Washington—handed the independence men the weapon they needed to guarantee their victory. On May 17, an American captured early in the Canadian campaign and sent to England for trial arrived in New York. He had been returned to Halifax and escaped from jail there. Sewn into his clothes were copies of the treaties George III had made with the German princes to hire their troops. Washington rushed the news to Congress, and it was soon racing through the streets of Philadelphia. It was conclusive proof that George III was an enemy of American freedom, trumpeted the independence men. And anyone who supported this murderous king was also an enemy.[14]

On May 20, the day scheduled for the meeting of the new enlarged assembly, four or five thousand Philadelphians braved a cold rain to gather in the State House yard under the aegis of the radical-led Philadelphia committee. Daniel Roberdeau, a defeated independence candidate and commander of the Philadelphia militia, was selected as chairman. John Adams' preamble and the resolution calling for new governments won tremendous applause. Stony silence greeted a recital of the instructions the assembly had given to the province's delegates in Congress. In the Pennsylvania State House, the assembly was unable to do business for lack of a quorum. Many moderates were frightened by the potential for violence in the crowd in the State House yard and thought that there was a good chance that they might go home wearing tar and feathers.

Although there was no violence, the attitude of the crowd was distinctly menacing. Their resolutions, each carried with a shout, bristled with hostility to the old order. They called the assembly "a body of men bound by oath and allegiance to our enemy," and accused many of its members of "pecuniary employment under the Proprietary." They therefore concluded that "a government modeled by them would be the means of subjecting us and our posterity to greater grievances than any we have hitherto experienced." They also said that the assembly was elected by men "in real or supposed allegiance to the King to the exclusion of many worthy inhabitants." [15]

Even more hostile was the letter sent the next day "to the public in all parts of the province." Interestingly, the word "independence" was omitted from it. The issue was declared to be union of the colonies versus the rule of assembly. The revolutionaries declared themselves "open in our affairs and . . . against private machinations." Then came another menacing snarl. "Let the men come forward who are endeavoring privately to undermine the Union. We dare them to do it." [16]

Pennsylvania's moderates fought back. A protest was circulated throughout the city and signed by a considerable number of people. It was supported by the Quakers, who felt that a declaration of independence would be a declaration of war. The protest argued that Congress did not mean by its resolution of May 15 to interfere in any colony's internal affairs. It also insisted that the present assembly could accomplish any needed change in the form of government, and reiterated that the only object to be sought is "an accommodation of the unhappy differences with Great Britain, an event which, though traduced and treated as rebel, we still profess earnestly to desire."

The county committee of Philadelphia, also controlled by moderates, sent a message to the assembly urging it to stand fast and defy the city committee. What alarmed most moderates was the aim of the radicals to demolish not only the assembly but the charter of the colony, which they regarded as a bulwark of their public liberties. The assembly tried to ride out the protest by making concessions. It widened voting rights and repealed the oath of allegiance to the King. It even began to draft new instructions for the state's delegates in the Continental Congress, tacitly freeing them to vote for independence. But it was too little and too late. The idea that the assembly and charter were mortal enemies of independence had taken root. The triumph of one meant the destruction of the other. This all-or-nothing approach would, within six months, threaten the United States of America with extinction.[17]

XXI

The Premature Child, Independence

On June 7, Richard Henry Lee arose in Congress and, in obedience to instructions from the Virginia convention, resolved "that these United Colonies, are, and of right ought to be, free and independent states: that they are absolved from all allegiance to the British Crown; and that all political connection between them and the state of Great Britain is, and ought to be, totally dissolved."

Lee added two additional resolutions to be acted upon by Congress as soon as independence was approved. First, that it was "expedient forthwith to take the most effectual measures for forming foreign alliances." Next—a call that many moderates felt should precede independence—"that a plan of confederation be prepared and transmitted to the respective colonies for their consideration and approbation."

Conservatives and moderates, led by John Dickinson, rose to the attack. John Adams must have been not a little dismayed to see Edward Rutledge of South Carolina among those condemning the idea. For two days, Rutledge, James Wilson of Pennsylvania, Dickinson, and Robert Livingston of New York dueled with New Englanders, Virginians, and Georgians. On Saturday, the eighth, Rutledge, summing up the debate in a letter to his fellow moderate, John Jay of New York, wrote, "No reason could be assigned for pressing into this Measure, but the reason of every Madman, a shew of our spirit. The Question was postponed; it is to be renewed on Monday when I mean to move that it should be postponed for three Weeks or Months." [1]

On Monday morning, June 10, Rutledge moved to delay a vote for three weeks, and Congress agreed. This would give time for delegates to visit their home states or write to sitting conventions for instructions. At the same time, pros and antis agreed it would be a good idea to prepare a declaration of independence. A committee was appointed— *Mr. Jefferson, Mr. J. Adams, Mr. Franklin, Mr. Sherman, Mr. R. R. Livingston.*

Dickinson, Rutledge, and the other opponents of independence and confederation claimed that they were "friends to the measures themselves," yet were against adopting them at this time. Wilson and Dickinson of Pennsylvania made a point of arguing that the assembly of the state "was now sitting" in a room just above the Congress. There had also been a call for a state convention. Both bodies should be given a chance to report on the sentiments of the people of Pennsylvania. But we can be certain that many of these men, like James Duane and Robert R. Livingston of New York, were hoping that delay would bring the arrival of the long awaited peace commissioners with concrete propositions for reconciliation with England. Livingston explained the strategy of the moderates as "well-timed delays, indefatigable industry, and a minute attention to every favorable circumstance." [2]

The Pennsylvania newspapers spent the month of June battling over independence. The *Evening Post,* a radical paper, published a sarcastic list called "What Patriots Fear."

"Should independence be declared, I fear I shall lose my office.

"I fear I shall lose the honor of being related to men in office.

"I shall lose the rent of my house for two years or three.

"The common people will have too much power in their hands.

"I fear the New Englandmen will turn into Goths and vandals and overrun this country." [3]

This last possibility was very much on the minds of some prominent congressmen. Edward Rutledge urged John Jay to return from New York as soon as possible. If he failed to come, Rutledge predicted that "ruin to some colonies will be the consequence." He dreaded "the idea of destroying all Provincial Distinctions and making every thing of the minute kind bend to what they call the good of the whole." This was simply a demagogic way of saying that "these Colonies must be subject to the government of the Eastern Provinces [New England]." Rutledge did not hesitate to spell out the full measure of his prejudices against New England. "I dread their overruling Influence in Council. I dread their low Cunning, and those leveling Principles which men without Character and Fortune in general possess, which are so captivating to the lower class of Mankind." [4]

But the independence men, particularly those "without doors," as

Continental Congressmen usually referred to the citizens of Philadelphia, were in no mood to tolerate delay. They were determined to destroy the old assembly and the charter, and establish a truly revolutionary government, which in turn would create the kind of revolutionary atmosphere in Philadelphia that would guarantee an overwhelming congressional majority for independence. Under orders from the independents, their followers in the assembly began to boycott it, and enough moderates were still frightened by threats of violence to make a quorum impossible.

On June 18, 108 members of the provincial conference of Pennsylvania met at Carpenters Hall. To make sure the voting went in the right direction, among the first motions carried was the rule that each county and the city of Philadelphia would have one vote each. This carried things rather far from the supposedly hallowed democratic principle of one-man-one-vote. It ignored the heavy proportion of the state's population in and around Philadelphia. But independence men predominated in the thinly populated western counties, and the arrangement guaranteed radical control of the conference.

On June 19, the delegates "resolved unanimously" in favor of the Congress's resolution of May 15 and declared the present government of the province "not competent to the exigencies of our affairs." It would be necessary to call a constitutional convention to form a new government. Without waiting around for this convention, the delegates gave the vote to every militia volunteer who was twenty-one years of age and had resided a year in the colony and paid his taxes. They then proceeded to a frontal assault not only on the old assembly but on its electors. Anyone declared an enemy of America by any county or city Committee of Inspection or Safety would not be allowed to vote, and persons who had previously voted to elect the assembly must take an oath vowing that they did not "bear allegiance to George III" and would not oppose the government established by the convention or any measure adopted by Congress "against the tyranny attempted to be established in these colonies by the court of Great Britain."

This oath disfranchised most moderates in Pennsylvania—which was precisely what the radicals wanted to do. They then progressed from Machiavellianism to idiocy by declaring that no one could be elected to the convention who did not declare his belief in the doctrine of the Trinity and the divine inspiration of the Scriptures.

The resolutions of the provincial conference made the independence men look as dangerous in fact as they had sounded in print. This impression was strengthened by a well-publicized poll of nearly 2,000 men in the four battalions of the city militia. Only four officers and twenty-five privates voted against independence. In two battalions, the vote was unanimous. The implied threat to the disarmed and already demoralized moderates was devastatingly clear.[5]

When the assembly of Pennsylvania adjourned for good on June 14, after once more failing to find a quorum, a bitter James Allen wrote in his diary that the "Tide [for independence] is too strong." With his wife and three children, he loaded his "Chariot, Phaeton, and Sulky" and departed for his country home in Northampton County.[6]

In some parts of America, the resolution calling for new governments and its explosive preamble began to produce that torrent for independence which caused such exultation in John Adams' letters. From Virginia, an ecstatic Richard Henry Lee wrote that "the British flag on the capitol was immediately struck and the Continental [Grand Union] flag hoisted in its room. The troops were drawn out, and we had a discharge of artillery and small arms." On June 14 and 15, the Connecticut and New Hampshire assemblies instructed their delegates to vote for independence.

Elsewhere, things were not so torrential. The Delaware assembly could not bring itself to mention the word independence, and simply authorized its delegates to adopt "such other measures" as they found necessary for "promoting the liberty, safety, and interests of America." Maryland remained paralyzed by a fear of a slave–poor white insurrection along the Eastern Shore. But the gentleman delegates did muster the courage to request Royal Governor Eden to leave the colony. They assured him that he could take with him all his papers, baggage, and furniture. They also resolved that the prayers for the King would be omitted in the churches "until our unhappy differences are ended." The Marylanders attempted to withdraw their delegates from Philadelphia with a guarantee that Congress would not discuss independence until they returned. Congress refused because, as John Adams put it, "it is now become public in the colonies that those questions [independence and confederation] are to be brought on the first of July." [7]

But Maryland and Delaware were to play only peripheral roles in the drama of the year 1776. The crucial states were New York, New Jersey, and Pennsylvania. In these, independence was still no torrent. It was closer to a trickle. The New York provincial congress responded to the Adams-inspired call for the creation of a new government by setting a date for the election of a new congress. It added that when and if a new government was formed, it would remain in force "until a future peace with Great Britain shall render the same unnecessary." When the General Committee of Mechanics in Union of New York declared it would give them "the highest satisfaction" if the state's delegates voted for independence, the provincial congress thanked the workingmen for their warm attachment "to the Cause of Liberty," but advised them that they had no authority to tell the state's elected representatives what to think about important issues.[8]

When the provincial congress got a letter from the New York congressional delegation on June 10 asking for instructions, John Jay took charge of the strategy of delay. He offered a series of resolutions "on the subject of independence" which sounded marvelous but guaranteed the state's immobility. The "good people" of New York, Jay insisted, had as yet not declared their minds on the subject, and for the moment it would be inconvenient to ask them about it. Instead, let the people write to their delegates in Congress directly. They might also give the provincial congress power to commit New York to independence and confederation. The congress adopted these resolutions and then voted to keep them a secret. There was no need to publish them until after the forthcoming election. Thus their prophecy of "a future peace with Great Britain" remained unchallenged. Meanwhile, Jay informed the state's delegates in Philadelphia that they did not have the authority to vote for independence because the people had not spoken and it would be "imprudent" to ask them about it "lest it should create a division." [9]

In New Jersey, where the strength of the independence party was to become crucial for the survival of the Revolution before the end of 1776, a new provincial congress, elected on May 28 in response to the call from Philadelphia, had a majority in favor of separation. When Governor William Franklin called a meeting of the old assembly, the congress voted 38 to 11 to order the people to disregard the summons and arrested the popular governor. Acutely aware that they were dealing with the son of the most distinguished living American, they offered him a chance to choose neutrality on his farm near Burlington. Franklin defied them, and he was declared "an enemy to the liberties of this country" and deported to Connecticut. The provincial congress then chose new delegates to Congress and instructed them to join in declaring "the United Colonies" independent of Great Britain—if necessary. They then began drafting a constitution.

This rush toward independence produced an alarming leakage in the attendance of the delegates at the New Jersey provincial congress. By the end of June, there were only thirty-five of the original sixty-five members sitting. This was hardly surprising. In many counties, the total vote cast for the independence slate did not exceed a hundred. Independence had a shaky foundation in New Jersey, and many delegates were obviously aware of it.[10]

In Philadelphia, Thomas Jefferson was toiling through many revisions of the Declaration of Independence. Franklin, the man who would have been given the job if he did not have a loyalist son under arrest in New Jersey, tactfully stayed out of it. John Adams, ruefully recognizing the vast unpopularity he had accumulated in the bruising debates and maneuvers over and around the issue of independence, had handed the job to Jefferson. The other two committee members, Robert R. Livingston of New York and Roger Sherman of Connecticut, were eliminated for more practical reasons. Livingston did not want a declaration of independence, and Sherman was no writer. But the larger reason was geography. Adams pushed Jefferson into the job for the same reason that he had proposed George Washington as commander in chief of the American army. He knew the deep suspicion and dislike which many men from the middle states and the South felt for him in particular and New Englanders in general. A declaration of independence emanating from Virginia, on the other hand, had an almost irresistible appeal.

Later, Jefferson said that he consulted "neither book nor pamphlet." He insisted that he had had no desire to find out "new principles or new arguments never before thought of." The declaration "was intended to be an expression of the American mind and to give to that expression the proper tone and spirit called for by the occasion."

This statement blurs the skill with which Thomas Jefferson made the Declaration of Independence both a statement of separation from England and a vehicle for social change. There was no single American mind in 1776 any more than such an entity exists today. If the Declaration had expressed the American mind as personified by John Jay of New York, Robert Morris of Pennsylvania, or Landon Carter of Virginia, it would have become a very different document from the one produced by the vibrant pen and soaring mind of Thomas Jefferson. A leader of the fight against aristocratic privilege and the established church in Virginia, Jefferson was in wholehearted agreement with his friend John Adams "that a more equal liberty than had prevailed in other parts of the earth must be established in America."

What concerned Jefferson and Adams and like-minded men was the way the American tradition of deference to leading families was tending to create a complacent arrogance and opulence that was perilously close to the style of the English aristocracy. Great landowners such as the Carters of Virginia and the Philipses of New York were making thousands of pounds a year from rents. Even more alarming were the landholdings of the English proprietors such as Lord Baltimore in Maryland, the Penns in Pennsylvania, Lord Fairfax in Virginia, Lord Granville in North Carolina. Exercising old land claims from the seventeenth century, these noblemen were reaping huge rents from Americans in these colonies. In Maryland and Pennsylvania, many Americans, such as the Allen family, had grown rich as their spokesmen.[11]

This was the social danger at which Jefferson struck in the Declaration. It was what John Adams was talking about when he told Patrick Henry it was time to bring "down nearer to the confines of reason and moderation . . . the insolent domination of a few, a very few, opulent monopolizing families." Let "the dons, the bashaws, the grandees, the patricians, the sachems, the nabobs, call them by what names you will . . . sigh and groan, and fret and sometimes stamp and foam and curse." This was the direction that America's revolution must take.[12]

So Jefferson, in his first draft, wrote: "We hold these truths to be sacred and undeniable; that all men are created equal and independent; that in that equal creation they derive rights inherent & inalienable, among which are the preservation of life, & liberty, & the pursuit of happiness." Most previous declarations of American rights had listed "life, liberty, and property" as the three primary concerns. Jefferson had no interest in abolishing the right to property; he was no proto-Marxist. He agreed with John Adams, who advised Massachusetts politicians, struggling to frame a new government, that "power always follows property . . . Such is the frailty of the human heart, that very few men who have no property have any judgement of their own."

What Jefferson and Adams were seeking was a containment of the power of property. Thus Adams sharply rejected the notion of one Massachusetts politician that the number of votes a citizen might be allowed to cast should be proportionate to the property he held. Jefferson, no more than Adams, wished "to confound and destroy all distinctions, and prostrate all rights to one common level." But there was in his view of America's future a more resounding optimism than John Adams could muster from his Puritan soul. So the Declaration grandly declared not for property but for the pursuit of happiness and announced that the purpose of the new government should be "the safety and happiness" of its citizens.[13]

Almost as interesting, from a psychological point of view, is Jefferson's opening line in his rough draft: "When in the course of human events it becomes necessary for a people to advance from that subordination in which they have hitherto remained . . ." Here was the underlying, the central cause of the American Revolution, stated so nakedly that Jefferson, after consulting with the members of his committee, changed it to read, "When in the course of human events it becomes necessary for one people to dissolve the political bands which have connected them with another . . ."

To reject openly the idea of subordination to the King would have been psychologically disastrous. It would have awakened the very realistic fears in the minds of many moderate congressmen that Americans might begin rejecting subordination all the way down the line. It was more effective psychologically to speak of dissolving political bands. The same astuteness—whether Jefferson's or the consultation of the entire committee we do not know—is evident in another change. Jefferson had originally written that Americans were to "assume among the power of the earth the equal and independent station to which the laws of Nature & of Nature's God entitle them." This was changed to "separate and equal station." Finally, Jefferson had written that "a decent respect to the opinions of mankind requires that they should declare the causes which impel them to the change." This last word was altered to read "separation." [14]

Again, the psychological difference is immense. Separation stressed the crucial fact driven home so relentlessly by Tom Paine in *Common Sense*—the three thousand miles of ocean between England and America, the differences between the Old World and the New, the contradiction of an island attempting to rule a continent. These changes reveal how sensitive Jefferson and his fellow committeemen were to the emotional problems surrounding the word "independence."

In the rest of the document, Jefferson followed the trail blazed by the numerous pamphleteers who accused the British of plotting to destroy America's freedom. But he added to it a touch from Tom Paine by blaming it all on George III. In twenty fierce indictments, he tried to kill the father of the country once and for all. But in these accusations, which ranged from erecting "a multitude of new offices," and sending "hither swarms of officers to harass our people & eat out their substance" to "suspending our own legislatures" and "imposing taxes on us without our consent," Jefferson still displayed his reformer's zeal. The twentieth indictment was a ferocious attack on the slave trade, which Jefferson also blamed on George III.

The King had "prostituted his negative for suppressing every legislative attempt [by Americans] to prohibit or restrain this execrable commerce." He was now "exciting those very people to rise in arms among us, and to purchase that liberty of which *he* has deprived them, by murdering the people upon whom *he* also obtruded them."

Jefferson closed with another shrewd psychological touch. He acknowledged the affection which many Americans still felt for the mother country. "We might have been a great people together," he wrote. The Americans had asked the British people for help. But they had not listened. So "we must endeavor to forget our former love for them, and to hold them as we hold the rest of mankind, enemies in war, in peace friends." [15]

On June 29, Congress learned that a British fleet of an estimated 150 ships had been sighted off Sandy Hook. They were transporting the army that Washington had driven out of Boston. Congress knew that another fleet and army was attacking Charleston, South Carolina. By now, they also knew the dimensions of the disaster in Canada. Jefferson's completed draft lay on the president's table. But no instructions to vote for independence had yet come from New York's provincial congress. Nor did the Pennsylvania delegation show any sign of listening to the agitation for independence in the streets of Philadelphia. Voting for the provincial convention that would form a new government was not scheduled until July 8. So the assembly was still the legal government of Pennsylvania, and their final instructions to their delegates, while removing the prohibition against voting for independence, carefully refrained from using the word. Instead, they were equivocally advised to "concur with the other delegates in Congress" in "such measures as shall be judged necessary for promoting the liberty, safety, and interests of America." A majority of the Pennsylvania delegation, still led by John Dickinson, insisted that the situation called for delay, not an immediate declaration.

At nine o'clock on July 1, with the temperature in the State House soaring toward the nineties, the delegates took their places and began the day with the usual accumulation of trivia. There were letters from George Washington, from Benedict Arnold, from Philip Schuyler, from the provincial convention in New Jersey, the convention of New

Hampshire—fourteen letters in all, dealing with matters large and small. Not until noon did Congress "resolve itself into a committee of the whole to take into consideration the resolution concerning independence." John Hancock surrendered the mace with which he presided at the president's chair and took his seat among the congressmen. Bulky Benjamin Harrison of Virginia became chairman of the committee of the whole. Everything said now was off the record. The goal was to take the sense of Congress, to thrash out differences, before voting on the record, where the public might see more than Congress wanted it to see.

The first speaker was John Dickinson. In a plum-colored coat, gaunt and trembling with emotion, he elaborated the last argument of the moderates—independence was premature. They had not yet heard from France. How did they know what their ancient enemy was up to? To declare independence was to put themselves irremediably beyond the protection of Great Britain. It would commit Americans to irrevocable war—a war that would ruin them and England financially. France would rise on the ruins. Let not the gentlemen from Boston be so confident that their city has escaped the scourge of war. A British fleet could burn it in a day. The Indians will ravage the frontiers of Pennsylvania, Virginia, the Carolinas, New York. Worse, the Americans did not even have a government. In an obvious reference to what was happening in Pennsylvania, Dickinson declared they were "destroying our house in winter and exposing a growing family before we have got another shelter." Finally, Dickinson flung a prophecy at New England. In twenty or thirty years, he predicted, if they rushed rashly into independence without first agreeing to a workable government, they would find the thirteen colonies splitting up—and he predicted that there would be "a separate commonwealth to the northward" with a "boundary on the Hudson River." [16]

A summer storm mounted above Philadelphia as John Adams rose to reply to Dickinson. He would have preferred to let Richard Henry Lee defend his own resolution, but Lee was in Virginia. While thunder rumbled and lightning flashed, Adams denied Dickinson's contentions and declared that a declaration of independence was not merely a necessity, it was—it would be—the salvation of America. Jefferson later recalled that Adams spoke "with a power of thought and expression that moved us from our seats." But because he spoke in a committee of the whole, no record was made of his words. Adams himself seemed to dismiss his performance. A few days later, he said he had merely repeated what had been "hackneyed in that room before, a hundred times for six months past." This was hardly an accurate statement. Six months before, no one dared mention the word independence in Congress.[17]

In the middle of Adams' speech, the New Jersey delegates, all determined independence men, led by imperious John Witherspoon, president of Princeton, arrived. They asked Adams to repeat his arguments for their benefit. He did so—a pro forma performance if there ever was one. The New Jersey men knew perfectly well how they were going to vote. John Witherspoon declared himself in full agreement with Adams' assertion that the colonies were ripe for independence. Looking at the New York delegation, he added, "Some colonies are rotten for the want of it."

It was hardly the kind of unanimity that Congress needed or wanted, and Benjamin Harrison hastily called for a vote. One by one the states were polled. The results were dismaying. The four New England states, New Jersey, Virginia, North Carolina, and Georgia voted for separation. But New York abstained. Delaware's two-man delegation, considered a certainty, divided, and Pennsylvania and South Carolina voted no.[18]

Disaster confronted the independence movement. Without Pennsylvania, New York, and South Carolina, a vote for a declaration would be suicide. Edward Rutledge temporarily rescued the situation by suggesting that an official vote be postponed until the following day. A night of frantic negotiation ensued. With great reluctance, Rutledge and the South Carolina delegates agreed to change their vote for the sake of unanimity. John Dickinson and his followers were told that they no longer represented the people of Pennsylvania. With even greater reluctance, they agreed. Tomorrow, Dickinson and Robert Morris would stay home. The Pennsylvania delegation would then vote for independence, three to two. A post rider was sent rushing to Delaware to find Caesar Rodney, the third member of the state's delegation. Much has been written about Rodney's ride through storm and wind and rain to reach Congress the next morning. But practically nothing has ever been said about what he was doing in Delaware in the first place. He was rallying local militia against a loyalist uprising.[19]

The next morning, the performance for the benefit of the public was played with historic smoothness. Rodney stumbled in, covered with mud, to vote Delaware into the independence column. South Carolina and Pennsylvania also joined the parade with majority votes. Only New

York continued to abstain. But the independence men told themselves this was a small cloud, at best. Exultantly, John Adams predicted that the second day of July would be "the most memorable Epocha in the history of America." This same day, across the river in Burlington, New Jersey, the state's provincial congress was adopting a new constitution by a vote of 26 to 9. The constitution widened voting rights but stipulated that no one could be elected to the assembly unless he was worth £500, and no one could serve on the governor's council unless he was worth £1,000—not exactly an endorsement of the Jefferson-Adams drive for equality. Most significant, the provincial congress stated that in the event of a reconciliation with England, the new constitution was null and void. So much for the torrent of independence in the state that would shortly become the cockpit of the Revolution.[20]

To Jefferson's great chagrin, the Continental Congress edited his Declaration rather severely. They eliminated most of his reproof to the English people for failing to join the Americans in a march to greatness. The congressmen could see no point in alienating what they still fondly believed was substantial support for America in the mother country. In pursuit of this illusion, they lost a chance to make a strong appeal to moderates and loyalist Americans.

Congress threw out completely Jefferson's indictment of George III for imposing slavery on America. In his old age, Jefferson claimed that this last excision was made because South Carolina and Georgia objected to it, and some northern states, who had participated in the slave trade, "felt a little tender" on the subject. Since the discussion took place in the committee of the whole, we have nothing but an old man's memory to rely on—and when Jefferson remembered this episode, he was anxious to remind Americans that they all shared in the responsibility for the continued existence of slavery.

It seems at least as probable that the charge was excised because it was patently ridiculous. To have accused George III of being responsible for the continued existence of slavery in America would have drawn hoots of laughter from every intelligent Englishman, and at least as much derision from American loyalists and moderates. On this point, Jefferson let his reformer's zeal—his desire to make the Declaration a blueprint for the changes he wanted in American society—distort his judgment.[21]

The final version of the Declaration of Independence was approved by Congress on July 4. The power of the document's prose outshone the date on which independence was voted, exploding John Adams'

hyperbolic prediction about July 2. Contrary to popular versions of the
nation's birthday (with or without music), no bells rang, and nobody
signed the Declaration on July 4. Not until August 2, when it was
"engrossed on parchment," according to the orders of Congress, did an
unceremonious and haphazard signing begin. Some members did not
get around to putting their names on it until September.

On July 8, the Declaration of Independence was read to the public
in the Philadelphia State House yard. The selection of this date was no
accident. It was the day that delegates were to be chosen for the Pennsylvania state convention, and the purpose was to reinforce the grip of
the radical independents and inspire their supporters. Christopher
Marshall, a fervent independence man, told his diary, "There were
bonfires, ringing bells with other great demonstrations of joy upon the
unanimity and agreement of the Declaration." A more moderate eyewitness, Nicholas Biddle, saw things a little differently. "There were
very few respectable people" among the crowd, he noted, and he suspected that among this minority were a number who were "much opposed" to the Declaration.[22]

The vote on July 8 showed anything but unanimity in Pennsylvania.
An extraordinary number of Pennsylvanians declined to swear an oath
abandoning their allegiance to George III and approving the destruction of the old assembly and the charter—an oath they had to take in
order to vote. Unwittingly, the independence men had created a refer-
endum on these issues, and the results were ominous. In a state with a
population of almost 300,000, only 6,000 voters went to the polls. With
the widened voting rights and a presumed enthusiasm for independence, the total should have been closer to 60,000. So much for the torrent of independence in the state that was the heart of the Union.[23]

The convention that met a week later was dominated by the radicals. Benjamin Franklin sat as president, lending his prestige to the
gathering. Astronomer and mathematician David Rittenhouse also participated. But neither of these Philadelphia geniuses seems to have exerted much influence on the proceedings. If they did, the results were
no tribute to their political judgment. Most of the engineering was in
the hands of James Cannon and Timothy Matlack. In the background
were Dr. Thomas Young and Thomas Paine.

It was the only time in the entire American Revolution when radicals dominated a government. They demonstrated their extreme distrust of power by emasculating the executive branch. Instead of a governor, there was a revolving council of fifteen. There was only one

house in the legislature, which was to be elected annually. Oddest of all was the provision that for seven years no change could be made in the constitution. Then a council of censors was to be elected to examine the record and decide whether the constitution should be amended.

The new revolutionary government of Pennsylvania appalled John Adams and many other men. A North Carolina congressman called it a beast without a head and said it made the mob the second branch of the legislature. One Pennsylvanian told a friend in the army that Paine and company had made the state "ridiculous in the eyes of the world." Moderates, conservatives, crypto-loyalists, and even many independents soon united in opposition to the new government. More than a few of them were probably thinking—though few dared to say it—that if this was what independence produced, for God's sake bring on the peace commissioners.[24]

Throughout New England and Virginia, the Declaration of Independence was greeted with acclamations. In South Carolina, there were all the externals of celebration. It arrived, by happy coincidence, on the day that the battered British fleet and army finally departed from Charleston Harbor. But behind the church bells and the parades, many men were still dubious about the wisdom of the step. These included South Carolina's delegates to the Continental Congress. They reported their decision to vote for independence in almost incredibly evasive fashion. It took them seven days to find the nerve to write a letter. For the first few paragraphs, they discussed trivia, such as resolutions of Congress in regard to the state's regiments and naval forces. Then, "enclosed also," they wrote, "are some of the occasional resolutions and a very important Declaration which the King of Great Britain has at last reduced us to the necessity of making."

Henry Laurens later recalled how he joined in a "procession for Promulgating the Declaration." He happened to be in mourning for a son who had recently died. It suited his mood. He saw the occasion as a "solemn and . . . awful renunciation of a union which I, at the hazzard of my life and reputation, most earnestly strove to conserve and support. In truth, I wept that day, as I [had] done for the melancholy catastrophe which caused me to put on black clothes—and felt much more pain. I thought and openly declared that in my private opinion, Congress had been too hasty in shutting the door against reconciliation."[25]

In New York City, at 6 P.M. on July 9, Washington had the Declaration read before each brigade of his army. The troops marched to their barracks—and the New York mob took charge of the celebration. Soldiers and citizens had been frequenting the public houses "to testify to our joy" for the previous several days. A huge crowd rampaged through the city, breaking the windows of prominent loyalists and shouting defiance to the British fleet in the harbor and the army on Staten Island.

Someone pointed to the massive equestrian statue of George III in the middle of Bowling Green. The King wore the dress of a Roman emperor. To emphasize his royalty, the statue was larger than life-size and was covered with gold leaf from the foot of the horse's hooves to the crown of laurels on the King's head. Sons of Liberty vaulted the iron fence around the statue and looped ropes around the horse's neck and belly and legs and around the King's throat and waist. Eager hands seized the ropes and began tugging. With an enormous crash, the fifteen-foot sculpture toppled to the ground. With great deliberation, one man sawed off the King's head. The business was done with scarcely a shout or even a sound from the crowd. They were in the grip of emotions that could not be expressed by words or noise.[26]

Thus the father of his country met metaphorical death at the hands of his American sons. But the army tents whitening the hillsides of Staten Island and the forest of man-of-war masts in the water around them suggested a very real possibility that George III had the power to rise from the grave and severely distress his slayers.

XXII

Everything Now
Begins to Look
Extremely Serious

Aboard the British flagship *Eagle* in New York Harbor, Lord Howe's secretary, Ambrose Serle, was predictably outraged by the Declaration of Independence. It confirmed what this very typical Englishman had believed for some time—the rebellion was the plot of a faction who had been aiming at independence all along. "The Congress have at length thought it convenient to throw off the Mask," Serle informed his journal. "Their Declaration of the 4th of July . . . is founded upon such Reasons only, as proved that Independence to have been their Object from the Beginning." Serle was particularly incensed by the Declaration's attack on George III. "A more impudent, false and atrocious Proclamation was never fabricated by the Hands of Man," he declared. "Hitherto, they have thrown all the Blame and the Insult upon the Parliament and ministry: now they have the audacity to calumniate the King and People of Great Britain." [1]

Serle's dudgeon no doubt rose higher when he learned that his boss, Lord Howe, remained determined to negotiate a settlement. His brother, the general, after eighteen months in America, was considerably less inclined to talk peace. He told the admiral that he considered the announcement of the peace commission a waste of time. Only after the defeat of the rebel army entrenched in New York and Long Island would there be any hope of effective negotiations. But Lord Howe was a stubborn man, and he declined to take his brother's advice. On Saturday, July 13, he sent ashore the first lieutenant of the *Eagle* with dispatches addressed to the Royal Governors of New Jersey, Pennsylvania, Maryland, Virginia, North Carolina, and South Carolina, announcing the appointment of himself and the general as peace commissioners and enclosing a proclamation for them to publish. There is something almost pathetic about this gesture. Not one of these Royal Governors still governed; only one, Pennsylvania's John Penn, who had declared himself a neutral, even remained on the soil of his colony. But Howe's instructions forbade him even to address a letter to illegal rebel assemblies or their elected officials.[2]

In an attempt to ignore the Declaration of Independence, Howe dated his letters and the proclamation "Eagle, off the coast of the Province of Massachusetts Bay, June 20th, 1776." Howe was well aware that there was no real point in writing letters to the Royal Governors. He left everything unsealed, so that the Americans at Perth Amboy could read them and forward them, he hoped, to the Continental Congress. He included in his packet letters to Benjamin Franklin and several other Americans. Howe sent a frigate to Rhode Island with similar letters addressed to the governors of New England. The American commander in Perth Amboy, Brigadier General Hugh Mercer, accepted the packet from the *Eagle's* lieutenant, and invited him to stay for breakfast.

Meanwhile, Howe sent another lieutenant under a flag of truce to New York with a letter addressed to George Washington. This lieutenant's reception was not so polite. As his boat approached the tip of Manhattan, he was hailed by three American guard boats and ordered to lay to and state his business. The lieutenant said he was trying to deliver a letter.

The colonel in command of the guard boat asked the lieutenant to whom the letter was addressed. He replied, "To George Washington, Esquire." The colonel thought this address was improper, and ordered the lieutenant's boat to wait while he went ashore for instructions. A few minutes later, he returned with Joseph Reed, now the adjutant general of the American army. The British lieutenant bowed courteously, doffed his hat, and said, "I have a letter, sir, from Lord Howe to Mr. Washington."

"Sir," Colonel Reed replied, "we have no person here in our army with that address."

"Sir," the British officer replied, "will you look at that address?" He took the letter from his pocket and handed it to Reed, who promptly handed it back to him.

"I cannot receive that letter," he said.

"I am very sorry and so will be Lord Howe," said the lieutenant.

Reed nodded politely. "Why, sir, I must obey orders."

"Oh yes, sir, you must obey orders, to be sure."

Reed gave the lieutenant some letters from British prisoners in New York, bowed, and pulled away. The lieutenant started to return to the *Eagle,* but suddenly put about and overtook Reed's boat again to ask him how Washington should be addressed.

"You are sensible, sir," Reed replied, "of the rank of General Washington in our army?"

"Yes, sir, we are. I'm sure Lord Howe will lament exceedingly this affair, as the letter is quite of a civil nature and not a military one. He laments exceedingly that he was not here a little sooner." [3]

The lieutenant's return with the undelivered letter was a blow to Lord Howe. It produced another explosion of indignation from his secretary, Ambrose Serle. "So high is the Vanity and the Insolence of these Men!" he fulminated in his journal. "The Truth is, the Punctilio of an Address would never have retarded the Reception of a Letter from a Person with whose high Rank and Commission they were well acquainted, and whose Bravery and Honor were so well known every where; if their Minds had been in the least disposed to the Duties of Humanity, Law, and Allegiance . . ." [4]

But Lord Howe refused to give up. A few days later, Washington sent General Howe a letter, complaining about the treatment of American prisoners in Canada. General Howe replied, addressing the letter to "George Washington, Esq., &ca, &ca." This letter too was refused. But the British used this refusal as a pretext to ask if "General Washington" would consider talking with Lieutenant Colonel James Patterson, the adjutant general of the British army. Washington said he would be perfectly willing to do so, and hopes for peace momentarily soared. Washington received Patterson in his full-dress uniform at the handsome Kennedy house, No. 1 Broadway. A guard of honor opened ranks as the British officer appeared. A light lunch and bottles of wine awaited the two soldiers inside.

Patterson declined the food and drink, and concentrated on trying to explain away the "Esq., &ca, &ca." He said it was often used in diplomatic correspondence when a man's precise rank or title was in doubt. Washington told him there was no doubt whatsoever about his correct title and noted that "etcetera etcetera" could mean "anything—or nothing." The American commander then discussed in rather warm terms the reports he had received of American prisoners being mistreated in Canada. Patterson said that the Canadian army was outside the Howes' jurisdiction, but assured Washington that the Howes would do everything in their power to correct the situation.

Patterson then gingerly approached the possibility of Lord Howe's talking peace with Washington. He tried to use the Howe name as clear proof that the King wanted peace. The Howes had no connections to the hated ministry, and presumably Washington knew their strong affection for America. Washington's reply was discouraging. He said he had no power to negotiate with any representatives of Great Britain. He was a soldier acting under orders of the Continental Congress. Moreover, as far as he knew, the Howes had no real power to make peace. All they could do was "grant pardons." The Americans felt they had committed no fault in defending their indisputable rights and therefore "wanted no pardons." [5]

Patterson returned to have dinner with the Howes aboard the *Eagle* and report the almost total failure of his mission. As self-righteous as ever, Ambrose Serle wrote in his diary, "There is this reflection on our Side, that we strove as far as Decency and Honour could permit, or Humanity itself demand, to avert all Bloodshed & to promote an Accommodation."

The Howes were not so bellicose. They waited to see what Congress would do with Lord Howe's proclamation and what response private citizens, particularly Benjamin Franklin, might make to his personal letters. On July 25, Lord Howe learned that Congress had adopted a resolution ordering copies of his circular letters and declarations to be published in the newspapers, "that the good people of these United States may be informed of what nature are the commissioners, and what the terms, with . . . which the insidious Court of Britain has endeavoured to amuse and disarm them, and that the few, who still remain suspended by a hope founded either in the justice or moderation of their great King, may now, at length, be convinced that the valour alone of their country is to save its liberties." [6]

Five days later, Benjamin Franklin's reply to Lord Howe's letter was also published in the newspapers. Franklin began by saying he was sorry for Howe and could foresee for His Lordship nothing but "Pain to be sent upon so fruitless a business." Howe's peace commission was only one more proof of "that opinion of our Ignorance, Baseness, and

Insensibility, which your uninform'd and proud Nation has long been pleased to entertain of us; but it can have no other Effect than that of increasing our Resentments." Franklin made it clear that in his opinion war had already begun. "It is impossible we should think of submission to a Government, that has with the most wanton barbarity and cruelty burnt our defenseless Towns in the midst of Winter and is even now bringing Foreign Mercenaries to deluge our Settlements with Blood. These atrocious Injuries have extinguished every remaining spark of Affection for that Parent Country we once held so dear."

In a neat psychological turn, Franklin declared that even if the Americans could forget and forgive these injuries, it was impossible for the British "to forgive the People you have so heavily injured. You can never confide again in those as Fellow Subjects, and permit them to enjoy equal Freedom, to whom you know you have given such just Cause of lasting Enmity. And this must impel you, were we again under your Government, to endeavour the breaking our Spirit by the severest Tyranny, and obstructing, by every means in your Power, our growing Strength and Prosperity." Franklin was probably thinking about Ireland. The British had pursued such a policy there since that unfortunate nation made the mistake of trusting England's promises of benevolent treatment when the Irish surrendered to them at the close of the previous century.

Franklin told Lord Howe there might be some possibility of a treaty between Britain and an independent America, but he was sure His Lordship had no power to negotiate one. Franklin was also convinced that Great Britain's "abounding pride and deficient wisdom" made such a negotiation impossible. With deep feeling that went beyond politics, Franklin reminded Howe of "the tears of joy that wet my cheek" when Howe gave him hopes during their negotiations in London early in 1775 "that a reconciliation might soon take place." Instead, he had found himself vilified as "the cause of the mischief I was labouring to prevent."

His esteem, even his affection, for Lord Howe, Franklin continued, "makes it painful for me to see you engaged in conducting a war," the purpose of which, to quote Howe's own letter, was "the necessity of preventing the American trade from passing into foreign channels." Franklin did not believe that "the obtaining or retaining of any trade, how valuable soever, is an object for which men may justly spill each other's blood." He considered the war against America "both unjust and unwise," and he was certain that "cool dispassionate posterity" will condemn to infamy those who advised it. He could only hope that when Lord Howe found a reconciliation hopeless on the terms he was permitted to propose, he would "relinquish so odious a command, and return to a more honourable private station." [7]

Ironically, while Lord Howe was losing this argument with Franklin by his naïve confession of Britain's chief interest, America's trade, his secretary, Ambrose Serle, was reaching a far different conclusion about that trade. "Events will shew," he informed his diary on July 27, "that our rage for Colonization, in Countries which yield exactly the same Produce with out own, has like the Spanish Colonization, done us more harm than good." By August 8, he was telling himself, "I almost wish that the Colonies had never existed. They have weakened our National Force; and are now a Force turned against us . . . They have been sapping the foundations of our Commerce for a long time, and are now intent (if possible) to demolish it entirely." [8]

On August 10, the ghost of an earlier attempt at peace appeared aboard the *Eagle*—Thomas Lord Drummond. He had returned from Bermuda, still technically a paroled prisoner of the American government. At dinner with Lord Howe, he gave him a summary of his aborted negotiations of last winter and spring. Lord Howe asked him to write out the set of propositions on which Drummond had based his talks. Howe saw that Drummond might be a way to communicate with George Washington, without capitulating to his demand to be addressed by his military title. Drummond might even be a way of breaking through the wall of silence Lord George Germain had built around Howe with his ridiculous instructions. Drummond could say things to which Howe might agree, he could deliver hints, details—such as the fact that the amount of money North felt he needed as a minmum to get his peace plan approved by Parliament was between 5 and 10 percent of the peacetime military budget, by no means an outrageous sum for a country as rich as America. In 1772–73, the cost of the Royal Army and Navy had averaged £3,500,000. Ten percent of this would cost the 2,250,000 Americans about seventy-five cents per person each year. [9]

On August 12, Lord Drummond sent Lord Howe "the sketch of the propositions referred to in my late conversations with Your Lordship, which propositions I have understood the colonies were disposed not many months ago to make a basis of a reconciliation with Great Britain." Lord Howe promptly responded. He thought the propositions "contained matter that upon a conference and cool discussion might be wrought into a plan of permanent union." He would therefore "with great satisfaction embrace the first opportunity that may be offered to talk with the Americans upon these grounds, to promote so desirable an event."

Drummond enclosed this letter with a copy of his propositions in a letter to Washington, and boarded a boat to deliver them in person. He wrote Washington that in the course of a conversation with Lord Howe he had realized "the powers he is vested with as well as his disposition for establishing an equitable and permanent peace are altogether misunderstood by the colonies." Drummond said he had showed Howe his propositions, and the admiral had "assured me he was willing to confer upon those grounds with any gentlemen of the greatest influence in the country." The Scot asked Washington for permission "to land at New York to go to Philadelphia in order to lay this matter before the general Congress." [10]

Washington and his aides let Lord Drummond sit out on the river for a long time while they debated what to do with him. They finally decided that he smelled of treachery and double dealing. Moreover, it was clear that Drummond had broken his parole, which forbade him to talk with anyone in arms against America, or even to go on board their ships. After hours on the water in the hot August sun, Lord Drummond got for his troubles a very stiff rebuke. Washington told him his "well-meant zeal . . . has transported you beyond that attention to your Parole, which comprehends the character of a man of Strict Honour." Thus Washington found himself "under the disagreeable Necessity of objecting to the mode of Negotiation proposed while Your Lordship's conduct appeared so exceptionable." He told Drummond he would forward the papers to the Continental Congress, and "the Result will be communicated as soon as possible." [11]

The next day, Washington sent the papers to John Hancock with a baffled comment. "I am exceedingly at a loss to know the Motives and Causes inducing a Proceeding of such a nature at this time and why Lord Howe has not attempted some Plan of Negotiation before." Washington's answer to his own question was a series of suspicions, the main one being that the British were procrastinating in the hope that the militia supporting the regular American army would grow weary and go home. But Lord Drummond refused to go away. On August 19, he was back with another letter. He begged Washington for a personal interview, so that he could explain away the parole problem. But Washington, more suspicious than ever, insisted again that Drummond had broken his word and declined to see him.[12]

Washington's attitude was in itself a summary of the impossible contradictions in which Lord Howe found himself trapped. A few days later, in a letter to his cousin Lund, the American commander succinctly pointed out these contradictions. First, he noted that the Howes now had between twenty and twenty-seven thousand men in their army. Yet Lord Howe was consistently painting himself as a "messenger of peace." If this was true, why was he "running the nation to some millions of pounds sterling" to make war? It seemed especially ridiculous to Washington that "before a blow is struck, they are willing to give the terms proposed by Congress before they, or we, had encountered the enormous expense that both are now run to." [13]

The real villains in this breakdown of communications were Lord George Germain and George III, with their restrictions on Howe's conduct. Another reason for the failure of this honest try for peace was Lord Drummond himself. In a letter that undoubtedly echoed prevailing American opinion, Joseph Reed wrote, "Lord Drummond does not seem to be a character of sufficient significance for such important business." At least as fatal to peace was the fact that the negotiation was conducted entirely between military men. Most of the British and most of the Americans were spoiling for a fight. Virtually admitting this— and at the same time the precarious state of the American army—Reed added, "As . . . our troops have arrived, I wish it [the negotiation] had not happened. The militia in three days will want to go home." [14]

Still Howe refused to quit. He wrote again to Bejamin Franklin and came close to disobeying his instructions by saying that he had enough power to settle with the colonists along the lines proposed in the last petition Congress sent to the King—the so-called Olive Branch Petition—in the summer of 1775. Franklin rejected this second letter even more bluntly than the first one. He told Howe that all talk of America submitting to Great Britain was futile. He might as well make the same suggestion to the French, because at one time British kings had ruled most of France.

While Lord Howe was fruitlessly negotiating, the results of George III's and Lord George Germain's strenuous efforts to make war gathered around him in New York Harbor. On August 1, Henry Clinton and the eight regiments he had picked up in North Carolina and led to the fiasco in Charleston Harbor returned to New York with several men-of-war. The ships looked more than a little weary, particularly Sir Peter Parker's flagship, *Bristol,* which limped in several days later minus its main- and mizzenmasts. On August 3, a small convoy of twenty-two warships and transports arrived, and on the twelfth, the main body of the expeditionary force—some 10,000 men, including 8,000 Hessians—arrived in over a hundred ships. General Howe now had close to 24,000 men, and in New York Harbor bobbed some four hundred transports and thirty men-of-war. It was the largest fleet ever seen in America and the largest army Great Britain had ever sent from her shores. Lord Howe and his brother were forced to consider the best way to use this magnificent war machine.

On August 20, the day Lord Howe received Franklin's second letter, all the captains in the fleet were ordered to report aboard H.M.S. *Eagle* for a consultation. In his journal, Ambrose Serle wrote, "Every thing now begins to look extremely serious." [15]

XXIII

Defenders of
Everything Dear
and Valuable

While the British commanders conferred, the Americans were living in a mixture of illusion and anxiety. Much of the illusion was in the lower ranks of the American army. From his camp on Long Island, Joseph Hodgkins, the Ipswich lieutenant in the Twelfth Massachusetts Regiment, wrote to his wife, "Our enemys are coming in almost every day and we expect that they will have 25,000 men when they al git in but I would not have you be uneasy about us for our numbers fair exceed theirs for we have 42,000 men now and they are coming in every day two brigades are coming from Philadelphia consisting of 53 battalions." Defending himself against a reproach from his wife for re-enlisting, Hodgkins echoed the continuing assumption that this would be a one-year war. "I think so much of this present campaign that I have not spent any time thinking about another."

Most Americans shared Hodgkins' opinion that "we have got pretty well fortified and I think they will meat with a warm reception." News that the British had been defeated at Charleston buoyed the spirits of the army when Washington announced the victory in general orders. Hodgkins told his wife, "Both fleet & army have been repulsed with grate loss by a small number of valient troops." [1]

Morale was also buoyed by good news from the back country of Virginia and the Carolinas. Three small armies of frontiersmen continued a tradition of victory that they had begun by defeating the

Shawnees in 1774. This time it was the much more formidable Cherokees, who were so totally defeated that all fears of an Indian onslaught
along the southern frontier vanished for the rest of the war. The
Creeks, the Choctaws, and other powerful tribes were intimidated by
the ruthless punishment meted out to the Cherokees. Their villages
and farms were burned, and they were forced to sue for peace on the
most humiliating terms, giving hostages for their good conduct and
ceding additional land to the victorious Americans.

From the Virginia tidewater came another piece of good news.
Early in July, Lord Dunmore had been driven from Gwynn's Island by
a cannonade from the shore. He loitered in the Chesapeake for a few
weeks trying to find another base, but hostility and gunfire met him
wherever he tried to land, and he finally sailed away in despair to join
the British in New York.

But the success of the main American army in New York was the
crucial factor in the continental struggle. At headquarters, anxiety, not
optimism, was the prevailing mood. George Washington was acutely
aware that his ranks did not approach the 42,000 men so confidently
numbered by Lieutenant Hodgkins. The regular American army—men
with some semblance of training and organization—barely exceeded
10,000 men. In theory, their numbers had been bolstered by calling out
some 19,000 militia. But the torrent for independence had somehow
missed half of these temporary soldiers, and they failed to march with
their companies. Those who responded to the call trickled into the
American camp throughout the summer, giving Washington no time to
train them or integrate them into his army.

On August 7, Washington had only 10,514 men fit for duty out of a
paper strength of 17,225. Hardly enough, he told Governor Jonathan
Trumbull of Connecticut, "to oppose an army of 30,000 experienced
veterans," especially when the Americans were so scattered—"some fifteen miles apart." [2]

On August 19, a head count ordered by Washington told him he
had 23,000 men. At this point, only three of fourteen militia regiments
promised by Connecticut's Governor Trumbull had arrived. On
August 26, Washington was forced to confess to John Hancock, the
president of Congress, that he did not know how many men he had
because of "the shifting and changing the regiments have undergone
of late." He believed his strength was "much the same . . . with the addition of nine Militia Regiments more from Connecticut averaging
about 350 men each." [3]

One reason for the uncertain strength of the American army was

visible in the journal of Second Lieutenant Isaac Bangs of the Second
Massachusetts Regiment. On July 14, he wrote, "Almost the whole regiment are sick with camp Distemper." On the twenty-fourth of the same
month, about half of his company were still "very low." This camp distemper, better known among the soldiers as the bloody flux, was dysentery. "Though it emaciates them very much yet it is not very mortal, as
not more than one in our regiment has died with this disorder," Bangs
noted. But no soldier with dysentery was a fighting man, and throughout the summer about 20 percent of Washington's troops were suffering from it. The problem was the primitive state of the American commissary and New York's foul water. The citizens of the town—those
who could afford it—never drank the water that came out of the public
pumps. They bought safe water from carts that toured the city.[4]

Another reason for illness in the army was a place called the Holy
Ground, named with fine New York irony because it belonged to Trinity Church. It was the city's red-light district. Again and again, the
officer of the day and his guard were summoned to break up riots in
this area. One New Englander in a letter to his wife described plunging
into "knots of men and women fighting, pulling caps, swearing, crying
'Murder!,' etc., [and hurrying] them off to the Provost Dungeon by half
dozens, there let them lay mixed till next day. Then some are punished
and some get off clear—Hell's work."

Harvard-educated Lieutenant Bangs visited the Holy Ground several times "out of curiosity." He thought "nothing could exceed them
[the whores] for impudence and immodesty; but I found the more I
was acquainted with them the more they excelled in their brutality."
Bangs found it "Strange that any man can so divest himself of Manhood as to desire an intimate connexion with these worse than brutal
Creatures. Yet it is not more strange than true that many of our
officers & soldiers have been so imprudent as to follow them . . . till
the Fatal Disorder seized them & convinced them of their error."[5]

Not only were the whores infecting as many as forty men in a single
regiment, they also were inclined to murder their customers. In the
previous week, Bangs wrote, two men had been killed by them and
another "castrated in a barbarous manner." The soldiers retaliated by
wrecking the houses where these acts of savagery took place.

Another American problem was alcohol. In general orders, Washington denounced the "gin shops . . . where liquors have been
heretofore retailed within or near the lines." They were forbidden to
sell another drop "to any soldier in the army," and the houses were to

be vacated and occupied by troops. Any soldier found "disguised with liquor"—Washington's eighteenth-century term for "drunk"—was to be punished "with the utmost severity." The general also ordered that "no sutler in the army shall sell to any soldier more than one-half pint of spirit per day." This final clause practically admitted the futility of Washington's prohibition campaign. Since the army condoned liquor to the point where sutlers were officially attached to regiments, it was next to impossible to regulate the amounts consumed. Who was going to testify against a sutler who sold more than the stipulated half pint?

Sheer exhaustion may have had something to do with the bad health of some soldiers. During most of the summer, when those fit for duty were little more than 7,000, Washington had set them the enormous task of fortifying New York Island (as Manhattan was usually called), Governor's Island, and Brooklyn Heights, which commanded the East River and the city of New York.

The men built no less than thirteen forts and batteries within the mile-long limits of the city itself, all equipped with cannon. North of the city were a half dozen more forts, including a formidable work where Gracie Mansion now stands. Every street leading from the river on either side of the city was barricaded, often with mahogany logs taken from West Indian cargo ships. City Hall Park, known as the Fields, or the Commons, was barricaded on all sides. A dozen other streets and squares were similarly obstructed, all with the purpose of making the city "a disputable field of battle" even if the British gained a foothold in it. Each of these forts involved immense efforts. Wells had to be dug in the larger ones, deep ditches dug around the outside, hundreds of spears sharpened and planted pointing outward from the works. Bricks made of turf were laid on the slopes of the raw earthworks to reinforce them.

On Brooklyn Heights, the effort was equally large. A strong fort was built at Red Hook on the westernmost tip of Long Island, its guns commanding the vital harbor waters on that flank. On the mile-long defense line from Wallabout Bay to the Gowanus marsh, three large forts and two redoubts were constructed. The largest, in the center of the line, was named Fort Greene, after Nathanael Greene, the commander on Long Island. A star-shaped structure mounting six cannon, its garrison consisted of an entire regiment. Deep ditches connected all the forts. For the better part of three months, a thousand men a day toiled on these defenses in the sultry summer heat. The working parties got so dirty they were issued double their usual ration of soap each day. More than once in their orders, Washington and other generals admitted that the work was "exceedingly heavy on the men." [6]

This emphasis on fortifications meant that the Americans were relying dangerously on the tactic that had seemingly served them so well at Bunker Hill—choosing a crucial site, fortifying it, and forcing the British to attack them in their entrenchments. Major General Charles Lee summed up this attitude when he told Congress that New York could be "made a most advantageous field of battle, so advantageous, indeed, that if our people behave with common spirit, and the commanders are men of discretion, it might cost the enemy many thousands of men to get possession of it." It did not seem to occur to Lee or anyone else that the British might have learned a very harsh lesson at Bunker Hill, and had no intention of repeating the mistake they made there. Worse, Lee, Washington, and most other American commanders had not been at Bunker Hill and did not realize that the British by no means displayed a lemming-like desire to attack the American entrenchments. The generals who had been there, particularly Israel Putnam, were inclined to glorify the results to boost their own reputations.

Washington and his lieutenants were aware that they were fortifying an island against an enemy with a formidable fleet. They knew that a shrewd general and an ambitious admiral might decide to land their army north of New York, along the Hudson, and come rampaging down on them. But the Americans convinced themselves that they had the guns and ingenuity to frustrate this possibility. From the Battery, for a mile along the Hudson shore, and from Paulus Hook on the Jersey shore, dozens of cannon bristled from the forts, ready to punish any ship that dared to come within range. Huge wooden obstructions called chevaux-de-frise were sunk in the river to block the channel. The combination was thought to be unchallengeable—until July 12.

On that day, five British ships—H.M.S. *Phoenix,* with forty-four guns, H.M.S. *Rose,* with twenty guns, the schooner *Trial,* and tenders *Charlotta* and *Shuldham*—appeared in New York's upper harbor with every sail hoisted and both tide and a southwest wind in their favor. Sandbags piled along the bulwarks protected their crews. At 4:10 P.M., as they drew opposite the city, the men-of-war opened fire. Their screaming round shot created chaos in New York. Women and children ran howling through the streets. With a tremendous crash, one American gun in the grand battery below Fort George exploded, killing six soldiers and mangling five others. The men working the gun had been so fascinated by the spectacle of the British ships they had forgotten to sponge the cannon, and when the next cartridge was rammed down, the powder had instantly ignited.[7]

Although signal guns had announced the British approach, more than half the American gunners were not at their posts, according to one disgusted Massachusetts officer. They were either drinking in the taverns or in their "usual place of abode"—the brothels of the Holy Ground. Many other soldiers, instead of manning the forts and batteries, ran along the shore watching the spectacle, arousing Washington to fury. The next day, he condemned their "weak curiosity," which, he said, "makes a man look mean and contemptible." [8]

By 4:30, the British ships had escaped the fire of the New York and New Jersey batteries unscathed. An hour later, they glided imperturbably past a similar cascade of metal from the guns of Fort Washington on northern Manhattan Island. The men-of-war took numerous balls through their rigging and one or two through their hulls, but only four men were wounded. The captain of the *Rose,* James Wallace, ordered a bowl of punch and a bottle of claret brought to the quarterdeck so he and his officers could toast their success. By the time the British anchored in Tappan Zee between Nyack and Tarrytown at 7 P.M., American illusions about the impregnability of their Hudson River defenses—and with it the entire theory of their defense of New York—had gone up in cannon smoke. The frigates and tenders had brushed aside the American underwater obstructions with ridiculous ease, and defied their batteries with impunity. If this could be accomplished by light ships, what would happen if the British moved up their battleships with their tiers of heavy guns that more than matched the Americans' land-based firepower?

Neither Washington nor anyone else in his army could bear to give up the strategy on which they had expended so many thousands of man-hours. Instead, militia was summoned from western Connecticut and from Westchester and Dutchess counties to guard the riverside. A brigade of militia from Massachusetts was ordered to reinforce them.[9]

Neither dysentery, venereal disease, liquor, the British navy, nor even the uncertain size of his army concerned Washington as much as the lukewarm attitude of New York's politicians toward the Revolution, and the alarming number of "internal as well as external enemies to contend with." When Washington arrived in New York, he was well aware, thanks to the caustic pen of Charles Lee, that the situation was, as the American commander later put it, "delicate." To assist him, Washington had persuaded Joseph Reed to return to the army as adjutant general. He told Reed that he feared he would "have a difficult card to play in this government [of New York]" and needed "your assistance and advice to manage it." [10]

Almost from the day he arrived in New York, on April 13, Washington had been forced to utilize all his tact and political skill to deal with the New York provincial congress. Unlike Lee's, his letters were models of politeness and deference. But beneath this velvet, the congress soon discovered there was a tough determination to take charge of the city. Under his firm pressure, the New York Committee of Safety soon banned all communication with the men-of-war in the harbor. Next, Washington persuaded the congress to appoint a local commander for the New York militia in the city. The provincial congress en masse had been attempting to exercise this command so that they could maintain maximum control over the situation. Once more the congress capitulated and assigned the job to Brigadier General John Morin Scott, an enthusiastic patriot, with the distinct understanding that he would serve under Washington.

But the rest of the state's militia generals remained outside Washington's control. Perhaps strangest of all was the authority the provincial congress gave to Brigadier General Nathaniel Woodhull, commander of the militia on Long Island. They authorized him to make "such dispositions of the Militia of your brigade, at any sudden invasion, as you, from time to time, shall think best, without delaying for directions from the Provincial Congress, Committee of Safety, or the Commander in Chief of the Continental forces of this colony." The fact that Woodhull was also president of the congress may have had something to do with this amazing grant of independence.[11]

As for the independence of the United States of America, Woodhull and the majority of his confreres in the congress continued to loathe the idea. With this attitude so dominant, it was hardly surprising that Washington got nowhere in his attempts to persuade the congress to crack down on the clandestine activities of loyalists in New York and on Long Island. In spite of the American commander's orders and constant patrols, the men-of-war in the harbor were still getting fresh food and frequent communications from the shore. As early as June 6, 1776, Governor Tryon had in his possession a thorough description of "the state of the forts and batteries and breastworks erected about the city of New York and Hudson River." [12]

The problem worried not only Washington but other general officers. Toward the end of June, four of his top generals submitted to

Washington a report in which they complained that the county committees on Long Island were frustrating their attempts to suppress the
loyalists. As fast as the army arrested them, the county committeemen
discharged them "on their giving bond as a security for their good behavior." This method, the generals said, was "very improper and inef-
fectual." They urged Washington to persuade the provincial congress
to do a better job and in the meantime to stop discharging loyalists
under arrest, no matter what the county committees said.[13]

Chief among these loyalists was Oliver De Lancey. Until the trouble
with England began, he was the most powerful politician in New York.
Since 1765, his family had dominated the assembly and aggregated to
themselves and their followers all the political plums worth picking. De
Lancey's wealth and power in New York were built on British connections, both in politics and in business. His sister Susanna had married a
British admiral, Peter Warren, who became a naval hero in earlier wars
with France. His late brother James was connected by marriage to the
Heathcotes, a powerful parliamentary family, and had been acting governor of New York for seven years. For twenty-one consecutive years,
Oliver De Lancey had been a member of the Governor's council. His
brother Peter was a formidable power in Westchester and was married
to the daughter of Cadwallader Colden, the lieutenant governor of
New York.

Partly because it was good politics, De Lancey had backed the first
American protests against British taxation and regulation. He publicly
declared he would spend the last cent he had to see American rights
and liberties secured. But he drew the line at armed resistance, and,
like most New Yorkers, was no friend of independence. Under much
prodding from Washington, the provincial assembly began summoning
people like De Lancey to appear before a special Committee of Seven
for interrogation. On the night of June 20, De Lancey left his handsome house in what was then a small village, Bloomingdale (in the
northwest corner of modern Central Park), hurried to the Hudson
River and a waiting rowboat, and within an hour or two was aboard the
Duchess of Gordon conferring with Governor Tryon.[14]

Not only was De Lancey's escape embarrassing to Washington, who
was supposed to be guarding Manhattan Island—it was a signal to
numerous wavering New Yorkers that the De Lanceys were choosing
the King's side. Not by accident did the Americans choose the following
day to reveal a powerful piece of anti-loyalist propaganda—a plot to
kidnap Washington, blow up the American magazines, and destroy the

one escape route from Manhattan, over Kingsbridge at the northern end of the island. The plot emerged from a crackdown on a group of counterfeiters in Cold Spring, Long Island, who had been reprinting paper money issued by the state of Connecticut. While in jail, one of the counterfeiters talked to two Continental Army soldiers who had been arrested for attempting to pass bogus bills. One of them, Thomas Hickey, was a member of Washington's guard. He boasted about a secret Tory corps organized with the help of money from Governor Tryon. More than seven hundred men were involved, including David Matthews, the mayor of New York, and several other members of Washington's guard.

The dimensions of this plot were so alarming the New York provincial congress never fully revealed them. Matthews was arrested and deported to Connecticut. Thomas Hickey was court-martialed, found guilty, and hanged. Rumors of the plot swept the city, and the New York mob took to the streets, beating and abusing loyalists luckless enough to fall into their hands.[15]

The rest of the conspirators were pardoned or ignored because, the provincial congress said, there was no law against treason to the embryonic United States of America. Only Hickey, who was tried under the articles of war, was liable to condign punishment. But the distinct lack of follow-through on the part of Washington and the congress suggests that they felt it was better to make an example of Hickey and play down the depth and breadth of loyalist feeling the plot revealed. Washington practically admitted as much in his report to the Continental Congress on the matter. He said he was hopeful that Hickey's "example will . . . deter others from entering into like traitorous practices." In the very next line, he refers to a resolve of the provincial congress denouncing "the disaffected on Long Island who have taken up arms." Washington "sent a party after them," but his men were unsuccessful. The loyalists "concealed themselves in a difficult Wood and morass." [16]

The Tory or Tryon plot, as it was alternately called, stimulated the voters to send to the provincial congress men ready to declare New York's support for independence. But enough waverers were still present to persuade the congress to approve a preamble lamenting the step as "a cruel necessity." Significantly, the president of the congress, Nathaniel Woodhull, declined to sign the document. It was a symptom of his personal reluctance—shared by so many of his fellow New Yorkers—to fight the kind of all-out war that Washington now saw was necessary.[17]

From the day the British fleet and army arrived in New York harbor, Washington had gone to work on the problem of how to frustrate and harass them. He put himself in William Howe's place, in command of an army which would soon number perhaps 30,000 men. Add to these the sailors in the fleet, and the British were faced with the problem of feeding some 60,000 men three meals a day. This was an enormous task when the men were fighting three thousand miles from home. From the intelligence reports he received during the siege of Boston, Washington knew better than anyone else in America the tons of food and the tens of thousands of pounds sterling the British were losing in the foul holds of their slow-moving supply ships. To force the enemy to rely as much as possible—perhaps exclusively—on the wretched salt beef and dried peas and tooth-cracking ship's bread from England would be a major step toward winning the war. The morale and the health of the regulars would inevitably suffer.

But how to achieve this goal? There was one obvious solution—a grim one. Staten Island and Long Island, which could not be defended with the limited number of men Washington had at his disposal, should be stripped of their livestock and grain immediately. Horses were particularly valuable to the enemy, Washington pointed out to the president of the provincial congress on July 3. It was practically impossible to ship them from England; most died en route. Without horses, the British artillery and supply wagons would be paralyzed, and this in turn would immobilize their army.[18]

Not until the first British ship arrived in the harbor was Washington able to get the provincial congress to agree to remove livestock from Staten Island. The man they appointed to do the job was so lackadaisical, Washington fired off a letter to Brigadier General Nathaniel Heard of New Jersey, ordering him to cross from Elizabethtown and take charge of the operation. But the New Jersey men were loath to invade a neighboring state, and dawdled until the very eve of the British landing on the island. The locals managed to drive most of their livestock into the woods. Fulfilling Washington's prophecy, the moment the British landed, they sent Cortlandt Skinner of New Jersey and other loyalists across the island buying stock and vegetables from the inhabitants.

Staten Island was a minor prize compared to Long Island, or "Nassau Island," as it was called in 1776. It contained between 80,000 and 100,000 head of horned cattle, and as many sheep. In Queens County alone there were 1,000 horses. The failure on Staten Island made Washington tougher about Long Island. He ordered a roundup of all

the cattle in Queens and Kings counties, and told local militia officers
to drive them east and north, as far away from the British as possible.
If they met any resistance from local Tories, they were to shoot the
animals without wasting time in argument.[19]

The Long Island militiamen, under the command of Nathaniel
Woodhull, simultaneous brigadier general and president of the provincial congress, declined to obey the general's order. They were not
under his direct command, thanks to the grant of independence that
the congress had made to Woodhull. Soon there was a committee on
Washington's doorstep, asking him to change his mind. Washington
"absolutely refused to retract" his order, reminding the committeemen
of "the unhappy consequences of not seasonably removing" the stock
from Staten Island.

The provincial congress, which had changed its name to the Convention of the Representatives of the State of New York, promised to
cooperate and borrowed $20,000 from Washington to finance the
operation. A week later, Nathaniel Woodhull informed Washington by
letter that they had changed their minds. He said removing the stock
would reduce the inhabitants to "the most deplorable and insuperable
difficulties and distresses." This was a nice way of saying it would cost
them a lot of money. He said it would take the greater part of the campaign to remove the 100,000 horned cattle and "a much larger number
of sheep and other stock." Instead, the convention had resolved to raise
900 militia, and order them to remove stock from places "which are
most exposed." If the British invaded the island with their army, it was
up to "Your Excellency" to "give a good account of them." This was
rather snide, coming from a fellow patriot.[20]

If Major General Charles Lee had received such a letter, he would
have exploded. But Washington really believed in the subordination of
military to civilian power. He wrote Woodhull a polite reply, hoping
that his halfhearted livestock roundup would "prove adequate." Early
in August, Washington again warned the New York politicians that the
enemy's army, "so largely augmented," was capable of seizing "the
whole stock on Long Island." He hoped the convention would not
"regret that they were not removed." The convention did not even
bother to answer this letter. Moreover, Woodhull used the same tactics
which had infuriated Charles Lee earlier in the year, and neglected to
sign his next letter to Washington, which discussed other business and
conspicuously omitted the matter of the cattle.

On the same day, President Woodhull quit the convention and put on his brigadier general's hat to take command of the Suffolk County militia and the cattle roundup. Before a single horse or cow was collected, Woodhull ordered two colonels to march some four or five hundred militia from Suffolk, Queens, and Kings counties to join the main American army at Brooklyn. This was an odd step to take, since it badly depleted the number of men available for Woodhull's all-important task. Perhaps by now Washington already smelled something fishy about Woodhull—and the whole convention for that matter. Their declension from lukewarm to cool coincided with Lord Howe's arrival and the circulation of his proclamation declaring his ardent desire for peace.

The prevalence of disloyalty in New York made some ranking American officers begin to wonder about the immense effort and alarming risks involved in defending the city. After the British navy proved they could run New York's batteries and proceed up the Hudson River at will, Adjutant General Joseph Reed told a friend, "I confess I do not see the propriety of risking the fate of America, which will much depend on that of this army and its military stores, to defend a city, the greater part of whose inhabitants are plotting our destruction." While Washington and the majority of his officers were still ready to gamble everything on a single battle, the cautious Reed was coming to a very opposite conclusion. "My opinion is, we should make it a war of posts, prolong, procrastinate, avoid any general action, or indeed any action, unless we have great advantages." [21]

Ominous as the situation appeared in New York, the news from New Jersey was even worse. The British army had scarcely landed on Staten Island when sixty men from the vicinity of Shrewsbury and Upper Freehold joined them. They reported there were five hundred more men in their neighborhoods ready to rise in support of the King the moment the Royal Army entered the state. Another forty-eight men crossed Raritan Bay from Perth Amboy. In Hunterdon County, a group of loyalists revolted against the revolutionary government and were suppressed only by superior force. In Monmouth County, it took four hundred militia to suppress another incipient counterrebellion.

The large contingent of New Jersey militia in the American army clamored to return to their native state. Washington was forced to yield to their demands. He dispatched 1,200 of them to Perth Amboy, under the command of Brigadier General Hugh Mercer of Virginia. The American plan called for a "Flying Camp" of 10,000 militiamen from Pennsylvania, Maryland, and Delaware in this little town at the mouth

of the Raritan River. They were supposed to defend the natural highway to Philadelphia and serve as a reserve for Washington's men if they
became hard pressed in New York.

This was one of those ideas that look marvelous on paper but in execution prove to be disastrous. For weeks, Maryland and Delaware sent
no militia to this post. The New Jersey men were no sooner in Perth
Amboy than they began fretting over the hot, dry July weather and
declaring that if they could not go home their harvests would be
ruined. By July 20, there was scarcely a single New Jersey militiaman in
Perth Amboy. They were replaced by 2,000 "Association" militiamen
from Philadelphia. Associators were volunteers, which made them, in
theory at least, better troops than the militiamen who were on the rolls
because the law required them to serve. Washington soon drafted the
Philadelphians into his New York army. Congress told the New Jersey
provincial congress to replace them with their state's militia.

The provincial congress issued a call, declaring that "the hour is
approaching, which will, in all human probability, decide the fate of
America. . . . Life, liberty, and property, all await the issue of the
present struggle. Arise, then, and exert yourselves!" Scarcely a man
responded to these noble words. On August 4, Hugh Mercer told
Washington that he only had 274 rank and file in his command. The
New Jersey provincial congress decided to adopt a desperate expedient—they divided the state's able-bodied men into two classes, each
of whom would serve alternate months. This was the kind of arrangement that would drive a general mad, but it persuaded the men to turn
out. Within a week, Mercer had nine regiments guarding the New Jersey shoreline from South Amboy to Fort Lee. More Philadelphia Associators also arrived, as well as troops from Delaware and Maryland,
bringing Mercer's strength to 5,000.[22]

But the troubles of the commander of the Flying Camp were by no
means over. The Philadelphia Associators soon became bored with digging fortifications around Perth Amboy. On August 4, Mercer was
lamenting that men were deserting not "singly, but by companies." The
men who stayed "were very abusive to their officers," and often refused
to obey their commands. A French engineer who was in charge of fortifying Perth Amboy wrote in near despair to a member of Congress
that the Americans were hopeless. They refused to dig trenches "until
they see the enemy upon them."

The "Cowardly infamous Spirit of Desertion," as it was called by the
New Jersey provincial congress, became so widespread that they passed

a law forbidding anyone to use ferries across the Delaware or the Hudson without a pass signed by a field officer. This device only prompted the recalcitrant militiamen to devise more ingenious ways of getting home. Epidemics of vague illnesses, such as sick headaches, stomach complaints, bad backs, and lame knees, swept the Flying Camp and harried officers signed passes to let the instant invalids go home.

While they were on duty, the members of the Flying Camp wreaked havoc on the surrounding countryside. They tore down fences for firewood, devastated corn and grain fields, raided hencoops, and generally made the civilians in eastern New Jersey pray for an early peace. One Philadelphia Associator noted a month after his regiment arrived in Perth Amboy that the countryside around the town "now exibeted an appearance meloncholly beyond description." When Continental Congressman Abraham Clark visited his home in Elizabethtown, he reported to a friend that "Staten Island hath not suffered from the British troops scarcely the tenth part of the damage this town hath from the Militia."

Although their own militiamen were by no means model soldiers, much of the New Jersey men's spleen was fastened on the Philadelphians. Toward the end of August, when most of them had either deserted or been released from duty, William Livingston, just elected New Jersey's governor, wrote a letter to a friend lamenting the lack of discipline among the state's militia. But they were not as bad as that "discipline hating, good-living loving 'to eternal fame damned' coxcombical crew we lately had here from Philadelphia." [23]

The militiamen were not entirely to blame for their depredations. The American system of supply for the Flying Camp ranged from primitive to nonexistent. One Philadelphia Associator told of being quartered in a two-room house with thirty-three other soldiers in addition to the owner's family of six. It was difficult if not impossible to maintain a high degree of altruistic fervor in such a situation. The weather was ferociously hot. Mosquitoes swarmed from New Jersey's marshes, and the British showed no interest in a climactic battle that would decide in an hour or two the fate of America. Everyone, from George Washington to the lowliest militia private on one month's temporary duty, was discovering that war was a tedious business.

The taverns, inns, and roadsides of New Jersey swarmed with straggling soldiers and loitering officers who seemed more interested in their next drink than in the pursuit of happiness and the defense of life, liberty, and property. Loyalist Nicholas Cresswell, on his way to

New York in the hope of getting passage to England, told his diary, "If my countrymen are beaten by these ragamuffins I shall be much surprised." A number of sensible patriots had intimations of disaster when they saw these disorderly vagrants. Congressman Abraham Clark told a friend, "I assure you, sir, I see—I feel, the danger we are in. I am far from exulting in our imaginary happiness; nothing short of the almighty power of God can save us." [24]

In New York, Washington may have been having similar thoughts. On August 15, his commander on Long Island, Nathanael Greene, a man who was emerging as his most competent subordinate, collapsed with a raging fever, a victim of the camp disorder. Five days later, he was still feeling very weak, and Washington decided to replace him with Major General John Sullivan, who had just arrived in the city, so disgruntled over being replaced as commander in chief in Canada that he had tried to resign in Philadelphia, and withdrew a formal letter only after considerable cajolery from President John Hancock. Sullivan was a touchy, unstable character, as he had amply proved in the Canadian theater. But he was the only major general available besides Israel Putnam of Connecticut.

A popular hero from the Seven Years' War, Putnam was fifty-eight, beefy, profane, and stupid. He had courage and could, as he proved at Bunker Hill, be an effective leader in a battle. But when it came to thinking, he was almost a total loss. Although his dig-in-and-let-them-attack strategy inflicted heavy casualties on the British at Bunker Hill, he had lost that battle because he had tried to operate without that most rudimentary tool of generalship, a staff. Now Washington discovered that "Old Put" was chagrined by the choice of Sullivan for the Long Island command. With some 9,000 Connecticut militia and regulars in his army, this was not good news. Old Put was a talkative fellow, and his discontent could, like the camp disorder, permeate the army.

Washington also had to worry about the impact of Lord Drummond's peace mission on the army. On August 20, the same day that he appointed Sullivan commander on Long Island, Washington was forced to deal with this threat in his general orders. He noted that "a report prevails and is industriously spread far and wide that Lord Howe has made propositions of peace." Washington flatly denied that such an offer had been made. "On the contrary, from the best intelligence . . . the army may expect an attack as soon as the wind and tide shall prove favorable." Washington therefore hoped that "every man's mind and arms, will be prepared for action, and when called to

1776

On July 16, New York celebrated the Declaration of Independence by pulling down the gilded lead statue of George III on Bowling Green. The torso was shipped to Connecticut and melted down for bullets. The head was given to soldiers, who set it up on a spike in the Blue Bell Tavern near modern 181st Street and Broadway. One dark night, loyalists stole it and gave it to the British when they drove the Americans out of New York. The head was sent to England "to convince them at home of the Infamous Disposition of the Ungrateful people of this distressed Country."

Admiral Richard Lord Howe had the illusion that he was a peacemaker. He persuaded his younger brother, William, the British army commander, to fight a limited war aimed at beating the Americans just badly enough to yield to the Admiral's personal charm and negotiate. But hard-liners in the British government had no intention of keeping Howe's promises of generous treatment. This rarely seen portrait *(left)*, painted by Gainsborough about 1765, is the closest likeness of the man whose good intentions almost seduced Americans into unconditional surrender in 1776.

"I thought that all London was afloat," said one American as a British fleet of over 400 ships gathered off Staten Island *(above)*. To oppose them, Washington put the hero of Bunker Hill, Major General Israel Putnam *(right)*, in command on Long Island. Putnam's attempt to repeat Bunker Hill there became a recipe for disaster.

American inclination to negotiate diminished sharply when it was learned that Charleston, South Carolina, had beaten off a British attack on June 28, 1776 *(right)*, led by Major General Henry Clinton *(above)* and Admiral Sir Peter Parker. American cannon on Fort Sullivan severely mauled the royal men-of-war, inspiring the cartoon *(below)* picturing "Miss Carolina" wearing the fort as a headdress.

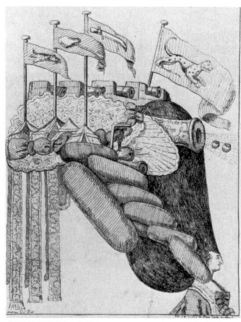

By September, the Americans, driven out of New York, resorted to scorched-earth tactics and tried to burn down the city on the twenty-first of that month (*above*). Unfortunately, the flames trapped spy Nathan Hale in the city. Some suspect he may have participated in setting the fire. He was hanged without ceremony (*left*) and forgotten by both sides.

Brigadier General Benedict Arnold *(right)* had almost as many enemies in the American army as he had in the British army. But without his leadership, the northern front might have collapsed. In October he turned admiral and fought a thunderous battle with a British fleet at Valcour Bay *(below)* on Lake Champlain. Arnold hoped to lure the British into the narrow bay a few ships at a time. Their superior fire power gave his fleet a terrible battering. But Arnold's pugnacity delayed the British invasion so long they retired to Canada for the winter, giving the Americans time to consolidate their shaky grip on upstate New York.

The American defense of New York was based on control of the Hudson River. But the British fleet proved able to move up and down the river with impunity. *Right:* H.M.S. *Phoenix* and *Rose* beat off American fire ships after sailing unscathed past American batteries. *Below, left:* The British launch their assault on Fort Washington, in which 2,900 Americans were captured. *Below, right:* British troops invade New Jersey. Desperate Americans tried to cripple the fleet with the world's first submarine, the *Turtle (left),* invented by Connecticut's David Bushnell.

Among Washington's worries as the Americans reeled from defeat to defeat were Major General Philip Schuyler *(below, left)*, who kept threatening to resign, Major General Charles Lee *(above, right)*, who was insubordinate and contemptuous of his military talent, his adjutant general, Joseph Reed *(above, left)*, who encouraged Lee, and loyalists who hoped for British victory.

Among them were William Franklin *(opposite page, top left)*, the son of Benjamin Franklin and Royal Governor of New Jersey; Frederick Philipse *(top right)*, owner of a huge swatch of land along the Hudson; Joseph Galloway *(center)*, ex-speaker of the Pennsylvania assembly; influential New York lawyer William Smith *(bottom left)*, who thought the "violent" on both sides were at fault; and wealthy William Byrd III *(bottom right)* of Virginia who had sons on both sides. Franklin and Philipse were jailed, Smith was allowed to retire to his farm as a neutral, Galloway defected to the British late in the year. Byrd committed suicide on January 1, 1777.

British contempt for Americans
grew as reports of the Royal
Army's victories reached England. This caricature of typical
Yankee soldiers and others like it
caused one American in London
to exclaim, "Four-fifths of the
English people despise us, and
look upon us as cowards."

dont think

Gen. a is still a Labourer in Vain

Tis Old Olivers Cause

I fear Our no Monarchy nor Laws

The sperit moves us in Sun—dry places &c:

yet I fear the Lord is not with us

DEATH or LIBERTY

Without these three men, America might have surrendered late in 1776 or early in 1777. Robert Morris *(top, right)* used his worldwide contacts as a merchant prince to funnel tons of gunpowder and other needed war materiel from the West Indies. The financial wizardry of Jacques Necker *(right, center)* enabled France to put up much of the money for these purchases. Benjamin Franklin *(bottom, right)* arrived in Paris late in 1776 to restore sagging French faith in the American cause.

Washington's Christmas-night victory at Trenton, dramatized above by John Trumbull, inspired Americans to resist a very effective British peace offensive. Thousands of New Jerseyans had already accepted pardons, promising to remain "in peaceable obedience to His Majesty." Washington was warned that Pennsylvania and New York would soon follow suit unless "something was attempted." When Washington outgeneraled Lord Cornwallis *(left)*, and won another victory at Princeton *(right)*, Lord Howe's hopes of pacifying America went glimmering.

Here is the mature Washington who shed the major illusion of 1776—that an outburst of patriotism would win the war in a single campaign—and evolved the strategy of retreat and delay, of attacking only when and where the British were weak, that eventually won the Revolution.

it, shew our enemies, and the whole world, that Free Men, contending on their own land, are superior to any mercenaries on earth . . ." [25]

As if he did not have enough to worry about, Washington had another problem deposited in his lap by Congress. Several members of that honorable body, including Thomas Jefferson and Benjamin Franklin, decided that it would be a simple matter to persuade the Hessians to desert. Franklin helped concoct a broadside telling them about the blessings of liberty currently being enjoyed in Pennsylvania and other colonies by many thousands of their former countrymen. The problem was how to get this message within reading distance of the Germans. Washington said he would try to figure out a way to do it. He asked Lieutenant Colonel Harmon Zedwitz of the First New York Regiment to translate into German the resolves of Congress and thus make them part of the propaganda package. The resolves seem to have had a strikingly contradictory effect on Colonel Zedwitz. He wrote a letter to Governor Tryon, telling him about the scheme and offering to serve as a British spy. His letter was intercepted, and the colonel was promptly court-martialed.[26]

The British soon fulfilled Washington's prediction of early battle. Lord Howe's men-of-war began moving up the bay and anchored in the Narrows. Through telescopes it was evident that their decks were crowded with soldiers. By the following morning, no less than 400 transports and 37 men-of-war had moved into this new anchorage. Early on August 22, some 75 attack flatboats and 11 batteaux began moving across the harbor. Their goal was Gravesend Bay, where frigates and bomb ships had already moved in close to shore to cover the landing. Behind the flatboats and batteaux came transports with a second wave. By noon, 15,000 British troops were on Long Island with scarcely a shot fired at them. The only troops in the vicinity of the bay were a rifle battalion of Pennsylvanians, who withdrew, burning grain and stacks of hay and killing cattle on farms in the area.

The Pennsylvanians retreated to the wooded hills overlooking the bay, part of the Heights of Guan, a row of hills almost parallel to the fortifications on Brooklyn Heights, about a mile and a half to the west. The British quickly occupied the village of Flatbush and surrounding terrain along the coast for about six miles. There was now nothing between the British and the rest of Long Island but a handful of Continentals and a few feeble companies of militia in Queens and Suffolk counties. Washington could only grind his teeth in frustration at the thought of the enemy possessing those tens of thousands of horses, cattle, sheep, and pigs which he had tried to persuade the New Yorkers to remove.[27]

A spy sent to Staten Island by William Livingston of New Jersey on the night of August 20 had warned Washington of the impending attack. Without consulting the New York convention, he had detached 200 men from the Twelfth Massachusetts Regiment, including Lieutenant Joseph Hodgkins, to destroy boats and collect all available cattle along the South Shore. These men were forty-two miles from the American lines, deep in Queens County "amongst a people that 9 tenths of them were our Secret Enemy," as Hodgkins described the Queens County loyalists.[28]

The New York convention finally ordered Brigadier General Woodhull to "use all possible diligence to prevent the stock and other provisions in Queens County from falling into the hands of the enemy." Washington's opinion of this too-little-and-too-late gesture was evident in a letter he wrote to Governor Trumbull of Connecticut on August 24. He asked Trumbull to send a thousand militiamen from Connecticut to eastern Long Island. Not only could they annoy the British rear and flanks, but they might prevent the enemy from getting their hands on cattle they badly needed. Reports from Washington's spies on Staten Island had convinced him that the British were "rather distressed on account of provisions." If only the Americans could deprive them of Long Island's rich provender, "much good will follow from it."

This was, at best, a cry of despair. Washington had sacrificed his scorched-earth policy to his deference to the civilian authority of New York's congress. It was a wildly impractical idea to ship a thousand men across Long Island Sound, waters controlled by the British fleet. The scheme revealed Washington's harassed and uncertain state of mind on the eve of battle.[29]

On the same day—August 24—Washington made a decision which revealed still deeper insecurities. He yielded to the pleadings of Major General Israel Putnam, and gave him command of the army on Long Island. This hardly improved the disposition of touchy John Sullivan. While it may have solved the problem of what to do about "the brave old man," as Adjutant General Reed called Putnam, who was "quite miserable" at being kept in New York, it put in charge of the Long Island army, which Washington now reinforced heavily, an incompetent general.

Worse, Putnam was told to "soothe and soften" Sullivan's hurt feelings as much as possible. Putnam's solution to this order was to accept the defensive dispositions made by Sullivan, a man who was "wholly unacquainted with the ground or country," without the slightest cavil. This was hardly surprising, since Putnam knew little more about Long Island than Sullivan. He had spent 95 percent of his time in New York, coming over to Long Island occasionally as a military tourist. Washington showed his distrust of both generals by personally visiting the scene and writing Putnam a sharp letter about the lack of discipline in the whole command.

Americans were wasting ammunition taking potshots at the British. Nothing had been done to form "a proper line of defense" outside the fortifications. It was vital to stop the men from wandering in all directions as they pleased. "Send out scouting parties and Partizan corps, by all means," Washington urged. But "under proper regulations." The distinction between a well-regulated army and a mob, Washington reminded Putnam, is "good order and discipline." The general denounced burning and looting houses, which the Americans did on a wide scale as they retreated, regarding the owners as loyalists and therefore fair game.

With a distinct lamentation in his words, Washington reminded Putnam that his men were not employed "as mere hirelings" but were defending "every thing that is dear and valuable," and that they should therefore "take uncommon pains to conduct themselves with uncommon propriety and good order." It was clear that the American army on Long Island was displaying none of these qualities. It was not a good omen.[30]

XXIV

The Great Bunker Hill Backlash

The night was uncommonly cold for Long Island in August. But William Glanville Evelyn, captain of the light infantry in the King's Own Regiment, was much too busy to think about the weather. The handsome, thirty-four-year-old Englishman was keenly aware that honor and even a little glory might be his before the night was over. He also knew that for an advance guard, the difference between glory and disaster was often an unstable compound of alertness and luck. With every step his eyes and ears probed the almost impenetrable darkness. Around him, his flankers prowled in an extended line with fixed bayonets, under orders to kill or capture but at all costs silence every living thing they met.

Just ahead of Captain Evelyn rode another captain, twenty-three-year-old Oliver De Lancey, Jr. He was an officer in the only British cavalry regiment in America, the Seventeenth Light Dragoons. He was, if possible, more excited than Captain Evelyn, for several reasons. This was his first taste of action. Captain Evelyn had fought at Lexington and Bunker Hill, where he had led a company of thirty-three men against the entrenched Americans and come back with five. More important to young De Lancey, he was fighting not only for his king but for his family. His father was Oliver De Lancey, Sr., whom we met in the previous chapter, slipping down the Hudson in his rowboat to join

Governor Tryon aboard the *Duchess of Gordon*. Colonel De Lancey and 60 loyalist volunteers now rode not far behind his son—part of a 10,000-man British column that was marching east, away from the Americans on Brooklyn Heights and its outlying hills. The army was being guided by three Long Island loyalists recruited by Oliver De Lancey, Sr.[1]

The finest soldiers in William Howe's command were in this long, silent column. Immediately behind the advance guard rode Major General Henry Clinton, heading a brigade of crack light infantry. A half mile behind him was energetic Major General Charles Lord Cornwallis, with four elite battalions of grenadiers, two regiments of regular infantry, and the famed Seventy-first Regiment, fierce Scottish Highlanders in traditional kilts, many with one-edged backswords (officially banned) in their belts. Fourteen pieces of artillery rolled in the center of this brigade.

Another half mile to the rear rode the commander in chief, General William Howe. With Major General Hugh Lord Percy's assistance, he led twelve more regiments of infantry and ten guns. Behind them was a supply train with a regimental guard and four more guns.

It was a calculated risk, marching this enormous column across terrain completely strange to both officers and men, while an enemy army crouched a few miles away in the sheltering hills. A sudden attack could smash the extended line into chaotic fragments. A wrong turn could send them plodding in circles, exhausting men who were expected to fight for their lives and British liberty in the dawn. William Howe was aware of the risk, and none too easy about it. Henry Clinton had spent the week talking Howe into making this march.

General Howe had no illusions about General Clinton. He knew the strange and often contradictory ambitions and frustrations which churned in his subordinate's hypersensitive soul. General Clinton was in a mood to gamble because he was burning to rescue his military reputation from the Charleston fiasco. At first, Howe had hesitated to take his advice. It was given in Clinton's arrogant, often condescending manner. As a soldier trained in the "German school," Clinton tended to look down on men like Howe who had seen no service in that theater of the Seven Years' War.

The British commander in chief finally decided to discount Clinton's motives and manner and accept his plan. It may have been risky. But it also dovetailed with the kind of battle that his brother, Lord Howe, wanted to fight. More than a few British army and navy officers had urged the Howes to land a large portion of the army above New York in Westchester, and trap Washington on Manhattan Island, finishing him off with a combination of siege and storm. But the Howes, though they had decided to fight, had no desire to annihilate Washington in one savage stroke. That would leave the Americans open to the ruthless peace by proscription which the British had inflicted on Scotland and Ireland after their rebellions in the past—a policy to which Lord George Germain and others in the British cabinet were clearly inclined.

Far better, the Howes reasoned, to drive the Americans back in a series of battles that would, they hoped, convince them that the British army was invincible. This would also give the Howes an opportunity to re-establish royal government in the territories abandoned by the Americans, and by the example of a mild, lenient policy, persuade the rebels that they had nothing to fear from submitting to the King's rule once more. Lord Howe was the architect of this strategy. Before the admiral arrived, General Howe had written several letters to Lord George Germain, stating without qualification that the rebellion could not be ended till the American army was defeated in a "decisive Action." [2]

Argumentative Henry Clinton had led the advance guard across the Narrows to Gravesend Bay on August 22. As soon as the British position was secured, Clinton began scouting the American defenses. The Americans were clustered around three roads that ran through the rugged Heights of Guan to Brooklyn. The first, facing the British left wing, ran along the Gravesend coast. The next two roads ran from the village of Flatbush through the center of the hills. It would cost hundreds, perhaps thousands, of men to fight through the thick woods around these passes. Moving up the roads in the face of musket and cannon fire would be mass suicide. As Clinton continued his scouting expedition, accompanied by another British general, Sir William Erskine, he stopped to talk with American loyalists, many of them farmers whose corn and grain had been burned and their cattle slaughtered by the retreating rebels. They told him—and he soon saw for himself—that there was a fourth pass through the Heights of Guan—the Jamaica pass—and, though it was hard to believe, it seemed to be unguarded by the Americans.

This was nothing less than the truth. The Jamaica pass was far out on the left wing of the American position, almost four miles from their Brooklyn lines. Obsessed by their Bunker Hill psychology, the Americans were convinced that the British would take the shortest routes to get at them. But a glance at his map of Long Island showed Clinton that this unguarded pass was an open door through which the British could turn the American left flank, and get in behind all those pugnacious troops on the heights of Guan who were briskly skirmishing with the Royal Army even as General Clinton concocted their destruction. Sir William Erskine, a tall, solemn Scotsman, was enthusiastic about Clinton's plan. He took it to Howe, who let other subordinate generals, notably James Grant, dismiss it "as savouring too much of the German school." [3]

Grant was almost typecast for the beefy, arrogant Englishman. A vehement anti-American, he had declared in the House of Commons "that the Americans could not fight and that he would undertake to march from one end of the continent to the other with five thousand men." Grant was confident that the British could batter their way right up the Gravesend and Flatbush passes. But Howe also talked with Oliver De Lancey, who assured him that the route that Clinton proposed was easy marching and there would be no difficulty about finding local guides to lead the column through the darkness. Howe decided to take the gamble. To minimize the risk, the Hessians and a British division under Major General Grant would stage feint attacks on the center and right wing of the American army to pin them down until the trap was sprung. The fleet would simultaneously make a demonstration against the enemy's batteries at Brooklyn and New York to further distract them.

At eight o'clock on August 26, Clinton's advance guard began their march from the village of Flatlands. They left all their tents behind them in the fields to convince the Americans that they were spending the night there. The Seventy-first Regiment formed a screen between the marching column and the Americans in the hills to guarantee against a collision with a rebel patrol. Any civilian found on the road by the roving flankers was swept into the column and made a temporary prisoner, whether he was a loyalist or a rebel.

Suddenly, the column's forward motion slowed, then ceased entirely. Officers strode among their companies, hissing orders against straggling, threatening deserters with instant death. Aides galloped forward from Howe and Cornwallis to ask Clinton what was happening. They found the column commander in tense conference with his loyalist guides, three nervous-looking men in the homespun of the Long Island farmer. They were explaining to him that directly ahead was a little salt creek, crossed by a bridge named after one Schoon-

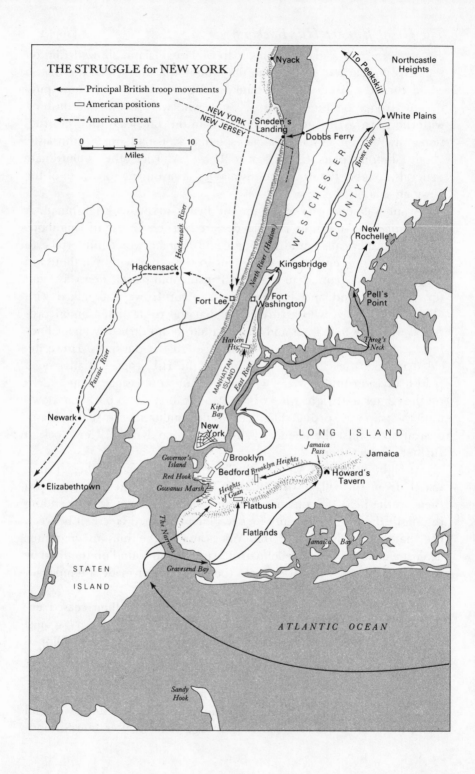

THE STRUGGLE for NEW YORK

⟵ Principal British troop movements
▭ American positions
⟵--- American retreat

0   5   10
Miles

Nyack

To Peekskill

Northcastle
Heights

NEW YORK
NEW JERSEY

Sneden's
Landing

Dobbs Ferry

White Plains

WESTCHESTER COUNTY

Bronx River

New
Rochelle

Hackensack River

Hackensack

North River (Hudson)

Kingsbridge

Fort
Washington

Fort Lee

Pell's
Point

Harlem
Hts.

Throg's
Neck

Passaic River

MANHATTAN ISLAND

East River

Kips
Bay

LONG ISLAND

Newark

New
York

Jamaica
Pass

Jamaica

Governor's
Island

Brooklyn

Red Hook

Bedford Brooklyn Heights

Howard's
Tavern

Gowanus Marsh

Heights
of Guan

Elizabethtown

Flatbush

The Narrows

Flatlands

Jamaica Bay

STATEN

ISLAND

Gravesend Bay

ATLANTIC OCEAN

Sandy
Hook

maker. It was such a natural position for defense, the rebels could not have failed to fortify it.

Clinton ordered Evelyn's company to open into a skirmish line and take the bridge by storm if necessary. In a moment, light infantrymen were moving forward. Not a man was permitted to load his musket. If there was an enemy in this chilly darkness, he must be silenced with the bayonet. Now they were close enough to the creek to see the starlight glinting in the shallow water. The little wooden bridge could be seen in dim outline, apparently deserted. But was a regiment of men with fingers on musket triggers just beyond it? There was only one way to find out. Evelyn and his men dashed across it, and plunged into the woods on the other side.

Nothing. There was no guard at Schoonmaker's Bridge. Evelyn sent a messenger racing back to the waiting Clinton. Once more orders were barked, muskets were shouldered, and the long column snaked forward again.[4]

But now Captain Evelyn and his light infantrymen and Captain De Lancey and his troopers, after another conference with the three loyalist guides, swung west, and the column abandoned the road. On they trudged (and rode) across farmland which had been cleared by industrious Dutch burghers decades before, squashing vegetables beneath their boots and cutting destructive swaths through fields of corn.

Between two and three in the morning, they emerged from this cross-country tour into the Jamaica road less than a quarter of a mile from the crucial pass. A startled Evelyn and De Lancey heard hoofbeats coming toward them from the southwest. Who was it? Anyone on a horse coming from this direction ought to be British. All parts of the Jamaica plain between the flanking column and the South Shore were—theoretically—under their control. De Lancey challenged the oncoming riders and ordered them to identify themselves. His American accent proved valuable. Out of the darkness came an ingenuous response: "Americans—friends." De Lancey put spurs to his horse and lunged into the darkness, followed by his dragoons. In a moment, five very frightened young American officers were surrounded by upraised sabers. They meekly surrendered and were escorted to General Clinton.[5]

He asked them what they were doing on the road. Were they spies? If so, they could expect sudden death. Like most of the Americans in the army, the captives were wearing civilian clothes. They swore that they were lieutenants in the American army, assigned by General Sullivan to guard the Jamaica pass. In their zeal, they had ridden beyond the pass and down the road toward Flatlands, never dreaming that the British would cut across the fields and appear on the road behind them.

Pretending skepticism, Clinton demanded to know exactly how many men the Americans had guarding the pass.

"None."

Clinton could not believe it at first. He warned his captives that if they were lying, the sudden-death-for-spies clause would be reinvoked. Trembling, the Americans insisted there was not a living soul at Jamaica pass but innkeeper William Howard and his family, asleep in their tavern.

Clinton ordered Captain Evelyn and his company to surround the tavern and take the Howards prisoners. In a few minutes, Clinton, young De Lancey, his father, and the loyalist guides were questioning the frightened innkeeper and his son. They confirmed the total absence of American troops in the pass. The exultant Clinton sent detachments of cavalry and light infantry down the road to confirm this fact and hold the position, then relaxed in the tavern to await William Howe and the rest of the army. The men were ordered to lie down in the fields on either side of the road and rest. It took two hours for a very nervous William Howe to arrive. Clinton exuded optimism. But Howe remained jittery while the army marched through the "deep winding cut" which could have been defended for hours by a few hundred well-placed American troops. By 7 A.M., the British were moving down the road toward the village of Bedford, still without a sign of American opposition, in spite of the fact that they were now closer to the American fortifications on Brooklyn Heights than the rebel regiments posted around the passes on the hills of Guan. As they resumed their advance, they fired two cannon—signals for the Germans in the center of the line and Grant, facing the American right wing, to begin their frontal assaults. Clinton later recalled that General Howe could not seem to believe what was happening. He urged Clinton to form a line of battle; he was sure the Americans would attack them on the march. Clinton scoffed at the notion. The fight was as good as over.[6]

As they entered the village of Bedford, they saw a group of Americans emerge from a wood perhaps a quarter of a mile away and head for another cluster of trees on the British left. Were they forming a line of battle as Howe feared? Clinton decided to find out. He took command of the British cavalry and charged them. The Americans ran into the woods without firing a shot. The excited cavalrymen were ready to pursue them, but Clinton recalled them to the main army and gave Howe a triumphant smile. There was no longer any doubt that they had achieved total surprise. With just a hint of mockery in his words, Clinton wished Howe "joy of future victory," took charge of the light infantry again, and went storming down the Jamaica road. The only obstacle was a small breastwork the Americans had thrown up in the village of Bedford. It was undefended.[7]

To the left, on the wooded heights, the crash of muskets and the thunder of cannon grew more intense. The Hessians were attacking. Clinton threw his 4,000 light infantrymen at the rear of the embattled Americans. It was the beginning of the end.

The Americans in the center of the hills still had no idea of their peril. They and their commander, Major General John Sullivan, thought the enemy were doing exactly what they were expected to do—charge straight at the muzzles of their waiting guns. On the right, the Americans were commanded by William Alexander, somewhat incongruously called Lord Stirling by his fellow rebels. A pugnacious brigadier general from New Jersey, he was the son of James Alexander, a brilliant Scotsman who was, among many things, a friend of Benjamin Franklin and the man who financed newspaper editor John Peter Zenger in his historic trial. William Alexander claimed the earldom of Stirling. There all comparison between him and Lord Drummond ended. Alexander's loyalty to the land of his birth—America—took precedence over this aristocratic dream, and he was sacrificing his title and risking the estate that made him one of the richest men in America by joining the rebellion. Most of the troops under him were from Maryland and Delaware—among the best equipped and most highly motivated regiments in the American army.[8]

Guarding the American left flank was Colonel Samuel Miles of Pennsylvania with a huge regiment of riflemen, divided into twelve companies. After the battle, he claimed that he had a hunch the British were moving down the Jamaica road. If so, he did nothing about it until the Hessians began attacking. He then marched his men away from this battlefront for an hour or so until they reached the road. There, to his "great mortification," he saw the rear guard of Howe's flanking column. About 9,500 of Howe's 10,000 men had got by him.[9]

For a moment, Miles thought about attacking the British from the rear. But his officers talked him out of it. The enemy were obviously all around them, and they were three miles from the Brooklyn lines. They decided instead to let the baggage guard pass and attempt a retreat. Before they went a quarter of a mile, they collided with British troops waiting for them in the woods. Behind him, Miles' lieutenant colonel, leading another part of the battalion Indian file, was also ambushed and his men dispersed. It was an ironic turn of affairs if there ever was one—the European-trained redcoats bushwhacking the Americans, supposedly so good at fighting Indian style. But the image of the Americans as shrewd guerrilla fighters and the British as stupid automatons who could only fight in parade-ground maneuvers is one of the myths of 1776.[10]

At the Bedford pass, Colonel Samuel Wyllys, commander of the Twenty-second Connecticut Regiment, heard the British attacking Miles. Wyllys decided to retreat, although no one had fired a shot at him and his men. By the time they reached the Jamaica road, the flanking column had long since passed it and was busy devouring Miles' men and attacking Sullivan's men while the head of the column drove hard for the Gowanus road, where they could cut off Stirling's line of retreat. Wyllys and his men, staying largely in the woods, managed to struggle back to the Brooklyn lines with little loss.

A harsher fate awaited Sullivan and his men at the Flatlands pass. As they turned to fight the British in their rear, the thunder of guns and drums announced a Hessian advance. Up from the Flatbush plain the mercenaries came, their green-coated jaegers, armed with short-barreled rifles, swarming ahead, followed by blue-coated grenadiers, big men made taller by high, elliptical brass caps. The golden lion of Hesse was rampant on their blue flags. It was an awesome sight, and not many Americans stayed around to contemplate it. A few riflemen stood their ground, but the Germans soon convinced themselves they had little to fear from these supposedly deadly sharpshooters. The moment a rifleman fired at them, they charged him with the bayonet. It took a full minute, perhaps two, to reload these tricky weapons, and long before that the sharpshooter was (sometimes literally) pinned to the tree behind which he was firing. The potency of the American rifle is another myth of 1776.[11]

As the Hessians pursued the fleeing Americans, they displayed a tendency to bayonet wounded men attempting to surrender. It was not entirely their fault. Washington had distributed before their camp some of the Continental Congress desertion propaganda, wrapped around packets of tobacco. The British, worried that some of the Germans might succumb, told their hired helpers that the Americans had taken a special hate to them, and planned to give them no quarter if captured. Since scarcely one of the Hessians could speak English, there was no possibility of an American explaining away this counter-propaganda. Thus there were dozens of short, nasty encounters in the woods, young Americans pleading for mercy, enraged young Germans sinking their bayonets into them, thinking to themselves that they were only doing unto the rebels what the rebels had hoped to do unto them. Numerous British officers, unaware that their own high command had created this ferocity, declared themselves shocked at the Hessians' savagery.[12]

It was the first of many calamities that were to befall Lord Howe's policy of conciliation. Men who saw their wounded friends bayoneted without mercy were not inclined to think conciliatory thoughts. Nor were the rest of their friends in the army after they heard eyewitness stories. The same was true of families and friends back home who got the bitter message by mail.

After 9 A.M., when Clinton took the undefended redoubt in Bedford village, chaos and random death were the order of the day all along the American front. Fleeing singly and in small groups, the Americans were riddled by volleys from left, right, front, and rear, summoned to surrender before hundreds of leveled muskets, hunted like animals by exultant dragoons on horseback. Captain Wade and Lieutenant Hodgkins of the Twelfth Massachusetts Regiment were among the fugitives. They were stationed at the Flatbush defile, confident that "the Road was so Fortified that they could not pass." Too late, they "perceived their plan was to surround us." They kept their posts "till the fire got a Cross the road in the rear betwixt us and our lines." Wade was stationed on the downside of the hill, and his words testify to the shock he got when "ascending the hill, found there ware a Vast Body of the Enemy Betwixt us and the Lines . . ." [13]

On the American right wing, Brigadier General Stirling and his Maryland and Delaware troops were still skirmishing heavily with the 5,000-man British division under General Grant. Although Grant heard the signal guns fired by Howe, he did not attack until he had replenished his men's ammunition and reinforced them with 2,000 marines from the British ships offshore. Frigates from the British fleet simultaneously maneuvered against an unfavorable wind to bombard the batteries at Red Hook and rake the Gowanus road. It was an unnerving situation for men in their first battle. But every man in the scarlet-coated Maryland and blue-coated Delaware regiments was a volunteer. They formed in a V formation on high but open ground and proudly maintained their position while British cannonballs smashed through their ranks.[14]

Although he was outnumbered four to one, Stirling was determined to fight the British in the standard European manner—another demolition of the myth of guerrilla-fighting Americans. For about four hours, from 6 A.M. to 10 A.M., the skirmishing and bombarding continued, the Americans growing more and more convinced that the British were afraid to attack them. But Grant was only waiting for the 4,000-man division led by Lord Cornwallis to reach the American rear.

Taking advantage of his superior manpower, Grant extended his attacking line to overlap the American flanks. Stirling sent a detachment of Connecticut and Pennsylvania troops into the woods on that flank to handle this threat. As they sought to take possession of a small hill, guns crashed and musket balls whizzed around them. It was part of the flanking column, moving forward to trap Stirling's brigade. It was a total reversal of Bunker Hill. This time the Americans were at the bottom of a hill and the British were entrenched on top of it. In a headlong charge, the Pennsylvanians knocked the British off the crest. Lieutenant Colonel James Grant, commander of the Fortieth Regiment (no relation to the general of the same name), rallied his men and led a counterattack. A blast of American fire cut down a half dozen of the attackers, including the colonel. But the Pennsylvanians were not on the hill fifteen minutes when out of the woods on their left came thousands of Hessians. The Germans were moving down the ridge, rolling up any and all American resistance. The Pennsylvanians recoiled from this overwhelming force and tried to retreat toward the Brooklyn lines. They found their route blocked by Cornwallis' grenadiers.[15]

The appearance of the Hessians made it clear to Stirling that Sullivan and his men had been routed. By this time, hundreds of fugitives had streamed into the American lines at Brooklyn Heights. Washington was there, and so was Putnam. Yet no one sent Stirling an order to retreat. Even at this late hour, no one in the American high command seemed to know what was happening.

With his men being hammered from front and flank, Stirling decided to retreat. Only then did he discover that a third of the British army was between him and the Brooklyn lines. At this point, the situation became confused for both sides. The chief cause was the Hessians. The British knew they were coming out of the woods on the American left. They wore blue coats faced with red. When a colonel of the British grenadiers saw a group of men wearing these uniforms blasting away at him, he ordered a marine lieutenant to tell the Hessians to stop shooting at their friends. The marine lieutenant took a sergeant, a corporal, and twenty men for company, and marched forward to obey. Only when he got within pistol shot did he discover that the Hessians were Delawares. He was taken prisoner. So were a half dozen Hessians lost in the woods who thought they were rejoining their regiment.

But this momentary comedy could not alter the impending tragedy. Looking around him, Stirling saw there was only one apparent retreat route, across the marshes on his right to Gowanus Creek, eighty yards wide at the mouth, with a strong tide running. But his men, floundering through muddy water up to their chests, would be incapable of defending themselves against the hotly pursuing enemy. They would die like wingless ducks in a hail of British musket balls. There was only one solution, and the grim-faced Stirling chose it, with unflinching Scottish fortitude. He detached 250 Marylanders under their commanding officer, Major Mordecai Gist, put himself, sword in hand, at their head, and launched a frontal assault on the 10,000 British and Germans surrounding them.[16]

The Marylanders' red coats ironically completed their imitation of a British bayonet charge. At first, the astonished King's men could not believe the sight of this handful of Americans, fifes shrilling and drums beating, coming toward them across the grassy field. Then they woke up and began blasting away at them with every available musket and two fieldpieces. Men crumpled. The American ranks wavered, broke. Stirling and Gist reformed them, and they returned to the attack—not once, but five more times. In the last effort, they almost reached the British lines. But by now an alarmed Cornwallis had rushed four regiments into the fight, and their firepower took a final toll. The Marylanders broke, and Stirling made no attempt to rally them again. They were surrounded by Hessians and British. But most of their comrades had made it safely through the marsh and across the creek. Now it was every man for himself. Only Major Gist and eight others escaped the ring of red- and blue-coated hunters.

Stirling, who had made himself a target for every enemy soldier in sight, surrendered his sword to the German commander, Lieutenant General Leopold von Heister. Around the same time, about a mile away, Major General John Sullivan was being flushed out of a corn field by a regiment of Hessians.[17]

The sacrifice of the Marylanders was agonizingly visible to the

Americans on Brooklyn Heights. Watching them attack against such fearful odds, George Washington choked, "Good God! What brave fellows I must this day lose." [18]

The Marylanders and Delawares crawled out of Gowanus Creek, their handsome uniforms covered with slime, looking, in the words of one eyewitness, "like water rats." Many of them had lost their guns. A high percentage of the refugees from Sullivan's front were in the same condition. Captain Nathaniel Wade told of "Crossing a Piece of Marsh and through a Creek Breast high." The appearance as well as the psychological state of these beaten men spread panic throughout the regiments inside the Brooklyn lines. For the first time, the Americans were forced to confront their foggy thinking and even foggier planning.[19]

In spite of all the digging they had done, the Americans suddenly saw that the Brooklyn lines were dangerously weak in several places. While the sound of firing rolled across the plain below them and groups of fugitives acted out their frantic dramas, hundreds of men were ordered to pile brush before the trenches that connected the huge forts. The most glaring omission was the lack of any defenses on the Jamaica road. Three New York militia regiments were ordered to defend this position. Their commander was shocked to discover that from high ground only forty yards outside the line they were digging a man would be able to "fire under my horse's belly whenever he pleased." [20]

Henry Clinton saw the weakness of the Jamaica road defenses at a glance, and advanced toward them, hoping Howe would let him smash the New Yorkers and drive them all the way to the Brooklyn ferry— which would have cut off the American retreat. Clinton gave Major General John Vaughan permission to assault Fort Putnam, the key to the American right wing. Before Vaughan could deploy his men, one of General Howe's aides came pounding up on horseback and ordered him to retreat. Vaughan exploded into a stream of oaths. He pointed to his exultant grenadiers and swore they could take the fort in five minutes.[21]

Inside the American lines, General Putnam raced up and down, roaring, "Don't fire, boys, until you can see the whites of their eyes!" Brandishing two pistols, Washington declared that he would shoot the first man who ran. It was Bunker Hillism rampant. But William Howe once more declined to play the Americans' game. If he had chosen to play it, he probably could have ended the Revolution that afternoon. Washington and his staff and almost every available general, plus 7,500 men, most of them Continentals, were in the Brooklyn lines. A two- or three-pronged thrust by the British, concentrating on the weak points in the American defenses, would have annihilated what little fighting spirit the shaken Americans had left. But this would have cost men, and Howe had won the first round with unbelievably few casualties: 5 officers and 56 men killed, 13 officers and 275 men wounded among the British troops, 2 men killed, 3 officers and 23 men wounded among the Germans—a total of 377. American killed, wounded, and missing totaled 1,407. Some 800 of these men were captives.[22]

From all parts of the front, regimental officers sent Howe requests to attack. Again and again he said no. There was an alternative to the frontal assault in the professional soldier's repertoire. If a general could not outflank an entrenched enemy, he could demolish him by "regular approaches." This was the standard military term for siege techniques. The process was all but certain. The attackers "approached" by digging trenches and gun emplacements of their own. They then zigzagged closer and closer to the defenders' lines, methodically silencing their artillery and enfilading their trenches until the defenders had only two choices, to surrender or to face annihilation from a final charge.

Washington, still thinking he had found the site of his climactic battle, kept his men awake all night, peering into the darkness for an attack that never came. The next morning, the American commander in chief, still not divining Howe's intentions, decided he needed reinforcements. Obliging of old George, the British must have thought as they saw two Pennsylvania regiments and the Fourteenth Massachusetts Regiment row from the tip of Manhattan Island to the Brooklyn ferry. The British frigates which had attacked the American fort at Red Hook the previous day made no attempt to interfere with this transfer.

Lord Howe had relapsed into a strange passivity. Aboard the frigate *Rainbow,* Captain George Collier wrote in his diary, "If we become masters of this body of rebels (which I think is inevitable) the war is at an end." Throughout the day, Collier expected orders from Lord Howe to make another attempt to place his ship and four other frigates in the East River between Brooklyn and New York. But the order never came. Around midday, the wind shifted to northeast, and it began to rain. Previous historians of these events have accepted at face value the statement of Lord Howe that the shift in the wind made such a movement impossible. But Captain Collier, writing in a journal that was discovered only a few years ago, obviously did not think so. He wrote that he and his fellow captains "have been in constant expectation of being ordered" to cut the one American escape route from Brooklyn.[23]

Inside the American defenses, the waiting men shivered in the bone-chilling rain, trying to keep their powder and guns dry. In some places in the crude trenches, the water was waist high. The Fourteenth Massachusetts, most of them tough sailors from Marblehead, skirmished sharply with the British along their front in the early morning. But once the rain began to fall, silence enveloped the front. The Americans remained braced for an attack. They thought the rain might inspire the British to come at them relying on the bayonet, betting wet American muskets would misfire. But the gray, rain-whipped day oozed into the night without a sign of movement from the enemy. From the British point of view, it was shrewd psychology. The Americans had nerved themselves for the climactic battle. "It seems the Day is Come . . . on which depends the Salvation of this Countery. . . . It is the Determination to Defend our Lines to the Last extremity," Lieutenant Joseph Hodgkins wrote to his wife, Sarah, on August 28.[24]

Only in front of Fort Putnam guarding the left flank of the American line did the British make an aggressive move, sending a heavy force of light infantry skirmishers forward at twilight. A seesaw fire fight erupted, with the Americans convinced that they had the better of it. But at the end of the shooting, the Americans did what the British wanted them to do—they pulled their outlying pickets inside the fort.

As dawn filtered through the gray drizzle on the morning of the twenty-ninth, the Americans saw a muddy hump about six hundred yards from the fort. It was a British redoubt. Behind it was a network of trenches. General Howe had begun his "regular approaches."

There was only one sensible thing for the Americans to do—retreat. But that word was not supposed to be in their lexicon. Washington, acutely sensitive about his reputation, and impelled by natural pugnacity as well as the prevailing Bunker Hillism, found himself incapable of suggesting it. He needed someone to rescue him from the impending catastrophe. The man who did the job was Thomas Mifflin, a handsome, self-assured Pennsylvania aristocrat who had rejected the neutralism and pacifism of his Quaker parents to become a violent independence man. Thirsting for action, he had abandoned his job as quartermaster and become a brigadier general. Mifflin had accompanied the two Pennsylvania regiments to Brooklyn, and on the night of the twenty-eighth he volunteered to "make the rounds"—patrol the American lines as officer in command, while Washington and Putnam got some sleep. As he rode from Wallabout Bay to Gowanus Creek, conferring with officers and talking to men during the night, Mifflin became more and more alarmed about the situation. John Shee, colonel of one of the Pennsylvania regiments, which was stationed on the extreme left along the shores of Wallabout Bay, told him that the militia posted near them were discouraged and talking surrender.

At 4:30 A.M. on the twenty-ninth, Washington arose to write a brief message to Congress. As he finished it, Mifflin reported what he had seen and heard. In his opinion, another day or two in the lines and the army might surrender en masse. "You must either fight or retreat immediately," Mifflin said. "What is your strength?"

"Nine thousand," Washington replied.

"It is not sufficient, we must retreat," Mifflin said.

Fortunately for the future of the United States of America, Washington had been thinking similar thoughts. A deserter from the Twenty-third Regiment had told him everyone in the British army expected the fleet to move between Brooklyn and New York. Brooklynites with knowledge of local navigation told the general that armed sloops and cruisers could easily navigate the waters between them and Governor's Island. Apparently no one in the American army had bothered to raise this question before.[25]

What the Americans were just learning the British had known for the previous four months. An intelligence report dated April 6, 1776, in the papers of Henry Clinton, stated that a ship or sloop could get between Governor's Island and Long Island with no nautical difficulty. But where were these ships or sloops? For two days, Admiral Howe, famed for the ferocity of his attacks on the French in other wars, declined to take the slightest advantage of this opportunity.[26]

Washington told Mifflin he would call a council of war. Would Mifflin propose a retreat at that meeting? This was rather too clever for Mifflin's taste. It was the beginning of an alienation between the two men that would eventually make Mifflin a chief plotter in the attempt to dump Washington as commander in chief during the travails of Valley Forge. Mifflin agreed, but he insisted on one provision, "lest his character should suffer." If a retreat was the council of war's decision, he wanted to command the rear guard. If they voted for an attack, he wanted command of "the van." Washington agreed, and aides were told to summon all the other general officers on duty in Brooklyn immediately.

The generals met in the comfortable summer house of Philip Livingston, who was representing New York in the Continental Congress. There was little debate. Only the New York militia brigadier general, John Morin Scott, opposed the idea of retreating, and he was swiftly persuaded by the others to change his mind. The generals listed eight reasons for abandoning the mile and a half of Long Island to which they were clinging. Orders were rushed to New York to collect every boat "from Hellgate on the Sound to Spuyten Duyvil creek that could be kept afloat and that had either sails or oars." [27]

These orders were executed with vigor. By nightfall, a formidable fleet had been collected along the East River docks. That these boats could be sailed down the East and Hudson rivers unnoticed by the British is unbelievable, in spite of the continuing rain and fog—unless the commander in chief of the British navy did not want to find out what the Americans were doing.

That night, Washington issued an order, signed by General Putnam. It directed the evacuation of all the sick and wounded to New York and announced that "troops are expected this afternoon from the flying camp in Jersey." To make room for these newcomers (who did not exist) "a proportionate number of regiments" were to be relieved and others shifted. All regiments were therefore ordered to be ready to move with their arms, accouterments, and knapsacks at 7 P.M.

The best troops, the Pennsylvanians, the Marylanders and Delawares, and a regiment of Connecticut Continentals, were left in the lines under Mifflin's command. Most of these men were stationed in the forts. Between these positions, when regiments were withdrawn, no one replaced them. Huge holes were left in the American line. It was an enormous risk. It probably would have led to disaster—if the Americans were fighting a general who really wanted to trap and destroy them. An aggressive commander would have had patrols probing the American lines throughout the night, advanced sentries alert and listening for the slightest movement.

All night, the Americans filed down to the Brooklyn ferry and boarded boats manned by Massachusetts and Connecticut sailors. Tons of equipment and cannon were loaded into these small craft. For the first two hours, everything went smoothly. Then the northeast wind began to blow, and the sloops and sailboats so industriously collected during the day became useless. Nothing but rowboats could be used. New York Brigadier Alexander McDougall, a merchant sailor in his youth, sent an aide to tell Washington that they could never get all the men and supplies over before morning. The aide was unable to locate the general, and meanwhile the embarkation continued. At eleven o'clock, the northeast wind died away, and a southwest zephyr began to blow—the best possible wind for sailboats moving between Brooklyn and New York. The water became "smooth as glass," and the sailors were emboldened to move out with as little as three inches of free-board.

Once more, one can only wonder where the British navy was while this providential breeze blew for the Americans. There is not a word in any American account of this tense night about a single one of these overloaded boats carrying defensive weapons. The British navy had dozens of cutters on which small swivel guns—light cannon—were often mounted. Even one of these swift-moving craft manned by expert oarsmen could have wreaked havoc on the plodding, defenseless American vessels.

But Admiral Howe was not interested in preventing an American retreat. On the contrary, he was once more pursuing a negotiated peace. Aboard his flagship *Eagle,* he had spent much of the previous day in earnest conversation with the two captured American generals, Lord Stirling and John Sullivan. He permitted Stirling to write a formal report on his brigade's conduct in the battle to Washington, but the New Jersey Scot, a very sophisticated man (in contrast to the propaganda image of him created by the British and loyalists—a drunken buffoon), remained unconvinced of the admiral's good intentions.

John Sullivan was a more naïve and enthusiastic character. His rustic New Hampshire background did not prepare him for dealing with persuasive English noblemen. He was soon eager to become His Lordship's peace missionary. But what peace would there have been to negotiate if most of Washington's army had been slaughtered on the swift waters of the East River or driven back, demoralized, to the Brooklyn shore? This was why no British cutters knifed through the night belching death and destruction at Washington's men.[28]

At dawn on August 30, most of the American rear guard were still manning the fortifications. Delays caused by the weather and the use of many boats to transport back to New York tons of food and ammunition, as well as most of the American cannon, had left these men exposed to death or capture. British army sentries would detect by the first light the absence of men and guns in long stretches of the American line. Aggressive British captains such as George Collier would not have waited for orders from Lord Howe to attack the American boats the moment they became visible—nor could Lord Howe have withheld such an order.

Benjamin Tallmadge of Connecticut, friend of Nathan Hale, was on duty with one of these regiments. As he recalled it later, they were acutely aware of their plight. "As the dawn of the next day approached, those of us who remained in the trenches became very anxious for our own safety." One is tempted to agree with Tallmadge's explanation for what happened next. "At this time a very dense fog began to rise and it seemed to settle in a peculiar manner over both encampments. I recollect this peculiar providential occurrence perfectly well, and so very dense was the atmosphere that I could scarcely discern a man at six yards' distance.

"When the sun rose, we had just received orders to leave the lines, but before we reached the ferry, the Commander in Chief sent one of his aides to order the regiment to repair again to their former station on the line. Colonel Chester [the commander] immediately faced to the right about and returned, where we tarried until the sun had risen, but the fog remained as dense as ever."

Tallmadge left his horse tied to a post at the Brooklyn ferry. When he and his men reached New York, the fog was still so thick that he decided to go back and rescue his steed. Washington, a horse lover himself, gave permission, Tallmadge commandeered a boat, recruited some volunteers and returned to Brooklyn, coaxed his horse into the boat, and was safely out on the river when the first British troops appeared at the ferry landing. "We were saluted merrily from their musketry and finally by their field pieces," Tallmadge said, but not a man was hit. Summing it up, the Connecticut officer declared, "In the history of warfare, I do not recollect a more fortunate retreat." [29]

In the British army on Long Island and aboard the British fleet, consternation and disbelief were the order of the day. Aboard H.M.S. *Rainbow,* Captain George Collier confided to his diary his "inexpressible astonishment and concern [that] the rebel army have all escapd across the River to New York! . . . Now I foresee they will give us trouble enough, and protract the war, Heaven knows how long." [30]

XXV

Jaw-Jaw Proves No Better than War-War

In New York City, Washington's exhausted, bedraggled regiments cast "a general damp" throughout the city. In the words of a neutralist observer, F. G. Shewkirk, pastor of the Moravian Church, "Many looked sickly, emaciated, cast down." The pastor's comments in his diary were a good example of the average civilian's attitude toward an army that retreats. "To the surprise of the city, it was found that all that could come back was back; and that they had abandoned Long Island, when many had thought to surround the King's troops and make them prisoners with little trouble."

If Washington's men looked "sickly," it was hardly surprising. Most of them had spent three days and three nights with no sleep, soaked to the skin in a chill northeast wind. The commander in chief was not in much better shape than his men. As he told the president of Congress the following day, he had hardly been off his horse for forty-eight hours. While he slept, his army started to dissolve. Many soldiers who had endured the travails of Long Island and others who saw the battered army return began having second thoughts about dying for their embryonic country. In militia regiments, most of them from Connecticut, whole companies talked it over, town-meeting style, and decided to go home.

Other Americans, enraged by the possibility of defeat and disgrace, decided to make personal profit their main preoccupation. One shocked New Yorker, a staunch patriot, wrote to his father, "Colonel Hand's Pennsylvania regiment plunder everybody . . . indiscriminately." British army engineer John Montresor had a house on an East River island which he also owned—the results of some twenty-four years of service in America. Hand's man "plundered and committed the most unwarrantable destruction upon it, fifty dozens of bottles were broken in the cellar, the paper tore from the rooms and every pane of glass broke to pieces. His furniture and clothes were brought over to Morisania and sold at public auction." Houses of loyalists, such as the De Lanceys, were sacked in equally ruthless fashion.

Washington condemned this plundering and tried in his general orders to reverse the plunge in morale of which it was a symptom: "Both officers and soldiers are informed that the Retreat from Long Island was made by the unanimous advice of all the General Officers, not from any doubts of the spirit of the troops." He explained that the British had "their Main Body" on Long Island and the Americans decided it was "unsafe" to fight them with only a part of their army. Now the situation was reversed. The whole American army was "collected together," while the enemy could receive little assistance from their ships. "Their army is, and must be divided into many bodies, and fatigued with keeping up a communication with their ships; whereas ours is connected, and can act together: they must effect a landing under so many disadvantages, that if officers and soldiers are vigilant, and alert, to prevent surprise and add spirit when they approach, there is no doubt of our success." [1]

Even green lieutenants such as Joseph Hodgkins could see that it was fatuous to declare that an enemy attacking an island "can receive little assistance from their ships." Five days after he read this statement from his commander in chief, Lieutenant Hodgkins wrote his wife a much more accurate—and discouraging—estimate of the American situation. "It is Verry Diffelt to gard Both sides of this Island against a Numeras Enemy and a large fleet of ships as Ever whas in america. It is Expected they will Land from Long-island over hear at a Place called hellgate. This place is not far from us only across the Island. There is a grate number of our people there and I hope thay will be able to anoy the Enemy but as for hindering there Landing I do not expect they can."

Nothing Washington said could diminish the damage that Bunker Hillism had inflicted on the American army, as Lieutenant Hodgkins' next lines made clear. "You may think that I write tu Discorredging. But only Considder aminute we have Ben all this Summer Digging & Billding of foorts to Cover our heads and now we have Ben obliged to Leave them and now we are hear and not one shovell full of Durte to Cover us But in all Probability we must met them in the oppen field." [2]

With this kind of gloom pervading his army, Washington awoke on Saturday, August 31, to find Major General John Sullivan arriving in New York under a flag of truce. The New Hampshireman told Washington that he wanted permission to go to Philadelphia bearing Lord Howe's olive branch and a request to confer with some members of Congress. With considerable reluctance, Washington let him go. "I have consented," he told the president of Congress, "as I do not mean or conceive it right to withhold or prevent him from giving such Information as he possesses, in this instance." This was far different from the rough handling Lord Drummond received only a few weeks earlier.[3]

Sullivan departed for Philadelphia to talk peace. On Manhattan Island, Washington began distributing his dispirited army for an all-out defense. He reorganized them into "three Grand Divisions" and ordered the center division "to march immediately to Harlem to prevent the enemy's landing on this Island." While he talked about acting with "union and firmness" in his general orders, Washington confided to the president of Congress that the situation was "truly distressing." The minds of "too great a proportion" of the troops were gripped "by apprehension and dispair." The militia were now marching off by whole regiments "instead of calling forth their utmost efforts to a brave and manly opposition." Within a week, 6,000 of the 8,000 men in Connecticut's thirteen militia regiments had vanished, and the harassed governor of that state had to find new men to replace them.[4]

In a long letter, Washington lectured Congress on the need for "a permanent standing Army" enlisted for the duration of the war. Then, without realizing that it was the first step toward the salvation of America, Washington began disengaging himself from Bunker Hillism. "Till of late I had no doubt in my own mind of defending this place, nor should I have yet, if the men would do their duty." Other men on his staff were taking an even more negative look at defending New York. On the same day that Washington wrote to Congress, Adjutant General Joseph Reed wrote to his wife, "My country will I trust yet be free, whatever may be our fate who are cooped up, or are in danger of being so, on this tongue of land, where we ought never to have been." [5]

Reed denounced the runaways and the cowards, in words that demolish the myth of 1776 as a golden age of heroism and idealism.
"When I look round, and see how few of the numbers who talked so
largely of death and honour are around me, . . . I am lost in wonder
and surprise. Some of our Philadelphia gentlemen who came over on
visits, upon the first cannon, went off in the most violent hurry. Your
noisy Sons of Liberty are, I find, the quietest in the field. . . . An engagement, or even the expectation of one, gives a wonderful insight
into character." [6]

Now, if ever, was the moment for an aggressive Royal Army to assault and destroy these rattled, discouraged Americans. Most of the
junior British generals were convinced that the war was practically
over. No less than three of them wrote home in the next few days
predicting an early American collapse. An officer in the Forty-second
Scottish Highlanders looked forward to profits as well as glory! "Rejoice, my friend, that we have given the rebels a d——d crush. . . . I
expect the affair will be over this campaign, and we shall all return covered with American laurels and have the cream of American lands
allotted us for our services." [7]

But no coup de grâce was struck. For two weeks, the British army
sat on Long Island and the British fleet rocked in New York harbor
without firing a shot, while Richard Lord Howe pursued the results of
Major General John Sullivan's peace mission to Congress. Aboard the
Rainbow, Captain George Collier fumed, "I know not what Mr. Washington and his army are doing, but ours have been totally inactive since
the retreat of the rebels, which has occasioned universal dissatisfaction
in the fleet and army. The enemy have now time to breathe and to
throw up fresh works to make our approach to the city more difficult." [8]

In Philadelphia, Major General Sullivan found the Continental
Congress in a poisonous mood. After the fight for independence had
ended in the heady rhetoric of the Declaration, the delegates had
turned to a committee of thirteen who reported on July 12 a draft of
"Articles of Confederation and Perpetual Union." The committee ordered eighty copies printed, expecting them to be "laid before the several states for their approbation" in a matter of days. But the delegates,
although they had managed to construct a shaky majority for independence, were, if anything, more disunited than they were before they
made that historic decision.

Two weeks after the Declaration, Robert Morris, still a power in

Congress thanks to his control of the Committee of Commerce, was telling one correspondent that he still opposed independence "because in my poor opinion it . . . will neither promote the interest or redound to the honour of America, for it has caused division when we wanted Union." Morris was reflecting the situation in Pennsylvania, where radicals were locked in political combat with moderates and conservatives over the constitution. Inevitably, the political atmosphere of this crucial province pervaded Congress.[9]

Some delegates began wondering if Congress should have "setled on a plan of confederation before declaring independence." It was soon apparent to most delegates that this "setling" was going to take time. As Josiah Bartlett wrote to his mentors in New Hampshire, "The sentiments of the members were very different on many of the articles."[10]

The more they argued, the more the delegates realized there were serious divisions between large states and small and between individual delegates about how much power each state should have in Congress and how much each should contribute to the national defense. The small states were afraid of being swallowed by the large states—notably Massachusetts and Virginia. Others were outraged by Virginia's claim that her boundaries extended to "the South Sea." John Adams infuriated small-staters when he informed them if they wanted equal power with the large states they must "pay equally."

By the end of July, Samuel Chase of Maryland was in despair. "What contract will a foreign state make with us when we cannot agree among ourselves?" he asked. Dr. John Witherspoon of New Jersey rose to lecture the delegates in hellfire style. His fellow delegate from the Garden State, Abraham Clark, leaped to his feet to cry, "We must apply for pardons if we don't confederate." Pennsylvania announced they would confederate with no one who claimed their boundaries ran to the South Sea. Connecticut, which claimed a large hunk of western Pennsylvania, sided with Virginia, avowing, "A man's right does not cease to be a right because it is large." A Maryland delegate swore that the "right to happiness and security" of the small colonies was endangered if the large states were not limited.

Another wrangle broke out over slavery. Northern delegates argued that Negroes should be counted as human beings when it came to deciding what proportion of taxes a state should pay. Numerous Southerners maintained, with Edward Rutledge of South Carolina, that they "would be happy to get rid of the idea of slavery" but as long as it existed, slaves were property, not people, and should not be taxed any more than land, sheep, cattle, or horses. This was too much for Benjamin Franklin to swallow in silence. He noted there was "some difference" between slaves and sheep: "Sheep will never make any insurrections."

By the middle of August, the delegates were deadlocked. A disgusted Edward Rutledge wrote that confederation "is of little consequence if we never see it again; for we have made such a Devil of it already that the colonies can never agree to it." Samuel Chase of Maryland and other influential delegates had gone home in disgust. The only hope, wrote Rutledge, was to call "a special Congress" composed of new members dedicated to nothing but hammering out a confederation. But a constitutional convention was out of the question in the middle of a war.[11]

Into this disunited, decimated Congress walked John Sullivan, bearing Washington's report of the defeat on Long Island and disarray in New York—and Lord Howe's olive branch. The timing could not have been better, from Lord Howe's point of view—or worse, from the point of view of John Adams and other unrepentant independents. *Sotto voce,* Adams said that he wished the first shot fired by the British on Long Island had gone through Sullivan's head. But with the anti-independence men still growling in the wings and independence men having second thoughts, it was impossible to dismiss Sullivan. A committee of three was appointed to meet Lord Howe. Franklin was the inevitable first choice, representing the middle states. John Adams spoke for New England, and Edward Rutledge, a latecomer to independence but temperamentally no moderate, represented the South.[12]

On September 11, the three men rode down to the shore of Raritan Bay on Perth Amboy and boarded Admiral Howe's barge, which soon carried them to Staten Island. Lord Howe had sent one of his flag officers in the barge. He had presented himself as a volunteer hostage who would stay in Perth Amboy as a guarantee that the Americans would not be seized as traitors. John Adams thought this was childish, and they took the officer back with them.

Lord Howe went down to the beach to greet the delegation. Looking at his returned officer, he said, "Gentlemen, you make me a very high compliment, and you may depend upon it I will consider it as the most sacred of things." Lord Howe had brought with him his other secretary, Henry Strachey, older and shrewder than Ambrose Serle. Introducing him, the admiral led the party up the hill to the stone mansion of Colonel Christopher Billopp, commander of Staten Island's loyalist militia. The Hessian regiment guarding the shore had converted it into a command post. In the course of this conversion, they had looted and wrecked it—another ironic commentary on the Howes' pacification plans.[13]

As they entered the house, a Hessian guard of honor, composed of grenadiers, "looking fierce as ten furies," John Adams thought, came to attention. The house smelled like a stable. Eighteenth-century military sanitation was primitive. Lord Howe had attempted to dispel the odors and disguise the wrecked condition of the house by spreading "a carpet of moss and green sprigs" in the "large handsome" dining room. John Adams thought the effect was not only wholesome but "romantically elegant."

The table was set "with good claret, good bread, cold ham, tongue and mutton." In this pleasant atmosphere, with the conversation limited to polite small talk, Howe, Strachey, the Hessian colonel in command of the area, and the three Americans enjoyed what we would call lunch but the eighteenth century called dinner. After coffee, the Hessian colonel departed, and so did most of the atmosphere. Its remnants were sustained for a while by Lord Howe, as he tried to convince the Americans that he had come not to make war but peace and had accepted the naval command only at the government's insistence. He had hoped to come with "a civil commission only," and his plan was "to have gone immediately to Philadelphia." He had even objected to his brother the general's being on the commission and again had yielded only to government pressure. He insisted that the last American petition to the King, sent in the summer of 1775, was a basis for negotiating "with candour . . . a plan of permanency." But, sighed the admiral, the Declaration of Independence had "changed the ground." There was no hope of his receiving power to treat with the colonies as independent states—he could not even confer with them as representatives of Congress. He was liable to "reproach" if they forced him to acknowledge their role as a committee from that body.

Benjamin Franklin told the admiral not to worry about this problem for the present. They would consider the conversation "held as amongst friends." Rutledge and Adams, not having had the pleasure of Lord Howe's acquaintance before, agreed to this idea somewhat curtly. Howe then went on to review his thinking on a negotiated peace. He reiterated "His Majesty's most earnest desire . . . to make his American subjects happy." The King was ready "to concur with his Parlia-

ment in the redress of any real grievances." Rather naïvely, Howe
added that it seemed to him the whole dispute revolved around the
way Great Britain should receive "aid" from America.

Franklin pointed out that America had never refused such aid to
Great Britain when it was sought as a special requisition, in time of war.
Howe acknowledged this truth and declared that America's money
"was the smallest consideration." It was "America's commerce, her
strength, her men" that England wanted.

Franklin laughed. "Ay, My Lord, we have a pretty considerable
manufactury of men," he said. Strachey bristled, thinking Franklin was
alluding to the American army. But Howe understood that the philosopher was referring to America's birth rate, which Franklin had accurately predicted in 1750 would double the population of the colonies
every twenty-five years. This fact, widely disseminated in England, had
had not a little to do with making British politicians regard Americans
as potential rivals whose growth and power must be controlled.

Earnestly, Lord Howe ended his discourse with an emotional plea
"to put a stop to these ruinous extremities, as well for the sake of our
country as yours—when an American falls, England feels it. Is there no
way of treading back this step of independency, and opening the door
to a full discussion?"

The Americans responded by throwing the cold water of reality on
Lord Howe's dream. Franklin reiterated much of what he had already
told His Lordship in his July 20 letter, that all former attachment to
Great Britain was "obliterated." As for discussing peace based on the
petition to the King—the Americans considered the Prohibitory Act the
answer to that petition. Britain now had no hope of ruling America—
except by force.

John Adams, with even more warmth, informed Lord Howe that
the Declaration of Independence was not a decision made by Congress
on its own authority. They had acted on instructions from *all* the colonies. Personally, he would never "depart from the idea of independency."

Rutledge, less acerbic than Adams and with no personal reasons for
resentment, such as Franklin had, gave the most effective reply. He
told Lord Howe that he was "one of the oldest members of Congress"—he had represented South Carolina "from the beginning."
There was no hope that the people of his state would ever "consent to
come again under the English government." Never again would the citizens of South Carolina tolerate crown officers who exercised their

royal powers to line their own pockets and jailed anyone who dared to oppose them. They had "taken the government into their own hands" and were "happy under that government" and would not return to the King's government even if Congress urged them to do it.

This did not mean war was inevitable. As an alternative, Rutledge urged Great Britain to consider "whether she would not receive greater advantages by an alliance with the colonies as independent states." He pointed out that she could still enjoy "a great share" of America's commerce. He was even sure that Americans would consent to a treaty of alliance to protect Great Britain's West Indian islands—something they could do "much more effectively and more easily" than England.

Lord Howe shook his head. "If such are your sentiments," he said, "I can only lament it is not in my power to bring about an accommodation." Howe reiterated that he would never receive from the British government the power to treat with the colonies as independent states.

Why not try to get it? Franklin asked. It would "take as much time" for Congress to find out if their constituents were willing to give up the idea of independence. In three months, Howe could get "fresh instructions from home."

Again the admiral shook his head. "It was vain to think" of his receiving such instructions.

There was a leaden pause, and then Franklin said, "Well, My Lord, as America is to expect nothing but upon total unconditional submission—"

Lord Howe flinched at that word "submission." He interrupted Franklin to insist that "Great Britain did not require unconditional submission." He did not want them to go away with such an idea.

Franklin nodded and continued. "—And Your Lordship has no proposition to make us, give me leave to ask whether, if we should make propositions to Great Britain (not that I know or am authorized to say we shall), you would receive and transmit them?"

Howe said that he could not avoid receiving papers that "might be put into his hands." He was not sure about "the propriety" of sending them home. But he would not absolutely decline to do it.

Hands were shaken all around, Lord Howe and secretary Strachey escorted the Americans to the admiral's barge, and the peace conference was over.[14]

The meeting had revealed, once more, that Lord Howe had good intentions—but grave deficiencies as a diplomat. In Parliament, he had been semi-famous for his turgid, almost incomprehensible speeches.

His military mind, trained by decades of rigid obedience to orders, was riveted on his instructions to the point of immobility. His dread of disobeying his orders and seeming to recognize Congress clashed fatally with his generous instincts. A more flexible man, operating three thousand miles from home, would have grasped Franklin's hint that Congress might consider making overtures to Parliament and agreed to transmit such offers, simultaneously suggesting a truce during the three to six months it would take them to be considered. In the admiral's mind, a "reproach" was tantamount to a blot on his honor. He seemed to regard the possibility of criticism from Parliament's politicians on a par with censure in a battle report. Lord George Germain and his victory-in-one-year ultras had clearly won their fight for control of the peace commissioner.

In Perth Amboy, Americans swarmed around Franklin, Adams, and Rutledge, trying to find out what had happened on Staten Island. Perth Amboy was heavily neutralist and loyalist, and most of these interrogators were hoping to hear that Lord Howe had made an offer that could lead to peace. But in spite of "every Stratagem" the committee remained silent.[15]

Proof of their sense of urgency, however, was the decision to send their youngest member, Edward Rutledge, back to Philadelphia immediately, to make an oral report to Congress. At ten o'clock that night in New Brunswick, he wrote a letter to George Washington, who was also very anxious to get a report. Rutledge told Washington that Howe "talked altogether in generals;—that he came out here to consult, advise, and confer with gentlemen of the greatest influence in the Colonies, about their complaints." Rutledge's conclusion: "Our reliance continues, therefore, to be, under God, on your wisdom and fortitude, and that of your forces." [16]

Adams and Franklin returned to Philadelphia the following day and submitted a written report which was a reasonably accurate summary of their conversation with Lord Howe. They said that His Lordship had nothing to offer but the same proposals he had made in his earlier letters and proclamations—pardon on submission and the vague promise that Americans' grievances would be considered after they surrendered.

Congress ordered the committee's report published. Many loyalists and neutralists, such as William Smith of New York, who had retreated from the embattled city to his country house in Haverstraw, were convinced that the Americans were lying and waited impatiently for Lord

Howe to issue a refutation of the committee's report. Smith noted that the Congress had withheld "any Declaration of their Opinion upon it, probably to feel the public Pulse." But he also noted glumly that Congress had voted to establish a standing army of eighty-eight battalions, "which shews their Intention to prepare for the Continuance of the war."

The hopes of Smith and other loyalists were vain. No one in Lord Howe's entourage saw any reason to refute the Franklin-Adams-Rutledge report. Aboard H.M.S. *Eagle,* the mood around the peace commissioner was grim. "They met, they talked, they parted," Ambrose Serle wrote, "and now, nothing remains but to fight it out against a Set of the most determined Hypocrites & Demagogues, compiled of the Refuse of the colonies, that ever were permitted by Providence to be the Scourge of a country." [17]

XXVI

American Sprinters vs. British Liberators

In Haverstraw, New York, William Smith agonized about the possibility—the probability, in his opinion—that Congress had rejected a genuine offer of peace. Smith linked Lord Drummond's mission and Lord Howe's commission and studied every detail of Howe's movements for the previous six months for evidence supporting his thesis. He could not believe that Howe had "waited two months" in England to obtain alterations in his official instructions and then arrived with "no formal powers . . . except for granting Pardons on submission." No, Smith said, "the powers waited for could be no other than such as directed a conference for peace. . . . Can the tables be so turned that the guilt of wasting human blood in future should be our's?" [1]

This, Smith said, "is a critical Moment. Was I a Delegate [to Congress] I should have moved for laying all the private Negotiations of last winter [Lord Drummond] before the Continent and for taking the sense of the Collective body. Lord Howe, I guess, and the Ministers too will make an appeal to the whole world upon this subject . . ."

In New York, other Americans were preparing a much different response to Lord Howe's pacific gestures. They were readying a secret weapon designed to blow up the admiral's flagship and send him, his secretaries, and several hundred British officers and seamen to the bottom of New York Bay. David Bushnell was ready to launch the first submarine attack in the history of warfare. He and his brother, Ezra, had brought their weird-looking ship, the *Turtle*, down from Saybrook, Connecticut, in a sloop early in the summer. Ezra Bushnell had continued to receive frequent leaves, which enabled him to return to

Saybrook and train to become the *Turtle*'s one-man crew. Soon the Connecticut inventor was satisfied that Ezra was "very ingenious and [has] made himself master of the business."

In New York, Bushnell explained his plan to Washington. Although the American commander was skeptical, he gave him money and the half dozen assistants he said he needed. But before any attack could be made, Ezra Bushnell came down with the camp disorder. The doctors predicted it would take him weeks to recover. David Bushnell was in despair. Where could he find a man with the right combination of strength and navigational knowledge to guide the *Turtle* across New York harbor on its deadly mission? He asked Israel Putnam for help. Old Put sent him to another Connecticut general, Samuel Parsons, who came from Lyme, just across the river from Saybrook. Parsons persuaded his brother-in-law, twenty-seven-year-old Sergeant Ezra Lee, to volunteer, along with two other soldiers whom history has failed to name.

Retreating to Saybrook, Bushnell concentrated on training Lee, who was also from Lyme and had a Connecticut River man's familiarity with small craft. Returning to New York early in September, Bushnell found the American army in disarray, the cause in grave peril. He went to Parsons and urged an immediate attack on Admiral Howe's flagship. What better way to cripple the British fleet? Parsons agreed. Because the British now controlled the East River, he arranged for a wagon to haul the *Turtle* overland from New Rochelle to Kingsbridge on the Hudson.

By September 6, the *Turtle* was concealed aboard a sloop docked at the South Ferry landing beneath two thirty-two-pounders of the Whitehall battery. Bushnell decided to attack that very night. The *Turtle* was lowered into the water at the foot of the wharf, and a cask of powder with an ingenious clock and gunlock firing mechanism was screwed into position over the rudder. A screw on the top of the *Turtle* would secure the explosives to the *Eagle.* Bushnell tested the *Turtle*'s complex mechanism, flooded its tanks and began to sink, pumped them out and rose. Everything was ready for the great attempt.

Two whaleboat crews appeared out of the night, Sergeant Lee entered the top hatch of the *Turtle* and screwed it shut, and the whaleboats pulled the submarine out into the bay. They could not get too near the British ships, which were surrounded by patrolling guard boats. They came "as nigh the ships as they dared," in Lee's words, "and cast me off." [2]

Almost instantly, Lee was in trouble. He found that someone had misjudged the tide. The *Turtle* did not have enough power to move against even a modest tide, and the tides in New York harbor were not modest. He soon found himself swept past his target. For two and a half hours, he had to paddle and crank to hold his own. Finally, "the tide slacked so that I could get along side of the man-of-war which lay above the transports."

There was just enough moonlight for Lee to see where he was going, but not enough for a lookout on the *Eagle* to notice the six or seven inches of the *Turtle* moving slowly through the calm water. With his top hatch open, Lee could "see the men on deck and hear them talk." Unnoticed, he reached the *Eagle*'s stern. Now came the moment of truth. Lee "shut down all the doors, sunk down and came under the bottom of the ship. Up with the screw against the bottom."

Consternation. "It would not enter." Again and again Lee drove his craft against the hull of the *Eagle* and cranked the screwing mechanism. Each time, the *Turtle* bounced away. What was wrong? In a panic, Sergeant Lee realized that the *Eagle* was sheathed in copper—an innovation which the British navy had been adding to its men-of-war for several years, to increase sailing speed and retard rot. Actually, it was not the copper that was frustrating Lee. Bushnell had foreseen a copper-sheathed hull, and his screwing mechanism was strong enough to pierce it. What Lee was trying to penetrate was the iron bar connecting the rudder hinge with the stern. "Had he moved a few inches," Bushnell wrote later, "which he might have done without rowing, I have no doubt he would have found wood where he might have fixed the screw." [3]

But Lee, rattled by his failure, tried to row to another position on the ship. He mismanaged the *Turtle*'s ballast, and the submarine shot to the surface east of the *Eagle,* with dawn breaking. Lee turned the water valve, and the *Turtle* "sunk again like a porpoise." Under the surface, he thought about trying again, but he realized that the time he had lost fighting the tide was liable to prove fatal to him. Ships' boats would soon be rowing throughout the fleet, carrying messages from the admiral to his captains and vice versa, ferrying sick ashore and provisions aboard. Lee decided that "the best generalship was to retreat as fast as I could." He had four miles to paddle, and he had to pass British-held Governor's Island.

Unfamiliar with New York harbor and no hand with a compass, Lee was "obliged to rise up every few minutes to see that I sailed in the right direction." Worse, the flood tide kept sweeping him toward Governor's Island. As he came abreast of the fort on the island, he saw "3 or 400 men . . . upon the parapet to observe me." Within minutes, a twelve-oared barge was pulling for him. When it was sixty yards away, Lee freed his magazine, automatically setting the clock-gunlock mechanism going. He hoped "that if they should take me they would likewise pick up the magazine, and then we should all be blown up together."

When the men in the barge saw this odd-looking package emerge from beneath the water, they decided it was an American secret weapon, and they hastily rowed back to Governor's Island. Lee paddled with all his strength in the opposite direction, and Americans on the Battery finally spotted him, sent out a whaleboat, and towed him in. A few minutes later, the magazine went off with a tremendous bang, "throwing up large bodies of water to an immense height." [4]

The explosion knocked people out of their beds in New York and threw the British fleet into a momentary panic. But it was a waste of 150 pounds of American gunpowder. Mournfully, Bushnell wondered why Lee had not "fastened the magazine under the stern of the ship above water as he rowed up to the stern and touched it before he descended." Lee seems to have been a brave man, but a literalist who was determined to make his attack under water, even when it was not necessary. But at least Sergeant Lee had brought the *Turtle* back in one piece. They would try again, Bushnell vowed. General Putnam, cheered by the immense explosion, assured the Connecticut genius that he would have the full cooperation of the American army.

Meanwhile, more important things were happening inside George Washington's head. For two days, he had been pondering a letter sent to him by Nathanael Greene, the first American general to shake off the obsession with Bunker Hill. Greene asked Washington to consider "whether a . . . speedy retreat from this island is necessary or not. To me it appears the only eligible plan to oppose the enemy successfully and secure ourselves from disgrace." He told Washington that the city and island of New York "are no objects for us." There was no reason to "bring them into competition with the general interests of America." Moreover, "part of the army has already met with a defeat; the country is struck with a panick. Any capital loss at this time may ruin the cause." The American philosophy, Greene said, should be "to study to avoid any considerable misfortune, and to take posts where the enemy will be obliged to fight us, and not we them." Greene urged Washington to burn New York City and the suburbs. Two-thirds of the property belonged to Tories anyway.[5]

The day after he received this letter, Washington got a very different message from Congress. "*Resolved,* that General Washington be acquainted, that the Congress would have especial care taken, in case he should find it necessary to quit New York, that no damage be done to the said city by his troops, on their leaving it: the Congress having no doubt of being able to recover the same, though the enemy should, for a time, obtain possession of it." [6]

The next day, September 7, Washington summoned a council of war and asked his generals what they thought. A majority, still convinced that Bunker Hill could be re-enacted, voted to stand and fight. They felt—and so did Washington—that Congress practically ordered them to do it. The next day, Washington wrote a curious letter to Congress, revealing how much he had changed his mind about playing the Bunker Hill game and simultaneously trying to change Congress's mind about not burning New York.

Instead of seeking one titanic all-or-nothing battle, Washington now thought "We should on all occasions avoid a general Action or put anything to the Risk, unless compelled by a necessity, into which we ought never to be drawn." New York, Washington informed Congress, was "a strong Post, but not an Impregnable one." Moreover, "every man of judgment" acknowledged it to be "untenable, unless the enemy will make the Attack upon lines, when they can avoid it and their movements indicate that they mean to do so." It was almost inevitable that the Americans would be compelled to retreat. He was "sensible a retreating Army is incircled with difficulties," and that "declining an Engagement subjects a General to reproach." But the "fate of America" was at stake, and he intended to pursue this policy. He therefore had a tough question to ask Congress. They had resolved that New York should not be destroyed. Were they willing to change their minds, now that "nothing seems to remain but to determine the time of their [the British] taking possession?" [7]

It was a mad way to fight a war—referring command decisions to a collection of military amateurs a hundred miles away. It was evidence of Washington's own inner uncertainty, as well as his deep devotion to the idea of civilian control of the army. Even as he wrote this letter, he rearranged the disposition of his troops to conform with his new strategic thinking. Only 5,000 men were left to defend New York City. Nine thousand—almost half the army—were stationed at Kingsbridge to cover the line of retreat. The rest of his men were posted between New York and this northern exit to contest a British attempt to land above the city. For his new headquarters, Washington chose a country house belonging to the Morris family. It is now known as the Jumel Mansion and still stands at 161st Street.

To avoid more cruel surprises such as the British flanking attack on Long Island, Washington organized a corps of rangers under the command of Lieutenant Colonel Thomas Knowlton of Connecticut. A tall, remarkably handsome man, Knowlton had fought well at Bunker Hill and distinguished himself during the siege of Boston. The corps was to number only 120 men, all volunteers, hand-picked by Knowlton himself.

Among the earliest to offer his services was Captain Nathan Hale. Five months of garrison duty in New York had left him bored and impatient. The very name ranger sounded like action to him. He welcomed the opportunity to operate in semi-independence from the regular army organization. Within a few days, one company of rangers was patrolling the Westchester shore of Long Island Sound. Others were operating along the Harlem and Hellgate shores. This was some comfort to Washington, but no guarantee against another British flank attack. The rangers could hardly oppose a landing in force.

It became apparent to Washington that he had to find out what the British were going to do next. He urged every general under his command to establish some "channel of information" that would give the Americans "intelligence of the enemy's designs." He even suggested persuading a Tory to spy "for a reasonable reward." By September 5, he had abandoned his tendency to be parsimonious, and was telling Major General William Heath to "leave no stone unturned, nor do not stick at expense" to get information. "I never was more uneasy than on account of my want of knowledge on this score." [8]

On September 8, some bits of information dribbled in from a spy on Long Island. Two other spies, working for Governor George Clinton of New York (no relation to Major General Henry Clinton), spent four days on Long Island, but brought back only a gross exaggeration of the strength of the British army. At this point, Washington may have turned to Knowlton and his rangers and asked him for help. Or Knowlton may have simply responded to the pleas Washington was making to almost every commanding officer who he thought could help. The rangers were a logical choice. At any rate, Knowlton called his officers together and asked for a volunteer to cross over to Long Island and operate as a spy. No one responded. Knowlton asked a veteran of the French and Indian War to do the job. He refused. "I am willing to go & fight them, but as far as going among them & being taken & hung up like a dog, I will not do it."

His reply revealed the attitude which most soldiers had—and most still have—toward spying. There was something repugnant about it. Everyone was therefore doubly startled when Captain Nathan Hale said, "I will undertake it."

Knowlton was a superb combat leader, but as an intelligence officer he was a disaster. His orders to Hale were vague to the point of being suicidal. He was simply told to cross to Long Island and learn as much as he could about the British army's fortifications and plans. He was given no invisible ink—although it had been invented three years earlier—or any code which might have enabled him to use innocent-looking letters to conceal information. No false orders were issued to explain Hale's withdrawal from his company. In fact, every officer in the rangers knew where he had gone. Hale himself discussed his mission with a close friend, William Hull, a captain in his former Connecticut regiment. Hull was appalled and tried to talk him out of it. No one could order him to become a spy. With ominous foresight, Hull pointed out that Hale's "nature was too frank and open for deceit and disguise." Moreover, "Who respects the character of a spy?"

Hale calmly replied that "every kind of service, necessary to the public good, becomes honorable by being necessary." Besides, he had been in the army a full year and had yet to render any "material service," Hale said.

On September 12, Hale, accompanied by Sergeant Stephen Hempstead, left the American camp and journeyed to Norwalk. They donned civilian clothes, and Hale assumed his disguise—a "Dutch schoolmaster," out of work because of the turmoil of war and seeking employment among the loyalists of Long Island. He persuaded the captain of an armed American sloop, the *Schuyler,* to take him across Long Island Sound and land him in Huntington. From there, he set out on foot for the British camps around Brooklyn, armed with nothing but his Yale diploma and his determination to do some "material service." [9]

While Hale spied, loyalists were executing an equally daring caper: the theft—or rescue—of George III's head. When the equestrian statue on Bowling Green was toppled and the head sawed off, the King's torso and the horse were shipped to Ridgefield, Connecticut, where they were melted into 42,088 bullets. The head received far more personal treatment. It was carried to the Blue Bell Tavern, which stood near the

northwest corner of present 181st Street and Broadway. There, no
doubt with a plethora of drunken toasts, it was mounted on a spike, the
traditional English treatment of traitors. Not far from the tavern was
the American bastion known as Fort Washington. In the overconfident
days before the British landed on Long Island, the Americans planned
to put the head on the flagstaff of the fort, thus guaranteeing, they
thought, a super Bunker Hill. There is no record that the head ever
achieved this perch. It apparently remained in or in front of the tavern.

Word of the King's downfall had been received with indignation at
British headquarters. Captain John Montresor, the veteran army engineer who had lived in New York for over twenty years, decided to do
something about it. He smuggled orders—and no doubt some
guineas—to John Corbie, who ran a tavern near Canal Street on the
Hudson not far from George Washington's original New York headquarters. Montresor told Corbie to rescue the King's head—and spare
no expense. Corbie hustled to the northern end of New York Island
and conferred with another innkeeper, English-born John Cock, who
ran a tavern on what is today the corner of 230th Street and
Broadway—just east of Kingsbridge.

Like Corbie, Cock had secretly switched to the British side—in spite
of the fact that he had been elected captain of the local militia company. One dark night early in September, they descended on the Blue
Bell Tavern, snatched the King's head, and lugged it back to Cock's
tavern, where they buried it, confident that the day was not far off
when they would be able to present it to Captain Montresor in person.[10]

British maneuvers around New York made this meeting seem more
and more imminent—and Washington's hopes of avoiding another surprise more and more dubious. Landing parties seized two large islands
in the East River, Buchanan's (now Wards) and Montresor's (now Ran-
dalls). Flatboats were seen moving up the Long Island shore. Frigates
moved past the American batteries in New York City, preparing to support a landing. All those enormous forts constructed in New York City
with so much labor were obviously about to be outflanked as totally as
the Americans had been on Long Island. Nathanael Greene circulated
among the generals a petition to Washington for another council of
war. This time, all but three of the ranking officers recommended an
immediate evacuation of Manhattan Island and a retreat across the
Harlem River into Westchester. To retain control of the Hudson, they

recommended leaving 8,000 men on the cliffs south of Kingsbridge in the huge earthwork called Fort Washington.[11]

Washington began evacuating tons of ammunition and supplies from New York City. This proved to be an agonizingly slow process. The American army was short of wagons and horses. Meanwhile, British guns dueled with American batteries at Hellgate, at the northern end of the island, and with a heavy battery at Horn's Hook (present-day Carl Schurz Park at Eighty-ninth Street). This led Americans to suspect that the British planned to land near the village of Harlem—present-day 125th Street. Washington posted some of his best troops there. Farther down the shore, he distributed Connecticut militia—a mistake which was soon to haunt him.

The British army had not been entirely idle while Lord Howe was talking peace with Benjamin Franklin and his friends. A contingent under the command of Oliver De Lancey, Sr., backed by the Seventy-first Regiment of Scottish Highlanders and the Seventeenth Light Dragoons, all under the command of Brigadier General Sir William Erskine, headed east down Long Island and were astonished by the welcome they received. Everywhere, there was a rush to declare loyalty to the King and abjure the rebellion. Among those captured was Brigadier General Nathaniel Woodhull, president of the New York convention. He had collected about 1,500 head of cattle from largely loyalist Kings County and driven them into equally loyalist Queens County, where he began collecting still more beef on the hoof. Instead of retreating farther down the island into Suffolk County, where he might have found some support as well as boats to ship his mooing charges to Connecticut, Woodhull revolved ineffectually around the west end of Queens County in the vicinity of Jamaica, where a party of the Seventeenth Light Dragoons, commanded by Captain Oliver De Lancey, Jr., captured him.[12]

Woodhull surrendered his men, his cattle, and himself without firing a shot. From the tone of several letters he wrote shortly before the event, it was evident that the president of the New York convention was strongly inclined to switch sides and was hoping—even planning—to be captured with a minimum of fuss. He made a feeble attempt to escape, but was trapped in a barn by one of the dragoons, and he surrendered after a brief scuffle in which he was wounded slightly on the arm and hand. The British gave him the best available medical treatment, but the wound became infected and Woodhull died. Lieutenant

Robert Troup, one of the five Americans captured in the Jamaica pass, wrote a wildly fabricated letter to the convention claiming that Woodhull had been butchered by his British captors. Troup was hoping to recoup the military reputation he had lost in the Jamaica pass. The convention ignored Troup, but forty years later his letter was resurrected, and the halfhearted if not totally traitorous Woodhull was elevated into a patriot martyr.[13]

The British did not need Woodhull's support to subdue Long Island. On August 29, Sir William Erskine issued a proclamation ordering "all Committee men and others acting under the authority of the Rebels" in Suffolk County to "cease and remain at their respective homes, that every man in arms lay them down forthwith and surrender themselves on pain of being treated as rebels." Erskine exhorted all persons to assist His Majesty's forces "by furnishing them with whatever lays in their power." In particular, he urged the farmers to bring him their cattle, and their wagons and horses for transporting the army's stores and baggage. Unless he saw "an immediate compliance respecting the cattle and the wagons," he would be under the necessity "of marching the forces under my command without delay into the county." [14]

The only Continental troops on Long Island—some 200 commanded by twenty-six-year-old Lieutenant Colonel Henry Beekman Livingston—were helpless to counteract the impact of this proclamation. The despairing young colonel wrote Washington on August 31 that the British cavalry regiment was considered "an insuperable obstacle" to independence. Within the next few days, whole towns petitioned Erskine for pardon and protection. Just as Washington had feared, cattle and horses flowed into the British camp. On September 6, Lord Howe's secretary, Ambrose Serle, wrote contentedly in his journal, "The Fleet & Army are now exceedingly well supplied with fresh provisions & vegetables from Long Island, which is a pleasing circumstance both for the health & spirit of the troops." [15]

With his men well fed, his rear pacified, and peace negotiations a failure, the question before the British commander in chief was what to do next. He had lost the chance to trap Washington and his entire army inside New York City. But even with Washington's army redistributed, Henry Clinton, the architect of the victory on Long Island, thought there was a chance to repeat the performance on an even grander scale. A direct move across the Bronx to Kingsbridge was his recommendation. He was sure that it would end the war. The Americans had lost "all confidence." An army in such a situation "trembles whenever its rear is threatened." [16]

Once again, Clinton was butting his head against the Howes' approach to the rebellion. They still did not want to trap and destroy Washington's army. Their spies told them that there were only about 5,000 men left in New York. This would be another very acceptable slice of Washington's force. They planned an attack aimed at trapping these men and acquiring New York City with a minimum of bloodshed.

After thinking about a landing in Harlem, Howe abandoned it on the advice of his brother's captains, because it was too close to the tide rips of Hellgate. Howe decided to concentrate his attack on Kips Bay, a fairly deep indentation in the Manhattan shore at present-day Thirty-fourth Street, with a V-shaped meadow rising beyond it. There were no cannon near it and no significant fortifications. The Americans would be forced to fight in the open—something Howe and his advisers were sure they could not do successfully against trained soldiers.

General Clinton was given charge of the advance guard, and Sunday morning, September 15, was chosen for D day. Clinton spent a large part of the night of the fourteenth trying to talk Howe out of the landing. He was sure that the result was going to be a slaughter. The tide in the East River ran so strong it would not be possible to get the flatboats across it at flood—the only time when the troops would be able to land on firm sand. Two hours later, they would be forced to flounder through mud and rock, "entirely exposed to the enemy's fire." Howe tried to calm him down by assuring him that a preliminary cannonade from the fleet's frigates would clear the beach. But Clinton was unconvinced. Early on the morning of the fifteenth, he wrote a harried memorandum to himself: "My advice has ever been to avoid even the possibility of a check. We live by victory. Are we sure of it this day? J'en doute. [I doubt it.] These people are assembled in force. . . . I like it not. No diversion, no demonstration but what a child would see through, little prospect of victory without buying it dear." [17]

Lower in the ranks, there was no such apprehension. Frederick MacKenzie, a captain in the Twenty-third Welsh Fusiliers, one of the army's elite regiments, wrote in his diary on the eve of the battle, "The troops are all in the highest health and spirits, and one may venture to say that their behavior when they attack the Enemy will fully answer the General's expectations. . . . We have no doubt of success." [18]

At 7:30 P.M. on Saturday, September 14, five British frigates,

H.M.S. *Phoenix, Roebuck, Carysfort, Rose,* and *Orpheus,* dropped anchor in Kips Bay. They were close enough to exchange insults with the Connecticut militia regiments on the shore. Sixteen-year-old Joseph Plumb Martin heard an American sentry call, "All is well." A sailor aboard one of the frigates replied, "We will alter your tune before tomorrow night." As dawn broke, Martin and his friends saw the five ships "within musket shot of us." They were spread out along the shore for about 1,100 yards. The *Phoenix* was close enough to Martin for him to read her name "as distinctly as though I had been directly under her stern." [19]

The militiamen shouted insults, waved their guns, and urged the British to try coming ashoré. But the sailors briskly went about loading their cannon and preparing their ships for action without replying. Two hours passed. The sun rose in the sky with summer fierceness. A hot, muggy haze enveloped Manhattan Island. The waiting Connecticut militiamen grew more and more restless.

Out of Bushwick Creek opposite Kips Bay came the British in their flatboats—more and more of them, until they looked to young Martin "like a large clover field in full bloom." With steady, rhythmic beats from their oarsmen, the boats began moving across the East River. In the lead boat was Henry Clinton. Beside him as his aide was Lord Rawdon, the young Irish nobleman who had brooded and frozen so bitterly last winter on Bunker Hill. Clinton had seven battalions of red-coated British light infantry and grenadiers and a brigade of British guards behind him in his boats, as well as three battalions of blue-coated Hessian grenadiers and green-coated jaegers. The Germans, convinced that they were about to be slaughtered—amphibious operations were new to them—began singing hymns. The irreligious British damned their officers and the enemy indiscriminately "with wonderful fervency," according to one earwitness.[20]

The American commander in chief of the East River lines was aging Major General Joseph Spencer of Connecticut, a man whom Alexander McDougall of New York described as "a fool." Spencer seems to have made no attempt to take charge of his sprawling regiments. Instead, individual commanders were allowed to play guessing games with the advancing British. The wind and tide bent the oncoming British line into a crescent, and carried it upstream. This made some colonels think the British were heading for Turtle Bay, the next cove above Kips Bay at present-day Forty-second Street. Others, watching the slow assemblage of the British flatboat armada, decided that the British were waiting for an ebb tide to land nearer New York at Stuyvesant's Cove near present-day Fifteenth Street.

At 11 A.M., when the British barges were about fifty yards from the offshore frigates, the eighty-six cannon on the men-of-war exploded. Joseph Martin, who had straggled into a nearby warehouse, thought his "head would go with the sound." He dived into his trench and lay there trying to decide "which part of my carcass was to go first." [21]

Midshipman Bartholomew James, who was aboard the *Orpheus*, later wrote it was "hardly possible to conceive what a tremendous fire was kept up by those five ships for fifty-nine minutes." In the *Orpheus* alone, James maintained, they blasted away 5,376 pounds of powder. Most of the round shot whistled over the heads of the men in the trenches. The British concentrated their fire on the Americans who had made the mistake of thinking the soldiers were going to land at Stuyvesant's Cove. With these reserves cut off, only the thin line of Connecticut militia cowering in their trenches opposed the 4,000 elite British troops in the attacking flatboats. Out of the shroud of powder smoke hanging over Kips Bay, these now loomed in three columns, the Hessians on the left, the British grenadiers on the right, and the light infantry in the center.

The Connecticut militiamen took one look at these murky, murderous shapes and started running. By the time the first British flatboat grounded several dozen yards from the beach and the men began floundering through the mud, only the local commander of the Connecticut militia brigade, Colonel William Douglas, and a handful of men over whom he had immediate control were still in the trenches. On paper, Douglas' brigade had numbered 1,300 men, but about 400 were sick. The cannonade and the feeling that they had been left in their paltry trenches unsupported were simply too much for the raw militiamen to endure.[22]

There were four New York regiments under the command of John Morin Scott stationed behind the Stuyvesant house near the foot of Sixteenth Street, and five more regiments of Connecticut militia under the command of Brigadier General James Wadsworth near the vicinity of what is now Twenty-third Street. They should have rushed to Douglas' support—but were as paralyzed by the cannonade and the awesome sight of the oncoming British attackers as the men confronting them at Kips Bay.

Henry Clinton could not quite believe it as his flatboats disgorged their men without a shot being fired at them. His light infantry, led by

Brigadier General Alexander Leslie, swarmed ahead of the grenadiers in open formation, bayonets ready. But there was no one to bayonet. By this time, the Connecticut militia were legging it north along the Boston Post Road. Behind the light infantry came the British grenadiers with their high black fur caps glistening in the morning sunlight. They reinforced the light infantrymen, and together they were soon in possession of General Howe's immediate objective—the gently sloping high ground around present-day Thirty-fourth Street, known as the Inclenberg. On its crest was a comfortable mansion which belonged to a Quaker named Murray.

On the left, the Hessian grenadiers moved behind their screen of jaegers to seize woods and fields belonging to a man named Watts. They were met by a round of musketry from the woods. A few hundred Americans were trying to make a stand there. The grenadiers charged with the bayonet, and it was Long Island all over again. Whimpering, pleading Americans were skewered trying to surrender. Others fought to the death in the hot green stillness. Perhaps sixty men died here, and another sixty managed to surrender, when the fury of the first bayonet charge dissipated. By 1 P.M., the British had absolute control of their beachhead and were cautiously expanding it north and south, still braced for an American counterattack.

No such event was forthcoming. George Washington and his staff, and other generals in the vicinity, including Parsons and the area commander, Spencer, both of Connecticut, tried to rally the fleeing Yankee militiamen. They hoped to organize a stand along the Bloomingdale road, around present Forty-first Street, where farmers' fields were divided by a number of stone walls and the corn stood high. They had two brigades of Connecticut troops—about 2,500 men, no one of whom had been anywhere near the Kips Bay beachhead. But when they saw the defenders of Kips Bay running helter-skelter up the road and across the fields, these regiments also collapsed. The sight of about 70 British light infantrymen on the crest of the Inclenberg, a good quarter of a mile away, completed their panic. In vain Washington roared, "Take the wall! Take the cornfield!" The men raced past him up the road or legged it into the fields around him.

Washington saw his military reputation vanishing, and he went berserk. He flung his hat to the ground and cried out in anguish, "Are these the men with which I am to defend America?" Cursing stupendously, he lashed runaways who were within reach of his riding crop. But neither oral nor physical fury had the slightest effect. Washington was left alone in a road littered by thrown-away muskets, knapsacks, canteens, and cartridge boxes.

Washington seldom let his volcanic temper get out of control. When he did, he was drained to the point of stupor by the immense explosion of emotional energy. Not by accident did the Indians who met him on the frontier in his twenties, before he had acquired his monumental self-control, christen him "Canotocarius"—"town burner." On the Bloomingdale road, the commander in chief slumped in his saddle staring dazedly around him. A ten-year-old with a toy sword could have taken him prisoner. Bewildered aides waited for him to do something. So did the equally bewildered British redcoats on the crest of the Inclenberg. Suspecting a trap, the British light infantrymen moved forward with maximum caution. Washington did not even seem to see them. Finally, one of his aides—perhaps Joseph Reed—rode up to the general, took the bridle of his horse, and led him up the road in the littered wake of his troops.[23]

By now, the east side of Manhattan Island from present-day Forty-second Street down to the New York City line was in control of the British and their German allies. They were also in control of the Hudson River up to Stryker's Bay at Ninetieth Street. Three men-of-war had moved up that stream while Clinton's men were landing at Kips Bay. The New Jersey and Pennsylvania militia manning the American fort at Paulus Hook (contemporary Jersey City) fled at a single broadside from these floating gun platforms, ending any hope of evacuating New York City by water. Inside New York were perhaps 4,000 men, including most of the American army's irreplaceable artillerymen. Sixty-seven heavy guns were also still in the city—about half the cannon in the American army. It was too late to move these out now. It would be a miracle if the men themselves escaped. Twelve exposed miles stood between them and the safety of the American positions on Harlem Heights, and there was only one route left for their exit—the Greenwich road which ran up the west side of the island through the village of the same name.

Israel Putnam was in command of these men. He would have preferred to stand and fight to the last man. But he received an explicit order from Washington to retreat, and with the help of energetic aide Aaron Burr he organized these stranded troops into a column and began a disorderly flight up the Greenwich road. From approximately 1:30 P.M., the British under Clinton had been sitting on and around the Inclenberg waiting for William Howe to arrive with the second division of the army. Clinton had no orders to advance, and Howe never sent him any while his men were being ferried across the tricky East River. This task took almost four hours, and by that time Putnam and his 4,000 retreaters had got well north of Thirty-fourth Street. According to an old New York legend that refuses to die, the British failed to draw a line of steel across the island because the mistress of the Murray mansion entertained the British high command with cakes and Madeira and witty conversation until they lost interest in winning the war. Mrs. Murray may have served some goodies to General Clinton and his staff, but the repast had nothing to do with their failure to advance.

Elsewhere inside the British beachhead, confusion was the order of the day, as Midshipman Bartholomew James of H.M.S. *Orpheus* soon discovered. He was sent with a ship's barge to tow ashore several flatboats which had been abandoned by their crews and were in danger of floating away. Ashore, James and his crew decided to collect souvenirs. They were picking up discarded American muskets, swords, canteens, and similar paraphernalia when a blast of musketry from the East River whistled around their ears. It was a boat from the *Orpheus,* firing at them, assuming they were rebels. "I made signs of friendship but all in vain," James recalled later, "and I was obliged to throw away my little affairs and take to my heels, as the enemy had done before."

On his arrival aboard the *Orpheus,* he found the second lieutenant amusing the captain with the story of how he had dispersed a body of rebels. James heatedly informed him that he and his sailors had been the target and bemoaned "the valuable swords and little trifles" which he had left behind him. The lieutenant decided he would like a few of these souvenirs and persuaded the good-natured captain to let him and James go ashore again. They soon procured no less than nine drums and some "fusees"—light muskets carried by officers. A midshipman from H.M.S. *Phoenix* joined them, and when the lieutenant wandered off in another direction, the two midshipmen went exploring.

In an orchard, they found a rebel prisoner who gratefully surrendered to them rather than put himself in charge of the Hessians who were "dispersed all round the woods," he told them. Feeling very martial, James and his fellow midshipman led a group of sailors deeper into the woods. They heard voices and leveled their muskets in the direction of the sound, assuming they were about to bag more prisoners. Instead, "up start two or three hundred Hessians, with flaming large brass caps on, and with charged bayonets advanced rapidly toward us." James and his fellow sailors were "alarmed prodigiously" and attempted through elaborate gestures to convince the Germans that they were friends. Unconvinced, the Hessians knocked them down and banged them around with the stocks of their muskets, calling them "rebels."

James pointed to his white cuffs as proof that he was part of the British navy. The Hessians pointed to a nearby American officer who was propped against a tree, dying, his leg shot off by a cannonball. He had on exactly the same uniform. The righteous Germans began bashing the sailors around again and were about to bayonet them when Brigadier General Robert Pigot came rushing up, recognized Midshipman James, and ordered the Hessians to cease and desist. "They made a thousand ridiculous apologies for their treatment," James said, "and we returned to our ships, in need of both cook and doctor, and totally weary of our expedition." [24]

Not until five o'clock did the British move south, the Hessians in the lead, and begin to occupy New York. There were still scattered pockets of Americans in the city. Among these were about 80 musketeers and artillerymen in the Bunker Hill redoubt near the present intersection of Grand and Centre streets. Israel Putnam's aides forgot to tell them that a retreat was in progress. As darkness fell, they finally abandoned their symbolically named fort and legged it toward the Hudson shore.

Captain Frederick MacKenzie urged his commanding officer, Brigadier William Smith, to station his men across the island from the Bowery to the Hudson River. But Smith, MacKenzie morosely noted in his diary, was "slow, and not inclined to attend to whatever may be considered as advice, and seemed more intent upon looking out for comfortable quarters for himself, than preventing the retreat of those who might be in the town." The brigadier "grew angry" and said MacKenzie "hurried him." He would place the brigade "as he thought proper." He proceeded to distribute his men in a vertical column for three miles along the road to New York. This enabled the garrison of the Bunker Hill redoubt and other fugitives to wait on the Hudson shore until after darkness fell, when boats arrived from New Jersey and carried them to safety.[25]

Downtown, the civilians were demonstrating whose side they were on. When it became apparent that the Americans were abandoning the city, Admiral Howe sent a party of marines to take possession of the fort on the Battery and hoist the Union Jack. A crowd of people swarmed around the seagoing soldiers, and as the flag soared aloft there was an explosion of cheers. The American Grand Union flag was trampled underfoot "with the most contemptuous indignation," reported Ambrose Serle, who was an eyewitness from the deck of H.M.S. *Eagle*. "Nothing could equal the Expressions of Joy, shewn by the Inhabitants," Serle wrote. "They even carried some of [the King's officers] upon their shoulders about the streets. They have felt so much of real Tyranny since the New England & other Rebels came among them, they are at a Loss how to enjoy their Release." [26]

XXVII

A Town Burner
Loses a Spy

In the American camp on Harlem Heights, gloom was thickening by the hour. At dawn, in the Morris mansion, George Washington wrote a report of the Kips Bay debacle to Congress. He had "used every means in my power" to rally the fleeing men, but "they ran away in the greatest confusion without firing a single Shot." If the enemy attacked the main body of the army on Harlem Heights, Washington hoped that they would "meet with a defeat . . . if the generality of our Troops would behave with tolerable resolution, But, experience, to my extreme affliction, has convinced me that this is rather to be wished for than expected." [1]

He closed his letter by remarking that he had "sent out some reconoitring parties to gain Intelligence." One of these parties was Knowlton's rangers. As Washington wrote, they were prowling through the well-tilled fields of Farmer Nicholas Jones in the vicinity of present 106th Street and West End Avenue. British pickets spotted them, and a skirmish began. Four hundred British light infantrymen were camped only a few hundred yards south, and they responded to the American challenge. For the better part of two hours, the two groups blasted away at each other. Then Knowlton saw the Forty-second Regiment—the famed Scottish Black Watch—advancing on the American left, bagpipes skirling. His men already outnumbered, Knowlton ordered them to retreat. The light infantrymen began a hot pursuit, and fighting continued along both sides of the Bloomingdale road all the way up to a deep depression known as the Hollow Way, near present-day 125th Street.

Adjutant General Joseph Reed, who had ridden forward to watch the skirmish, found Washington at the American army's advance posts around West 135th Street, and urged him to reinforce Knowlton. At that moment, the pursuing British appeared on a rise known as Claremont, close to where Grant's Tomb stands now. Over the heads of the retreating Americans, and floating up to the ears of the men on Harlem Heights, came the sound of British bugles blowing the whoo-whoop call of a fox hunt, meaning the fox was dead and the chase was over. Reed and many other Americans, already writhing at the sight of another retreat, felt this was the ultimate mortification. "I never felt such a sensation before," Reed told his wife a few days later. "It seemed to crown our disgrace." [2]

Reed told the wary Washington that they should teach the British a lesson for this display of arrogance. Washington, dreading the possibility of a full-scale battle with his men still shaken by the previous day's disaster, reluctantly consented. He told Knowlton to take his rangers and three rifle companies of the Third Virginia Regiment under Major Andrew Leitch through the woods and along the slopes of Vanderwater's Heights—now Morningside Heights—and try to cut off the British light infantrymen. At the same time, another party—many of them volunteers—descended into the Hollow Way. The British came down from their high ground to meet them, and a hot skirmish began.

Meanwhile, Knowlton's men were making good progress along the British flank, and it looked for a while as if they might gain their rear and cut them off. At present 123rd Street, where they were to swing west, some members of the Third Virginia Regiment could not resist the sight of the unsuspecting British and began firing at them. The well-trained light infantrymen whirled to defend their flank, and their first volley hit Major Leitch with three bullets as he stood on a ledge urging the men to move rapidly past him. Thomas Knowlton immediately replaced him in this exposed position, and a musket ball hit him in the back. He fell into the arms of one of his captains, who asked him if he was badly hurt. Knowlton nodded and said, "I do not value my life if we do but get the day." [3]

Men carried him to Joseph Reed, who lifted him on his horse and rode to the rear. With only captains to command them, the Americans launched an amazingly ferocious attack on the stunned British light infantrymen. Washington poured another 800 men into the Hollow Way and added some Maryland and Connecticut militia regiments. The British were soon fighting for their lives. Washington threw in more men to support both the flank and frontal attackers. The British commander of the light infantry, Brigadier General Alexander Leslie, ordered the Forty-second Regiment into the fight and called for help from nearby German units.

At first, the fighting was in the open—by American choice. They were still eager to prove that they could best the British European style. Lieutenant Joseph Hodgkins told his wife how the enemy had pursued the Americans "Down the Hill with all speed to a Plain spot of ground then our Brigade marched out of the woods then a very hot Fire began on Both sides and Lasted for upward of an hour." The pressure grew too great on front and flanks, and the British light infantry retreated into some woods that lined the sloping hill along which Broadway now runs.

The elated Americans pursued them vigorously. A spirited charge by parts of two Maryland regiments drove the British out of the woods to the edge of a buckwheat field at the top of the slope. There the British met reinforcements—the Second and Third Battalions of light infantry with two pieces of field artillery.

By now, even some of the men who had fled from Kips Bay were in the fight, displaying new self-confidence. One of these Connecticut men, Sergeant Ebenezer Leffingwell, was sent to the rear by his company officer to get more ammunition. He collided with Adjutant General Joseph Reed, who thought he was repeating the Kips Bay performance and ordered him back to the front. When Leffingwell argued with him, Reed drew his sword and threatened to kill him. Leffingwell threw up his musket and fired point-blank at Reed's head. The musket flashed in the pan and did not go off. Reed seized a musket from a nearby soldier and fired at Leffingwell. This gun, too, failed to go off. Reed then attacked Leffingwell with his sword, cut off his thumb, and forced him to surrender.

For another hour, perhaps two, the fight swayed back and forth on the edge of the buckwheat field between present 120th and 119th streets. Then the British, low on ammunition, began falling back again, often breaking and running quite unceremoniously while the Americans pursued them with whoops and musket bullets. As the British got down below 111th Street, frigates anchored in Stryker's Bay on the Hudson began firing. They had no hope of hitting anything. It was

further evidence the British were anxious to persuade the Americans
to cease and desist. The naval cannon and the sight of heavy reinforcements of German and British grenadiers persuaded the Americans to
break off the pursuit.

The Americans were enormously heartened by this small skirmish,
in which the British suffered about 180 casualties and the Americans
130. "We whar informed By two Prisonors that thay found that they
had not the Milisha to Deal with at this Time," Joseph Hodgkins told
his wife. "This whas the first time we had any Chance to fite them and I
dout not if we should have another opportunity But we should give
them another Dressing." Hodgkins was sure the British had 500 killed
and as many wounded.[4]

British overconfidence produced by two successive American routs
had led light infantry junior officers to give Washington the semblance
of a victory to restore confidence to his shaken army. Perhaps the best
example of this new attitude was noted by Joseph Plumb Martin of
Connecticut, whose regiment had been among the Kips Bay sprinters.
They remained on the Harlem Heights battlefield until almost sunset,
expecting the British to counterattack. "The men were very much fatigued and faint, having had nothing to eat for 48 hours," Martin
recalled. One man, standing next to the lieutenant colonel, complained
of his hunger. The colonel put his hand into his coat pocket, took out a
piece of an ear of Indian corn burnt as black as a coal. "Here," he said,
"eat this and learn to be a soldier."

In his journal, Captain Frederick MacKenzie of the Royal Welsh
Fusiliers called the Harlem Heights skirmish "an unfortunate business." He added that it gave Howe "a good deal of concern." The general demonstrated this concern by placing his army on a strict defensive. He began fortifying a line from Stryker's Bay on the Hudson
River to Horn's Hook on the East River. He also issued strict orders
against abusing the inhabitants of New York, whom he described as
"loyal, good subjects." He expected "soldiers whose valour has freed a
people from the worst kind of Slavery, will be careful that no act of
theirs prevent the enjoyment of all the blessings that attend British liberty." No man was to take anything under the pretense that it was rebel
property. Nor were they to "pull roots or enter gardens without the
owner's leave."[5]

Having thus—he hoped—assured the good behavior of his troops,
the general and his brother decided that it was time for another peace-
making effort. Instead of appealing to the rebel leaders, this time they

decided to go over their heads to the people. On September 19, the admiral and the general issued a joint declaration urging any and all
Americans to confer with them on "the means of restoring public tranquillity and establishing a permanent union." They declared that the
King was prepared to revise royal instructions and acts of Parliament to
achieve this happy goal. They urged Americans "to reflect seriously
upon their present conditions and expectations and to judge for themselves whether it be more consistent with their honour and happiness
to offer up their lives as a sacrifice to the unjust and precarious cause in
which they are engaged" or "to return to their allegiance, accept the
blessings of peace, and to be secured in a free enjoyment of their liberty and properties upon the true principles of the constitution." [6]

This noble-sounding document was a diplomatic disaster. Most people read it as the Howes' reply to the Franklin-Adams-Rutledge committee report to Congress on their conference with Lord Howe. At
Haverstraw, William Smith fumed to his diary, "What egregious Blundering to publish an Address in such general terms. . . . This paper
confirms the Assertion of the Committee that His Lordship had nothing to offer." [7]

Most members of the British army and navy thought little of the
Howes' declaration. Captain Andrew Snape Hammond of H.M.S. *Roebuck,* an admirer of Admiral Howe, wrote to a friend, "It has long been
too late for Negotiations, yet it is easy to be perceived My Lord Howe
came out with a different Idea." [8]

Privately, the Howes were already growing pessimistic about their
peace overtures. The day after they issued their proclamation, they
wrote a joint letter to Lord George Germain claiming they were "not
without hopes of its producing some good." But they admitted, "We do
not yet perceive any symptom of that disposition of allegiance, and submission to legal government which would justify us in expecting to see
the public tranquillity soon restored." [9]

Within twenty-four hours, this pessimism was more than justified by
new proof of the rebel Americans' determination. Shortly after midnight on September 20, a cry that every eighteenth-century city dweller
dreaded was heard in New York's streets: "FIRE." The wind was blowing briskly from the south, and the flames, which broke out first in a
wooden house near Whitehall ferry slip, swept north with devastating
rapidity. Most of New York's houses had shingle roofs, and the wind
carried burning flakes to other houses, many of them empty, setting
them ablaze. Lord Howe ordered hundreds of seamen from the fleet

ashore to fight the blaze, and two regiments of the army's Fifth
Brigade, stationed just north of the town, rushed to help. But they had
no experience as firemen, and there was little they could do. Water was
scarce, the fire engines were found to be practically useless, and there
was a shortage of buckets.

The British soon discovered that the wind was not the only reason
for the rapid spread of the flames. The Indian who had dubbed
George Washington "Town Burner" had prophetic powers. Troops
and sailors caught a number of Americans running from empty houses
seconds before they burst into flame. At one point in the roaring chaos,
they heard a cry of pain and saw a woman who had been carrying
buckets of water up to the fire engines clutching a bloody arm. A
man—some later said it was her husband—had stabbed her. The seamen seized him, and the woman said that he had been cutting the
handles of the fire buckets. He was killed by the enraged sailors and
hung up by the heels. Several other Americans caught setting fires met
equally brutal deaths. Their bodies were thrown into the flames.

Later witnesses swore that they saw two men on the roof of Trinity
Church. As an Episcopal church, it was a symbol of British authority,
and hence a logical target of New York and New England rebels, who
were mostly Presbyterians and Congregationalists. The church was
soon ablaze, its wooden spire creating "a lofty pyramid of fire." [10]

General Howe refused to commit his whole army to fighting the
flames, fearing it might be part of a plan to attack his forward positions. At daybreak, the fire was still burning out of control, and he sent
a brigade of the foot guards to help. By this time, the fire had blazed
for a mile up the Hudson shore. Captain Frederick MacKenzie, who
reached the city around this time, wrote in his diary that it was "almost
impossible to conceive a scene of more horror and distress . . . the
sick, the aged, women and children half naked were seen going they
knew not where, taking refuge in houses which were at a distance from
the fire, but from whence they were in several instances driven a second and even a third time by the devouring element, and at last in a
state of despair lying themselves down on the common."

Only by pulling down dozens of houses and creating firebreaks did
the soldiers and sailors finally confine the blaze. Somewhere between
400 and 600 houses—a quarter of the city—were destroyed. The British began a house-to-house search for more American incendiaries.
Sentries were urged to be on the alert and to search and challenge
every stranger. Admiral Howe's secretary, Ambrose Serle, who went

ashore to see the damage later in the day, said it took him some time to convince one soldier that he was "no Rebel." Serle commended the man for "the steady Performance of his duty." [11]

This increased vigilance was Captain Nathan Hale's undoing. Events had fatally outrun the amateur spy's movements, almost from the moment he had landed on Long Island. The British attack at Kips Bay made his original mission meaningless. With courage that approached foolhardiness, Hale apparently decided to enter New York and see what he could find out about British plans from inside their lines there. This was infinitely more risky than moving along the well-traveled roads of Long Island. No one knows when Hale arrived in New York, but he spent enough time there to note British troop dispositions and the field fortifications Howe's men were constructing. According to tradition, he carefully wrote down all this information and concealed the papers in his shoes.

A man aggressive enough and daring enough to be selected as an officer in Knowlton's rangers should have had little difficulty slipping through the British sentries that night and reaching the safety of the American lines on Harlem Heights. But the inferno that exploded in New York drove Hale out of the city before he had time to formulate a plan. He reportedly took refuge in a tavern, the Cedars, north of the city, and was trapped there when the British searched the place for incendiaries. The story that he was turned in by a Tory cousin is probably untrue. Some loyalist may have pointed him out as suspicious. That night, almost everyone looked suspicious to the enraged supporters of the King.

Hale admitted everything. He was escorted to General Howe's headquarters in the Beekman mansion, which stood near the corner of present First Avenue and Fifty-first Street. Howe, already infuriated by the flames engulfing New York and jumpy over a possible American attack, wasted no time. Hale again admitted he was an American officer operating as a spy. Howe ordered him hanged without even the formality of a trial.

Hale spent the night in the greenhouse of the Beekman mansion. The next day, he was escorted to the British artillery park by Provost Marshal William Cunningham, a man who had already proved himself something of a sadist guarding American prisoners in Boston. Hale asked Cunningham for a clergyman. The provost marshal refused the request. Hale asked for a Bible. The answer was the same curt no.

At the artillery park, Cunningham was called away on other business, and Hale was left standing with his guard. Perhaps the provost marshal was hoping he would break down. Captain John Montresor, the engineer who had rescued George III's head, was sitting in the marquee of his tent only a few feet away. Montresor invited the condemned man to sit down beside him in the marquee. Hale remained amazingly composed. He asked Montresor for pen and paper and wrote two letters, one to his brother Enoch, the other to Colonel Knowlton. Hale did not know that his commanding officer was already dead and buried on Harlem Heights. Montresor was moved by Hale's "gentle dignity, the consciousness of rectitude and high intentions."

The two men talked for a few moments, and then Cunningham summoned Hale to his fate. The official hangman, a mulatto named Richmond, put the noose over his head. Hale mounted a ladder propped against the tree that served as his gallows. Cunningham asked the spy if he had any final words. Even the most vicious criminals in the eighteenth century were given this privilege. The blindfolded Hale replied, in an unshaken voice, "I only regret, that I have but one life to lose for my country." On an order from the provost marshal, he stepped off the ladder into eternity.[12]

Hale's sacrifice, and especially his last words, have provided inspiration for thousands of Fourth of July orators. But in 1776 they inspired practically no one. When Montresor handed over Hale's letters to Provost Marshal Cunningham, he refused to deliver them. "The rebels should never know they had a man who could die with so much firmness," he said.

A few days later, Montresor met a party of American officers under a flag of truce to discuss an exchange of prisoners. Among the Americans was Captain William Hull. Montresor told Hull the story of Hale's death. Apparently he was still moved by it. Hull, appalled by his friend's fate, which he still considered disgraceful, if not dishonorable, told no one about it for another fifty years, when he finally confided it to his daughter. Badly as the Americans needed heroes, in 1776 Nathan Hale was closer to being an unknown soldier.[13]

XXVIII

Indecisive Generals and Hard-Drinking Heroes

On Harlem Heights the day after Hale died, Colonel Henry Knox, commander of the American artillery, wrote a doleful letter to his brother. "The General is as worthy a man as breathes, but he cannot do every thing nor be every where. . . . There is a radical evil in our army—the lack of officers." Most of the army's officers, Knox said, were "a parcel of ignorant, stupid men who might make tolerable soldiers, but are bad officers. . . . As the army now stands, it is only a receptacle for ragamuffins." [1]

The following day, Washington stole "from the hours allotted to Sleep" time to write a very long letter to John Hancock, the president of Congress, pleading with him to end the dependence on short-term militia, and take steps to create a decent officer corps, the soul of every army. Washington told Congress a fact of life which political purists found—and still find—difficult to accept. After the waning of the idealistic emotions that first prompt people to support a cause, it was vain to hope that most men (or women) could be "influenced by any other principles but those of Interest." To expect anything else "was to look for what never did, and I fear never will happen." In particular, he urged Congress to pay officers enough "to live like, and support the Characters of gentlemen." Too many officers were being "driven by a scanty pittance to low, and dirty arts . . . to filch the publick." [2]

Washington told of one officer who had robbed a supposedly Tory house "of a number of valuable goods; among which (to shew that nothing escapes) were four large Pier looking Glasses, a women's

Cloaths and other Articles which one would think, could be of no earthly use to him. He was met by a major of brigade who ordered him to return the Goods, as taken contrary to Genl. Orders." The officer not only refused to do so, but with the aid of some thieving companions swore he would defend his spoils "at the hazard of his life." The major had to call out a full company of men to subdue the thief, who was court-martialed and cashiered.[3]

Above all, Washington begged Congress to enlist enough men for the duration of the war to give him a standing army. He knew how jittery this term made some politicians. But "the evils to be apprehended from one," he argued, "are remote." While the result of not having one "is certain and inevitable Ruin." [4]

In the diaries of British officers, there was ample evidence that Washington was telling the turth. On September 24, the same day that Washington wrote to Congress, Captain MacKenzie noted "near 80 deserters came in one day lately." Three days later, he noted, "many deserters came in." The American army was continuing to dissolve. MacKenzie concluded in his diary that "there can be no doubt that much greater numbers leave them to return to their own homes." [5]

This was exactly what was happening on Harlem Heights. Among the Connecticut militia regiments, one dwindled to 14 men, another to 30. Several others had fewer than 50 soldiers in their ranks. Other regiments were mutinous. When Sergeant Leffingwell, the man attacked and arrested by Adjutant General Reed for cowardice, was condemned to death, his comrades in his Connecticut regiment warned their officers that if Leffingwell was executed, his would not "be the only blood that would [be] spilt." The Connecticut officers intervened with Reed, who in turn persuaded Washington to pardon the man.[6]

"If the enemy should make a vigorous push," Joseph Reed wrote to his wife, "I would not answer for our success at any time." He commented on reports he had heard from Philadelphia that there was a considerable party "for absolute and unconditional submission." Noting that "Jemmy Allen [James Allen, of Pennsylvania's powerful anti-independence Allen family] was here the other day with a view to discover I suppose what prospects we had, so that the party might take their measures accordingly." Allen's brother William had resigned his commission as lieutenant colonel of the Second Pennsylvania Regiment because he did not agree with the Declaration of Independence. Reed had only one consolation. Allen went away uncertain of what was really happening. The American army still looked fairly formidable. "A person must be in the secret to know the worst of our affairs," Reed wrote.[7]

On the Hudson River, that tenacious Connecticut genius David Bushnell was having another go at the British fleet with his submarine. This time, his target was one of the frigates that had come up the river during the attack on Kips Bay. Hoping to avoid the previous error, Bushnell told Sergeant Lee to attach the torpedo on the waterline. Alas, this produced comic-opera results. Lee was spotted by an alert British sailor and was forced to dive. Under the surface, the cork which was supposed to tell him his depth stuck in the gauge. He went all the way to the bottom of the river and was swept away by the tide. It took him hours to crank and pedal his way to safety.

Annoyed by this attack and by an earlier assault by fire ships, the British decided to rid the Hudson of the gaggle of American sloops and war galleys which flitted about the river above Fort Washington. One of these ships, the galley *Crane,* was the floating refuge of Bushnell's *Turtle.* The Americans thought they were protected by the guns of the fort and another set of chevaux-de-frise sunk in the channel. On October 9, The British frigates attacked, broke through the underwater barrier, and streamed past the belching guns of Fort Washington unscratched. They went to work on the American river fleet, capturing or sinking almost everything larger than a rowboat. Among the victims was the *Crane,* which took the *Turtle* to the bottom with her. Submarine warfare would have to wait another century.[8]

The British army remained on an inert defensive. Even a mere captain could see the folly of a frontal assault on Harlem Heights. On September 29, Captain MacKenzie noted that the American army had spent the entire previous night under arms in expectation of an attack. "I believe they may be easy on that head, for I am of opinion Genl Howe will never attack them in front in their present position. He certainly intends something very different." [9]

But MacKenzie was not correct about another supposition which he, as a professional soldier, assumed to be the reason why he and his fellow Britons were risking their lives in America. "The grand point in view is certainly to beat and disperse this their principal army, which, if once effected, little more will remain to be done." On the day that MacKenzie wrote this in his diary—October 8—a British council of war decided on a plan of attack designed to do the precise opposite. Destroying Washington's army was still not part of the Howes' plans.

While a distracted Washington was writing to his cousin, Lund

Washington, that "if the men will stand by me (which by the by I despair of) I am resolved not to be forced from this ground while I have life," Howe put Henry Clinton and 5,000 men aboard flatboats in the East River and, under the guidance of his brother's ships and sailors, moved them through the perilous waters of Hellgate in a thick fog to land them unopposed on Throg's Neck, a point of land near the junction of the East River and Long Island Sound (present-day Fort Schuyler Park in the Bronx). At the council of war, Clinton had urged a landing at or near New Rochelle on Long Island Sound. From there, they could quickly cut the main road to New England and be only a short march from White Plains, the key position in Westchester County, astride a network of roads. With ships in the Hudson already cutting off all Washington's waterborne supplies, his army would have no choice but to starve, disperse, or fight under very disadvantageous circumstances.[10]

Admiral Howe had objected to New Rochelle because he feared an autumn storm could wreck his fleet in that unsheltered place. Throg's Neck was chosen largely to placate the admiral. It had no strategic advantages, beyond signaling Washington that the British were outflanking him again and he had better abandon New York. The country between the Neck and Kingsbridge was rough and broken by stone fences which made it easy to defend. William Duer, a member of the New York convention, remarked that if he had had the power to land the British army on the worst possible place on the continent, Throg's Neck would have been his choice.[11]

The Americans destroyed the only route off Throg's Neck to the mainland—a causeway and bridge. They moved up cannon and began fortifying the shore. For four days, Clinton and his men, bitten by mosquitoes which swarmed through the marshes, sat there waiting for orders. In New York, Captain MacKenzie noted in his diary the rumor that the army was paralyzed because the rebels had destroyed a bridge. "I am of opinion there must be some other obstacle to prevent the Army from advancing than the destruction of a single bridge," the captain wrote. It was a logical conclusion for a man who had seen the same army cross the wide, swift-running East River and land in the face of an entrenched enemy. That these troops could be balked by a creek fordable at low tide made no sense—or it made sense only if one understood what was going on at British headquarters.

On October 18, Admiral Howe and his brother withdrew Clinton and his men from Throg's Neck and landed them at Pell's Point in present-day Pelham. There the British met some stiff resistance from Brigadier General John Glover's four Massachusetts regiments. Although they were only skeleton organizations, totaling barely 750 men, they inflicted heavy losses, particularly on the German regiments as they advanced inland. Among the British casualties was Captain William Glanville Evelyn, who had led the advance guard of the flanking column on Long Island. Evelyn's company charged Glover's men as they crouched behind "bendstone" walls. His men drove the Americans from one wall, but another party of Americans were waiting behind the next wall, and as Evelyn vaulted over the abandoned wall, he was hit by three bullets; one grazed his left arm, the second tore open his left thigh, the third shattered his right leg above the knee. Carried back to New York, he refused amputation, in spite of repeated urging by British army doctors. Leg wounds were frequently fatal in the eighteenth century because they became infected. Within three weeks, the handsome young captain, who had survived blizzards of American bullets at Bunker Hill, was dead.[12]

Once the British beachhead around Pell's Point was secure, Howe extended it northward to New Rochelle and sat down to await reinforcements. He had just learned that 8,000 Hessians had arrived at Sandy Hook. There was not the slightest attempt to advance toward White Plains and seize the high ground. Howe had 240 light dragoons in his army, more than enough to reconnoiter the eighteen miles between him and that strategic village and discover that it was defended by nothing but a handful of militia.

In the American camp, a mercurial figure was striding about playing his favorite game, uproar. Major General Charles Lee had been summoned from South Carolina by the jittery Continental Congress to rescue George Washington and his fellow generals. By the time Lee left South Carolina, many of the revolutionary leaders there were looking on him with jaundiced eyes. One called him "very clever but . . . . a strange animal." Another also admitted his cleverness but denounced his arrogance and overweening confidence in his own opinions. But to Congress Lee was the only American general in sight who had won a recent victory. The success with which South Carolinians, aided by North Carolinians and Virginians, smashed the Cherokee Indian uprising along their frontiers added to these laurels, although he had practically nothing to do with this back-country fighting.

When they summoned Lee to New York, neither Congress nor the men whom he was supposedly coming to rescue realized that the hawk had become a dove. The fierce advocate of independence and all-out war was now telling influential civilians that it was time to make peace with the British. Charles Carroll of Maryland, one of those senators whom Lee had denounced as a namby-pamby, heard this with astonishment when Lee stopped at his plantation for dinner on his way to Philadelphia. Congress must have been equally amazed when Lee told them that "one or two persons . . . should converse with the Howes" about peace terms.[13]

Lee's passage north was reported by newspapers in such glowing terms that several members of the American army were inclined to be sarcastic. One wrote that "General Lee was hourly expected as if from Heaven, with a legion of flaming swordsmen." But another soldier told his wife that Lee was worth ten thousand men and most of the army could not wait for him to arrive. This was an ominous commentary on their loss of confidence in George Washington.

Lee immediately began urging Washington to get off Manhattan Island. He also told Washington that he ought to threaten to resign if Congress kept interfering with his military decisions. This was hardly disinterested advice—the new American commander would have been Charles Lee. On October 16, while Howe's army still fought mosquitoes on Throg's Neck, Lee persuaded a council of war to vote for retreat. But Congress had urged Washington to keep the Hudson River closed to British ships. The generals decided to leave some 2,000 men behind in Fort Washington to handle this problem.

The new retreat was a nightmare. There were still not enough horses to haul wagons and guns. Some cannon were dragged by hand. The American army was a long, exposed line of 13,000 weary, dispirited men. Six miles away by a straight road, at Eastchester, were William Howe's elite light infantry and grenadiers. Unquestionably, they could have smashed Washington's army to pieces in a single day's march. Or Howe could have led these light troops to unassailable positions in the hills above White Plains. Instead, he did nothing while Washington's army crawled painfully to these same hills and took possession of them.

Perhaps Howe, knowing the psychological impact of a retreat on an amateur army such as Washington's, was hoping that the American force would dissolve. More probably, he thought the Americans would flee north, leaving the rich granary of Westchester County in British control. It was clear that he did *not* wish to trap Washington's army in a position where an all-out fight would be their only alternative. But the

Americans startled him by drawing up in a line of battle on the hills above White Plains, daring the British to attack.

Lieutenant Colonel Charles Stuart, an aggressive young soldier, who, like MacKenzie, thought he was fighting to destroy the American army, told his father in England that "a more glorious scene cou'd not have presented itself to a General of spirit and determination. Their position was strong, but the superior discipline of the British Troops and a judicious attack wou'd at once have routed and chastised them. . . . I speak as a soldier whose mind glow'd with hopes of a victory whose consequences would have stopped the effusion of human blood and subdued this country." [14]

Washington, under the pressure of Charles Lee's aggressive advice, was leaning toward Bunker Hillism again—with sagacious variations. The American position was extremely strong. They held three miles of high ground. Behind them were the higher hills of Northcastle, to which they could, at least theoretically, retreat. Many Americans were again seized by that old idea of one titanic clash that would decide everything. On October 26, Joseph Reed wrote to his wife, "The business of this campaign, and possibly the next, may probably be determined this week. To the protection of that Being who blessed our early days and first connexion, I must commend you and the dear children." [15]

The American position had one potentially fatal weakness. In advance of their right wing was a height known as Chatterton's Hill, which dominated the entire American front. Charles Lee was not slow in noting this fact and reporting his concern to Washington. Lee pointed to the hills north of White Plains. "Yonder," he said, "is the ground we ought to occupy."

Before a decision could be made, Howe attacked. The British artillery blasted the Americans all along the line. On Chatterton's Hill, a regiment of militia broke and fled when a cannonball smashed a man's thigh. A reinforcement of regulars was rushed to Chatterton's summit, but it was too little and too late. In a superbly executed maneuver, Germans and British stormed up the hill. The militia fled once more, many of them without firing a shot. After some brief but stiff resistance, the regulars were forced to retreat.

The entire right wing of the American line was now vulnerable to a flank assault. Colonel Charles Stuart, whose regiment had helped seize Chatterton's Hill, reported, "The rebels . . . [showed] much consternation on their right flank being turned." An aggressive general who wanted to finish the war would have and could have attacked all along the line immediately, rolling up the American right flank and possibly surrounding the wreckage of the army by seizing the high ground in its rear. Instead, Howe did nothing. The baffled British and Germans sat on Chatterton's Hill and elsewhere along the battle line, waiting for orders that never came. The next day, Charles Stuart wrote, "We were ordered to encamp, to our astonishment, as the hill we had taken commanded the rebel position; moreover not a shot was fired." [16]

For three days, Howe did nothing but construct batteries. Washington demonstrated his lack of enthusiasm for Bunker Hillism by moving most of his stores and his sick and wounded to the heights of Northcastle. The men lay in the lines shivering, without tents or blankets, while first snow and then rain fell upon them.

Everyone in the British army could see that the Americans were retreating. "I perceived . . . that the enemy were marching off their stores and that the greater part of their army were gone," Charles Stuart wrote. "Is it through incapacity or by design of our C—— that so many great opportunities are let slip, I am inclin'd to Adopt the latter," wrote another officer. Recalling a British general who believed in going for the enemy's jugular, he added, "O thou spirit of the Great Wolf[e], the more I see, the more I think of thee, and the more I revere thy most sacred memory." [17]

Years later, when his conduct was examined by a committee of the House of Commons, William Howe said that he had "political reasons, and no other, for declining to explain" why he had not assaulted the whole American front on the twenty-eighth. This was the closest he ever came to admitting the restraints which his brother's policy placed on his conduct of the war in 1776.[18]

On the night of November 1, the American infantry withdrew from White Plains and took new positions in the Northcastle hills. Howe did not show the least inclination to pursue them. A staff officer, Lord Rawdon, naturally inclined to side with the general, thought this was a wise decision, noting that the Americans were "indefatigable in fortifying" their position. If Howe had made even a cursory investigation, he would have found that the American fortifications were nothing more than cornstalks covered with loose earth. Apparently Washington did not dare ask his men to dig any more real fortifications.

As it was, the American army was dissolving at an ever more alarming rate. Washington's secretary, Robert Harrison, reported to Congress, "Several gentlemen who have come to camp within a few days have observed large numbers of militia returning home on the different roads." After Kips Bay, it was the Connecticut militia who deserted en masse. Now it was the New Yorkers, an even more discouraging sight since they were fighting to defend their own state. Perhaps most alarming was the fact that the enlistments of a large percentage of the American army would expire early in December.

Congress chose the worst possible way to raise new regiments. State governments were ordered to send committees to the army. These politicians were supposed to confer with Washington about which officers should be reappointed in the new regiments so that they could "proceed immediately to enlist such men as are now in the service and inclined to re-enlist during [for the duration of] the war." By November 1, not a single state committeeman had appeared in the camp—which meant that not a single officer had been appointed, nor did most officers, good or bad, know where they stood in regard to future service.[19]

One New York officer, speaking mostly for militia under his command, wrote, "One month more disbands a very considerable part of our army. How a new one will be recruited, God only knows. This I know, many are disgusted with the service." On November 3, Washington was reduced to pleading with the deserters in general orders. He was "sorry to find that there were some soldiers, so lost to all Sense of Honour and Honesty, as to leave the Army when there is the greatest necessity for their services." [20]

It is obvious that if Howe had pursued Washington into the Hudson highlands, using the British navy's command of the river to land above the Americans and harry them relentlessly, the Continental Army would have collapsed. It probably would have collapsed if Howe had simply remained in White Plains, poised to attack. In that position, he cut most of Washington's communications with his chief food supply, the state of Connecticut, while the ships in the Hudson interdicted the supplies from upstate New York.

Washington had other woes. His men were robbing the local Westchester population with the same assiduity that they had looted New York. In the diary of John Smith, a sergeant in a Rhode Island regiment, stealing is taken almost for granted. On October 22, when the American army was stumbling toward White Plains, in deadly peril of being destroyed by the enemy, Smith recorded that "Amaziah Blackmore, a sergeant in Capt. Blackmores company, went to Eastchester amongst the diserted houses to see would he Could Plunder." The sergeant was accompanied by a lieutenant and a fifer. They collided with thirty Hessians on a similar mission and were captured. The sergeant managed to escape by kicking off his shoes and running away at the right moment. But he must have brought back good reports of the pickings. At nightfall, Smith recorded, "Capt. Baley & Lieut Richmond went Down & plundred Some houses at E: Chester of . . . furniture to the value of $400 & one colt." Brigadier General John Nixon thought this was such fine work he made a present of the colt to Captain Baley.[21]

They were clearly not the only ones operating in this fashion. In a scorching paragraph in his orders of the day, Washington condemned "officers" who were seizing horses from nearby farms and sending them into the country for their private use. "Can it be possible, that persons bearing Commissions, and fighting in such a Cause can degrade themselves into Plunderers of Horses?" Washington asked.[22]

On the night of November 4, strange sounds began emanating from the British camp. American sentries heard the rumble and clank of wheels, the clop of horses' hooves. The army was placed on full alert for an attack. But when dawn broke, they saw with unbelieving eyes that the British were retreating.

Exultation replaced anxiety in the American camp. They told themselves they had won the war of maneuver against General Howe. In a letter to Benjamin Franklin, Charles Lee declared, "We have by proper positions brought Mr. Howe to his *ne plus ultra*. He has therefore apparently given [up] all hopes of taking us prisoners, as I believed he lately sanguinely promised himself." In a confidential letter to his brother Jack, Washington was not quite so exultant. "We have, I think, by one Manouvre and another, and with a parcel of ———— but it is best to say nothing more about them. Mixed, and ungovernable Troops spun the campaign out to this time without coming to any decisive action, or without letting Genl How obtain any advantage which, in my opinion, can contribute much to the completion of the business he has come upon." [23]

In these words can be seen the slow death of Washington's belief, hope, and expectation that the war would be decided in 1776—and the birth of the strategy that would eventually win the Revolution: delay, delay, and more delay.

The British retreat inspired some Americans to a peculiar bit of nonheroics. They burned the village of White Plains. The perpetrators were some fine fellows from the Sixteenth Massachusetts Regiment, under the command of Major Jonathan Austin. Ignoring a specific order from Washington that forbade burning any house or barn without permission from a general officer, the Yankees first looted the center of the little village where some thirteen or fourteen houses clustered. Such tactics were not likely to improve New Yorkers' low opinion of New Englanders. Mrs. Nathaniel Adams, the wife of a loyalist blacksmith, begged Major Austin to spare her house. Austin replied, "You are all damn Tories," and drove her into the November night without even giving her time to dress her children. Austin and his men then set the looted houses afire, burning almost all of them and the courthouse. A furious Washington ordered an immediate court-martial, and Austin was cashiered, largely on the testimony of Mrs. Adams.[24]

Such distractions explain in part why Washington, having mastered one fundamental lesson in the art of war, now demonstrated a melancholy failure to master an even more vital necessity for a successful leader—a reliance on his own usually sound judgment. Watching the British retreat to New York, he asked himself where Howe was going. The answer, which he even stated in a letter to Congress, was the strong probability that the British planned to invade New Jersey, and also to "bend their force against Fort Washington and invest it immediately." To counter these moves, Washington decided to divide his army, leaving Charles Lee and about 11,000 men in Westchester, while he marched with another 2,500 into New Jersey.[25]

But what to do about the 2,000 men in Fort Washington? Nathanael Greene, who was in immediate command of these troops, and of regiments stationed in Fort Lee, on the New Jersey shore opposite Fort Washington, had been corresponding with Washington about it. Greene's attitude was influenced by the presence of a large number of New Jersey and Pennsylvania militia at Fort Lee. The morale of these men was already alarmingly low. Greene was even more unnerved when he paid a visit to New York militia guarding the Westchester shore at King's Ferry, north of Fort Washington. There he found that an entire regiment under the command of Colonel Ann Hawkes Hay had mutinied. They told Hay that "General Howe had promised them peace, liberty and safety; and that is all they want." These words had a cutting irony in them. They were an exact quote from the petition of the First Continental Congress to the King. "This spirit and temper should be checked in its infancy," wrote the jittery Greene. He sent Hay reinforcements to cow the New Yorkers and threatened to order them across the river to do heavy digging at Fort Lee.[26]

This counterrevolutionary turmoil made Greene extremely reluctant to abandon Fort Washington. In the eyes of the unstable militiamen, this would be another retreat. Greene clung to this resolution even after six battalions of Hessians under the command of Lieutenant General Wilhelm von Knyphausen seized high ground around Kingsbridge, and relaid the bridge that the Americans had destroyed. Although Fort Washington was obviously menaced by these self-confident Germans and he was uncertain how much territory the Americans could hold outside the fort itself, Greene's response was to reinforce the isolated garrison.

Now known as Washington Heights, the hill on which the fort stood had been dubbed Mount Washington by the Americans. It was about a mile long and 230 feet high, and it was flanked by steep cliffs running down into the Harlem and Hudson rivers. Below it, through a narrow valley, ran the road to Kingsbridge and upstate New York. Cannon on Mount Washington not only could harass British ships in the Hudson but could close land communication with the rich farms of Westchester. These were worthwhile goals, but whether they could be achieved indefinitely with Fort Washington surrounded by the British army and navy was a serious question. There was no well in the fort, no bombproof trenches, no fuel, and only the most primitive sanitation. Water had to be hauled up from the Hudson. Shorn of the support of Washington's army in Westchester, the fort was a military absurdity.

But Bunker Hillism still gripped significant portions of the American army, notably the man who had made his reputation there, Israel Putnam. Even the normally sensible Greene, who had played a key role in saving Washington from fighting to the death inside New York City, remained mesmerized by the natural strength of Fort Washington's position. On November 9, he declared, "I cannot conceive the garrison to be in any great danger. The men can be brought off at any time." [27]

Yet two days earlier Greene had informed Washington that vessels attempting to supply the fort with flour from New Jersey had been attacked by British barges and tenders, which drove the American boats ashore and were prevented from burning them only by the most determined resistance. Washington pointed out to Greene on November 8 that the British navy was sailing up the Hudson with impunity through the obstructions and cannon fire from Forts Lee and Washington. He was therefore "inclined to think it will not be prudent to hazard the men and Stores at Mount Washington."

But Washington left it up to Greene "to give such Orders as to evacuating Mount Washington as you Judge best." This was not the language of a commanding general, and Greene airily dismissed it. He argued that it was costing the British "double the number of men to invest it that we have to occupy it. . . . Upon the whole, I cannot help thinking the garrison is of advantage." After conferring with Colonel Robert Magaw, the commander of the fort, he was convinced that it could be held until "December expires." [28]

While the Americans debated, William Howe paused at Dobbs Ferry with most of his army, detaching three brigades under Lord Percy to assist General Knyphausen in attacking Fort Washington. The British knew exactly what they were doing, thanks to some help from defecting Americans. On November 3, an American officer named William Demont deserted to the British stationed on Manhattan Island. He brought with him the plans for Fort Washington and its outworks.[29]

Washington began crossing the Hudson with his 2500-man share of the army. The presence of the British navy at the lower ferries of the river forced him north to the highlands. The sixty-five-mile march took three full days. He did not arrive at Fort Lee until November 13. When he reached this position, he was upset to discover that the New Jersey militia were not turning out to defend the state. Washington expected at least 5,000 New Jerseyans, ready to fight for their home soil. Instead, there were only a handful, which meant that 3,500 men under Greene and the 2,500 he brought with him were his entire army.

By this time, militia morale in New Jersey had deteriorated almost totally. When Matthias Williamson accepted a commission as brigadier general of the state's militia on September 15, he had warned Governor William Livingston that the system of monthly rotation was not working. Fewer and fewer men turned out with each rotation, and Williamson expected his forces "to dwindle away to a mere nothing in three or four relieves more." [30]

This made the Fort Washington garrison—which now numbered 2,600 men—all the more vital. Greene, Putnam, and Hugh Mercer, the general in command of the Flying Camp in New Jersey, were all in favor of fighting for the fort. Washington, though he remained dubious, permitted them to continue reinforcing the garrison.

Washington had other things on his mind. On November 15, he was up at dawn to ride to Hackensack to confer with New Jersey authorities about the defense of that state and the organization of a supply depot in the town. About 5:30, a dispatch rider arrived with a report from General Greene. The British had demanded the surrender of Fort Washington. Colonel Magaw had replied that they were "determined to defend the post or die." By the time Washington returned to Fort Lee, it was dark. He learned that Generals Greene and Putnam were at Fort Washington, conferring with Colonel Magaw. So uneasy was Washington, he immediately boarded a boat to join them. Halfway across the river, he met Greene and Putnam returning. The Bunker Hill hero had dominated the conference. The men in the fort were in high spirits and eager to make a stand. Since there was nothing that Washington could discover in the dark to contradict these assertions, he ordered his oarsmen to come about and return to New Jersey with his two major generals.

At dawn on the sixteenth, Washington crossed the river with Putnam, Greene, and Hugh Mercer to survey the situation. While they were on the river, firing broke out in the vicinity of Fort Washington. By the time they struggled up the cliff to the heights, the British attack was rolling forward and had already overrun the fort's outer defenses on the southern slopes. The generals walked down to Washington's old headquarters, the Morris house, where they watched the British assault. There was nothing they could do now about withdrawing the garrison, nor was there any criticism to be made of Colonel Magaw's defensive preparations. So, after a few awkward minutes as spectators, the generals returned to their boat and were rowed back across the Hudson. They did not leave a moment too soon. Within fifteen minutes of their departure from the vicinity of the Morris mansion, the British were in possession of the ground.[31]

Howe's attack was nothing less than a military masterpiece. From every available height within range of Fort Washington, artillery poured fire on the American positions. From Kingsbridge on the north, Lieutenant General Wilhelm von Knyphausen led a column of Hessians, supported by a brigade of British guards who stormed across the Harlem River. From the south, a brigade of British light infantry and a brigade of Hessians moved through McGowan's pass to smash the American outworks on that side of Mount Washington. Other light infantry regiments and the Forty-second Black Watch crossed the Harlem River in flatboats and outflanked the American defenders on the south. Militia, posted to defend the riverbank, fled when the colonel commanding them was killed.

The most spectacular fighting was between the Hessians and Pennsylvania riflemen at the northern end of Mount Washington, a half mile from the fort. Led by Colonel Johann Rall and his regiment, the Germans clawed their way up the almost vertical slope, clinging to bushes and outjutting rocks like alpinists while the Pennsylvanians poured rifle fire and blasts of grape and round shot from three cannon down on them. For two hours, the Germans inched their way up the face of the mountain, with Rall in the lead roaring encouragement to his men and defiance to the flying American lead to which he seemed almost miraculously impervious. Then the American fire began to dwindle. The myth of the potent American rifle was once more laid bare. The long, thin barrels easily became fouled. On the heights, one man after another found he could no longer load his gun. By this time, another column of Germans, under the personal command of Lieutenant General von Knyphausen, was attacking the flank of the hill. The Americans broke and ran for the fort with the Germans on their heels. The Pennsylvanians found the entrance to the fort crammed with refugees fleeing British attackers from the south. The pentagonal earthwork was soon so crowded that some men were forced to remain outside in the ditch. By now, 2,637 men and 221 officers were jammed into and around the fort.[32]

Knyphausen ordered one of his captains to tie a white cloth to the end of a musket barrel and advance to the fort to demand its surrender. The Americans, who had been told they were to fight to the death, blazed away at the captain and his drummer boy as they walked toward them. But they were bad shots, and the captain was soon face to face with Colonel Magaw, who asked for four hours to confer with his officers. By that time, darkness would have fallen and the Americans might have been able to evacuate the garrison to New Jersey. The German captain, well aware of this possibility, gave him a half hour.

Magaw, his bravado of the previous day totally dissipated, wrestled with his conscience. At this point, a messenger from Washington arrived—a daring young American captain from Rhode Island named John Gooch. He had rowed across the Hudson and dodged his way up the cliff to the fort through the surrounding Hessians. The message was simply an exhortation to hold out until darkness—hardly a solution to Magaw's dilemma.

The Pennsylvania colonel told Gooch that this was impossible. The British and Germans were planning to storm the fort. There was little doubt that the Germans, who had suffered heavy casualties fighting their way up the northern cliffs, would take full advantage of the military tradition that defenders of a fort who refused to surrender could be massacred to the last man. With a sigh, Magaw told Gooch that it was too late. He had begun to negotiate, and if he refused the enemy's terms, he would be exposing his men to almost certain slaughter. Gooch got out of the fort and somehow escaped potshots and bayonets from the surrounding Hessians to take this despairing message back to Washington.[33]

Magaw accepted the German terms, and at 4 P.M. the Americans surrendered. They left behind them in the fort forty-three cannon, plus tons of ammunition and supplies. According to the terms, the Americans were supposed to retain their private property. As they marched out, the Hessians stripped the clothes off their backs. Finally, the British intervened and ordered the prisoners to take a different route. The British were amused at the ragtag appearance of the American prisoners. "Few of them . . . appear to have washed themselves during the Campaign," Captain Frederick MacKenzie wrote in his diary. "A great many of them were lads under fifteen, and old men . . . Their odd figures frequently excited the laughter of our Soldiers." [34]

Washington had a somewhat higher opinion of the Pennsylvanians. "The loss of such a number of Officers and Men," he told Congress, "many of whom have been trained with much more than common attention, will I fear be severely felt." Washington could not tell Congress exactly how many men had been captured. On the morning of the attack, someone, perhaps Greene, or more probably Putnam, had sent several hundred additional men across the river to be swallowed by the waiting enemy. Washington was in danger of becoming a parody of a general, and many people knew it.

On the day that Fort Washington fell, Charles Lee wrote to Adjutant General Joseph Reed, "I confess I cannot conceive what circumstances give to Fort Washington so great a degree of value and importance as to counterbalance the probability or almost certainty of losing fourteen hundred of our best Troops." Before the end of the day, Reed was telling Lee that the fort had surrendered. Reed said he wrote at Washington's orders, and was conveying a question from the general: What did Lee think of retaining his present post in Westchester "under all circumstances?" [35]

Lee was having his own troubles. On the same fateful November 16, he had addressed a plea to the "Officers and Soldiers of the Massachusetts militia," whose time of service had expired. They constituted about half his army. He asked them in the name of "the sacred cause in which They are engag'd" to remain "a few days longer." Lee denounced "some few" officers who "unhappily have been elected to sta-

tions their characters disgrace." These officers have "laboured to dis-
suade the soldiers" from staying. Although Lee threatened to make the
names of the officers known as "enemies and Pests to their Country,"
they—and their men—went home en masse. Even in Massachusetts, the
torrent for independence was drying up with fearful rapidity.[36]

Ebenezer Huntington, brother of the Continental Army officer who
had been so exultant when the British evacuated Boston, described to
his father the desertion of the Massachusetts militia. They "would not
stay tho their eternal salvation was to be forfeited if they went home.
The persuasion of a Cisero would not any more effect their tarrying
than the Niagara Falls would the kindling of a fire." The captain's
conclusion: "I am . . . in Great Fear for our political salvation." [37]

Meanwhile, Lee was writing to Congressman Benjamin Rush, one
of the militant independence men who had helped overthrow the government of Pennsylvania, that "the affair at Fort Washington cannot
surprise you in Philadelphia more than it amazed and stunned me. I
must entreat that you will keep what I say to yourself; but I foresaw,
predicted, all that has happened. . . . My last words to the General
were—Draw off the garrison, or they will be lost."

Having stabbed Washington in the back, Lee proceeded to demolish
Congress. "I confess your apathy amazes me. You make me mad . . .
Such a total want of sense pervades all your counsels that Heaven alone
can save you." Then came words that revealed Lee to be—potentially,
at least—the most dangerous man in the American army. "Had I the
powers I could do you much good—might I but dictate one week—but
I am sure you will never give any man the necessary power—did none
of the Congress ever read the Roman History?" [38]

In Hackensack, George Washington was writing to his brother Jack,
"I am weary almost to death with the retrograde motion of things."
The letter was a jeremiad about everything from the failure of his
officers to give him the right advice—or take his advice—to the failure
of Congress to create a decent army. All year he had begged them to
do something. Now it was too late. The different states were quarreling
about appointments and nominating as officers men "not fit to be
shoeblacks." In ten days, he would not have two thousand regulars on
the New Jersey side of the Hudson to oppose Howe's whole army "and
very little more on the other to secure the Eastern Colonies and the Important Passes leading through the Highlands to Albany."

The defense of New York, on which Washington had staked his
reputation—and at times his life—was over. It had been an almost un-

mitigated disaster. Three hundred and twenty-nine officers and 4,100 men had been taken prisoner. Several thousand more—no one knows how many since most were militia—had died of disease. Another 600 had been killed or wounded. But even these losses were not as damaging as the thousands of Americans, most of them from New York, Connecticut, and Massachusetts, who had simply picked up their muskets and gone home to spread the word that the American army was a mess and anyone who risked his life in it was out of his mind.

For a nation fighting a war on paper money, with severely limited technology, the military equipment lost in New York was almost as disastrous. Two hundred and eighteen cannon had been captured by the British. Thousands of tents and blankets and entrenching tools and other hard-to-replace equipment had been lost in the frequent retreats.

The only fortification left in American hands from the dozens constructed in their wrongheaded defense of New York was the earthwork on the New Jersey shore originally named Fort Constitution, and renamed Fort Lee when that General rejoined the main army. It was a forlorn relic, which no longer served any defensive purpose. But Washington, stewing in his rage and despair at Hackensack, wasted three days before issuing an order to evacuate the place. Even then, loath to report another retreat to Congress, he said only the removal of the fort's cannon and stores "had been determined on." Most of the men in the fort were New Jersey and Pennsylvania militia from the remnants of the Flying Camp. The Pennsylvanians were particularly dispirited, because so many of their friends had been captured in Fort Washington.

Early on the morning of November 20, a local farmer rushed into General Greene's headquarters at Fort Lee and informed him that some four to five thousand British had crossed the Hudson at Dobbs Ferry, landed without opposition, and were marching toward the fort. Greene asked Washington, still at Hackensack, what to do. Washington proved that all vestiges of Bunker Hillism had been scoured from his mind and soul. He leaped on his horse and galloped to Fort Lee. Without debating or conferring, he told Greene to get his men together and retreat, instantly. It was not simply a question of defending the fort. The Hackensack River formed a neck of land that was almost as isolated by water as Manhattan between the East and Hudson rivers. All the British had to do was seize the one bridge over the Hackensack and another 2,000 Americans were in their bag. There was no time, Washington growled, even to strike a tent or douse the fires under the pots in which the men were cooking dinner. The only thing loaded into the few available wagons under his grim eye was ammunition.

Missing their dinner put the militiamen in a nasty mood. They broke into the fort's supplies of rum, and several hundred of them got drunk. Washington ignored them. He told the drummers to beat the order to fall in. Enough men responded to form a column, and he led them toward Hackensack Bridge. Along the route, they passed thousands of cattle in the Hackensack meadows, driven from Pennsylvania and western New Jersey to feed the American army. There was no time for a roundup. Washington could only try not to think about how many roast-beef dinners he was giving the British commissary. Instead of scorching the earth before the advancing enemy, the Americans were making gourmets of them.

About two hours later, Nathanael Greene returned to Fort Lee, and found three or four hundred militiamen staggering around the place. He ordered them to form ranks and follow the rest of the column. Most of them did. But at least a hundred ran into the nearby woods, and as soon as Greene departed, they returned and continued drinking until the British army appeared. Most of them ran away again. But when the British light infantrymen charged with bayonets ready and muskets loaded through the gates of the fort, they found twelve of these heroes of 1776 too drunk to walk.[39]

XXIX

An Admiral
Loses a Battle
and Saves a Country

If the future looked bleak for Washington's army, hopeless was the
only word that adequately described the prospects of the erstwhile conquerors of Canada. The remnants of that American army had
staggered back to Fort Ticonderoga at the southern end of Lake
Champlain in late July. Their numbers had dwindled to some 3,500
men, and, in the words of Colonel Anthony Wayne, they were "still
Destitute of almost every necessary fit for a soldier, shoes, stockings,
shirts and coats are articles not easily done without—yet they cannot be
Obtained." Of the 2,000 Pennsylvanians who marched confidently
north with Wayne, barely 900 were still alive. Worse, the army was
riven with dissension.[1]

Congress had appointed Major General Horatio Gates to command
the army in Canada, replacing the erratic John Sullivan. When the
army retreated out of Canada, Major General Philip Schuyler, in command at Albany, asserted his seniority and insisted that Gates was now
his second in command. This divided the army into pro-Gates and pro-
Schuyler factions. To compound the disarray, Schuyler had been accused of being a traitor by the Berkshire County, Massachusetts, Committee of Safety in a memorial sent to George Washington on June 7. It
was part of the continuing feud between Schuyler and New England
men over the New Hampshire Grants. Because the claims of the New

Yorkers rested on a royal decision, New Englanders suspected that Schuyler and others like him were inclined to swing to the British side.

While he was not disloyal, Schuyler was hardly an enthusiastic independence man. Within a few months, he would admit to a loyalist friend that he hoped Congress would "bargain away the Bubble of Independency for British Liberty well secured." But the touchy aristocrat resented accusations that he was a Tory. "There never was a man so infamously scandalized and ill-treated as I am," he lamented to Washington.[2]

Gates' partisans included Commissary General Joseph Trumbull of Connecticut, who gave a nice sample of the prevailing virulence by warning Gates that he was "commanded by a person who will be willing to have you knocked in the head . . . if he can have the money chest go in his power." Both Gates and Schuyler were severely criticized for the decision to retreat from Crown Point to Ticonderoga—with Shuyler taking a somewhat worse beating. Schuyler renewed his favorite threat—resignation. Next, he demanded an investigation by Congress. When they dragged their feet throughout the summer—absorbed by the ruinous debate over confederation—Schuyler wrote Washington in September, declaring he could "no longer suffer the public odium." On September 14, he resigned and announced he was coming to Congress as a New York delegate to make his New England accusers eat their words.[3]

The New York convention urged Congress to reject Schuyler's resignation. The general himself showed how little stock he put in it by scolding Congress a few weeks after he resigned for shipping some powder to the Northern Department, consigned to General Gates and not to him. When Congress resolved to send a committee to Albany to investigate the military situation and instructed them to confer with General Gates, Schuyler was furious and called the resolution an insult. He threatened to publish his correspondence with Congress if they did not treat him with more respect. "Whatever may be the consequences . . . I cannot sacrifice my honor to any consideration whatever," he insisted.[4]

Among the consequences of this prima-donna quarreling was the very real possibility that the British army commanded by Generals Guy Carleton and John Burgoyne would spend the winter in Albany. Throughout the spring and summer, Schuyler and the independence men in that crucial city had been spending much of their time breaking up plots for loyalist uprisings and arresting loyalist leaders and sympathizers. With the British army to protect them, there is no doubt that the loyalists could have created an effective counterrevolution in and around Albany—a movement which could have swept down the Hudson River valley wrecking the supply lines of the American army in New York and swinging New York State out of the independence column.

Among the most restless citizens were the tenants of Livingston Manor. They lived like serfs on this 160,000-acre demesne and had little sympathy for a revolution supported by their landlord and his family. Early in 1776, militia companies from three neighboring counties entered the Manor and disarmed and arrested a large number of "suspected persons." Another problem was the presence of numerous retired British officers in northern New York. After the Declaration of Independence, the Albany County committee made them swear they would not bear arms against the United States of America. How many regarded this as a binding oath was a serious question.[5]

Another source of potential disaffection was the moderate policy of Guy Carleton. On August 11, Carleton had released all the men captured in the assault on Quebec. The enlisted men had promised him "not to take up arms against His Majesty, but to remain peaceable and quiet in our respective places of abode." They thanked Carleton for his "clemency and goodness to us whilst in prison" and assured him that "you may depend upon our fidelity." The officers had refused to make such a promise, but had signed a parole promising not to fight again until they were exchanged for captive British officers of the same rank.[6]

Throughout the summer and fall, there were signs of rising resistance among the loyalists and war weariness among the patriots. Mr. Coenraedt Hooghtieling complained to the Albany County committee that a company of rangers had eaten "two gamins, two sides of pork, and forty-odd fowls." Some of the rangers paid for the food, some refused, and they made his wife cook it all for them. In the Albany jail were thirty-four loyalists too stubborn to be intimidated and too dangerous to let go.

In recaptured New York City, loyalists issued a "Declaration of Dependence" and petitioned Lord Howe to restore civil government. With regret, the admiral said he was unable to do it because only a small portion of the colony had been reclaimed from the rebels. The collapse of the American Cause in northern New York would have remedied this legal defect.

Among the men who did the most to sustain American resistance was, paradoxically, Philip Schuyler. In spite of his frequent relapses into self-pity and his uncertainty about independence, Schuyler continued to give the Americans the prestige of his name in northern New York. Supply was a major problem in frontier warfare, and Schuyler's considerable business acumen and experience in this department were also invaluable. Most important, Schuyler proved himself a match for the British in the struggle for the allegiance of the most powerful confederation of Indian tribes in America, the Iroquois.

The great white father of the Iroquois, Sir William Johnson, had died in 1774. His power had been inherited by his son, John, and his nephew, Guy. With a tough combination of threats and harassment, Schuyler had broken the Johnsons' nerve, and they had fled to Canada in the late spring, after word of the British evacuation of Boston dispirited loyalists and Indians. This left Schuyler free to negotiate with the Iroquois. In early August, he achieved a diplomatic victory of the first rank in a treaty session at German Flats. Schuyler urged the Iroquois to stay neutral in the white man's quarrel. Lavishly dispensing gifts that ranged from guns to trinkets, and encouraging the 1,200 assembled Indians to consume "incredible" amounts of food and rum, he convinced the Iroquois sachems that peace with the Americans could be almost as profitable as war for the British.[7]

In early October, the British began a campaign to undo Schuyler's Iroquois diplomacy. Their agent was Joseph Brant, a Mohawk war chief and reputed son (or adopted son) of the late Sir William Johnson. In the spring of 1776, Brant had gone to England to protest the policy of Governor Guy Carleton, who refused to invite the Iroquois or the Indians of Canada to join the war against the Americans. Lord George Germain, delighted at the chance to make trouble for Carleton, countermanded this humane policy. Germain also saw to it that young Brant was flattered and fawned over by members of the cabinet. They gave him expensive presents, invited him to their great estates, and arranged to have his portrait painted by Sir Joshua Reynolds.

Brant returned from England in time to watch William Howe belabor Washington around Long Island, New York, and Westchester, and then departed for his homeland. Traveling by night, he eluded all the Americans guarding the Hudson highlands and the outreaches of Albany, and easily reached the safety of the Susquehanna River village of Onoquaga, where a number of Iroquois tribes lived. Brant gathered the young braves around him and began telling them of his trip to England, the favors and honors fatherly King George had showered on him there, which Brant offered as proof of England's power and friendship. He denounced the Iroquois's decision to remain neutral and called the Americans the enemy of all Indians. He assured them that he spoke for Guy Johnson, inheritor of Sir William Johnson's title as Indian superintendent, who also urged them to take up the hatchet for the King. The speech was received with violent enthusiasm in Onoquaga, and Brant departed on a tour of other Iroquois villages to inspire them with similar bloody thoughts.[8]

Obviously, for the rebel Americans everything depended upon keeping the British army in Canada at bay. This task had been handed by the wily Gates and quarrelsome Schuyler to Brigadier General Benedict Arnold. His strategy—to create a fleet and control the waters of Lake Champlain—was the Americans' only hope. Throughout the summer, Generals Carleton and Burgoyne had continued to receive reinforcements. In September, some 3,000 German troops arrived, bringing their strength to nearly 16,000 men. On land, there was nothing to oppose this formidable force but the 3,500 semi-clothed and dispirited men camped around Fort Ticonderoga.[9]

But there was no road down 135-mile-long Lake Champlain, and a march along its swampy, forested shores was an impossibility for an army transporting heavy cannon and tons of ammunition and supplies. There was only one thing for the British to do—build a fleet that would give them control of the lake. They had two advantages—plenty of money and the presence of the British navy in the St. Lawrence to supply them with skilled carpenters and sailors to man the ships after they were built.

A naval captain, Thomas Pringle, was put in charge of the dockyard at St. John's. Seasoned timber was shipped from the dockyards at Quebec and Montreal. Hammers and saws, adzes and axes were soon busy creating an inland armada. Carleton was no gambler. He was determined to sweep the Americans off the lake with an overwhelming superiority in ships, men, and guns. His program called for 24 gunboats, each armed with a single cannon, ranging from twenty-four-pounders to nine-pounders; two schooners, the *Maria* and the *Carleton,* mounting fourteen and twelve six-pounders; a huge raft called the *Thunderer* with six twenty-four-pounders, six twelve-pounders, and two howitzers; and a full-rigged ship, the *Inflexible,* with eighteen twelve-pounders. To these were added 680 flat-bottomed boats to transport the army.[10]

To match this firepower, Arnold had to summon legerdemain that

more than matched his performance before Quebec. He had no seasoned timber—considered a necessity for seaworthy wooden ships. His
fleet would have to be built from trees felled the previous day—green
wood that warped and leaked. At first, getting anything at all built was
a problem. On July 18, there were only about 20 carpenters at work in
the improvised American shipyard at Skenesborough (now Whitehall)
on Champlain's southern shore. Arnold bombarded Schuyler with demands for more carpenters, shipwrights, blacksmiths, and tools. Then
came calls for seventy bolts of thick sailcloth, a hundred pounds of sew-
ing twine, three barrels of tar, five dozen sheepskins for sponges, 200
swivel guns, and ammunition for nine-, twelve-, eighteen-, and twenty-
four-pounders.

The hard-working Schuyler and his secretary, Richard Varick,
found all this matériel somehow and got it transported to Skenesborough—a feat in itself. Varick told Arnold he had procured "twenty-
six anchors and cables from the skippers of the Hudson River who are
exceedingly averse to parting with any of their rigging except that
which is worn out and at exorbitant rates." Spurred by a direct order
from the Continental Congress, 50 ship carpenters arrived from Rhode
Island. They demanded and got outrageous wages for 1776—five dollars a day—and they declined to accept Continental currency. It was
hard money or no work.[11]

Arnold sent recruiters to the seaports of New England to find
sailors for his fleet. They came back with scarcely a man. Every sailor
capable of hauling on a rope was shipping or had shipped out aboard a
privateer, with dreams of a fortune dancing before his salt-stung eyes.
Arnold had to man his ships with soldiers drafted from the army. He
called them "a miserable set." Few of them "were ever wet with salt
water," he growled. As for the marines—armed with muskets to repel
boarders or to do some boarding of their own—they were "the refuse
of every regiment." [12]

Arnold not only supervised the creation of the fleet, he designed
most of the ships. They were crude but reasonably effective for sailing
on Lake Champlain's waters. The gondolas, or "gundelos," were flat-
bottomed open boats, between 50 and 60 feet long and 15 feet wide.
They had a single twelve-pounder mounted in the bow and two nine-
pounders amidships. Two square sails on a 60-foot mast and sixteen
oars, eight to a side, provided the power. There was a stove made of
brick in the waist and a 10-foot platform on the stern for the ship's
officers and helmsman. Row galleys were larger, perhaps 72 feet, and

they had two masts, each rigged with a high-pointed lateen sail in the Spanish style. They had fourteen oars on each side and six to eight guns to keep their 80-man crews busy.

By mid-August, driving carpenters and axemen twelve and four-teen hours a day, Arnold had ten ships afloat, and he soon added three more—a total of five galleys and eight gondolas. To this he could add the ships he already had on the lake—the three schooners and a sloop captured from the British.[13]

Arnold accomplished this near miracle while simultaneously in-volved in a most unbecoming wrangle with his fellow officers. While re-treating from Montreal, he had seized a large quantity of food, cloth, and other goods for the army, including six tons of bullets and shot. He was authorized to do so by Franklin and the other members of the congressional mission to Canada. Some of the goods were seized from known loyalists, others purchased from putative American sympa-thizers. The man placed in charge of this load of semi-booty, Colonel Moses Hazen, had already encountered Arnold's waspish temper and imperious style and liked neither. He allowed American soldiers to plunder Arnold's packages and crates. Merchants' names and labels were destroyed, making it impossible for Arnold to settle his accounts.

Arnold demanded a court-martial for Hazen. But others in the army had also learned to dislike Arnold. They packed the court-martial board and rejected Arnold's chief witness, the major who had escorted the goods from Montreal and delivered them to Hazen. When Arnold protested with his usual vigor, the court-martial board demanded an apology. Arnold challenged the entire board to (presumably) a series of duels, declaring he would "by no means withhold from any gentleman of the Court the satisfaction his nice honour may require." The board retaliated by demanding Arnold's arrest.

Major General Gates was called upon to play Solomon in this dis-play of acrimony. Was he going to put his best general-admiral in jail with the British invasion fleet ready to appear over the horizon? He wisely preferred to send Arnold north with his galleys and gondolas and buck the whole hassle on to Congress, who he knew would take months to decide anything.[14]

Afloat, Arnold had to weather one more example of American dis-sension—the most incredible yet. In May, 1776, before things began to fall apart in Canada, Major General Schuyler had appointed one Ja-cobus Wynkoop commander of the handful of American vessels then on Lake Champlain. Wynkoop was a pompous fool who spent most of his time talking about his heroic exploits in the Seven Years' War. Prowling the quarterdeck of his ex-flagship, the schooner *Royal Savage,* Wynkoop felt intense resentment when he saw Arnold flying an admiral's pennant from the mast of the galley *Congress.*[15]

Ten days later, Arnold ordered two schooners north to investigate a report that the enemy was advancing. As the ships headed out of the bay at Crown Point, the *Royal Savage* fired a blast at them from her bow guns and ordered them to heave to. Wynkoop sent Arnold a note which read, "I know no orders but what shall be given out by me, except sailing orders from the Commander in Chief." Arnold leaped into a rowboat and was soon aboard the *Royal Savage,* practically skinning Wynkoop alive. "You must be out of your senses," he roared. Wynkoop protested to Gates, who ordered him arrested and returned to Ticonderoga as a prisoner.

Arnold realized that "the Commodore," as he wryly called the Dutchman, was trying to undo both Gates and Arnold by appealing over their heads to Schuyler. But Dutch fellow feeling did not extend in Schuyler's mind to losing the war, and he backed Arnold and Gates, leaving Wynkoop to join Wooster, Sullivan, and several other victims of the Canadian fiasco demanding vindication from Congress.

Arnold sailed to the head of Lake Champlain and arrayed his fleet across the mile-wide channel, daring the British to come out and fight. The British dragged some heavy guns to a hill overlooking the channel and forced the Americans to retreat several miles. Earlier in the summer, Arnold had sent a number of patrols up the lake to discover just what the British were building at St. John's. These scouts did not learn very much. The three largest British ships were built at shipyards in the St. Lawrence, and then sailed to the Chambly rapids, broken into some thirty sections, and hauled overland to St. John's. The last of these to arrive was the 180-ton three-masted *Inflexible,* whose eighteen twelve-pounders had enough firepower to demolish Arnold's entire fleet unassisted.[16]

Arnold, with that persistent energy which was his forte, continued to send out patrols from his ships. On September 17, an American lieutenant returned with two prisoners from the British Twenty-ninth Regiment. They described a "ship on the stocks capable of carrying twenty guns, nine- and twelve-pounders"—the *Inflexible.* For the first time, the Americans realized they were faced with annihilation.[17]

With that ruthless realism which has always been another attribute of a great soldier, Arnold decided to retreat and adopt a defensive strategy. Falling back down the bay, he ordered two boats "to sound round the island Valcour." About halfway down the lake, two-mile-long Valcour hugged the western shore of Champlain, not far from present-day Plattsburgh. Between the shore and the rugged pine-covered island was a channel a mile wide and some three miles long. On the north, it was unassailable, full of rocky shoals. On the south, there was plenty of deep, clear water, and Arnold anchored his fleet across the mouth of the bay. He ordered his men to create a network of anchor cables which would enable them to maneuver their ships within the bay to the utmost advantage. Foreseeing that his unsalted sailors would be vulnerable to small-arms fire from the shore, he had them build walls of pine and cedar planks around the decks of their low-slung craft.

Arnold was using to maximum advantage American knowledge of Champlain seamanship. The British could only hope to attack his fleet in Valcour Bay by sailing into the prevailing north wind. Not until it was too late would they see Arnold's network of anchor cables. There was a good chance that he could destroy the enemy fleet piecemeal as they struggled to form a line of battle in the narrow channel.[18]

Arnold's boldness in sailing up the lake had already produced what was to become a vital dividend. Not a few English officers were eager to launch the offensive early in September. All their ships were ready except the *Inflexible*. Everyone, British and Americans, knew that time was almost as crucial as firepower on the northern frontier. There were only some two months of campaigning weather left before ice began to form and snow began to fall. Champlain often froze for as long as sixty-eight days. If the British were going to capture Ticonderoga, much less move on to Albany, speed was essential. The weather watchers argued that their heavier gunned, better manned fleet could take care of Arnold's green-timber ships without the *Inflexible*. But Carleton, after looking at Arnold's battle line, did not agree. He insisted on waiting another four weeks while the *Inflexible* was put together at St. John's.[19]

Not until October 5 did the British move out of the Richelieu River past Île-aux-Noix into Lake Champlain. The *Inflexible* led the awesome procession. Behind the fleet were several hundred Indians in huge birchbark canoes, which carried as many as thirty war-painted braves. Behind this bizarre mixture of the modern and the primitive came the army in its 680 flatboats, their red coats an immense blaze of color on the autumn lake.

While the Americans waited in Valcour Bay for the advancing British, they heard about Washington's evacuation of Long Island and New York. At first, Arnold could not believe it. He wrote to Gates, revealing a wild overestimation of Washington's army. "It appears to me our troops or officers are panick-struck, or why does a hundred thousand men fly before one-quarter of their number? Is it possible my countrymen can be callous to their roles or hesitate one moment between slavery and death?" With an optimism that seemed to defy reality, Arnold looked over his matchbox fleet and make-believe sailors and reiterated his confidence that "the Being in whose hands are all human events, will doubtless turn the scale in favor of the just and oppressed." [20]

At dawn on October 11, the poorly clad American soldier-sailors shivered beside their guns. An icy wind was blowing from the north, frothing the lake with whitecaps, and sending the autumn leaves skittering from the elms and silver birches. Suddenly the British fleet appeared at the mouth of the bay, their sails taut in the bitter wind. To the astonishment of the Americans, they sailed past without a sign of recognition. Arnold waited until the *Inflexible* and the heavy gun raft *Thunderer* were well past the mouth of the bay. Then he ordered the *Royal Savage* and three row galleys to attack the enemy's smaller ships.

From the deck of his flagship *Congress,* Arnold started counting British gunboats. There were twenty-four of them, three or four times the number he expected. They could surround his attacking ships like packs of terriers and tear them apart. Arnold signaled an immediate return to Valcour Bay. Unfortunately, the schooner *Royal Savage* could not sail into Champlain's wind any better than the British ships. The galleys, relying on their oars, had no difficulty. Lagging behind, the *Royal Savage* came under fire from a dozen gunboats, and her panicky crew ran her aground on the southern tip of Valcour Island. The cannon fire awoke Carleton and the British naval commander, Captain Pringle, to the presence of the American fleet. They swung the *Inflexible* and *Thunderer* about, but had a terrible time beating upwind in the narrow lake. The schooner *Maria* had the same problem. Only one major British ship, the schooner *Carleton,* was able to get into firing range.

As Arnold had hoped, the *Carleton*'s commander, Lieutenant James Richard Dacres of the Royal Navy, was contemptuous of the Americans. He ignored the fact that he was alone and began dueling with Arnold's entire fleet. The Americans used their network of anchor cables to maneuver their guns into a deadly arc, and poured metal into the *Carleton.* Double-shotted blasts of ball and canister swept across her decks. For a few minutes, it looked as if the *Carleton* might have to strike her colors. A falling spar knocked Lieutenant Dacres unconscious, and the crew wavered. But a nineteen-year-old midshipman, Edward Pellew, crept out on the bowsprit with lead flying all around him and set up a jib sail. Still the *Carleton* failed to move. But Pellew clung to the bowsprit until two longboats from other ships came alongside, threw him hawsers, and towed the *Carleton* out of range.

Sailors from the *Thunderer,* the unwieldy raft that could have destroyed the entire American fleet, were furious because their clumsy craft could not get within range. They rowed to the *Royal Savage* and boarded her, hoping to turn her guns on the American fleet. The American crew rushed back aboard from shore and drove the British to their boats. The British gunboats turned their cannon on the stranded ship and drove the Americans ashore again. The *Thunderer*'s sailors reboarded and fired a broadside or two at the Americans. Cannon fire from nearby ships drove them off the bloodstained deck, dragging dead and wounded with them. The Americans tried to recapture the *Savage,* and a boarding party from the *Maria* met them, cutlasses in hand, driving them ashore again.

Aboard the *Congress,* Benedict Arnold, his hair singed, his face blackened with powder, ran from gun to gun aiming the eight- and twelve-pounders. He was the only man aboard who knew how to fire cannon. The British gunboats bored in on the flagship, blasting her with their twelve-pound guns. A dozen balls crashed through the hull. Mangled men fell writhing to the deck. Arnold kept on aiming his guns.

Aboard the *Washington,* David Waterbury found himself the only officer not dead or wounded. From the shore, British Indian allies howled threats and insults and peppered the Americans with musketry and blazing arrows. But Arnold's wooden walls protected his sailors from this harassment.

For six hours, from about 12:30 until dusk, the two fleets blazed away at each other. In the narrow channel, the crash of guns bounding off the rocky 180-foot Valcour cliffs was, according to one German officer, "tremendous." Even Arnold admitted it was "very warm." The British and Germans manning the open gunboats suffered severely from the American fondness for combining grapeshot and round shot.

One gunboat took a direct hit in its ammunition locker and exploded. Most of the gunboats retreated to 700 yards, where their heavier cannon could still damage the Americans in comparative safety.

As the October light began to fail, H.M.S. *Inflexible* finally got into the battle. She moved boldly into the center of the American line, where the *Carleton* had taken such punishment, and unleashed five broadsides which sent dozens of twelve-pound shot and clouds of deadly grape and chain across the already bloody American decks. The gondola *Philadelphia* sagged deep in the water, her gunwales awash. The *Congress,* with seven hits along the waterline, also seemed to be sinking. The galley *Washington* was not in much better shape. But the indomitable Arnold kept enough guns firing to persuade the *Inflexible* to retreat to the safe 700-yard range. As darkness fell, the armed raft *Thunderer* finally got close enough to fire a few ponderous shots from its six twenty-four-pounders. But the battle was over for the time being.[21]

Although the British had learned to respect the Americans as inland-sea fighters, they were sure that tomorrow would bring them total victory. While the ships fought, British troops and Indians had occupied not only Valcour Island but the Champlain shore, cutting off one obvious American retreat route. Tomorrow they would renew the battle at dawn, with the *Thunderer* and *Inflexible* leading the attack. The Americans would have only two alternatives: surrender or annihilation. Captain Pringle ranged his ships in a crescent across the mouth of Valcour Bay. Knowing Arnold's fondness for night attacks, he ordered his men to remain awake and alert.

Aboard the *Congress,* Arnold was holding a grim council of war. Shortly after darkness fell, the *Philadelphia* had sunk. Water was rising steadily in the galleys *Congress* and *Washington.* On the gondola *New York,* every officer was dead but the captain. Casualties among the officers on every ship were high. They had stood upright on their exposed decks throughout the fight as an example to the men. Gloomiest of all was the report from every ship that ammunition and powder were virtually exhausted. While the Americans talked, Indian whoops and howls drifted out of the darkness around them. Then, with a crash and a roar, the *Royal Savage* exploded and began burning fiercely. The British, suspecting that the Americans might try to free her in the darkness, had sent a final boarding party with orders to destroy her.[22]

All Arnold's personal papers and baggage were devoured by those flames. But he showed not a trace of concern. His mind was riveted on persuading his fellow officers to accept a desperate plan. A fog was rising on the lake. It would thicken during the early hours of the night. There was enough water between the shore and the western end of the British blockade to escape. Each ship would carry a hooded lantern in a canvas sack on her stern. Oarlocks were to be greased and muffled with rags. Every rope running through a block or sheave was also greased.

The galley *Trumbull,* commanded by Colonel Edward Wigglesworth, led the way. The smaller gondolas and schooners followed him, and the galleys *Washington* and *Congress* brought up the rear of this tense procession. Through the mist, the flames of the *Royal Savage* flickered eerily. The Americans could hear hammers falling, saws rasping aboard the British ships, as carpenters repaired the damage of the day. But no voice cried out, no cannon boomed or musket barked to challenge the American runaways. British overconfidence, this time personified by Captain Thomas Pringle of the Royal Navy, was America's salvation once more.

The Americans staggered down the lake for eight miles and hauled their battered ships ashore at Schuyler's Island, where they tried to make them seaworthy again. They were forced to give up on two galleys, and sank them, shifting their men and guns to other ships.

At dawn, the British primed their guns, hoisted their sails, and prepared to renew the battle. They blinked in disbelief as light filtered across Valcour Bay. The Americans were gone. A furious Carleton ordered an immediate pursuit. Arnold's men depended mostly on oars to move their waterlogged craft. Champlain's tricky winds frustrated both hunter and hunted, and for the rest of the day and night of October 12–13 the two fleets drifted and rowed without making any real progress. At dawn on October 13, the Americans had only got six miles from Schuyler's Island. They were still some twenty-eight miles from Crown Point. The British fleet was in sight, eight miles behind them. Arnold's men toiled at the sweeps, groggy from exhaustion. They had had neither food nor sleep for two days. On their part of the lake, a southerly breeze slowed them to a crawl, while a northeast gust sent the British booming toward them under full sail, the *Inflexible* leading the battle line like a great, angry bird of prey.

By 11 A.M., the British were close enough to open fire. Aboard *Congress,* Arnold ordered his helmsman to come about. He signaled the galley *Washington* to join him. Together, they took on the British fleet to give the smaller ships a chance to escape. The *Washington* was so full of water it was wallowing, but Brigadier General David Waterbury obeyed Arnold's order. The schooner *Maria* and a half dozen other British ships surrounded *Washington* and pounded her to a blood-soaked wreck. Waterbury was forced to strike his colors. The rest of the British ships, led by the *Inflexible*, attacked *Congress*. They were soon joined by the *Maria* and the other victors over the *Washington*.

For two and a half hours, Arnold and his men exchanged broadsides with the entire British fleet. He was supported at long range by four gondolas that were too waterlogged to escape. It seemed only a question of time before Arnold would be forced to join the *Washington* in surrender. Twenty-seven of his seventy-three-man crew were dead or wounded. But the impromptu American admiral doggedly limped up and down his shattered decks, aiming and firing the *Congress*'s guns. Then he barked an order to his exhausted men, and they staggered to their oars. Arnold signaled the crippled gondolas, and the five American ships rowed through a hole in the British cordon to windward, where the enemy had trouble following them.

In an hour of frantic effort, they beached their ships on the shore of Buttonmould Bay, ten miles from Crown Point. Arnold had small arms and ammunition carried ashore, then ordered the ships burned. He personally put the torch to the *Congress*. Carrying their wounded, the Americans staggered through the forest to a rendezvous with their five surviving ships opposite Crown Point. After crossing the lake, Arnold ordered all the buildings in this already semi-ruined fort set ablaze and retreated to Ticonderoga, ten miles south.

On October 14, Guy Carleton informed Lord George Germain that "the Rebel fleet upon Lake Champlain has been entirely defeated." After detailing the battle, Carleton added words that were to have enormous significance. "The season is so far advanced that I cannot yet pretend to Your Lordship whether anything further can be done this year." [23]

Carleton shared the Howes' reluctance to smash the Americans into submission. He thought it would be enough to establish beyond question the superiority of the British army and navy, and wait for the Americans to open negotiations for peace. He even told General John Burgoyne that he saw no reason to be elated by the victory at Valcour Bay. They had been forced to spill the blood of fellow Englishmen, fellow subjects of His Majesty, a fact which should prompt mourning rather than rejoicing. Burgoyne and numerous other officers in the British army did not agree and urged Carleton to attack Fort Ticonderoga immediately.

Carleton sailed down the lake to within sight of the massive bastion at the intersection of Lake George and Lake Champlain and skirmished with American patrols. If he had been willing to risk a frontal assault, he probably could have taken the fort. He outnumbered the defenders almost five to one, and the Americans had been deplorably slow about preparing the place for defense. They seemed to have bet everything on the success of Arnold's fleet. Only after they received the news of its destruction did they begin, in the words of Colonel Jeduthan Baldwin, "mounting all the cannon we had carriages for & all the Carpenters & Smiths making New ones, our men prepairing to receive the enemy."[24]

On October 28, the British army moved to within three miles of Ticonderoga. Captain John Lacey of Pennsylvania recalled in his memoirs that "collem after collem presented their fronts along the lines, with fixed byonet, whose glissining firearms reflecting the bright raise of the sun presented a lustre from their tablits more radient than the sun itself." Lacey said that the sound of drums beating to arms, the boom of the alarm cannon, and the cry of sergeants urging men to turn out "would make even a coward brave." But he added that "these were . . . the times that trye men's souls" and more than one "sunshine and summer soldier srunk from the expected conflict." More than a few officers, he said, "never appeared to head their men, leaving that task to their subalterns to perform."[25]

So timid were the Americans they let a small British foraging party drive off a hundred and fifty head of cattle only several hundred yards from their walls without putting up a fight. Disease continued to rack the garrison. Dr. Beebe recorded an autopsy performed on one dead soldier in his regiment. His "difficulty" was found to be worms. General Waterbury and the 106 men who had surrendered with him arrived at the fort, paroled by Carleton on their promise not to take up arms again. Gates refused to let Waterbury and his fellow captives land lest they spread reconciliation fever. They were kept out on the lake like pariahs, and ordered to sail on to Skenesborough.

Not even the presence of Arnold was of much use to the dispirited army. The colonels with whom he had been feuding all summer industriously propagated the slander that he was responsible for all the Canadian disasters, and Valcour Island was one more proof of his incompetence. Colonel William Maxwell, commander of a New Jersey regiment, wrote to Governor Livingston, "General Arnold, our evil genius to the north, has, with a good deal of industry, got us clear of all

our fine fleet." Maxwell, who was no sailor, thought Arnold had allowed himself to be surrounded "between an island and the mainland
. . . a pretty piece of admiralship." If they had their fleet, Maxwell
lamented, "we would give ourselves little concern about the enemy." [26]

The Americans at Ticonderoga concealed their weakness and disarray with blasts of cannon fire at British ships and soldiers when they
approached the fort. As far as Guy Carleton could see, they were ready
to fight hard. Storming the place would be a bloody business, and he
had repeatedly expressed his abhorrence of this fratricidal war. In the
ruins of Crown Point, he conferred with Burgoyne and the British
officers who were recommending an attack, or at least a feint, to see if
the rebels could be driven out by panic. Carleton also conferred with
his Indian allies. They told him that snow would soon be falling. Already the wind from Canada was ominously cold and stiff, whipping
Champlain's waves to dangerous heights. Canoes and small boats, even
the King's large ships, might not survive the lake's November storms.

For a while, Carleton toyed with leaving a garrison at Crown Point,
and even began rebuilding the fire-ravaged barracks. But the number
of men needed to guarantee the security of the post created insoluble
supply problems. He finally decided to return to Canada with all his
ships, soldiers, and sailors. Behind his back, several high-ranking
officers maligned him in letters home, saying he had listened "to the
whim of a drunken Indian." Germain would welcome these attacks,
and use them to accuse Carleton of virtual dereliction of duty.

But Carleton, aside from his reluctance to spill more blood in 1776,
knew the Candian winter. As he told Germain, "Troops cannot encamp
in [the] advanced season without perishing from cold alone." They had
to be sheltered in barracks or houses. There were no barracks in the
vicinity of Ticonderoga. If there had been more time, Carleton would
have been unable to refuse an attack on Ticonderoga in the face of
demands for action from Burgoyne and other officers. "If we could
have begun our . . . expedition four weeks earlier," lamented the commander of the German troops. It had taken exactly four weeks to
launch the *Inflexible* at St. John's—the ship that Carleton decided he
had to have in his fleet when he saw Arnold and his galleys patrolling
the entrance to Lake Champlain. The impromptu admiral and his
green fleet had bought Americans a precious year to solidify their tenuous grip on northern New York.[27]

XXX

Revolutions
Break Hearts

While the navies and armies fought and maneuvered and Parliament and Congress passed laws and resolves, individuals tried to cope with the mounting convulsion in their own often hapless ways. For thousands of people, the Declaration of Independence was the beginning of a long personal agony. It forced them to choose between two sovereign nations. John Morton, an old friend of Benjamin Franklin and the Pennsylvania delegate who had provided the vote that swung the state into the independence column, summed up the anguish in a letter. "The contest is horrid. Parents against children, children against parents." He might have added, "friends against friends, neighbors against neighbors." [1]

In North Carolina, James Cotton, a magistrate and wealthy planter in Anson County, was arrested for urging his neighbors to fight for the King. Militiamen came to take him to the county Committee of Safety for trial and probable imprisonment. He got his captors drunk, fled into the woods, and hid in a cave. There he remained for weeks, fed surreptitiously by a few friends, while a detachment of militia camped on his farm, ravaged and burned his fields, barns, and other outbuildings, and insulted and tormented his wife and children. His wife died as a result of this ordeal, and his children were parceled out to neighbors. Cotton gave up all hope of an early victory and traveled 700 miles through the back-country wilderness to join the British army in St. Augustine, Florida. [2]

In New York, one of the richest men in the province, Frederick

Philipse III, whose estate consisted of 90,000 acres and extended for twenty-four miles up the Hudson in Westchester County, was arrested when he convened a large number of the freeholders of the county and prevailed on them to enter into an association to preserve the peace and support the legal government. He was deported to Connecticut, leaving his wife and nine children behind him. Philipse's good friend, George Washington (he had almost married Philipse's sister), obviously embarrassed by the situation, gave the guards orders which, Philipse admitted, "are remarkably kind and favourable to us." Philipse nevertheless was bitter. "If this be the liberty we are contending for—" he wrote to his wife, en route to Connecticut. There was no need for him to finish the sentence.[3]

In their modest house opposite the church on the village green at Washington, Connecticut, Joel and Leman Stone decorated their bedrooms in ominously opposite fashion. Joel's room displayed British warships and flags, while Leman preferred eagles surrounded by thirteen stars. In 1775, Joel was hauled before a patriot committee and accused of assisting British prisoners confined in Connecticut. His accusers lacked proof, but early in the year 1776 he discovered, as he later told it, "that it was perfectly impracticable any longer to conceal my sentiments from the violent public." When he heard that the British army had landed on Staten Island, he decided to flee to their protection. He got away only hours before local militia arrived at his house with a warrant for his arrest.[4]

In Wallingford, Connecticut, Moses Dunbar, already alienated from his family, all of whom were devout Congregationalists, by his decision to join the Episcopal Church, was attacked by a mob of forty men for speaking out on behalf of the King. He tried to negotiate with the local Committee of Safety, offering to enter into a voluntary confinement within the limits of his farm. But he was thrown into the New Haven jail for fourteen days. Released, he went home to find his life threatened once more by his neighbors. In despair, he abandoned his motherless children—his wife had died in May—and fled to the protection of the British army in New York.[5]

In the upstate village of Kinderhook, New York, Peter Van Schaack made an exhaustive study of all the acts of Parliament, the rulings of the Privy Council, the Board of Trade, and other government agencies to see if there was any justification for the charge that there was a conspiracy in England to deprive Americans of their freedom. Van Schaack failed to find a "preconcerted plan of enslaving us." At the same time, he admitted that "men of the greatest abilities and the soundest integrity" had taken up arms to fight the British. But such a decision was "too serious a matter, implicitly to yield to the authority of any characters however respectable." With a truly American independence, Van Schaack maintained that "every man must exercise his own reason and judge for himself."

In spite of his doubts, Van Schaack was chosen by the electors of Kinderhook to represent them on the Committee of Safety for Albany County. But he refused to sign a pledge to take up arms against the mother country and was instantly in disfavor with his fellow patriots. Retiring to Kinderhook, he was assailed by a series of physical afflictions. His two sons died. His wife became seriously ill with consumption. He went blind in one eye and the sight began to fail in the other eye. But none of these misfortunes deterred his fellow Americans from persecuting him.

The Albany Committee of Safety accused Van Schaack of maintaining "an equivocal neutrality." When he refused to take an oath of allegiance to the state of New York, they exiled him to Boston. By this time, he was almost completely blind and his wife was dying. It was a commentary on the weakness of the Revolution in northern New York that the Committee of Safety found it necessary to exile a blind man simply because he disagreed with them.[6]

Perhaps the most poignant personal story involved a name that loomed larger than any other American's, even Washington, during 1776—Benjamin Franklin. When John Morton lamented that the contest was turning fathers against sons and sons against fathers, he was thinking of Franklin and his son William, the Royal Governor of New Jersey, by that time under arrest in Connecticut as an enemy of his country while his father voted for independence. But the real victims of this tragic clash were not the father and the son, although the pain they suffered was acute. Behind the public men stood two lesser figures, Elizabeth Downes Franklin, William's wife, and William Temple Franklin, William's son, Benjamin's grandson.

Born in St. Thomas Parish, Barbados, in 1728, the daughter of a prosperous planter, Elizabeth had received "a refined education" in the West Indies and in England. She had married William Franklin in fashionable St. George's Church in London's Hanover Square on September 2, 1762, after a long courtship. She was not the woman Benjamin Franklin wanted his son to marry. Elizabeth was a rather fragile, dependent person, perhaps because she had lost her father at the age of three. Benjamin tried to reconcile himself to William's choice. In a letter to a friend, he described her as "a very agreeable West Indian lady."

West Indians were by instinct far more loyal to the mother country than continental Americans. Only the presence of a British fleet on station protected them from assault and capture by the nearby French and Spanish, and there was a British regiment permanently stationed on almost every island to prevent slave insurrections. Without educational or natural resources—the islands were sweltering, unhealthy sugar factories—most planters sent their children to England to be educated and followed them as soon as finances permitted.

Also like most West Indians, Elizabeth had expensive tastes. She brought her husband a modest inheritance. Whether it remained invested in sound British stocks or was taken to America with them we do not know, but William found it impossible to live on his annual salary of £750 a year, and was soon borrowing heavily from his father to furnish his house and buy clothes in the style to which Elizabeth Franklin was accustomed. Neither this talent for spending money, her blind emotional loyalism, nor her piety—she was a devout adherent of the Church of England and had converted William—endeared Elizabeth to her father-in-law. Perhaps even more serious was another failure in the eyes of the elder Franklin, who once dreamed of founding a great American family—Elizabeth was childless. She and William had married late. She had been thirty-four, he thirty-one.[7]

William Temple Franklin was sixteen or seventeen years old in 1776. The date of his birth is somewhat obscure because, like his father, he was illegitimate, the son of an unknown mother, born a year or two before William's marriage. Between Temple and his father there was a discord harsher and much more obvious than the one that grated beneath the surface between William and Benjamin. Benjamin had insisted on his son's following his example and taking responsibility for the boy. But William at the time had no visible means of support, so Benjamin had assumed the financial burden. Reluctantly, Franklin permitted William to keep the boy's existence a secret from his wife. Both feared that Elizabeth, with her strong religious predilections, might have found the offense unforgivable. Besides, there was a good chance that the child would not grow to manhood. Scarcely one in four babies did in the eighteenth century.[8]

Through friends, the elder Franklin arranged for Temple to be nursed and cared for by a family outside London. As the boy grew older, the grandfather paid for his education and regularly brought him to the city for visits. But not until he was in his early teens did Franklin tell Temple that he was his grandson. Until that time, Temple thought he was the child of an English Franklin cousin who had died shortly after his birth. If the Revolution had not exploded, Temple would probably have remained in England for the rest of his life, perhaps never knowing the true story of his parentage. Benjamin himself would probably have remained in London, too, a contented citizen of the Empire. After the death of his wife, Deborah, in 1773, there was little reason for him to return to America. But by 1775, Franklin was a totally disillusioned ex-admirer of the Empire, and he returned home a determined independence man. He took Temple with him, even more determined that no grandson of his would grow up an Englishman.

Strained relations between Temple and his father were inevitable at first. The knowledge that William had virtually abandoned him, except for agreeing to pay at some future date the costs of raising him—by now he owed Franklin an estimated £1,500, which the grandfather obviously had no hope or intention of collecting—must have been disturbing. But Elizabeth Downes Franklin's warmth and affection swiftly healed this wound. At forty-eight, she had no hope of having a child and was almost pathetically eager to welcome Temple as her own long-lost son. For Temple, who had never known a mother's love, Elizabeth's acceptance was a deeply gratifying and important experience. William, too, exerted his by no means inconsiderable charm on the sixteen-year-old boy, with encouraging results. Temple accepted his new parents without a word of reproach or reluctance, and spent the summer of 1775 enjoying himself immensely in their company.

But always in the background, like an irrepressible somber theme, was the Revolution. As the tide turned toward independence, Benjamin, representing Pennsylvania in the Continental Congress, and William, His Majesty's Royal Governor of New Jersey, became more and more estranged. Benjamin refused to allow William to visit him in Philadelphia. When Benjamin made an infrequent appearance in Perth Amboy, the argument between father and son raged into the night. To the elder Franklin, convinced that America could not lose the war if Britain chose to fight, William was throwing away the great opportunity of his life. Few men in America could equal his military and political experience. If he joined his country's cause, there was no office to which he could not aspire—president of the Continental Congress, a general's rank in the army, and, after the war, the opportunity to become one of the leaders—perhaps the leader—of the new nation. William was the same age as George Washington. His generation was leading the Revolution. How could he *not* join them?

William's answer was always the same. Independence was a chimera that would turn into a flesh-and-blood monster called anarchy. America was succumbing to a madness bred in New England by quarrelsome fanatics whose Puritan ancestors had murdered one king and almost destroyed England. Although Benjamin had long since outgrown the narrow doctrines of his Massachusetts boyhood, he was anything but pleased to hear his own son denigrating the Yankees, tauntingly calling them frauds and hypocrites. Their independent spirit was bred into Benjamin Franklin's bones. He had defended them against the sneers and denunciations of British ministers and had paid a bitter personal price for acting as Massachusetts' London agent.[9]

Complicating and intensifying this family struggle was the presence of Temple. He soon became a prize over which Benjamin and William and, finally, Elizabeth Franklin fought. For the first year, William had a large advantage over his father in this contest. The Governor's palace, called Proprietary House, and the surrounding Perth Amboy countryside were much more enjoyable to an active teen-ager than Franklin's crowded house in Philadelphia, where his daughter, Sally, his son-in-law, William Bache, and their three children were also living. When Temple returned to Philadelphia to enter college for the 1775–76 school year, he wrote his father and stepmother a lively letter thanking them for a delightful summer. He added, tentatively, that he was not sure Elizabeth really wanted to hear from him.

Elizabeth responded with gentle tenderness to this youthful uncertainty. She told Temple she was "in hopes that long before this you were convinced of my regard, & that I sincerely interest myself in everything that relates to you." She signed her letter, "Yours very affectionately." More letters flowed back and forth between Temple and William and Elizabeth, with her tone becoming more and more maternal. As 1776 began, she was writing, "I am afraid dear William will begin to think me a very ill-bred woman & a very unkind mama for so long neglecting to answer his obliging letter of the 4th of last month."

Early in 1776, the patriots of New Jersey decided to intimidate William Franklin. They surrounded his mansion with a regiment of militia at 2 A.M. and demanded his surrender. William used Elizabeth's reaction to win Temple's sympathy. He began by practically committing her to his son's care.

I hope you will never be wanting in a grateful sense of her kindness to you. I should be able to keep up my spirits in struggling through all the present and expected difficulties if it was not on her account. Her constitution is naturally weak and delicate and the late brutal treatment she has received, and her anxious concern for me, had nearly deprived her of her life. She is not yet perfectly recovered of the fright she was put into this day fortnight, by being awakened with a violent knocking at the door, about two o'clock in the morning, and seeing the house surrounded by a large party of men armed with guns and bayonets. Her spirits continue so agitated, that the least sudden noise almost throws her into hysterics, and I am really apprehensive that another alarm of the like nature will put an end to her life. Having for some time past foreseen these consequences, I have endeavoured to prevail on her to go either to Barbados or England, where she has friends and relations who will treat her with that kindness and respect with which she has always treated mine. But she is not willing to leave me on any consideration, especially to go on a voyage to sea and I cannot accompany her. She has no relations of her own in this country to whom she can resort, or from whom she can receive any comfort in a time of distress; and, she cannot but take notice that mine do not at present seem disposed to give themselves any concern about her, omitting even those inquiries and outward forms of complaisance and civility which she daily receives from strangers.[10]

When William was deported to Connecticut in June, he wrote to Temple:

God bless you, my dear boy; be dutiful and attentive to your grandfather to whom you owe great obligations. Love Mrs. Franklin for she loves you and will do all she can for you if I should never return more. If we survive the present storm we may all meet and enjoy the sweets of peace with greater relish.

I am ever

Your truly affectionate father

While William was en route to Connecticut, the British army landed on Staten Island. The Americans rushed troops to defend the vulnerable New Jersey shoreline. One of the most obvious possible invasion routes was Perth Amboy, and the town became an armed camp. This did not make life any easier for Elizabeth Franklin, alone in Proprietary House except for a few servants. The militia regarded the governor's mansion as a symbol of royal authority and a prime target for insults and depredations. On July 16, Elizabeth wrote a plaintive letter to Temple, which gives a doleful picture of how vindictive and undisciplined some Americans were in 1776.

MY DEAR SON

. . . Our little Town now Swarms with unruly Soldiers, & more
are pouring in every Day; they have been extremely rude, Insolent
& abusive to me, & have terrified me almost out of my Senses, but
the Day before yesterday, General Mercer, sent two of his officers
down to acquaint me that he had given Strickt orders that none of
his Men should for the future come down to my House, or treat any
of my Family with disrespect. Yesterday, the orders were obeyed,
but today a party of them came down pluckt all the Green Apples
of the Trees, & threw them about the Orchard, & was going to steal
your Dog. —It is certainly very disagreeable Living here at present
but I cannot think of removing, for in the first place I have no
House to remove my Family to, & if I had I could not move so
much Furniture as we have without being at a vast expense, & run
the Risk of having great part of it Shatter'd to pieces, as it must go
by Land; therefore I am resolved to stay, & trust to the Almighty
God, for Protection.—

I have had no letter from your dear injured, persecuted father
since you left me, but I had a visit from two gentlemen that saw him
at New Haven and they told me that he was much fatigued with his
horrid journey and had a little fever on him. I don't expect to hear
from him whilst he is a prisoner for I suppose the good *Saints* think
it is too great indulgence to suffer *Sinners* to correspond with each
other tho' bound together by the strongest ties of affection and
marriage. The Lord have mercy on poor me, for my heart is almost
broke for troubles of all sorts surround me.

The New Jersey government's decision to deport most of Perth Amboy's numerous loyalists to the interior of the state deepened her isolation.

This day all the gentlemen of my acquaintance except the Chief
Justice, Mr. Elliot, and the parson are taken away and made prisoners in other parts of the country. Even our doctor who has several patients now very ill. . . . Next to my husband I lament the loss
of the doctor for I am at present one of his patients, having been
for some time in a very bad state of health.

God bless you, my dearest boy, and may you live and inherit the
virtues of the best of men, your dear father and my beloved husband, and may the Almighty protect him and give him grace and
spirit to bear his persecution patiently, and may he never deviate
from the character he has always supported of being an honest,
upright, conscientious man.

Pray present my duty to my father and Aunt Mecom. My love
attends you, the rest of the family.[11]

Deeply concerned, Temple went to his grandfather and wangled permission to go to Perth Amboy and stay with Elizabeth. The permission was given with great reluctance, but Temple was angrily insistent on going. He wrote a letter to Elizabeth Franklin telling her he was on his way. She wrote back asking him to bring some money. "I fear I may want it before I hear from my dear persecuted prisoner." She had tried to collect money owed to Governor Franklin, but with no success.

The elder Franklin sent Elizabeth sixty dollars and a letter expressing his sympathy for her plight. He reminded her that hundreds, even thousands, were suffering in the revolutionary upheaval.

Elizabeth replied on August 6, "My troubles do indeed lie heavy on my mind, tho' many people may suffer still more than I do, yet that does not lessen the weight of mine, which are really more than so weak a frame is able to support. I will not distress you by enumerating all my afflictions, but allow me, dear sir, to mention that it is greatly in your power to relieve them."

She begged Franklin to use his influence to arrange for William to live in Perth Amboy under house arrest. "Consider, my dear and honoured sir, that I am now pleading the case of your son, and my beloved husband. If I have said or done anything wrong, I beg to be forgiven." [12]

The letter shows a total noncomprehension of how dangerous William Franklin was to the shaky revolutionary cause in New Jersey. Benjamin neither replied to his daughter-in-law nor did anything on behalf of his stubborn loyalist son. When Elizabeth heard nothing from her father-in-law, and William, imprisoned in Litchfield, Connecticut, without pen or paper, remained unable to communicate with her, she became more and more distressed. She asked Temple to take a letter to his father by hand. The boy wrote to his grandfather in Philadelphia asking permission. On September 19, Franklin replied:

DEAR BILLY—
I received yours of the 16th in which you propose going to your father if I have no objection. I have considered the matter and cannot approve of your making such a journey at this time, especially alone, for many reasons which I have not time to write.

Benjamin suggested that Elizabeth write to her husband, care of Governor Jonathan Trumbull of Connecticut, assuring him that her letter related only to private family matters. Franklin added a postscript to his letter, revealing another side of the family's turmoil. His sister, Jane Mecom, and his daughter Sally disapproved of the harsh line he was taking with Elizabeth and William. The postscript said that Sally and her aunt "desire I should express more particularly their love to Mrs. Franklin."

Temple was not happy with this letter. On September 21, 1776, he wrote a warm reply.

> Hon. Sir.
>
> I am very sorry to find that my intended visit to my father does not meet with your approbation; and it likewise makes my Mother very uneasy as she will not now be able to communicate the situation of her family concerns and get that advice she is desirous of having and without which she knows not how to act.
>
> The method you recommend of enclosing her letter sealed to Governor Trumbull she has tried . . . but has had no accounting of their being received either opened or unopened tho' there has been sufficient time for that purpose. She likewise knows not how to take the liberty of enclosing a letter to a gentleman with whom she is totally unacquainted and who has not shown any favour to her husband during his imprisonment, but on the contrary has rather been severe.
>
> In my going you might perhaps imagine I should give such intelligence to my father as would not be thought proper for him to know. But I can assure you, Sir, that I am entirely ignorant of everything relating to public affairs except the petty news which is talked of by everybody and is in all the public prints.[13]

He went on to explain that Elizabeth would not leave Proprietary House without express orders from William. With winter coming on and no money to buy fuel or food, Elizabeth's situation was becoming critical.

Three days later, Franklin replied.

> Dear Grandson,
>
> You are mistaken in imagining that I am apprehensive of your carrying dangerous intelligence to your father, for while he remains where he is he could make no use of it if you were to know & acquaint him with all that passes. You would have been more in the right if you would have suspected me of a little tender concern for your welfare on acct of the length of the journey, your youth and inexperience, the number of sick [soldiers] returning on that road with the infectious camp distemper which makes the beds unsafe, together with the loss of time in your studies, of which I fear you begin to grow tired.[14]

Benjamin enclosed several franked envelopes addressed to Governor Trumbull for Elizabeth to use. He said he was also writing the governor asking him to handle Elizabeth's mail discreetly.

This exchange of letters made it clear to Franklin that Temple was in danger of becoming a loyalist. The reference to his studies indicates that the grandfather had hoped and expected that Temple would stay in America and become a useful citizen of the new country. With his usual mixture of candor and guile, Franklin smoothly altered this plan.

On September 28, he wrote Temple another letter:

DEAR TEMPLE—

I hope you will return hither immediately & that your mother will make no objection to it, something offering here that will be much to your advantage if you are not out of the way. I am so hurried that I can only add

Ever your affectionate grandfather

In a P.S., he added, "My love to her."

The "something offering" was the opportunity to be Benjamin Franklin's private secretary in France. A worried Congress, badly shaken by Washington's defeats around New York, had decided to send a three-man mission to France to seek desperately needed aid and negotiate a commercial treaty. Benjamin Franklin was an inevitable choice to head this mission.

There is no historical evidence of the anguish with which William Temple Franklin must have greeted his grandfather's offer. To accept it meant he was leaving alone and helpless in Proprietary House the gentle, affectionate woman whom he had learned to call mother. Yet his father had told him to be obedient to his grandfather to whom he owed "great obligations."

In such a situation, it would be too much to expect a seventeen-year-old boy to resist the blandishments of Benjamin Franklin, describing the adventure, the incomparable opportunity for learning, the chance to win political fame that went with the mission to France. Temple accepted his grandfather's offer. On October 25, he and Franklin and six-year-old Benjamin Franklin Bache (Sally's son) boarded U.S.S. *Reprisal* and sailed for France.

At Perth Amboy, Elizabeth Franklin, ignorant of what was happening, continued to write letters addressed to "My dear son," and signed, "Your ever affectionate mother." William Franklin also wrote to Temple urging him to "let your mother know that I am well and long much to have a letter from her." When Temple did not reply, Elizabeth began to suspect the worst. Her last letter has a farewell ring to it. "I am truly miserable indeed, to be here in a strange country without a friend or protector. . . . God bless you, my dear boy, & make you worthy of the name you bear, is the sincere prayer of your ever affectionate mother." [15] A year later, Elizabeth would die a refugee in British-occupied New York without seeing her "dear persecuted prisoner" or her "dear boy" again.

When Elizabeth died, Benjamin Franklin's sister, Jane Mecom, a perceptive woman, remarked, "Temple will mourn for her much." She was right. Temple would live another fifty years. He never achieved a satisfactory relationship with a woman and frequently declared he loathed the very idea of marriage.

XXXI

The Luckiest Friday the Thirteenth in History

In the main British army commanded by William Howe, confidence soared higher and higher. Lord Rawdon wrote to a friend in England, "I have not been mistaken in my judgment of this people. The southern people will no more fight than the Yankees. The fact is that their army is broken all to pieces, and the spirits of their leaders and their abettors is also broken. . . . I think one may venture to pronounce that it it well nigh over with them." [1]

Across the Hudson at British headquarters, Generals Howe and Clinton were talking and thinking in opposite directions once more. Clinton was in a nasty mood. He was furious with Howe for his persistent refusal to take his advice since Long Island. Clinton had exploded to Lord Cornwallis while the British were withdrawing from White Plains, "I cannot bear to serve under him [Howe] and had rather command three companies by myself than hold my post [as] I have done last campaign in his army!" Cornwallis, whether out of a desire to cause trouble for Clinton, and thus acquire for himself the opportunity to lead the advance guard and win most of the glory in forthcoming battles, or out of a mistaken notion that he could persuade Howe to soothe Clinton's discontent, repeated this nasty comment to the British commander in chief. It practically guaranteed Howe's resistance to anything else Clinton suggested. Which was just as well for the future of the United States, because Clinton now suggested to Howe a plan that would have ended the American Revolution. [2]

Howe had chosen Clinton as the commander of an expedition

which had long been on the books—the capture of Newport, Rhode Island, and its sheltered harbor. Militarily, the plan made little sense— Clinton was ordered to do no more than occupy the island on which Newport stood. But it secured for Admiral Lord Howe an ice-free harbor for his fleet, an absolute necessity in the admiral's view. New York harbor often froze. The admiral was supposed to keep men-of-war on patrol off the American coast throughout the winter. This would become difficult if half his ships were stuck in New York's ice.

All very good, Clinton agreed. But couldn't the admiral wait a week or two while Clinton took the 6,000 men assigned to the occupation of Newport, loaded them on their waiting transports, and used them to capture Philadelphia, by sailing either up the Delaware or up the Chesapeake? Howe said no, although there was sitting on his desk a report from the British negotiator-spy, Gilbert Barkly, whom Lord North had sent to Philadelphia a year ago. Barkly assured Howe the Delaware was undefended up to Chester and gave him road directions for marching from there.[3]

Then put me and the men ashore on the Jersey coast, Clinton begged. He guaranteed that he would cut off Washington's retreating army while Cornwallis pursued him from Fort Lee. Then a leisurely march to Philadelphia, occupy that city, disperse the Continental Congress—and the war was over. There would be no need for Lord Howe to keep his cruisers out of the ice to patrol the coast. They could sit in New York or in the Delaware River off Philadelphia—or in the Bay of Biscay, for that matter. Smash the rebellion now and forget about Rhode Island, Clinton argued.

It did not take a general to see such possibilities in the military situation. Captain Frederick MacKenzie wrote in his diary, "This is now the time to push these rascals, and if we do, and not give them time to recover themselves, we may depend upon it they will never make head again. A body of troops landed at this time at Amboy might, in conjunction with those already in Jersey, push on to Philadelphia, with very little difficulty." The New Jersey loyalist, Howe's assistant adjutant general Stephen Kemble, made a similar comment in his diary.[4]

The only American opposition to a British landing at Amboy was a brigade of about 1,000 commanded by Lord Stirling. They were guarding the passes through the Watchung Mountains from Amboy and Elizabethtown and patrolling much of New Jersey's long Atlantic coast. They were little more than an enlarged scouting party, strung out in a hopelessly thin line.

Howe still said no to Clinton's proposal. It was not part of the Howe plan for winning the war. But the unexpected ease with which Cornwallis had seized Fort Lee—and the realization that Washington had divided his army, leaving New Jersey almost defenseless, did interest Howe in another way. Here was an opportunity to enlarge at a very cheap rate the conquered territory which His Majesty's peace commissioners could administer with a nice mixture of justice and mercy, thus convincing these obstreperous Americans that the blessings of British liberty were preferable to independence.

Howe ordered Clinton to take the 6,000 men assigned to him and head for Rhode Island. Simultaneously, he gave Charles Lord Cornwallis, now his second in command, orders to pursue Washington as far as New Brunswick, but there to halt, no matter what was happening. Howe knew Cornwallis was an impetuous, aggressive fighter. He reined him in with a strict order not to proceed beyond this town on the Raritan, which marked the border line of East Jersey. The Garden Colony, as it was known even then, had originally been divided into West and East Jersey, and the names and approximate shape of the districts were common usage. East Jersey with its rich farmlands would be a handsome addition to the Royal Army's conquest for 1776. It would practically eliminate Howe's supply problems, already eased by the capture of Long Island. The stunning successes at Fort Washington and Fort Lee had imbued Howe himself with not a little arrogance. Telling Clinton of his plan to take hold East Jersey, he talked about creating a series of fortified posts from Passaic to Elizabethtown. Clinton warned him that they would be targets for American raids. Howe smiled. "We can take liberties with these people."

"The military dictionary contains no such word as liberties," Clinton replied, relapsing into his pedagogical know-it-all German style that set Howe's teeth on edge. If Howe failed to destroy Washington's army, Clinton said, he should withdraw his troops to Staten Island until the spring.

Howe looked sullen and told Clinton he was probably right. But he was just getting rid of him. On November 26, Clinton led 6,000 Germans and British aboard the transports and departed for Newport, taking with him another talented general, Hugh Lord Percy, as his second in command.[5]

In New Jersey, Charles Lord Cornwallis began a cautious pursuit of Washington and his retreating army. Howe had reinforced Cornwallis heavily. He now had almost 10,000 men. Washington, according to a

tabulation which he sent Congress on November 23 from Newark, had
5,410 troops more or less under his command. He was counting the
1,000 men of Stirling's brigade, strung out to the south, and some
2,000 militia who had the right to go home on December 1 and undoubtedly would do so. The Pennsylvania militia were also declaring
that they intended to go at the same time, although they had contracted to stay until January 1.[6]

There was only one hope of regaining control of the situation, and
Washington saw it clearly. He must reunite his army. Across the Hudson in Westchester County, Charles Lee still had between 7,000 and
9,000 troops—enough to enable the Americans to make a stand on the
Raritan River. But Washington was dogged by a painful sense of inferiority in his dealings with Lee. First, he had an aide write that it would
be "advisable" for Lee to join him in New Jersey. Even after the retreat
from Fort Lee, Washington could not give Lee an order. He said that
he was "of opinion and the gentlemen about me concur in it, that the
public interest requires your coming over to this side [of the Hudson]."

In White Plains, Lee was thinking other thoughts. In a letter to
James Bowdoin, president of the council of Massachusetts, he declared,
"Before the unfortunate affair at Fort Washington, it was my opinion
that the two armies—that on the east and that on the west side of North
River—must rest each on its own bottom; that the idea of detaching
and reinforcing from one side to the other, on every motion of the
enemy was chimerical; but to harbour such a thought in our present
circumstances is absolute insanity." He did his best to frighten Bowdoin
about the possibility of the British invading New England or seizing the
Hudson River highlands. In either eventuality, he said he would "never
entertain a thought of being succoured from the western army. I know
it is impossible. We must therefore depend upon ourselves. To Connecticut and Massachusetts, I shall look for assistance." [7]

General Lee was on his way to setting up an independent command
for himself. On this same November 21, he got a letter from Joseph
Reed which was unlikely to change his mind. Reed began by saying that
he wished to have Lee with them at the "principal Scene of Action." Although he claimed that he did not wish to praise Lee "at the Expence
of any other," he proceeded to do just that by writing that it was "entirely owing to you that this Army & the Liberties of America . . . are
not totally cut off. You have Decision, a Quality often wanting in Minds
otherwise valuable." He was not alone in this opinion, Reed said.
"Every Gentleman of the Family [Washington's staff], the Officers &
soldiers generally have a Confidence in you." [8]

Then Reed went from flattery to politics. Deploring the "very awful & alarming State" of American affairs, he told Lee that "as soon as the Season will admit I think yourself & some others should go to Congress & form the Plan of a new army." George Washington was conspicuously absent from this delegation. This was deference with a vengeance. It was inevitable as long as Washington hesitated to give Lee an order. Reporting his plans to Congress, Washington dictated to aide Tench Tilghman, "I have wrote to Genl Lee and Ordered him to come over with the Continental regiments immediately under his command." In the final draft of the letter, he struck out the words "and Ordered him."

Lee refused to come. Instead, he sent orders to Major General William Heath, who was guarding the Hudson highlands with 4,000 men at Peekskill, to detach 2,000 of his men and send them to Washington's aid. Heath refused, saying that his orders did not admit "of moving any part of the troops from the posts assigned to me, unless it be by express order from his Excellency, or to support you in case you are attacked." The mild-mannered bald-headed Heath, a Massachusetts farmer before the war, seemed the last person one might expect to stand up to the imperious Lee with his European reputation. But stand he did, rejecting a direct order to take 2,000 men and march into New Jersey. Lee raged that Heath had "formed an opinion to yourself that shou'd General Washington remove to the Streights of Magellan, the instructions he left with you upon a particular occasion, have to all intents and purposes invested you with a command separate from and independent of any other superior." Lee continued in this cutting vein for some time, then declared that "the Commander in Chief is now separated from us" and that he [Lee] therefore commanded "on this side of the Water [and] I must & will be obey'd." [9]

It was Lee who hoped to set up the independent command, and he worked hard at converting James Bowdoin of Massachusetts into his political backer. In another letter to him, Lee expatiated upon the dangers of indecision both in Congress and in "our military councils." He told Bowdoin that affairs were in such a crisis, "even the resolves of Congress must no longer too nicely weigh with us. We must save the community in spite of the ordinances of the Legislature. There are times when we must commit treason against the laws of the State for the salvation of the State. The present crisis demands this brave, virtuous kind of treason." He asked Bowdoin to add four companies to every Continental regiment being recruited in Massachusetts, plus "a formidable body of Militia" to replace the Continental troops which he was "ordered to convey over the river." If Massachusetts and Connecticut supported him, he assured Bowdoin, "I will answer for their success."

In Newark, Washington was appalled by Lee's orders to Heath, which endangered the vital highland passes. He quickly countermanded them. Lee was not the only general with whom Washington had to cope. Israel Putnam was wandering through New Jersey telling everyone—Tories included—that the Cause was lost. This defeatism soon reached the British high command. Ambrose Serle reported it to correspondents in England.

"Putnam about five or six days ago was at the house of a Mr. K, a gentleman of considerable property in the Jerseys, who was since released by the Retreat of him and his followers; and, being asked in a free Manner what He and his Colleagues thought of American Affairs since their repeated Defeats and the Capture of their strongest Holds, delivered himself in the following words; 'We all think that our cause is nearly ruined; that as our army is just disbanding and because their Time mostly expires on the 1st of December, and the King's Troops are severely pushing us, we shall not be able to get another together; and that, if we could, they could make no Sort of Resistance in the plain Country to the Southward, against such an Army as is brought against us.' "

Obviously, Bunker Hillism was still intact in Putnam's muddled head. Without hills and time to build forts on them, he could see no hope. It was not very good for American morale to have the third ranking general in the army talking this way.[10]

While the high command was falling apart and desertion continued to fritter away the edges of the army camped around Newark, Thomas Paine, the man who had assured the Americans that they could beat the British without sweat or debt, began writing a series of articles in a much more dolorous tone. Paine had been playing amateur soldier all summer, first in the New Jersey Flying Camp and then as aide to Nathanael Greene at Fort Lee. He had been an eyewitness of the retreat from there and the disaster at Fort Washington that preceded it. Paine went back to Philadelphia to finish the articles, which he called *The American Crisis*.

"These are the times that try men's souls," he began. "The summer soldier and the sunshine patriot will, in this crisis, shrink from the service of his country; but he that stands it *now* deserves the love and thanks of man and woman. Tyranny, like Hell, is not easily conquered;

yet we have this consolation with us, the harder the conflict, the more glorious the triumph."

Paine insisted that the Americans were far from beaten. " 'Tis surprising to see how rapidly a panick will sometimes run through a country. All nations and ages have been subject to them. . . . Yet panicks, in some cases, have their uses. They produce as much good as hurt. Their duration is always short; the mind soon grows through them, and acquires a firmer habit than before."

Paine added to this sonorous prose a narrative of the retreat from Fort Lee to Newark. "Both officers and men," he wrote, "though greatly harassed and fatigued, frequently without rest, covering, or provision . . . bore it with a manly and a martial spirit. All their wishes were one, which was, that the country would turn out and help them drive the enemy back." [11]

No mention here of drunken militiamen or quarreling, despairing generals or whole regiments refusing to obey orders. One wonders what effect an investigative reporter who ferreted out these truths about the American army would have had on the conduct of the war. Would it have been better for the American people to know that Charles Lee was on his way to creating a military dictatorship backed (he hoped) by New England bayonets? Would it have helped to know that in almost every battle they had fought thus far in 1776, the American troops had run away? Would a searching appraisal of George Washington, indicting him for indecision, have been good medicine for the infant nation?

Fortunately, those questions did not have to be answered in 1776. Paine's exhortation was delivered to the *Pennsylvania Journal* while the remnants of the Flying Camp militiamen and the rest of Washington's excuse for an army retreated from Newark on November 28. As the American rear guard trudged out of the town, Cornwallis' advance guard entered it. But the British did not pursue the Americans. They once more displayed their predilection for occupying territory rather than destroying the rebel army. They stayed overnight in the little village.

On November 29, Washington's troops stumbled into New Brunswick, where they discovered that Lord Stirling's men had been repeating the example of the militia at Fort Lee—breaking into the liquor supplies and getting drunk. Everywhere there were symptoms of what one Pennsylvania lieutenant called "barrel fever"—black eyes and bloody noses. The next day, November 30, was the last day of service for half of Washington's army—and they showed no inclination to stay around. Scouts reported that the British were collecting wagons, horses, cattle, and sheep, which Washington took "as proof of their intent to march a Considerable distance." There was no sign of the New Jersey militia turning out in force. On paper they could muster 16,000 men. Thus far, Washington had barely 1,000. The numerous loyalists among them were working "to influence some and intimidate others." [12]

On that same day, a letter arrived from Major General Charles Lee, addressed to Adjutant General Joseph Reed. He was in Burlington conferring with Governor William Livingston and the legislature of New Jersey on ways to turn out the state's reluctant militia. Assuming it was army business, Washington opened the letter and read—with a mixture of chagrin and embarrassment and sadness—the response of his second in command to his adjutant general's flattery. Lee began by agreeing that he, too, lamented "that fatal indecision of mind which in war is a much greater disqualification than stupidity or even want of personal courage." He went on to discuss Washington's orders in a now familiar vein. "The General recommends in so pressing a matter as almost to amount to an order to bring over the Continental Troops under my command." This, Lee said, "throws me into the greatest dilemma." He complained that his troops were unequipped for a march—and then with no apparent awareness of the contradiction discussed his intention to strike at some elements of the British army which he thought were in "so expos'd a situation as to give the fairest opportunity of being carried off." [13]

By now, nothing that he could have discovered about Lee would have surprised Washington. He had formed a fairly good estimate of his unstable character. But to find out that Reed, the man who was his closest confidant in the army, one of the few to whom this naturally taciturn man felt he could speak freely, was criticizing him behind his back—this was a bitter revelation which would have driven more than one man to a distracted fury—especially a man in Washington's situation. But Washington was discovering with almost every passing day that he was alone, and in that loneliness he found a strength which he did not suspect he possessed. The discovery that he could no longer depend upon Reed was only a small increment to the essential loneliness he had been experiencing since he saw the American flag go down at Fort Washington. There, Greene and Putnam had proved themselves unreliable—Putnam even a menace. Lee never was dependable.

The command decisions would henceforth have to be made by him—alone. He would have to make the best of this loneliness. He would have to make the best of his fellow Americans as they were—quarrelsome, self-interested, suspicious of each other, a majority of them with only a halfhearted commitment to independence.'

Washington resealed Lee's letter and sent it on to Joseph Reed with a brief note, apologizing for opening it, because he thought it was "upon the business of your office." Then he turned to the problems of the day. He wrote a letter to Governor William Livingston, asking him to station guards at all the ferries across the Delaware to arrest members of the Pennsylvania militia who were "deserting in great numbers" although they had enlisted until January 1. "I will not . . . despair," he told Livingston.[14]

A calm, tough realism now informed Washington's letters to Congress. Gone was much of the deference and all of the apologies for retreating. Gone, too, was any pretense of optimism. Within twenty-four hours, he told them, "Our force will be reduced to a mere handfull." The next day, he sent another grim bulletin: "The enemy are fast advancing, some of 'em are now in sight. All the men of the Jersey Flying Camp under Genl. Herd . . . have refused to continue longer in service." There was no hope of stopping the enemy. "Our Force is totally inadequate to any attempt." He told Congress to start collecting boats to transport his men across the Delaware, and to scour the river for any other craft the British might use. In another letter to Governor Livingston, he asked that particular attention be paid to the Durham boats—the big, awkward craft used to carry produce down the river. "One such boat would transport a Regiment of Men."

At 7:30 that night—December 1—Washington informed Congress that the 10,000-man British column was advancing toward the one bridge across the Raritan. He had only 3,000 men. It was insanity to fight them. With his new bluntness, Washington told the politicians that "we shall retreat to the West side of Delaware." Under fire from Hessian jaegers, Washington's engineers managed to destroy most of the bridge. There were several fords within a few miles' march where the river could be crossed. The December weather remained amazingly mild, though rainy. There was nothing to prevent Cornwallis from continuing his pursuit of Washington's disappearing army—except the order Howe had given him to stop in New Brunswick.[15]

Cornwallis sent an aide racing back to New York, asking for permission to continue the chase. Howe responded that he would join him and make a decision upon the spot. The trip from New York to New Brunswick could easily be made by a man on horseback in a single day. It took Howe four days to leave New York. Moreover, though he brought with him reinforcements under Major General James Grant, he came as a peacemaker, not a conqueror, distributing along his line of march copies of another proclamation issued by himself and his brother.

It ordered the dispersal of all armed groups and called on Congress to abandon its pretensions to being the voice of a legal government. Next came a statement that stunned British army officers and loyalists. The Howes offered to pardon and guarantee against "forfeitures, attainders and penalties" anyone who appeared before a British official within the next sixty days and signed a statement promising that he would "remain in a peaceable Obedience to His Majesty." [16]

This was the most daring gesture made by the Howes. While it conformed to the letter of their instructions—it was still dealing with the Americans in terms of pardon and submission—it went considerably beyond the spirit of these instructions by offering to return to repentant rebels their forfeited estates. The British officers and loyalists who looked forward to acquiring these estates were outraged. On the day before the proclamation was issued, Lord Howe's secretary, Ambrose Serle, had filled his diary with a diatribe against the Americans, based on conversations with loyalists. He had concluded that "by their Fears alone are [the Americans] to be governed, and not by a Resort to any more generous affections" and had deplored the possibility of making "foolish agreements . . . with a defeated though subtle foe." This is evidence of how isolated the Howes were in their attitude toward America.

Serle demonstrated his pique at the proclamation the following morning when he went aboard *Eagle* to tell Lord Howe that the terms were impracticable. He argued that people in the southern colonies would not hear about it for thirty days, and in the back country they would be seven or eight hundred miles from a royal officer—with the rebels patrolling all the rivers, roads, and seaports. But Serle was a pompous, vindictive fool and Lord Howe ignored him. Serle's real motives were revealed in another entry in his diary on that same December 1. He complained that the proclamation "may save from the Halter a Set of Villains in N. York, who have been principal Factors of this atrocious Rebellion and disoblige most of its loyal and suffering inhabitants." [17]

The Howes were not thinking about the southern colonies. The proclamation could always be renewed or extended for them at a propitious time. They were concentrating on New York and particularly on New Jersey, where they thought—with considerable accuracy, it soon proved—that the proclamation would have great impact. More and more, it became evident to them that New Jersey was ripe for a return to royal allegiance—and was a perfect place in which to sow the seeds of reconciliation. The population was heterogeneous—Dutch in the north along the Hackensack River, Yankee south of them, but heavily Quaker and with a scattering of German settlements in the west along the Delaware. William Franklin had been a popular Royal Governor, and more than a few people disapproved of the way he was arrested, abused, and imprisoned. Everything indicated a heavy percentage of loyalist and neutralist sentiment among the populace—and the latest historical research on New Jersey loyalism bears out the Howes' conclusions. About half the state were either secret or active loyalists.

If New Jersey succumbed to royal government and its rebels became peaceable farmers on their restored estates, it would be an irresistible argument to moderates and anti-independence men in New York and Pennsylvania. With these three colonies pacified, the rebellion would be dismembered. New England and the southern colonies could then be seduced or reduced, depending on their will to resist, almost at leisure.

The decision to wait in New York and give the proclamation a few days to circulate through New Jersey left Cornwallis and the British army sitting in New Brunswick during the warmest December weather in the memory of any American. Ambrose Serle thought the fifth, sixth, and seventh days of December "equal in Warmth & Pleasantness to those of August in England." If Cornwallis had been unleashed, he would have used this perfect campaigning weather to pin Washington against the Delaware, or force him to retreat in disorder down the New Jersey side of the river, leaving Philadelphia defenseless. Instead, Washington had four precious days to ship his army's baggage wagons across the river, and complete the removal of all boats from the New Jersey to the Pennsylvania shore.[18]

The American commander wrote letter after letter to Charles Lee, urging him to join him. But he was still afraid to give Lee a positive order. On December 3 at Trenton, Washington got a letter from Lee, written on November 30, reporting he was bringing "four thousand firm and willing troops" into New Jersey. The enemy detachment which he was going to attack—and for which he had wasted four valuable days—had "contracted themselves into a compact body very suddenly." But Lee claimed that he had used the wasted time to persuade most of his army to follow him. When he got to New Jersey, he told Washington, "I could wish you would bind me as little as possible." He wanted his freedom not from an exaggerated opinion of his "parts," but from a belief that "detached Generals cannot have too great latitude." [19]

With only a thin screen of politeness, Lee was telling Washington that he had no intention of joining him. The second in command of the American army was displaying ever more ominous tendencies. "Good God, have I come from gathering laurels in many other parts of the world to lose them in America?" he asked rhetorically in the presence of his aides. He told James Bowdoin of Massachusetts that he was now against a volunteer American army. "When the soldiers of a community are composed of volunteers, war becomes quite a distinct profession. The arms of a Republic get into the hands of its worst members. Volunteers [were] composed in general of the most idle, vicious and dissolute part of every society." Lee recommended drafting men from the militia to fill up the Continental regiments. It was another step in the evolution of the general into the military dictator.[20]

By this time, even Congress was beginning to wonder about General Lee. They ordered Washington to send an express rider to find him and get an exact count of his strength. Washington dispatched Major Walter Stewart of Pennsylvania with another letter, in which he still refrained from a confrontation with his second in command. He would give Lee no instructions as to his route. He understood that Lee "must be governed by Circumstances, this has been the language of all my Letters since I had Occasion to call for your aid." But he insisted that "the sooner you can join me with your division, the sooner the Service will be benefited." This was the understatement of the year.

Despite repeated calls from the state's leaders, the New Jersey militia refused to turn out. Only Colonel Jacob Ford, Jr., of Morris County managed to muster a respectable number of men. From Sussex, Essex, and other counties came only handfuls, single individuals instead of organized companies. The New Jersey legislature had responded to the exhortations of Joseph Reed by issuing one last summons to the militia and disbanding. There were reports of as many as three to four hundred people a day flocking to the British army posts at New Brunswick, Elizabethtown, and elsewhere to take advantage of the Howes' offer of amnesty. With the pardon came a certificate of protection which—in theory—would insure the bearer against robbery and insult by the Royal Army and their loyalist associates.[21]

But Lee and his wandering army continued to be Washington's biggest worry. If he knew what was happening elsewhere, he would have been even more worried. Congress, roused from its internecine squabbling by the crisis, had ordered Philip Schuyler, commander of the Northern Department, to detach as many men as he could spare to reinforce Washington. Schuyler dispatched seven regiments under the command of Horatio Gates—about 800 men. While on the march, Gates received a message from the Council of Safety of the state of New York, who had no particular affection for George Washington, urging him to place his men under Lee's command. The wary Gates, who may already have been thinking of himself as a potential candidate for commander in chief of the American army, refused to do so.

On December 4, Lee wrote another outrageous letter to Washington. He told him that he was going to take command of "the Northern Army"—Gates' men—and would soon have "five thousand good troops in good spirits." He urged Washington "to communicate this to the corps immediately under your command. It may encourage them." Surely this was the ultimate condescension. On his march through New Jersey, Lee said he planned "to clothe my people at the expense of the Tories which has a double good effect—it puts them in spirits and comfort, and is a correction of the iniquity of the foes of liberty." Giving permission to his largely New England army to plunder New Jerseyans was one more sign of Lee's political inclinations.[22]

Lieutenant Joseph Hodgkins of the Twelfth Massachusetts Regiment was in Lee's army. His regiment had almost ceased to exist. Three-quarters of the men and their colonel had declined to make the march, claiming illness or some other disqualification. Included in these stay-behinds was Hodgkins' friend and captain, Nathaniel Wade. In fact, so many men from various New England regiments joined what a sergeant called "the lame & lasy & the Faint Hearted" that the skeleton regiments from various states were consolidated into a New England brigade, headed by Rhode Islander Daniel Hitchcock. He was coughing blood and obviously dying of consumption, but he was one of those indomitable few who declined to quit. Even those who marched with him, such as Hodgkins, had no intention of serving beyond January 1, when their enlistments expired. Hodgkins told his wife he was looking forward to "the pleasure of facing you & all frinds in a fue weaks more if nothing extraordinary happens." His dismay at the order to march into New Jersey is visible in his next letter, from Peekskill. "This march whas Very unexpected to us all & the traveling verry Bad." [23]

The reception Lee's men encountered as they marched toward the New Jersey border was anything but encouraging. In Ramapo, New York, Sergeant Smith of Rhode Island wrote in his diary, "The inhabitents Abused us Caling us Damd Rebels & would not sell Us any thing for money the Soldiers Killd their fowles & one Stole a hive of Bees at Noon Day & Caried it off with him." In New Jersey, the Sergeant was sent to buy a hot breakfast for three officers on "a verey Cold Day." He went "to every house in my way for 10 or 11 miles but Got none till noon." Lieutenant Hodgkins told his wife "the Contry is full of them Cursed Creaters Called Torys." [24]

Charles Lee now turned from condescension to lying to Washington. On December 8, he wrote, "If I was not taught to think that your army was considerably reinforced, I should immediately join you." Lee did not say who had taught him to think this. All of Washington's letters had said the precise opposite. Since Washington was so strong, Lee thought he could "make a better impression" by hanging on the British rear, disrupting their communications and attacking the garrisons at New Brunswick and elsewhere. When a messenger from Washington arrived a few hours after Lee wrote this letter, and told him how many men Washington had, Lee dashed off a second note, saying he was "certainly shocked to hear that your force is so inadequate." But that was all right. He did not think the British planned to advance to Philadelphia. He still thought he could do Washington "more service" by attacking the enemy's rear. At any rate, he would "look about me tomorrow, and inform you further." [25]

This made little sense to Washington, who was watching the British juggernaut from the front. Howe and Cornwallis advanced from New Brunswick on December 6 and were in Princeton the following day. Washington did not even think about fighting. He shipped the last of his men and supplies across the Delaware at Trenton as fast as the big Durham boats could carry them. As usual, Howe showed no interest in trying to do Washington any serious damage. An aggressive advance might at the very least have trapped part of the American rear guard against the river. One British officer was so irked he said that Howe seemed to calculate exactly how long it would take Washington to get his men out of the state before moving on to Trenton. But at this point—December 8—Howe clearly had hopes of pushing on to Phila-delphia. He sent Cornwallis hustling up the Delaware to Coryell's ferry, twelve miles above Trenton, in search of boats. He found the banks bare and American cannon barking at him from the Pennsylvania side.

This stripping the Delaware of boats is usually described as a great American coup—a stroke of guerrilla genius that stopped the British advance. But Washington knew this was a silly idea on December 9, 1776. If the British wanted to cross the river, he told Congress, there was nothing he could do to stop them. For one thing, they could easily bring their attack flatboats overland by wagon from New York. In fact, intelligence reports had led him to think they were doing just that. With a well-trained army engineering corps, and hundreds of carpen-ters in the British fleet, it would have been a simple matter for Howe to build boats or rafts in or around Trenton. The town had a hardware store and three blacksmith shops to give him all the nails and iron he needed. His chief engineer, with the help of some loyalists, found 48,000 feet of already cut boards only a few yards away from the house Howe was using as headquarters.

"It will be impossible for our Small Force to give them any consider-able opposition in the Passage of the river," Washington admitted to Congress. "Indeed they may make a feint at one place, and by a Sud-den removal carry their Boats higher or lower, before we can bring our Cannon up to play upon them." There were eight fords within a day's march of Trenton at which the British could cross, establish a beach-head, and then ferry the rest of their army over at their leisure. Wash-ington spent the rest of the letter giving Congress advice on how to for-tify Philadelphia.[26]

As Washington saw it, the only hope of saving Philadelphia was Charles Lee. Although Nathanael Greene had told him that Lee would never join the army unless he gave him a positive order, Washington still hesitated to affront his second in command. On December 10, he wrote, "I cannot but request and entreat you and this too, by the advice of all the Genl Officers with me, to march and join me with all your whole force." [27]

Lee sat at Morristown looking about him. On December 9, he told Heath to order three regiments of the seven that were marching under Gates' command to join him there. "I am in hopes," he wrote, "to reconquer (if I may so express myself) the Jerseys. It was really in the hands of the enemy before my arrival." Two days later, he was rushing another letter to Heath, reporting, "We have no rum for the soldiery, and very little flour." The same day, he told Washington he could not march because his men had no shoes. He talked of crossing the Delaware at two different places but gave no indication of when. Washington had sent him a route and did everything but draw a line on a map for him, but Lee as usual ignored him.

On the twelfth, Lee began marching south toward Burlington. It began to snow and continued all night. His ragged men, most of them without blankets and shoes, were suffering so badly it became obvious that they were incapable of any serious offensive operations. He changed direction and began marching north to the crossing of the Delaware that Washington had suggested. In a letter to Horatio Gates, Lee took out his spleen on the American commander in chief. "Entre nous, a certain great man is most damnably deficient—He has thrown me into a situation where I have my choice of difficulties—if I stay in this Province I risk myself and Army and if I do not stay the Province is lost forever—I have neither guides, Cavalry, Medicines, Money, Shoes or Stockings . . . Tories are in my front, rear and on my flanks—the Mass of the People is strangely contaminated—In short unless something which I do not expect turns up We are lost." [28]

Lee wrote this letter at a tavern in Basking Ridge, New Jersey, where he was spending the night. His army was camped three miles away. With him, Lee had only his guard of fifteen men, an aide, Major William Bradford, Major James Wilkinson, who was acting as a courier from and to General Gates, and two French volunteers.

The British were well aware that Lee was moving through New Jersey. Cornwallis decided to find out what he was doing. On December 11, he ordered Lieutenant Colonel William Harcourt, commander of the Seventeenth Light Dragoons, to take twenty-five men and find Lee. They moved toward Morristown with a burly red-headed cornet (second lieutenant) named Banastre Tarleton commanding the advance guard of six men. They got plenty of information from British sympathizers along the way, and rode to within a mile of Lee's army, where they captured two sentries "without firing a Gun." Tarleton, who was to become one of the most aggressive cavalry leaders of the war, threatened the captives with "instant death," and they told him that Lee was sleeping some distance from his army and "his Guard was not very large." Next, Tarleton captured an American light horseman carrying a message from Lee to Major General John Sullivan, who had been exchanged and was second in command of Lee's army. "The Fear of the Saber" persuaded this captive to point out exactly where Lee was staying.

Harcourt asked one of his captains if he thought they were strong enough. The captain said yes, and the lieutenant colonel ordered Tarleton to charge the inn. Howling like fiends, whirling their sabers, the six dragoons thundered straight at the front door of the tavern, where two sentries were stationed. The guards took one look at these fearsome figures, dropped their guns, and ran for their lives. The dragoons rode around the house like plains Indians, firing into every door and window. An old woman ran out to the road and fell on her knees in front of Tarleton, screaming for mercy. Lee was inside, she said.

Lee's guard, quartered in an outbuilding, came tumbling into the yard and were mowed down by a charge from the rest of the British dragoons. The officers inside the tavern with Lee tried to defend the place with handguns. These weapons were even less accurate than a musket, and they hit no one. One of the French officers tried to make a dash out the back door and was flattened by a saber stroke on the head. The old lady, who was Mrs. White, the owner of the tavern, kept screaming that Lee was in the house and they could have him, but please not to burn down her tavern. This chaos lasted seven or eight minutes, then Lee's aide, Major Bradford, peered out of the front door, ducked a blast of British bullets, and shouted that the general would surrender.

A few moments later, Lee himself came downstairs, so agitated he was not even wearing a cloak or hat. Bradford ran back into the tavern and got these for him, and the second in command of the American army was ordered to mount behind a dragoon. Riding hard, and taking unguarded roads suggested to them by local loyalists, the horsemen were soon inside British lines at Hillsborough, where a battalion of the Seventy-first Regiment was stationed. Major General Charles Lee was a prisoner of war. "This coupe de Main has put an end to the campaign," the excited young Tarleton told his mother in a letter. A German officer confided the same opinion to his journal: "Victoria, we have got our hands on General Lee, the only Rebel General we had to fear." It was Friday, the thirteenth, an apparently unlucky day for the Americans.[29]

But only the timid consider thirteen an unlucky number. Lee's capture was in fact, the luckiest thing that happened to the infant United States in 1776. Having mesmerized the legislatures of New England and buffaloed the leaders of the South, he was in a position to demand the supreme command of the Revolution—and he was clearly in a mood to do so on the day he was seized. If he had succeeded, Lee would almost certainly have turned the American Revolution into something very different from what it became under George Washington's leadership. Lee combined the abstract political passion of a Robespierre and the ruthlessness of a professional soldier in an alarming combination. But the most important effect of Lee's capture was personal. The removal of his outspoken, overbearing presence freed George Washington from the diffidence and inferiority he felt as long as Lee was looking over his shoulder.

Lee's capture was not the only fortunate event that took place on December 13, 1776. The snow that began falling on the twelfth and continued into the morning of the thirteenth changed William Howe's mind about crossing the Delaware. There were reports from Philadelphia that the city was in a panic and Congress was preparing to flee. Thanks to an intercepted letter from Washington, Howe knew that the enlistments of most of the American army expired on January 1 and there was very little hope of recruiting another one. Moreover, thoroughly pacifying New Jersey with the admiral's pardons and his bayonets was undoubtedly the best way to prove to the Americans that reconciliation was possible through the mediation of the brothers Howe. Then there was Mrs. Loring, who was waiting for Sir William in his warm, comfortable New York headquarters. The combination of political and fleshly temptations was too much for the general. He announced, on that same fateful Friday the thirteenth, that the campaign of 1776 was over.

With Lee captured, Howe decided that the American army could be dismissed. Washington's performance thus far in 1776 inclined Howe to return to the opinion he had stated to Henry Clinton—the British could "take liberties" with these demoralized amateur soldiers. So Howe distributed his men in a chain of posts along the Delaware from Burlington to Trenton and garrisoned others at Princeton, Hillsborough, New Brunswick, Amboy, Elizabethtown, Newark, Hackensack, Bergen, and Paulus Hook. In command of this scattered army he placed Major General James Grant at New Brunswick. Then he and Lord Cornwallis rode back to New York, arriving there on December 17. On the twentieth, Howe reported the close of the campaign to Lord George Germain. Commenting on the New Jersey garrisons, he remarked, "The chain, I own, is rather too extensive." But he went on to justify it by arguing that the presence of British troops was needed to protect and encourage the "many loyal inhabitants" of New Jersey.[30]

On the other side of the Delaware, on December 13, Washington was getting another hoodoo off his back—the Continental Congress. On the twelfth, he had received a letter from Congress which amply demonstrated their panic. It enclosed a resolution which requested Washington to contradict the "scandalous report" spread by the enemies of America that the Congress was about to disperse. The resolution then went on to declare that Congress would not "adjourn from the city of Philadelphia in the present state of affairs, unless the last necessity shall direct it." Since the last necessity was looming large, the resolution practically contradicted itself. Washington informed the panicked politicians that publishing the resolve in the army's orders "will not lead to any good end, but on the contrary, may be attended by some bad consequences." Whether or not Congress should leave Philadelphia "must be governed by circumstances and events." [31]

Washington was starting to take charge of the war. The next day, the thirteenth, Congress passed a resolution that admitted its own incompetence. "Until the Congress shall otherwise order, General Washington [shall] be possessed of full power to order and direct all things relative to the department, and the operations of war." It underscored the admission by decamping from the nation's capital to Baltimore. The capture of Charles Lee may have had something to do with this final capitulation to panic.

Washington began acting like a leader. In response to a panicky letter from Governor Jonathan Trumbull asking for help in Connecticut, he replied that all he could send him was Benedict Arnold. He was drawing together every available man to fight Howe on the Delaware— and already he was thinking in terms not of defense but offense. He was hoping "to attempt a Stroke upon the Forces of the Enemy, who lay a good deal scattered and to all appearance in a state of Security." The same day, not knowing that Lee was a captive, he sent Brigadier General Lord Stirling to find him and bring him across the Delaware. He told Stirling to talk with Lee about "what probable mode of attack can be attempted" by his army, and made it clear he was ready to cooperate with it. Next, he turned his attention to the dangers of a loyalist uprising in his rear. The militia of Bucks County had "not only refused to obey" the general summons to turn out but, Washington was told, "exulted in the approach of the Enemy and our late misfortunes." He asked the Pennsylvania Council of Safety "whether such people are to be trusted with Arms in their Hands?" [32]

With most of his army due to depart on January 1, the only hope for the future was to raise a new army as fast as possible. There were good officers in his ranks who had not been appointed by the idiotic system of state commissioners which Congress had inflicted on him. Washington decided to utilize them to raise an additional sixteen regiments—betting they would come through for him faster than the political appointees. "If any good officers offer to raise men up on Continental pay," he informed Congress, "I shall encourage them to do so and regiment them when they have done it." Well aware that this was a large departure from his previous servility, Washington added, "It may be thought that I am going a good deal out of the line of my duty to adopt these Measures. . . . A Character to lose, an Estate to forfeit, the inestimable Blessing of liberty at Stake, and a life devoted must be my excuse." Confidentially, he wrote to his cousin Lund that if this attempt to enlist a new army failed, "I think the game will be pretty well up." To his brother Jack he confessed, "No man, I believe, ever had a greater choice of difficulties and less means to extricate himself from them." Yet, with Americans switching sides all around him, he remained convinced that the cause was just, and this conviction sustained his faith that it would not fail. "I cannot entertain an idea that it will finally sink tho it may remain for some time under a cloud." [33]

XXXII

Farewell
to Illusions

This faith and Washington's new firmness seemed frail things to most Americans at the close of 1776. Everywhere they looked, gaping holes were appearing in the façade of unity created by the Declaration of Independence. In Delaware, loyalists and anti-independence moderates controlled the legislature and fired Caesar Rodney and Thomas McKean as their delegates to the Continental Congress. In two-thirds of the state, newly elected judges and other officials were all outspoken supporters of George III. North Carolina's first election after independence had revealed dismaying divisions between radicals and moderates. The election had erupted into a mini–civil war in some districts, with violence and corruption of every sort used to win votes. The losers were disgruntled and disillusioned and the loyalists were rubbing their hands and chortling "I told you so." New Jersey was gone. Long Island had capitulated almost to a man. The loyalists were organizing secret companies of militia in Westchester and Dutchess counties, north of New York City. General Clinton and his expedition had captured Newport and a hefty chunk of Rhode Island without firing a shot. Worst of all, in Pennsylvania the Revolution was mortally ill, making a mockery of any hope of a defense in depth. John Dickinson, dean of the anti-independence men, wrote to his brother, Philemon Dickinson, brigadier general in command of New Jersey's nonexistent militia, telling him not to accept any more Continental dollars for bonds and mortgages. A number of other leading Pennsylvanians, including several Allens and Joseph Galloway, for many years speaker of the state's assembly, had slipped across the Delaware to join the Royal Army, expecting an advance on the capital and the total collapse of American resistance.[1]

Throughout the fall, Pennsylvania moderates and conservatives had continued to feud with the radical independents over the state's constitution. The moderates had taken a leaf from the radicals' book and held mass meetings in the Philadelphia State House yard. Streams of letters, petitions, and delegations poured into the Pennsylvania back country to arouse hostility to the constitution in that part of the state.

In Philadelphia, the anti-constitutionalists won a victory in early November elections and began using the weapon the radicals had used to wreck the old assembly—the boycott. But the most significant political symptom was the absence of enthusiasm for either side. The November vote was even lighter than the vote for the delegates to the constitutional convention. Months of agitation had left Pennsylvanians with an acute case of social dyspepsia. Most of them wanted out—out of politics, out of the Revolution.[2]

Among the few Pennsylvanians who did not bolt to the British or waver into neutralism was Robert Morris. He was still an opponent of independence and said so in letters to Horatio Gates. He was also a realist of the Washington school. He had volunteered to remain behind in Philadelphia to represent the Continental Congress. Once he had removed his family and books to safety in the country, he went to work with a strange combination of pessimism and calm.

"I fear our forces not equal to the task before them, and unless that task is performed, Philadelphia, nay, I say Pennsylvania, must fall," he told one correspondent. "The task I mean is to drive the enemy out of New Jersey." But Morris added that his mind was now "at ease and his time was now given up to the public" although he had "many thousands of pounds worth of effects here without any prospect of saving them."

Morris lamented that the Americans had faltered in the crisis. "Our people knew not the hardships and calamities of war when they . . . dared Britain to arms; every man was then a bold patriot, felt himself equal to the contest, and seemed to wish for an opportunity for evincing his prowess; but now, when we are fairly engaged, when death and ruin stare us in the face, and when nothing but the most intrepid courage can rescue us from contempt and disgrace, sorry am I to say it, many of those who were foremost in noise shrink cowardlike from the danger and are begging pardon without striking a blow." For the moment, he said, "this tendency is not general; but dejection of spirits is an epidemical disease, and unless some fortunate event or other gives a turn to the disorder, in time it may prevail throughout the community."

Morris accurately diagnosed the reason for the threatening collapse. "Alas, our internal enemies have by various arts and means frightened many, disaffected others, and caused a general languor to prevail over the minds of almost all men . . ." [3]

In New Jersey, Brigadier General Alexander McDougall wrote from Morristown on December 22, "This state is totally deranged, without Government or officers, civil or military, in it, that will act with any spirit. Many of them have gone to the enemy for protection, others are out of the state, and the few that remain are mostly indecisive in their conduct. . . . When I anticipate the bad consequences that will result to the common cause from the submission of this state, it renders me almost unfit for any business." [4]

Samuel Tucker of Trenton, former president of the New Jersey provincial congress, fled at the approach of the British army. After hiding for several days, he tried to return home to care for a sick wife. Captured by a roving band of armed loyalists, he capitulated and asked for protection from General Howe. Richard Stockton, one of the signers of the Declaration of Independence, fled from Morven, his handsome house in Princeton, to the shelter of a friend in Monmouth County. There the loyalists seized him and hustled him off to brutal captivity in New York which would break him in health and spirit. John Hart, another signer, fled from his farm at Hopewell and lived in the snow-filled woods for weeks to avoid capture. His wife died of exposure, and he himself never recovered his health.

Loyalist farmers rushed to sell provisions to the British army, and loyalist militia companies sprang up everywhere. Many other fighting men joined the New Jersey volunteers under Cortlandt Skinner, the state's former attorney general, who had received a brigadier general's commission from Howe. In the eighteen months of New Jersey's revolutionary government, more than a few loyalists had been harried and persecuted. Now they settled scores. In Monmouth County, the going for rebels was particularly rough. One loyalist said that it was in his power to have ropes about five or six necks. Now, he gloated, watch the Whigs run to the Tories for protection. [5]

Well-known loyalists in Monmouth were appointed commissioners to accept the submission of the rebels. They posted a notice calling on every able-bodied man between sixteen and fifty to turn out on December 30 to take an oath of allegiance. In Bergen and other northern counties where the loyalists were in the majority, the same thing was happening. Washington wrote to his brother Jack that "the Conduct of the Jerseys has been most Infamous." But this was a momentary emotion. Washington did not expect heroism from defenseless civilians. In another letter, he told General Heath that "the defection of the people in the lower part of Jersey, has been as much owing to the want of an Army to look the Enemy in the face, as any other cause."

Washington decided to give the New Jersey men at least a semblance of support. When the three regiments from the northern army whom Charles Lee had diverted to Morristown arrived there five days after Lee was captured, Washington let Alexander McDougall keep them there to support the fairly good turnout of militia in that area. He sent Brigadier General William Maxwell, a native of New Jersey, to bolster New Yorker McDougall's leadership of these New Jerseyans. In the north, Major General William Heath advanced into Bergen County with 500 or 600 men, where he was joined by General George Clinton with some 600 New York militia. They moved down the Hackensack Valley, arresting loyalists, seizing arms and supplies collected for them, and disrupting British hopes to pacify the region. On the east side of the Watchung Mountains, in Springfield, New Jersey, another militia army gathered under the command of Colonel Jacob Ford, Jr., of Morristown.[6]

All these little armies were soon annoying the British. From Woodbridge, New Jersey, on the shore just across from Staten Island, an area that General Howe presumed was pacified, a company of militia captured some 400 cattle and 200 sheep collected by British commissaries. The Reverend James Caldwell, pastor of the Elizabethtown Presbyterian Church and one of the fiercest rebels in New Jersey, reported that the militia under Colonel Ford had "taken off many of the most active Tories and struck fear into the British garrison at Elizabethtown." Several pitched battles were fought between German and British regulars and these militia bands.

As early as December 14, a Hessian officer wrote in his diary, "It is now very hard to travel in New Jersey. The peasant *canaille* meet our people singly and in groups without weapons, but have their muskets lying hidden in some nearby bushes, ditch, or the like; when they think they can achieve their purpose successfully and see one person or only a few who belong to our army, they shoot at their heads, then throw their muskets away again at once, and act as if they knew nothing about it." [7]

Near Elizabethtown, a British commissary, George Brindley, was ambushed and badly wounded as he rode through the country buying forage. In New Brunswick, Lieutenant Colonel William Harcourt of the Sixteenth Dragoons wrote a mournful letter to a British admiral, telling him how his son, a cornet in the regiment, had been killed when "fired upon by a party of the Rebels, who had concealed themselves on each side of the road." Before he retired to New York, General Howe had issued a warning that "small, straggling Parties, not dressed like Soldiers and without Officers, not being admissible in War, who presume to molest or fire upon Soldiers or peaceable Inhabitants of the Country, will be immediately hanged without Trial as Assassins." The day after Howe issued this order, five dragoons were ambushed on a road not far from Trenton. By December 18, Major General James Grant was issuing an order in New Brunswick that no officer or dragoon or forage wagon should leave headquarters without an escort. Ambrose Serle noted in his diary that "two troops of light horse went over [to New Jersey] this Afternoon, in order to assist the Commissaries and foraging Parties in future." [8]

Part of the reason for this upsurge of resistance in New Jersey was the indifference of lower-ranking British officers to the depredations their men wreaked on local citizens. Prohibitions against plundering issued by Howe and Cornwallis were ignored. When Howe went into winter quarters on December 14, he mentioned this problem in his orders. "The Commander in Chief calls upon the Commanding Officers to exert themselves in preserving the greatest Regularity and strictest Discipline in their respective Quarters, particularly attending to the Protection of the Inhabitants and their Property in their several Districts." There is a pleading note in these words, which suggests that Howe knew how little attention had been paid to his previous orders.[9]

Watching the British army in action, many New Jerseyans became convinced that Howe's orders were mere window dressing. An eyewitness described the redcoats looting the town of Piscataway. "The men of the village had retired on the approach of the enemy. Some women and children were left. I heard their lamentations as the soldiers carried off their furniture, scattered the feathers of beds to the winds [in search of valuables] and piled up looking glasses, with frying pans in the same heap, by the roadside. The soldier would place a female camp follower as a guard upon the spoil, while he returned to add to the treasure." Houses, gristmills, barns of Whigs frequently caught fire in mysterious circumstances. The homes and farms of prominent rebel leaders were ruthlessly stripped. Such conduct made men who had committed themselves to the rebel cause have grave doubts about the sincerity or the value of Howe's promise of protection upon submission.[10]

But too much stress should not be placed upon these British outrages. The Americans too had their plunderers. The Reverend James Caldwell, discussing the problem of keeping the Morris and Essex county militias in a compact body, remarked that they were "rather fond of plunder and adventure [and] kept a continual scouting which kept out [too] many detached parties." Caldwell was uncertain what to do about "the arms, horses, or other property taken with any of the enemy. The parties who take them think themselves entitled to these things." [11] The militia had repeatedly demonstrated by this time in the year 1776 that they were incapable of serious resistance against a regular army. There has been a tendency to romanticize guerrilla warfare in recent years. In no part of New Jersey were militia guerrillas seriously threatening British control. Colonel Joseph Reed, who was at Bristol on the Pennsylvania side of the Delaware collecting information about the enemy, reported that in Burlington County the British and Germans were "scattered through all the farmers' houses, eight, ten, twelve and fifteen in a house, and rambling over the whole country." Not exactly the conduct of troops who were under the constant menace of guerrilla attack.

Reed reported that the spirits of the Pennsylvania militia at Bristol were "very high." But he put no stock in their transitory emotions. "Something must be attempted before the sixty days expire which the Commissioners have allowed," he told Washington, "for however many affect to despise it, it is evident that a very serious attention is paid to it, and I am confident that unless some more favourable appearance attends our arms and cause before that time, a very great number of the militia officers here will follow the example of those of Jersey and take benefit from it." [12]

These words from one of the most astute politicians of the revolutionary era are the best possible proof of how close the Howes were to succeeding with their policy of reconciliation through the use of controlled force. There is no mention here of an outraged populace plundered to distraction and arising in wrath to smite their persecutors.

Reed's exhortation was quite unnecessary. Washington had been thinking about a strike at the British and German garrisons for over a week when his ex-confidant and advisor wrote this letter. He had already selected the German garrison at Trenton as the most likely target, and was utilizing every device in his power to guarantee his success. Day after day, strong patrols crossed the Delaware to attack the German outposts around the village. Dragoons carrying letters and dispatches were ambushed so regularly the German commander at Trenton, Colonel Johann Rall, finally sent a letter with an escort of a hundred men and a cannon to the British commander at Princeton, Brigadier General Alexander Leslie.

If even a handful of Hessians appeared on the riverbank outside the town, they were greeted by a blast of cannon fire from the Pennsylvania shore. A hundred Germans did rotating duty at the drawbridge over Crosswick's Creek—a vital point because it linked the garrisons at Trenton and Bordentown. They were constantly harassed. One officer noted bitterly in his diary, "We have not slept one night in peace since we came to this place." The twenty British dragoons stationed at Trenton were so intimidated that they were afraid to patrol without infantry protection, "for they never went out patrolling without being fired upon, or having one wounded or even shot dead." They were thus rendered useless as scouts.[13]

Washington was intimidating the Germans into staying within a small perimeter around Trenton. He was also considerably reducing the arrogance with which they had fought Americans in and around New York. After a long voyage and a hard campaign, the men were looking forward to some months of peace in comfortable winter quarters. This was standard procedure in European armies. Instead, they were in constant danger, and their morale declined steadily. Only their commander, Colonel Rall, persisted in despising the Americans. He ignored instructions to fortify the town, and dismissed pleas by some of his junior officers to let them and their men build redoubts voluntarily.

While distinguishing himself at Fort Washington, Rall had conceived an immense contempt for the Americans. In this he was echoed by the British commander in chief in New Jersey, Major General Grant. On December 24, Grant wrote a soothing letter to Rall telling him that the American army had "neither shoes nor stockings, are in fact almost naked, dying of cold, without blankets and very ill supplied with Provisions." When one junior officer asked permission to build some fortifications at the Trenton ferry, Rall exclaimed, *"Lasst sie nur kommen! Keine Schanzen! Mit dem Bajonet wollen wir an sie!"* (Let them come! We want no trenches! We'll go after them with the bayonet!") [14]

On Monday, December 23, Dr. William Bryant, a leading loyalist, told Rall he had just heard from a Negro who had crossed the river that the Americans were drawing rations for a march of several days— obviously part of a plan to attack Trenton.

"This is all idle! It is woman's talk," answered Rall.

Dr. Bryant was dismayed. He had a twenty-two-man picket guard stationed in his house and was not anxious to see his property become a battleground.[15]

Perhaps the most important thing Washington was doing to the headstrong Rall was a secret. Not long after Rall arrived in Trenton, a man named John Honeyman, a former British soldier who lived at Griggstown in Somerset County, appeared in the village, proclaiming his loyalty to the King. Honeyman told Rall he was a butcher and a dealer in cattle, and the delighted German commander hired him to obtain meat for himself and his men. He had been performing a similar service for other British and German regiments in New Jersey, which certified him for Rall as a trustworthy man.

Actually, Honeyman was George Washington's personal spy. Washington had hired him in November on one of his early visits to Hackensack. To protect his family from retaliation by angry Americans, Washington supplied Honeyman with a letter which read, "The wife and children of John Honeyman of Griggstown, the notorious Tory now within the British lines and probably acting the part of a spy" should be "protected from all harm and annoyance." But the order specifically added that this was to furnish "no protection for Honeyman himself."

On December 22, after spending about a week in Trenton, getting a thorough picture of the German garrison's routine and the disposition of their pickets, Honeyman wandered into the countryside, ostensibly looking for cattle which local farmers had hidden in the woods. He carried a rope and cart whip which he frequently cracked. The sound attracted an American patrol, who captured him at gun point, tied him up with his own rope, and ferried him across the river.

Honeyman was marched to Washington's headquarters. The American commander's face grew stern. He ordered the room cleared, declaring he wanted to interrogate this infamous turncoat personally, offering him a chance to save his life if he recanted and told everything he knew.

A half hour later, Washington flung open the door of his office and ordered his aides to put Honeyman under close arrest. The guard was ordered to shoot him if he tried to escape. Tomorrow morning, Washington sternly declared, the Tory would be court-martialed and hanged.

That night, Honeyman, using a key slipped to him by the American commander, escaped from the guardhouse and legged it past the American sentries with musket balls whistling around him. He found a boat tied up to the Delaware bank and got across the river in darkness. Sometime on December 24, he stumbled into Trenton and told Colonel Rall the exciting story of his capture. Rall naturally wanted to know what Honeyman had seen and heard about the American army. The spy assured Rall that the Americans were falling apart. They were frozen, half naked, without the food or basic equipment, such as shoes, to make a winter march. This eyewitness report confirmed what Grant had told the German colonel. It renewed his conviction that the Americans were incapable of launching a major attack.

In that half-hour talk with Washington, Honeyman had told the American commander everything he needed to know about the German garrison at Trenton. Dr. Benjamin Rush, who visited Washington not long after Honeyman escaped, was one of the many whom the American commander fooled with his furious denunciation of incompetent guards and sentries. As he ranted, the general was scribbling something on numerous scraps of paper. Rush picked one up and read without realizing it the password for the attack on Trenton—"Victory or death." [16]

The following day, Washington sent a letter to Joseph Reed at Bristol. He wanted to know if Reed and the Pennsylvania militia had moved across the river to support Colonel Samuel Griffen of New Jersey, who was heading a haphazard collection of local militiamen and two companies of Virginia regulars. Washington had no faith in Griffen, and he made it clear in the words following his inquiry. "Christmas Day at night, one hour before day, is the time fixed upon for our attempt on Trenton. For Heaven's sake, keep this to yourself, as the discovery of it may prove fatal to us; our numbers, sorry am I to say, being less than I had any conception of; but necessity, dire necessity will, nay must, justify my attack." He ordered Reed and the Pennsylvanians, with Griffen's help if available, to "attack as many of their posts as you possibly can, with a prospect of success; the more we attack at the same instant, the more confusion we shall spread and a greater good will result from it." [17]

By the time Reed got this letter, he had already visited Griffen and his troops at Mount Holly. He found the militia colonel seriously ill from exposure, and his men's morale low. When Hessians under Colonel Carl von Donop advanced against them from Bordertown, Griffen's men made no pretense of putting up a fight, although their numbers were almost equal. They retreated hastily down the Delaware to Moorestown.[18]

Reed rode to Philadelphia to see if he could persuade Israel Putnam to scrape together what troops and militia were available in the city, to join the foray into New Jersey. The adjutant general and the hero of Bunker Hill conferred at midnight on Christmas Eve. Putnam told Reed that he dared not let his handful of troops out of the city. There was grave danger of a loyalist insurrection if he did so. Back at Bristol, Reed and the militia general in command, Brigadier John Cadwalader, counted their men. They had 1,000 militia and 500 New England troops. They would have to do what they could with these men, although most of the regulars were without blankets or shoes.[19]

Farther up the river, Washington's men were not in much better shape. But he still remained determined to attack. He ordered Brigadier General James Ewing to assemble some 600 to 800 Pennsylvania militia opposite Trenton and try to cross the river at this point and seize the bridge at Assunpink Creek, cutting off the German retreat route down the bank of the Delaware. Washington and 2,400 regulars were to cross at McKonkey's ferry, nine miles above Trenton. Late on Christmas Day, as the troops were being assembled, he received a letter from Reed telling him that Putnam's support was out of the question. Next came a letter from Cadwalader, warning him that he could do little or nothing with his militiamen and exhausted regulars. "Notwithstanding the discouraging accounts I have received," Washington replied, "I am determined . . . to cross the river and make the attack upon Trenton in the morning." [20]

At 2 P.M., the first American regiments began marching toward McKonkey's ferry. By nightfall, the 2,400 men were assembled. The ugly fifty-foot-long Durham boats were gathered at the riverbank. Orders were issued to each brigade detailing their routes and points of attack.

Before he marched, Washington wrote a remarkably serene letter to Robert Morris. "I agree with you, that it is vain to ruminate upon, or even reflect upon the Authors or Causes of our present Misfortunes. We should rather exert ourselves, and look forward with Hopes that

some lucky Chance may yet turn up in our favour. Bad as our prospects are, I should not have the least doubt of Success in the End, did
not the late Treachery and defection of those who . . . by using their
influence with some, and working on the fears of others, may extend
the Circle so as to take in whole Towns, Counties, nay Provinces." [21]

It is one more proof of how close Americans were to accepting submission to a British army that seemed invincible, on terms that were
perilously close to unconditional surrender.

Looking back across the year 1776, Washington may have wondered if it was all a dream. Was it less than nine months ago, on March
17, that he had been the toast of the continent, the hero who had
driven the British army out of Boston? All the illusions with which the
Americans had begun the year were shattered now. The silly idea that
the British, once driven off the continent, could not obtain another
foothold. The complacent idea that untrained militia could fight
professional British regulars as equals. The overconfident idea that amateur American generals operating as a council of war could match
British generals, trained and experienced in strategy and tactics. The
absurd idea that Bunker Hill was the key to America's military future.
The naïve idea that the sheer nobility of the cause would inspire people
to fight and die for it, even when the chances of success looked hopeless. The blind idea that the British had nothing to offer the Americans
but brute force, rule by the bayonet, when they had their own philosophy—"the blessings of British liberty"—as a viable alternative to the
rights of man. Gone, gone were all these illusions.

Gone, too, were the great military reputations that had over-
shadowed Washington at the beginning of the year—Lee with his European laurels, Putnam with his Bunker Hill heroics. Gone was Congress
with its fatuous attempts to mingle things political and military. Reality
now was these 2,400 ragged, shivering men in ranks on the road and in
the fields behind the ferry landing. Most of them had only another five
days to serve, and they had made it clear that they intended to go home
the moment their contracts expired. They were symbols of the rest of
America on this gloomy Christmas Day, saying in effect to the Virginia
farmer turned soldier, "Show us what you can do—or else."

In response, Washington had reached deep into his American self,
and conceived a plan that was rooted in his primary experience as a soldier, when he fought the French and Indians on the frontier. Gone
were pretensions about fighting the enemy in the open on equal terms.

What he hoped to do in Trenton was quintessentially American—a lesson learned in the harsh and bitter decades of struggle against a savage foe.

If Washington and his men failed, America would never again be permitted to pursue a separate destiny. She would be as mercilessly a part of England and Europe as Ireland—and with perhaps as many sorrows to tell. Never again would the British make the mistake of allowing the Americans enough freedom to mount a revolution. Worse, the success of the Howes' propaganda and the defection of New Jersey made it clear that Americans would probably never want to risk a revolution again. They would prefer what Lord Howe promised—British liberty, carefully circumscribed and controlled by the King and his aristocratic supporters. If this eruption of stealth and savagery faltered on the other side of the Delaware tonight, Americans would be meek, humble, second-class citizens of the omnipotent Empire for a hundred—perhaps two hundred—years.

The big man on his horse by the ferry, watching his regiments board the bulky Durham boats, did not know or think all this, of course. He was neither a historian nor a philosopher. But he was something else, much more remarkable. He was a leader, his own man, fighting for that equally rare thing—a good cause. It was a cause that transcended the failures and imperfections of those who supported it, but it could not survive, no matter how good, how noble, how transcendent it was; its nobility would vanish, dismissed as foolish idealism by hardheaded men in power—if it did not receive the leadership it deserved. This was what George Washington was finally giving it. He was crossing this ice-filled river, leading these men down the snowy roads to Trenton, to give new faith to those unstable militiamen who were "rather too fond of plunder and adventure," to all the bewildered and uncertain people of New Jersey, sitting in their snowbound houses, wondering how long they should wait before they went to the nearest British officer to "promise and declare that I will remain in a peaceable obedience to His Majesty."

XXXIII

Double-Talk in London and Paris

In London on October 31, George III opened Parliament with a regal procession to the House of Lords. Peter Oliver, former chief justice of Massachusetts, was awed by the sight of His Majesty "in the elegant state coach, which is glazed all around, and the body elegantly gilt, with a gilt crown on the top, with other decorations, drawn by eight dun horses, the finest I ever saw, and kept in such order that their skin and hair appeared like a rich velvet." Oliver was equally impressed by "the amazing string of coaches and the vast crowd of spectators in the streets and in the windows of houses, ladies richly dressed . . . the whole, united with the apparent joy of countenances, exhibited an idea of the grandeur and importance of a British monarch."

The King took his seat on the throne before the assembled peers in the House of Lords and invited the House of Commons to join them. They came preceded by their speaker, who was preceded by his mace bearer and followed by his train bearer. The speaker was "richly dressed in his gold laced robes and made a magnificent appearance," Peter Oliver thought. The King then delivered his speech with, in Oliver's predictable opinion, "that dignity, propriety of accent and pronunciation which commanded attention and created esteem." [1]

George III exuded confidence in an early victory over the Americans. He reported their defeat on Long Island and called for unanimous support in prosecuting the war to a triumphant conclusion. He also expressed confidence that Europe would remain at peace—which everyone understood meant that France and Spain would not enter the war.

Little more than three weeks earlier, the King and his ministers were by no means so sanguine. During the summer and early fall of 1776, uneasiness and forced optimism were the prevailing moods of the men in power. Bad news from the American South—the repulse in Charleston Harbor, the defeats inflicted on the southern Indians by the frontiersmen of the region, cast a pall. Lord Howe, preoccupied with assisting his brother's army in its carefully controlled campaign, could spare few ships for blockade duty. As a result, the seas off the American coast were thick with privateers picking off British ships at a prodigious rate. Reports poured in from the West Indies about the continuously growing American trade with the Dutch and French West Indies. The government's chief ministers, while they continued to talk confidently for public consumption, were beset by anxiety. All of them—particularly Lord George Germain—had staked their political existence on a quick end to the war in America. If it dragged on, France and Spain were almost certain to strike a blow at England. Intelligence reports from Europe confirmed rumors that both the Spanish and the French were embarked on an ominous expansion of their battle fleets.

For a while, Prime Minister Lord North seemed to symbolize, perhaps even to prophesy, the fate of the government. On September 23, while riding on his country estate, he was thrown from his horse and his right arm was fractured. One American loyalist, the Reverend Henry Caner, former pastor of King's Chapel in Boston, who had reached London in June and by now was thoroughly disillusioned with England's attitude toward the Americans, wrote to a friend, "Lord North lately fell from his horse and broke his arm: many people here wish it had been his Neck." The painful accident brought the King out for a personal visit to North. But not even this seemed to raise the prime minister's spirits. George III remained obstinately optimistic, and told the government's chief political operator, John Robinson, that he differed greatly with Lord North "as to bad news being likely from New York." [2]

Fortunately for the government, the opposition was in as much disarray as the ministers. The reason was the Declaration of Independence. It seemed to confirm the government's chief accusation against the Americans—that they had been plotting this move since they first began screaming "No taxation without representation." A gloomy Edmund Burke wrote to a schoolmaster friend in Ireland, "I do not know how to wish success to those whose victory is to separate us from a large and noble part of our empire. Still less do I wish success to injustice, oppression, and absurdity." Lord Shelburne, who had said he was ready to bet his head that Americans were not independentists, decided to keep it on his shoulders by saying nothing for a while.[3]

After canvassing supporters, Lord Rockingham talked about boycotting Parliament as the only consistent way to maintain a united opposition. If he brought his people into the House of Commons, he was afraid they might start quarreling in public. Stephen Sayre, the American-born banker who had been arrested by the North government on a trumped-up charge of treason, tried to persuade Rockingham to join in a huge public demonstration which he and others were trying to organize in the City of London. But Rockingham would have none of it, and without the support of someone of his stature the idea withered.[4]

Beyond the narrow world of the politicians, England remained complacent and hopeful. War contracts kept employment high. Stocks remained firm. An abundant harvest for the second successive year kept food prices low. The Declaration of Independence struck the average Englishman as an act of outrageous impertinence that confirmed all the nasty things the government pamphleteers had been saying about the Americans. The ministry arranged for the publication of a number of vigorous rebuttals to it. The most trenchant came from the pen of loyalist Thomas Hutchinson, who carefully refuted each of Thomas Jefferson's indictments of George III and reiterated the government's favorite argument—plotters in each of the thirteen colonies had been fomenting independence for years. With this sort of diet for the public, Lord George Germain was able to tell Lord Howe on October 10 that the country appeared "to be more universally bent on the Assertion of their Dominion over America than I have ever known them upon any other point." [5]

In Paris, a new man was rising to power in the political-financial ferment created by the Revolution in America. Foreign Minister Vergennes's policy of secret aid to the Americans required France to rearm against the possibility of an English declaration of war. This, in turn, required huge amounts of money. Where was it to come from? The dismissal of Turgot had created a vacuum in French finances. Without reforms, new taxes could not be imposed on the already rebellious people.

Louis XVI and his advisers decided to imitate the English, and finance their adventure capitalist style. Turgot had been committed to spending no more than the surplus of what France produced, in the style of a frugal shopkeeper or careful housewife. There was no magic in his formula. To replace him, and achieve her new ambitions, France needed a wizard. They found him in the person of Jacques Necker.

Necker was a Protestant, scion of one of those Huguenot families who had been driven out of France by the intolerant policies of previous kings. The Huguenots had settled in cities such as Geneva, Amsterdam, and London and created a financial network of immense power. Thellusson Necker & Co. was one of the greatest of these Protestant banks, and through it Necker had intimate connections in every major city in Europe. Although he had been born in Geneva, his English contacts were good enough to enable him to make a fortune speculating on the London stock exchange during the Seven Years' War. He made another fortune helping to finance French trade with India in a remarkably peaceful semi-partnership with the English East India Company. Necker was the quintessential international financier, a man whom French traditionalists instinctively despised. He and his circle were considered without loyalty to any country.

Like Beaumarchais, Necker got his job because he had performed some very important secret diplomacy for Louis XVI. The Count de Guines, French ambassador in London, had been recalled for his clumsy handling of the delicate issues raised by the American revolt. Guines left behind him stupendous debts from equally inept stock speculations on the London market. Defending himself in French courts, he claimed to have been framed by his secretary and an insidious ring of English bankers. The courts found in his favor. But his bankers, Huguenots named Baurieu and Chollet, insisted on being paid, and threatened to make matters very uncomfortable for the French Crown by papering Europe with lawsuits against Louis XVI. At the King's request, Necker hastened to London and soothed his fellow Huguenots with soft promises of letting them handle some of the millions that would soon be passing through his hands as the man in charge of France's finances.

Early in October, Louis XVI appointed a yes-man named Taboureau des Reaux as controller general of France. Necker was named director of the royal treasury. As a Protestant, he could not be named controller general. But it was understood by everyone, including Taboureau des Reaux, that Necker was the boss. Turgot wrote to one of the *philosophes* that it was a parody of the Holy Trinity. Prime Minister Maurepas presided like an absent-minded God the Father, Taboureau was a meek and mild God the Son, and Necker breathed life into everything as the Holy Spirit, "and you only have to read the Acts of the Apostles," Turgot added, "to see what a commotion that produces." [6]

Necker began playing wizard. Taking over a state bank created in the last weeks of Turgot's ministry, he put it into the hands of an international consortium heavily dependent on Protestant financial power, but also involving traditional French Catholic financiers, who could not resist the opportunity to speculate in the tidal wave of paper that Necker soon produced. By the time he resigned in 1781, Necker had saddled the Crown of France with 500 million livres of government loans. Most of the creditors were Protestant bankers in Geneva with no sympathy, much less loyalty, to the French monarchy. It was a debt Louis XVI would pay with his head.

But for the time being, Louis thought he had the money to give his cabinet and court what they and the nation apparently wanted— revenge against England. Millions of Necker's make-believe livres were poured into preparations for war. French shipyards sprang to life, recruits trooped aboard refitted men-of-war, the ranks of skeleton army regiments were filled. An emboldened Count de Vergennes received the unofficial American representative in France, Silas Deane, and on August 31 wrote another of his position papers, declaring that there was no longer any question that France should join the Americans in war against England. The reason for this last outburst of bravado was the American Declaration of Independence, which gave the French an electric shock.

But a stronger shock was on its way—a British product that would numb the French into timid passivity. On October 10, a packet boat reached England with William Howe's report of his victory on Long Island. England exploded in a paroxysm of joy. Bonfires burned on street corners, church bells clanged, and innumerable glasses were raised to toast those noble heroes, Admiral Lord Richard and General William Howe. The King made General Howe a Knight of the Bath—a relatively trivial honor—but bolstered it by writing him a personal letter congratulating him and assuring him that a government sinecure would be forthcoming in the near future.[7]

The opposition was shattered by the news. Charles James Fox was one of the few who advocated continued resistance to the North machine. He urged Rockingham not to secede from Parliament. "I hope that it will be a point of honour among us all to support the American pretensions in adversity as much as we did in their prosperity, and that we shall never desert those who have acted *unsuccessfully* upon Whig principles." Fox begged Rockingham to come to Parliament and lead the opposition. "I cannot help conjuring you, over and over again, to consider the importance of this crisis."

Rockingham decided to keep his party in Parliament. He told Burke that he hoped that they could state their case "with dignity and solemnity." But he confessed to deep discouragement, and reproached himself for imagining "that this country can or will be served by anything like honesty, integrity or policy." The public was like "a silly echo" of what the Court sounded, "while the still voice of reason" was lost as in a vacuum.[8]

After the King's speech, it was traditional for Parliament to make a reply. The opposition mustered its decimated ranks to restrain the government's iron fist. Led by Charles James Fox, they moved to amend the majority reply, which was a total endorsement of the prevailing policy, with a plea for a suspension of hostilities and a generous peace.

Fox arraigned the government for talking of restoring law and liberty to America. Why was it ever disturbed? he asked. It reigned there "till the abominable doctrine of gaining money by taxes infatuated the heads of our statesmen." How was this "blessed system of law and liberty" to be established? By the bayonets of disciplined Germans? He scorned the government's repeated assurances that France and Spain had no intention of helping the Americans. Most dangerous was the ministry's argument that England had to choose between conquest or surrender. "If we are reduced to that I am for abandoning America," Fox said. It would take a standing army to "break the spirits" of the Americans, "to trample on the rights and live on the spoils cruelly wrung from the sweat and labor of their fellow subjects." Such an army would be a menace to the liberties of England.

Edward Gibbon said that he had never heard a more masterly speech in his life. Burke called it "a noble performance." But he noted that the ministry did not even bother to answer it. The House of Commons' response to Fox's eloquence was a vote to approve the majority response to the King's speech and the government's policy, 242 to 87.[9]

While the North government was riding high in Parliament, twenty armed boats moved up the Thames from Deptford and Woolwich, taking every sailor from cabin boys to mates from every ship on the river. The streets of London and other ports were scoured by naval officers backed by club-swinging seamen. The navy had ordered a general press to fill the ranks of the European fleet as a precaution against the

French rearmament program. A waterman from the Lord Mayor of London's own barge was seized, and His Honor, outraged, ordered every naval officer arrested who set foot inside the city. Three officers were jailed, but they found among the aldermen a government supporter who signed their press warrants. Nor did the Lord Mayor get back his bargeman. When the case came before Lord Mansfield, the chief justice, he ruled that pressing was legal. His Lordship piously added, "A pressed sailor is not a slave. No compulsion can be put upon him except to serve his country; and, while doing so, he is entitled to claim all the rights of an Englishman." [10]

The government's grim determination filled many American loyalist refugees in England with dismay. "Would to God," cried Samuel Curwen, "that moderate and just views of the real interests of both countries might possess the minds of those who direct the public measures here." The mild-mannered Curwen found himself more and more outraged by the aspersions he heard heaped on Americans. After talking to a British officer who had returned from America in mid-December and hearing Americans called "cowards and poltroons" and having every bad quality "the depraved heart can be cursed with," Curwen wrote, "It is my earnest wish [that] the despised Americans may convince these conceited islanders that without regular standing armies, our Continent can furnish brave soldiers . . . by some knock-down irrefragable argument; . . . not till then may we expect generous treatment." Curwen confessed that it "picques my pride . . . to hear us called *our colonies* and *our plantations,* as if our property and persons were absolutely theirs." [11]

As more reports of victories reached England, the government's confidence soared. Edward Gibbon spent an evening with Lord George Germain and found him "in high spirits." The historian of the decline of Rome came away convinced that "whatever force can effect will be performed" by the Howes. Friends wrote to British soldiers and sailors in America, reporting "the general joy."

The most successful paper in England, the *Morning Post,* hitherto one of Lord North's roughest critics, switched sides and began praising everyone on the government bench, even Lord George Germain. The *Post* editor, a dissolute ex-clergyman named Henry Bate, had been purchased from the secret-service fund for £200 a year. In January, the *Post* had been calling North "merely an office creature" and vowing that the government's military talents were "well adapted to convert a flower into a thistle." Now Bate reported that Charles James Fox had "fixed his price with administration" and sneered at the "cowardice of the panic smitten Yankies, at Long Island." [12]

But only a small band of Howe partisans were enthusiastic about the admiral's attempts to reconcile the Americans. More than a few of the King's ministers and the hard-liners in Parliament were infuriated by Howe's statement that the King was ready to revise all acts of Parliament that the colonials found objectionable. Ex-Governor Thomas Hutchinson of Massachusetts reported that one minister, Lord Townshend, called at his house "in a perfect rage." From his denunciations of Lord Howe, Hutchinson concluded, "They [the Howes] may make what agreement they will, but Parliament must finally approve it." [13]

Lord John Cavendish, leader of the Rockingham opposition in the House of Commons, asked that body to consider revising all the acts that had "aggrieved" America. After all, he asked, with delicious naïveté, hadn't Lord Howe announced that the government was prepared to do this? Why not prove England's sincerity to the Americans and do it without waiting for them to surrender? The motion was rejected with angry contempt by the government's supporters.

Charles James Fox accused North, Germain, and their supporters of vicious misrepresentation. In America, he said, the government was distributing literature that spoke of "peace, conciliation and parental tenderness." In England, nothing was heard but "subjugation, unconditional submission and a war of conquest . . . taxes are to be obtained, charters are to be modified or annihilated at pleasure . . ." [14]

Some members of the opposition were so alarmed by the authoritarian tendencies they perceived in the government that they actually began discussing the possibility of fleeing England to save their heads. The Duke of Richmond, whom Burke had tried in vain to arouse in January, went to France in the late summer and began trying to validate an old family claim to the dukedom of Aubigny. This required the approval of the Parlement of Paris and required an immense amount of trouble and bribery. Writing to Edmund Burke, Richmond complained "that beside the real business itself, the visits, formalities, solicitations, dinners, suppers" involved in wooing the Parlement were draining him dry of both money and energy. But he felt he was not wasting his time. In the not too distant future, "a retreat to this country" may be "a happy thing to have." [15]

France was on Prime Minister Lord North's mind, too. He and his secretaries of state made sure that the reports of British victories in America reached Paris as fast as possible. The news transformed

Foreign Minister Vergennes from belligerent to cautious neutral again. As a study in international hypocrisy, his letter to the British ambassador, Lord Stormont, is worth quoting in full.

MONSIEUR:
I am indeed touched at the attention shown me by your Excellency in admitting me to share your joy at the satisfactory news of the success of British arms in Connecticut and New York. I beg your Excellency to accept my many thanks at this testimonial of your friendship and my sincere felicitations upon an event so calculated to contribute to the reestablishment of peace in that part of the globe. I shall impart the communication made me to the King and now take it upon myself to assure you that His Majesty will always receive with pleasure news of whatever may contribute to the satisfaction and glory of the King your master.[16]

Vergennes ordered an immediate halt to selling arms and ammunition to the Americans. Four ships loaded with war matériel by Beaumarchais's secret company, Hortalez & Co., were about to embark. Not even his personal influence with Louis XVI could rescind the cancellation of their clearance papers. Vessels with French papers could sail for American ports carrying clothing, cordage, blankets, and drugs. But Vergennes intimated that there would be no protest forthcoming from France if English cruisers intercepted them. In the West Indies, a similar Gallic coolness chilled William Bingham and other American agents. Bingham's credit as an American government representative dried up. But he risked his own cash to keep the gunpowder and muskets coming.

Silas Deane was discouraged to the point of hysteria by this French retreat from the Revolution. Throughout the fall, he had bombarded Vergennes with proposals and warnings to act boldly on America's behalf. All were ignored. On November 23, Deane's desperation became so intense he sent Vergennes a draft of a treaty calling for a perpetual union of France, Spain, and America. Together, the allies would wrest Canada and all of the West Indian islands from England and sign a compact vowing never to trade with England under any circumstances. In return, France and Spain were to dispatch fleets to defend the coast of America. Vergennes saw no need to comment on this wild idea.

The French foreign minister did make one effort to restore the prestige of the sinking Americans. With the aid of the minister of war, he persuaded the Count de Broglie, one of France's best and most

famous generals, to offer himself to Congress as a combination supreme commander and dictator for three years. Baron de Kalb was
dispatched to Philadelphia to interest the Americans in the idea. In a
letter outlining his proffered services, the Count stipulated a "large pecuniary consideration" but insisted that the outlay would "reimburse
the cost a hundred fold in a single campaign." It was a striking example
of French non-comprehension of the American Revolution.[17]

Then came news that created vast excitement in both Paris and
London. Benjamin Franklin had landed at the small fishing port of
Auray in Brittany and was proceeding overland to Paris. More than a
few people in London, particularly George III, were convinced that
Franklin was the evil genius behind the entire Revolution. There is no
question that in May of 1775, when he returned from England, if
Franklin had come breathing peace and moderation, he would have
had an enormous impact on the Continental Congress. Instead, he had
said he was for independence.

Government writers in London began planting stories in the newspapers asserting that Franklin had fled the collapsing American cause.
Opposition politicians, among whom Franklin had many admirers, defended him. "I will never believe," said Edmund Burke, "that he is
going to conclude a long life, which has brightened every hour it has
continued, with so foul and dishonorable a flight." Burke's mentor,
Lord Rockingham, agreed and said that he considered the presence of
Franklin at the French Court "much more than a balance for the few
additional acres" which the English had gained by the conquest of
Manhattan Island.[18]

Both Burke and Rockingham feared that Franklin was more than
capable of persuading France and Spain to enter the war on the American side and strike Great Britain a mortal blow. The British ambassador in Paris, Lord Stormont, agreed, calling Franklin "a very dangerous engine." For a while, Burke and Rockingham thought that it might
be the opportune moment for a peace mission to Paris. They debated
the possibility that their "party might be made a sort of Mediators." But
the Declaration of Independence, they finally decided, made such a
move politically suicidal.[19]

Ironically, Franklin was in France against his better judgment. He
did not think America should seek French aid. "A virgin state," he said
in one of those homely metaphors to which he loved to reduce politics,
should not go about "suitoring" for alliances. Franklin wanted to retain
the diplomatic advantage of letting France do the suitoring. They had

already begun the romance with the Bonvouloir mission. But a panicky Congress decided to abandon all pretense of America's being able to go it alone. Instead, they initiated something called "militia diplomacy"—a bad choice of terms if there ever was one, considering the performance of the militia thus far in 1776. Franklin was hurried to France with orders for other American diplomats to storm the foreign ministries of Spain and Prussia, who had shown little or no interest in aiding the Americans. These portfolio militiamen met nothing but rebuffs and humiliation. But in France Franklin began turning Congress's bad judgment into one of the keystones of eventual victory.

Franklin assured the French that all this talk of British victories was nonsense. "I see that you have had bad news of our affairs in America," he wrote to a friend in Paris. "They are not true. The British, with the assistance of their ships, have gained a footing in two islands, but they have not extended their foothold on the continent, where we hold them at a respectful distance. Our armies were one or two miles apart when I left, and both entrenched. In different skirmishes which had occurred lately between parties of five hundred and a thousand men on each side, we have always had the advantage, and have driven them from the field with loss, our fire being more destructive than theirs."

This was making a great deal of the Harlem Heights skirmish and ignoring the Long Island and Kips Bay routs. The surrender of Fort Washington, the retreat from Fort Lee, and the capitulation of New Jersey had occurred after Franklin sailed. The Sage closed his letter with a comment on the American activity at sea which was closer to the truth. "We have seriously molested their commerce, taking large numbers of their ships in the West Indies, which are daily brought into our ports." [20]

Unlike Silas Deane, who went into frenzies when the French clamped down on American aid, Franklin had spent twenty years hobnobbing with the men who ran the British Empire and had no illusion that statesmen were motivated by anything but national self-interest. Franklin also knew he was not going to get French aid on a platter—and although he never commented on it, he must have been appalled by the maudlin supplications and bizarre treaties with which Deane had been showering the French.

In his first interview with Vergennes, Franklin made it clear that he considered a French-American connection a two-way street. America was not a beggar nation, forlornly hurling herself into the arms of France. She had an immensely profitable trade—which she was willing to divert from England to France by signing a commercial treaty. Franklin did not say a word about a military or a diplomatic alliance. Vergennes wrote to the French ambassador in Madrid after the interview. The canny foreign minister suspected that Franklin "had not told me everything." The offer of a commercial treaty was so "modest" Vergennes suspected there were "political considerations" behind it.[21]

Eight days later, Franklin followed up this interview with a bold letter in which he asked Vergennes for what he knew he could not get— eight ships of the line completely manned to help the Americans deal with the British fleet. He also dangled before Vergennes American military cooperation to help conquer the British West Indies once the war on the American continent was won. Without her American and West Indian colonies, Franklin pointed out, England would be stripped of "much the greatest part of that commerce which has rendered her so opulent, and be reduced to that state of weakness and humiliation which she has, by her perfidy, her insolence, and her cruelty, both in the East and the West, so justly merited." Next, Franklin politely pointed out that the exportation of "the private purchase made by Mr. Deane" had been forbidden. He was referring to the four ships loaded with ammunition, muskets, cannon, and other vital war supplies "sold" to Deane by Beaumarchais. Pretending Deane was persona non grata for some reason, Franklin told Vergennes he wished to buy in the name of the American Congress "twenty or thirty thousand muskets and bayonets and a large quantity of ammunition and brass field pieces, to be sent under convoy." [22]

Vergennes replied to this blunt propositioning orally via his undersecretary, Alexandre Gerard. He said no to the eight ships and the idea of convoying arms and ammunition to America. But the King wished to prove his good will. Henceforth, he would open his ports to American vessels in distress—and permit the Americans to purchase arms and supplies on credit. The government advanced two million livres to the Americans, and the financiers of the Farmers General advanced another million. What more can one ask? demanded the Count de Vergennes.[23]

Franklin had an answer to that—war. But for the time being, he was willing to let events take their course. In a letter to the Committee of Secret Correspondence, he explained the loans as "the inclination of the wealthy here to assist us." Franklin was aware that France swarmed with British secret-service agents, and there was no possibility of concealing the loans from George III. But Franklin had already decided that the more the English knew about France's secret aid, the better it was for America. The information might goad the English into declaring war on France. Franklin did not care who declared war on whom. His mission was to get France into the war on the American side. Moving the French a step closer to this goal in the face of a deluge of bad news from America was an amazing achievement.

But in the power politics of the eighteenth century, appearances meant a great deal. The French had been careful not to challenge Britain openly. Lord North, Lord George Germain, and George III read the reports of their secret agents—on which they reportedly spent about £80,000 a year—and decided to say nothing about France's aid for the time being. Their decision was based on a fresh spate of good news from America. On December 19, they learned from Lord Howe's dispatches that the Americans had abandoned Manhattan Island and that Rhode Island would soon be occupied. On December 30 came another dispatch from Sir William Howe, reporting in restrained but modestly triumphant style the progress of the Royal Army from Pell's Point to White Plains to Fort Washington, Fort Lee, Newark, and New Brunswick, a military tour de force with less than a thousand casualties.

Even more exciting was the news that Americans by the hundreds were taking oaths of allegiance to the King. Revolutionary committees were dissolving in a spume of royal apostrophes, and Washington's army seemed to be going the same way. The Continental currency was collapsing. There was every sign that the war was almost over.

George III chortled that the news exceeded "the most sanguine expectations." Everyone heaped praise on General Howe for doing so much at such small cost. Throughout the nation, but most especially in the great houses to which the lords and ladies and their retainers had retired for the holidays, people drank in the New Year with more toasts to the Howes. Lord George Germain confidently declared that the news meant "a continuance of Peace in Europe." It guaranteed the failure of Franklin's mission to Paris, he said.[24]

But Lord George Germain did not have a single kind word for Lord Howe's proclamation of November 30. It arrived along with an angry blast from Royal Governor William Tryon, who called it a betrayal of the loyalists. Lord George agreed. He called the proclamation "poor Encouragement for the friends of government who have been suffering under the Tyranny of the Rebels." He said it was a "sentimental manner of making war." Germain told the Howes that they did not have permission to offer such a sweeping pardon again. Those

Americans who failed to respond within the sixty-day limit would have
to face the kind of punishment that Lord George was looking forward
to giving them.[25]

So the year ended, in Paris and in London, with the men in power,
the kings and their ministers, waiting tensely for more news from
America. If the next dispatches reported a British army in Philadelphia, George Washington a prisoner of war, his army shattered and
dispersed, the Count de Vergennes would count his losses and find a
way to repossess the guns and ammunition that the Americans were
buying on credit. Lord George Germain would become the most powerful man in the British government, a wronged, brooding figure with
the Sackville tendency to extremes, motivated by a passionate loyalty to
George III, the man who had rescued him from political and moral
oblivion. No wonder men like Burke and Fox and Richmond feared
for British liberty. As for the Americans, the British had never been
inclined to be merciful to an enemy they did not respect. The Irish
were considered second-class human beings. There were signs that
Americans were falling into the same category. An American agent in
London wrote to a friend, "The state of politics here is in every way
disagreeable. Four-fifths at least of the English people despise us, and
look upon us as cowards . . ."[26]

A great deal—in fact, it is hardly an exaggeration to say everything—depended on those ragged, shivering men led by the tall, grim-
jawed soldier from Virginia whom we left struggling across the ice-
filled Delaware at midnight on December 25, 1776.

XXXIV

Gallant and Spirited Behavior—at Last

At first, everything seemed to be going wrong. A mixture of sleet and snow slashed out of the black sky on a northeast wind. The Delaware was high, and the current was running with unusual swiftness. Chunks of ice smashed against the Durham boats, driving them downstream and making them difficult to maneuver. Eighteen cannon had to be dragged by hand aboard the boats. Washington crossed early and sat down on a box by the ferry landing on the New Jersey shore, an image of patience and resolution to the weary men who filed past him. It was 4 A.M. before the last cannon was debarked and the regiments placed in order of battle. By this time, sleet was blowing on the bitter wind.

Nine miles downriver, at the Trenton ferry crossing, the militiamen and their commanding officer, Brigadier General James Ewing, looked at the ice-filled river and the sleet-filled air, and decided to stay in their tents. Another dozen miles down the river, John Cadwalader and his largely militia division were also baffled by the ice in the river and marched to another ferry south of Bristol. By this time, most of the night was gone—it was 5 A.M. before the first of Cadwalader's troops began even to board boats on the Pennsylvania side. But Washington had already written them off—as he had written off so many others. Everything depended on the 2,400 men under his command.

Sunrise was expected about 7:20. There would be enough light to see at about seven o'clock. Could they cover nine miles in this sleet storm and still achieve surprise? At the little crossroads town of Birmingham, five miles below McKonkey's ferry, the army split in two.

Half, led by Major General John Sullivan, took the river road. The other half, led by Major General Nathanael Greene, with Washington beside him, took the upper, or Pennington, road. Both columns had the same distance to march. Washington ordered all his officers to set their watches by his watch, and urged them to remind their men of the password, "Victory or death." There is not much doubt that Washington himself was prepared to die at Trenton if the assault failed.

The northeast wind sent the sleet driving into the soldiers' backs. The road became a blaze of ice beneath their feet. About two miles from Trenton, Captain John Mott, who lived on the river road and was serving as a guide for Sullivan's men, looked at the musket he was carrying. He had covered the firing pan with a handkerchief to keep the priming powder dry. But the sleet had soaked through the cloth. The gun was useless. A quick check of the guns in the line of march revealed that most were in the same condition. Sullivan sent a nervous message to Washington. He replied, "Tell the General to use the bayonet. . . . The town must be taken." [1]

When both columns were about two miles from Trenton, dawn began to break. But only a minimum of light penetrated the thick gray clouds that continued to whirl snow and sleet around the marching men. Washington rode near the center of Greene's column. Just as the first light appeared, the column came to a halt in the road. Washington rode to the head of the column and found Greene conferring with a captain from the Fifth Virginia Regiment. Early on Christmas Day, he had been sent across the river on patrol without Washington's knowledge or approval. The man who sent him, Brigadier General Adam Stephen of Virginia, was unreliable and something of a blowhard. The captain, Richard Anderson, whose son would make history defending Fort Sumter, proudly informed Washington that he had had a fierce skirmish with the Hessian picket guard earlier that night.

Washington turned on Stephen in a fury. "You, sir, may have ruined all my plans by having put them on their guard!" He ordered the captain and his men to join the vanguard and rode back down the line of march, pausing at several points to encourage the men.[2] "Soldiers, keep by your officers, for God's sake, keep by your officers," he said several times in a voice that seemed to a young Connecticut artilleryman "deep and Solemn." At one point on the icy road, his horse's hind feet slipped from under him, and for a moment it looked as if Washington and the horse would topple down a "Slanting slippery bank." But one of Washington's big hands seized the horse's mane and heaved the animal's head erect with a single motion of his powerful arm. To the watching men, it seemed a symbolic gesture of command. The young Connecticut artilleryman remembered it forty years later.[3]

Inside Trenton, Colonel Rall, lulled by the reassurances of Washington's spy, John Honeyman, and his general contempt for the American rebels, was asleep. He had received a warning from Major General Grant on Christmas Day that the Americans might make an attack. When Captain Anderson and his Virginians assaulted the picket and then melted into the woods, Rall concluded that the attack had been made and he had no more to worry about. He had spent the night playing cards at the House of Abraham Hunt, a New Jerseyan who managed to keep on good terms with both loyalists and rebels. Around midnight, a loyalist from Bucks County came to Hunt's door and asked to see the Hessian colonel. Hunt's Negro servant told the man that the colonel was busy. The farmer scribbled a note telling Rall that the Americans were crossing the Delaware, and fled into the night. Rall slipped the note into his pocket without reading it and went back to his card game.

Other members of Rall's regiment were better soldiers. They were on duty during the night of December 25–26. This meant that they slept with their uniforms on and their muskets by their sides. At 4 A.M., they prepared to send out a patrol with two cannon—a daily procedure. Rall was sleeping off his celebration and incapable of giving any orders. The lieutenant in charge of the patrol asked another officer, Major Friedrich Ludwig von Dechow, for orders. The major looked at the sleet-filled snow and told the lieutenant to go back to bed. There would be no patrol this morning. It would be impossible for the shoeless, coatless American army to survive, much less attack, in such weather.[4]

At about eight o'clock, Washington's two columns came out of the woods at a "long trot" to attack both ends of the rectangular little town of a hundred houses. The Hessian picket guards were driven in, firing their guns and shouting the alarm: *"Der Feind. Der Feind. Heraus."* ("The enemy. The enemy. Turn out.") By the time the Americans reached the town itself, the three German regiments were forming up and almost ready to fight. But the American artillery raked the two principal streets, and infantrymen seized many of the houses and blasted the Germans with musketry. The mercenaries got only two of their cannon into action, and these were captured in a headlong charge led by Captain William Washington of Virginia, the American com-

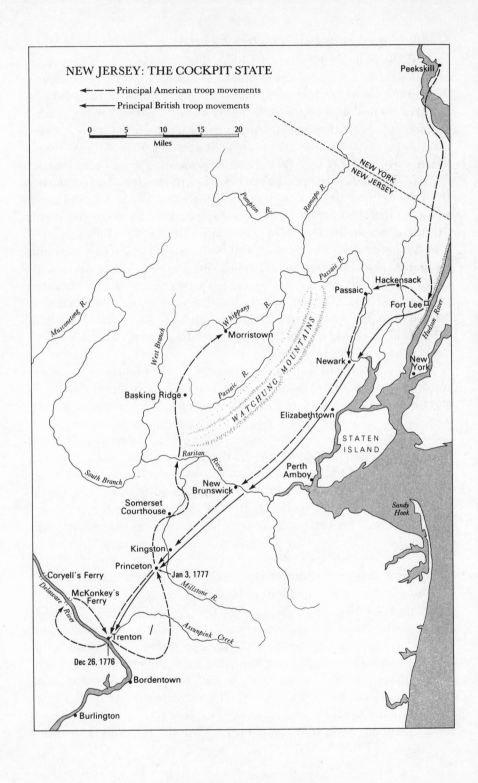

NEW JERSEY: THE COCKPIT STATE

←– – – Principal American troop movements

←——— Principal British troop movements

0   5   10   15   20
Miles

Peekskill

NEW YORK
NEW JERSEY

Pompton R.

Ramapo R.

Passaic R.

Passaic

Hackensack

Fort Lee

Hudson River

Muscanetcong R.

West Branch

Whippany R.

Morristown

WATCHUNG MOUNTAINS

Newark

New York

Passaic R.

Basking Ridge

Elizabethtown

STATEN ISLAND

South Branch

Raritan   River

New Brunswick

Perth Amboy

Sandy Hook

Somerset Courthouse

Kingston

Princeton

Coryell's Ferry

McKonkey's Ferry

Delaware River

Jan 3, 1777

Millstone R.

Trenton

Assunpink Creek

Dec 26, 1776

Bordentown

Burlington

mander's second cousin, and Lieutenant James Monroe, the future president. The gun crews had been decimated by counterfire from the battery commanded by Captain Alexander Hamilton of New York.[5]

For about an hour, a tremendous brawl raged through Trenton's streets. Howling like Indians, firing from house windows and doors, the Americans kept the German ranks in a continuous state of confusion. One historian has not inaccurately described it as a kind of large-scale riot, with swirling snow and sleet adding to the chaos. The Hessians fought desperately at first. But their attempts to attack with the bayonet were frustrated by the impromptu American tactics and by blasts of grapeshot from Henry Knox's cannons.

The Knyphausen regiment broke first and fled across Assunpink Creek on the bridge that Ewing's militia was supposed to have closed by crossing at the Trenton ferry. Twenty British dragoons stationed in the town used this same escape route. Then Sullivan's men seized the bridge, and the only way out of Trenton was through the swift, icy waters of the creek. A few Germans took this route, although the water was neck-deep.

Colonel Rall, befuddled by liquor and the whirling snow, was unable to comprehend the American attack. He never organized his three regiments into a unified fighting force. With two remaining regiments, his own and the von Lossbergs, he tried to fight his way out of the northern end of the town up the Princeton road. Washington blocked him with hundreds of men and cannon. The despairing colonel ordered his men to fall back to an orchard near the creek, where he may have considered making a last stand. A moment after he gave this order, grapeshot ripped into his side, and Rall, mortally wounded, toppled from his horse. His men half-carried half-walked him into a nearby church. The demoralized officers and men of the two regiments surrendered. At around the same time, remnants of the Knyphausen regiment surrendered to Sullivan's men.

Washington had finally won an unqualified, undebatable victory against troops who had created a myth of invincibility among many Americans. Eight hundred and sixty-eight German officers and men were captives, and 106 were killed or wounded. Between three and four hundred had managed to escape only by ingloriously running for their lives. The Americans had only four men wounded, not a man killed.[6]

Washington's first reaction to this victory was typical of the man. The news was brought to him on the high ground north of Trenton, where he had set up a command post. The bearer was eighteen-year-old Major James Wilkinson, who told him that the Hessians in the southern end of the town, mostly the Knyphausens, had surrendered. When Washington was deeply moved, he often reached out to touch or embrace those around him. The handshake in the eighteenth century was not the bone-crushing contest of strength which later generations of American males have made it. When Washington referred to it, he often used the phrase "taking my hand." This was what he did now with the boyish major. He took his hand and said, "This is a glorious day for our country." [7]

The next day, in his general orders to the army, Washington's emotion was still visible. "With the utmost sincerity and affection," he thanked the officers and soldiers "for their gallant and spirited behavior" at Trenton. "With inexpressible pleasure," he declared that "he did not see a single instance of bad behavior in either officers or privates." As a reward, he was putting a price on all the cannon muskets, horses, and other matériel captured, and distributing the equivalent in cash among the men who crossed the river.[8]

In this tribute, and in this report to Congress, Washington omitted some bad behavior on the part of the Americans as soon as the battle was over. A large number of the victors broke into the Hessian supply of rum and got drunk. To prevent the army from getting completely out of hand, Washington ordered forty hogsheads of rum stove in and dumped into the street. This widespread intoxication and the knowledge that there were enough British and Hessians at Princeton and Bordentown to smash his army even if it was in fighting trim made Washington decide to get his prisoners and his men back across the Delaware as fast as possible.

Some of his officers wanted to advance farther into New Jersey or down the river toward the Hessians in Bordentown. But between liquor and exhaustion, the men were in no shape to attempt such a feat. It took most of the day to get everyone back across the Delaware. Elisha Bostwick, a Connecticut soldier from Nathan Hale's old regiment, gave a glimpse of some of the problems in his diary. He was in one boat loaded with Hessian prisoners. "The ice," he wrote, "Continually Stuck to the boats driving them downstream. The boatmen endevering to clear off the ice pounded the boat, and stamping with their feet beconed to the prisoners to do the same and they all set to jumping at once with their cues flying up and down . . ." [9]

By the time the army stumbled into their tents, many of them had been on their feet for thirty-six hours. Captain William Hull, Nathan Hale's close friend, sank into a chair in his quarters and asked for a dish of hasty pudding. He fell asleep eating it and awoke the next morning with the spoon still in his hand. No less than 1,000 of the 2,400 men were reported unfit for duty on December 27.

That same day, Washington received a letter from Brigadier General John Cadwalader, who thought the American commander was still in Trenton. After explaining why he had not been able to cross the river to cooperate with Washington—the ice on the Jersey shore made it impossible to unload his artillery—Cadwalader reported that he was going to lead his men across that day. They had been reinforced by more militia from Philadelphia, stimulated by the news of the Trenton victory. New Jersey militia were also turning out. Cadwalader thought he would have 1,800 men under his command—enough to attack the Hessian regiments at Bordentown. "I should be glad to hear from you before we set out," he wrote. It was almost a dare to the American commander to maintain the offensive he had begun.

Later that day, another letter arrived from Cadwalader reporting that he had occupied the town of Burlington. By now, Cadwalader knew Washington was back on the Pennsylvania side. He reported that the Hessians had retreated with "great precipitation" from Bordentown, seizing "all the wagons in their reach." As the Americans moved up the road from Burlington to Bordentown in the Hessians' wake, they saw a sight which summed up the precarious plight of the Revolution in New Jersey. Ahead of them on the road, almost every house had a red rag nailed on the door. The inhabitants were hastily ripping off these symbols of royal allegiance before the Americans reached them.[10]

Cadwalader told Washington that if he crossed the river again and joined him in pursuing the Hessians, it would "keep up the panic." This was precisely what Washington wanted to do, but his men were exhausted and his commissary reported a dismaying lack of supplies. There would not be enough food on hand to issue more than short rations for two days. Men were not going to march in winter weather on empty stomachs. Even more agonizing was the knowledge that the enlistments of most of the victors of Trenton were expiring on January 1. It would be dangerous to cross the river and have these men deserting—much more dangerous than the Trenton adventure. But Washington had committed himself to living dangerously and he was not going to stop now.

Washington recognized Trenton for exactly what it was—"a lucky stroke," as he called it in one letter. To Congress, he described it as "an enterprise against a Detachment of the Enemy." If he was going to capitalize on it, he had to do more than lurk on the Pennsylvania side of the Delaware. New Jersey was the prize for which both armies were contending. Although his lack of military education made him somewhat weak on battlefield tactics, Washington's grasp of the strategy and politics of war was superb.

Washington did everything in his power to make the most of the Trenton victory. The captured Germans were marched through Philadelphia on December 31. Practically the entire population of the city— at least those who had not fled—turned out to see them. One spectator noted the startling contrast between the Germans, "well-clad," and the American guards, "mostly in light summer dress, and some without shoes." A German soldier recorded the experience in his diary. "Large and small, old and young stood there seeing what kind of people we were. . . . Old women screamed fearfully and wanted to choke us because we had come to America to deprive them [of] their liberty. . . . The American troops who guarded us had orders from Washington to march us all over the city, so that all should see us." Even before this triumphal parade, Philadelphians were telling Washington that Trenton had "given such amazing spirit to our people that you might do anything or go anywhere with them." [11]

At British headquarters in New Brunswick and New York, meanwhile, all was shock and consternation. The commander in New Jersey, Major General Grant, wrote, "I did not think that all the Rebels in America would have taken that brigade prisoners." Charles Lord Cornwallis had already placed his baggage aboard a ship in New York harbor. He was sailing home to spend the winter with his ailing wife. Howe revoked his leave and sent him hustling across New Jersey to Princeton with orders to concentrate every available man there. While he was en route, the German-British high command was in almost laughable disarray. Brigadier Alexander Leslie was ordered to advance toward Trenton with his brigade, leaving von Donop in charge at Princeton. Leslie took with him Colonel Thomas Stirling, commander of the Forty-second Regiment, who had been acting as von Donop's interpreter. The German colonel was soon writing to Grant, "I am now obliged to guess the meaning of your letters by the sense of the paragraphs, not being able to understand your language fully. . . . The

same thing happens to me when the country people come to me to give
me news of the movements of the army of Washington." [12]

On December 30, Washington's men plodded through snow six
inches deep to the Trenton ferry landing. The Delaware was choked by
ice. It was a daylong struggle to transport the army to the New Jersey
shore. As darkness fell, some regiments were still shivering in the cold
on the Pennsylvania side. Before he marched, Washington had sent
orders to every general in the vicinity of New Jersey, from Cadwalader
to Heath in the New York highlands to Alexander McDougall at Morristown and William Maxwell at Springfield, "to watch the motions of
the Enemy, and if they incline to retreat (or advance) harass their Rear
and Flanks." He urged them to assure the militia "that nothing is wanting but for them to lend a hand" to drive the enemy "from the whole
province of Jersey." [13]

On the same day that he crossed the Delaware, Washington ordered
each regiment that was slated for discharge on the thirty-first to muster
before him. Most of them were New England men, not a good omen. It
was common knowledge in the army that the southern regiments
looked upon all New Englanders with contempt. Now a Southerner was
speaking to them in the soft accents of Virginia from the saddle of a
big horse. A Southerner who had in the not too distant past made some
rather nasty comments about New Englanders himself. He was telling
them that he wanted and needed their help. As one man recalled it
years later, Washington said, "You have done all I asked you to do, and
more than could be reasonably expected; but your country is at stake,
your wives, your houses, and all that you hold dear." If they agreed to
serve another six weeks, they could not only rescue the cause—they
could earn themselves a ten-dollar bounty.

Continental money had not yet started to depreciate seriously. This
was a substantial sum for men who were earning only six dollars a
month. In fact, Washington told Congress that he considered it "a most
extravagant price." But the Pennsylvania militiamen had been offered
the same amount of money by their state to turn out for about the
same length of time, and they had not endured the military agonies of
Long Island and New York and the retreat across New Jersey.

Every man prepared to stay and serve—step forward now, Washington pleaded. The regimental drums beat briskly. Not a man moved.
Washington rode down the line and, as one man recalled it, pleaded,
"in the most affectionate manner," for the men to stay. Washington was

no orator, and the man's use of the word "affectionate" referred to the intensity of the general's emotions. Friends exchanged glances. The total sincerity, the absolute commitment of the man before them, reached deep into their souls. Phrases like "the cause of liberty" and "your country" suddenly had a new resonance. Grudgingly, local resentment and self-preservation fighting against it, they began to respond to one of the most mysterious yet crucial powers in a society of free men—the power of leadership. The drums beat again. One man stepped forward. Then another. "I will stay if you will," said a man to a friend beside him. They both stepped forward. In a few minutes, everyone except the invalids had volunteered.[14]

Washington did not have time to appeal to every regiment. He passed on this task to subordinate generals and colonels. They were not as successful. In the end, only slightly more than half the New Englanders volunteered. The largest defection came from John Glover's Marblehead regiment, the men on whom Washington depended to cross the Delaware. They were eager to get home and ship out on privateers to make their fortunes.[15]

The most successful appeal was made by Quartermaster General Thomas Mifflin to the New England brigade station at Bristol. If we add this to his advice on Long Island, Mifflin is one of the forgotten heroes of 1776. A gifted orator, he had already turned out several thousand Pennsylvania militiamen. Now, wearing a rose-colored blanket made into an overcoat, he urged the New Englanders to stay another month or six weeks. He not only offered them a ten-dollar bounty, but assured them that they could keep any booty they captured. This was at best a half-truth. He added some outright lies. Reinforcements were on the way and so were warm clothing and better food. Over half of the men volunteered.

There was a crowd of civilian spectators watching the scene, and they gave the soldiers a round of applause. Sergeant John Smith of Rhode Island called it "clapping of hands for Joy amongst the spectators." The civilians applauded the soldiers all the way to their quarters, telling them, "we had Done honour to our Country viz New England." The men were probably more pleased when "the General ordered us to heave [have] a gill of Rum per man." [16]

To pay the bounty, Washington rushed a letter to Robert Morris in Philadelphia. These New Englanders were not going to accept promissory notes. They wanted cash in hand. Washington begged Morris to "borrow money where it can be done . . . upon our private Credit.

Every Man of Interest and every Lover of his Country must strain his Credit upon such an Occasion." He also requested from Morris £150 in hard money. Washington needed this to pay "a certain set of people who are of particular use to us." He meant spies, who were not inclined to risk a noose for paper dollars. Borrowing on his large credit as a merchant prince, Morris rushed 50,000 paper dollars to Washington, and £124.7.6 in hard money, most of it Spanish silver dollars. Eight years later, when Washington was settling his accounts with Congress, he remembered the amount of hard money precisely, adding, "The time and circumstances of [its receipt] being too remarkable ever to be forgotten by me." [17]

With his men paid and the spine of his army stiffened by the approximately 1,400 regulars who had agreed to accept the bounty, Washington merged his division and Cadwallader's men and found himself in command of some 5,000 soldiers, three-fifths of them militia and most of these Pennsylvanians who had yet to fire a shot in battle. He concentrated this unstable force on a hill behind Assunpink Creek just across from the village of Trenton. The militiamen were in high spirits—too high. They talked of chasing the British into the Hudson River. Unstable and undisciplined, they roamed out of the army's camp to potshot at British sentries on the road to Princeton day and night. The British grew so jumpy they illuminated the road with a row of bonfires for several miles.[18]

Like the militia harassments before the victory of Trenton, the impact of this guerrilla fighting should not be romanticized. In Princeton, Cornwallis was studying his maps and gathering intelligence from the numerous loyalists in the vicinity. He knew exactly where George Washington and his army were. With 8,000 seasoned veterans, he was preparing to smash him. If he succeeded, Trenton would be revenged, New Jersey would be repacified, and the marauding militimen would pin red ribbons to their doors and swear an oath of allegiance to the King.

On this last day of the year, Washington received a letter from Congress informing him that he had been made a dictator for six months. This was a tribute to the success of Trenton and Congress's growing realization that they were not an assembly of generals. They gave Washington "full, ample, and complete powers to raise and collect together, in the most speedy and effectual manner" the sixteen extra battalions of infantry he had already told them he planned to recruit. They also gave him the power to "displace and appoint all officers under the rank of brigadier general" and "to take, wherever he may be, whatever he may want for the use of the army, if the inhabitants will not sell it" and "to arrest and confine persons who refuse to take the Continental currency, or are otherwise disaffected to the American Cause."

Here was the power that Charles Lee had hinted that he would like to possess. What was Washington's response? He wrote soberly to Congress that he by no means felt himself "free from all *civil* obligations by this mark of confidence." Instead, he would "constantly bear in mind that as the sword was the last resort for the preservation of our liberties, so it ought to be the first to be laid aside when these liberties are firmly established." It would be difficult, perhaps impossible, to choose the single instance on which George Washington made his greatest contribution to the American republic. But if the task was attempted, this response should certainly rank near the top of any list. Instinctively, he was creating a workable compromise between the ideal of civilian control of an army and the need for an army's leaders to have enough autonomy to make the command decisions that create victory. The essence of that compromise is built on Washington's example—on mutual trust between citizen and soldier.[19]

Washington told Congress that he would get to work on reforming the army. But he could not hope to make as much "progress as if I had a little leisure time upon my hand." Within twenty-four hours of writing these words, Washington and his men were fighting for their lives. Lord Cornwallis arrived in Princeton on January 1. The next morning, he led 7,000 German and British regulars from Princeton, leaving behind some 1,200 men in three regiments to protect his rear and garrison the town. Washington had stationed a number of regiments along the Princeton road, and they gave the British very stiff resistance, fighting from fence to fence and wood to wood and slowing the British advance to a crawl.

Two ominous events took place in the course of this fighting retreat. The commander of the American field force was Mathias Alexis de Fermoy, a Frenchman born in Martinique who persuaded Congress to appoint him a brigadier general on November 5, 1776. For some unknown reason—possibly that he was too drunk to make sense—he abandoned his troops and retreated to Trenton, leaving a Pennsylvania Irishman, Colonel Edward Hand, in command. Hand fought his men brilliantly, at one point forcing the British to form into a line of battle as if they were facing Washington's entire army. But one regiment behaved badly—a Pennsylvania German battalion which broke and fled as the fighting began to envelop the village of Trenton. The commander, Colonel Nicholas Haussegger, surrendered without making the slightest resistance. He had decided the war was lost and had passed the word to his men. As a pseudo-captive, he was to spend most of his time trying to persuade American prisoners to join the British army.[20]

It was 4 P.M. by the time the British cleared the town of Trenton and the last Americans crossed the bridge over Assunpink Creek. The sun was already low in the January sky. The British had been marching and fighting all day. Cornwallis allowed a few daring soldiers to attempt to seize the bridge, but when they were driven off by cannon fire, he decided against making an attack. It would be almost dark before he could get his weary men into position. Tomorrow, he told his staff, would be time enough to "bag the fox." Brigadier Sir William Erskine did not agree. Looking across the creek at the American army, he said, "If Washington is the general I think him to be, he will not be there tomorrow morning." Cornwallis scoffed, and ordered his men to cook their suppers.[21]

Where, the British commander probably asked himself, could Washington go? If he tried to retreat across the Delaware, the rear half of his army could be smashed with ease. If he retreated to the southern end of New Jersey, he was in another trap. It never occurred to Cornwallis that Washington was planning an attack.

XXXV

All Liberty Mad Again

Early in the evening of January 2, Washington called a council of war. What should they do, stand and fight? This seemed a suicidal choice. North of Trenton were several fords across Assunpink Creek. Loyalists had undoubtedly pointed them out to the British. The King's men would thus be able to develop their favorite maneuver, a flank attack that would rip the American army apart while a frontal assault pinned them against the Delaware. To lower-ranking officers in the army, this was all the future seemed to hold. "The most sanguine among us could not flatter himself with any hopes of victory," one young lieutenant recalled. "The fate of this extensive continent seemed suspended by a single thread." [1]

The Washington who could not make up his mind, the man who waited for others to advise him, would have sat there and allowed Cornwallis to cut that thread. This was a different man, a warrior leader who lived on risk. But the risk was carefully calculated, and he was using danger to inspirit his men and lure the British into the over-confidence that Cornwallis was displaying. Washington haters—there have been some in every generation, including the men of 1776—later claimed that the American position on high ground south of Assunpink Creek was a cul-de-sac from which only the grace of God and the advice of others extricated him.

This is nonsense. Washington had around him men who knew the countryside well. Joseph Reed, for instance, had lived for several years in Burlington, had been born in Trenton, and had gone to college at

Princeton. He also had with him some bold and wide-ranging cavalry, the Philadelphia troop of light horsemen. Only the day before, they had ridden almost to Princeton and captured a party of British dragoons who were "attacking and Conquering a Parcel of Mince Pyes." These Philadelphians, who had been commanded by Reed, used the Quaker Bridge, several miles beyond the British left flank, which led to a little-used "lower road" to Princeton. The man who had pledged himself henceforth to avoid at all costs risking the fate of the nation in a single battle would never have placed himself and his army with their backs to the Delaware if he did not know about that road.[2]

It is significant that there was not "one dissenting voice" in the council of war over which Washington presided. The hard decisions had been made in advance by the commander in chief. All the baggage wagons and supplies would be sent south to Burlington. The American army would move out in the darkness across the Quaker Bridge and along the lower or Quaker Road to Princeton. They would attack and destroy the British garrison there and then push on to New Brunswick, where they would, with luck, capture that town as well, the main British supply depot for New Jersey.

It was a tremendously risky plan. Washington was placing his entire army between two British armies, one commanded by Howe in New York, the other by Cornwallis at Trenton, each of which outnumbered him. But it had its advantages, too. Foremost, both an advantage and a necessity, was, as Washington put it later, "that it would avoid the appearance of a retreat." That, he said, was "the one thing I was sure of." As for "the hazard of the whole army's being cut off," that was "unavoidable." [3]

There was another major worry—the muddy roads would make it difficult to haul even light cannon. The generals decided that the artillerymen would have to solve that problem somehow. When the council of war broke up and they strode across the fields toward their brigades, they found the ground beneath their feet surprisingly firm. The wind had shifted to the north, the temperature had plunged to 21 degrees, and there was a very good chance that the road to Princeton would be frozen by the time they marched.

In each brigade, staff officers went from regiment to regiment and ordered the men to build their campfires higher until there were several dozen veritable bonfires blazing on the heights south of the creek. Then, one by one, the regiments were ordered to fall in and march. Several times, the orders were given in such a low whisper the colonels in command missed half the directions. Five hundred men were left behind to guard the bridge and feed the fires. As an afterthought, Washington told them to keep warm by clanging picks and shovels on the freezing earth. This gave the listening British sentries the impression that the Americans were busy building earthworks.

The cannon moved smoothly over the frozen earth, their wheels wrapped in cloths to muffle the sound. It was an utterly black night. The road passed through a large tract of desolate land known as "the Barrens," full of stunted oaks twisted in weird shapes. Somewhere in this eerie stretch of country, a cry went up that the Hessians were all around them. About a thousand Pennsylvania militia, the same bravos who had been talking about chasing the British into the Hudson River a few days before, bolted and did not stop running until they got to Burlington. This left Washington with little more than 4,000 men.[4]

The pace was slow. At first, the route was full of stumps over which men stumbled, cursing, and which became major obstacles to the artillery. On the Quaker Road, there were sheets of ice that had the artillery horses, many of which lacked shoes, sliding and slipping helplessly. There were frequent nerve-racking halts, during which many men fell asleep standing up.

As dawn broke, the American advance guards were crossing Stony Brook bridge, still three miles from Princeton. Washington halted his troops in a field on the other side of the swift little creek. Buckets of rum were passed among the half-frozen men, and they were formed into two columns. One, under the command of John Sullivan, wheeled to the right to attack Princeton from the rear. The second column, led by Nathanael Greene, headed for the main or Post Road from Trenton. They had orders to destroy its bridge over Stony Brook and them move up this road on the double to attack the town.[5]

Inside the village of fifty-two houses, three British regiments were awake and alert, and two of them were preparing for battle. During the night, Cornwallis had ordered them to join him for the assault on Washington, bringing with them some needed supplies. Two of these regiments, the Seventeenth and the Fifty-fifth, commanded by Lieutenant Colonel Charles Mawhood of the Seventeenth, were already on the road to Trenton, escorted by a troop of some thirty mounted dragoons. Mawhood was riding at the head of his own Seventeenth Regiment on a small pony, two pet spaniels scampering along the side of the road in front of him. Most of the Fifty-fifth Regiment was a mile or so behind him, guarding the wagon train. It was a beautiful morning. A stark winter sun was rising into an icy blue sky. Hoarfrost glittered on trees, grass, fences. Ahead of Colonel Mawhood and his marching troops, the countryside looked utterly serene.[6]

Serenity vanished moments later. Mawhood spotted the advance brigade of Greene's column coming up the Quaker Road, which intersected at a rough right angle with the Post Road. At almost the same moment, the British were spotted by the commander of his advance guard, Brigadier General Hugh Mercer of Virginia. The composition of the brigade, which deserved the name only because it was commanded by a brigadier, was a commentary on the shattered state of the American army. There were twenty Virginians led by twenty-one-year-old Captain John Fleming—all that was left of their regiment; a "fragment" from Colonel William Smallwood's Maryland regiment under another captain; Colonel John Haslet with the last of his Delaware regiment, four officers and two privates; and a New Jersey militia artillery company commanded by one of the few who had responded to Washington's call, Captain Daniel Neil. Two hundred Pennsylvania riflemen, fighting as volunteers, brought the brigade's strength to about 350 men.[7]

When Mawhood saw Mercer's men, he blinked in disbelief, but did not lose his head. He was a first-class professional soldier. He ordered his men back across the Stony Brook bridge which they had just crossed. At this point, Mawhood thought he was fighting an American patrol or some wandering militia. He had not yet seen the American army. Mercer had not got a good look at Mawhood either, and thought he was attacking a small detachment. The British commander decided to seize the nearest piece of high ground, on which stood an orchard protected by a hedge fence and the house and barn of William Clark's farm. Mercer, cutting across the fields to get onto the Post Road between the British and Princeton, headed for the same hill, and got there first. But he had with him only 100 Pennsylvania riflemen and Captain Fleming with his 20 forlorn Virginians. They were stunned to collide with the 350 men of Mawhood's superbly disciplined regiment. Taking cover in the orchard, the Americans began blasting away at the British who were lying prone behind a fence in the field just beyond them. Mawhood had two light cannon on a rise behind his men. Captain Neil arrived with his cannon to duel them, and Colonel John Haslet came puffing up with the rest of Mercer's tiny brigade. A hot mini-battle erupted between the two equal forces.

The British charged with the bayonet. Once more the myth of the omnipotent American rifle was exploded. The bulk of Mercer's force, the Pennsylvania riflemen, could not load their clumsy guns fast enough to stop them, and they had no bayonets to help them at close quarters. They broke and ran. A cannonball shattered the leg of Mercer's horse as he tried to rally his men. On foot, he faced over a dozen howling redcoats and went down with seven bayonets in him. Captain Neil was bayoneted standing by his gun. Colonel Haslet toppled with a bullet in his brain. Captain Fleming and his Virginians, among the few Americans with bayonets, were cut to pieces trying to make a stand. One lieutenant was bayoneted thirteen times.[8]

Up from the Quaker Road to help Mercer's shattered brigade came John Cadwalader and over 1,000 Philadelphia militia. Mawhood ordered his men to fall back to a fence and ditch on low ground at the foot of William Clark's hill, and posted his artillery behind them once more. Cadwalader led his Philadelphia militiamen in a charge at the entrenched British. It was an ironic reversal of the roles, and Cadwalader discovered that frontal assaults did not work for the Americans any more than they usually did for the British. Men dropped on all sides from the blasts of enemy fire, and the militiamen fled into the woods, abandoning one of their cannon.

At this point, Washington, who had left the main column the moment he heard the firing, reached the scene, accompanied by aide Colonel John Fitzgerald and other staff officers. They rode among the broken clumps of regiments cowering in the woods, urging them to form for another try. Meanwhile, the New England brigade, commanded by Major Israel Angell of Rhode Island, arrived on the battlefield. They had been the rear guard of the army on the march from Trenton. They now made the ten-dollar-per-man bounty they had received the best investment in American history. With professional grimness, they moved into line of battle on the American right. The Philadelphia militiamen took heart and reformed. Washington personally led them toward the British in a steady advance. Scarcely a shot was fired until both sides were only thirty yards apart.

"Halt and fire," Washington shouted. The British obeyed his command as instantaneously as the Americans. A cloud of smoke enveloped the battlefield. Colonel John Fitzgerald put his hat in front of his eyes. Washington was on his horse between those blazing muskets. The smoke cleared, and Fitzgerald saw the big man still erect in the saddle. He raced to his side, his eyes brimming with tears. "Thank God Your Excellency is safe," he cried.

Washington, again displaying deep emotion, took his hand. "Bring up the troops," he said, "the day is our own." [9]

American cannon hammered at the thin British line, and rebel infantry, who outnumbered them now perhaps five to one, lapped around both of Mawhood's flanks. His men were falling fast. "A resolution was taken to retreat, i.e., run away as fast as we could," recalled one of Mawhood's junior officers.[10]

Colonel Mawhood led the retreat with a compact body of men. They cut their way through the Americans and escaped by back roads to the British post at Maidenhead. Other officers were less successful in rallying the men around them, and the flight soon became a rout. All warrior now, Washington joined the pursuit. Memories of a certain insulting bugle call leaped into his mind, and he roared, "It is a fine fox chase, my boys." He was so carried away by the sight of vaunted British regulars on the run, littering the road behind them with muskets and knapsacks and canteens in a style heretofore displayed only by Americans in 1776, that he came close to getting himself captured. The British light dragoons of Mawhood's escort had stayed on the road during the fight around the orchard. About a mile beyond the Stony Brook bridge, they swung about, drew their sabers, and defended the road as Mawhood's men streamed past them. Washington was on his way to a collision with this blocking force when one of his aides caught up with him to shout a warning. The general galloped back to the battlefield.

There he learned that Major General John Sullivan and his column had swept the remaining British out of Princeton. About half the Fortieth Regiment had tried to barricade themselves in Nassau Hall. But a cannon shot from Captain Alexander Hamilton's battery persuaded them to surrender. The rest of that regiment and some of the Fifty-fifth Regiment had made a brief stand at a ravine south of the town, then fled down the road to New Brunswick. En route to the town, Washington ordered a detachment of Pennsylvania militia to destroy the Post Road bridge over Stony Brook immediately. They were still at work when the vanguard of the British army from Trenton appeared on the road "in a most infernal sweat, running, puffing, and blowing, and swearing at being so outwitted." The light infantrymen in the advance guard opened fire on the Pennsylvanians and charged them with the bayonet. Major John Kelly either fell or dived into the icy brook, taking a light infantryman with him. He dragged him out by the neck and made him his prisoner.[11]

The dripping Irish militia major and his men retreated while the

British advance guard hesitated on the banks of the stream, cursing the ruined bridge. Not until their commander, Brigadier General Alexander Leslie, arrived did they ford the brook and advance on Princeton.

By this time, the Americans had thoroughly looted the little village. The men were acting on Brigadier General Mifflin's promise that they could keep what they captured. Washington had confirmed this promise, but had warned "the order about plunder and Stores does not extend to Tory property." He knew that soldiers were not judges of civilian loyalties, and he did not want "the effects of many good staunch worthy persons . . . fallen a sacrifice." But he was too busy counting captives, worrying about the wounded, and rounding up his divided army to control his men at Princeton. The soldiers told themselves the town was "chiefly inhabited by Tories," and they stole everything from Bibles to teapots.

Within an hour, the bark of muskets at the Post Road bridge told the Americans it was time to go. They set fire to British magazines and headed down the road to New Brunswick. The British moved cautiously into the town around noon. With no Americans to fight, the angry redcoats vented their spleen on Princeton's civilians. They wrecked Richard Stockton's home, Morven, throwing his furniture and valuable library into a bonfire on the lawn. By the time the British were through, one dismayed American said the village looked as if it had "been desolated with the plague and an earthquake." [12]

On the road, George Washington was making a difficult decision. Could his exhausted men march the nineteen miles to New Brunswick over roads covered by fresh snow? Nearer to Princeton was the British post of Somerset Courthouse, where 1,300 redcoats were reportedly stationed. But New Brunswick was the real prize. The main British supply depot was crammed with food, guns, and ammunition. To destroy it would be a victory of the first magnitude. Washington looked at his exhausted men, most of whom had had nothing to eat since the previous morning, and began to have second thoughts about New Brunswick.[13]

By the time they crossed the Millstone River at Kingston and destroyed the bridge to further delay British pursuit, men were dropping out of the line of march by the dozen. At Kingston, the road forked, running on the right to New Brunswick and on the left to Somerset Courthouse. Washington and several of his generals sat on their horses at the fork, studying the men. For a moment, the American com-

mander allowed one of the primary illusion of 1776 to seize him again.
As he put it in a later report to Congress, if he had had "Six or Eight
hundred fresh troops [for] a forced March," he could have pushed on
to New Brunswick and "destroyed all their Stores, and Magazines,
taken . . . their Military Chest containing 70,000£ and put an end to
the War." [14]

It was still an attractive dream, this vision of victory in a single year.
It had seduced both the British and the Americans. But Washington
had learned too much to let it lure him again. New Brunswick was
beyond the strength of his men. His saw "the danger of loosing the advantage we had gaind by aiming at too much." The reluctant order was
given, and the troops swung left at the fork and trudged on to Somerset Courthouse. They arrived there to discover 400 New Jersey militiamen, who informed them that the 100 (instead of 1,300) British
troops stationed in the town had just departed with twenty baggage
wagons. Although the militia outnumbered them four to one, they had
let them go without firing a shot when the British rejected a feeble
demand for surrender. Washington's men were too exhausted to pursue them.

The American army began dissolving again. A blundering quartermaster had put all the blankets belonging to the Philadelphia militia in
the baggage wagons that had been sent to Burlington. This meant
these city-bred young men had to sleep on the bare ground in sub-zero
cold. They began going home in droves. The next day, Washington led
his men forward again to the village of Pluckemin, and had to call a
halt there to gather up no less than 1,000 stragglers who had fallen out
of the line of march, disabled by cold, weariness, and minimum rations.
He rested there for two days and on the sixth marched his men into
Morristown.

Geography made this village a perfect base camp. The town sat on a
high triangular plateau, backed against Thimble Mountain, and was
protected on the east by the rugged Watchung Mountains whose few
passes could be defended by a relative handful of men. From Morristown, Washington told Congress, he could "watch the motions of the
enemy and avail myself of every favourable circumstance."

By that time, his scouts and spies had assured him that he had no
need to worry about British pursuit or attack. Cornwallis had yielded to
panic and marched his army all night from Princeton to New Brunswick, where he put them in order of battle on the hills around the
town. When no American attack was forthcoming, it dawned on most

members of the British army that they had been outfought, outgeneraled, and—worst of all—made to look ridiculous. One of Howe's officers moaned that the British had been "boxed about in Jersey as if we had no feelings." The confidence of the average regular in the invincibility of the British army—and an early end to the war—plummeted.

Even more devastating was the impact of Washington's success on the loyalists of New Jersey. The British high command decided they could no longer guarantee the safety of isolated garrisons. So they withdrew from Elizabethtown, Hackensack, and other communities and formed a fortified defensive line along the Raritan River, with heavy concentrations of troops at Perth Amboy and New Brunswick. Instead of occupying the entire state, they now controlled barely a fifth of it—and even within that fifth, militia and parties of rangers from Washington's army roamed, attacking dragoons and foraging parties. Elsewhere in the state, the American rebels were in charge. Loyalists were arrested, imprisoned, and fined. Their farms were looted by the New Jersey militia to such a disgraceful point that Washington practically ordered Governor William Livingston to put a stop to it.

Proving he could play the reconciliation game as expertly as the Howes, Washington issued a proclamation calling on all those who had accepted the British offer of pardon to visit the nearest military headquarters and swear "allegiance to the United States." New Jersey Continental Congressmen, hungry as their militiamen for revenge on the loyalists and defectors, protested that Washington was wielding legislative power that Congress had never intended to grant him. Congress swallowed hard and backed Washington, declaring the proclamation a "military necessity." [15]

The Howes' dream of making New Jersey the first state to submit to the King's peace went glimmering. Gloomily reversing his entire policy (without admitting it, of course), Howe told Lord George Germain that the enemy's success in New Jersey had "thrown us further back than was at first apprehended, from the great encouragement it has given the Rebels. I do not now see a prospect of terminating the war, but by a general action." [16]

General Howe informed Lord George that he could not hope to end the war in the following year without an additional 15,000 men. There was no possibility of persuading Parliament to vote the extra money for such a quantum leap in the army—nor much hope of recruiting that many men in England, once the news of Trenton and

Princeton appeared in the newspapers and popular enthusiasm for the war went into a steep decline. The First Lord of the Admiralty, Lord Sandwich, was even more apoplectic when he received a demand from Lord Howe for eight additional ships of the line. The stage was set for a confrontation between the Howes and the hard-liners in the government, which exploded eighteen months later.

In France, the news of Trenton and Princeton persuaded the Count de Vergennes to revoke his prohibition against the Americans' purchasing arms and ammunition. He gave permission for Beaumarchais's four ships, crammed with weapons and gunpowder, to sail. It was almost a declaration of war. The British ignored it, thereby admitting that a war with France was the last thing they wanted. This encouraged the wary Vergennes to expand his secret support of the Americans into a formal alliance early in 1778. Until the moment this became public, the North government continued to lie industriously to Parliament about French aid.[17]

Outside of New Jersey, the news of Trenton and Princeton had an electric effect on the morale of the United States. Loyalist Nicholas Cresswell, who had wandered from Virginia to New York and back to Virginia again, wrote gloomily in his diary, "The minds of the people are much altered. A few days ago they had given up their cause for lost. Their late successes have turned the scale and now they are all liberty mad again. Their recruiting parties could not get a man, except he bought him [an indentured servant] from his master no longer since than last week, and now men are coming in by companies. . . . They have recovered their panic and it will not be an easy matter to throw them into that confusion again." [18]

For another loyalist, far more American than the English-born Cresswell, the news of Trenton created a much deeper, more personal gloom. On January 1, 1777, William Byrd III arose at dawn and faced the future. It looked as unbearably bleak and cold as the weather. The war was certain to continue for at least another year now—which meant there was no hope of his selling any of the tobacco and wheat lying in his warehouses and granaries. Worse, the war would henceforth be waged with grim determination by both sides. There would be no more talk of a truce, no more peace proclamations. Soon men like him would be required to take an oath of loyalty to the new government—or face the confiscation of their lands. His son Otway remained in the American army; his son Thomas remained in the British army. It was too much for a weak man to bear. Carefully dressing himself, William Byrd

went to Westover's armory. There he selected an expensive pistol, methodically loaded it, placed it against his temple, and pulled the trigger.

Ambrose Serle, Lord Howe's secretary, told his diary, "The Rebels
presume upon their late Successes." More significant was Serle's discovery that a leading loyalist in New York had "a correspondent to the
Southward among the Rebels." They had a secret agreement that when
the time came to desert the royal cause, or vice versa, they would advise
each other by a "private Mark" on their letters. "This is making loyalty
a sure Game," wrote Serle.[19]

So the year 1776 ended with both sides stripped of their illusions
and faced with the grimmest of all truths—it was easier to start a war
than to end one. Both sides had been forced to abandon the myth of
their invincibility. Both had been forced to confront the realities of
human nature, on the battlefield and in the struggle for allegiance to
their causes. For the Americans, it had been a shock to discover that it
was easy to persuade people to cheer for life, liberty, and the pursuit of
happiness, but it was another matter to persuade them to take large
risks or make real sacrifices for these ideals. A dismaying number of
Americans in 1776 seemed more interested in achieving what might be
called instant equality by looting their loyalist countrymen.

Nevertheless, the articulation of these ideals in America in 1776 had
set in motion a revolution in the thoughts and feelings of average men
that is still shaking the world today. The goal of British aristocrats in
their war against America—the achievement of a "proper subordination" of America to England, which would have also guaranteed subordination at home and reinforced this aristocratic idea around the
world—was forever frustrated by the events of this enormous year.
Seventeen seventy-six was truly, in the words of Pastor Shewkirk of the
Moravian Church in New York, "a time of shaking."

Seventeen seventy-six was also a tragic year. Americans fighting in
the name of liberty persecuted, robbed, and sometimes killed fellow
Americans who chose to remain loyal to the old order, with its more
circumscribed, yet sincere, commitment to freedom. Seventeen seventy-
six was also a heroic year. Richard Montgomery, Benedict Arnold,
George Washington led the list of men with the courage to mean literally that shout which opened the year at Quebec and closed it at
Trenton—victory or death. Seventeen seventy-six was also a disgraceful
year. Americans revealed a capacity for cowardice, disorganization, incompetence, and stupidity.

In recent years, historians have spent a great deal of time studying the evolution of the American government which began in 1776. There has been a general agreement that perhaps the most notable thing about this government was the institutionalization of a point of view about human nature—a view that saw men as potentially corrupt, fallible, limited, and hence in need of a strong government with built-in checks and balances. While this philosophy derived in part from the prevailing thought patterns of educated Americans in the eighteenth century, not enough attention has been paid, in this writer's opinion, to the revolutionary experience itself, especially to the chaos and failures of 1776. The need for a strong executive, the awareness that government had to deal with the interests as well as the idealism of men—in a word, the central realism of America's political structure—can be traced to the often bitter lessons learned in 1776.[20]

We have celebrated the heroic side of 1776 for a long time. Perhaps after two hundred years we are ready to look steadily at the dark side of the story as well. Perhaps by facing it, absorbing it, contemporary and future Americans will be spared the paroxysms of shock and dismay, the cries of despair and predictions of imminent doom which emanate from so many mouths whenever we discover some of our contemporary politicians or soldiers or plain citizens are fallible or corrupt. Instead of these seizures of infantile emotion, perhaps we can begin to accept such failings as part of our limited human natures and learn from the mistakes, without losing hope or faith in the future. This was what that quintessentially mature man George Washington did in 1776. This is what a mature nation can and should do in 1976.

At the same time, this new realism about 1776 might also help us eliminate once and for all two types of thinking. One comes from men and women who fear power so pathologically they want to dilute it to the point of paralyzing our leaders. This attitude almost destroyed George Washington—and the nation—in 1776. The other extreme might be called the Charles Lee variation. These people pontificate about freedom and human rights but have absurd ideas about how much others should sacrifice for these ideas—or their version of them. When this sacrifice is not forthcoming, they denounce the inefficiencies, delays, and frustrations of a free society in which power is distributed and responsibility shared and fall in love with forcing their version of justice on everyone with power that grows from the barrel of a gun. Washington and the men around him endured the failures and fumblings of 1776 without abandoning their commitment to the free society they were defending. At times in 1776, this required an act of faith that defied present realities. It is a faith which Americans of 1976—and 2076—no matter what their discouragements, must never abandon.

Notes

I. Soldiers Far from Home

1. Peter Force, ed., *American Archives: Consisting of a Collection of Authentick Records, State Papers, Debates and Letters and Other Notices of Public Affairs . . .* 4th ser. (Washington, D.C., 1837–46), vol. 4, pp. 288–89. Cited hereafter as *Archives*.

2. George Dangerfield, *Chancellor Robert R. Livingston* (New York, 1960), p. 62.

3. Thomas P. Robinson, "Some Notes on Major General Richard Montgomery," *New York History,* 37 (1956), 391.

4. Force, *Archives,* vol. 4, pp. 906–7.

5. Willard M. Wallace, *Traitorous Hero: The Life and Fortunes of Benedict Arnold* (New York, 1954), p. 26.

6. Kenneth Roberts, ed., *March to Quebec: Journals of the Members of Arnold's Expedition* (New York, 1938), Sentner journal, p. 231.

7. Force, *Archives,* vol. 4, p. 466.

8. Roberts, *March to Quebec,* p. 232.

9. Ibid., p. 274.

10. Ibid., p. 562.

11. Peter D. McClelland, "The Cost to America of British Imperial Policy," *American Economic Review,* 59 (1969), 382ff.

12. Sheldon S. Cohen, ed., *Canada Preserved: The Journal of Captain Thomas Ainslie* (New York, 1968), p. 33.

13. Ibid., p. 22. Also see Allen French, *The First Year of the American Revolution* (Boston, 1934), p. 613, n. 55. At least one of Montgomery's officers talked loosely about this badly kept secret.

14. Roberts, *March to Quebec,* Stocking journal, p. 563.

15. Ibid., Henry journal, p. 375.

16. Isaac Q. Leake, *Memoirs of the Life and Times of John Lamb* (Albany, N.Y., 1857), p. 119.

17. Roberts, *March to Quebec,* Dearborn journal, p. 149.

18. Ibid., Sentner journal, p. 233.

19. Ibid., Henry journal, p. 376.
20. Ibid., Fobes journal, pp. 590–91.
21. French, *First Year of the Revolution,* p. 615. For more information on Coffin, see James H. Stark, *The Loyalists of Massachusetts* (Boston, 1910), pp. 233–46.
22. Wallace, *Traitorous Hero,* p. 84.
23. Don Higginbotham, *Daniel Morgan: Revolutionary Rifleman* (Chapel Hill, N.C., 1961), pp. 45–46.
24. Roberts, *March to Quebec,* Dearborn journal, pp. 149–50.
25. Ibid., Stocking journal, p. 564.
26. Major Henry Caldwell, letter of June 15, 1776, from the manuscripts relating to the early history of Canada, Literary Historical Society of Quebec, 2nd ser., vol. 5, pp. 9–13.
27. Roberts, *March to Quebec,* Dearborn journal, p. 150.
28. Cohen, *Ainslie Journal,* p. 36.
29. Roberts, *March to Quebec,* Sentner journal, p. 234.
30. Ibid., Thayer journal, p. 278.

II. Their Country—Rights and Wrongs

1. R. R. Palmer, *The Age of the Democratic Revolution,* (Princeton, 1959), vol. 1, p. 156.
2. *Historical Statistics of the United States* (Washington, D.C., 1960), pp. 756ff.
3. I. R. Christie, *Crisis of Empire* (New York, 1966), p. 110.
4. *Historical Statistics,* p. 757.
5. Jackson Turner Main, *The Social Structure of Revolutionary America* (Princeton, 1965), pp. 43ff.
6. R. G. Albion and L. Dodson, eds., *Journal of Philip Vickers Fithian* (Princeton, 1934), p. 63.
7. Main, *Revolutionary America,* pp. 42–45, 66, 226–27.
8. Michael G. Kammen, ed., *Politics and Society in Colonial America* (New York, 1973), p. 75.
9. John Adams, *Defence of the Constitution of the United States* (Philadelphia, 1797), vol. 1, pp. 110–11.
10. Bernard Bailyn, *The Ideological Origins of the American Revolution* (Cambridge, Mass., 1967), chaps. 3 and 4. For those who wish to explore this idea in depth, this book is essential reading.
11. Oliver M. Dickerson, *The Navigation Acts and the American Revolution* (Philadelphia, 1951), pp. 224, 231.
12. Thomas Fleming, ed., *Benjamin Franklin: A Biography in His Own Words* (New York, 1972), p. 234.

III. A General and His Illusionary Army

1. Philip G. Davidson, *Propaganda and the American Revolution, 1763–1783* (Chapel Hill, N.C., 1941), p. 165.
2. James Kirby Martin, *Men in Rebellion: Higher Governmental Leaders and the Coming of the American Revolution* (New Brunswick, N.J., 1973), p. 155.
3. Douglas Southall Freeman, *George Washington: A Biography* (New York, 1948–57), vol. 2, p. 155.
4. John C. Fitzpatrick, ed., *The Writings of George Washington from the Origi-*

nal Manuscript Sources, 1745–1799 (Washington, D.C., 1931–44), vol. 2, p. 500. Cited hereafter as *GW Writings.*

5. John Shy, *Toward Lexington: the Role of the British Army in the Coming of the American Revolution* (Princeton, 1965), p. 379. Shy has much detail on the bad conduct of British officers in America and American fear of their influence.

6. *GW Writings,* vol. 4, p. 207.

7. Ibid., p. 211.

8. Fithian (Albion and Dodson, eds.), in his journal of his tour of the Pennsylvania back country in 1775, gives a vivid picture of the patriotic fervor there.

9. *GW Writings,* vol. 4, pp. 124–25.

10. Edmund C. Burnett, ed., *Letters of Members of the Continental Congress* (Washington, D.C., 1921–36), vol. 1, pp. 256, 279.

11. Jared Sparks, ed., *The Correspondence of the American Revolution: Being Letters of Eminent Men to George Washington* (Boston, 1853), vol. 1, p. 127.

12. Ibid., pp. 149–51.

13. *The Lee Papers,* Collections of the New-York Historical Society (1871), vol. 1, pp. 234–36.

14. Sparks, *Letters to Washington,* vol. 1, pp. 111–13.

15. Freeman, *Washington,* vol. 4, p. 10.

16. James Thomas Flexner, *George Washington in the American Revolution* (Boston, 1968), vol. 2, p. 59.

17. William B. Clark, *George Washington's Navy: Being an Account of His Excellency's Fleet in New England Waters* (Baton Rouge, La., 1960). This is the best and most detailed telling of the story of Washington's privateers.

18. David Bushnell, "General Principles and Construction of a Sub-marine Vessel," *Transactions of the American Philosophical Society,* 4 (Philadelphia, 1799), 303–7. See also David Thompson, "David Bushnell and the First American Submarine," *U.S. Naval Institute Proceedings,* 68 (1942), 467–78.

19. North Callahan, *Henry Knox: General Washington's General* (New York, 1958), pp. 41ff.

20. Force, *Archives,* vol. 4, p. 484.

21. Herbert T. Wade and Robert A. Lively, *This Glorious Cause: The Adventures of Two Company Officers in Washington's Army* (Princeton, 1958), pp. 41–42.

22. Ibid., pp. 184, 187, 191.

23. *Report of the Royal Historical Manuscripts Commission on the Manuscripts of Mrs. Stopford-Sackville* (London, 1904–10), vol. 1, p. 15. Cited hereafter as *Stopford-Sackville Manuscripts.*

24. Force, *Archives,* vol. 4, p. 484, Nathanael Greene to Samuel Ward.

25. Henry P. Johnston, *Nathan Hale, 1776* (New Haven, 1914), pp. 76–82.

26. French, *First Year of the Revolution,* p. 475.

IV. All the King's Unhappy Men

1. *The Kemble Papers,* Collections of the New-York Historical Society (1883–84), vol. 1, pp. 288–89.

2. French, *First Year of the Revolution,* p. 532.

3. Margaret Wheeler Willard, ed., *Letters on the American Revolution, 1774–1776* (Boston, 1925), p. 189.

4. Ann Hunter and Miss Bell, eds., *The Journal of General Sir Martin Hunter* (Edinburgh, 1894), p. 12.

5. French, *First Year of the Revolution,* p. 652.

6. Wallace Brown, *The King's Friends: The Composition and Motives of the American Loyalist Claimants* (Providence, R.I., 1965), pp. 30–31.

7. *Kemble Papers*, vol. 1, pp. 64–65.

8. French, *First Year of the Revolution,* p. 328.

9. *Hunter Journal*, p. 14.

10. Troyer S. Anderson, *The Command of the Howe Brothers during the American Revolution* (New York, 1936), pp. 48–49.

11. French, *First Year of the Revolution*, p. 538.

12. Force, *Archives*, vol. 4, p. 336.

13. Anderson, *Command of the Howe Brothers*, p. 111, citing *Stopford-Sackville Manuscripts*, vol. 2, p. 9. It is significant that Howe wrote this letter to his brother, to whom he would be more frank and honest than he would be to a government minister.

V. A Not Very Merrie Mother

1. Lloyd's *Evening Post*, January 1, 1776, no. 2888, British Museum Photographic Service, catalogue 6366.

2. Palmer, *Age of the Revolution*, pp. 153–55. At the same time, the administration of public finances was incredibly inefficient. The accounts for the paymaster of the forces during the Seven Years' War, which ended in 1763, had not been completely audited when the Revolution began in 1775 (J. E. D. Binney, *British Public Finance and Administration* [Oxford, 1958], p. 153).

3. Dickerson, *Navigation Acts*, p. 90.

4. Steven Watson, *The Reign of George III, 1760–1815* (Oxford, 1960), pp. 335–36.

5. T. S. Ashton, *The Industrial Revolution* (London, 1947), p. 92.

6. *The Annual Register; or, A View of the History, Politics, and Literature for the Year 1776* (London, 1776), pp. 161–62.

7. Ibid., pp. 53–54.

8. *Morning Chronicle*, no. 2065, p. 3, British Museum.

9. *Post*, no. 995, p. 2; *Chronicle*, no. 2066, p. 6, British Museum.

10. *Post*, no. 996, p. 1, British Museum.

11. Ibid., p. 2. For a good discussion of the role of the British newspapers during the Revolution, see Solomon Lutnick, *The American Revolution in the British Press, 1775–1783* (Columbia, S.C., 1967).

12. Robert H. Hopkins, *The True Genius of Oliver Goldsmith* (Baltimore, 1969), p. 113.

13. This proprietary attitude toward liberty dovetailed neatly with the assumption that the Americans were conspirators aiming at independence. Conspirators were *de facto* against liberty. See Ira D. Gruber, "The American Revolution as a Conspiracy: The British View," for a good discussion of how this became a rooted conviction after the war began in 1775 (*William & Mary Quarterly*, 3rd ser., 29 [Jan., 1972], 360–72). J. M. Bumsted argues convincingly that the British had prepared themselves to believe this by predicting repeatedly that Americans would opt for independence the moment they thought they could get away with it ("Things in the Womb of Time: Ideas of American Independence, 1633 to 1763," *William & Mary Quarterly*, 3rd ser., 31 [Oct., 1974], 533–64).

VI. Father (of the Country) at Work

1. Sir John Fortescue, *The Correspondence of King George III* (London, 1928), vol. 3, pp. 306–27.

2. James Lee McKelvey, *George III and Lord Bute: The Leicester House Years* (Durham, N.C., 1973).

3. E. A. Reitan, "The Civil List in Eighteenth-Century British Politics: Parliamentary Supremacy versus the Independence of the Crown," *Historical Journal*, 9 (1966), 318–27.

4. Ibid., p. 322.

5. William T. Laprade, ed., *Parliamentary Papers of John Robinson, 1774–1784* (London, 1922), pp. 9–17.

6. Ibid., p. 26.

7. Reginald Blunt, *Thomas Lord Lyttelton: The Portrait of a Rake, with a Brief Memoir of His Sister, Lady Lucy Valentia* (London, 1936), pp. 161–62.

8. For my view of George III, I am indebted to Richard Pares, "George III and the Politicians," *Royal Historical Society London Transactions*, 5th ser., 1 (1951), 127–51, and Walter R. Fryer, "King George III: His Political Character and Conduct, 1760–1784: A New Whig Interpretation," *Renaissance and Modern Studies*, 6 (1962), 168–201. I agree with these and other historians, such as Herbert Butterfield, that George III was not the dark reactionary pictured by a previous generation of historians. But he was also not the injured innocent who appears in the pages of Sir Lewis Namier, particularly in his essay, "King George III: A Study of Personality," in his *Personalities and Powers* (New York, 1954). John Brooke, in his generally excellent biography of George III (New York, 1972), also tries to exonerate the King.

9. Lewis Namier and John Brooke, *The History of Parliament* (London, 1964). The introduction to this invaluable work (vol. 1) is the best available discussion of the election process and make-up of the House of Commons in 1776.

10. Bailyn, *Ideological Origins of the Revolution*, p. 168.

11. Fleming, *Benjamin Franklin*, p. 260.

VII. Father's Dangerous Friends

1. Walter R. Fryer, "The Study of British Politics between the Revolution and the Reform Act," *Renaissance and Modern Studies*, 1 (1957), 91–114.

2. Robert Gore-Browne, *Chancellor Thurlow* (London, 1953), pp. 85–87.

3. Charles R. Ritcheson, *British Politics and the American Revolution* (Norman, Okla., 1954), p. 187.

4. Gerald S. Brown, *The American Secretary: The Colonial Policy of Lord George Germain, 1775–1778* (Ann Arbor, Mich., 1963), is the basis for most of the preceding sketch.

5. Alan Valentine, *Lord George Germain* (New York, 1962), p. 25.

6. Arthur Young, *A Tour in Ireland* (Dublin, 1780); reprint (Shannon, Eire, 1970), vol. 2, pp. 40–56.

7. Brown, *American Secretary*, pp. 24–25.

8. Valentine, *Lord George Germain*, p. 93.

9. Piers Mackesy, *The War for America, 1775–1783* (Cambridge, Mass., 1964), p. 55.

10. Alan Valentine, *Lord North* (Norman, Okla., 1967), vol. 1, pp. 380–82.

VIII. Another King, Another Country

1. Edward J. Lowell, *The Hessians and the Other German Auxiliaries of Great Britain in the Revolutionary War* (New York, 1884), pp. 1–26.

2. Ernst Kipping, *The Hessian View of America, 1776–1783* (Monmouth Beach, N.J., 1971), p. 7.

3. Lowell, *Hessians in the Revolutionary War,* p. 24.

4. Derek Jarrett, *The Begetters of Revolution: England's Involvement with France, 1759–1789* (Totowa, N.J., 1973), p. 203. Much of what follows in this chapter is drawn from this remarkable book, which abounds in fresh historical insights.

5. Douglas Dakin, *Turgot and the Ancien Régime in France* (London, 1939), pp. 121–23, for a good description of the factions in the Court.

6. J. F. Bosher, *French Finances, 1770–1785* (Cambridge, 1970). This book gives an astonishing picture of the power of the tax merchants.

7. Dakin, *Turgot,* p. 131.

8. Palmer, *Age of the Revolution,* p. 73.

9. See Palmer, *Age of the Revolution,* particularly chap. 14, "The French Revolution: The Aristocratic Resurgence."

10. Jarrett, "Begetters of Revolution," p. 145.

11. Dallas D. Irvine, "The Newfoundland Fishery: A French Objective in the War of American Independence," *Canadian Historical Review,* 13 (Sept., 1932), 276.

12. Ibid., p. 277.

13. Georges Lemaitre, *Beaumarchais* (New York, 1949), pp. 48ff.

14. Namier and Brooke, *History of Parliament,* vol. 3, p. 640.

15. Louis D. Lomenie, *Beaumarchais and His Times,* trans. Henry S. Edwards (New York, 1857), pp. 267–70.

16. Irvine, "Newfoundland Fishery," p. 278.

17. James H. Hutson, "The Partition Treaty and the Declaration of American Independence," *Journal of American History,* 58 (March, 1972), 880ff.

18. Samuel F. Bemis, *The Diplomacy of the American Revolution* (Bloomington, Ind., 1957), pp. 25–27.

19. Dakin, *Turgot,* p. 262.

IX. Politicians in Search of a Policy

1. Francis Wharton, ed., *The Revolutionary Diplomatic Correspondence of the United States* (Washington, D.C., 1889), vol. 1, pp. 334–35.

2. Ronald Hoffman, *The Spirit of Dissension: Economics, Politics, and the Revolution in Maryland* (Baltimore, 1973), pp. 154–55.

3. Force, *Archives,* vol. 4, pp. 1626ff., for all of the preceding material on Congress.

4. W. C. Ford, ed., *Warren-Adams Letters,* Collections of the Massachusetts Historical Society (1917, 1925), vol. 1, pp. 199–200.

5. Force, *Archives,* vol. 4, p. 1681.

6. Merrill Jensen, *The Founding of a Nation* (New York, 1968), pp. 653–54.

7. Ibid., p. 652.

8. Charles Francis Adams, ed., *Familiar Letters of John Adams and His Wife, Abigail Adams, during the Revolution, with a Memoir of Mrs. Adams* (New York, 1876), p. 82.

9. *Warren-Adams Letters,* vol. 1, p. 190.

10. Winthrop D. Jordan, "Familial Politics: Thomas Paine and the Killing of the King, 1776," *Journal of American History,* 60 (Sept., 1973), 294–308.

11. Merrill Jensen, ed., *Tracts of the American Revolution, 1763–1776* (New York, 1967), pp. 436–39. Paine's remarks about naval warfare proved particularly fatuous. Most of America's tiny regular navy (five ships) commanded by Commodore Esek Hopkins failed to capture a single twenty-gun British frigate in an April battle off Block Island.

12. Johnston, *Nathan Hale,* p. 86.

X. Petticoat Despotism and Other Democratic Terrors

1. Page Smith, *John Adams* (New York, 1962), vol. 1, p. 240.

2. Jensen, *Tracts of the Revolution,* pp. 450ff., and *Warren-Adams Letters,* vol. 1, p. 234.

3. Adams, *Familiar Letters,* p. 97.

4. Lyman H. Butterfield, ed., *The Adams Papers,* vol. 3, *Diary and Autobiography of John Adams* (New York, 1964), pp. 361–63.

5. Ibid., p. 365.

6. Ibid., vol. 2, pp. 229–30.

7. Ibid., vol. 3, pp. 366–68.

8. Edmund C. Burnett, *The Continental Congress* (New York, 1941), pp. 147–48.

9. Force, *Archives,* vol. 5, p. 472.

XI. The Cautious Men of Gotham

1. Bruce Bliven, Jr., *Under the Guns* (New York, 1972), pp. 101–3.

2. John R. Alden, *General Charles Lee: Traitor or Patriot?* (Baton Rouge, La., 1951), pp. 17ff.

3. Ibid., p. 84.

4. *Lee Papers,* vol. 1, p. 257.

5. Ibid., p. 259.

6. Ibid., p. 272.

7. The largely neglected story of Lord Drummond's peace mission has been constructed from the following sources: Herbert A. Meistrich, "Lord Drummond and Reconciliation," *Proceedings of the New Jersey Historical Society,* 81 (1963), 256–77; the Drummond Papers, Scottish Public Record Office, Edinburgh; and William B. Willcox, *Portrait of a General: Sir Henry Clinton and the War of Independence* (New York, 1964), pp. 70ff. See also Alden, *General Charles Lee,* and *Lee Papers.*

8. William H. W. Sabine, ed., *Historical Memoirs of William Smith* (New York, 1956), vol. 1, pp. 258–59. Smith's voluminous diary is another primary source for the story of Lord Drummond's peace mission.

9. Sabine, *William Smith Memoirs,* vol. 1, pp. 261–63.

10. Willcox, *Portrait of a General,* p. 74.

11. In his autobiography, written when he was an old man, Adams still dismissed Drummond's peace mission as "a very airy Phantom . . . so flimsy a veil, that the purblind might see through it" (*Adams Papers,* vol. 3, pp. 367–68).

12. Sabine, *William Smith Memoirs,* vol. 1, p. 64.

13. Ibid., p. 265.

14. Ibid., p. 267.

15. *Lee Papers*, vol. 1, p. 338.

16. Ibid., p. 359.

17. William H. W. Sabine, *Murder, 1776, and Washington's Policy of Silence* (New York, 1973), p. 74.

XII. Nervous Masters, Restless Slaves, and a Flaming Argument

1. Hoffman, *Spirit of Dissension*, p. 154.

2. William Eddis, *Letters from America* (London, 1792), pp. 245ff.

3. Jensen, *Founding of a Nation*, pp. 693–94.

4. Benjamin Quarles, *The Negro in the American Revolution* (Chapel Hill, N.C., 1961), p. 22.

5. Force, *Archives*, vol. 3, p. 1385.

6. Quarles, *Negro in the Revolution*, p. 24.

7. Ivor Noel Hume, *1775: Another Part of the Field* (New York, 1966), pp. 398–99.

8. Force, *Archives*, vol. 4, p. 465.

9. Ibid., pp. 224, 228–29.

10. Noel Hume, *Another Part of the Field*, pp. 445–46.

11. Force, *Archives*, vol. 4, p. 538.

12. Alden Hatch, *The Byrds of Virginia* (New York, 1969), pp. 212–15.

13. Samuel Thornely, ed., *The Journal of Nicholas Cresswell, 1774–1777* (New York, 1924), pp. 134–36.

14. "The Diary of Landon Carter," *William & Mary Quarterly*, 16 (1907), 149–50.

XIII. King George and Broadswords

1. John R. Alden, *The South in the Revolution* (Baton Rouge, La., 1957), pp. 159–61.

2. Malcolm Ross, *The Cape Fear* (New York, 1965), p. 116. See also Carl Bridenbaugh, *Myths and Realities: The Societies of the Colonial South* (New York, 1963), p. 121, for the surprisingly high population figures for the back country. In North Carolina, 40 percent of the population lived there.

3. Robert O. DeMond, *The Loyalists in North Carolina during the Revolution* (Durham, N.C., 1940), p. 50.

4. Hugh F. Rankin, *The North Carolina Continentals* (Chapel Hill, N.C., 1971), pp. 34–40.

5. Alden, *The South in the Revolution*, pp. 197–98. For a fuller account, see Rankin, pp. 47–50.

6. Alden, *The South in the Revolution*, p. 211.

XIV. How to Celebrate a Non-Victory

1. *GW Writings*, vol. 4, p. 348. For problem of councils of war, see Don Higginbotham, *The War of American Independence* (New York, 1971), p. 211.

2. Wade and Lively, *This Glorious Cause*, pp. 193–94.

3. Jeannette D. Black and William G. Roelker, eds., *A Rhode Island Chaplain*

in the Revolution: Letters of Ebenezer David to Nicholas Brown (Providence, R.I., 1949), pp. 7–14; "Letters of Ebenezer Huntington," *American Historical Review*, 5, no. 4 (1900), 708.

4. *GW Writings*, vol. 4, p. 320.

5. Ibid., p. 359.

6. W. C. Ford, ed., *Correspondence and Journals of Samuel Blachley Webb* (New York, 1893), vol. 1, p. 131.

7. French, *First Year of the Revolution*, pp. 656–57.

8. Edward Bangs, ed., *Journal of Lieutenant Isaac Bangs* (Cambridge, Mass., 1890), p. 9.

9. Flexner, *Washington in the Revolution*, p. 75. Also Freeman, *Washington*, p. 23. In *GW Writings*, vol. 4, p. 358, Washington tells Philip Schuyler he wants Howe to "risk an engagement."

10. Ibid.

11. Bangs, *Journal*, p. 11.

12. French, *First Year of the Revolution*, pp. 660–61.

13. Archibald Robertson, *Diaries and Sketches in America* (New York, 1930), p. 74. *Kemble Papers*, vol. 1, pp. 71, 311–12.

14. French, *First Year of the Revolution*, p. 661.

15. Freeman, *Washington*, p. 43.

16. French, *First Year of the Revolution*, p. 665.

17. Robertson, *Sketches in America*, p. 80.

18. Richard Frothingham, *History of the Siege of Boston* (Boston, 1903), p. 312.

19. French, *First Year of the Revolution*, p. 671.

20. *GW Writings*, vol. 4, p. 448.

21. Frothingham, *Siege of Boston*, p. 320.

XV. Discouraged Peacemakers and Revenue-Hungry Gentlemen

1. George H. Guttridge, *The Correspondence of Edmund Burke* (Chicago, 1961), vol. 3, pp. 264–65.

2. James Prior, ed., *The Miscellaneous Works of Oliver Goldsmith* (New York, 1857), vol. 4, pp. 112–13.

3. Ross J. S. Hoffman, *The Marquis: A Study of Lord Rockingham, 1730–1782* (New York, 1973), p. 13. I am indebted to this first thorough study of Rockingham for much of what precedes and follows.

4. Guttridge, *Burke Correspondence*, vol. 3, pp. 183, 189–95.

5. Ibid.

6. Ibid., pp. 215–16.

7. Hoffman, *Rockingham*, pp. 288–89.

8. Guttridge, *Burke Correspondence*, vol. 3, pp. 217–19.

9. Ibid., p. 244.

10. John W. Derry, *Charles James Fox* (New York, 1972), p. 50.

11. Namier and Brooke, *History of Parliament*, vol. 2, p. 457.

12. Force, *Archives*, vol. 6, pp. 314–15.

13. Edmund Fitzmaurice, *Life of William Earl of Shelburne, with Extracts from His Papers and Correspondence* (London, 1876), vol. 1, pp. 14–15.

14. Force, *Archives*, vol. 6, pp. 278–387.

XVI. Profitable Islands in the Sun

1. Orlando W. Stephenson, "The Supply of Gunpowder in 1776," *American Historical Review*, 30 (Jan. 1925), 271–81.
2. Richard W. Van Alstyne, *Empire and Independence: The International History of the American Revolution* (New York, 1967), p. 82.
3. Wharton, *Diplomatic Correspondence*, vol. 2, p. 238.
4. Helen Augur, *The Secret War of Independence* (New York, 1955), p. 71.
5. Ibid., p. 49.
6. Ibid., pp. 59–61.
7. J. Franklin Jameson, "Saint Eustatius and the American Revolution," *American Historical Review*, 8 (1904), 687.
8. Ibid., pp. 690–91.
9. Van Alstyne, *Empire and Independence*, p. 86.
10. Augur, *Secret War of Independence*, p. 87.
11. Ibid., p. 94. See Robert C. Alberts, *The Golden Voyage: The Life and Times of William Bingham* (Boston, 1969), in which an estimate of 250 ships is given for the West Indies. For the blow against slavery, see David Brion Davis, *The Problem of Slavery in the Age of Revolution, 1770–1823* (New York, 1975), pp. 51–52.
12. Augur, *Secret War of Independence*, pp. 95–96. See Samuel Eliot Morison, *John Paul Jones* (Boston, 1959), pp. 66–70, for problem of prize money.
13. Jameson, "Saint Eustatius and the Revolution," p. 686.
14. Alberts, *Golden Voyage*, pp. 20–34.
15. Jameson, "Saint Eustatius and the Revolution," pp. 691–92.
16. Ibid., p. 691.
17. Alberts, *Golden Voyage*, pp. 33–34, 52.

XVII. A Retreating, Raged, Starved, Lousey, Thevish, Pockey Army

1. Wallace, *Traitorous Hero*, p. 91.
2. Force, *Archives*, vol. 5, pp. 12, 845–46.
3. Ibid., pp. 845–46, 869–70.
4. *GW Writings*, vol. 4, pp. 519–20.
5. Malcolm Decker, *Benedict Arnold* (Tarrytown, N.Y., 1932), p. 143.
6. Benjamin Franklin Papers, Yale University, document 24762.
7. Cohen, *Ainslie Journal*, pp. 89–91.
8. Ibid., p. 95.
9. Frederick R. Kirkland, ed., "Journal of a Physician on the Expedition against Canada, 1776," *Pennsylvania Magazine of History and Biography*, 59 (Oct., 1935), 325–27.
10. Ibid., pp. 328–29.
11. Wallace, *Traitorous Hero*, pp. 92–95.
12. Kirkland, "Journal of a Physician," pp. 329–30.
13. Ibid., pp. 331–32. Beebe was a Yale classmate (1771) of Major John Brown, who had quarreled bitterly with Arnold at Quebec and was the ringleader of the group that had refused to attack the place until Montgomery shamed them into it.
14. Charles J. Stillé, *Major General Wayne and the Pennsylvania Line* (Philadelphia, 1893), p. 28.

15. Ibid., pp. 29–31, based on Wayne's letter of June 13 to Benjamin Franklin.

16. James Wilkinson, *Memoirs of My Own Times* (Philadelphia, 1816), vol. 1, p. 51.

17. Thomas W. Baldwin, ed., *The Revolutionary Journal of Colonel Jeduthan Baldwin, 1775–1778* (Bangor, Maine, 1906), p. 60.

18. Wallace, *Traitorous Hero,* p. 96.

19. Baldwin, *Revolutionary Journal,* p. 55.

20. Kirkland, "Journal of a Physician," pp. 11–12. The dying Woedtke asked Chaplain Ammi R. Robbins to give him the sacrament. He was denied even this consolation by Robbins, a strict Presbyterian. *Journal of the Reverend Ammi R. Robbins* (New Haven, 1850), p. 32.

21. Wallace, *Traitorous Hero,* pp. 96–98.

22. Sparks, *Letters to Washington,* vol. 1, p. 237.

XVIII. A Commodore Loses His Breeches

1. *Lee Papers,* vol. 1, pp. 381–82.

2. Hoffman, *Spirit of Dissension,* p. 163.

3. *Lee Papers,* vol. 1, p. 379.

4. Agnes Hunt, *The Provincial Committees of Safety of the American Revolution* (Cleveland, 1904), pp. 114–15.

5. *Lee Papers,* vol. 1, p. 425.

6. Ibid., vol. 2, p. 20; Alden, *General Charles Lee,* p. 117.

7. Willcox, *Portrait of a General,* pp. 83–84.

8. *Lee Papers,* vol. 2, pp. 222–24.

9. Edward McCrady, *The History of South Carolina in the Revolution* (New York, 1902), vol. 1, p. 109.

10. Alden, *General Charles Lee,* p. 121.

11. Willcox, *Portrait of a General,* p. 87.

12. William Moultrie, *Memoirs of the American Revolution* (New York, 1802), p. 141.

13. Ibid., pp. 142–44, Alden, *General Charles Lee,* pp. 122–23.

14. *Lee Papers,* vol. 2, p. 10.

15. Willcox, *Portrait of a General,* pp. 87–88.

16. Moultrie, *Memoirs of the Revolution,* p. 174.

17. Ibid., p. 175. Most of what follows is based on Moultrie's *Memoirs,* with additional material from *The Lee Papers,* from Alden, *General Charles Lee,* and Willcox, *Portrait of a General.* See also John Drayton, *Memoirs of the American Revolution* (Charleston, S.C. 1821), vol. 2, pp. 293–306.

18. *Lee Papers,* vol. 2, p. 223.

19. Ibid., pp. 102–3.

XIX. A Sailor Sights an Olive Branch

1. Ira D. Gruber, *The Howe Brothers and the American Revolution* (Chapel Hill, N.C., 1972), p. 52.

2. Thomas Fleming, *The Man Who Dared the Lightning* (New York, 1971), pp. 266–85, has a detailed account of these negotiations.

3. Ritcheson, *British Politics and the Revolution,* p. 201.

4. Gruber, *Howe Brothers,* pp. 61, 67.

5. Ibid., p. 46.
6. Ibid., pp. 69–70.
7. William Knox, "Account of First Peace Commission of 1776," Knox Papers, William Clements Library, Ann Arbor, Mich.
8. Edward H. Tatum, Jr., ed., *The American Journal of Ambrose Serle* (San Marino, Calif., 1940), Introduction, p. xii.
9. Valentine, *Lord North*, vol. 1, pp. 408–10.
10. Knox, "Account of First Peace Commission."
11. Anderson, *Command of the Howe Brothers*, p. 151.
12. Thomas Hutchinson, ed., *Diary and Letters of Thomas Hutchinson* (Boston, 1884–86), vol. 2, pp. 32–33.
13. Gruber, *Howe Brothers*, pp. 78–79.
14. Viola F. Barnes, "Francis Legge, Governor of Loyalist Nova Scotia," *New England Quarterly*, 4 (1931), 420–47, and Emily P. Weaver, "Nova Scotia during the Revolution," *American Historical Review*, 10 (1905), 52–71.
15. Tatum, *Serle Journal*, p. 26.
16. Ibid., pp. 28–29.

XX. Labor Pains, Real and Imaginary

1. *Warren-Adams Letters*, vol. 1, p. 224.
2. Jensen, *Founding of a Nation*, p. 678.
3. Hutson, "The Partition Treaty," pp. 891ff.
4. Burnett, *Letters of Members of Congress*, vol. 1, p. 449.
5. Burnett, *Continental Congress*, p. 169. A New Hampshire delegate, obviously a wishful thinker of the John Adams school, called this resolution "the last strugles of expiring faction." Burnett remarks that it required "a robust faith" to believe this.
6. David Freeman Hawke, *In the Midst of a Revolution* (Philadelphia, 1961), pp. 29–30, 60–61. This is by far the best extended account—in fact, the only recent one—of the too little known political upheaval in Pennsylvania during 1776. I have relied on it heavily for my necessarily briefer narrative.
7. Charles L. Lincoln, *The Revolutionary Movement in Pennsylvania, 1760–1776* (Philadelphia, 1901), p. 249.
8. William B. Reed, *The Life and Correspondence of Joseph Reed* (Philadelphia, 1847), vol. 1, p. 184.
9. Burnett, *Continental Congress*, p. 165.
10. Ibid., p. 157.
11. Hawke, *In the Midst of a Revolution*, pp. 120–21.
12. *Adams Papers*, vol. 3, p. 386; Jensen, *Founding of a Nation*, p. 685.
13. Hawke, *In the Midst of a Revolution*, p. 127; "The Diary of James Allen," *Pennsylvania Magazine of History and Biography*, 9 (1885), 186–87.
14. David Freeman Hawke, "Dr. Thomas Young: 'Eternal Fisher in Troubled Waters,'" *New-York Historical Society Quarterly*, 54 (Jan., 1970), 7–29. For eighteenth-century Philadelphia, see Sam Bass Warner, Jr., *The Private City: Philadelphia in Three Periods of Its Growth* (Philadelphia, 1968), pp. 16–21; for Hessian treaties, see Freeman, *Washington*, vol. 4, pp. 97–99.
15. Hawke, *In the Midst of a Revolution*, pp. 135–37. The South Carolina visitor thought the people behaved "in such a tyrannical manner that the least opposition was dangerous."
16. Lincoln, *Revolutionary Movement*, pp. 255–56.

17. Hawke, *In the Midst of a Revolution,* pp. 151ff. Mr. Hawke points out that the assembly was also hampered by the myth, devoutly believed by John Adams, that it was dominated by the Quakers.

XXI. The Premature Child, Independence

1. Burnett, *Letters of Members of Congress,* vol. 1, pp. 476–77.
2. Jensen, *Founding of a Nation,* p. 697.
3. Catherine Drinker Bowen, *John Adams and the American Revolution* (Boston, 1950), p. 593.
4. Burnett, *Letters of Members of Congress,* vol. 1, pp. 517–18.
5. Hawke, *In the Midst of a Revolution,* pp. 174–75; Lincoln, *Revolutionary Movement,* pp. 249ff.; Jensen, *Founding of a Nation,* p. 691.
6. "Diary of James Allen," p. 187.
7. Jensen, *Founding of a Nation,* pp. 694–95. Chase read Adams' letter to the Maryland convention and it finally voted for independence on June 28.
8. Ibid., pp. 697–98.
9. Ibid., p. 698.
10. John E. Pomfret, *Colonial New Jersey* (New York, 1973), p. 262.
11. James H. Hutson and Stephen G. Kurtz, eds., *Essays on the American Revolution* (Chapel Hill, N.C., 1973), pp. 266–67.
12. Smith, *John Adams,* pp. 248–49.
13. Arthur M. Schlesinger, Sr., contends that Jefferson used "pursuit" in its eighteenth-century meaning—the practice of happiness rather than the quest for it ("The Lost Meaning of the Pursuit of Happiness," *William & Mary Quarterly,* 3rd ser., 21 [July, 1964], 325–27). It seems to me that Jefferson blended both meanings. But it is worth recalling the eighteenth-century meaning. Certainly Jefferson never intended to commit the American people to the pursuit of that will-o'-the-wisp, personal happiness. For further discussion of the subject, see Dumas Malone, *Jefferson, the Virginian* (Boston, 1948), pp. 227–28.
14. Carl Becker, *The Declaration of Independence* (New York, 1922), Vintage Book ed., pp. 135ff. This chapter, "Drafting the Declaration," exhaustively discusses Jefferson's various changes. I have focused on the ones I deem important to one of the main themes of this book, the reluctance with which Americans accepted the idea of independence.
15. Ibid., pp. 169–70.
16. J. H. Powell, ed., "Speech of John Dickinson Opposing the Declaration of Independence, 1 July 1776," *Pennsylvania Magazine of History and Biography,* 65 (1941), 458–81.
17. Smith, *John Adams,* p. 269.
18. Burnett, *Continental Congress,* p. 182.
19. Harold B. Hancock, "The Kent County Loyalists," *Delaware History,* 6 (1954), 3–24. The loyalists of Kent County gathered 5,000 signatures on a petition to the assembly denouncing independence. The Whigs could only muster 300, but the loyalist bearer of the petition was captured and the petition destroyed. This triggered the uprising. The only people Rodney consulted about independence were the local light infantry regiment. Two-thirds of them were predictably for it. The perplexed Rodney asked his brother Thomas, who had played a leading role in quelling the uprising, what he should do. Thomas favored independence. "That then shall be my vote," said Caesar.

20. Pomfret, *Colonial New Jersey*, pp. 263–64.

21. John H. Hazelton, *The Declaration of Independence: Its History* (New York, 1906), pp. 170–80.

22. Leonard Baker, *John Marshall* (New York, 1974), p. 38, citing the autobiography of Charles Biddle.

23. Allan Nevins, *The American States during and after the Revolution* (New York, 1924), p. 149.

24. Ibid., p. 153; Hawke, *In the Midst of a Revolution*, p. 178. "Good God," John Adams exclaimed, "the people of Pennsylvania in two years will be glad to petition the Crown of Britain for reconciliation in order to be delivered from the tyranny of their Constitution."

25. McCrady, *South Carolina in the Revolution*, pp. 178–79.

26. Bangs, *Journal*, p. 57.

XXII. Everything Now Begins to Look Extremely Serious

1. Tatum, *Serle Journal*, p. 31.

2. Gruber, *Howe Brothers*, p. 93.

3. Freeman, *Washington*, vol. 4, p. 139. For different dialogue describing the same incident, see Gruber, *Howe Brothers*, p. 94.

4. Tatum, *Serle Journal*, p. 33.

5. Freeman, *Washington*, vol. 4, pp. 139–40.

6. *Journals of the Continental Congress*, vol. 5, pp. 592–93.

7. Fleming, *Benjamin Franklin*, pp. 274–77.

8. Tatum, *Serle Journal*, p. 48.

9. Meistrich, "Lord Drummond," pp. 272–73. Figures from *Annual Register*, 1772–73.

10. Washington Papers, 4th ser., reel 37, Drummond to Washington, August 17, 1776, with enclosures. Library of Congress, Washington, D.C.

11. *GW Writings*, vol. 5, p. 449.

12. Ibid., p. 451.

13. Ibid., p. 458.

14. *Reed Correspondence*, vol. 1, p. 217.

15. Tatum, *Serle Journal*, p. 70.

XXIII. Defenders of Everything Dear and Valuable

1. Wade and Lively, *This Glorious Cause*, p. 209.

2. *GW Writings*, vol. 5, p. 390.

3. Ibid., pp. 490–91.

4. Bangs, *Journal*, p. 60.

5. Freeman, *Washington*, vol. 4, p. 85; Bangs, *Journal*, p. 29.

6. Henry P. Johnston, *The Campaign of 1776 around New York and Brooklyn*, Memoirs of the Long Island Historical Society, vol. 3 (1878), p. 79.

7. Lieutenant Bangs says they were drunk (*Journal*, p. 59).

8. Ibid., p. 60.

9. Richard J. Koke, "The Struggle for the Hudson," *New-York Historical Society Quarterly*, 40 (April, 1956), 125–34.

10. Freeman, *Washington*, vol. 4, pp. 105–6.

11. Sabine, *Murder, 1776*, p. 26.

12. Freeman, *Washington*, vol. 4, p. 88, n. 87.

13. Johnston, *Campaign of 1776*, pp. 81–82.

14. Patricia U. Bonomi, *A Factious People: Politics and Society in Colonial New York* (New York, 1971), pp. 146–47.

15. John Campbell, *Minutes of a Conspiracy against the Liberties of America* (Philadelphia, 1865). This is an extensive and very confused account of the Hickey conspiracy. See also Freeman, *Washington*, vol. 4, pp. 118ff.

16. *GW Writings*, vol. 5, pp. 193–94.

17. Sabine, *Murder, 1776*, p. 30.

18. *GW Writings*, vol. 5, p. 215.

19. Thomas W. Field, *The Battle of Long Island* (Brooklyn, 1869), p. 336.

20. Sabine, *Murder, 1776*, p. 34.

21. *Reed Correspondence*, vol. 1, p. 213.

22. Leonard Lundin, *Cockpit of the Revolution: The War for Indpendence in New Jersey* (Princeton, 1940), pp. 122ff.

23. Ibid., p. 129n.

24. Thornely, *Cresswell Journal*, p. 159; Force, *Archives*, 5th ser., vol. 1, p. 786.

25. *GW Writings*, vol. 5, p. 469.

26. Lyman H. Butterfield, "Psychological Warfare in 1776: The Jefferson-Franklin Plan to Cause Hessian Desertions," *Proceedings of the American Philosophical Society*, 94 (June, 1950), 233–41.

27. Johnston, *Campaign of 1776*, pp. 148–54.

28. Wade and Lively, *This Glorious Cause*, p. 214.

29. Sabine, *Murder, 1776*, p. 42; *GW Writings*, vol. 5, p. 486.

30. Freeman, *Washington*, vol. 4, pp. 154–55; *GW Writings*, vol. 5, p. 489.

XXIV. The Great Bunker Hill Backlash

1. G. D. Scull, ed., *Memoir and Letters of Captain W. Glanville Evelyn of the Fourth Regiment ("King's Own") from North America, 1774–1776* (Oxford, 1879), pp. 89–90; Johnston, *Campaign of 1776*, pp. 177–78; Sabine, *Murder, 1776*, pp. 49–50.

2. Gruber, *Howe Brothers*, p. 83.

3. Willcox, *Portrait of a General*, p. 105.

4. Field, *Battle of Long Island*, p. 159.

5. Scull, *Evelyn Memoir*, pp. 89–90; Johnston, *Campaign of 1776*, pp. 178–79; Sabine, *Murder, 1776*, p. 50.

6. Field, *Battle of Long Island*, p. 160; Willcox, *Portrait of a General*, p. 106.

7. William B. Willcox, ed., *The American Rebellion: Sir Henry Clinton's Narrative of His Campaigns, 1775–1782* (New Haven, 1954), pp. 42–43.

8. Field, *Battle of Long Island*, pp. 170–73.

9. Johnston, *Campaign of 1776*, p. 181.

10. Ibid., p. 182.

11. Field, *Battle of Long Island*, p. 187.

12. Ibid., pp. 402–3, citing Force, *Archives*, 5th ser., vol. 1, p. 1259.

13. Wade and Lively, *This Glorious Cause*, p. 78.

14. Field, *Battle of Long Island*, pp. 178–79; Johnston, *Campaign of 1776*, pp. 166–70.

15. Ibid., pp. 170–71.

16. Ibid., pp. 186–87.

17. Ibid., pp. 188–89.

18. Freeman, *Washington*, vol. 4, p. 166.

19. George M. Scheer, ed., *Private Yankee Doodle* (Boston, 1962), p. 26.

20. Johnston, *Campaign of 1776*, p. 37, Document section, letter of Brigadier General John Morin Scott to John Jay.

21. Field, *Battle of Long Island*, p. 215; Willcox, *Portrait of a General*, pp. 106–7.

22. Freeman, *Washington*, vol. 4, p. 167n. The exact American casualty figures have never been determined because of the general confusion in the American army.

23. Louis L. Tucker, ed., " 'To My Inexpressible Astonishment': Admiral Sir George Collier's Observations on the Battle of Long Island," *New-York Historical Society Quarterly*, 48 (Oct., 1964), 304.

24. Wade and Lively, *This Glorious Cause*, p. 215.

25. Johnston, *Campaign of 1776*, pp. 216–17.

26. Freeman, *Washington*, vol. 4, p. 174n.

27. Johnston, *Campaign of 1776*, p. 218.

28. Gruber, *Howe Brothers*, p. 116.

29. *Memoir of Colonel Benjamin Tallmadge* (New York, 1858), p. 11.

30. Tucker, Collier diary, p. 304.

XXV. Jaw-Jaw Proves No Better than War-War

1. Lewis Morris, Jr., *Letters to General Lewis Morris*, Collections of the New-York Historical Society (1875), pp. 440–43; *GW Writings*, vol. 5, p. 502.

2. Wade and Lively, *This Glorious Cause*, pp. 216–17.

3. *GW Writings*, vol. 5, p. 507.

4. Ibid., vol. 6, p. 32.

5. Ibid., vol. 6, p. 5; *Reed Correspondence*, vol. 1, p. 230.

6. Reed Papers, letter to his wife, Sept. 6, 1776, New-York Historical Society.

7. Gruber, *Howe Brothers*, p. 115; Force, *Archives*, 5th ser., vol. 1, p. 1260.

8. Tucker, Collier diary, p. 305. Some historians have confused the diary with a biography of Collier published in the *Naval Chronicle*, 32 (1814), which has even more sarcastic comments about "our brave veterans . . . on the banks of the East River like Moses on Mount Pisgah, looking at their promised land little more than a half mile distant."

9. Lynn Montross, *The Reluctant Rebels: The Story of the Continental Congress* (New York, 1950), p. 171.

10. Burnett, *Continental Congress*, p. 219.

11. Ibid., pp. 223–29.

12. Ibid., p. 203.

13. *Adams Papers*, vol. 3, p. 419.

14. P. L. Ford, "Lord Howe's Commission," *Atlantic*, 77 (1896), 759–62. This contains notes which Henry Strachey made of the conversation. Other details have been drawn from John Adams' account in his autobiography, cited above as *Adams Papers*, vol. 3.

15. Sabine, *William Smith Memoirs*, vol. 2, p. 12.

16. Sparks, *Letters to Washington*, vol. 1, pp. 287–88.

17. Tatum, *Serle Journal*, p. 101.

XXVI. American Sprinters vs. British Liberators

1. Sabine, *William Smith Memoirs*, vol. 1, pp. 13–14.
2. Henry P. Johnston, "Sergeant Lee's Experience with Bushnell's Submarine Torpedo in 1776," *Magazine of History*, 29 (1893), 262–66.
3. Bushnell letter in *Transactions of the American Philosophical Society*, 4 (1799), 310.
4. Johnston, "Sergeant Lee's Experience," p. 264.
5. Force, *Archives*, 5th ser., vol. 2, pp. 182–83.
6. Freeman, *Washington*, vol. 4, p. 184.
7. *GW Writings*, vol. 6, pp. 27–33.
8. Ibid., pp. 18–19.
9. John Bakeless, *Turncoats, Traitors, and Heroes* (New York, 1959), pp. 112–15.
10. William A. Tieck, *Riverdale, Kingsbridge, Spuyten Duyvil* (Old Tappan, N.J., 1968), pp. 31–35.
11. Freeman, *Washington*, vol. 4, p. 188.
12. Henry Underdonk, Jr., *Revolutionary Incidents of Suffolk and Kings County* (New York, 1849), pp. 43ff.
13. Sabine, *Murder, 1776*, pp. 59–105. Sabine proves in exhaustive detail that Woodhull was anything but a patriot and may well have been a traitor.
14. Underdonk, *Revolutionary Incidents*, pp. 44–45.
15. Tatum, *Serle Journal*, p. 94.
16. Willcox, *Portrait of a General*, p. 108.
17. Willcox, *American Rebellion*, p. 46n.
18. *Diary of Frederick MacKenzie* (Cambridge, Mass., 1930), vol. 1, p. 45.
19. Martin, *Men in Rebellion*, p. 31.
20. Willcox, *Portrait of a General*, p. 111.
21. Martin, *Men in Rebellion*, p. 34.
22. Freeman, *Washington*, vol. 4, p. 193.
23. Flexner, *Washington in the Revolution*, vol. 2, pp. 122–23. Freeman does not accept Washington's emotional collapse. As usual, he hates to see a flaw in his hero. But there is considerable evidence for it. Nathanael Greene wrote that Washington was "so vexed at the infamous conduct of his troops that he sought death rather than life." General George Weedon told John Page, president of the Virginia council, that "it was with difficulty his friends could get him to quit the field, so great was his emotions." For the details of the rout as I have described them, see Johnston, *Campaign of 1776*, pp. 234ff.
24. *The Journal of Rear Admiral Bartholomew James* (London, 1896), pp. 31–33.
25. *MacKenzie Diary*, pp. 49–50.
26. Tatum, *Serle Journal*, pp. 104–6.

XXVII. A Town Burner Loses a Spy

1. *GW Writings*, vol. 6, pp. 57–59.
2. Johnston, *Campaign of 1776*, 250–51.
3. Bruce Bliven, Jr., *The Battle for Manhattan* (New York, 1956), p. 96.
4. Wade and Lively, *This Glorious Cause*, pp. 84–85.
5. *MacKenzie Diary*, p. 51.
6. Anderson, *Command of the Howe Brothers*, p. 160.

7. Sabine, *William Smith Memoirs*, vol. 1, p. 216.

8. Gruber, *Howe Brothers*, p. 125.

9. Ibid., p. 162.

10. *MacKenzie Diary*, pp. 58–61.

11. Tatum, *Serle Journal*, p. 112. Details of my description of the fire are also drawn from Serle, p. 111.

12. Bakeless, *Turncoats, Traitors, and Heroes*, pp. 118–21. There are several explanations of Hale's capture, which Colonel Bakeless explores carefully in this account. I prefer this one and have added to it the hitherto unmentioned complicating factor of the American decision to burn New York. William Henry Shelton, in "What Was the Mission of Nathan Hale?," *Journal of American History*, 9 (1915), 269–89, argues that Hale was part of the team that burned New York. It is an interesting speculation, but difficult to prove.

13. As late as 1826, a man who knew Hale well wrote, "Why is it that the delicious Captain Hale should be left & lost in an unknown grave & forgotten?" George Dudley Seymour, *Documentary Life of Nathan Hale* (New Haven, 1941), p. 423.

XXVIII. Indecisive Generals and Hard-Drinking Heroes

1. Callahan, *Henry Knox*, pp. 72–73.

2. *GW Writings*, vol. 6, p. 109. American captains received only $20 a month—half the British pay—and a British officer could buy most of what he needed at a reduced rate from government suppliers, stretching his money twice as far.

3. Ibid., p. 115.

4. Ibid., p. 112.

5. *MacKenzie Diary*, p. 64.

6. Martin, *Men in Rebellion*, p. 46, n. 7.

7. *Reed Correspondence*, vol. 1, p. 243.

8. Johnston, "Sergeant Lee's Experience," p. 265; *MacKenzie Diary*, p. 75.

9. Ibid., p. 66.

10. Gruber, *Howe Brothers*, p. 129.

11. Frederick Shonnard, and W. W. Spooner, *History of Westchester County* (New York, 1900), p. 368. Duer expressed amazement that the loyalists "who are capable of giving the most Minute Description of the Grounds in the County of Westchester" would not have given the British better advice.

12. George Athan Billias, *General John Glover and His Marblehead Marines* (New York, 1960), pp. 110ff.; Scull, *Evelyn Memoir*, p. 13.

13. Hoffman, *Spirit of Dissension*, p. 181; *Lee Papers*, vol. 2, p. 259.

14. Stuart-Wortley, Mrs. E., *A Prime Minister and His Son* (London, 1925), p. 88.

15. *Reed Correspondence*, p. 246.

16. Stuart-Wortley, *Prime Minister and His Son*, pp. 88–89.

17. Ibid., p. 88; "Diary of William Bamford," *Maryland Historical Magazine*, 27 (March, 1933), 16–17.

18. *Narrative of William Howe* (London, 1779), p. 7.

19. Freeman, *Washington*, vol. 6, pp. 209, 234.

20. *GW Writings*, vol. 6, p. 238.

21. "The Military Journal of Sergeant John Smith," *Mississippi Valley Historical Review*, 20 (1933–34), 247–70.

22. *GW Writings,* vol. 6, p. 234.

23. Ibid., p. 242.

24. Catherine S. Crary, ed., *The Price of Loyalty* (New York, 1973), p. 171.

25. *GW Writings,* vol. 6, p. 250.

26. Force, *Archives,* 5th ser., vol. 3, p. 523.

27. Flexner, *Washington in the Revolution,* vol. 2, p. 147.

28. Freeman, *Washington,* vol. 4, pp. 245–47; Christopher Ward, *The War of the Revolution* (New York, 1952), vol. 1, pp. 268–70.

29. *MacKenzie Diary,* pp. 95–96.

30. Lundin, *Cockpit of the Revolution,* p. 130.

31. Freeman, *Washington,* vol. 4, pp. 250–51.

32. Johnston, *Campaign of 1776,* p. 281; Ward, *War of the Revolution,* vol. 1, p. 272.

33. Freeman, *Washington,* vol. 4, p. 151n.

34. *MacKenzie Diary,* p. 112. Captain MacKenzie also has a thorough description of the British attack on Fort Washington (pp. 104–11), on which I have relied heavily for many details.

35. *Lee Papers,* vol. 2, p. 283.

36. Ibid., pp. 282–83.

37. Huntington letters in *American Historical Review,* 5 (1900), 715.

38. *Lee Papers,* vol. 2, pp. 288–89.

39. "Journal of an Unknown Pennsylvania Soldier," *New York Public Library Bulletin,* 8 (1904), 549; Force, *Archives,* 5th ser., vol. 3, p. 1071; "Letter of a British Officer," *Morning Chronicle,* Jan. 8, 1777. This writer says they captured 200 drinkers at Fort Lee. There must have been a hot pursuit of those who took to the woods. He tells how the surrendered drinkers whined to their captors, "Brother soldier, we'll have a dram." Henry Steele Commager and Richard Morris, eds., *The Spirit of Seventy-Six* (New York, 1958), vol. 1, p. 496, letter of Francis Lord Rawdon: "In the fort they found but twelve men, who were all dead drunk."

XXIX. An Admiral Loses a Battle and Saves a Country

1. Stillé, *Wayne and the Pennsylvania Line,* pp. 37–38.

2. Don R. Gerlach, "Philip Schuyler and 'The Road to Glory': A Question of Loyalty and Competence," *New-York Historical Society Quarterly,* 44 (1965), 357.

3. Ibid., pp. 359, 364.

4. Ibid., p. 367.

5. James Sullivan, ed., *Minutes of the Albany Committee of Correspondence* (Albany, N.Y., 1923), vol. 1, p. 336.

6. John Codman, *Arnold's Expedition to Quebec* (New York, 1901), p. 307. See also Roberts, *March to Quebec,* pp. 287–88, 537.

7. Barbara Graymont, *The Iroquois in the American Revolution* (Sryacuse, N.Y., 1972), pp. 106–8.

8. Ibid., pp. 109–11.

9. Mackesy, *War for America,* p. 94.

10. Ibid., pp. 95–96. See also Lorenzo Hagglund, *A Page from the Past* (Lake George, N.Y., 1949), p. 9.

11. Ibid., pp. 6–7.

12. Wallace, *Traitorous Hero,* p. 111.

13. Hagglund, *Page from the Past*, pp. 7–8.

14. Wallace, *Traitorous Hero*, pp. 99–105.

15. Ibid., p. 108.

16. Mackesy, *War for America*, p. 96.

17. T. W. Hubbard, "Battle at Valcour Island: Benedict Arnold as Hero," *American Heritage*, Oct., 1966, p. 88.

18. Ibid.

19. Mackesy, *War for America*, p. 96.

20. Wallace, *Traitorous Hero*, p. 112.

21. Hubbard, "Battle at Valcour Island," pp. 88–89. See also *Journal of Captain Georg Pausch* (Albany, N.Y., 1886), pp. 82–85, and Wallace, *Traitorous Hero*, pp. 114–15. Also Force, *Archives*, 5th ser., vol. 3, pp. 253–54, Arnold's letter to Schuyler, which has many details of the battle.

22. Hagglund, *Page from the Past*, pp. 13–14. He gives a vivid description of how the *Philadelphia* sank. The captain inadvertently sent too many men forward, and a twenty-four-pound-shot hole in the bow went completely under water. The gondola sat on the bottom in sixty feet of water until 1935, when it was discovered and raised.

23. Hubbard, "Battle at Valcour Island," p. 91; James M. Hadden, *A Journal Kept in Canada . . ."* (Albany, N.Y., 1884), pp. 28–29.

24. Baldwin, *Revolutionary Journal*, p. 81.

25. "Memoirs of John Lacey," *Pennsylvania Magazine of History and Biography*, 25 (1901), 510–12.

26. Wallace, *Traitorous Hero*, p. 120.

27. Mackesy, *War for America*, p. 96. Lieutenant Hadden notes in his *Journal* (p. 34) that the British thought there were 12,000 to 16,000 Americans in Ticonderoga.

XXX. Revolutions Break Hearts

1. Burnett, *Letters of Members of Congress*, vol. I, p. 114.

2. DeMond, *Loyalists in North Carolina*, pp. 109–10.

3. Crary, *Price of Loyalty*, pp. 142–45.

4. Ibid., pp. 161–65.

5. Ibid., pp. 23–34.

6. Henry C. Van Schaack, *Life of Peter Van Schaack* (New York, 1842), pp. 53–73. Early in 1777, Van Schaack was permitted to return to care for his dying wife. When she expired in 1778, he was exiled again.

7. Vernon O. Stumpf, "Who was Elizabeth Downes Franklin?" unpublished essay, American Philosophical Society.

8. William H. Mariboe, "The Life of William Franklin," unpublished doctoral dissertation, University of Pennsylvania, 1962, pp. 102ff.

9. The conflict between William and his father is treated extensively in my *Man Who Dared the Lightning*, pp. 291–343.

10. Benjamin Franklin Papers, American Philosophical Society, Philadelphia.

11. Ibid.

12. Ibid.

13. Ibid.

14. Albert H. Smyth, ed., *The Writings of Benjamin Franklin* (New York, 1905–7), vol. 6, pp. 468–69.

15. Benjamin Franklin Papers, American Philosophical Society.

XXXI. The Luckiest Friday the Thirteenth in History

1. Commager and Morris, *Spirit of Seventy-Six,* p. 496.
2. Willcox, *Portrait of a General,* pp. 114–15.
3. Geoffrey Seed, "A British Spy in Philadelphia, 1775–1777," *Pennsylvania Magazine of History and Biography,* 85 (1961), 3–37.
4. *MacKenzie Diary,* p. 113.
5. Willcox, *Portrait of a General,* pp. 116–20.
6. *GW Writings,* vol. 6, p. 303n.
7. *Lee Papers,* vol. 2, pp. 291–92.
8. Ibid., pp. 293–94.
9. Ibid., pp. 299, 314.
10. Tatum, *Serle Journal,* pp. 152–53.
11. M. D. Conway, ed., *The Writings of Thomas Paine* (New York, 1891–96), vol. 1, pp. 170–73.
12. *GW Writings,* vol. 6, pp. 320–21.
13. *Lee Papers,* vol. 2, pp. 305–6.
14. *GW Writings,* vol. 6, pp. 313–15.
15. Ibid., pp. 318–20.
16. Tatum, *Serle Journal,* pp. 451–52; Gruber, *Howe Brothers,* pp. 146–47.
17. Tatum, *Serle Journal,* p. 151.
18. Ibid., p. 155. Stephen Kemble makes a similar comment in his journal. *Kemble Papers,* vol. 1, p. 101.
19. *Lee Papers,* vol. 2, p. 322.
20. Ibid., pp. 323–24.
21. Gruber, *Howe Brothers,* pp. 149–50.
22. *Lee Papers,* vol. 2, pp. 329–30.
23. Wade and Lively, *This Glorious Cause,* p. 227.
24. Smith, "Military Journal," p. 263.
25. *Lee Papers,* vol. 2, pp. 336–37.
26. *GW Writings,* vol. 6, pp. 338–39.
27. Ibid., pp. 340–41.
28. *Lee Papers,* vol. 2, pp. 340, 344, 348.
29. Robert D. Bass, *The Green Dragoon* (New York, 1957), pp. 19–22; Ernst Kipping and Samuel S. Smith, eds., *At General Howe's Side: The Diary of General William Howe's Aide de Camp, Captain Friedrich von Muenchhausen* (Monmouth Beach, N.J., 1974), p. 7.
30. Force, *Archives,* 5th ser., vol. 3, pp. 13–17.
31. *GW Writings,* vol. 6, p. 353.
32. Ibid., p. 366; Burnett, *Continental Congress,* p. 233.
33. *GW Writings,* vol. 6, pp. 402–3, 398–99.

XXXII. Farewell to Illusions

1. Force, *Archives,* 5th ser., vol. 3, p. 1255.
2. Nevins, *American States,* p. 155. Only about 1,500 people voted. In the city and county of Philadelphia, the anti-constitutionists won by 2 to 1. For "sickly Constitution," see Stillé, *Wayne and the Pennsylvania Line,* p. 45.
3. Wharton, *Diplomatic Correspondence,* pp. 231–36.
4. Lundin, *Cockpit of the Revolution,* pp. 57–58.
5. Ibid., p. 163.
6. Ibid., pp. 182–83.

7. *Lee Papers,* vol. 2, pp. 346–47, letter from the Reverend James Caldwell.

8. Tatum, *Serle Journal,* p. 157; Lundin, *Cockpit of the Revolution,* pp. 179–80.

9. Ibid., p. 172.

10. Ibid., p. 174.

11. *Lee Papers,* vol. 2, pp. 346–47. Joseph Reed told his wife, "It is of little consequence which army passes. It is equally destructive to friend and foe" (*Reed Correspondence,* vol. 1, p. 248).

12. Ibid., p. 272.

13. Lundin, *Cockpit of the Revolution,* pp. 187–88.

14. William S. Stryker, *The Battles of Trenton and Princeton* (Cambridge, Mass., 1898), p. 107.

15. Ibid., p. 111.

16. Bakeless, *Turncoats, Traitors, and Heroes,* pp. 166–69. See also Stryker, *Battles of Trenton and Princeton,* pp. 87–89, for another account of Honeyman's exploit.

17. Ibid., p. 342. This letter is not included in Fitzpatrick, *GW Writings.* See Freeman, *Washington,* vol. 4, p. 308n, for its authenticity.

18. Stryker, *Battles of Trenton and Princeton,* pp. 70, 73–74.

19. Freeman, *Washington,* vol. 4, p. 308.

20. Ibid., p. 309.

21. *GW Writings,* vol. 6, pp. 436–37.

XXXIII. Double-Talk in London and Paris

1. Hutchinson, *Diary,* vol. 2, pp. 109–10.

2. Valentine, *Lord North,* vol. 1, pp. 423–24.

3. Guttridge, *Burke Correspondence,* vol. 3, p. 286.

4. Hoffman *Rockingham,* pp. 336–37.

5. Gruber, *Howe Brothers,* pp. 161–62.

6. Jarrett, *Begetters of Revolution,* pp. 156ff. Many Englishmen were deeply impressed by Necker's legerdemain, including Edward Gibbon and Edmund Burke.

7. Gruber, *Howe Brothers,* p. 163. Germain, with his talent for pursuing vendettas and causing quarrels, told Howe that the King had given a similar distinction to General Carleton "before he had any claim to it by his operations in Canada." He went on to tell Howe that he had wangled a guarantee from the King that a government sinecure would soon be forthcoming. Otherwise, "I should have been unhappy to have seen your services and those of General Carleton put upon the same footing" (Germain to William Howe, *Stopford-Sackville Manuscripts,* vol. 1, p. 43.

8. Hoffman, *Rockingham,* pp. 338–39.

9. Force, *Archives,* 5th ser., vol. 3, p. 1004.

10. George Otto Trevelyan, *The American Revolution* (New York, 1922), vol. 3, p. 196.

11. Andrew Oliver, ed., *The Journal of Samuel Curwen, Loyalist* (Cambridge, Mass., 1972), p. 284.

12. Lutnick, *The Revolution in the British Press,* p. 25.

13. Hutchinson, *Diary,* p. 119.

14. Force, *Archives,* 5th ser., vol. 3, pp. 1006–10.

15. Trevelyan, *American Revolution,* vol. 3, pp. 162–63.

16. Edward S. Corwin, *French Policy and the American Alliance of 1778* (Princeton, 1916), pp. 86–87.

17. Gruber, *Howe Brothers*, p. 169; Alberts, *Golden Voyage*, pp. 40–41. For Deane's diplomacy, see Van Alstyne, *Empire and Independence*, pp. 100–103.

18. Hoffman, *Rockingham*, pp. 340–41.

19. Guttridge, *Burke Correspondence*, vol. 3, p. 310.

20. Fleming, *Benjamin Franklin*, pp. 282–83.

21. Alfred Owen Aldridge, *Benjamin Franklin, Philosopher and Man* (Philadelphia, 1965), p. 269.

22. Wharton, *Diplomatic Correspondence*, vol. 2, pp. 245–46.

23. Ibid., p. 250.

24. Gruber, *Howe Brothers*, pp. 171–72.

25. Ibid., p. 173.

26. Jarrett, *Begetters of Revolution*, p. 149. For a bloodcurdling view of how the British rationalized their barbarism in Ireland, see Nicholas P. Canny, "The Ideology of English Colonization: From Ireland to America," *William & Mary Quarterly*, 3rd ser., 20 (Oct., 1973), 575–98, especially p. 582, where a British pamphleteer proudly describes how Colonel Sir Humphrey Gilbert forced those who surrendered to approach him down a lane of "the [severed] heddes of their dedde fathers, brothers, children, kinsfolke and freinds."

XXXIV. Gallant and Spirited Behavior—at Last

1. Stryker, *Battles of Trenton and Princeton*, p. 140.

2. Ibid., 373–74.

3. William S. Powell, ed., "A Connecticut Soldier under Washington: Elisha Bostwick's Memoirs of the First Years of the Revolution," *William & Mary Quarterly*, 3rd ser., 6 (1949), 102.

4. Stryker, *Battles of Trenton and Princeton*, pp. 125, 145–46.

5. Washington praised the conduct of the Hessian sentries, telling the president of Congress, "For their Numbers, they behaved very well" (*GW Writings*, vol. 6, p. 442). For the charge against the cannon, see Ward, *War of the Revolution*, vol. 1, p. 321.

6. These are figures given by the Hessian high command. Washington reported 918 captives, no doubt including some of the number the Hessians counted as wounded. See Samuel B. Smith, *The Battle of Trenton* (Monmouth Beach, N.J., 1965), p. 31.

7. Freeman, *Washington*, vol. 4, p. 321.

8. Ibid., pp. 325–26.

9. Powell, "A Connecticut Soldier," pp. 102–3. For the decision to retreat and the Americans getting drunk, see Stryker, *Battles of Trenton and Princeton*, p. 206.

10. *Reed Correspondence*, vol. 1, p. 280.

11. Stryker, *Battles of Trenton and Princeton*, pp. 213–14; Freeman, *Washington*, vol. 4, p. 326.

12. Stryker, *Battles of Trenton and Princeton*, p. 426.

13. *GW Writings*, vol. 6, p. 449.

14. Freeman, *Washington*, pp. 332–33; Powell, "A Connecticut Soldier," p. 103.

15. Freeman, *Washington*, vol. 4, p. 333. In a letter to the officer in command of the troops at Morristown, where four Continental regiments were

operating, Washington told a pardonable lie, saying the New Englanders had re-enlisted "to a man" (*GW Writings*, vol. 6, p. 455).

16. Stryker, *Battles of Trenton and Princeton*, p. 253; Smith, "Military Journal," pp. 269–70.

17. *GW Writings*, vol. 6, pp. 457–58, including note.

18. Lundin, *Cockpit of the Revolution*, pp. 201–2.

19. *GW Writings*, vol. 6, p. 461.

20. Stryker, *Battles of Trenton and Princeton*, pp. 263–64.

21. Ibid., pp. 268–69.

XXXV. All Liberty Mad Again

1. Stryker, *Battles of Trenton and Princeton*, pp. 481–82.

2. Ibid., 269–72. See also Samuel S. Smith, *The Battle of Princeton* (Monmouth Beach, N.J., 1967), pp. 10–11, for details of Reed's reconnaissance.

3. *GW Writings*, vol. 6, pp. 468–69.

4. Smith, *Battle of Princeton*, p. 19.

5. Ibid. In one case, the rum was spiked with gunpowder.

6. Ward, *War of the Revolution*, vol. 1, p. 312.

7. Smith, *Battle of Princeton*, p. 20.

8. Stryker, *Battles of Trenton and Princeton*, pp. 281–82.

9. Freeman, *Washington*, vol. 4, pp. 353–54.

10. W. H. Wilkin, *Some British Soldiers in America* (London, 1914), p. 224.

11. Stryker, *Battles of Trenton and Princeton*, pp. 449–51, letter of Henry Knox to his wife.

12. Smith, *Battle of Princeton*, pp. 28–29.

13. Stryker, *Battles of Trenton and Princeton*, pp. 438–42, from the journal of Captain Thomas Rodney.

14. *GW Writings*, vol. 6, p. 470.

15. Freeman, *Washington*, vol. 4, pp. 389–91. For looting by the militia, see Lundin, *Cockpit of the Revolution*, p. 219.

16. Gruber, *Howe Brothers*, p. 157.

17. Van Alstyne, *Empire and Independence*, p. 120.

18. Thornely, *Cresswell Journal*, p. 176.

19. Tatum, *Serle Journal*, pp. 171–72.

20. Jack P. Greene, ed., *The Reinterpretation of the American Revolution* (New York, 1968), pp. 72–73.

Select Bibliography

Adams, Charles Francis, ed. *Familiar Letters of John Adams and His Wife, Abigail Adams, during the Revolution.* New York, 1876.

Adams, John. *Defence of the Constitution of the United States.* 3 vols. Philadelphia, 1797.

Alberts, Robert C. *The Golden Voyage: The Life and Times of William Bingham.* Boston, 1969.

Albion, R. G., and L. Dodson, eds. *Journal of Philip Vickers Fithian.* Princeton, 1934.

Alden, John R. *General Charles Lee: Traitor or Patriot?* Baton Rouge, La., 1951.

———. *The South in the Revolution.* Baton Rouge, La., 1957.

Aldridge, Alfred Owen. *Benjamin Franklin, Philosopher and Man.* Philadelphia, 1965.

Anderson, Troyer S. *The Command of the Howe Brothers during the American Revolution.* New York, 1936.

Annual Register, The; or, A View of the History, Politics, and Literature for the Year 1776. London, 1776.

Ashton, T. S. *The Industrial Revolution.* London, 1947.

Augur, Helen. *The Secret War of Independence.* New York, 1955.

Bailyn, Bernard. *The Ideological Origins of the American Revolution.* Cambridge, Mass., 1967.

———. *The Ordeal of Thomas Hutchinson.* Cambridge, Mass., 1974.

Bakeless, John. *Turncoats, Traitors, and Heroes.* New York, 1959.

Baker, Leonard. *John Marshall.* New York, 1974.

Baldwin, Thomas W., ed. *The Revolutionary Journal of Colonel Jeduthan Baldwin, 1775–1778.* Bangor, Maine, 1906.

Bangs, Edward, ed. *Journal of Lieutenant Isaac Bangs.* Cambridge, Mass., 1890.

Bass, Robert D. *The Green Dragoon.* New York, 1957.

Becker, Carl. *The Declaration of Independence.* New York, 1922.

Bemis, Samuel F. *The Diplomacy of the American Revolution.* Bloomington, Ind., 1957.

Billias, George Athan. *General John Glover and His Marblehead Marines.* New York, 1960.

Binney, J. E. D. *British Public Finance and Administration.* Oxford, 1958.

Black, Jeannette D., and William G. Roelker, eds. *A Rhode Island Chaplain in the Revolution: Letters of Ebenezer David.* Providence, R.I., 1949.

Bliven, Bruce, Jr. *The Battle for Manhattan.* New York, 1956.

———. *Under the Guns.* New York, 1972.

Blunt, Reginald. *Thomas Lord Lyttelton: The Portrait of a Rake with a Brief Memoir of His Sister, Lady Lucy Valentia.* London, 1936.

Bonomi, Patricia U. *A Factious People: Politics and Society in Colonial New York.* New York, 1971.

Bosher, J. F. *French Finances, 1770–1785.* Cambridge, 1970.

Boudinot, Elias. *Journal of Historical Recollections of American Events during the Revolutionary War.* Philadelphia, 1894.

Boustead, Guy M. *The Lone Monarch.* London, 1940.

Bowen, Catherine Drinker. *John Adams and the American Revolution.* Boston, 1950.

Bridenbaugh, Carl. *Myths and Realities: The Societies of the Colonial South.* New York, 1963.

Brooke, John. *King George III.* New York, 1972.

Brown, Gerald S. *The American Secretary: The Colonial Policy of Lord George Germain, 1775–1778.* Ann Arbor, Mich., 1963.

Brown, Peter. *The Chathamites.* London, 1967.

Brown, Wallace. *The King's Friends: The Composition and Motives of the American Loyalist Claimants.* Providence, R.I., 1965.

Brown, Weldon A. *Empire or Independence: A Study in the Failure of Reconciliation, 1774–1783.* Baton Rouge, La., 1941.

Burnett, Edmund C. *The Continental Congress.* New York, 1941.

———, ed. *Letters of Members of the Continental Congress.* 8 vols. Washington, D.C., 1921–36.

Butterfield, Lyman H., ed. *The Adams Papers: Diary and Autobiography of John Adams.* Vol. 3 of 4 vols. New York, 1964.

Callahan, North. *Henry Knox: General Washington's General.* New York, 1958.

Campbell, John. *Minutes of a Conspiracy against the Liberties of America.* Philadelphia, 1865.

Christie, I. R. *Crisis of Empire.* New York, 1966.

Clark, Dora Mae. *British Opinion and the American Revolution.* New Haven, 1930.

Clark, George L. *Silas Deane: A Connecticut Leader in the American Revolution.* New York, 1913.

Clark, William B. *George Washington's Navy: Being an Account of His Excellency's Fleet in New England Waters.* Baton Rouge, La., 1960.

Codman, John, II. *Arnold's Expedition to Quebec.* New York, 1901.

Cohen, Sheldon S., ed. *Canada Preserved: The Journal of Captain Thomas Ainslie.* New York, 1968.

Commager, Henry Steele, and Richard Morris, eds. *The Spirit of Seventy-Six.* 2 vols. New York, 1958.

Cone, Carl B. *Burke and the Nature of Politics.* Lexington, Ky., 1957.

Conway, M. D., ed. *The Writings of Thomas Paine.* 4 vols. New York, 1891–96.

Corwin, Edward S. *French Policy and the American Alliance of 1778.* Princeton, 1916.

Crary, Catherine S., ed. *The Price of Loyalty.* New York, 1973.

Dakin, Douglas. *Turgot and the Ancien Regime in France.* London, 1939.

Dangerfield, George. *Chancellor Robert R. Livingston.* New York, 1960.

Dartmouth, Earl of. *Report on the Manuscripts of the Earl of Dartmouth.* London, 1896.

Davidson, Philip G. *Propaganda and the American Revolution, 1763–1783.* Chapel Hill, N.C., 1941.

Davis, David Brion. *The Problem of Slavery in the Age of Revolution, 1770–1823.* New York, 1974.

Decker, Malcolm. *Benedict Arnold.* Tarrytown, N.Y., 1932.

DeMond, Robert O. *The Loyalists in North Carolina during the Revolution.* Durham, N.C., 1940.

Denton, William Allen. *Whig Loyalism: An Aspect of Political Ideology in the American Revolutionary Era.* Paterson, N.J., 1969.

Derry, John W. *Charles James Fox.* New York, 1972.

Dickerson, Oliver M. *The Navigation Acts and the American Revolution.* Philadelphia, 1951.

Drayton, John. *Memoirs of the American Revolution.* 2 vols. Charleston, S.C., 1821.

Drinkwater, John. *Charles James Fox.* New York, 1928.

Drummond Papers. Scottish Public Records Office, Edinburgh.

Eddis, William. *Letters from America.* London, 1792.

Ellis, Kenneth. *The Post Office in the Eighteenth Century.* London, 1950.

Field, Thomas W. *The Battle of Lond Island.* Brooklyn, N.Y., 1869.

Fifoot, C. H. S. *Lord Mansfield.* Oxford, 1936.

Fitzmaurice, Edmund. *Life of William Earl of Shelburne with Extracts from His Papers and Correspondence.* London, 1876.

Fitzpatrick, John C., ed. *The Writings of George Washington from the Original Manuscript Sources, 1745–1799.* 39 vols. Washington, D.C., 1931–44.

Fleming, Thomas, ed. *Benjamin Franklin: A Biography in His Own Words.* New York, 1972.

———. *The Man Who Dared the Lightning.* New York, 1971.

Flexner, James Thomas. *George Washington.* 4 vols. Boston, 1965–72.

Force, Peter, ed. *American Archives.* 4th ser., 6 vols.; 5th ser., 3 vols. Washington, D.C., 1837–53.

Ford, W. C., ed. *Correspondence and Journals of Samuel Blachley Webb.* New York, 1893.

———, ed. *Warren-Adams Letters.* 2 vols. Collections of the Massachusetts Historical Society, 1917–25.

Fortescue, John. *The Correspondence of King George III.* 6 vols. London, 1928.

Freeman, Douglas Southall. *George Washington: A Biography.* 7 vols. New York, 1948–57.

French, Allen. *The First Year of the American Revolution.* Boston, 1934.

Frothingham, Richard. *History of the Siege of Boston.* Boston, 1903.

Gardiner, C. Harvey, ed. *A Study in Dissent: The Warren-Gerry Correspondence, 1776–1792.* Carbondale, Ill., 1968.

Gipson, Lawrence Henry. *Jared Ingersoll: A Study of American Loyalism in Relation to British Colonial Government.* New Haven, 1920.

Gore-Browne, Robert. *Chancellor Thurlow.* London, 1953.

Graymont, Barbara. *The Iroquois in the American Revolution.* Syracuse, N.Y., 1972.

Greene, Jack P. *The Quest for Power: The Lower Houses of Assembly in the Southern Royal Colonies, 1689–1776.* Chapel Hill, N.C., 1963.

———, ed. *The Reinterpretation of the American Revolution.* New York, 1968.

Gruber, Ira D. *The Howe Brothers and the American Revolution.* Chapel Hill, N.C., 1972.

Guttmacher, Manfred S. *America's Last King.* New York, 1941.

Guttridge, George H., ed. *The Correspondence of Edmund Burke.* Chicago, 1961.

Hadden, James M. *A Journal Kept in Canada . . .* Albany, N.Y., 1884.

Hagglund, Lorenzo. *A Page from the Past.* Lake George, N.Y., 1949.

Hardy, Basil Cozens, ed. *The Diary of Sylas Neville, 1767–1788.* London, 1950.

Harrell, Isaac S. *Loyalism in Virginia.* Durham, N.C., 1926.

Hatch, Alden. *The Byrds of Virginia.* New York, 1969.

Hawke, David Freeman. *In the Midst of a Revolution.* Philadelphia, 1961.

———. *Paine.* New York, 1974.

Hazleton, John H. *The Declaration of Independence: Its History.* New York, 1906.

Higginbotham, Don. *Daniel Morgan: Revolutionary Rifleman.* Chapel Hill, N.C., 1961.

———. *The War of American Independence.* New York, 1971.

Historical Statistics of the United States. Washington, D.C., 1960.

Hobhouse, Christopher. *Fox.* London, 1934.

Hoffman, Ronald. *The Spirit of Dissension: Economics, Politics and the Revolution in Maryland.* Baltimore, 1973.

Hoffman, Ross J. S. *The Marquis: A Study of Lord Rockingham, 1730–1782.* New York, 1973.

Hopkins, Robert H. *The True Genius of Oliver Goldsmith.* Baltimore, 1969.

Howe, William. *The Narrative of William Howe.* London, 1779.

Hunt, Agnes. *The Provincial Committees of Safety of the American Revolution.* Cleveland, 1904.

Hunter, Ann, and Miss Bell, eds. *The Journal of General Sir Martin Hunter, G.C.M.G., G.C.E., and Some Letters of His Wife, Lady Hunter.* Edinburgh, 1894.

Hutchinson, Thomas, ed. *Diary and Letters of Thomas Hutchinson.* 2 vols. Boston, 1884–86.

Hutson, James H., and Stephen G. Kurtz, eds. *Essays on the American Revolution.* Chapel Hill, N.C., 1973.

James, Bartholomew. *Journal of Rear Admiral Bartholomew James.* London, 1896.

Jarrett, Derek. *The Begetters of Revolution: England's Involvement with France, 1759–1789.* Totowa, N.J., 1973.

Jensen, Merrill. *The Founding of a Nation.* New York, 1968.

———, ed. *Tracts of the American Revolution, 1763–1776.* New York, 1967.

Johnston, Henry P. *The Campaign of 1776 around New York and Brooklyn.* Long Island Historical Society, vol. 3. 1878.

———. *Nathan Hale, 1776.* New Haven, 1914.

Kammen, Michael G., ed. *Politics and Society in Colonial America.* New York, 1973.

Kemble, Stephen. *The Kemble Papers.* 2 vols. Collections of the New-York Historical Society, 1884–85.

Kipping, Ernst. *The Hessian View of America, 1776–1783.* Monmouth Beach, N.J., 1971.

———, and Samuel S. Smith, eds. *At General Howe's Side: The Diary of General William Howe's Aide de Camp, Captain Friedrich von Muenchhausen.* Monmouth Beach, N.J., 1974.

Knox, William. Knox Papers. William Clements Library, Ann Arbor, Mich.

Laprade, William T., ed. *Parliamentary Papers of John Robinson, 1774–1784.* London, 1922.

Leake, Isaac Q. *Memoirs of the Life and Times of John Lamb.* Albany, N.Y., 1857.

Leder, Lawrence H., ed. *The Meaning of the American Revolution.* Chicago, 1969.

Lee, Charles. *The Lee Papers.* 2 vols. Collections of the New-York Historical Society, 1871.

Lemaitre, Georges. *Beaumarchais.* New York, 1949.

Lincoln, Charles L. *The Revolutionary Movement in Pennsylvania, 1760–1776.* Philadelphia, 1901.

Lomenie, Louis D. *Beaumarchais and His Times,* trans. Henry S. Edwards. New York, 1857.

Lowell, Edward J. *The Hessians and the Other German Auxiliaries of Great Britain in the Revolutionary War.* New York, 1884.

Lundin, Leonard. *Cockpit of the Revolution: The War for Independence in New Jersey.* Princeton, 1940.

Lutnick, Solomon. *The American Revolution in the British Press, 1775–1783.* Columbia, S.C., 1967.

Macalpine, Ida, and Richard Hunter. *George III and the Mad Business.* London, 1969.

McCrady, Edward. *The History of South Carolina in the Revolution.* 2 vols. New York, 1902.

McKelvey, James Lee. *George III and Lord Bute: The Leicester House Years.* Durham, N.C., 1973.

MacKenzie, Frederick. *The Diary of Frederick MacKenzie.* 2 vols. Cambridge, Mass., 1930.

Mackesy, Piers. *The War for America, 1775–1783.* Cambridge, Mass., 1964.

Main, Jackson Turner. *The Social Structure of Revolutionary America.* Princeton, 1965.

Malone, Dumas. *Jefferson, the Virginian.* Boston, 1948.

Mariboe, William H. "The Life of William Franklin," unpublished doctoral dissertation, University of Pennsylvania, 1962.

Martelli, George. *Jemmy Twitcher: A Life of the Fourth Earl of Sandwich.* London, 1962.

Martin, James Kirby. *Men in Rebellion: Higher Governmental Leaders and the Coming of the American Revolution.* New Brunswick, N.J., 1973.

Montross, Lynn. *The Reluctant Rebels: The Story of the Continental Congress.* New York, 1950.

Morison, Samuel Eliot. *John Paul Jones.* Boston, 1959.

Morris, Richard B. *The American Revolution Reconsidered.* New York, 1967.

Moultrie, William. *Memoirs of the American Revolution.* New York, 1802.

Namier, Lewis. *Personalities and Powers.* New York, 1954.

———, and John Brooke. *The History of Parliament.* 3 vols. London, 1964.

Nelson, William H. *The American Tory.* Oxford, 1961.

Neuenschwander, John A. *The Middle Colonies and the Coming of the American Revolution.* Port Washington, N.Y., 1973.

Nevins, Allan. *The American States during and after the Revolution.* New York, 1924.

Noel Hume, Ivor. *1775: Another Part of the Field.* New York, 1966.

O'Connell, Maurice R. *Irish Politics and Social Conflict in the Age of the American Revolution.* Philadelphia, 1965.

Oliver, Andrew, ed. *The Journal of Samuel Curwen, Loyalist.* 2 vols. Cambridge, Mass., 1972.

Palmer, R. R. *The Age of the Democratic Revolution.* Princeton, 1959.

Pares, Richard. *George III and the Politicians.* London, 1951.

Pausch, Georg. *Journal of Captain Georg Pausch.* Albany, N.Y., 1886.

Pomfret, John E. *Colonial New Jersey.* New York, 1973.

Prior, James, ed. *The Miscellaneous Works of Oliver Goldsmith.* 4 vols. New York, 1857.

Quarles, Benjamin. *The Negro in the American Revolution.* Chapel Hill, N.C., 1961.

Rankin, Hugh F. *The North Carolina Continentals*. Chapel Hill, N.C., 1971.

Reed, William B. *The Life and Correspondence of Joseph Reed*. 2 vols. Philadelphia, 1847.

Reid, Loren. *Charles James Fox: A Man for the People*. London, 1969.

Report of the Royal Historical Manuscripts Commission on the Manuscripts of Mrs. Stopford-Sackville. 2 vols. London, 1904–10.

Report on American Manuscripts in the Royal Institution of Great Britain. London, 1904.

Report on Manuscripts in Various Collections. London, 1909.

Ritcheson, Charles R. *British Politics and the American Revolution*. Norman, Okla., 1954.

Robbins, Ammi R. *Journal of the Reverend Ammi R. Robbins*. New Haven, 1850.

Roberts, Kenneth, ed. *March to Quebec: Journals of the Members of Arnold's Expedition*. New York, 1938.

Robertson, Archibald. *Diaries and Sketches in America*. New York, 1930.

Robson, Eric, ed. *Letters from America, 1773–1780, Being the Letters of a Scots Officer, Sir James Murray, to His Home during the War for American Independence*. Manchester, England, 1951.

Ross, Malcolm. *The Cape Fear*. New York, 1965.

Sabine, Lorenzo. *The American Loyalists*. Boston, 1847.

Sabine, William H. W., ed. *Historical Memoirs of William Smith*. New York, 1956.

———. *Murder, 1776, and Washington's Policy of Silence*. New York, 1973.

Sachs, William S., and Ari Hoogenboom. *The Enterprising Colonials: Society on the Eve of the Revolution*. Chicago, 1965.

Scheer, George M., ed. *Private Yankee Doodle*. Boston, 1962.

Scull, G. D., ed. *Memoir and Letters of Captain W. Glanville Evelyn of the Fourth Regiment ("King's Own") from North America, 1774–1776*. Oxford, 1879.

Seymour, George Dudley. *Documentary Life of Nathan Hale*. New Haven, 1941.

Shonnard, Frederick, and W. W. Spooner. *History of Westchester County*. New York, 1900.

Shy, John. *Toward Lexington: The Role of the British Army in the Coming of the American Revolution*. Princeton, 1965.

Smith, Page. *John Adams*. 2 vols. New York, 1962.

Smith, Samuel S. *The Battle of Princeton*. Monmouth Beach, N.J., 1967.

———. *The Battle of Trenton*. Monmouth Beach, N.J., 1965.

Smyth, Albert H., ed. *The Writings of Benjamin Franklin*. 10 vols. New York, 1905–7.

Sosin, Jack M. *Agents and Merchants: British Colonial Policy and the Origins of the American Revolution*. Lincoln, Nebr., 1965.

Sparks, Jared, ed. *The Correspondence of the American Revolution: Being Letters of Eminent Men to George Washington*. 4 vols. Boston, 1853.

Stark, James H. *The Loyalists of Massachusetts*. Boston, 1910.

Stillé, Charles J. *Major General Wayne and the Pennsylvania Line*. Philadelphia, 1893.

Stryker, William S. *The Battles of Trenton and Princeton*. Cambridge, Mass., 1898.

Stuart, Charles. *New Records of the American Revolution*. London, 1927.

Stuart-Wortley, Mrs. E. *A Prime Minister and His Son*. London, 1925.

Sullivan, James, ed. *Minutes of the Albany Committee of Correspondence*. Albany, N.Y., 1923.

Swain, Joseph Ward. *Edward Gibbon the Historian*. New York, 1966.

Tallmadge, Benjamin. *Memoir of Colonel Benjamin Tallmadge, Prepared by Himself*. New York, 1858.

Tatum, Edward H., Jr., ed. *The American Journal of Ambrose Serle.* San Marino, Calif., 1940.

Thornely, Samuel, ed. *The Journal of Nicholas Cresswell, 1774–1777.* New York, 1924.

Tieck, William A. *Riverdale, Kingsbridge, Spuyten Duyvil.* Old Tappan, N.J., 1968.

Trevelyan, George Otto. *The American Revolution.* 4 vols. New York, 1922.

Uhlendorf, Bernard A., trans. and annotator. *Revolution in America: Confidential Letters and Journals, 1776–1784, of Adjutant General Major Baurmeister of the Hessian Forces.* New Brunswick, N.J., 1957.

Underdonk, Henry, Jr. *Revolutionary Incidents of Suffolk and Kings County.* New York, 1849.

Valentine, Alan. *Lord George Germain.* New York, 1962.

——. *Lord North.* 2 vols. Norman, Okla., 1967.

Van Alstyne, Richard W. *Empire and Independence: The International History of the American Revolution.* New York, 1967.

Van Schaack, Henry C. *The Life of Peter Van Schaack.* New York, 1842.

Wade, Herbert T., and Robert A. Lively. *This Glorious Cause: The Adventures of Two Company Officers in Washington's Army.* Princeton, 1958.

Wallace, Willard M. *Traitorous Hero: The Life and Fortunes of Benedict Arnold.* New York, 1945.

Ward, Christopher. *The War of the Revolution.* 2 vols. New York, 1952.

Warner, Sam Bass, Jr. *The Private City: Philadelphia in Three Periods of Its Growth.* Philadelphia, 1968.

Watson, Steven. *The Reign of George III, 1760–1815,* in The Oxford History of England. Oxford, 1960.

Wharton, Francis, ed. *The Revolutionary Diplomatic Correspondence of the United States.* Washington, D.C., 1889.

Wilkin, W. H. *Some British Soldiers in America.* London, 1914.

Wilkinson, James. *Memoirs of My Own Times.* 3 vols. Philadelphia, 1816.

Willard, Margaret Wheeler, ed. *Letters on the American Revolution, 1774–1776.* Boston, 1925.

Willcox, William B., ed. *The American Rebellion: Sir Henry Clinton's Narrative of His Campaigns, 1775–1782.* New Haven, 1954.

——. *Portrait of a General: Sir Henry Clinton and the War of Independence.* New York, 1964.

Young, Arthur. *A Tour in Ireland, with General Observations on the Present State of That Kingdom, Made in 1776, 1777, 1778.* Dublin, 1780.

Index

H